ARBITRATION ACT 1996

Related titles

Arbitration Law
by Robert Merkin
(looseleaf)

Introduction to Arbitration
by Harold Crowter
(1998)

So you Really Want to be an Arbitrator
by D. Mark Cato
(1999)

Arbitration Practice and Procedure: Interlocutory and Hearing Problems
Third edition
by D. Mark Cato
(2002)

International Arbitration: A Handbook
Third edition
by Philip Capper
(2004)

Arbitration Law
by Robert Merkin
(2004)

Arbitration Law Handbook
by Ben Horn and Roger Hopkins
(2007)

A Practical Guide to International Arbitration in London
by Hilary Heilbron QC
(2008)

ARBITRATION ACT 1996

BY

ROBERT MERKIN, LLB, LLM
Lloyd's Law Reports, Professor of Commercial Law
University of Southampton

Consultant
BARLOW LYDE & GILBERT LLP

AND

LOUIS FLANNERY, LLB, FCI Arb
Solicitor Advocate

Partner
STEPHENSON HARWOOD

FOURTH EDITION

informa

LONDON
2008

Informa Law
Mortimer House
37–41 Mortimer Street
London W1T 3JH
law.enquiries@informa.com

First published
as *Arbitration Act 1996: An Annotated Guide* 1996
Second edition 2000
Third edition 2005
Fourth edition 2008

British Library Cataloguing in Publication Data
A catalogue record
for this book is available
from the British Library

ISBN 978-184311-778-0

Typeset in 10/12pt Times by
Interactive Sciences Ltd, Gloucester
Printed in Great Britain by
MPG Books, Bodmin, Cornwall
Printed on paper from sustainable sources

PREFACE TO THE FOURTH EDITION

It seems only a short while ago that we were both reading the proofs of the third edition, in early 2005. So much case law has emerged in a period barely longer than three years that a fresh look at the Act and its detailed provisions has become necessary. We have endeavored to cover all the major decisions emanating from the English Courts, a wealth of which have emanated from the judiciary in the Commercial Court and the Technology and Construction Court, where most arbitration-related matters are now heard. In addition, several issues of principle concerning the Act have been aired by the Court of Appeal, and, in three cases since the third edition was published, by the English House of Lords (*Premium Nafta*—i.e. *Fiona Trust*, *West Tankers* and *Lesotho Highlands*, the decision of which appeared only weeks after the appearance of the third edition). We have also included where possible, and where it was regarded as necessary, references to important and relevant decisions from other common law jurisdictions.

We both give thanks to the usual unnamed suspects in our respective families.

The text was submitted for publication in September 2008, but we have incorporated at the proof stage cases decided up to the end of October 2008, including the Court of Appeal decision in *IPCO Nigeria* v. *NNPC*.

ROB MERKIN
LOUIS FLANNERY
October 2008

CONTENTS

TABLE OF CASES

TABLE OF LEGISLATION

Page numbers shown in **bold** indicate where text is reproduced

PART I

BACKGROUND TO THE ARBITRATION ACT 1996

Pressure for reform

The Arbitration Act 1996 is a combination of consolidation and reform of the legal principles enshrined in the Arbitration Acts 1950, 1975 and 1979, the Consumer Arbitration Agreements Act 1988, and the common law. English arbitration law has evolved slowly, with common law principles being laid down and those principles subsequently being adopted, and on occasion modified, by statutory intervention. One of the major difficulties with a structure based on common law and statute proved to be the absence of a definitive code of arbitration law, the result being that arbitration has necessarily been the provenance of those skilled in the law rather than those with business expertise (who may be far more suited to the resolution of complex technical disputes). The Arbitration Act 1996 was intended to be both a fresh start and the closest thing to a definitive code of arbitration law that has ever been enacted in England. There has been mixed success. It is certainly the case that pre-1996 authorities have ceased to be of major significance other than as illustrative guidance. However, it would be wrong to treat the 1996 Act as a "code" in the Continental sense:[1] the legislation is far from exhaustive, and in the years since its passing there have been several hundred decided cases, many of which lay down fundamental principles concerning the scope and application of the 1996 Act. The pace of the decisions does not appear to have abated, and what has happened goes significantly beyond the sort of short-term dislocation or bedding-down that typifies the passing of new legislation. As a result, the position some 12 years on from the implementation of the 1996 Act is that the law can be devised only from a reading of the legislation itself and of the numerous cases decided under it. To the extent that the 1996 Act was intended to be a "one-stop shop" it can be regarded as a comprehensive failure.

The moves which led ultimately to the Arbitration Act 1996 are directly traceable to those which led to the Arbitration Act 1979. The earlier Act was in essence a statement of party autonomy as opposed to the previous tradition of judicial intervention. The 1979 Act abolished the long-established case stated procedure, whereby the courts were free to review an award if an error of law or fact appeared on the face of the award, and in its place established a structure under which errors of fact could not be the subject of an appeal and errors of law could be appealed only under stringent conditions. The 1979 Act also, within limits, permitted the parties to contract out of any right of appeal to the courts.

1. Codification of a sort was briefly flirted with in England in a 30-year period running from the 1880s, with the work of Sir Mackenzie Chalmers. His classic pieces of "codified" legislation—including the Bills of Exchange Act 1882, the Sale of Goods Act 1893 and the Marine Insurance Act 1906—operated as a snapshot of the decided cases in those years. None purported, or proved, to be an exhaustive statement of the law.

Examination of the debates on the Bill which led to the Arbitration Act 1979 reveals the concern that English law, by providing frequent and numerous opportunities for judicial intervention in the progress of an arbitration and as regards the ultimate award, had developed in a fashion inconsistent with the perceived advantages of arbitration, namely, privacy, speed, low costs, finality and the ability to select the individuals who are to resolve any dispute. The argument that if the parties could not achieve their ends by arbitrating in England, they would arbitrate elsewhere, proved to be conclusive, not just in the passing of the 1979 Act itself but—after an uncertain start—in the subsequent judicial attitude to that Act which witnessed a pronounced judicial retreat from intervention.

The 1979 Act was, however, only a partial answer to the problem, and other matters addressed by the 1978 Report of the DAC were left unaddressed. The 1979 Act said nothing about the procedural aspects of arbitrations, and to this extent the 1950 Act remained interventionist in a number of respects. In particular: it was necessary to have recourse to the courts where one of the parties to an arbitration refused to co-operate with the proceedings or where for other reasons the proceedings could not run smoothly; the courts retained residual power to strike down an arbitration agreement and to dismiss the arbitrators; and the courts gradually developed a fresh interventionist power, based on "procedural mishap", enabling the remission of an award to the arbitrators where "something had gone wrong" in the arbitration, often the fault of the applicant himself. In the event the scope of procedural mishap did not become fully clear until after its abolition by the Arbitration Act 1996, and it proved that Parliament's decision to abolish this jurisdiction was fully justified. Moreover, there were doubts as to whether the parties could agree to abandon strict rules of evidence and adversarial procedures. There were minor statutory modifications promoting autonomy, particularly the Courts and Legal Services Act 1990, but the basic structure remained unchanged.

The problems were highlighted by the adoption in June 1985 by the United Nations of a Model Law on Arbitration, drafted by UNCITRAL, the international trade law committee of the United Nations. The Model Law is a succinct code of arbitration law, designed by its terms for international commercial arbitration but capable of adaptation for a domestic code. The principal features of the Model Law are party autonomy over the arbitration proceedings, the absence of any appeal procedure, the restriction of judicial intervention in the proceedings to default powers and the free enforceability of the award other than in cases of want of jurisdiction or clear unfairness in the procedure. A large and increasing number of countries have adopted the Model Law verbatim as their arbitration law, at least as regards international commercial arbitration. The Model Law was modified in 2006. The text of the modified version is set out in Appendix 7 to this work.

Proposed English adoption of the Model Law

The question of whether the UNCITRAL Model Law was appropriate for adoption in England was put to the Departmental Advisory Committee on Arbitration Law chaired by Lord Mustill. The DAC, reporting in 1989, rejected calls for the adoption of the Model Law into English law. Instead, the Committee recommended that there should be a new Arbitration Act, incorporating the best features of existing law but redrafted in more user-friendly terms, filling in the many gaps in the legislation which had been resolved, if at all, by case law. The DAC felt that, wherever possible, the new Act should reflect the Model

Law, but that wholesale adoption would be detrimental. The DAC's reasons were as follows:

(a) as the Model Law applied only to international commercial arbitration, its adoption would lead to different regimes in English law for purely domestic disputes and for international commercial disputes;[1]
(b) adopting the Model Law, being so different from established principles of English law, would cause a good deal of short-term dislocation in the English arbitration market while new procedures and principles were absorbed by practitioners of the art;[2]
(c) the Model Law was designed primarily for those jurisdictions with little or nothing in the way of developed principles of arbitration law, whereas England in this respect possessed a mature tried-and-tested system; and
(d) evidence to the DAC did not demonstrate any generalised call for root and branch reform.

The DAC was also of the view that the Model Law was in some respects arguably less suited to the modern arbitral process than existing English law. The particular features of the Model Law which were perceived as less beneficial than existing English law were identified by the DAC as including the following:

(a) the loss of any right of appeal on a point of law which would lead to loss of the necessary ultimate protection for the parties;[3]
(b) the requirement for a written or reasoned award, which would run contrary to the established English flexibility in this regard;
(c) the ability of a tribunal to rule on its own jurisdiction, which would merely increase potential delays in the proceedings;[4]
(d) the imposition of rigid time limits for the exchange of pleadings;
(e) the power of the tribunal to appoint experts, which was seen as causing delay and increasing costs;
(f) the recognition of "equitable" arbitration based on business principles rather than strict rules of law, which would lead to uncertainty;
(g) the need for any arbitration agreement to be signed by the parties, which ran counter to established practice in certain trades;
(h) the use of three-arbitrator panels rather than the traditional English tribunal of an umpire and two arbitrators;
(i) the absence in the Model Law of the convenient English rule that, if each party is to appoint an arbitrator and one fails to do so, the other can treat his arbitrator as the sole arbitrator;
(j) the introduction of a formal process for challenging the validity of an arbitrator's appointment, which again was seen as an open invitation to delay;

1. This is the position in a number of jurisdictions which have adopted the Model Law.
2. As commented above, and given that the 1996 Act is very close to the Model Law in a number of respects, this prediction has been proved right.
3. Views on this were and remain mixed. Some sectors (e.g., insurance and reinsurance) demand finality, whereas others (e.g., marine cargo and related sectors) regard arbitration as the starting point for the dispute resolution process.
4. An accurate prediction in the light of experience under the 1996 Act.

(k) less efficient procedures for the appointment of a substitute arbitrator where an appointed arbitrator cannot or will not act;
(l) the absence from the Model Law of any power to extend contractual time limits for the commencement of arbitration proceedings;
(m) the restriction of the power of remission to cases in which the award could be set aside; and
(n) the absence of any power of summary enforcement.

It might be noted in passing that the Arbitration Act 1996 adopts from the Model Law points (b), (c), (e), (f), (h), (k) and (m) in the above list, and restricts the right of appeal in accordance with point (a). Point (g) was subsequently addressed by the amendments to the Model Law adopted in 2006. Only points (d), (i), (j), (l) and (n) distinguish English law from the Model Law.

Having ruled out wholesale adoption of the Model Law, the DAC 1989 Report considered a number of other options, ranging from enactment of a modified version of the Model Law to no change at all. The Committee's ultimate conclusion was that there was an urgent need for fresh legislation enacting the principles of the most favourable aspects of the Model Law and thereby rendering English law more accessible to overseas traders, but primarily having the purpose of clarifying and modernising English law. The Report was accepted by the Government, with the result that while legislation was promised, it was clear that it was not a priority in the legislative programme.

First steps towards legislation

Following the Report of the DAC, and faced with the likelihood that there would be no legislative action, a number of private organisations, including individual lawyers and arbitrators, commissioned and contributed to a privately-drafted Bill produced by Mr Arthur Marriott. The "unofficial" Bill, along with detailed explanatory notes, was published and circulated for comment in November 1990. The Bill was based on the Model Law, although substantial parts of the Model Law were not reproduced in it. The language of the Bill was intended to be more "user-friendly" than that found in a traditional Act.

In April 1992, the DAC, by this time under the chairmanship of Steyn J, recommended that the Department of Trade and Industry (DTI) should take over the work on the Bill and publish its own proposals. This proposal was accepted by the Secretary of State, and work commenced. The result was that in February 1994 the DTI published a Consultation Paper which incorporated a draft Bill. The Paper contained detailed commentary on the rationale of the various clauses of the Bill and on the provisions of the clauses themselves. The February 1994 Bill upheld the 1989 decision not to incorporate the Model Law wholesale into English law, but nevertheless reflected a desire to move closer to the Model Law both in terms of the structure and ordering of the Bill and in terms of matters dealt with by the Model Law on which English law had previously been silent. Other stated aims of the February 1994 Bill included:

(a) the production of legislation which was more accessible in terms of language and scope of coverage;

(b) emphasis on the importance of party autonomy, and in particular the ability of the parties to adopt different forms of procedure for determining their dispute; and
(c) the facilitation of the incorporation of standard form and institutional arbitration rules into arbitration agreements.

Consultation nevertheless demonstrated that the Bill was deficient in a number of respects, both in failing to clarify its intentions (most importantly, as regards the intention to confer upon arbitrators a wider power to adopt a non-adversarial procedure) and in leaving untouched various contentious areas of law (including "equity" clauses and the appointment of the arbitral tribunal where there are more than two parties to an arbitration agreement). The result of the consultation was the abandonment of the February 1994 Bill in that form, and work was commenced on a revised version.

In July 1995 the DAC, by that time under the chairmanship of Saville J, published a further Consultation Paper including the draft of a new Arbitration Bill. As before, the adoption of the Model Law as a whole was rejected, but the July 1995 Bill moved closer to the Model Law than previous DTI versions. Most of the provisions of the Model Law appeared in one or other form in the Bill, although there were various aspects of the Bill which were thought to be helpful to the smooth running of arbitrations but which did not appear in the Model Law and which were the basis of the original decision in 1989 not to adopt the Model Law. The July 1995 Bill, which, like its predecessors, was a combination of consolidation and modification, was stated by the Consultation Paper to have the following objectives:

(a) to restate the major aspects of the current law on arbitration in a clear and accessible way so that it is readily understandable by all those who are considering using arbitration in England and Wales;
(b) to introduce changes that will help to facilitate speedy and cost-effective dispute resolution—one particular feature of this was the introduction of the general concept that there can be an appeal from a decision of the court exercising powers of assistance only with the permission of the court; and
(c) to increase the scope for party autonomy by preparing legislation which, with some exceptions, comes into play only where the parties have failed to agree what should happen, and which strengthens the powers of arbitrators in order to give effect to the parties' intention to restrict access to the courts.

One notable feature of the Bill was its search for finality. In those cases in which recourse to the court was required, the court's decision could not be appealed without the permission of the court itself. By this method, the Bill limited the danger that applications to the court for assistance might become major pieces of litigation in their own right. The Bill applied to all arbitrations, and continued the English tradition of having a single regime applicable to domestic and international arbitrations: the Model Law, by contrast, is confined to international and commercial arbitration. The only distinction drawn in English law at that time was between consumer and commercial arbitrations, the former being governed by the Consumer Arbitration Agreements Act 1988 which in most cases negatived the effect of an arbitration clause agreed to before the dispute had arisen.

The July 1995 Bill was not intended to be in final form. In particular, the provisions of Part II of the Arbitration Act 1950, and of the Arbitration Act 1975, on the enforcement of foreign awards, were not at that stage incorporated into the draft, the intention being that this would occur on the formal introduction of the Bill into Parliament. Also, there were a number of issues on which further views were sought. In accordance with the Government's intended timetable, an Arbitration Bill was given its First Reading in the House of Lords on 12 December 1995. The Bill that was finally presented to Parliament adopted most of the principles of the July 1995 version, but almost every clause in the Bill was redrafted in order to achieve legal clarity and precision. Moreover, the December 1995 version witnessed a number of important changes of policy from the earlier draft. In particular, a statement of overriding objectives was added. Significantly, the concept of party autonomy proved in the course of consultation not to be as popular among arbitrators and practitioners as had previously been thought to be the case, and the December 1995 Bill opted for arbitrator autonomy: in other words, the choice of procedure was to be one primarily for the arbitrators and not for the parties. The Bill took a further step to reduce the delays involved where recourse to the court was required, by adopting the principle that the arbitration might proceed while the matter before the court is being considered by it.

The Government stressed at Second Reading in the House of Lords that the purposes of legislating were: to provide a single source for arbitration law; to ensure that the law was expressed in a clear and accessible manner; and to set out the law in a logical fashion. By achieving these aims, London would continue to be an attractive forum for the resolution of disputes by arbitration. Rejuvenated arbitration law was also regarded as an important mechanism for keeping disputes out of the courts, leaving the courts free to deal with those matters not appropriate for or capable of resolution by private means. The Bill was welcomed by everybody who spoke in the Parliamentary debates on it, with vital contributions from a distinguished array of Law Lords and ex-Law Lords including Lords Mustill, Wilberforce, Ackner, Donaldson and Roskill. The clarity and all-embracing nature of the Bill brought particular praise.

Parliamentary progress

The Bill was first introduced in the House of Lords, and then proceeded to the House of Commons, in line with the usual practice for non-controversial legislation. It had originally been the Government's intention to subject the Bill to the Public Bill Committee Procedure at Committee stage in the House of Lords, but objections were raised to this on Second Reading in the House of Lords, on the basis that it would result in unacceptable delay. Nevertheless, the Government stuck to its original intentions. Minor amendments were made to the Bill, but for the most part the Arbitration Act 1996 reflects the December 1996 Bill. The Parliamentary Progress of the Bill was as follows:

- — HL First Reading: 12 December 1995, HL Hansard, cols 116–164 (general discussion);
- — HL Second Reading: 18 January 1996, HL Hansard, cols 760–794 (general discussion);
- — HL Committee: 28 February 1996, HL Hansard, CWH1–30 (minor amendments, clarification of power to award security for costs, provisions relating to county courts);
- — HL Report: 18 March 1996, HL Hansard, cols 1076–1087 (minor amendments, amendments to provisions on scope of Bill);

- HL Third Reading: 2 April 1996, HL Hansard cols 151–159 (amendments to consumer arbitration agreements provisions);
- HC First Reading: 2 April 1996;
- HC Second Reading: 2 May 1996, Hansard, cols 1308–1320;
- HC Standing Committee A: 14 May 1996 (amendments to county court provisions);
- HC Third Reading: 10 June 1996;
- Royal Assent: 17 June 1996;
- In force, 31 January 1997.

One important, and unusual, feature of the 1996 Act is an almost complete absence of cross-referencing to other legislation. Thus, relevant provisions of the Limitation Act 1980 and the Civil Jurisdiction and Judgments Act 1982 were re-enacted in the Act so that they were available to readers of the Act. The Act does not, however, seek to codify the vast bulk of common law authority which had developed under earlier legislation and which to some extent remains applicable, so that anyone reading the Act will continue to receive only a part—albeit a substantial part—of the story. The DAC's February 1996 Report indeed states, at paragraph 9, that full codification would have been undesirable, as it would have inhibited the gradual evolution of the law. Thus, there is nothing in the Act concerning the complex and developing rules on exactly when an arbitration award and material produced for the arbitration is confidential and unable to be used in subsequent related judicial or arbitration proceedings.[1]

In February 1996 the DAC Report was published (referred to in this book as the DAC Report) setting out the objectives of the Bill and raising for consideration various matters which had come to light on Second Reading in the House of Lords. In January 1997, shortly before the Act was brought into force, a Supplementary Report was published (referred to in this book as the DAC Supplementary Report) highlighting the features of the Act and pointing out any variations between the DAC's original recommendations and the final version of the Act. The comments made by the DAC in these Reports are incorporated at the appropriate places in the following commentary. The text of the Reports is published as an appendix to this work (Appendices 8 and 9). In reading the DAC Report care should be taken to note that it refers to clauses rather than sections and that various matters considered by the DAC Report did not ultimately find their way into the final legislation. Any differences are highlighted in the notes to the sections of the Act itself. These minor matters aside, the Reports have come to be regarded by the courts as an authoritative source on the interpretation of the Act and are cited with some regularity in judgments.

Implementation

The Arbitration Act 1996 was brought into force by the Arbitration Act 1996 (Commencement No 1) Order 1996,[2] although various provisions authorising the making of statutory instruments came into force on 16 December 1996.

1. DAC Supplementary Report, January 1997, para. 44.
2. SI 1996 No 3146. There is brief commentary on the commencement provisions appended to the DAC Supplementary Report, January 1997, paras 70–74.

The substantive provisions of the Act took effect on 31 January 1997, and apply to arbitration proceedings commenced on or after that date.[1] The date on which the arbitration agreement itself is made is immaterial to the application or otherwise of the 1996 Act. The earlier legislation accordingly applies only to: arbitral proceedings commenced before 31 January 1997; applications to the court commenced or made before 31 January 1997; and applications to the court commenced or made before 31 January 1997 relating to arbitration proceedings commenced before 31 January 1997. With the increasing passage of time since the Act came into force, it has become unlikely in the extreme that there are any arbitral proceedings or applications still on foot to which the earlier legislation applies. Sections 85 to 87 have not been brought into force and will almost certainly not be. These sections draw a distinction between domestic and non-domestic agreements, familiar under the earlier legislation, and confer upon the court discretion to refuse to stay domestic proceedings commenced in breach of an arbitration agreement and remove the power of the parties to enter into an arbitration clause in a domestic agreement which excludes judicial review for error of law. As the sections have not been bought into force, the law is the same as regards both domestic and non-domestic agreements: the court has no discretion to refuse to stay judicial proceedings in the face of a valid arbitration agreement (section 9); and the parties may oust the power of the court to rule on a point of law or to review an award by reason of error of law (sections 45 and 69).

Arbitration claims

Applications to the court under the earlier legislation fell within RSC Ord. 73, a provision which was complex and required different forms of application for different matters. RSC Ord. 73 was recast to take account of the Arbitration Act 1996, and the revised version came into force on 31 January 1997 along with the Act itself. The new version set out a single procedure for all "arbitration applications". With effect from 25 April 1999, the date on which the Rules of the Supreme Court were replaced by the Civil Procedure Rules 1998 (CPR) under the Woolf Reforms, RSC Ord. 73 was replaced by CPR Part 49 and Practice Direction 49G. Practice Direction 49G re-enacted in substance the amended version of RSC Ord. 73 with modifications to take account of the replacement of the RSC by the CPR. Part I of Practice Direction 49G applied to an arbitration application made on or after 31 January 1997, whereas Part II of Practice Direction 49G re-enacted with consequential modifications the version of RSC Ord. 73 in force prior to 31 January 1999 and applied to arbitration applications made before that date. This temporary edifice was demolished and replaced with effect from 25 March 2002 by Part 62 of the CPR, as supplemented by a Practice Direction to Part 62. The broad effect of Part 62 is to bring arbitration claims in line, so far as possible, with the generality of the content of the CPR. Section I of Part 62 governs all applications to the court under the Arbitration Act 1996, Section II governs all applications under earlier arbitration legislation (now, of course, almost exclusively redundant) and Section III regulates applications for the enforcement of arbitration awards.

1. Sections 91 (orders in respect of consumer arbitrations), 105 (orders allocating jurisdiction between courts), 107 (repeal of legislation) and 108–110 (short title and commencement).

The full text of CPR Part 62 and its Practice Direction are set out in the Appendices to this work.[1] References to them will be made at appropriate places in the annotations, although the provisions may be outlined as follows.

CPR Part 62 applies to any "arbitration claim", which includes:

- (i) any application under the 1996 Act;
- (ii) any application affecting:
  - (a) the validity or otherwise of an arbitration agreement; or
  - (b) whether an arbitration tribunal is properly constituted; or
  - (c) what matters have been submitted to arbitration in accordance with an arbitration agreement;
- (iii) a claim to declare that an award by an arbitral tribunal is not binding on a party; and
- (iv) any other application affecting arbitration proceedings (whether started or not) or an arbitration agreement.[2]

An arbitration claim is to be made by means of an arbitration claim form issued in the appropriate court.[3] Notice must be given to any other party to the arbitration by making them a defendant and serving a copy of the arbitration claim form in accordance with CPR Part 62.[4] Under the Act, where notice of any application or claim is required to be given to an arbitrator, it may be given by sending a copy of the arbitration claim form and any evidence in support.[5] An arbitration claim form must, most importantly, include a concise statement of the remedy claimed and the questions to be referred to the court, give details of any award to be challenged, show that the statutory requirements for a claim set out in the 1996 Act have been met, specify the sections of the 1996 Act under which the claim is brought, identify the defendants against whom a costs order is sought and specify the person on whom the claim form is to be served (unless it is without notice).[6] Service must be within one month of the date of issue.[7] Where the arbitration is taking place within the jurisdiction, the court may permit service of an arbitration claim form at the address of a party's solicitor or representative acting for him in the arbitration.[8] Otherwise, application may, where appropriate, be made for the service of the claim form outside the jurisdic-

1. Copies of the relevant forms may be accessed online at www.courtservice.gov.uk/cms/media/n8.pdf.
2. CPR r. 62.2: for amendment of the claim form, see *ED & F Man Sugar Ltd* v. *Lendoudis* [2007] 2 Lloyd's Rep 579. Although the categories here seem to suggest that an application may be made otherwise than under the 1996 Act, CPR r. 62.4(1)(d) makes it clear that all arbitration claims under the Act are within Section 1 of Part 62.
3. CPR r. 62.3 and para. 2.2 of the Arbitration Practice Direction (CPR PD 62).
4. CPR r. 62.6(3). The requirement to make any other party to the arbitration a defendant to the arbitration claim is dependent upon the requirement to give notice in the section of the Act relied upon, but since every application under the Act requires notice to be given (at least) to the other party or parties to the arbitral proceedings, they will always be named defendants in the arbitration claim form.
5. CPR r. 62.6(2).
6. CPR r. 62.4(1).
7. CPR r. 62.4(2). A person who wishes to know whether an arbitration claim form has been issued may apply to the court to search the court's records: CPR r. 5(4) and CPR PD 66, para. 5.1, and see *Advance Specialist Treatment Engineering Ltd* v. *Cleveland Structural Engineering (Hong Kong) Ltd* [2000] 2 All ER (Comm) 189.
8. CPR PD 62, para. 3.1.

tion.[1] The arbitrator is to be made a party where the claim is for his removal or is in respect of his remuneration.[2] In any other case under the Act where an application is to be made on notice to the tribunal, any arbitrator may apply to be added as a defendant or may make written representations to the court.[3] Arbitration claims are allocated to the multi-track procedure under the CPR, and automatic directions as to the filing and serving of evidence and time limits for compliance will operate unless the court orders otherwise.[4] Unless the court orders otherwise, substantive hearings of claims involving points of law are to be in public and all other hearings (including applications for a stay of existing proceedings under section 9 of the 1996 Act) are to be in private:[5] judgments themselves are public documents unless there is some compelling reason based on the need for confidentiality for a judgment not to be published.[6] The court may order the claimant to provide security for costs in respect of an arbitration claim.[7]

The court to which an arbitration application is made is determined by the High Court and County Court (Allocation of Arbitration) Proceedings Order 1996[8] as supplemented by CPR PD 62, paragraph 2.3. Under these provisions, arbitration claim proceedings are to be commenced in the Admiralty and Commercial Registry of the High Court, the Technology and Construction Court in London, any District Registry of the High Court where a mercantile list is established, the TCC List in a District Registry or the Central London County Court Mercantile List. The exceptions relate to applications for a stay of judicial proceedings, which are to be heard in the court in which the proceedings themselves are pending, and proceedings for the enforcement of an arbitration award, which may be commenced in any court. Once an arbitration application has been made, one division of the High Court may nevertheless transfer the application to another division or to the Central London County Court, and vice versa. The criteria which must be taken into account in any decision as to whether a transfer should be made are: the value of the claim; the nature of the dispute; whether the proceedings raise questions of importance to third parties; and the balance of convenience. In the Central London County Court Mercantile List, if the financial substance of the dispute is £200,000 or more, other than in exceptional circumstances the proceedings should be issued in the High Court unless the proceedings do not raise questions of general importance to persons who are not parties.[9]

1. CPR r. 62.5. It is not clear whether permission is required to serve the arbitration claim form out of the jurisdiction on defendants situated in an EU or Lugano Convention country, since ordinarily no such permission is required under CPR r. 6.19. It is presumed that permission under CPR r. 62.5 is required only in cases where CPR r. 6.19 does not apply. One aspect of the problem is that arbitration is excluded from the scope of the Brussels Regulation and Lugano Convention. For that reason, it is uncertain whether a purely arbitration related court application falls within CPR r. 6.19. In case there is any doubt, an application for permission ought to be applied for out of an abundance of caution. In such cases, care should be taken to extend the time for service of the claim form. An application to this effect may be included in the application for permission for service out.
2. CPR r. 62.6(1).
3. CPR r. 62.7, incorporating CPR PD paras 6.1 to 6.7.
4. CPR PD 62, para. 4.1.
5. CPR r. 62.10. See: *Department of Economics Policy and Development of the City of Moscow* v. *Bankers Trust Co* [2004] 2 Lloyd's Rep 179; *Arab National Bank* v. *El Sharif Saoud Bin Masoud Bin Haza'a El-Abdali* [2004] EWHC 2381 (Comm).
6. *Department of Economics Policy and Development of the City of Moscow* v. *Bankers Trust Co* [2004] 2 Lloyd's Rep 179.
7. CPR Part 25.
8. SI 1996 No 3215, as amended by the High Court and County Courts (Allocation of Arbitration Proceedings) (Amendment) Order 1999, SI 1999 No 1010 and by the Civil Procedure (Modification of Enactments) Order 2002, SI 2002 No 439. See the Appendix for the full text of the amended Order.
9. High Court and County Courts (Allocation of Arbitration Proceedings) Order 1996, Art. 5.

Appeals

The 1996 Act has as one of its key underlying objectives the speed and finality of arbitration proceedings, with an implicit desire to avoid time-consuming and costly satellite litigation in the form of applications to the court and appeals from court decisions. Accordingly, the majority of those sections under which an arbitration application may be made set out specific provisions governing appeals. The unifying feature is that an appeal may be made to the Court of Appeal only with the permission of the judge and not with the permission of the Court of Appeal,[1] and it has been confirmed by the courts that there is no possibility of an application to the Court of Appeal for permission to appeal where this is refused by the judge under the 1996 Act itself.[2] That said, the Court of Appeal does have residual power to hear an appeal under section 16 of the Supreme Court Act 1981 in the highly exceptional case where the judge has not made a valid decision at all,[3] and seemingly also where the relevant provision of the 1996 Act applies unless the parties have agreed to the contrary and the question is whether such an agreement has been entered into.[4] However, a number of sections which confer the right to apply to the court make no mention of a right of appeal. In *Inco Europe Ltd* v. *First Choice Distribution*[5] the House of Lords held that the 1996 Act had not removed a right of appeal from High Court decisions under section 9 of the 1996 Act (stay of proceedings), and it may be assumed that the same right extends to those sections of the Act which make no reference to a right of appeal.[6] There are also numerous sections which confer various rights and obligations on the parties but which make no reference to any application to the court: it was held by the Court of Appeal in *Virdee* v. *Virdi*[7] that if application is required to the court to give effect to those sections, there is also a right of appeal to the Court of Appeal against the judge's refusal to give permission for a further appeal.

1. *Henry Boot Construction (UK) Ltd* v. *Malmaison Hotel (Manchester) Ltd* [2001] 1 QB 388; *Athletic Union of Constantinople* v. *National Basketball Association* [2002] 1 Lloyd's Rep 305.

2. The affected sections are: s. 12, extension of time for commencement of arbitration proceedings; s. 17, power of court to appoint a sole arbitrator; s. 18, power of court to appoint an arbitral tribunal; s. 23, removal of arbitrator; s. 25, grant of relief to an arbitrator who has resigned; s. 32, determination of preliminary point of jurisdiction; s. 42, enforcement of arbitrators' peremptory order; s. 44, application for exercise of interim powers; s. 45, determination of preliminary point of law; s. 50, extension of time for making award; s. 56, determination of fees and expenses where an award is withheld; s. 67, jurisdictional appeal; s. 68, serious irregularity appeal; s. 69, permission to appeal against error of law and permission against ruling on appeal on error of law appeal; s. 70, appeal against supplementary order following appeal; s. 77, service of documents; s. 79, extension of time limits.

3. *Aden Refinery Co Ltd* v. *Ugland Management Co Ltd* [1986] 2 Lloyd's Rep 336; *North Range Shipping Ltd* v. *Seatrans Shipping Corporation* [2002] 2 Lloyd's Rep 1; *BLCT (13096) Ltd* v. *J Sainsbury plc* [2004] 2 P & CR 32; *CGU International Insurance plc* v. *AstraZeneca Insurance Co Ltd* [2007] 1 Lloyd's Rep 142; *ASM Shipping Ltd* v. *TTMI Ltd of England* [2007] 1 Lloyd's Rep 136; *Republic of Kazakhstan* v. *Istil Group (No 2)* [2007] 2 Lloyd's Rep 548.

4. So held in *Sumukan* v. *The Commonwealth Secretariat* [2007] 2 Lloyd's Rep 87, in respect of s. 69. If this ruling is of general application then it will also apply to: s. 17, power of court to appoint a sole arbitrator; s. 18, failure of appointment procedure; s. 25, consequences of arbitrator's resignation; s. 32, preliminary ruling on jurisdiction; s. 42, enforcement of peremptory orders; s. 44, exercise of interim powers; s. 45, preliminary ruling on point of law; s. 50, extension of time for making an award; s. 69 appeal on point of law; s. 77, authorisation of alternative form of service; s. 79, extension of time limits.

5. [2000] 1 WLR 586.

6. The relevant provisions are: s. 9, stay; s. 10, interpleader; s. 13, disapplication of statutory limitation period; s. 28, repayment of excessive fees by arbitrators; s. 64, recoverability of fees and expenses by arbitrators; s. 66, enforcement of award; s. 72, jurisdiction; s. 80, extension of time for statutory time limits.

7. [2003] EWCA Civ 41.

The Arbitration Act 1996 and the Model Law

As previously indicated, the Arbitration Act 1996 moves English law far closer to the UNCITRAL Model Law than had originally been proposed by the DAC in 1989. The Act differs from the Model Law in a number of respects, the most important of which are the following:

- (a) the 1996 Act applies to all classes of arbitration, whereas the Model Law (Articles 1 and 2) is confined to international commercial arbitration;
- (b) Article 7(2) of the Model Law requires an arbitration agreement to be signed: there is no equivalent provision in the Arbitration Act 1996. However, the Model Law was amended in 2006 by the addition of an alternative version of Article 7 which does not require signature;
- (c) where an action is brought in the English courts in respect of a matter which is the subject of a valid and subsisting arbitration clause, the English court can only stay its own proceedings; the Model Law (Article 8(2)) requires the court to refer the matter to arbitration;
- (d) the 1996 Act provides that, in default of agreement, there is to be a sole arbitrator: the Model Law (Article 10(1)) specifies a tribunal of three arbitrators as the default panel;
- (e) where each party is required to appoint an arbitrator, English law has retained the power of a party to treat his arbitrator as the sole arbitrator where the other party has failed to make an appointment: there is no equivalent provision in the appointment rules in Article 11 of the Model Law;
- (f) Article 13 of the Model Law requires a party who wishes to oppose the appointment of an arbitrator to do so within 15 days: under the 1996 Act, a challenge can be made at any time, subject to general principles of waiver;
- (g) the Model Law (Article 19) allows the parties to choose the procedure for the arbitration, with the arbitrators having default powers in the absence of agreement. Under the 1996 Act, the arbitrators have this right subject only to contrary agreement by the parties;
- (h) the Model Law (Article 23) lays down strict rules for the exchange of pleadings: there is no equivalent provision in the Arbitration Act 1996, which permits the arbitrators to decide how to proceed;
- (i) the Model Law does not contain any provision for the extension of agreed time limits for the commencement of proceedings; and
- (j) the Model Law does not contain any mechanism for summary enforcement of awards.

As the Act is intended to reflect the Model Law in a number of respects, the text of the Model Law is appended to this work.

PART II

THE ARBITRATION ACT 1996

ARRANGEMENT OF SECTIONS

Part I—Arbitration pursuant to an arbitration agreement

JURISDICTION OF THE ARBITRAL TRIBUNAL

30. Competence of tribunal to rule on its own jurisdiction.
31. Objection to substantive jurisdiction of tribunal.
32. Determination of preliminary point of jurisdiction.

THE ARBITRAL PROCEEDINGS

33. General duty of the tribunal.
34. Procedural and evidential matters.
35. Consolidation of proceedings and concurrent hearings.
36. Legal or other representation.
37. Power to appoint experts, legal advisers or assessors.
38. General powers exercisable by the tribunal.
39. Power to make provisional awards.
40. General duty of parties.
41. Powers of tribunal in case of party's default.

POWERS OF COURT IN RELATION TO ARBITRAL PROCEEDINGS

42. Enforcement of peremptory orders of tribunal.
43. Securing the attendance of witnesses.
44. Court powers exercisable in support of arbitral proceedings.
45. Determination of preliminary point of law.

THE AWARD

46. Rules applicable to substance of dispute.
47. Awards on different issues.
48. Remedies.
49. Interest.
50. Extension of time for making award.
51. Settlement.
52. Form of award.
53. Place where award treated as made.
54. Date of award.
55. Notification of award.
56. Power to withhold award in case of non-payment.
57. Correction of award or additional award.
58. Effect of award.

COSTS OF THE ARBITRATION

59. Costs of the arbitration.
60. Agreement to pay costs in any event.
61. Award of costs.
62. Effect of agreement or award about costs.
63. The recoverable costs of the arbitration.
64. Recoverable fees and expenses of arbitrators.
65. Power to limit recoverable costs.

POWERS OF THE COURT IN RELATION TO AWARD

66. Enforcement of the award.
67. Challenging the award: substantive jurisdiction.
68. Challenging the award: serious irregularity.
69. Appeal on point of law.
70. Challenge or appeal: supplementary provisions.
71. Challenge or appeal: effect of order of court.

PART I ARBITRATION PURSUANT TO AN ARBITRATION AGREEMENT

Introductory

General principles

1. The provisions of this Part are founded on the following principles, and shall be construed accordingly—

(a) the object of arbitration is to obtain the fair resolution of disputes by an impartial tribunal without unnecessary delay or expense;
(b) the parties should be free to agree how their disputes are resolved, subject only to such safeguards as are necessary in the public interest; and
(c) in matters governed by this Part the court should not intervene except as provided by this Part.

NOTES

This section lays down the general principles upon which the Act is based. Its provisions had no previous precedent in statutory arbitration law. It is made clear by the closing words of the first paragraph, and, indeed, by the DAC's Report, paragraphs 18 to 22, that, in the case of any ambiguity in the Act, the three stated principles are to have overriding effect. The Act does not seek to define arbitration as such, but rather defines its most important features. Principle (a) has specific significance, as it forms part of the general duty of the arbitrators in their handling of the arbitration (section 33(1)(b)). It was commented by Lord Lester during the Second Reading of the Bill in the House of Lords that the word "impartial" did not necessarily imply "independent", and that in the case of statutory arbitrations—governed by Part II of the Act—where arbitration is compulsory rather than purely consensual, the absence of an independent arbitrator and a public hearing might be contrary to the guarantee of judicial independence in Article 6 of the European Convention on Human Rights even though the Act goes to great lengths to secure impartiality. Lord Lester pressed the point further by the introduction of an amendment to section 97 on statutory arbitrations, requiring the independence of arbitrators. The Government's response to this point was that the DAC had itself concluded that impartiality ought to be enough, as in certain areas of arbitration—particularly where expert arbitrators are required—it might be difficult to find qualified arbitrators who are wholly uninterested in the issue, and accordingly that it should be enough that they act impartially. The point is developed further in the comments on section 24(1)(a) of the Act (removal of an arbitrator for want of impartiality).

The specific problem of compulsory statutory arbitrations and Article 6 of the European Convention on Human Rights[1] is to be addressed on a case-by-case basis, by means of statutory instruments made under section 97, as is explained in the notes to sections 97 and 98 below. To date no statutory instruments have been introduced. Nevertheless, the relationship between Article 6 and arbitration has been given detailed consideration by the courts and the following propositions may be put forward: (i) an arbitration agreement contained in standard rules does not infringe Article 6, as the agreement[2] constitutes a waiver of the right to a public hearing[3] by a judge[4] and the parties are in any event protected by rights of appeal; (ii) an order for security for costs may in principle infringe Article 6 if it has the effect of preventing the claimant from pursuing his claim;[5] (iii) arbitration clauses may be incorporated from one document or contract into another without infringement of Article 6;[6] (iv) an oral hearing in the arbitration is not always necessary as long as the procedure adopted is otherwise fair;[7] (v) limited reasons are necessary for any refusal by the court to give permission to appeal against an award on the basis of error of law,[8] although the right to appeal may be legitimately waived by agreement;[9] and (vi) the prohibition on the giving of permission to appeal by the Court of Appeal is consistent with Article 6 as long as the Court of Appeal can intervene where the judge failed to reach any valid decision on whether permission to appeal should be granted.[10]

Principle (b) was stated in the DAC 1996 Report (paragraph 19) as encompassing two distinct limbs: the parties should be held to their agreement; and the parties should be free to agree how their disputes are to be resolved. As will be seen in later discussion of the Act, the second limb of principle as so formulated is a little misleading, as autonomy over the procedure will generally vest in the arbitrators rather than the parties. Moreover, there are particular matters over which the provisions of the Act are paramount and override the intentions of the parties. In particular, the mandatory provisions of section 33—which require the arbitrators to conduct the proceedings in accordance with the rules of natural justice and in a manner proportional to the dispute—operate as an implied limit on principle (b), as it is thought that an arbitration which does not comply with these minimum requirements can scarcely be described as such.[11]

Principle (c) reflects a general desire to minimise judicial intervention in the running of arbitrations where the parties or the arbitrators can resolve issues for themselves, in the interests of speed, finality and reduced costs, and replicates the principle underlying Article 5 of the Model Law. The provision builds upon the process commenced in the Arbitration Act 1979 limiting rights of appeal against arbitration awards. It is also in one respect a restatement of the law under the 1950 Act, as

1. Now incorporated into English law by the Human Rights Act 1998.

2. As long as the agreement is legitimate and not induced by duress, misrepresentation or mistake: this reservation was recognised in *Stretford* v. *Football Association* [2007] 2 Lloyd's Rep 31.

3. *Department of Economics Policy and Development and Policy of the City of Moscow* v. *Bankers Trust Co* [2004] 2 Lloyd's Rep 179.

4. *Stretford* v. *Football Association* [2007] 2 Lloyd's Rep 31; *Shuttari* v. *Solicitors Indemnity Fund* [2007] EWCA Civ 244; *Entico Corporation Ltd* v. *United Nations Educational Scientific and Cultural Association* [2008] 1 Lloyd's Rep 673; *El Nasharty* v. *J Sainsbury plc (No 2)* [2008] 1 Lloyd's Rep 360.

5. *Nasser* v. *United Bank of Kuwait* [2002] 1 All ER 401; *El Nasharty* v. *J Sainsbury plc (No 2)* [2008] 1 Lloyd's Rep 360.

6. *Welex AG* v. *Rosa Maritime Ltd* [2002] 2 Lloyd's Rep 701.

7. *North Range Shipping Ltd* v. *Seatrans Shipping Corporation* [2002] 2 Lloyd's Rep 1; *BLCT (13096) Ltd* v. *J Sainsbury plc* [2004] 2 P & CR 32.

8. *North Range Shipping Ltd* v. *Seatrans Shipping Corporation* [2002] 2 Lloyd's Rep 1.

9. *Sumukan* v. *Commonwealth Secretariat* [2007] 2 Lloyd's Rep 87.

10. *North Range Shipping Ltd* v. *Seatrans Shipping Corporation* [2002] 2 Lloyd's Rep 1; *CGU International Insurance plc* v. *AstraZeneca Insurance Co Ltd* [2007] 1 Lloyd's Rep 142; *Republic of Kazakhstan* v. *Istil Group Ltd* [2007] 2 Lloyd's Rep 548 (CA).

11. *Cf.* the DAC Report, para. 155.

laid down by the House of Lords' decision in *Bremer Vulkan Schiffbau und Maschinenfabrik* v. *South India Shipping Corporation*,[1] to the effect that the courts have no residual jurisdiction over arbitrations other than that laid down in the legislation, but goes further than the position established under the 1950 Act which, by section 22, gave a blanket power to the courts to remit an award for procedural mishap, a power which was by implication repealed in 1996.[2] Doubts were expressed by Lord Wilberforce on Second Reading that the Act perhaps did not go quite as far as it might in restricting the role of the courts, but the general view expressed in the debates was that the Act retains for the courts the essential minimum of assistance to and supervision of arbitrations. For the most part decisions under the 1996 Act are consistent with this broad objective. The House of Lords has affirmed the principle of non-intervention whenever the legislation has come before it, most importantly in *Premium Nafta Products Ltd* v. *Fili Shipping Ltd*,[3] where it was confirmed that the interpretation of the scope of arbitration clauses should be generous and not hampered by fine linguistic distinctions, and in *Lesotho Highlands Development Authority* v. *Impregilo SpA*,[4] where the ambit of the appeal provisions in sections 68 and 69 was restated in narrow terms.

The concluding words of principle (c) restrict non-intervention to matters governed by Part I of the 1996 Act. This leaves open the possibility that matters not governed by Part I remain subject to some form of residual judicial intervention so that, for example, supportive powers not conferred on the courts by Part I but nevertheless open to the courts in ordinary proceedings may be exercised. This suggestion is contrary to the spirit of the legislation, and even if correct is to be exercised in exceptional circumstances only.[5] It was accordingly held by Thomas LJ in *Emmott* v. *Michael Wilson & Partners Ltd*[6] that a dispute as to the duty of confidentiality attaching to documents generated in the arbitration which one party wishes to use in judicial proceedings should be resolved by the arbitrators (assuming the arbitration is still ongoing) and not by the courts.

One matter which has given rise to particular difficulty is whether the English courts can intervene to grant an "anti-arbitration" injunction, restraining a person from pursuing arbitration proceedings or even restraining an arbitrator from acting in such proceedings. If such a power does exist, it would appear to arise under the general power of the court to grant injunctive relief in section 37 of the Supreme Court Act 1981 rather than under the Arbitration Act 1996 itself.[7] If the arbitration has its seat in England or Wales and is governed by the 1996 Act, then section 1(c) and the mechanisms in the Act itself for determining jurisdictional disputes[8] may well preclude an injunction absolutely or at the very least in all but the most exceptional of cases,[9] for example, where there is some sort of fraudulent or unconscionable conduct on the part of the person initiating or pursuing the arbitration.[10] If the arbitration has its seat outside England and Wales then, assuming that the court has jurisdiction over the party in question or the arbitrator, as the case may be, the power is again to be exercised in exceptional circumstances only, given that the arbitrator is almost certain to have the power under the relevant curial law to determine his own jurisdiction and there is unlikely to be

1. [1981] 1 All ER 289 at 324.

2. See *Bandwidth Shipping Corporation* v. *Intaari* [2008] 1 Lloyd's Rep 7, which confirms that the old supervisory jurisdiction has not survived the 1996 Act.

3. [2008] 1 Lloyd's Rep 254. See also: *Wedlake Bell* v. *Jones* [2007] EWHC 1143 (Ch); *Steamship Mutual Underwriting Association (Bermuda) Ltd* v. *Sulpicio Lines Inc* [2008] EWHC 914 (Comm); *Greene Wood & McClean* v. *Templeton Insurance Ltd* [2008] EWHC 1593 (Comm).

4. [2005] 2 Lloyd's Rep 310.

5. *Vale do Rio Doce Navagaçao SA* v. *Shanghai Bao Steel Ocean Shipping Co Ltd and Sea Partners Ltd* [2000] 2 Lloyd's Rep 1; *Hiscox Underwriting Ltd* v. *Dickson Manchester & Co Ltd* [2004] 2 Lloyd's Rep 438.

6. [2008] 1 Lloyd's Rep 616.

7. So that it is not an arbitration claim within CPR Part 62: *Albon* v. *Naza Motor Trading SDN BHD (No 4)* [2007] 2 Lloyd's Rep 420, affirmed on other grounds [2008] 1 Lloyd's Rep 1.

8. See ss. 30–32, 67 and 72, below.

9. *Electrim SA* v. *Vivendi Universal SA (No 2)* [2007] 2 Lloyd's Rep 8. See also *ASM Shipping Ltd of India* v. *TTMI Ltd (No 2)* [2007] 2 Lloyd's Rep 155.

10. *Republic of Kazakhstan* v. *Istil Group Inc (No 2)* [2008] 1 Lloyd's Rep 382. See also *J Jarvis & Sons Ltd* v. *Blue Circle Dartford Estates Ltd* [2007] EWHC 1262 (TCC).

any justification for intervention by the English courts[1] in the absence of fraudulent or unconscionable conduct.[2]

It was suggested by Lord Roskill on Second Reading that a fourth general principle should be inserted, namely, that arbitrations, documents used in them and any resulting awards are private and confidential.[3] This matter had been considered by the DAC in its 1996 Report, and its proposed solution was an amendment to what subsequently became section 81(2) of the Act, creating an express saving for the common law rules on privacy and confidentiality. This approach, which was ultimately not adopted by the Government, rather begs the question of exactly what those rules might be. The principles of privacy and confidentiality, long assumed but until recently not the subject of detailed authority, was established in a series of cases decided shortly before the introduction of the Bill, in particular *Dolling-Baker* v. *Merrett*,[4] *Hassneh Insurance* v. *Mew*,[5] *Insurance Company* v. *Lloyd's Syndicate*[6] and *London and Leeds Estates Ltd* v. *Paribas Ltd (No 2)*.[7] In those cases, it was made clear that confidentiality, which operated as an implied term in the arbitration agreement, could be lifted in exceptional circumstances only, in particular in the interests of justice being done in subsequent proceedings involving a party to the arbitration. The DAC did not see any need to take up Lord Roskill's suggestion to codify those principles, despite the fact that in Australia a rather different view has been taken of this issue and confidentiality there has to some extent been eroded.[8] The DAC was concerned particularly with two issues: the fact that arbitral confidentiality is part of a wider concept of the protection of confidential information which it would be difficult to deal with in the abstract; and the difficulty of setting out effective sanctions for breach of the parties' obligation of non-disclosure. The Government agreed with the DAC's view, and itself pointed out that there were exceptions to confidentiality in the case of New York Convention awards, which are enforceable in public proceedings, and, as is shown in the cases, in the common law itself: the Government's view was, therefore, that the matter should be resolved by the courts in the usual developmental fashion. Since the passing of the Act, the courts have considered the principles applicable to confidentiality on a number of occasions and have confirmed that the principle applies to documents generated for the purposes of the arbitration, evidence in the arbitration and the award itself. In the leading authority, the Court of Appeal in *Emmott* v. *Michael Wilson & Partners Ltd*,[9] Lawrence Collins LJ identified the various situations in which the issue might arise:

(1) where a party to litigation sought disclosure of documents generated in an arbitration;[10]
(2) where a party to an arbitration sought a witness summons from the court to obtain material used in another arbitration;[11]
(3) where the issue was whether court documents relating to an arbitration should be published;[12] and

1. *Weissfisch* v. *Julius* [2006] 1 Lloyd's Rep 716. In *Intermet FZCO* v. *Ansol Ltd* [2007] EWHC 266 (Comm) injunctive relief was refused, but on the traditional grounds that there was no vexatious conduct and there had been significant delay in making the application.
2. See: *Albon* v. *Naza Motor Trading SDN BHD (No 4)* [2008] 1 Lloyd's Rep 1.
3. These two terms are in principle distinct: privacy relates to personal information whereas confidentiality relates to business information. To some extent, however, the terms overlap.
4. [1991] 2 All ER 891.
5. [1993] 2 Lloyd's Rep 243.
6. [1995] 2 Lloyd's Rep 272.
7. [1995] 2 EG 134.
8. *Esso Australia Resources Ltd* v. *Minister for Energy and Minerals* [1994] ADRLJ 214: *Commonwealth of Australia* v. *Cockatoo Dockyard Pty Ltd* (1995) 36 NSWLR 662.
9. [2008] 1 Lloyd's Rep 616.
10. *Science Research Council* v. *Nassé* [1980] AC 1028; *Dolling-Baker* v. *Merrett* [1990] 1 WLR 1205.
11. *London and Leeds Estates Ltd* v. *Paribas Ltd (No 2)* [1995] 1 EGLR 102; *South Tyneside Borough Council* v. *Wickes Building Suppliers Ltd* [2004] EWHC 2428 (Comm).
12. *Glidepath BV* v. *Thompson* [2005] 2 Lloyd's Rep 549; *Department of Economic Policy and Development of the City of Moscow* v. *Bankers Trust Co* [2004] 2 Lloyd's Rep 179.

(4) where a party to an arbitration had an interest (commercial or otherwise) in disclosing documents generated in an arbitration (including the award itself) to third parties, for example, in a reinsurance case,[1] or where the documents are relevant to some other arbitration.[2]

Ali Shipping Corporation v. *Shipyard Trogir*[3] and *Emmott* have confirmed that the duty of confidentiality in relation to arbitration awards and documents used in arbitrations takes effect as a term implied in arbitration agreements as a matter of law and not on the basis of the presumed intention of the parties, although it is subject to exceptions. The implied term precludes the parties from using or disclosing for any other purpose documents prepared for or disclosed in the arbitration, including evidence or the award. That classification is important, because if the question of the scope of the duty arises while the arbitration is still in existence, the arbitrators alone have jurisdiction to resolve that question[4]: the court can become involved only if the arbitration has come to an end and one or other of the parties wishes to use the documents for his own purposes.

The duty is subject to limited exceptions:

(a) the parties may waive the implied term, as where one party refers to arbitral documents in later proceedings and the other then seeks disclosure of those documents: this was the position in *Emmott* itself. There may also be consent implied from the circumstances;[5]
(b) legal compulsion, where the court orders the production of arbitration documents for use in later proceedings,[6] for example, an appeal[7] or where there is a subsequent dispute between the parties involving the same facts;[8]
(c) where there is a duty to the public requiring disclosure;[9] and
(d) where disclosure is reasonably necessary for the protection of an arbitrating party's rights as against a third party.[10]

Scope of application of provisions

2.—(1) The provisions of this Part apply where the seat of the arbitration is in England and Wales or Northern Ireland.

1. *Hassneh Insurance Co of Israel* v. *Mew* [1993] 2 Lloyd's Rep 243; *Insurance Co* v. *Lloyd's Syndicate* [1995] 1 Lloyd's Rep 272.
2. *Hassneh Insurance Co of Israel* v. *Mew* [1993] 2 Lloyd's Rep 243; *Insurance Co* v. *Lloyd's Syndicate* [1995] 1 Lloyd's Rep 272.
3. [1998] 2 Lloyd's Rep 643.
4. The view of Thomas LJ in *Emmott* v. *Michael Wilson & Partners Ltd* [2008] 1 Lloyd's Rep 616.
5. See on this point *The Owners, Masters and Crew of the Tug "Hamtun"* v. *Owners of the ship "St John"* [1999] 1 Lloyd's Rep 883, in which Aikens J held that it was customary in the salvage market for the level of salvage awarded in an arbitration to be made available to later arbitrators and the courts, in order to achieve a level of consistency. Consent was thus implicit from the custom and practice of the market.
6. *Dolling-Baker* v. *Merrett* [1990] 1 WLR 1205; *London & Leeds Estates* v. *Paribas (No 2)* [1995] 1 EGLR 102; *Ali Shipping Corporation* v. *Shipyard Trogir* [1998] 2 Lloyd's Rep 643; *South Tyneside Borough Council* v. *Wickes Building Suppliers Ltd* [2004] EWHC 2428 (Comm).
7. *Department of Economics Policy and Development of the City of Moscow* v. *Bankers Trust Co* [2004] 2 Lloyd's Rep 179.
8. There is an issue estoppel where an issue arising in a subsequent arbitration formed a key part of the reasoning in the first arbitration: *Associated Electric & Gas Insurance Services Ltd* v. *European Reinsurance Co of Zurich* [2003] 1 All ER (Comm) 253; *Department of Economics Policy and Development of the City of Moscow* v. *Bankers Trust Co* [2004] 2 Lloyd's Rep 179; *Emcor Drake & Skull Ltd* v. *Costain Construction Ltd and Skanska Central Europe AB* [2004] EWHC 2439 (TCC); *Westland Helicopters Ltd* v. *Sheikh Salah Al-Hejailan* [2004] 2 Lloyd's Rep 523.
9. *London & Leeds Estates* v. *Paribas (No 2)* [1995] 1 EGLR 102. This ground is to be understood as applying only where the interests of justice so require: *Ali Shipping Corporation* v. *Shipyard Trogir* [1998] 2 Lloyd's Rep 643.
10. *Hassneh Insurance Co of Israel* v. *Mew* [1993] 2 Lloyd's Rep 243; *Emmott* v. *Michael Wilson & Partners Ltd* [2008] 1 Lloyd's Rep 616.

(2) The following sections apply even if the seat of the arbitration is outside England and Wales or Northern Ireland or no seat has been designated or determined:

(a) sections 9 to 11 (stay of legal proceedings), and
(b) section 66 (enforcement of arbitral awards).

(3) The powers conferred by the following sections apply even if the seat of the arbitration is outside England and Wales or Northern Ireland or no seat has been designated or determined:

(a) section 43 (securing the attendance of witnesses), and
(b) section 44 (court powers exercisable in support of arbitral proceedings);

but the court may refuse to exercise any such power if, in the opinion of the court, the fact that the seat of the arbitration is outside England and Wales or Northern Ireland, or that when designated or determined the seat is likely to be outside England and Wales or Northern Ireland, makes it inappropriate to do so.

(4) The court may exercise a power conferred by any provision of this Part not mentioned in subsection (2) or (3) for the purpose of supporting the arbitral process where—

(a) no seat of the arbitration has been designated or determined, and
(b) by reason of a connection with England and Wales or Northern Ireland the court is satisfied that it is appropriate to do so.

(5) Section 7 (separability of arbitration agreement) and section 8 (death of a party) apply where the law applicable to the arbitration agreement is the law of England and Wales or Northern Ireland even if the seat of the arbitration is outside England and Wales or Northern Ireland or has not been designated or determined.

NOTES

Section 2 defines the scope and application of the legislation. The Arbitration Acts 1950 to 1979 did not define the arbitrations to which their rules applied,[1] the matter being left to common law principles of jurisdiction. The English courts took the view that they could exercise supervisory powers only over those arbitrations subject to English law or with their seat within the jurisdiction. This was made clear by the House of Lords in *Channel Tunnel Group Ltd* v. *Balfour Beatty Construction Ltd*,[2] where their Lordships refused to grant an injunction to support an arbitration governed by ICC Rules and to be held in Belgium. Their Lordships ruled that the High Court had no jurisdiction to interfere with an arbitration held abroad and not governed by English law, as this would be to confer extraterritorial effect on English arbitration legislation. In determining jurisdiction, the courts developed the concept of the "seat" of an arbitration, the seat being regarded as the place in which the arbitration was actually based. This concept recognised that arbitrations, particularly international arbitrations, take place in a number of different jurisdictions, for the convenience of the arbitrators or witnesses or to facilitate inspection of any property forming part of the dispute. Consequently, an arbitration which had its seat in England was recognised as being within the English legislation even though various parts of the arbitration were conducted abroad.[3]

1. Other than as regards the enforcement of arbitration awards, as all awards wherever made are in principle enforceable in England.
2. [1993] AC 334.
3. *James Miller Partners Ltd* v. *Whitworth Street Estates (Manchester) Ltd* [1970] AC 583; *Naviera Amazonica Peruana SA* v. *Compania Internacional de Seguros del Peru* [1988] 1 Lloyd's Rep 116; *Union of India* v. *McDonnell Douglas* [1993] 2 Lloyd's Rep 48; *Sumitomo Heavy Industries* v. *Oil and Natural Gas Commission* [1994] 1 Lloyd's Rep 45; *Bay Hotel and Resort Ltd* v. *Cavalier Construction Co Ltd* [2001] UKPC 34.

An arbitration which did not have a seat, but which "floated", was generally regarded as invalid by the English courts at least for the purpose of the provision of curial support, although the arbitration would be saved if it was conducted under the rules of a recognised arbitral authority such as the ICC or UNCITRAL and the English courts accepted jurisdiction to award security for costs in exceptional circumstances[1] and to enforce any arbitration award emanating from such proceedings.[2]

The basis on which the Act should apply to arbitration proceedings was subjected to a good deal of thought, and in the event a series of major changes were made at Report Stage in the House of Lords, attempting to clarify the highly complex and almost incomprehensible provisions contained in earlier versions of the Bill.[3] Those complexities were ultimately resolved by the final version of section 2(1).[4] The applicability of the Act is firmly fixed by reference to the seat of the arbitration being in England and Wales or Northern Ireland. It is here to be emphasised that the seat of the arbitration is not necessarily the same place as that in which some or all of the arbitration is physically conducted: the seat is a juridical concept. This approach confirms the view expressed in the DAC Report (paragraph 23) that it would be wrong in principle for the Act to apply merely because the arbitration is physically located in England. All of Part I of the Act is applicable where the seat is domestic in this sense, irrespective of the law applicable to the arbitration agreement and of the place where the arbitration is physically conducted, although the parties are free to contract out of those provisions of Part I of the Act which are non-mandatory either directly or, in accordance with section 4(5), indirectly by choosing rules of some other law in their stead. The seat of an arbitration is to be determined in accordance with section 3. It will be appreciated that section 2 operates on the basis that there is a seat: a "floating" or "delocalised" arbitration without a seat was not recognised by English law prior to the Act, and this remains the case: this point is explained in the Notes to section 3 of the Act.

The remainder of section 2 lays down exceptional cases, where the Act applies to an arbitration even though its seat is outside England and Wales or Northern Ireland. In other cases the English court cannot intervene.[5]

Section 2(2) states that certain aspects of the Act apply where the seat of the arbitration is outside the jurisdiction or if the seat has yet to be determined, and (by implication) whether or not the law governing the procedure is English law. Consequently, if the seat is abroad, the English courts must:

(a) grant a mandatory stay of their proceedings where the matter is governed by a valid arbitration clause which applies to the case (sections 9 to 11); and
(b) enforce any award made abroad, in accordance with obligations under the New York Convention and general common law principles (section 66).

Both of these obligations are imposed by the New York Convention.[6]

Section 2(3) deals with the case where the assistance of the English court under its powers in sections 43 (securing the attendance of witnesses) and 44 (general powers exercisable in support of arbitral proceedings) is required to ensure the proper functioning of, or to protect, the arbitration.

Section 43, as applied by section 2(3)(a), entitles the court to provide assistance for securing the attendance of a witness, provided that the witness is in the United Kingdom and the arbitral proceedings are being conducted in England and Wales or Northern Ireland. What is thus contemplated is an arbitration which may have its seat elsewhere, but whose proceedings (i.e., hearings) are conducted within the jurisdiction. It is unclear whether the mere transitory holding of a hearing within the jurisdiction, aimed purely at enlisting the court's power under section 43 as regards a person within the UK, is enough to bring section 43 into play. It might be thought that the most

1. *Bank Mellat* v. *Helliniki Techniki SA* [1984] 1 QB 291; *Coppee-Lavalin SA/NV* v. *Ken-Ren Chemicals and Fertilizers Ltd* [1994] 2 Lloyd's Rep 109.

2. *Dallal* v. *Bank Mellat* [1986] 1 All ER 239.

3. The earlier drafts are discussed in previous editions of this work. That discussion is no longer necessary here.

4. See the discussion in the DAC Supplementary Report, paras 6–10.

5. *Weissfisch* v. *Julius* [2006] 1 Lloyd's Rep 716; *C* v. *D* [2008] 1 Lloyd's Rep 239. It was this consideration which influenced the court in *Braes of Doune Wind Farm (Scotland) Ltd* v. *Alfred McAlpine Business Services Ltd* [2008] 1 Lloyd's Rep 608 to refuse to find that the parties had agreed that the seat and the curial law should be different.

6. DAC Supplementary Report, para. 14.

sensible approach would be to treat this question not as one of jurisdiction under section 43, but rather one of judicial discretion under the proviso to section 2(3).

In the light of the proviso to section 2(3), the exercise of jurisdiction under section 44 is most likely to be used in the situation in which the seat of the arbitration is within the jurisdiction, since in other cases there is likely to be less justification for the English courts to become involved.[1] As was pointed out in the DAC Supplementary Report (paragraph 15), there may be situations in which it would be quite wrong for an English court to intervene, in particular where this would produce a conflict with the courts of some other jurisdiction. Section 2(3) to this extent appears to codify *Channel Tunnel*. One, and perhaps the most, important effect of this provision is to provide access to the English courts for the parties to overseas arbitrations as regards freezing injunctions or search orders in order to act against assets within the jurisdiction. This had been recommended by the DAC, in paragraph 25 of its Report, which also noted that it was necessary for an amendment to be made to the Rules of Court to ensure that permission for service of a claim form abroad can be given by the High Court where the purpose of the English action is to obtain interim relief in support of a foreign arbitration. That modification was made by the revised version of RSC Ord. 73 effective from January 1997, subsequently replaced by CPR r. 62.5. Under CPR r. 62.5, the court may give permission for an arbitration claim form to be served outside the jurisdiction where an interim remedy is sought from the English courts in respect of an arbitration with its seat outside the jurisdiction, whether or not any other remedy is sought from the English courts.[2]

The obvious conclusion to be drawn from section 2(3)(b) is that the parties should not agree that the seat is to be in one jurisdiction and the law governing the procedure is to be that of another jurisdiction.[3] Put another way:[4]

(a) where the seat is in England and the procedural law are English law, the Act applies in its entirety;[5]

(b) where the seat is England, the Act applies irrespective of the chosen or applicable procedural or curial law by virtue of section 2(1), and the court must apply the mandatory parts of the Act listed in Schedule 1 to the Act—as regards the non-mandatory aspects of the Act, under section 4(5) any express or implied choice of another law operates to oust the Act insofar as that choice applies to those non-mandatory aspects.[6] In the absence of such a choice, the fact that some other law is found to be applicable will not have the effect of disapplying the non-mandatory aspects of the Act;

(c) where (which is rare) the seat is abroad but the procedural or curial law is English law (by express choice—English law would almost certainly refuse to make such an implication), the procedures in section 44 of the Act are available (so that, for example, interim relief can be granted in respect of a foreign arbitration) but the English courts can refuse to act by virtue of the proviso to section 2(3) if the necessary link with the domestic jurisdiction is missing;

1. *Mobil Cerro Negro Ltd* v. *Petroleos de Venezuela SA* [2008] 1 Lloyd's Rep 684.

2. It is not clear whether permission is required to serve the arbitration claim form out of the jurisdiction on defendants situated in a Brussels Regulation or Lugano Convention country, since ordinarily no such permission is required under CPR r. 6.19. It is presumed that permission under CPR r. 62.5 is required only in cases where CPR r. 6.19 does not apply, i.e. where CPR r. 6.20 would otherwise apply. Since arbitration is excluded from the scope of the Brussels Regulation and Lugano Convention, it is uncertain whether a purely arbitration related court application falls within CPR r. 6.19. In case there is any doubt, an application for permission ought to be applied for out of an abundance of caution. In such cases, care should be taken to extend the time for service of the claim form. An application to this effect may be included in the application for permission for service out.

3. *Braes of Doune Wind Farm (Scotland) Ltd* v. *Alfred McAlpine Business Services Ltd* [2008] 1 Lloyd's Rep 608.

4. The following paragraph was cited with approval by Clarke J in *ABB Lummus Global Ltd* v. *Keppel Fels Ltd* [1999] 2 Lloyd's Rep 24.

5. This means that neither party can have resort to the courts of any other jurisdiction to challenge the award, so that if the seat and the curial law are both provided by England, there cannot be an application to the courts of New York to challenge the award on the basis that the substantive contract was governed by New York law and that the arbitrators had erred: *C* v. *D* [2008] 1 Lloyd's Rep 239, which also holds that such an application can be restrained by anti-suit injunction. See also *A* v. *B* [2007] 1 Lloyd's Rep 237 and *A* v. *B (No 2)* [2007] 1 Lloyd's Rep 358.

6. See *Dubai Islamic Bank PJSC* v. *Paymentech Merchant Services Inc* [2001] 1 Lloyd's Rep 65.

(d) where both the seat of the arbitration and the procedural or curial law are those of a foreign jurisdiction, there is on the whole no basis upon which the Act can apply other than in respect of stay and enforcement, in accordance with section 2(2), although in appropriate circumstances it will be possible to obtain protective interim relief from the English courts in respect of the foreign arbitration.[1]

Section 2(4) allows the court to apply any of the provisions of Part I of the Act where there has been no choice or determination of seat, provided that it is appropriate for the court to exercise jurisdiction, which will normally mean some connection with England and Wales or Northern Ireland. This situation will arise in particular where the parties have delegated the choice of seat either to the arbitrators or to an arbitral institution (e.g., the ICC or the LCIA) and they have not at the time of the application had the opportunity to consider the matter. It once again follows that a choice of English procedural law to govern the arbitration proceedings would on its face merit judicial application of the Act in such circumstances, particularly as in such a case the seat—once designated by the arbitrators—is likely to be England.[2] An example given by Lord Fraser, speaking for the Government in the Report Stage in the House of Lords, was the use of section 12 to extend time for the commencement of arbitration proceedings in a case where the arbitration had at that point no ascertained seat. As was pointed out in the Report Stage in the House of Lords, there is little objection to the English courts applying the Act in this situation, as there is likely not to be any other jurisdiction with which English orders might produce a conflict,[3] and indeed Lord Fraser commented that it might be appropriate to use section 2(4) only where there is no procedural law which might apply to the arbitration.

Section 2(5) states that the English courts may apply section 7 (separability of arbitration agreement) or section 8 (death of a party) where the law applicable to the arbitration agreement is that of England and Wales or Northern Ireland, and the seat is abroad or has not been designated. The effect of these provisions is considered in the notes to sections 7 and 8. In the absence of this provision, it would have been necessary to revert to the common law on separability or death to determine the validity of the arbitration agreement, a result which the DAC in its Supplementary Report described as "absurd" (paragraph 19).

The seat of the arbitration

3. In this Part "the seat of the arbitration" means the juridical seat of the arbitration designated—

(a) by the parties to the arbitration agreement, or
(b) by any arbitral or other institution or person vested by the parties with powers in that regard, or
(c) by the arbitral tribunal if so authorised by the parties,

or determined, in the absence of any such designation, having regard to the parties' agreement and all the relevant circumstances.

NOTES

The seat of the arbitration is significant for a number of reasons:

(a) if the seat is in England, the Act applies to the arbitration (section 2);
(b) the seat may determine whether or not any award is enforceable under the New York Convention (e.g., under the basis of the reciprocity reservation under Article I.3); and
(c) an award is deemed to be made in the place of the seat of the arbitration (sections 53 and 100(2)(b)) and if the award is made in England, it is subject to English review powers,

1. An application under s. 44 of the 1996 Act for an order for examination of witnesses in England in support of an arbitration was refused in *Commerce and Industry Insurance Co of Canada* v. *Lloyd's Underwriters* [2002] 1 Lloyd's Rep 219, on the basis that the purpose of the application was not merely to provide evidence but rather to operate as a fishing expedition.
2. DAC Supplementary Report, para. 16.
3. *Cf.* the DAC Supplementary Report, para. 17.

whereas if it is an award made outside England, it will be entitled to enforcement in England as a foreign award in accordance with either section 66 or (if a New York Convention award) section 101 of the Act.

As noted above, the concept of the seat of an arbitration had been recognised by the English courts before 1996. The "juridical" seat of the arbitration is defined by section 3 as the seat or place expressly or impliedly designated as such: the seat may be identified by express agreement, impliedly by choice of English law or procedure for the arbitration, by the arbitrators themselves or by an arbitral institution (if applicable) under powers delegated by the parties, or, in default of all of the above, by implication from the surrounding circumstances. The seat provides the focus for the arbitration, but it is not necessary for the entire proceedings to be conducted in a particular place for that place to be regarded as the seat.[1] Indeed, the Act assumes that there is no necessary connection between the seat and the location of the proceedings from time to time, as sections 2(3)(a) and 43 permit the court to secure the attendance before the arbitrators of a witness who is in the United Kingdom provided that the proceedings are being conducted in England and Wales or Northern Ireland, even though the seat of the arbitration is elsewhere.

In many cases the seat will be the subject of express agreement, as contemplated by section 3(a), or designated by the relevant arbitral institution under section 3(b) or, if the power is delegated to them, by the arbitrators under section 3(c). An express choice of seat will generally be taken to mean what it says, although if the parties have chosen English law to govern the procedure of the arbitration and they have also chosen some other country as the seat of the arbitration, the outcome could be that neither jurisdiction has effective control over the arbitration—in that scenario the 1996 Act would have no application at all. This occurred in *Braes of Doune Wind Farm (Scotland) Ltd* v. *Alfred McAlpine Business Services Ltd*,[2] in which Scotland was nominated as the seat but English law governed the procedure, and the court's view was that the agreement was intelligible only if the word "seat" was to be taken as referring to the physical location of the arbitration and not its juridical seat, the outcome being that the seat of the arbitration was England.

A theoretical difficulty arises under section 3(c) if one party contests the validity of the arbitration agreement, although it has been held that the agreement and the arbitrator's designation of the seat are to be presumed to be valid for the purpose of determining the seat of the arbitration.[3] The seat is usually, though not always, defined in terms of a city (e.g., London) rather than a country.

If there is no express agreement as to the seat, and if neither the arbitral institution nor the arbitrators have been given the power to determine the seat, then (despite the absence of any such express reference) the court may itself ascertain the seat by reference to the parties' agreement and to all other relevant circumstances. This general statement in effect means that common law rules continue to apply to the determination of the issue. Under those rules, there is a presumption that the seat follows any express choice of procedural law,[4] and, indeed, the converse proposition—that any express choice of seat will dictate the applicable procedural law—is also valid. In *ABB Lummus Global Ltd* v. *Keppel Fels Ltd*[5] Clarke J accepted the close link between the seat and the curial law, and held that only in exceptional cases was it appropriate for the two to be regarded as different, so that an agreement to arbitrate in London was all but conclusive that the seat of the arbitration was England. Other relevant considerations in the determination of the seat include: the nationality of the parties; the location of the dispute; the procedures adopted in the arbitration; and (for those arbitrations which have been concluded) the place where the award was issued.[6]

1. *James Miller Partners Ltd* v. *Whitworth Street Estates (Manchester) Ltd* [1970] AC 583; DAC Report, para. 26.
2. [2008] 1 Lloyd's Rep 608.
3. *Arab National Bank* v. *El Sharif Saoud Bin Masoud Bin Haza'a El-Abdali* [2004] EWHC 2381 (Comm); *C* v. *D* [2008] 1 Lloyd's Rep 239.
4. *Naviera Amazonica Peruana SA* v. *Compania Internacional de Seguros del Peru* [1988] 1 Lloyd's Rep 116.
5. [1999] 2 Lloyd's Rep 24. See also *Braes of Doune Wind Farm (Scotland) Ltd* v. *Alfred McAlpine Business Services Ltd* [2008] 1 Lloyd's Rep 608.
6. *Dubai Islamic Bank PJSC* v. *Paymentech Merchant Services Inc* [2001] 1 Lloyd's Rep 65; *Arab National Bank* v. *El Sharif Saoud Bin Masoud Bin Haza'a El-Abdali* [2004] EWHC 2381 (Comm); *Halpern* v. *Halpern* [2006] 2 Lloyd's Rep 83, affirmed [2007] 2 Lloyd's Rep 56.

In the event of a dispute as to the seat of the arbitration, the English court will assert jurisdiction over the question where the dispute has its closest connection with England.[1]

Prior to the 1996 Act the English courts refused to recognise an arbitration which did not have a seat but which was regarded as "floating" or "delocalised",[2] and this position is unaffected by the 1996 Act.[3] Under the 1996 Act the recognition of delocalised arbitration is confined to the situation in which the seat has not been ascertained at the time when the application for assistance is made to the English court, in accordance with section 2(4) above.[4] In practice entirely delocalised arbitrations are rare, as any arbitration which is governed by the rules of an arbitral body will be recognised as taking place under those rules and support may be granted accordingly.[5]

Mandatory and non-mandatory provisions

4.—(1) The mandatory provisions of this Part are listed in Schedule 1 and have effect notwithstanding any agreement to the contrary.

(2) The other provisions of this Part (the "non-mandatory provisions") allow the parties to make their own arrangements by agreement but provide rules which apply in the absence of such agreement.

(3) The parties may make such arrangements by agreeing to the application of institutional rules or providing any other means by which a matter may be decided.

(4) It is immaterial whether or not the law applicable to the parties' agreement is the law of England and Wales or, as the case may be, Northern Ireland.

(5) The choice of a law other than the law of England and Wales or Northern Ireland as the applicable law in respect of a matter provided for by a non-mandatory provision of this Part is equivalent to an agreement making provision about that matter.

For this purpose an applicable law determined in accordance with the parties' agreement, or which is objectively determined in the absence of any express or implied choice, shall be treated as chosen by the parties.

NOTES

Section 4, which had no counterpart in earlier legislation, is to be read with Schedule 1. It allows the parties to contract out of the Act only to a limited extent where the Act is otherwise applicable by virtue of the seat of the arbitration being England and Wales or Northern Ireland. The provisions listed in Schedule 1 are in these circumstances mandatory. The DAC Report, paragraph 30, emphasised that the mandatory provisions of the Act are irrelevant where the seat of the arbitration is outside England and Wales or Northern Ireland, even if the parties to the arbitration are UK nationals or UK-domiciled. In other contexts, the word "mandatory" refers to domestic laws which are to be applicable to persons domiciled in the UK in all circumstances (the word being used in that sense in Articles 3 and 7 of the Rome Convention 1980 relating to choice of law). UK legislation which is mandatory in this wider context includes the Unfair Terms in Consumer Contracts

1. *Tonicstar Ltd* v. *American Home Assurance Co* [2005] Lloyd's Rep IR 32.
2. *Bank Mellat* v. *Helliniki Techniki SA* [1984] QB 291; *Coppee-Lavalin SA/NV* v. *Ken-Ren Chemicals and Fertilizers Ltd* [1994] 2 Lloyd's Rep 109.
3. *Dubai Islamic Bank PJSC* v. *Paymentech Merchant Services Inc* [2001] 1 Lloyd's Rep 65; *Halpern* v. *Halpern* [2006] 2 Lloyd's Rep 83, affirmed [2007] 2 Lloyd's Rep 56.
4. DAC Report, para. 27.
5. *Bay Hotel and Resort Ltd* v. *Cavalier Construction Co Ltd* [2001] UKPC 34. The Rules of Arbitration of the LCIA (1998 Rules, Art. 16.1), the ICC (1998 Rules, Art. 14.1) and the AAA (2008 Rules, Art. 13.1) all delegate the determination of the seat (in the absence of agreement between the parties) to the arbitral institution concerned (though under the AAA Rules the determination is subject to the power of the tribunal to determine the seat within 60 days of its constitution). The UNCITRAL Rules of Arbitration (1998) delegate the determination to the arbitral tribunal (Art. 16.1).

Regulations 1999, as extended by Part II of the Arbitration Act 1996 to consumer arbitration agreements.

The mandatory provisions of the 1996 Act apply whatever the parties may have agreed (section 4(1)) whereas the remaining provisions are simply default provisions which may be ousted by agreement (section 4(2)), provided that the agreement is in writing in accordance with section 6.

Section 4(3) makes it clear that the parties are free to adopt the procedural rules laid down by an arbitral or other body. This statement is probably superfluous, but it is nevertheless important in terms of emphasising the principles underlying the Act: a similar provision appeared in the Marriott Bill of 1992, as a response to pressure from those involved in the practice of arbitration.

Under section 4(4), where an arbitration has its seat in England but English law does not govern the proceedings, the earlier part of section 4 is applicable, so that the mandatory provisions of the Act govern the position. As regards non-mandatory aspects of the Act, the choice of another law in respect of any of them operates as an agreement to exclude those parts of the Act.

As explained in the Notes to section 2, there is a strong presumption in favour of the curial law and the seat being the same, but if the parties should happen to agree that the curial law[1] is of some other jurisdiction but that the seat is England, the mandatory parts of the 1996 Act will continue to apply by virtue of section 4(5)[2] whereas the non-mandatory parts are ousted.

Agreements to be in writing

5.—(1) The provisions of this Part apply only where the arbitration agreement is in writing, and any other agreement between the parties as to any matter is effective for the purposes of this Part only if in writing.

The expressions "agreement", "agree" and "agreed" shall be construed accordingly.

(2) There is an agreement in writing—

(a) if the agreement is made in writing (whether or not it is signed by the parties),
(b) the agreement is made by exchange of communications in writing, or
(c) if the agreement is evidenced in writing.

(3) Where parties agree otherwise than in writing by reference to terms which are in writing, they make an agreement in writing.

(4) An agreement is evidenced in writing if an agreement made otherwise than in writing is recorded by one of the parties, or by a third party with the authority of the parties to the agreement.

(5) An exchange of written submissions in arbitral or legal proceedings in which the existence of an agreement otherwise than in writing is alleged by one party against another party and not denied by the other party in his response constitutes as between those parties an agreement in writing to the effect alleged.

(6) References in this Part to anything being written or in writing include its being recorded by any means.

NOTES

Section 5(1), based on the original version of Article 7 of the Model Law, requires an arbitration agreement to be in writing or at least evidenced in writing, and also any other agreement referred

1. The law chosen to be applicable to the substantive contract is irrelevant: *XL Insurance* v. *Owens Corning* [2000] 2 Lloyd's Rep 500; *C* v. *D* [2008] 1 Lloyd's Rep 239.

2. See *ABB Lummus Global Ltd* v. *Keppel Fels Ltd* [1999] 2 Lloyd's Rep 24, in which Clarke J accepted that, had he reached the conclusion that the seat of the arbitration was England but the governing law was Singapore law (in fact he held that the governing law was English law), an application to the court under s. 32 would have remained possible as the section is mandatory.

to by the Act must be in writing or evidenced in writing: the latter miscellaneous class of agreements consists mainly of agreements by the parties to exclude particular aspects of the Act, in accordance with section 4(2), and of agreements determining various procedural aspects of the arbitration. The need for writing in relation to the arbitration agreement as a precondition of the application of Part I of the Act is taken from section 32 of the Arbitration Act 1950. The DAC Report, paragraph 33, indicated that it had considered the suggestion that the writing requirement be abandoned, but rejected this on the basis that the loss of recourse to the courts was too important a right to be lost by oral agreement and that writing would remove any disputes as to exactly what had been agreed between the parties. The Committee also noted that the writing requirement has not in practice given rise to any great difficulty.

The Act does not specify that variations to any agreements must be in writing: by contrast, the July 1995 Bill stated that any variation to the arbitration agreement itself had to be in writing, and while on the face of things it might be assumed that the omission of this provision means that writing is not required for amendments, the DAC's Report, paragraph 35, indicates that variations to an arbitration agreement constitute "any other agreement between the parties" within section 5(1) and are required to be in writing to be enforceable. An agreement to terminate arbitration proceedings apparently need not be in writing (which was the DAC's intention—see paragraph 40 of the Report), and section 23(4), indeed, specifically so assumes, albeit that the point is there made in the limited context of the termination of the arbitrators' authority.

An arbitration agreement which is not in writing is outside the Act, but remains enforceable at common law. There is an express saving for the common law in this regard in section 81.

Section 5(2) of the Act indicates what constitutes writing or evidence in writing for the purposes of the writing requirement in section 5(1). There was no definition in the 1950 Act of what amounted to writing, although section 7 of the Arbitration Act 1975 provided guidance in relation to the form of arbitration agreement required as a condition of enforcement of an award under the New York Convention. That definition, which was not exhaustive, referred to exchanges of letters and telegrams, but is not separately reproduced in the 1996 Act. In the July 1995 Bill an extensive definition of "writing" was provided, referring to any letter, telemessage, telex, fax or any other means of communication providing a record of the agreement. That elaborate definition, derived from Article 7(2) of the Model Law, has been modified by the 1996 Act, and has been replaced by section 5(2)(b), which allows documents exchanged between the parties to be joined in order to establish the existence of an agreement and follows Article II.2 of the New York Convention. The DAC's Report, paragraph 34, makes it clear that the decision to abandon the original definition of writing was intended to widen rather than narrow the concept.[1]

There is no need under section 5(2)(a) of the Act for any agreement, including the arbitration agreement, to be signed by the parties,[2] even though Article 7(2) of the Model Law so requires. Signature does not accord with commercial practice, particularly in the shipping industry. Section 5(2)(c), permitting an agreement to be evidenced in writing, is a safety net provision, and means that an agreement might be found to exist from the sketchiest of documents.[3] These provisions should be read with section 5(6), which states that any form of recording is sufficient to constitute writing or evidence in writing: this is doubtless intended to refer particularly to electronic recording, whether on computer or any other form of electronic or magnetic medium. An email has been held to constitute writing for this purpose.[4]

1. The absence of a full definition of "writing" was noted by HHJ Bowsher QC in *American Design Associates* v. *Donald Install Associates* November 2000, unreported. For the concept of joinder of documents to produce an arbitration agreement, see *Welex AG* v. *Rosa Maritime Ltd* [2003] 2 Lloyd's Rep 509, but contrast: *Cigna Life Insurance Co of Europe NV* v. *Intercaser SA de Seguros y Reaseguros* [2001] Lloyd's Rep IR 821; *Stanstead Shipping Co Ltd* v. *Shenzen Nantian Oil Mills Co Ltd* 2000, unreported; *American International Speciality Lines Insurance Co* v. *Abbott Laboratories* [2004] Lloyd's Rep IR 815.

2. The earlier legislation had been so construed: *Excomm Ltd* v. *Ahmed Abdul-Qawi Bamaodah, The St Raphael* [1985] 1 Lloyd's Rep 403.

3. *Petredec Ltd* v. *Takumaru Kaiun Co, The Sargasso* [1994] 1 Lloyd's Rep 162, *Fahem Co* v. *Mareb Yemen Insurance Co* [1997] 2 Lloyd's Rep 738; *West of England Ship Owners Mutual Protection and Indemnity Association (Luxembourg)* v. *Hellenic Industrial Development Bank SA* [1999] 1 Lloyd's Rep 93.

4. *Bernuth Lines Ltd* v. *High Seas Shipping Ltd, The Eastern Navigator* [2006] 1 Lloyd's Rep 537.

Section 5(3) permits oral agreements insofar as they adopt written arbitration terms, provided, of course, that the existence of such an agreement can be proved.[1] The DAC Report, paragraph 36, expressed the view that many such agreements are entered into, and gives various examples of what might be caught by this provision, including: a salvage agreement based upon Lloyd's Open Form, which contains an arbitration clause; and a contract for the sale of goods which is oral (in that the parties have not formally agreed on fixed terms) but may be assumed to have been made on the standard terms of the buyer by reference to the fact that the seller has performed the contract. In this respect, the Act goes further than Article 7(2) of the Model Law.[2]

Section 5(4) was a provision new to the December 1995 Bill. While its positive purpose (as stated by the DAC in its February 1996 Report, paragraph 37), is to promote some flexibility in ascertaining when an agreement is in writing, it has the negative effect of preventing a written or other recording of a conversation between the parties being treated as an agreement between them where the recording was made without the authority of the parties. It follows that an attendance note made by one party, or by a third party (e.g., a lawyer) cannot be treated as an agreement in its own right unless all parties have agreed that it shall have that status. It would also seem logical that section 5(4) prevents an unauthorised recording being treated as supplementary evidence of the existence of an agreement, although this is far from clear.

Section 5(5) adopts the principle in Article 7(2) of the Model Law that an exchange of statements of claim in arbitration proceedings is sufficient to constitute a written arbitration agreement.[3] It is also the case that the mere fact that submissions are exchanged may of itself create an *ad hoc* arbitration agreement where none previously existed, for example, because the original agreement was invalid or the parties have acted under a mistake as to its scope.[4] The DAC has emphasised in its February 1996 Report, paragraph 38, that it is not enough that one party asserts in his submissions that there is an arbitration agreement and the other party fails to make any response at all:[5] what is required is a response by the other party, but a failure by him in that response to deny the existence of an arbitration agreement. Paragraph 39 of the Report points out that the use of the word "submissions" makes it clear that informal written communications between the parties do not suffice, as this would make it too easy for an arbitration agreement to be established in the absence of true consensus: formal submissions are required.

The Arbitration Agreement

Definition of arbitration agreement

6.—(1) In this Part an "arbitration agreement" means an agreement to submit to arbitration present or future disputes (whether they are contractual or not).

(2) The reference in an agreement to a written form of arbitration clause or to a document containing an arbitration clause constitutes an arbitration agreement if the reference is such as to make that clause part of the agreement.

1. *Cf. Zambia Steel Building Supplies Ltd* v. *Clark Eaton Ltd* [1986] 2 Lloyd's Rep 225; *Jarvis Sons plc* v. *Galliard Homes Ltd* [2000] BLR 33.

2. And, indeed, the position under the 1950 Act: *Jardine Birshe Ltd* v. *Cathedral Works Organisation (Chichester) Ltd* [1996] ADRLN 14.

3. English authority under the 1950 Act was on balance in favour of the same solution. In *Altco Ltd* v. *Sutherland* [1971] 2 Lloyd's Rep 515 Donaldson J had been of the view that the agreement remained oral, but the contrary appears to have been decided in *Jones Engineering Services Ltd* v. *Balfour Beatty Building Ltd* [1994] ADRLJ 133.

4. As in *The Amazonia* [1990] 1 Lloyd's Rep 236. See also: *LG Caltex Gas Co Ltd* v. *China National Petroleum Technology and Development Corporation* [2001] BLR 325; *Athletic Union of Constantinople* v. *National Basketball Association* [2002] 1 Lloyd's Rep 305; *JSC Zestafoni G Nikoladze Ferroalloy Plant* v. *Ronly Holdings Ltd* [2004] 2 Lloyd's Rep 335.

5. *Cf. Grovedeck Ltd* v. *Capital Demolition Ltd* [2000] BLR 181.

NOTES

Section 6(1) defines "arbitration agreement" in terms similar to those of the original version of Article 7(1) of the Model Law and re-enacts, with minor differences,[1] section 32 of the Arbitration Act 1950. The features of the definition are as follows:

(a) an arbitration agreement need not be in writing to be valid, but if it is not in writing the 1996 Act does not apply to it[2] and it is governed by the common law: the common law is expressly preserved by section 81;

(b) section 6(1) refers to "disputes" whereas section 32 of the 1950 Act referred to "differences". It is unclear whether as a matter of pure linguistic definition these words have any different meaning, although Danckwerts LJ in *F & G Sykes (Wessex) Ltd* v. *Fine Fare Ltd*[3] expressed the opinion that the term "difference" was wider in that it encompassed a failure to agree. The Act has rendered the issue immaterial by defining "dispute" in section 82(1) as referring to any difference, thereby possibly extending the common law meaning of "dispute";[4]

(c) section 6(1) encompasses both arbitration clauses (contract terms) and submission agreements (agreements to arbitrate made after a dispute has arisen).[5] It extends also to an agreement under which the parties have an option to refer a matter to arbitration,[6] in which case once made the reference can be withdrawn only with the consent of both parties.[7] Various parts of the Act apply only to arbitration clauses and not to submission agreements;[8] and

(d) section 6(1) makes it clear that a non-contractual dispute can be referred to arbitration. This is merely a declaratory provision, and there are many cases in which other forms of dispute have been held to be within the scope of arbitration agreements, for example, restitutionary actions[9] and claims in tort.[10]

The 1996 Act, unlike the July 1995 Bill, does not expressly state that an agreement need not name the arbitrator: such a clause was, rightly, regarded as superfluous in the light of the established principle that any reference to an arbitration agreement, however slight, will be enforceable.[11] In any

1. Described by the DAC Report, para. 41, as "more informative".
2. Under s. 5(1).
3. [1967] 1 Lloyd's Rep 53, at p. 60, a distinction cited with approval by the Court of Appeal in *Amec Civil Engineering Ltd* v. *Secretary of State for Transport* (2005) 101 Con LR 26.
4. *Cf.* the DAC Report, para. 41.
5. As to which, see, e.g.: *Hussmann (Europe) Ltd* v. *Al Ameen Development and Trading Establishment of Saudi Arabia* [2000] 2 Lloyd's Rep 83; *XL Insurance Ltd* v. *Owens Corning* [2000] 2 Lloyd's Rep 500.
6. *Alec Lobb Partnership Ltd* v. *Aintree Racecourse Co Ltd* [2000] BLR 65; *King* v. *Brandywine Reinsurance Co (UK) Ltd* [2004] 2 Lloyd's Rep 670, affirmed on other grounds [2005] 1 Lloyd's Rep 655.
7. *Whiting* v. *Halverson* [2003] EWCA Civ 403.
8. E.g., s. 12 (extension of time limits).
9. *Government of Gibraltar* v. *Kenney* [1956] 2 QB 410.
10. *Woolf* v. *Collins Removal Service* [1948] 1 KB 11; *Almare Societa di Navigazione SpA* v. *Derby Co, The Almare Prima* [1989] 2 Lloyd's Rep 376; *Aggeliki Charis Compania Maritima* v. *Pagnan SpA, The Angelic Grace* [1994] 1 Lloyd's Rep 168; *Fahem Co* v. *Mareb Yemen Insurance Co* [1997] 2 Lloyd's Rep 738; *Asghar & Co* v. *The Legal Services Commission and the Law Society* [2004] EWHC 1803 (QB). Whether an arbitration clause does extend to a claim in tort will depend upon its proper construction: *Chimimport plc* v. *G D'Alesio SAS, The Paola D'Alesio* [1994] 2 Lloyd's Rep 366; *Domansa* v. *Derin Shipping and Trading Co, The Sletreal* [2001] 1 Lloyd's Rep 362; *National Insurance and Guarantee Corporation Ltd* v. *M Young Legal Services Ltd* [2005] 2 Lloyd's Rep 46.
11. *Tritonia Shipping Inc* v. *South Nelson Forest Products Corporation* [1966] 1 Lloyd's Rep 114; *Hobbs, Padgett Co (Reinsurance) Ltd* v. *J C Kirkland Ltd* [1969] 2 Lloyd's Rep 547; *Swiss Banking Corporation* v. *Novorossiysk Shipping, The Petr Schmidt* [1995] 1 Lloyd's Rep 202; *Paul Smith Ltd* v. *H & S International Holdings Inc* [1991] 2 Lloyd's Rep 127; *Mangistaumunaigaz Oil Production Association* v. *United World Trading Inc* [1995] 1 Lloyd's Rep 66. *Alec Lobb Partnership* v. *Aintree Racecourse Co Ltd* [2000] BLR 65; *McNicholas plc* v. *AEI Cables* 1999, unreported. Contrast *Frota Oceanica Brasiliera SA* v. *Steamship Mutual Underwriting Association (Bermuda) Ltd, The Frotanorte* [1996] 2 Lloyd's Rep 461; *Cott UK Ltd* v. *FE Barber Ltd* [1997] 3 All ER 540; *Sonatrach Petroleum Corporation* v. *Ferrell International Ltd* [2002] 1 All ER (Comm) 627; *Atlanska Plovidba* v. *Consigaciones Asturianas SA* [2004] 2 Lloyd's Rep 109. Contrast *MH Alshaya Co WLL* v. *Retek Information Systems Inc* 2000, unreported, where, wholly exceptionally (and, arguably, incorrectly) an arbitration provision was found to be incompatible with the contractual arrangements entered into by the parties.

event, sections 15 *et seq.* of the Act provides adequate default provisions for the appointment of an arbitrator where none has been identified.

In all cases there must be a binding "agreement" in accordance with the general law.[1] In particular, an agreement which is "subject to contract" is not binding,[2] the parties must be of full capacity[3] and the arbitration agreement itself must be one not vitiated by misrepresentation, mistake or undue influence.[4] Further, the arbitration obligation must not have been brought to an end by agreement (including the acceptance of a repudiatory breach of the clause),[5] variation,[6] frustration or the operation of a statutory insolvency procedure. There can be an arbitration agreement even though only one of the parties is obliged[7] or entitled[8] to submit disputes to arbitration. An option to submit to arbitration, once exercised, takes effect as a binding arbitration agreement.[9] An arbitration clause may also be limited to particular disputes arising between the parties, for example, quantum where liability is admitted or established, or disputes which can be remedied only in ways open to the arbitrators.[10]

It is an unfortunate feature of contract drafting that contradictory clauses are not infrequently found side by side. One illustration is the conjunction of an arbitration clause accompanied by an exclusive or non-exclusive jurisdiction clause nominating the courts of an identified jurisdiction. The view of the English courts is that the arbitration clause takes priority, and that the jurisdiction provisions relate purely to curial issues.[11] Similarly, where—as is often the case in insurance agreements issued to US corporations by the London Market—there is an arbitration clause in conjunction with a service of suit clause under which the insurers agree to submit to the jurisdiction of any court of competent jurisdiction in the US if the assured wishes to bring an action, the service of suit clause is to be regarded as confined to providing a forum for enforcement which cannot be denied by the insurers.[12]

Not every agreement which provides for dispute resolution by a third party amounts to arbitration, and the 1996 Act applies only to arbitration proper. A distinction has to be drawn between

1. See, e.g. *Gurney Consulting Engineers* v. *Pearson Pension Property Fund Ltd* [2004] EWHC 1916 (TCC); *Glidepath Holdings BV* v. *Thompson* [2005] 2 Lloyd's Rep 549. See also *Glaxosmithkline UK Ltd* v. *Department of Health* [2007] EWHC 1470 (Comm) where a suggestion that participation in arbitration was "voluntary" was rejected.

2. *Jarvis Sons plc* v. *Galliard Homes Ltd* [2000] BLR 33. Thus, an agreement that there can be arbitration if both parties subsequently concur in a reference is a mere agreement to agree and not a binding arbitration clause: *Badrick* v. *British Judo Association*, July [2004] EWHC 1891 (Ch).

3. A company which has been removed from the register of companies ceases to be a party to an arbitration agreement, but if it is restored to the register any arbitration agreement to which it was a party prior to dissolution is revived: *Union Trans-Pacific Co Ltd* v. *Orient Shipping Rotterdam BV* [2002] EWHC 1451 (Comm).

4. *Irvani* v. *Irvani* [2000] 1 Lloyd's Rep 162.

5. *The Leonidas D* [1985] 1 WLR 925; *Bremer Vulkan Schiffbau und Maschinenfabrik* v. *South India Shipping Corporation Ltd* [1981] AC 909; *Villa Denizcilik Sanayi ve Ticaret AS* v. *Longen SA, The Villa* [1998] 1 Lloyd's Rep 195; *Huyton SA* v. *Peter Cremer GmbH & Co* [1999] 1 Lloyd's Rep 620; *Traube* v. *Perelman* [2003] EWHC 2822 (Ch); *Downing* v. *Al Tameer Establishment* [2002] 2 All ER (Comm) 545; *Indescon Ltd* v. *Ogden* [2005] 1 Lloyd's Rep 31; *BEA Hotels NV* v. *Bellway LLC* [2007] 2 Lloyd's Rep 493.

6. If the main agreement is varied, it is a matter of the construction of the variation and, indeed, of the arbitration clause itself whether the arbitration clause applies to the agreement as varied: *Oriental Maritime (Pte) Ltd* v. *Ministry of Food, Government of Bangladesh* [1989] 2 Lloyd's Rep 371; *El Nasharty* v. *J Sainsbury plc* [2004] 1 Lloyd's Rep 309.

7. *Pittalis* v. *Sherefettin* [1986] 2 All ER 227; *Nine Gladys Road Ltd* v. *Kersh* [2004] EWHC 1080 (Ch).

8. *NB Three Shipping Ltd* v. *Harebell Shipping Ltd* [2005] 1 Lloyd's Rep 509.

9. *Whiting* v. *Halverson* [2003] EWCA Civ 403.

10. *Vertex Data Science Ltd* v. *Powergen Retail Ltd* [2006] 2 Lloyd's Rep 591.

11. *Paul Smith* v. *H & S International Holding Inc* [1991] 2 Lloyd's Rep 127; *Shell International Petroleum Co* v. *Coral Oil Co Ltd (No 1)* [1999] 1 Lloyd's Rep 72; *Axa Re* v. *Ace Global Markets Ltd* [2006] 1 Lloyd's Rep 682.

12. *Ace Capital Ltd* v. *CMS Energy Corporation* [2008] 1 Lloyd's Rep 93.

arbitration and expert determination (requiring determination of a particular factual matter, for example, the quality of goods),[1] between arbitration and mediation[2] (a process with a non-binding outcome) and between arbitration and a judicial process.[3] The rules of an association which lay down a procedure for resolving internal disputes may or may not amount to arbitration, depending upon the substance of the agreed procedure.[4] A clause may be one for arbitration even though that word is not used,[5] and equally the description of a clause as one providing for arbitration is not conclusive if the procedure does not have the characteristics of arbitration.[6] The primary characteristics of arbitration are: a tribunal selected by the parties and required to operate impartially; a procedure whereby each party can state its case; an obligation on the tribunal to resolve the dispute according to the law; and a procedure designed to determine the substantive rights of the parties by means of a binding decision.[7]

If the subject matter of the arbitration clause is as a matter of law not justiciable, for example, because it involves an unenforceable wager[8] or illegality,[9] the clause does not qualify as an arbitration clause and is null and void. Subject to the constraints of public policy and of disputes not capable of private resolution, for example, because they involve the rights of children, the criminal law or inalienable statutory rights,[10] most matters are arbitrable.

Section 6(2), reflecting Article 7(2) of the Model Law, did not effect any change in the law,[11] but merely emphasises a point which is thought not to be widely appreciated, namely, that it is perfectly proper for the parties to incorporate an arbitration clause by reference to another document, for example, a set of standard arbitration rules.[12] Where there is a reference to arbitration rules, the general principle is that the version of the rules current when the arbitration is commenced is the applicable version even though there have been changes since the arbitration agreement was made.[13]

A note of caution should perhaps be expressed here, as there is a good deal of authority for the proposition that an arbitration clause contained in one contract will not be regarded as having been incorporated into another contract simply by the second contract stating that it is made on the same

1. *Jones* v. *Sherwood Services Ltd* [1992] 1 WLR 277; *Cott UK Ltd* v. *Barber* [1997] 3 All ER 540; *Veba Oil Supply and Trading GmbH* v. *Petrotrade Inc* [2002] 1 Lloyd's Rep 295; *Macro* v. *Thompson (No 3)* [2002] BCLC 36; *Bernhard Schulte* v. *Nile Holdings Ltd* [2004] 2 Lloyd's Rep 352; *Halifax Life Ltd* v. *Equitable Life Assurance Society* [2007] 1 Lloyd's Rep 528; *AIC Ltd* v. *ITS Testing Services (UK) Ltd, The Kriti Palm* [2007] 1 Lloyd's Rep 555; *Owen Pell Ltd* v. *Bindi (London) Ltd* [2008] EWHC 1420 (TCC).

2. *Flight Training International* v. *International Fire Training Equipment Ltd* [2004] 2 All ER (Comm) 568.

3. *Al Midani* v. *Al Midani* [1999] 1 Lloyd's Rep 923.

4. *Walkinshaw* v. *Diniz* [2000] 2 Lloyd's Rep 165 (arbitration); *Exeter City AFC* v. *Football Conference Ltd* [2004] 4 All ER 1179 (dispute resolution mechanism not amounting to arbitration).

5. *David Wilson Homes Ltd* v. *Survey Services Ltd* [2001] BLR 267.

6. *AIG Europe SA* v. *QBE International Insurance Ltd* [2001] 2 Lloyd's Rep 268.

7. *Walkinshaw* v. *Diniz* [2000] 2 Lloyd's Rep 165.

8. *O'Callaghan* v. *Coral Racing Ltd* (1999, unreported). See further the Notes to s. 7.

9. See the Notes to s. 7, below.

10. On this basis it has been held that a dispute as to the winding up of a company cannot be resolved by arbitration: *Exeter City AFC* v. *Football Conference Ltd* [2004] 4 All ER 1179, doubting *Re Vocam (Europe) Ltd* [1998] BCC 396.

11. *Sea Trade Maritime Corporation* v. *Hellenic Mutual War Risks Association (Bermuda) Ltd, The Athena (No 2)* [2007] 1 Lloyd's Rep 280.

12. *Roche Products* v. *Freeman Process Systems* (1996) 80 BLR 102; *Secretary of State for Foreign and Commonwealth Affairs* v. *Percy Thomas* (1998) 65 Con LR 11; *Axa Re* v. *Ace Global Markets Ltd* [2006] Lloyd's Rep IR 683; *Sea Trade Maritime Corporation* v. *Hellenic Mutual War Risks Association (Bermuda) Ltd, The Athena (No 2)* [2007] 1 Lloyd's Rep 280; *Heifer International Inc* v. *Christiansen* [2007] EWHC 3015 (TCC). Insofar as *Ben Barrett* v. *Henry Boot* [1995] CILL 1026 suggests a stricter approach, it is probably no longer good authority.

13. *Jayaar Impex Ltd* v. *Toaken Group Ltd* [1996] 2 Lloyd's Rep 437; *China Agribusiness Development Corporation* v. *Balli Trading* [1998] 2 Lloyd's Rep 76; *Ranko Group* v. *Antarctic Maritime SA, The Robin* [1998] ADRLN 35.

conditions as the first: the principle is that the obligation to arbitrate is distinct, and will not be carried by general words of incorporation unless the wording and intention are absolutely clear.[1] The DAC Report, paragraph 42, was not fully supportive of a narrow attitude to incorporation, and noted that there were inconsistent comments—particularly in *Aughton* v. *M F Kent Services*—as to whether an arbitration clause could be regarded as incorporated only if it was expressly referred to in the words of incorporation (Sir John Megaw) or whether the text was the lesser one of whether an intention to incorporate could be gleaned from the words used (Ralph Gibson LJ). The DAC favoured the view of Ralph Gibson LJ, but refused to be drawn:

> It seemed to us . . . that although we are of the view that the approach of Ralph Gibson LJ should prevail in all cases, this was really a matter for the Court to decide. The wording [of section 7(2)] we have used certainly leaves room for the adoption of the charterparty rule [i.e., the Ralph Gibson LJ analysis] in all cases, since it refers to references in a document containing an arbitration clause as well as a reference to the arbitration clause itself. Thus the wording is not confined to cases where there is a specific reference to the arbitration clause, which Sir John Megaw (but not Ralph Gibson LJ) considered was a requirement for effective incorporation by reference.

The effect of section 6(2) was considered by HHJ Jack QC in *Trygg Hansa Insurance Co Ltd* v. *Equitas*.[2] HHJ Jack QC rejected the argument that section 6(2) has effected any change in the law, and in particular that it had expressly adopted the rather broader approach in Article 7(2) of the Model Law: his view was that the DAC had chosen to leave the point open, and that the balance of authority favoured the proposition that an arbitration clause is to be regarded as incorporated only if there is express reference to it in the words of incorporation. Although the decision was reached in the context of reinsurance, it would appear to be of general application. Accordingly, in the absence of express words which incorporate the arbitration clause, there will be incorporation only where the intention to incorporate is otherwise unequivocal.[3] The wording of the arbitration clause itself is relevant only in a negative sense: an arbitration clause which contemplates that it may be incorporated from contract A into contract B will not operate to effect incorporation into contract B as this is a matter for contract B itself,[4] although if contract B does purport to incorporate the arbitration clause then the wording of the arbitration clause may prevent its incorporation where it makes no sense in contract B unless it can be "manipulated" to be given effect.

The existence and validity of the arbitration agreement are, subject to contrary agreement, matters for the arbitrators to determine in the first instance.[5]

1. The cases are largely derived from bills of lading, construction and reinsurance disputes. The leading bills of lading authorities are: *Thomas Co* v. *Portsea Steamship Co Ltd, The Portsmouth* [1912] AC 1; *The Elizabeth H* [1962] 1 Lloyd's Rep 172; *The Merak* [1964] 2 Lloyd's Rep 527; *The Annefield* [1971] 1 All ER 394; *The Rena K* [1979] 1 All ER 397; *The Varenna* [1983] 2 Lloyd's Rep 592; *The Federal Bulker* [1989] 1 Lloyd's Rep 103; *The Nerano* [1994] 2 Lloyd's Rep 50; *The Heidberg* [1994] 2 Lloyd's Rep 287; *The Delos* [2001] 1 Lloyd's Rep 703; *Michael S Evryalos Maritime SA* v. *China Pacific Insurance Co Ltd, The MV Michael S* 2001, unreported. The leading construction decisions are: *Modern Buildings Wales Ltd* v. *Limmer and Trinidad Co Ltd* [1975] 2 All ER 549; *Aughton* v. *M F Kent Services Ltd* [1992] ADRLJ 83; *Giffen* v. *Drake and Scull* 33 Con LR 84; *Laxair Ltd* v. *Edward W Taylor* (1993) 65 Build LR 87; *Alfred McAlpine Construction Ltd* v. *RMG Electrical Ltd* [1998] ADRLJ 53; *Jardine Birshe Ltd* v. *Cathedral Works Organisation (Chichester) Ltd* [1996] ADRLN 14. The reinsurance authorities are: *Pine Top Insurance Co Ltd* v. *Unione Italiana Anglo-Saxon Reinsurance Co Ltd* [1987] 1 Lloyd's Rep 476; *Excess Insurance Co* v. *Mander* [1995] LRLR 583; *Trygg Hansa Insurance Co Ltd* v. *Equitas* [1998] 2 Lloyd's Rep 439.
2. [1998] 2 Lloyd's Rep 439.
3. *American Design Associates* v. *Donald Install Associates*, November 2000, unreported; *AIG Europe SA* v. *QBE Insurance International Ltd* [2001] 2 Lloyd's Rep 268; *American International Speciality Lines Insurance Co* v. *Abbott Laboratories* [2004] Lloyd's Rep IR 815.
4. The authorities were discussed in *Siboti K/S* v. *BP France SA* [2003] 2 Lloyd's Rep 364, distinguishing *The Merak* [1964] 2 Lloyd's Rep 527 and applying *The Federal Bulker* [1989] 1 Lloyd's Rep 103 and *The Varenna* [1983] 2 Lloyd's Rep 692.
5. Sections 30 to 32. See below.

Separability of arbitration agreement

7. Unless otherwise agreed by the parties, an arbitration agreement which forms or was intended to form part of another agreement (whether or not in writing) shall not be regarded as invalid, non-existent or ineffective because that other agreement is invalid, or did not come into existence or has become ineffective, and it shall for that purpose be treated as a distinct agreement.

NOTES

As a matter of practice, an agreement to arbitrate may take the form of an arbitration clause within a main agreement, or an entirely distinct contract contained in separate documentation.[1] Whether or not the arbitration agreement is physically distinct, section 7 provides that the agreement to arbitrate is as a matter of law severable from the main obligation and stands or falls in its own right. In other words, the arbitration clause will remain valid even if the substantive agreement is (for example) declared to be void for illegality. This reflects the position as it was under the common law and also embodied in Article 16(1) of the Model Law. As the section makes clear, the main agreement containing the arbitration clause need not itself be in writing, a point which was clarified following a recommendation by the DAC.[2]

The concept of severability was not fully recognised in England until the 1993 decision of Steyn J, affirmed by the Court of Appeal in *Harbour Assurance Co (UK) Ltd* v. *Kansa General International Insurance Co Ltd*,[3] a landmark judgment which presented the pragmatic and intellectual justifications of severability, for example, the need to bring England into line with other jurisdictions, the need to give full effect to an arbitration clause in line with business expectations, and the need to avoid the prospect of a party avoiding an obligation to arbitrate by the mere assertion that the underlying agreement was void. Prior to that decision, the main barrier to the ability of the arbitrators to rule on the validity of the main contract had been the House of Lords ruling in *Heyman* v. *Darwins Ltd*,[4] in which it had been said that an argument that the main agreement was itself void or for some other reason unenforceable would prevent reliance on the arbitration clause, as the clause formed part of the agreement and could not survive independently of it. *Heyman* itself had taken the first tentative steps towards the concept of severability, by rejecting an argument originally accepted by Viscount Haldane LC in *Jureidini* v. *National British and Irish Millers Insurance Co*[5] that a breach of contract which led to the termination of that contract precluded reliance on the arbitration clause.[6] Having established that an arbitration clause is capable of surviving termination, the courts gradually moved to a full concept of separability by a series of decisions which held that an arbitration clause could, if appropriately worded, apply to questions of voidability,[7] frustration,[8] voidness[9] and, ultimately, illegality.[10] In the light of the decision of the House of Lords in *Fiona*

1. Of course, the more common form is a clause in a wider contract.
2. DAC Report, para. 358; see also the DAC Supplementary Report, para. 20.
3. [1993] 1 Lloyd's Rep 455.
4. [1942] AC 356.
5. [1915] AC 499.
6. This aspect of *Jureidini* was laid to rest by the Privy Council in *Super Chem Products Ltd* v. *American Life and General Insurance Co Ltd* [2004] Lloyd's Rep IR 446.
7. *Overseas Union Inc* v. *AA Mutual International Ltd* [1988] 2 Lloyd's Rep 63, although see the doubts expressed as late as 1988 in *Ashville Investments Ltd* v. *Elmer Contractors Ltd* [1988] 2 All ER 577.
8. *Government of Gibraltar* v. *Kenney* [1956] 2 QB 410, rejecting the earlier view in *Hirji Mulji* v. *Cheong Yue Steamship Co Ltd* [1926] AC 497.
9. *Harbour Assurance Co (UK) Ltd* v. *Kansa General International Insurance Co Ltd* [1992] 1 Lloyd's Rep 81, a landmark judgment of Steyn J which presented the pragmatic and intellectual justifications of severability, e.g. the need to bring England into line with other jurisdictions, the need to give full effect to an arbitration clause in line with business expectations, and the need to avoid the prospect of a party avoiding an obligation to arbitrate by the mere assertion that the underlying agreement was void.
10. *Harbour Assurance Co (UK) Ltd* v. *Kansa General International Insurance Co Ltd* [1993] 1 Lloyd's Rep 455, taking the step which Steyn J felt to be constrained by the authority of *David Taylor Son Ltd* v. *Barnett Trading Co* [1953] 1 Lloyd's Rep 181.

Trust & Holding Corp v. *Privalov & ors*,[1] these decisions plainly hold good under the 1996 Act. Whereas previously the only question was whether the wording of the clause was sufficiently wide to cover the issue,[2] it is now clear in the light of *Fiona Trust* that nice distinctions in the formulation of the arbitration clause as to, for example, scope are no longer relevant, in that very clear words would be needed before a court was satisfied that it had been accorded some sort of residual jurisdiction to consider, for example, restitutionary or tortious claims arising out of an agreement, whereas strictly "contractual" claims were within the sole province of the arbitrators. Furthermore, to be outside the scope of the arbitration clause, the issue of illegality would have to be directed at the arbitration clause itself, which would obviously be rare. Even before *Fiona Trust*, in *Vee Networks Ltd* v. *Econet Wireless International Ltd*[3] Colman J had held that section 7 empowered the arbitrator to decide whether or not a contract of supply was void for being *ultra vires* the customer. *El Nasharty* v. *J Sainsbury plc*[4] was decided as the House of Lords decision in *Fiona Trust* was emerging, and (in reliance in part on the decision in *Fiona Trust*) confirmed that a challenge to the existence of an arbitration agreement based on duress had to be based on facts specific to the arbitration agreement, and not simply parasitic upon a challenge to the validity of the contract containing it.[5] Issues as to the variation[6] and rectification[7] of the main agreement may on the same basis be determined by the arbitrators.

This section is not mandatory and, in accordance with the opening words of section 7, is subject to contrary agreement in writing. However, it is clear from the decision in *Fiona Trust* that such agreement would have to be clearly expressed so as to make it beyond doubt that the parties had agreed to reserve to the court the right to hear any claims at all in connection with the underlying agreement.

There is an important modification of the separability principle as regards contracts which plainly have no effect. In *Harbour* the Court of Appeal noted that there were categories of illegality which rendered contracts void, with the result that there could be nothing to arbitrate. In *Soleimany* v. *Soleimany*[8] Waller LJ repeated this proposition (albeit in the context of an application to enforce a foreign arbitral award) as regards contracts which were palpably illegal or contrary to public policy, such as an agreement between criminals to divide the proceeds of their activities. These *dicta* were relied upon by the Court of Appeal in *O'Callaghan* v. *Coral Racing Ltd*,[9] in which it was held that a wagering contract rendered illegal[10] or void[11] by the Gaming Act 1845 was simply non-existent and the arbitration clause in it was itself of no effect. However, this was a decision under the 1950 Act, and it is now possibly doubtful in the light of *Fiona Trust* whether the case would be decided the same way under the 1996 Act.

The firm recognition of the separability of the arbitration clause leads to the further proposition that the arbitrators are free to determine their own substantive jurisdiction under the main agreement itself, in respect of issues such as the validity of the arbitration clause, the validity of their own appointments and the issue as to what matters have been submitted to arbitration: section 30 of the Act. However, the Act, consistently with the common law, does not permit the arbitrators to have the final word on their own jurisdiction, and sections 30 to 32 lay down a special procedure, based on Article 16 of the Model Law, for challenges to the arbitrators' assertion or denial of jurisdiction.

1. [2008] 1 Lloyd's Rep 254.
2. Formerly, if a clause was confined to disputes arising "under" the contract, the arbitrators were only able to consider strictly contractual issues, whereas if, e.g., the clause referred to disputes "arising out of" a contract a wider jurisdiction was conferred, e.g. to consider tortious or restitutionary claims. This distinction has been swept away by the decision in *Fiona Trust*.
3. [2005] 1 Lloyd's Rep 192. See also *Continental Enterprises Limited* v. *Shandong Zhucheng Foreign Trade Group Co* [2005] EWHC 92 (Comm).
4. [2008] 1 Lloyd's Rep 361.
5. Note that the issue in *El Nasharty* did not turn on the scope of the arbitration clause, which was a widely-drafted standard ICC arbitration clause.
6. *Joseph Finney plc* v. *Vickers* 2001, unreported; *El Nasharty* v. *J Sainsbury plc* [2004] 1 Lloyd's Rep 309.
7. *Macepark (Whittlebury) Ltd* v. *Sargeant* 2002, unreported.
8. [1998] 3 WLR 811.
9. 1999, unreported.
10. *Per* Hirst LJ, Sir Christopher Slade concurring.
11. *Per* May LJ, Sir Christopher Slade concurring.

Separability and the right to determine jurisdiction are distinct concepts[1] in that the former is concerned with the right of the arbitrators to rule on the validity of the main contract whereas the latter is concerned with the right of the arbitrators to determine whether they have any power to sit as arbitrators. However, in many cases, both questions are in issue and to that extent the two notions will commonly overlap in the same proceedings.

The English courts are entitled to apply the principle of severability to a case coming before them where the seat of the arbitration is England and Wales or Northern Ireland, and even where the seat is elsewhere provided that the law applicable to the arbitration clause is that of England and Wales or Northern Ireland (see section 2(5)). Accordingly, in the latter case, if judicial proceedings are commenced in England, and if the question whether there is a valid arbitration clause is in play, for example, in the light of the termination, illegality or voidness of the main agreement, English law as contained in section 7 will determine whether the arbitration clause remains or is in existence so that, if appropriate, a stay can be granted under section 9. In the light of the decision in *Fiona Trust*, the circumstances in which a stay would be refused will be much rarer (see the Notes to section 9).

Whether agreement discharged by death of a party

8.—(1) Unless otherwise agreed by the parties, an arbitration agreement is not discharged by the death of a party and may be enforced by or against the personal representatives of that party.

(2) Subsection (1) does not affect the operation of any enactment or rule of law by virtue of which a substantive right or obligation is extinguished by death.

NOTES

Section 8(1) is no longer mandatory and operates subject to any contrary agreement. If a party to an arbitration has died after the proceedings have commenced and he has appointed an arbitrator, the authority of the arbitrator is not revoked by his death.[2]

Section 8(2) confirms that any earlier principle bringing a cause of action or obligation to an end on death does not apply to arbitrations. This terminology has been used in substitution for the old wording "cause of action".[3]

Both limbs of section 8 apply to an arbitration which does not have its seat in England and Wales or Northern Ireland, but where the arbitration agreement itself is governed by English law (section 2(5)), as in such a case the English courts are free to determine the validity of the arbitration clause.

Stay of Legal Proceedings

Stay of legal proceedings

9.—(1) A party to an arbitration agreement against whom legal proceedings are brought (whether by way of claim or counterclaim) in respect of a matter which under the agreement is to be referred to arbitration may (upon notice to the other parties to the proceedings) apply to the court in which the proceedings have been brought to stay the proceedings so far as they concern that matter.

(2) An application may be made notwithstanding that the matter is to be referred to arbitration only after the exhaustion of other dispute resolution procedures.

1. The DAC Report, para. 43, regarded the two concepts as "quite separate".
2. Section 23(2).
3. DAC Report, para. 48.

(3) An application may not be made by a person before taking the appropriate procedural step (if any) to acknowledge the legal proceedings against him or after he has taken any step in those proceedings to answer the substantive claim.

(4) On an application under this section the court shall grant a stay unless satisfied that the arbitration agreement is null and void, inoperative, or incapable of being performed.

(5) If the court refuses to stay the legal proceedings, any provision that an award is a condition precedent to the bringing of legal proceedings in respect of any matter is of no effect in relation to those proceedings.

NOTES

Section 9 broadly re-enacts earlier legislation which provided for a stay of judicial proceedings brought in contravention of an arbitration agreement. These sections were necessary in the light of the common law rule that an arbitration agreement could not oust the jurisdiction of the courts.[1] The earlier legislation drew a distinction between domestic and non-domestic arbitration clauses. In the case of a domestic arbitration agreement, governed by section 4 of the Arbitration Act 1950, the court had a discretion to stay, whereas in the case of a non-domestic arbitration agreement, governed by section 1 of the Arbitration Act 1975, the grant of a stay was mandatory (in accordance with Article 1 of the New York Convention 1958). Although section 86 has the effect of taking domestic agreements outside section 9(4), thereby reproducing the effect of the old law, it has not been brought into effect and is never likely to be (see the Notes to section 85). Consequently, under section 9(4) the court must stay its proceedings in all cases and regardless as to whether the seat of the arbitration is in or outside England and Wales.[2]

Section 9 reflects Article 8 of the Model Law, although it remains the case that section 9 is negative and merely stays judicial proceedings. By contrast, Article 8 of the Model Law is positive and requires the matter to be referred to arbitration by the court on refusing to stay its proceedings.[3]

Section 9(1), which, like its predecessors, applies to both arbitration clauses and submission agreements, confers upon a party who is being sued in a court[4] (and not in any other form of tribunal) the right to apply to the court for a stay in respect of that matter. This is to be done in the form of an application notice,[5] served on the other parties to the proceedings.[6] Normally the proceedings in respect of which the stay is sought will have been brought in breach of the terms of the arbitration clause, but such a breach is not necessary. Thus, section 9 is equally available where the arbitration clause confers upon one party (or, for that matter, both parties) the right to refer any dispute to arbitration and he has chosen to exercise that option,[7] in which case he may restrain pre-emptive judicial proceedings brought—at the time perfectly legitimately—by the other party.[8]

The power to stay relates only to matters which fall within the scope of the arbitration agreement. Where the parties have cross-claims arising out of disputes under a single contract, the various claims and counterclaims will normally all be covered by the arbitration clause and can be resolved in a single set of proceedings. There may, however, be circumstances in which either the claim or the counterclaim, but not both, is subject to arbitration. The approach adopted by the courts here is that, if the claim is to be arbitrated, but the respondent has a counterclaim arising out of the same or a closely related transaction ("transaction set-off") but falling outside the scope of the arbitration cause, the arbitrator nevertheless has jurisdiction to resolve the counterclaim on the basis that it

1. *Doleman & Sons Ltd* v. *Osset Corporation* [1912] 3 KB 257.
2. See s. 2(2).
3. Noted by Lord Mustill in *Channel Tunnel Group Ltd* v. *Balfour Beatty Construction Ltd* [1993] AC 334.
4. Even if there are co-defendants: *Wealands* v. *CLC Contractors Ltd* [1999] 2 Lloyd's Rep 739.
5. CPR r. 62.3(2). The application is made in the standard form in accordance with CPR Part 23.
6. CPR r. 62.8.
7. *Whiting* v. *Halverson* [2003] EWCA Civ 403.
8. *NB Three Shipping Ltd* v. *Harebell Shipping Ltd* [2004] EWHC 2001 (Comm); *Ashgar* v. *Legal Services Commission* [2004] EWHC 1803 (Ch).

operates as a defence to the claim itself.[1] By contrast, if the counterclaim arises out of an entirely separate transaction ("independent set-off") the arbitrator has no jurisdiction to resolve the counterclaim because it does not operate as a defence to the claim itself and indeed the award can be enforced without reference to the counterclaim.[2]

There are three alterations in section 9(1) from the position under the earlier legislation. First, it was stated in those provisions that any party to an arbitration agreement could seek a stay, and it was arguable that the term "any party" might include a party who was not himself being sued in the judicial proceedings. This construction was rejected by the Court of Appeal in *Etri Fans Ltd* v. *NMB (UK) Ltd*,[3] and that decision has been confirmed by the wording of section 9(1), which requires the applicant for a stay to be one who is sued.

Secondly, under the earlier provisions there was a reference to any person claiming "through or under" a party to arbitration proceedings as having the right to seek a stay, a provision which was held to include assignees but to exclude others with lesser derivative rights, for example, mortgagees.[4] This provision remains in being, but has been transferred to section 82(2) of the Act and now applies for all purposes under the Act and not simply the right to seek a stay.[5]

Thirdly, section 9(1) expressly applies to counterclaims. Indeed, there are circumstances in which the claim is not subject to the arbitration clause, but the counterclaim will be.[6] For a recent example, see *Prekons Insaat Sanayi AS* v. *Rowlands Castle Contracting Group*.[7]

Section 9(2) allows an application for a stay to be made even though the matter cannot be referred to arbitration until some other condition has been met. The clause codifies *dicta* of Lord Mustill in *Channel Tunnel Group Ltd* v. *Balfour Beatty Construction Ltd*.[8] The purpose of the provision is to permit alternative dispute resolution mechanisms—mediation, conciliation, adjudication and the like—to be exhausted. It would seem that, as a matter of law, an agreement to attempt to settle in good faith prior to the commencement of arbitration proceedings is unenforceable on the basis that it is void for uncertainty.[9] In *Halifax Financial Services Ltd* v. *Intuitive Systems Ltd* the court doubted whether it had jurisdiction to stay judicial proceedings in order to allow a non-binding ADR procedure to be exhausted, although this decision was distinguished and confined to the narrowest possible limits by Colman J in *Cable & Wireless plc* v. *IBM UK Ltd*[10] and it is now accepted to be the case that a stay can be granted to support an ADR process even if it is not enforceable as a matter of strict contract law. Whatever the position in judicial proceedings under the CPR, the position in arbitration is, under section 9(2), that no application may be made until any agreed procedure has been exhausted, and it might be thought that the section would be substantially weakened by confining it to pure arbitration clauses which make no provision for preliminary ADR.

Section 9(3) provides in effect that no application may be made before the applicant first lodges his acknowledgement of service. In English civil proceedings, the usual form of acknowledgement of service provides the defendant with three choices: admitting the claim (in whole or in part); stating an intention to defend the claim; and stating an intention to challenge the jurisdiction of the court. The safest option is probably to tick the box indicating that the defendant wishes to challenge the jurisdiction of the court, though such challenges are those more usually made under CPR Part

1. *Modern Engineering (Bristol) Ltd* v. *Gilbert-Ash* [1974] AC 689; *Ronly Holdings* v. *JSC Zestafoni G Nikoladze Ferroalloy Plant* [2004] 2 Lloyd's Rep 335; *Benford Ltd* v. *Lopecan SL* [2004] 2 Lloyd's Rep 618.

2. *Glencore Grain Ltd* v. *Agros Trading Ltd* [1992] 2 All ER 288; *Aectra Refining and Marketing Inc* v. *Exmare NV, The New Vanguard* [1995] 1 Lloyd's Rep 191; *Ronly Holdings* v. *JSC Zestafoni G Nikoladze Ferroalloy Plant* [2004] 2 Lloyd's Rep 335; *Metal Distributors (UK) Ltd* v. *ZCCM Investment Holdings plc* [2005] EWHC 156 (Comm); *Econet Satellite Services* v. *Vee Networks* [2006] 2 Lloyd's Rep 243.

3. [1987] 2 All ER 763.

4. *Bonnin* v. *Neame* [1910] 1 Ch 732.

5. See, more generally, the comments on s. 82(2).

6. *Delta Reclamation Ltd* v. *Premier Waste Management Ltd* [2008] EWHC B16 (QB).

7. [2007] 1 Lloyd's Rep 98.

8. [1993] AC 334. See the DAC Report, para. 53, and *cf. Cable & Wireless plc* v. *IBM UK Ltd* [2002] 2 All ER 1041.

9. *Walford* v. *Miles* [1992] 2 AC 128; *Paul Smith Ltd* v. *H S International Holding Inc* [1991] 2 Lloyd's Rep 127; *Halifax Financial Services Ltd* v. *Intuitive Systems Ltd* [1999] 1 All ER (Comm) 303.

10. [2002] 2 All ER 1041, and see also *Flight Training International* v. *International Fire Training Equipment Ltd* [2004] 2 All ER (Comm) 568.

11, for example, in favour of another more appropriate court rather than by way of seeking a stay of the proceedings to arbitration. No application may be made after the applicant has taken any steps in the judicial proceedings, a term which appeared in the earlier legislation and which was held to refer to any attempt to defend the claim on its merits rather than on jurisdiction.[1] In *Patel* v. *Patel*[2] the Court of Appeal held that the applicant had not taken a step in judicial proceedings merely by seeking to have a default judgment against him set aside and swearing two affidavits stating his intention to seek a stay of proceedings and also that he intended to apply for permission to defend the proceedings and issue a counterclaim. The court's view was that (a) if the claimant succeeded in setting aside the judgment, there would be no need for him to seek permission to defend, so that the affidavit was to that extent otiose and (b) the stated intention to seek a stay overrode the stated intention to seek permission to defend. Where in existing proceedings where original claims are brought that fall within the ambit of an arbitration clause, yet no stay is sought by the defendant, he may not succeed in staying additional claims brought by way of amendment if such claims are substantially the same as or very closely related to the original claims.[3] Where it is alleged in the context of a section 9 application that the applicant has answered the substantive claim in foreign court proceedings, English conflict rules provide that, if the steps in question are not regarded as a submission by the foreign court, they will not be so regarded so far as the English court is concerned.[4] Furthermore, an act which would otherwise constitute a step in the proceedings will not do so where the applicant has specifically stated at the same time that he intends to apply for a stay.[5] For example, an application for summary judgment followed by an application for a stay will not constitute a step in the proceedings if it is clear from the context that the summary judgment application was conditional on the stay application failing. The key question is whether the step in question is such that it impliedly affirms the correctness of the legal proceedings and the willingness of the applicant to go along with a determination by the court instead of by an arbitral tribunal.[6]

Section 9(4) sets out the rule that a stay is to be granted, unless the conditions in section 9(4) are met. In all cases (i.e. domestic and non-domestic agreements), the stay will be refused in any of three situations set out in section 9(4) and repeated almost verbatim from Article II.3 of the New York Convention. The list, which is exhaustive,[7] was previously set out in section 1 of the Arbitration Act 1975.

The list covers three separate matters: (a) the agreement is null and void; (b) the agreement is inoperative; and (c) the agreement is incapable of being performed. The phrase "null and void" refers to the situation in which there is simply no arbitration agreement between the parties[8] or, in exceptional circumstances, the situation in which there is no agreement to which the arbitration clause can relate.[9] The phrase "inoperative" may relate to the scope of the arbitration clause,[10] the arbitrability of the subject matter, the termination or cancellation of the arbitration clause[11] and the

1. See, e.g., *Pitchers Ltd* v. *Plaza (Queensbury) Ltd* [1940] 1 All ER 151; *Turner & Goudy* v. *McConnell* [1985] 2 All ER 34; *David McLean Housing Contractors Ltd* v. *Swansea Housing Association Ltd* [2002] BLR 125; *El Nasharty* v. *J Sainsbury plc (No 2)* [2008] 1 Lloyd's Rep 360.

2. [1999] 1 All ER (Comm) 923. The earlier contrary decision in *Russell Bros* v. *Breen*, 1997, unreported, probably cannot stand in the light of *Patel* v. *Patel*. See also *London Central and Suburban Developments* v. *Banger* [1999] ADRLJ 119 (step in proceedings need not comply with Civil Procedure Rules); *Capital Trust Investments Ltd* v. *Radio Design* [2002] 1 All ER (Comm) 514.

3. *Ahad & anr* v. *Uddin* [2005] EWCA Civ 883.

4. *Thyssen Inc* v. *Calypso Shipping Corp SA* [2000] 2 Lloyd's Rep 243.

5. *Patel* v. *Patel* [1999] 1 All ER (Comm) 923 at 925.

6. *Eagle Star* v. *Yuval* [1978] 1 Lloyd's Rep 357.

7. See, e.g., *SCOR* v. *Eras International Ltd* [1992] 1 Lloyd's Rep 570.

8. *Sun Life Assurance Co of Canada* v. *CX Reinsurance Co Ltd* [2004] Lloyd's Rep IR 86.

9. *Soleimany* v. *Soleimany* [1998] 3 WLR 811 (illegality). See also *Stretford* v. *Football Association* [2007] 2 Lloyd's Rep 31 (CA), where it was held that an arbitration clause was not null and void by reason of an alleged infringement of the right to a fair trial under Art. 6 of the ECHR (incorporated into English law by the Human Rights Act 1988). The right to a public hearing will have been waived by freely entering into an agreement to arbitrate.

10. *Al-Naimi* v. *Islamic Press Agency* [2000] 1 Lloyd's Rep 522; *El Nasharty* v. *J Sainsbury plc* [2004] 1 Lloyd's Rep 309.

11. *Traube* v. *Perelman*, 2001, unreported; *Downing* v. *Al Tameer Establishment & Anr* [2002] EWCA Civ 721; *Delta Reclamation Ltd* v. *Premier Waste Management Ltd* [2008] EWHC B16 (QB).

identities of the parties to the arbitration clause.[1] The phrase "incapable of being performed" covers the case in which one of the parties has been prevented by some external cause from performing his obligation, and not merely that he is insolvent.[2] As to the scope of the arbitration clause, following the House of Lords decision in *Fiona Trust & Holding Corp* v. *Privalov & ors*,[3] there will be far fewer successful resistances to section 9 stay applications based on the width of an arbitration clause, since such clauses are now to be accorded as wide an interpretation as possible, in accordance with the principle that the parties will be taken to have intended to resolve all their disputes in one forum except where clear words are used to indicate the contrary.[4]

The date on which the validity or applicability of the arbitration clause is to be tested is that on which the judicial proceedings were first commenced: if the clause is not enforceable at that date a stay is to be granted even if by the time of the application for a stay the clause has been reinstated.[5]

In the 1975 Act an additional matter was listed, namely, that there was no dispute between the parties. This does not appear in the New York Convention and was omitted from the 1996 Act on the basis that they were, in the words of the DAC Report, paragraph 55 "confusing and unnecessary, for the reasons given in *Hayter* v. *Nelson*".[6] It was thus considered possible for one party to assert that the parties were not in dispute and that there was no jurisdiction to grant a stay of judicial proceedings. However, this view of the DAC's comments was rejected by Clarke J[7] and a majority of the Court of Appeal in *Halki Shipping Corporation* v. *Sopex Oils Ltd*.[8] In *Halki* the Court of Appeal held that *Hayter* v. *Nelson* had decided that a dispute existed even where it was clear from the outset that one party was right and the other wrong, and that the only basis for the refusal of a stay of judicial proceedings was the reference in section 1 of the 1975 Act to the absence of a dispute between the parties. Adopting the *Hayter* v. *Nelson* approach, and combining it with a complex historical analysis, Clarke J and a majority of the Court of Appeal held that the repeal of section 1 of the 1975 Act had changed the law, and that a court could not refuse to stay its proceedings—normally proceedings brought for summary judgment—simply because the claimant argued that the defendant had no defence. The quality of the defence is not, therefore, an issue that can be assessed by a court where there is an arbitration clause and accordingly the court cannot give summary judgment even though the outcome of the case is all but inevitable, but must stay its proceedings where the matter is arguable so that the arbitrators can resolve the issue between the parties. Given that the obligation to stay arises only where there is a "dispute" between the parties, it is necessary to determine whether matters have reached that stage. The general definition of dispute requires the making of a claim by one party and its rejection by the other. Whether this has occurred in the course of lengthy correspondence and negotiation between the parties is not always immediately obvious. The making of a formal claim with a time limit for response is perhaps the simplest method of requiring the other party to define his position, but even if this approach is not used a failure by the other party to respond to a claim does not necessarily deny the existence of a dispute,[9] particularly where there are clear unresolved disagreements following the conclusion of negotiations.[10] A dispute may also be found to arise even though negotiations are still in progress, at least where it is clear that these are being protracted in an attempt to forestall proceedings.[11] By

1. *Anglia Oils Ltd* v. *Owners of the Marine Champion* [2002] EWHC 2407 (Adm).
2. *The Rena K* [1978] 1 Lloyd's Rep 545.
3. [2008] 1 Lloyd's Rep 254.
4. See the judgment of Lord Hoffmann in *Fiona Trust* at [13].
5. *Traube* v. *Perelman* July 2001, unreported (Jacob J). See also *A* v. *B* [2007] 1 Lloyd's Rep 237.
6. [1990] 2 Lloyd's Rep 265.
7. Albeit with some uncertainty as to what the DAC had intended to say. The learned judge followed his own reasoning in *Hume* v. *AA Mutual International Insurance Co Ltd* [1996] LRLR 19.
8. [1998] 1 Lloyd's Rep 49, affirmed [1998] 1 Lloyd's Rep 465. See also *Wealands* v. *CLC Contractors Ltd* [1999] 2 Lloyd's Rep 739.
9. *Ellerine Brothers (Pty) Ltd* v. *Klinger* [1982] 2 All ER 737, *per* Templeman LJ at p. 743. See also: *Marc Rich Agriculture Trading SA* v. *Agrimex Ltd* [2000] 1 All ER (Comm) 951; *Fastrack Contractors Ltd* v. *Morrison Construction Ltd* [2000] BLR 168.
10. *Black Peppiatt Ltd* v. *Norwest Holst Construction Ltd* [2003] BLR 316; *Amec Civil Engineering Ltd* v. *Secretary of State for Transport* [2004] EWHC 2339 (TCC), affirmed [2005] EWCA Civ 291; *Collins (Contractors) Ltd* v. *Baltic Quay Management (1994) Ltd* 2004, unreported.
11. *CIB Properties Ltd* v. *Birse Construction Ltd* 2004, unreported.

contrast there is no dispute if a response to the claim is under consideration,[1] if the issues are purely hypothetical or arise between the parties and a third party who is not subject to the arbitration clause.[2] It is unclear from *Halki* whether an admission of liability and *quantum* by the respondent gives the claimant the right to bring judicial proceedings for summary judgment or whether it remains necessary for the claimant to commence arbitration proceedings and to seek a summary award. However, in *Glencore Grain Ltd* v. *Agros Trading Co*,[3] the Court of Appeal held that a dispute did not cease to be a dispute simply because liability was admitted, as the claimant was entitled to obtain an arbitration award which he could then enforce under the New York Convention.

If there is a dispute between the parties relating to the jurisdiction of the arbitrators, for example, whether there is an agreement to go to arbitration, or a dispute which triggers the arbitration clause, then provided that the arbitrators have the power to determine their own jurisdiction—which is assumed to be the case under section 30—the court has a series of options. It may:

(1) decide on the basis of affidavit evidence that there is an arbitration agreement and that the disputes in question fall within its scope (in which case a stay must be granted by reason of the mandatory language in section 9(4)); or
(2) grant a stay but leave the jurisdictional issue to be determined by the arbitrators under section 30; or
(3) order an issue to be tried under CPR r. 62.8(3) as to, for example, the existence or validity of the arbitration clause;[4] or
(4) decide that there is no arbitration agreement or that the claim falls outside its scope and dismiss the application to stay.[5]

In the light of the decision in *Fiona Trust*, the presumption may now be that the arbitral tribunal will usually be the first port of call in any jurisdictional determination, even one that if proved correct would mean that the underlying contract were held to be void, for example, for illegality. However, the law is unclear as to the precise circumstances in which the court would proceed with, for example, option (3). A trial of a preliminary issue was ordered by Lightman J in *Albon* v. *Naza Motor Trading (No 3)*.[6] In *Albon*, Lightman J indicated (having read the Court of Appeal decision in *Fiona Trust*) that in fact the court would have no jurisdiction to grant a stay under section 9(1) unless satisfied that there was a valid arbitration agreement which extended to the dispute in question, and that until so satisfied, any power to stay the proceedings, for example, in order to allow the question of the validity of the arbitration agreement to be determined by the arbitral tribunal, was a power exercisable only under the court's inherent jurisdiction but not under section 9, and would be exercised only in an exceptional case, unless "virtually certain" that an arbitration agreement existed. In practice it is not easy to see any real difference between (a) an allegation that the underlying contract containing the arbitration clause had been procured by bribes and was, therefore, voidable (as in *Fiona Trust*, stay ordered) and (b) an allegation that the contract containing the arbitration agreement was a complete forgery (*Albon*, no stay but trial as to issue of forgery ordered). What is clear, following *Fiona Trust*, is that any application under section 9 founded upon an allegation that the contract containing the arbitration clause was procured by fraud, or was in some

1. *Cruden Construction Ltd* v. *Commissioner for the New Towns* [1995] 2 Lloyd's Rep 387; *Carillion Construction Ltd* v. *Devonport Royal Dockyard* [2003] 1 BLR 79.
2. *Carvill America Ltd* v. *Camperdown UK Ltd* [2004] EWHC 2221 (Comm).
3. [1999] 2 Lloyd's Rep 410.
4. It is considered unlikely that the court would order a trial to determine, e.g., whether the disputes in question fell within the scope of the arbitration clause as this would not involve complicated issues of fact. A trial is only likely to be ordered where there are disputed issues of fact that cannot be resolved by affidavit evidence and which relate, e.g., to the existence of the arbitration clause. However, applying the principles laid down by Lord Hoffmann in *Fiona Trust* v. *Privalov & Ors* [2008] 1 Lloyd's Rep 254, it would seem that an order for a trial of an issue going to jurisdiction will be rarely made, particularly as the arbitrators have the power under s. 30 to determine their own jurisdiction except in what must be the rarest circumstances of the parties having pre-agreed to deprive them of such power.
5. The above options were first set out in *Birse Construction Ltd* v. *St David Ltd* [1999] BLR 194 *per* HHJ Humphrey Lloyd QC, and have been approved by the Court of Appeal on several occasions, most recently in *Fiona Trust* v. *Privalov ors* [2007] 2 Lloyd's Rep 267.
6. [2007] 2 Lloyd's Rep 1.

way tainted by illegality, will fail unless it can be shown that there is a clear basis for an attack directed at the arbitration clause itself.[1]

The burden of proving that any of the grounds in section 9(4) has been made out is borne by the claimant (i.e. the respondent to the application), and if the applicant can raise only an arguable case in favour of validity, a stay should be granted.[2]

It might be noted that an arbitration agreement with a consumer is generally unenforceable, under section 89, and it follows that where that provision applies the court must refuse to stay its proceedings, even though the consumer may have participated in the arbitration proceedings.

Section 9(5) has no counterpart in earlier legislation, and is designed to deal with arbitration clauses in *Scott* v. *Avery*[3] form. Under a clause of this type arbitration is a condition precedent to judicial proceedings, and the parties may bring an action against each other only on the arbitrators' award, so that the contract becomes one solely to pay the sum awarded in arbitration. A *Scott* v. *Avery* clause necessarily ousts the general rule that judicial proceedings can be brought on a matter which has been made the subject of an arbitration agreement. Section 9(4) contains a more general principle that a *Scott* v. *Avery* clause is automatically overridden where a stay is refused.[4] A *Scott* v. *Avery* clause is, therefore, no longer an absolute bar to judicial proceedings. Section 9(5) also has the effect noted by the DAC in its February 1996 Report, paragraph 57, of avoiding the situation in which the arbitration clause is for some reason unworkable but there can be no access to the courts: the DAC noted that "a situation in which a party can neither arbitrate nor litigate must be avoided".

There is no express right of appeal against a decision on stay, but it was held by the House of Lords in *Inco Europe Ltd* v. *First Choice Distribution*[5] that a right of appeal exists. Permission to appeal may presumably be given by either the trial judge or the Court of Appeal.

Independently of the court's duties under section 9 of the 1996 Act, the court has a general discretion to stay its proceedings under section 49(3) of the Supreme Court Act 1981. That power may be exercised where an arbitration is to take place in some other jurisdiction involving one of the parties to the English judicial proceedings and the outcome of that arbitration would effectively determine the issues in dispute in the English action.[6] A stay may also be appropriate where the arbitration is not governed by the 1996 Act (e.g., because the arbitration agreement is not in writing), where the dispute resolution process is not arbitration as such but is nevertheless one which should be given the opportunity to be operated,[7] or where there is an arbitration agreement falling within the 1996 Act but the dispute itself in part falls outside the agreement but will be determined by the outcome of the arbitration.[8]

If an application for a stay under section 9(1) succeeds, the effect will be that the action is stayed forever (contrast the position in terms of, for example, a stay pending provision of security for costs). For that reason, the usual costs rule is that the claimant will be ordered to pay the defendant's costs of the action—this is the standard wording in the court pro forma for an order for a stay under section 9(1) of the 1996 Act.[9] It is also now settled that costs will usually be awarded against the claimant on an indemnity basis.[10]

1. See also *El Nasharty* v. *J Sainsbury plc* [2008] 1 Lloyd's Rep 360.
2. *Hume* v. *AA Mutual International Insurance* [1996] LRLR 19, as approved in *Downing* v. *Al Tameer Establishment & Anr* [2002] EWCA Civ 721. A stay is now of course much more likely following the decision in *Fiona Trust* v. *Privalov & Ors* [2008] 1 Lloyd's Rep 246. But for a different view see *Albon* v. *Naza Motor Trading (No 3)* [2007] 2 Lloyd's Rep 1 as discussed above.
3. (1856) 5 HL Cas 811.
4. The 1996 Act allows a *Scott* v. *Avery* clause to be overridden in a number of other circumstances: (i) s. 13(3), which disregards a *Scott* v. *Avery* clause for limitation purposes; (ii) s. 71(4), where it is alleged that the arbitrators did not have jurisdiction to make their award, that there has been serious irregularity in the proceedings or affecting the arbitrators or the award or that there has been an error of law. These provisions are new but reproduce the effect of the repealed provisions of the Arbitration Act 1950.
5. [2000] 1 Lloyd's Rep 467.
6. *Reichhold Norway ASA* v. *Goldman Sachs International* [1999] 1 All ER (Comm) 40.
7. See above.
8. *T & N Ltd* v. *Royal and Sun Alliance plc* [2004] Lloyd's Rep IR 102 (stay refused).
9. Court Form No PF167.
10. *A* v. *B (No 2)* [2007] 1 Lloyd's Rep 358.

Reference of interpleader issue in arbitration

10.—(1) Where in legal proceedings relief by way of interpleader is granted and any issue between the claimants is one in respect of which there is an arbitration agreement between them, the court granting the relief shall direct that the issue be determined in accordance with the agreement unless the circumstances are such that proceedings brought by a claimant in respect of the matter would not be stayed.

(2) Where subsection (1) applies but the court does not direct that the issue be determined in accordance with the arbitration agreement, any provision that an award is a condition precedent to the bringing of legal proceedings in respect of any matter shall not affect the determination of that issue by the court.

NOTES

Interpleader arises where a party A, who is under an obligation to party B or to party C, but it is not clear which, invokes the protection of the court by asking it to determine whether B or C is the obligee. This situation will most commonly arise where A is in possession of property or money to which both B and C claim an immediate right to possession: accounting to the wrong party will leave A open to an action by the other. In those circumstances, A has the right to apply to the court for interpleader relief, usually in the form of an order that B and C either withdraw their competing claims, or set their competing claims against one another. Section 5 of the Arbitration Act 1950 provided that, if the issue between B and C was one to which an arbitration agreement applied, the court could stay its own proceedings and order that the issue be decided in accordance with the arbitration agreement. Section 10 re-enacts this provision, with drafting modifications and two substantive changes.

The first change is found in section 10(1), which draws a distinction between cases in which the court would have refused to stay its proceedings (as set out in section 9(4)) and cases in which it would not have refused to stay its proceedings. In the former case the court is to direct that the matter is to be dealt with by arbitration, while in the latter case it may deal with the case itself. This reflects the New York Convention 1958, which requires each contracting state to provide in its domestic law that its courts are to grant a mandatory stay in the case of a non-domestic arbitration agreement: the UK had failed to implement this obligation in the case of interpleader, and section 10(1) of the Act corrects that default. The point is largely academic, given that section 86 has not been brought into force so that domestic and non-domestic agreements are to be treated in the same way.

The second change is in section 10(2), which allows a *Scott* v. *Avery* clause to be disregarded where the court deals with the matter itself under section 10(2). This is consistent with section 9(5), discussed above.

There is no express right of appeal against a court decision on the matters dealt with by section 10, but it was held by the House of Lords in *Inco Europe Ltd* v. *First Choice Distribution*[1] that a right of appeal exists. Permission to appeal may presumably be given by either the judge hearing the application or the Court of Appeal.

Retention of security where Admiralty proceedings stayed, &c

11.—(1) Where Admiralty proceedings are stayed on the ground that the dispute in question should be submitted to arbitration, the court granting the stay may, if in those proceedings property has been arrested or bail or other security has been given to prevent or obtain release from arrest—

(a) order that the property arrested be retained as security for the satisfaction of any award given in the arbitration in respect of that dispute, or

1. [2000] 1 Lloyd's Rep 467.

(b) order that the stay of these proceedings be conditional on the provision of equivalent security for the satisfaction of any such award.

(2) Subject to any provision made by rules of court and to any necessary modification, the same law and practice shall apply in relation to property retained in pursuance of an order as would apply if it were held for the purposes of proceedings in the court making the order.

NOTES

This section re-enacts, with minor and immaterial drafting differences, that part of section 26 of the Civil Jurisdiction and Judgments Act 1982 which applies to arbitration.[1] Prior to the passing of section 26, a vessel could be arrested only as security for a judgment and not for an arbitration award. The cases reached the position that a vessel which had been arrested to secure pending court proceedings had to be released if the proceedings were stayed in the light of an arbitration clause, although the arrest could be maintained if the court took the view that the proceedings would ultimately result in a judgment.[2] Given that a judgment was likely where the owner of the vessel was insolvent, the effect of the rule was that an arrest could be maintained in the case of an insolvent owner. The 1982 Act removed the basic difficulty by allowing the maintenance of the arrest, or the provision of security, for the satisfaction of an arbitration award.

There is one difference between section 26 of the 1982 Act and the replacement provision in the 1996 Act. Under the earlier provision the court was empowered to make the maintenance of the arrest conditional on, for example, the prompt pursuit of the arbitration proceedings. That power gave rise to no difficulty in the case of a domestic arbitration, but where the arbitration was non-domestic the New York Convention prevented the grant of a stay being made subject to any conditions, so that the court was required either to discharge the vessel or to maintain the arrest. In the light of this difficulty, section 26(2) has not been re-enacted in section 11 of the Act.

The maintenance of an arrest under section 11 remains discretionary.[3] Arrest may be discharged if security is provided, either by the respondent or—in practice—by his P & I Club, generally in the form of letters of credit issued by a bank and with the claimant as named beneficiary.[4]

Commencement of Arbitral Proceedings

Power of court to extend time for beginning arbitral proceedings

12.—(1) Where an arbitration agreement to refer future disputes to arbitration provides that a claim shall be barred, or the claimant's right extinguished, unless the claimant takes within a time fixed by the agreement some step—

(a) to begin arbitral proceedings, or

(b) to begin other dispute resolution procedures which must be exhausted before arbitral proceedings can be begun,

the court may by order extend the time for taking that step.

(2) Any party to the arbitration agreement may apply for such an order (upon notice to the other parties), but only after a claim has arisen and after exhausting any available arbitral process for obtaining an extension of time.

1. DAC Report, para. 60.
2. *The Tuyuti* [1984] 2 All ER 545.
3. For the exercise of the discretion, see *The Bazias 3* [1993] 1 Lloyd's Rep 101.
4. See *Mousaka Inc* v. *Golden Seagull Maritime Inc (No 2)* [2002] 1 Lloyd's Rep 797, in which it was held that letters of credit were not discharged by a ruling that the arrest was invalid, as they were autonomous contracts independent of legal proceedings between the parties to the dispute.

(3) The court shall make an order only if satisfied—

(a) that the circumstances are such as were outside the reasonable contemplation of the parties when they agreed the provision in question, and that it would be just to extend the time, or

(b) that the conduct of one party makes it unjust to hold the other party to the strict terms of the provision in question.

(4) The court may extend the time for such period and on such terms as it thinks fit, and may do so whether or not the time previously fixed by agreement or by a previous order has expired.

(5) An order under this section does not affect the operation of the Limitation Acts (see section 13).

(6) The leave of the court is required for any appeal from a decision of the court under this section.

NOTES

Section 12 can be traced back to the Arbitration Act 1934, and its purpose was to ensure that a party to a standard form arbitration agreement was not caught out by time limits in a document which, in the ordinary course of business, would not be read by him.[1] Moreover, there may have been some form of pressure exerted to agree to the clause in the first place. The removal, since 1988, of consumers from the binding effect of arbitration agreements is certainly an argument in favour of a less interventionist approach being taken to such clauses in the modern context, and this is indeed the approach adopted by the 1996 Act.[2]

Section 12 is mandatory and its operation may not be excluded by agreement in writing. The parties cannot, therefore, agree that the time limits laid down by them shall not be extended by the court.[3] One remaining doubt concerns the use of clauses which confer upon the arbitrators the right to extend time: such a clause did not preclude the operation of the earlier provision, section 27 of the 1950 Act,[4] but there is a possible argument to the effect that an implicit substitution of the judicial power to extend time is intended where such a clause is used. This argument would nevertheless seem to be negatived by section 12(2), which contemplates that there may be an arbitral process for the extension of time, and that the existence of such process does not necessarily preclude application under section 12. The same point arises under section 50, which allows the court to extend the agreed time for the making of an award subject to any agreement to the contrary.

The power under section 12(1) applies only to agreements to refer future disputes rather than to submission agreements,[5] and the use of the phrase "claim shall be barred, or the claimant's right extinguished" means beyond all doubt that section 12(1) applies both to clauses which, after time has run, bar arbitration and clauses which bar any remedy whatsoever.[6]

1. For the history, see the DAC Report, para. 65.
2. The DAC specifically decided against including a third ground in s. 12(3), namely, that the bargaining position of the parties was unequal, as it regarded other consumer protection measures as adequate to prevent abuse: DAC Report, paras 70–71.
3. That was also the position under s. 27 of the Arbitration Act 1950: *Pittalis* v. *Sherefettin* [1986] 2 All ER 227.
4. *Comdel Commodities Ltd* v. *Siporex Trade SA* [1990] 2 All ER 552.
5. An agreement which confers an option to arbitrate remains an agreement to refer future disputes: *Navigazione Alta Italia SpA* v. *Concordia Maritime Chartering AC, The Stena Pacifica* [1990] 2 Lloyd's Rep 234.
6. The 1950 Act referred only to claims being barred, but it was nevertheless held by the courts that s. 27 of the 1950 Act applied to both types of clause: *Consolidated Investment Contracting Co* v. *Saponaria Shipping Co Ltd, The Virgo* [1978] 3 All ER 988. For the distinction, see: *Evergos Naftiki Eteria* v. *Cargill plc, The Voltaz* [1997] 1 Lloyd's Rep 35; *Metalfer Corporation* v. *Pan Ocean Shipping Co Ltd* [1998] 2 Lloyd's Rep 632.

Section 12(1)(b) allows time to be extended for the commencement of dispute resolution procedures which must be exhausted before arbitral proceedings can take effect: the earlier provision was confined to extending time in relation to "some other step to commence arbitration proceedings", and the cases decided under it drew a difficult distinction between steps to commence proceedings (normally to appoint an arbitrator) and steps to establish the existence of a dispute between the parties, for example, giving written notice of a claim. In a number of cases it was held that steps of the latter type were not sufficiently proximate to the commencement of proceedings to be protected by section 27.[1] It is the case under the 1996 Act that any step which must lead to arbitration is within section 12(1)(b). It remains uncertain just how far this goes, for section 10(1) presupposes the existence of an established dispute. Take, for example, a rent review clause which permits the rent to be reviewed every three years, provided that the landlord proposes a new rent within a given period, and that if the tenant opposes the proposal the matter may be referred to arbitration. If the landlord fails to give notice of his intention to raise the rent within the due time, it is difficult to accept that section 12(1)(b) applies to his failure to give notice, as there is no dispute and the notice can scarcely be described as "dispute resolution procedures" in the absence of a dispute. It remains the case, therefore, that section 12(1)(b) requires difficult distinctions to be drawn. The DAC Report paragraph 74 treats the change as "small" and aimed at mediation and other alternative dispute resolution procedures.

Section 12(2) requires the applicant to have sought from the arbitrators any relief which they are empowered to grant under the arbitration agreement as a condition precedent of application to the High Court. The DAC Report, paragraph 74, indicated that, if the arbitrators have refused to extend time, it would be "difficult if not impossible" to persuade the court to do so.[2]

Section 12(3)(a) sets out the first of the two situations in which time can be extended. Two conditions have to be satisfied before time can be extended: (1) the circumstances could not reasonably have been contemplated when the arbitration agreement was made; and (2) extending time would be "just". The Arbitration Act 1950, section 27, authorised the extension of time limits where failure to do so would result in "undue hardship". The large number of authorities on the phrase "undue hardship" illustrate that the courts had taken a very liberal view of their powers, a tendency put down by the DAC Report, paragraphs 67 to 69, to a view that the courts possessed some form of residual supervisory jurisdiction over arbitration. Relevant factors in the exercise of discretion under the 1950 Act included the amount at stake, the length of the delay, the reason for the delay and comparative prejudice to the parties.[3] Condition (2), that it would be "just" to extend time (originally, "substantial injustice" by not extending time in the July 1995 Bill), is unfortunate, as it has the potential to give rise to a good deal of time-consuming speculation as to whether "undue hardship" means anything different to "just", although it might be thought that the wording indicates that section 12 is to be applied generously in order to allow disputes to go to arbitration rather than to be resolved in any other way. It might be noted that the phrase "substantial injustice" has been retained in sections 50 (extension of time for making an award) and 79(3)(b) (extension of time limits imposed by the default provisions of Part I of the Act).

Whether or not any meaningful change has been effected in the first part of section 12(3)(a), it is clear that the addition of the further requirement in section 12(3)(a) is intended to restrict significantly the operation of section 12. The form of wording chosen for section 12(3)(a) was stated by the Departmental Advisory Committee in its July 1995 Report to be "designed to reflect the

1. *Babanaft International Co SA* v. *Avant Petroleum Inc, The Oltenia* [1982] 3 All ER 244; *Mariana Islands Steamship Corporation* v. *Marimpex Mineraloel-Handelsgesellschaft mbH Co KG, The Medusa* [1986] 2 Lloyd's Rep 328. Contrast *Pittalis* v. *Sherefettin* [1986] 2 All ER 227 and *Jadranska Slobodna Plovidba* v. *Oleagine SA, The Luka Botic* [1983] 3 All ER 602, in each of which the various steps were closely interrelated and could not be distinguished.

2. See *Marc Rich Agriculture Trading SA* v. *Agrimex Ltd* [2000] 1 All ER (Comm) 951.

3. These principles were laid down in *Moscow V/O Exportkhleb* v. *Helmville Ltd, The Jocelyne* [1977] 2 Lloyd's Rep 121. Of the many cases illustrating a generous approach, see: *Tradax Internacional SA* v. *Cerrahogullari TAS, The M Eregli* [1981] 2 Lloyd's Rep 169; *Garrick Shipping Co* v. *Euro-Frachtkontor GmbH, The World Agamemnon* [1989] 2 Lloyd's Rep 316 (size of claim); *Unitramp SA* v. *Jenson Nicholson Pte Ltd, The Baiona* [1991] 2 Lloyd's Rep 121 (fault of claimant's legal advisers); *Phoenix Shipping (Pty) Ltd* v. *General Feeds Inc* [1997] 2 Lloyd's Rep 703 (fault of claimant's legal advisers).

overall philosophy of Part I of the Act so that, in effect, the parties can only escape from their arbitration bargain if events arise which can, in effect, clearly be said to fall outside that bargain". The unforeseeable is thus required to have taken place before the High Court has jurisdiction to extend time. It is apparent that the authorities under section 27 are largely unreliable. The post-Act authorities have borne out the restricted view of section 12(3)(a) adopted by the Court of Appeal. In the first of the cases, *Vosnoc Ltd* v. *Transglobal Projects Ltd*,[1] HHJ Jack QC held that a mistake by the claimant, which led to the belief that a notice had validly commenced arbitration proceedings when this was not in fact the case, was sufficient to allow an extension of time.[2] However, in all subsequent authorities a far stricter approach has been adopted and extensions have been refused in *Cathiship SA* v. *Allansons Ltd, The Catherine Helen*,[3] *Grimaldi Compagnia di Navigazione SpA* v. *Sekihyo Lines Ltd*,[4] *Harbour and General Works Ltd* v. *The Environment Agency*,[5] *Thyssen Inc* v. *Calypso Shipping Corp SA*[6] *Monella* v. *Pizza Express*[7] and *Van Oord ACZ Ltd* v. *The Port of Mostyn*,[8] in each case the claimant or his lawyers having mistaken the existence or operation of the arbitration clause. It is doubtful, therefore, whether *Vosnoc* represents the law. As was said by Colman J in *Harbour and General Works*:

> [I]t would appear quite impossible to characterise a negligent omission to comply with a time bar, however little delay were involved, as without more, outside their [the parties'] mutual contemplation. Narrowly overlooking a time bar due to an administrative oversight is far from being so uncommon as to be treated as beyond the parties' reasonable contemplation. The process of identifying and evaluating in the balance the disparity between the prejudice to the claimant on the one hand and the degree of fault on his part on the other will not normally be a relevant exercise in determining whether there were circumstances beyond the reasonable contemplation of the parties.

What is required for the extension of time is, therefore, an event which the parties could not have contemplated at all when the arbitration agreement was entered into,[9] for example, the fact the claimant company in the arbitration had been restored to the register of companies, thereby automatically reviving the arbitration proceedings brought by it and triggering the time limits for the appointment of an arbitrator.[10]

The alternative ground upon which time can be extended, in section 12(3)(b), relates to the conduct of the other party. A standstill agreement, express or implied, doubtless justifies an application under section 12(3)(b) if the time bar is subsequently pleaded in breach of that agreement. Mere inaction by the respondent is not enough to bring section 12(3)(b) into play,[11] although deliberate obstruction of the claimant's attempts to serve will justify an order for the extension of time under section 12(3)(b).[12]

1. [1998] 1 Lloyd's Rep 711.
2. Although the court was apparently mistaken on this point: see the Notes to s. 13, below.
3. [1998] 2 Lloyd's Rep 511.
4. [1998] 2 Lloyd's Rep 638. See also: *Fox & Widley* v. *Guram* [1998] 1 EGLR 91.
5. [2000] 1 All ER (Comm) 50.
6. [2000] 2 Lloyd's Rep 243.
7. [2004] 1 EGLR 43.
8. 2003, unreported.
9. *Grimaldi Compagnia di Navigazione SpA* v. *Sekihyo Lines Ltd* [1998] 2 Lloyd's Rep 638; *Cathiship SA* v. *Allansons Ltd, The Catherine Helen* [1998] 2 Lloyd's Rep 511; *Fox & Widley* v. *Guram* [1998] 3 EG 142; *Verity Shipping SA* v. *Chartworld Shipping Corporation, The Skier Star* [2008] 1 Lloyd's Rep 652.
10. *Union Trans-Pacific Co Ltd* v. *Orient Shipping Rotterdam BV* [2002] EWHC 1451 (Comm). See also *Borgship Tankers Inc* v. *Product Transport Corp Ltd, The Casco* [2005] EWHC 273 (Comm), where it was suggested that a change in the established law as to the meaning of an arbitration clause could amount to circumstances beyond the contemplation of the parties.
11. *Vosnoc* v. *Transglobal Projects Ltd* [1998] 1 Lloyd's Rep 711; *Grimaldi Compagnia di Navigazione SpA* v. *Sekihyo Lines Ltd* [1998] 2 Lloyd's Rep 638; *Cathiship SA* v. *Allansons Ltd, The Catherine Helen* [1998] 2 Lloyd's Rep 511; *Harbour and General Works Ltd* v. *The Environment Agency* [2000] 1 All ER (Comm) 50.
12. *Van Oord ACZ Ltd* v. *The Port of Mostyn* 2003, unreported.

It is to be emphasised that, even if either of the grounds in section 12(3) is made out, the court retains an overriding discretion as to whether or not to extend time:[1] the word "shall" in this context means "may".

Section 12(4) is self-explanatory. In practice most applications are made when time has expired.

Section 12(5) states that extension of time is without prejudice to the operation of "the Limitation Acts", a phrase which by section 13(4)(a) includes all statutory time limits (thereby preventing the extension of statutory time limits under legislation such as the Carriage of Goods by Sea Act 1971)[2] and also the Foreign Limitation Periods Act 1984, which governs the position where the law applicable to the agreement is a foreign law: the DAC in its July 1995 Report felt that there should be a clear reference to the 1984 Act, for the avoidance of doubt. Time limits under the Act itself can be extended by the court under its general powers contained in sections 79 and 80(5).

Section 12(6) confirms one of the underlying purposes of the Act, namely, to minimise judicial intervention and to ensure that such recourse to the courts as is permitted by the Act is not used to delay the arbitration proceedings. The "court" means the trial judge and not the Court of Appeal.[3]

Application to extend time is by means of an arbitration claim form. Notice, in the form of a copy of the arbitration claim form and any supporting evidence, must be given to the other parties to the arbitration, and they are to be made parties to the application.[4] The claim form may, under CPR r. 62.4(3), include in the alternative an application for a declaration that time for commencing the arbitration has not expired so that there is no need for time to be extended. This provision is problematical in that the arbitrators themselves will generally have jurisdiction to determine whether the proceedings have been validly commenced in time, so that if the arbitrators have yet to resolve the question the arbitration application to the court will be premature. Guidelines to overcome this problem were laid down by Mance J in *Grimaldi Compagnia di Navigazione SpA* v. *Sekihyo Lines*.[5] If the respondent agrees that the time bar issue can be resolved by the court, no problem arises. However, if the respondent objects, two alternative possibilities arise: either (a) the claimant can agree to the arbitrators determining the time bar issue, with the arbitration application being stayed pending the outcome; or (b) the claimant can request the court to proceed to decide the arbitration application concurrently with the arbitrators resolving the time bar issue itself, and the court may decide to do so on the assumption that the time bar is applicable.

Application of Limitation Acts

13.—(1) The Limitation Acts apply to arbitral proceedings as they apply to legal proceedings.

(2) The court may order that in computing the time prescribed by the Limitation Acts for the commencement of proceedings (including arbitral proceedings) in respect of a dispute which was the subject matter—

(a) of an award which the court orders to be set aside or declares to be of no effect, or

(b) of the affected part of an award which the court orders to be set aside in part, or declares to be in part of no effect.

1. *Vosnoc* v. *Transglobal Projects Ltd* [1998] 1 Lloyd's Rep 711. Contrast *Thyssen Inc* v. *Calypso Shipping Corporation SA* [2000] 2 Lloyd's Rep 243 (conduct of applicant not justifying an order).

2. See *Kenya Railways* v. *Antares Co Pte Ltd, The Antares* [1987] 1 Lloyd's Rep 424.

3. *Henry Boot Construction (UK) Ltd* v. *Malmaison Hotel (Manchester) Ltd* [2001] 1 QB 388; *Athletic Union of Constantinople* v. *National Basketball Association* [2002] 1 Lloyd's Rep 305; *Virdee* v. *Virdi* [2003] EWCA Civ 41.

4. CPR r. 62.6(2)–(3).

5. [1998] 2 Lloyd's Rep 638.

the period between the commencement of the arbitration and the date of the order referred to in paragraph (a) or (b) shall be excluded.

(3) In determining for the purposes of the Limitation Acts when a cause of action accrued, any provision that an award is a condition precedent to the bringing of legal proceedings in respect of a matter to which an arbitration agreement applies shall be disregarded.

(4) In this Part "the Limitation Acts" means

(a) in England and Wales, the Limitation Act 1980, the Foreign Limitation Periods Act 1984 and any other enactment (whenever passed) relating to the limitation of actions;

(b) in Northern Ireland, the Limitation (Northern Ireland) Order 1989, the Foreign Limitation Periods (Northern Ireland) Order 1985 and any other enactment (whenever passed) relating to the limitation of actions.

NOTES

This section re-enacts, with drafting but not substantive changes,[1] relevant parts of section 34 of the Limitation Act 1980. The provision must be read in conjunction with sections 14 and 76 of the 1996 Act, which, taken together with section 13, reproduce all of section 34 of the Limitation Act dealing with consensual arbitrations. Section 13 is concerned only with statutory time limits. Contractual time limits may be longer or shorter, and are governed by section 12 of the Act.

Section 13(1) applies the Limitation Act 1980 to arbitration proceedings. The most important aspect of this is that the time limit for commencing arbitration proceedings is the same as for judicial proceedings; in a contract case, the relevant period is six years from the date of the breach.[2] The various ways in which an arbitration may be commenced are set out in section 14, and it is to be emphasised that the steps required by section 14 must have occurred within the limitation period.

In an action for the enforcement of an arbitration award itself, section 7 of the Limitation Act 1980 provides that the action must be brought within six years of the date on which "the cause of action accrued". It was held in *Argomet Motoimport Ltd* v. *Maulden Engineering Co (Beds) Ltd*[3] that the date of accrual is the date on which the award ought to have been honoured, and not the date on which the original cause of action giving rise to the arbitration proceedings arose. This sensible decision is left intact by the Act. In most cases, the award itself will provide the time within which, for example, payment of damages should be made (often 28 days), and it is upon expiry of this period that the cause of action on the award arises.

There is one respect in which the Limitation Act 1980 cannot be applied to arbitration proceedings. In *Kenya Railways* v. *Antares Pte Ltd, The Antares*[4] it was held that section 35 of the Limitation Act 1980, which allows a new claim to be added to an action, backdated to the date of the commencement of the original action, cannot operate in the case of an arbitration, because, if the new claim falls outside the arbitrator's terms of reference, he has no jurisdiction over it.

Section 13(2) deals with the case in which an arbitration award is set aside, nullified or modified by the court. In order to allow the matter to go back to arbitration without falling foul of a statutory time bar, section 13(2) empowers the court to disregard, for limitation purposes, the lapse of time between the commencement of the original proceedings and the date of the court's order, so that the entire process may begin again. There is no express right of appeal against a court decision on this

1. DAC Report, para. 76, makes it clear that no substantive change was intended.
2. Limitation Act 1980, s. 5. The period is 12 years if the contract is in the form of a specialty: Limitation Act 1980, s. 8.
3. [1985] 2 All ER 436. See also *International Bulk Shipping Services Ltd* v. *Minerals & Metals Trading Corpn of India & Ors* [1996] 2 Lloyd's Rep 474 (party entitled to reasonable time from date of award to honour it).
4. [1987] 1 Lloyd's Rep 424.

matter, but it was held by the House of Lords in *Inco Europe Ltd* v. *First Choice Distribution*[1] that a right of appeal exists. Permission to appeal may presumably be given by either the trial judge or the Court of Appeal.

Section 13(3) is concerned with the conceptual difficulty raised by *Scott* v. *Avery* clauses.[2] Such clauses make arbitration a condition precedent to legal proceedings, and restrict each party's right to an action on the award itself. A *Scott* v. *Avery* clause makes a nonsense of the limitation rules, as the action cannot accrue until the award has been made, so that logically there is no limitation period at all for the commencement of the arbitration proceedings. This problem is overcome by section 13(3), by requiring the *Scott* v. *Avery* provision to be disregarded in determining when the cause of action to be arbitrated arose. In other words, the usual rules of limitation apply.

The purpose of section 13(4) is to indicate that the relevant limitation legislation is: any specific statute applicable to the contract itself (e.g., the Carriage of Goods by Sea Act 1971); the Limitation Act 1980 where the law applicable to the contract is English law; and the limitation rules of another law where that law is the law applicable to the contract, in accordance with the Foreign Limitation Periods Act 1984.[3]

Commencement of arbitral proceedings

14.—(1) The parties are free to agree when arbitral proceedings are to be regarded as commenced for the purposes of this Part and for the purposes of the Limitation Acts.

(2) If there is no such agreement the following provisions apply.

(3) Where the arbitrator is named or designated in the arbitration agreement, arbitral proceedings are commenced in respect of a matter when one party serves on the other party or parties a notice in writing requiring him or them to submit that matter to the person so named or designated.

(4) Where the arbitrator or arbitrators are to be appointed by the parties, arbitral proceedings are commenced in respect of a matter when one party serves on the other party or parties notice in writing requiring him or them to appoint an arbitrator or to agree to the appointment of an arbitrator in respect of that matter.

(5) Where the arbitrator or arbitrators are to be appointed by a person other than a party to the proceedings, arbitral proceedings are commenced in respect of a matter when one party gives notice in writing to that person requesting him to make the appointment in respect of that matter.

NOTES

This section is of the greatest significance for the purpose of determining whether the limitation period applicable to the claim has been satisfied, as under section 13(1) of the 1996 Act the Limitation Act 1980 extends to arbitration proceedings. The steps set out in section 14 for commencing the arbitration must, therefore, have been taken within the limitation period if the claim is not to be time-barred. It reflects Article 21 of the Model Law. The parties are free to agree what steps are necessary to commence the arbitration, but if they fail to do so then the Act provides default provisions which apply to the most common situations. Under the arbitration rules of both the ICC and LCIA, there are specific provisions concerning the commencement of the arbitral

1. [2000] 1 Lloyd's Rep 467.
2. Similar provisions are dotted throughout the Act.
3. A foreign limitation period can be disapplied by the English court in a case of "undue hardship": Foreign Limitation Periods Act 1984, s. 2. See: *Jones* v. *Trollope & Colls Cementation Overseas Ltd* (1990) *The Times*, 26 January; *Hellenic Steel Co* v. *Svolamar Shipping Co Ltd, The Komninos S* [1990] 1 Lloyd's Rep 541.

proceedings for limitation purposes.[1] A clause which provides that if there is no agreement on an arbitrator within 14 days of the notice of arbitration then an arbitration notice may be served, does not amount to an agreement as to when the arbitration has been commenced within section 14(1).[2]

In the absence of agreement the arbitration is to be treated as having commenced when any of the events set out in section 14 have occurred, that is, service of a notice in writing:[3]

(a) requiring the other party to submit the matter to a named or identified sole arbitrator (section 14(3));
(b) where there is a sole arbitrator to be appointed by the parties, requiring the other party to agree to an appointment (section 14(4));
(c) where each of the parties is to appoint an arbitrator, requiring the other party to make an appointment (section 14(4));
(d) where an arbitrator is to be appointed by some other person not a party to the proceedings, requiring that person to make the necessary appointment (section 14(5)—it is unclear why section 14(5) refers to "gives notice" while sections 14(3) and 14(4) talk of "serves notice", although the distinction is not significant and the DAC Report, paragraph 359, recommended that there should be consistency by the use of the word "serve", a recommendation not taken up by the draftsman[4]). The term "service" is defined by section 76 of the 1996 Act. Under that section, the parties are free to agree on how service is to be effected, failing which the section provides various default rules to ensure that service is always possible. If the parties have agreed on a form of service, the court does not have the power to disregard the agreement and to allow service in some other form.[5]

The word "matter" has been used, in distinction to the previous term "dispute": the DAC Report, paragraph 76, pointed out that this was necessary so that section 14 could apply not just to disputes but also to claims.

Section 14 does not preclude the commencement of the arbitration proceedings in some other way, although an application to the court for the stay of judicial proceedings brought by the other party does not amount to the commencement of arbitration proceedings, as the grant of a stay does not of itself operate as a reference of the matter to arbitration by the court.[6] The meaning of the word "requires" has given rise to some difficulty. In some cases decided under earlier legislation it had been held that the notice had to impose an obligation on the other party, so that a polite request or statement of intention will not suffice to commence the proceedings[7] unless there was agreement to that effect. This differs from the Model Law, Article 21 of which provides that a request is enough. Other cases indicated that a request would suffice provided it was clear that arbitration proceedings were to be commenced.[8] The conflict in authority continued after the passing of the 1996 Act. In *Vosnoc Ltd* v. *Transglobal Projects Ltd*[9] HHJ Jack QC held that a notice which simply stated that the dispute was to be referred to arbitration did not "require" the appointment of an arbitrator and

1. The ICC Rules (1998 edition) provide in Art. 4.2 that the date on which the Request for Arbitration (containing certain specified information) is received by the ICC Secretariat in Paris shall "for all purposes, be deemed to be the date of the commencement of the arbitral proceedings". Art. 1.2 of the LCIA Rules (1998 edition) similarly provides that the date of receipt by the Registrar of the Request for Arbitration (again containing certain specified information) shall be treated as the date on which the arbitration has commenced for all purposes. Art. 3.2 of the UNCITRAL Rules provides that arbitral proceedings shall be deemed to commence on the date on which the notice of arbitration is received by the respondent. In each case it is probably open to a respondent to argue that the arbitration only commences in accordance with the provision in question once a document complying with the Rules has been served.
2. *Taylor Woodrow Construction* v. *RMD Kwikform Ltd* [2008] EWHC 825 (TCC).
3. Email suffices: *Bernuth Lines Ltd* v. *High Seas Shipping Ltd, The Eastern Navigator* [2006] 1 Lloyd's Rep 537.
4. Noted by the DAC in its Supplementary Report, para. 21.
5. *Van Oord ACZ Ltd* v. *The Port of Mostyn* 2003, unreported.
6. *Channel Tunnel Group Ltd* v. *Balfour Beatty Construction Ltd* [1993] AC 334.
7. *Cf. Surrendra Overseas Ltd* v. *Government of Sri Lanka* [1977] 1 Lloyd's Rep 653.
8. *Nea Agrex SA* v. *Baltic Shipping Co Ltd, The Aghios Lazaros* [1976] 2 Lloyd's Rep 47; *The Sargasso* [1994] 1 Lloyd's Rep 162.
9. [1998] 1 Lloyd's Rep 711.

thus did not operate to commence the arbitration. This view has, however, been rejected on a number of occasions, and the better view is that a notice suffices if it is clear that the claimant intends to commence arbitration and that the respondent is to make an appointment: this was so held by Clarke J in *West of England Ship Owners Mutual Protection and Indemnity Association (Luxembourg) Ltd* v. *Hellenic Industrial Development Bank SA*[1] and *Allianz Versicherungs-Aktiengesellschaft* v. *Fortuna Co Inc, The Baltic Universal*[2] and by Rix J in *Charles M Willie Co (Shipping) Ltd* v. *Ocean Laser Shipping Ltd, The Smaro*[3] and by Thomas J in *Seabridge Shipping AB* v. *Orsleff's EFTS A/S.*[4] A statement that arbitration may be commenced is not, however, sufficient.[5] In *Charles M Willie* Rix J noted that the requirements of section 14 were not exhaustive, in that they were applicable only to the commencement of proceedings for statutory limitation purposes, and that proceedings might be commenced in other ways in order to satisfy contractual requirements. In *Seabridge Shipping* Thomas J expressed the view that section 14 was exhaustive but that its requirements should be construed in a broad and flexible fashion.

Even where a notice has the effect of imposing a requirement on the other party to submit a dispute to arbitration, the dispute in question must be clearly identified in the notice. In any event, the dispute must be an existing one and not a potential future dispute.[6]

If an arbitration is commenced in the name of the wrong party (as where the name of the claimant has changed or there has been a merger), the notice is nevertheless valid as long as the error was due to oversight rather than fundamental error: in the former case the error can be corrected simply by amending the relevant documents.[7]

The Arbitral Tribunal

The arbitral tribunal

15.—(1) The parties are free to agree on the number of arbitrators to form the tribunal and whether there is to be a chairman or umpire.

(2) Unless otherwise agreed by the parties, an agreement that the number of arbitrators shall be two or any other even number shall be understood as requiring the appointment of an additional arbitrator as chairman of the tribunal.

(3) If there is no agreement as to the number of arbitrators, the tribunal shall consist of a sole arbitrator.

NOTES

Section 15 lays down what is described by the DAC in its Report on the July 1995 Bill as a "new and comprehensive arrangement" to replace the "incomplete regime" contained in sections 6 to 9 of the Arbitration Act 1950. Section 15 is based on, but does not exactly reproduce, Article 10 of the Model Law.

Section 15(2) deals with the typical case in which each party is to appoint one arbitrator, leaving an even number of arbitrators. In such a case the presumption, which may be ousted by contrary agreement, is that a third arbitrator is to be appointed who is to be the chairman: the manner in which a three-arbitrator panel is to reach its decisions is set out in section 20 of the Act. The presumption in favour of a chairman reverses the position under section 8(1) of the Arbitration Act 1950, where

1. [1999] 1 Lloyd's Rep 93.
2. [1999] 1 Lloyd's Rep 497.
3. [1999] 1 Lloyd's Rep 225. See also the decision of Mance J in *Villa Denizcilik Sanayi ve Ticaret SA* v. *Longen SA, The Villa* [1998] 1 Lloyd's Rep 195, decided before *Vosnoc*.
4. [1999] 2 Lloyd's Rep 685.
5. *Taylor Woodrow Construction* v. *RMD Kwikform Ltd* [2008] EWHC 825 (TCC).
6. *Great Ormond Street Hospital NHS Trust* v. *Secretary of State for Health* (1997) 56 Con LR 1.
7. *AMB Generali Holding AB Manches* v. *Seb Tryg Holding Akt* [2006] 1 Lloyd's Rep 318; *Harper Versicherungs AG* v. *River Thames Insurance Co Ltd* [2006] 2 Lloyd's Rep 263.

the presumption was in favour of the appointment of an umpire rather than a third arbitrator[1] and there was no statutory implied power vested in the two appointed arbitrators to appoint a third arbitrator.[2] An umpire may be appointed only where there is express agreement between the parties to this effect.[3] The parties are free to contract out of the need for a chairman or umpire, in which case, in accordance with section 22, the arbitrators act by majority.

Section 15(3) is the governing position where the arbitration agreement is expressed in vague terms.[4] The presumption in favour of a single arbitrator may be ousted by proof of market custom or practice pointing in some other direction, given that a typical commodity arbitration will involve the appointment of two arbitrators, one by each party, with a third arbitrator or umpire to be appointed by the arbitrators themselves,[5] although in the absence of any contrary custom or practice the presumption in favour of a sole arbitrator holds good.[6] By contrast, Article 10(2) of the Model Law provides that, in default of agreement, the panel is to consist of three arbitrators. In large commercial disputes, particularly shipping and commodities, the usual panel is of three, and it is perhaps a little surprising that the Act has retained the old, and perhaps outmoded, presumption in favour of a sole arbitrator. This matter was commented on by Lord Byron in the Second Reading of the Bill. The DAC's February 1996 Report, paragraph 79, pointed out that a default provision which laid down a three-arbitrator panel would produce unnecessary expense. The DAC also commented that a sole arbitrator overcame the problem which might arise if there were more than two parties to the arbitration, as three arbitrators might then be inappropriate. Consultation also proved to be in favour of the pre-existing position.

Procedure for appointment of arbitrators

16.—(1) The parties are free to agree on the procedure for appointing the arbitrator or arbitrators, including the procedure for appointing any chairman or umpire.

(2) If or to the extent that there is no such agreement, the following provisions apply.

(3) If the tribunal is to consist of a sole arbitrator, the parties shall jointly appoint the arbitrator not later than 28 days after service of a request in writing by either party to do so.

(4) If the tribunal is to consist of two arbitrators, each party shall appoint one arbitrator not later than 14 days after service of a request in writing by either party to do so.

(5) If the tribunal is to consist of three arbitrators—

(a) each party shall appoint one arbitrator not later than 14 days after service of a request in writing by either party to do so, and

(b) the two so appointed shall forthwith appoint a third arbitrator as the chairman of the tribunal.

(6) If the tribunal is to consist of two arbitrators and an umpire—

1. A third arbitrator merely has a casting vote (although see the Notes to s. 20 in respect of the chairman of the arbitration panel), whereas an umpire may decide the issue alone. Neither of the terms "chairman" or "umpire" is defined by the Act, although their powers are set out in ss. 20 and 21, respectively.

2. *Fletamentos Maritimos SA* v. *Effjohn International BV* [1995] 1 Lloyd's Rep 311.

3. See s. 21.

4. See the Notes to s. 6.

5. *Cf. Laertis Shipping Corporation* v. *Exportadora Espanola de Cementos Portland SA, The Laertis* [1982] 1 Lloyd's Rep 613. Art. 10(2) of the Model Law sets out a presumption in favour of three arbitrators. As already commented, it is perhaps surprising that the 1996 Act did not do the same, recognising what is commercial practice in the marine and commodity markets, although clearly not in the rent review and construction sectors.

6. *Villa Denizcilik Sanayi ve Ticaret AS* v. *Longen SA, The Villa* [1998] 1 Lloyd's Rep 195; *Atlanska Plovidba* v. *Consignaciones Asturianas SA* [2004] 2 Lloyd's Rep 109.

(a) each party shall appoint one arbitrator not later than 14 days after service of a request in writing by either party to do so, and

(b) the two so appointed may appoint an umpire at any time after they themselves are appointed and shall do so before any substantive hearing or forthwith if they cannot agree on a matter relating to the arbitration.

(7) In any other case (in particular, if there are more than two parties) section 18 applies as in the case of a failure of the agreed appointment procedure.

NOTES

The 1996 Act contains straightforward provisions for the appointment of arbitrators. The great merit of the drafting is that, unlike the earlier law, a distinction is drawn between the initial appointment of arbitrators by an agreed procedure or a procedure provided for by the Act (section 16), the default powers which are exercisable where the procedure agreed or laid down by the Act breaks down (sections 17 and 18), and the filling of casual vacancies (section 27). Section 16 is concerned with the first of these matters, and draws upon Article. 11 of the Model Law.

Section 16 applies also to the appointment of substitute arbitrators where there is a casual vacancy or where an arbitrator has been removed by the court under section 24 of the Act: see section 27(3) of the Act.

Section 16(1) makes an express statement, corresponding to art. 11(2) of the Model Law, which did not previously appear in the arbitration legislation but which nevertheless reflected the position. Where the rules of an arbitration body, or standard arbitration rules, are used—as is normally the case—the matters set out in section 16 will generally be dealt with expressly. In particular, an external body, whether trade association or arbitration institution, may be given the power to make the necessary appointments. If that body fails to act, the default powers in sections 17 and 18 come into play. Section 16(1) is to be read as being applicable to the appointment of replacement arbitrators.[1]

Section 16(2) introduces the provisions which apply in the absence of agreement. There are separate provisions for one arbitrator, two arbitrators, three arbitrators, and two arbitrators and an umpire, with a fallback provision in the event that any form of tribunal is chosen or if the points dealt with in the three specific provisions are for some reason not applicable. The provisions are based on the Model Law Article 11(3)–(4), although the Model Law makes no provision for two-arbitrator panels or for panels including an umpire. If the obligations imposed on the parties are not met, the remedial powers in sections 17 and 18 become available. In each case 28 days' notice (reduced from 30 in the July 1995 Bill in order to avoid the possibility of a deadline expiring on a weekend) must be given to the defaulting party to comply with the applicant's request to make an appointment: this period is borrowed from Article 11 of the Model Law.

Section 16(3) applies to sole arbitrators, and requires the parties to make a joint appointment within 28 days after receipt of written notice[2] served on one of the parties by the other. The main effect of section 16(3) is to impose a time limit for agreement, after which other steps become available under section 18, although that time limit can be extended under the general power conferred upon the court by section 79: the DAC Report, paragraph 81, nevertheless expressed the view that the court would not in the ordinary case be expected to extend time under section 79. Where there is a default by one party, the other's remedy is to apply to the court for relief under section 18(3) on the basis that the agreed procedure has failed: it was held by Mance J in *Villa Denizcilik Sanayi ve Ticaret AS* v. *Longen SA, The Villa*[3] that, if the parties did not agree within the specified time, then the procedure was to be regarded as having failed unless the arbitration was abandoned.

1. *Federal Insurance Co* v. *Transamerica Insurance Co of Europe SA* [1999] 2 Lloyd's Rep 286.
2. This word has been construed widely, and the notice requirement has been held to be satisfied as long as it identifies the dispute and makes it clear that there is to be a reference to arbitration: *Atlanska Plovidba* v. *Consignaciones Asturianas SA* [2004] 2 Lloyd's Rep 109.
3. [1998] 1 Lloyd's Rep 195.

Section 16(4) deals with two-arbitrator tribunals,[1] and requires each party to make an appointment within 28 days. If one of the parties fails to do so, the other may treat his arbitrator as the sole arbitrator (section 17(1)).

Section 16(5) deals with three-arbitrator panels, one of the arbitrators being the chairman.[2] Each of the parties must appoint an arbitrator within 14 days (reduced from 30 days in the July 1995 Bill) from receipt of a request by the other, and the two appointees must themselves appoint the third arbitrator "forthwith". If either party fails to act in time, the other may treat his arbitrator as the sole arbitrator (section 17(1)), and if the arbitrators themselves are appointed but have failed to appoint the third arbitrator forthwith, either party may apply to the court to make the appointment (section 18(2)–(3)).

Section 16(6) deals with the case in which the tribunal is to consist of two arbitrators and an umpire. The appointment of the two arbitrators follows the provisions of section 16(5): if either party fails to appoint his arbitrator within 14 days of receipt of a notice from the other, that other may, under section 17(1), treat his appointee as the sole arbitrator. Once the arbitrators themselves have been appointed, the question arises as to the appointment of the umpire. Section 16(6) sets out the time at which the umpire must be appointed. The effect of section 16(6) is to allow an appointment at any time after the arbitrators themselves have been appointed, and to require an appointment before any substantive hearing has taken place or forthwith if the arbitrators have failed to agree on one or more issues.[3] The use of the phrase "a matter" makes it clear that disagreement need not be on all matters (an amendment introduced in the light of the DAC's comments in its February 1996 Report, paragraph 360[4]). The section differs from the position under section 8(1) of the Arbitration Act 1950, which empowered the arbitrators to appoint an umpire before disagreement, and only required them to do so after disagreement: the change reflects section 21(3), which requires the umpire to attend the hearing before any disagreement has arisen. Any failure to appoint in accordance with these provisions may be corrected by an application by any party to the court under section 18(3). The Act does not deal with the formalities of appointment, and there is a good deal of authority—which doubtless remains good law—as to the manner in which the arbitrators make their decision and how the appointment is actually effected.[5] The right of the umpire, once appointed, to participate in the hearing is governed by section 21, discussed below.

Section 16(7) governs all matters outside section 16(3)–(6), for example, a tribunal of four or more arbitrators. It provides for an application to the court for directions. The generality of the wording of section 16(7) indicates that it also applies to the forms of tribunal referred to in section 16(3)–(6) where the point is other than one relating directly to appointment. For example (and this is arguably the only example), section 16(7) would appear to apply to the appointment of an arbitrator as chairman in the absence of any agreement between the parties as to which of the arbitrators is to take on this role: this point is discussed in more detail in the Notes to section 20 of the Act.

In exercising its powers, the court must take account of the considerations set out in section 27 of the Act.

1. The fact that s. 15(2) requires the appointment of a third arbitrator to a two-arbitrator panel seemingly takes an agreement for two arbitrators outside this subsection and within s. 16(5). The result is that s. 16(4) applies only to two-arbitrator panels where the parties have specifically agreed that there was not to be a third arbitrator, thereby ousting s. 15(2) by agreement. The situation to which s. 16(4) applies is thus one which would be rarely if ever found in practice.

2. Where the parties have agreed that there is not to be a chairman, the arbitrators act by a majority. *Quaere*, however, the position where the parties have agreed that the chairman is to be one of the original appointees. These situations might arise where there has been an express agreement for three arbitrators, rather than a deemed agreement under s. 15(2), as where s. 15(2) applies the third arbitrator is to be the chairman.

3. Quite what this means is unclear, for the arbitrators can scarcely disagree on any substantive matter until they have commenced the hearing: it may be that the disagreement can relate to procedural issues as well. The simplest practical interpretation of s. 16(6)(b) is that the umpire must be appointed before the hearing commences.

4. Noted in the DAC Supplementary Report, para. 22.

5. See, e.g., *Re Hopper* (1867) LR 2 QB 367, requiring a choice to be made by the use of judgment rather than fortuity, and *Eads* v. *Williams* (1854) De GM G 674, requiring the choice to be made by both arbitrators.

It might be noted as a general point that, unless they are precluded by agreement from so doing, the arbitrators have the power themselves to determine whether the panel has been properly constituted and whether its members are qualified in accordance with the agreement of the parties.[1]

Power in case of default to appoint sole arbitrator

17.—(1) Unless the parties otherwise agree, where each of two parties to an arbitration agreement is to appoint an arbitrator and one party ("the party in default") refuses to do so, or fails to do so within the time specified, the other party, having duly appointed his arbitrator, may give notice in writing to the party in default that he proposes to appoint his arbitrator to act as sole arbitrator.

(2) If the party in default does not within 7 clear days of that notice being given—

(a) make the required appointment, and
(b) notify the other party that he has done so,

the other party may appoint his arbitrator as sole arbitrator whose award shall be binding on both parties as if he had been so appointed by agreement.

(3) Where a sole arbitrator has been appointed under subsection (2), the party in default may (upon notice to the appointing party) apply to the court which may set aside the appointment.

(4) The leave of the court is required for any appeal from a decision of the court under this section.

NOTES

The default powers set out in sections 17 and 18 are, as pointed out by the DAC in its July 1995 Report, very much drafted as such, and apply only where there is no other method for resolving the problem under the agreement itself. Sections 17 and 18 are based on the Model Law, Article 11(4), but additionally contain the long-established right in English arbitration law of one party in certain circumstances to make the necessary appointment on behalf of himself and the defaulting party. The potential loss of this right militated against the wholesale adoption by England of the Model Law.

Section 17(1) allows a party to appoint an arbitrator as the sole arbitrator where the other party has failed to make the necessary appointment himself. This subsection avoids the cost of an application to the court and applies in any situation in which a party to the arbitration agreement has to make an appointment of an arbitrator, that is:

(a) where it is agreed that there is to be a two-arbitrator panel and each party has to appoint his own arbitrator;
(b) where it is agreed that there is to be a three-arbitrator panel and each party has to appoint his own arbitrator to facilitate the appointment of the third arbitrator; and
(c) where it has been agreed that there is to be a two-arbitrator and one-umpire panel, and each party is to appoint his own arbitrator to facilitate the appointment of the umpire.

The right of a party to have his arbitrator treated as the sole arbitrator in the case of default by the other party does not apply where the arbitration agreement provides—either by agreement or under the default presumption in section 15(3)—that there is to be a sole arbitrator. In such a case, it will be necessary to seek the assistance of the court under section 18.[2]

1. Arbitration Act 1996, s. 30(1)(b). See the notes to that section.
2. If the parties have agreed that there is to be a sole arbitrator, s. 17 is inapplicable: *Mylcrist Builders Ltd* v. *Buck* [2008] EWHC 2172 (TCC).

There is no obligation upon a party to use the section 17 procedure: he may, instead of seeking to have his own arbitrator appointed as sole arbitrator, apply to the court under section 18 for the matter to be resolved.

The procedure to be employed under section 17 is set out in section 17(1)–(2), although it may be varied by agreement. If party A has given notice to party B to appoint his arbitrator,[1] party B has 14 days to act, in accordance with section 16(4)–(6) (as the case may be). If party B has failed to comply with that time limit,[2] or states his refusal to do so before that time limit has expired,[3] party A may appoint an arbitrator if he has not done so already, and give notice to party B that he intends to treat that arbitrator as the sole arbitrator. If party B does not, within seven clear days[4] of the notice being given, make the required appointment and inform party A that he has done so, party A may go ahead and appoint his arbitrator as the sole arbitrator. The party in default is required to inform the other that he has made an appointment (section 17(2)(b)), an obligation which the DAC Report, paragraph 83, thought would remove much of the expense and delay previously flowing on from uncertainty as to the actual conduct of the party in default.

Party B as the defaulting party does have the right under section 17(3) to apply to the court to have the appointment overturned. The application is to be made to the court by way of arbitration claim. Notice, in the form of a copy of the arbitration claim form and any supporting evidence, must be given to the other parties to the arbitration, and they are to be made defendants to the application.[5] There is no authority on the circumstances in which the court will exercise its discretion either way, and the DAC Report, paragraph 85, rejected the argument that it would be appropriate to lay down criteria in place of case-by-case judicial consideration: section 19 does provide that the court is to have regard to the qualifications required of arbitrators by the parties, and it is thought that section 19 is applicable to the exercise of the court's discretion under section 17(3).[6] In any event, by virtue of section 17(4), there is an appeal from any decision of the court only with the permission of the judge and not the Court of Appeal,[7] thereby seeking to confine initial procedural disputes to a single tier of appeal in all but exceptional cases: Article 11(5) of the Model Law goes beyond this, and bans further appeal absolutely.

As commented earlier, the absence in the Model Law of the default power originally contained in section 7(b) of the Arbitration Act 1950 was one reason for the DAC under Lord Mustill rejecting a wholesale adoption of the Model Law in England. The DAC in its February 1996 Report, paragraph 84, notes that consultation had demonstrated a general desire for the retention of the power, as it is used widely, provides a cheap alternative to application to the court and acts as a deterrent to a party wishing to adopt delaying tactics.[8]

Failure of appointment procedure

18.—(1) The parties are free to agree what is to happen in the event of a failure of the procedure for the appointment of the arbitral tribunal.

1. *Glidepath Holdings BV* v. *Thompson* [2005] 2 Lloyd's Rep 549. The notice requirement may be ousted by agreement: see *Minermet SpA Milan* v. *Luckyfield Shipping Corporation SA* [2004] 2 Lloyd's Rep 348, in which the Gencon arbitration clause was held to have this effect.
2. Time may be extended by means of an application to the court under s. 79, but this power may be exercised only if there would be a substantial injustice by a failure to extend time. This may be difficult to prove where the parties were both fully aware of what the position would be in the event of default and where the arbitration can proceed perfectly validly with a sole arbitrator: *Minermet SpA Milan* v. *Luckyfield Shipping Corporation SA* [2004] 2 Lloyd's Rep 348.
3. This is the significance of the word "refuses" in s. 17(1): DAC Report, para. 86.
4. The expression "seven clear days" means that at least that number of days must intervene between the day on which the act is done and that date: s. 78(4). For this purpose, Saturdays, Sundays and public holidays are excluded (s. 78(5)). Care should therefore be taken to allow the appropriate number of days before confirming any default appointment under this section.
5. CPR r. 62.6(2)–(3).
6. See the Notes to s. 19 for an explanation of this point.
7. *Virdee* v. *Virdi* [2003] EWCA Civ 41.
8. An approach noted with approval by Moore-Bick J in *Minermet SpA Milan* v. *Luckyfield Shipping Corporation SA* [2004] 2 Lloyd's Rep 348.

There is no failure if an appointment is duly made under section 17 (power in case of default to appoint sole arbitrator), unless that appointment is set aside.

(2) If or to the extent that there is no such agreement any party to the arbitration agreement may (upon notice to the other parties) apply to the court to exercise its powers under this section.

(3) Those powers are—

(a) to give directions as to the making of any necessary appointments;
(b) to direct that the tribunal shall be constituted by such appointments (or any one or more of them) as have been made;
(c) to revoke any appointments already made;
(d) to make any necessary appointment itself.

(4) An appointment made by the court under this section has effect as if made with the agreement of the parties.

(5) The leave of the court is required for any appeal from a decision of the court under this section.

NOTES

Section 18, by virtue of section 18(1), applies to all cases in which the appointment procedure has failed, other than those which have been disposed of under section 17 by the appointment of a sole arbitrator: if section 17 has not been used, or if the court has set aside the appointment of the sole arbitrator in accordance with section 17(3), section 18 will again be applicable. This provision is again based on the Model Law. The most important situations in which section 18 will apply are where:

(a) the tribunal is to consist of a single arbitrator and one party has failed to agree to an appointment; and
(b) a third party charged with the obligation to make an appointment has failed to do so—this extends to failure by the arbitrators themselves to appoint a third arbitrator or an umpire.

The default powers operate only where the agreed appointment procedure has failed. If the agreed procedure has not been implemented in the first place, it cannot be said to have failed and the court has no jurisdiction to intervene under section 18.[1]

In any case of failure of the appointment procedure, assuming that the parties have not agreed on any default procedure, an application may be made to the court under section 18(2) for the making of any necessary appointment or for directions on how the matter is to proceed. Notice, in the form of a copy of the arbitration claim form and any supporting evidence, must be given to the other parties to the arbitration, and they are to be made parties to the application.[2] The various powers open to the court are contained in section 18(3). The court is not required to exercise its powers under section 18, and some guidance may be obtained from decisions under section 10 of the 1950 Act, although it should be borne in mind that the approach under the 1996 Act is focused on holding the parties to their agreement so that an application will be granted other than in exceptional circumstances[3] and in particular will not be refused today simply because arbitration may be inconvenient given the existence of third party and other claims outside the scope of the arbitration

1. *Secretary of State for Foreign and Commonwealth Affairs* v. *Percy Thomas Partnership* (1998) 65 Con LR 11 (decided under earlier legislation).

2. CPR r. 62.6(2)–(3).

3. *West of England Ship Owners Mutual Protection and Indemnity Association (Luxembourg) Ltd* v. *Hellenic Industrial Development Bank SA* [1999] 1 Lloyd's Rep 93; *R Durtnell and Sons Ltd* v. *Secretary of State for Trade and Industry* [2000] BLR 771.

clause.[1] The court will thus refuse to act where the delay by the applicant has been such as to cause serious prejudice to the respondent[2] or if the claim would obviously be time-barred.[3] More recently it has been said that delay is not of itself determinative, and that the real question is whether the dispute could be fairly resolved in the arbitration.[4] The power to appoint an arbitrator has been exercised on the claimant's application even though there are judicial proceedings affecting the same dispute in existence in some other jurisdiction and the English court has refused to grant an anti-suit injunction to prevent the defendant from participating in those proceedings.[5] Assuming that the court decides to intervene, the Act does not specify how the court's discretion is to be exercised, although the court will incline to appoint a tribunal constituted as agreed between the parties in the arbitration clause.[6] Under section 19 of the Act the court is required to take account of any agreement by the parties as to the arbitrators' qualifications, any failure by the applicant to apply with reasonable diligence, and the need to ensure a fair hearing with the minimum of expense or delay. The power to revoke existing appointments, under section 18(3)(c), reflects the danger that, if party A has appointed his own arbitrator and the court appoints an arbitrator for party B, party B has a legitimate complaint that he has not been treated fairly: the DAC in its February 1996 Report, paragraph 88, noted that in France an arbitration award had been set aside in these very circumstances.

If an appointment is made, under section 18(4) it takes effect as if it had been agreed to by the parties. An appeal, under section 18(5), is possible only with the permission of the court, consistently with section 17(4). The Model Law does not afford any possibility of appeal to the courts, but the DAC Report, paragraph 89, suggested that a right of appeal should be given as there might well be questions of important general principle which would benefit from the laying down of judicial guidelines.

Section 18 applies also to failure in the appointment procedure of a substitute arbitrator following a casual vacancy or a removal under section 24 of the Act: see section 27(3) of the Act.

Section 18(5) requires the permission of the court for any appeal. The "court" means the trial judge and not the Court of Appeal.[7]

Court to have regard to agreed qualifications

19. In deciding whether to exercise, and in considering how to exercise, any of its powers under section 16 (procedure for appointment of arbitrators) or section 18 (failure of appointment procedure), the court shall have due regard to any agreement of the parties as to the qualifications required of the arbitrators.

1. See, under the earlier legislation, *Petredec Ltd* v. *Tokomaru Kaiun Co Ltd, The Sargasso* [1994] 1 Lloyd's Rep 162.
2. *Frota Oceanica Brasiliera SA* v. *Steamship Mutual Underwriting Association (Bermuda) Ltd, The Frotanorte* [1996] 2 Lloyd's Rep 461, which makes it clear that inexcusable and inordinate delay is not required, as would be the case for a striking out for want of prosecution. In that case the delay was described as "awe inspiring". See also *Secretary of State for Foreign and Commonwealth Affairs* v. *Percy Thomas Partnership* (1998) 65 Con LR 11. Contrast *R Durtnell and Sons Ltd* v. *Secretary of State for Trade and Industry* [2000] BLR 771; *Atlanska Plovidba* v. *Consignaciones Asturianas SA* [2004] 2 Lloyd's Rep 109.
3. In *West of England Ship Owners Mutual Protection and Indemnity Association (Luxembourg) Ltd* v. *Hellenic Industrial Development Bank SA* [1999] 1 Lloyd's Rep 93, the court appointed an arbitrator as the time-bar defence was arguable rather than established and the court's view was that the matter should be resolved by the arbitrator once appointed.
4. *Atlanska Plovidba* v. *Consignaciones Asturianas SA* [2004] 2 Lloyd's Rep 109, *per* Moore-Bick J.
5. *Through Transport Mutual Insurance Association (Eurasia) Ltd* v. *New India Assurance Co Ltd (No 2)* [2005] 2 Lloyd's Rep 378, in which an anti-suit injunction was refused because the defendant was exercising subrogation rights under Finnish legislation and thus was not in breach of the arbitration clause even though bound by it.
6. *Villa Denizcilik Sanayi ve Ticaret AS* v. *Longen SA, The Villa* [1998] 1 Lloyd's Rep 195.
7. *Henry Boot Construction (UK) Ltd* v. *Malmaison Hotel (Manchester) Ltd* [2001] 1 QB 388; *Athletic Union of Constantinople* v. *National Basketball Association* [2002] 1 Lloyd's Rep 305; *Virdee* v. *Virdi* [2003] EWCA Civ 41.

NOTES

The criterion set out in this section, relating to the qualifications of arbitrators, is to be taken into account by the court in deciding whether or how to act on application to it under section 18, where there has been a failure of the agreed procedure for the appointment of arbitrators. Section 19 states also that it applies to the exercise of judicial powers under section 16, but the court does not in fact have any powers under section 16, and it is thought that this should be taken to be a reference to section 17(3), which permits the court to set aside the appointment by one party of a sole arbitrator where the other party has failed after notice to appoint his own arbitrator. The section is based on Article 11(5) of the Model Law, the purpose of which is to preserve as much of the parties' agreement as possible.[1] There is no possibility of appeal from the judge's order under this section unless the judge gives permission to appeal, so even if there has been a clear failure by the judge to take into account agreed qualifications the decision cannot be corrected by the Court of Appeal itself giving permission to appeal.[2]

Under the July 1995 Bill the court was additionally required to take into account any delay by the applicant, and the need for the fair determination of disputes by an independent tribunal, and the section 19 criteria were relevant also to an order replacing the arbitrators with an umpire, under section 21(5), and the removal of an arbitrator under section 24. The additional criteria have been removed, and the remaining criterion is plainly inapplicable to sections 21(5) and 24 applications.

Chairman

20.—(1) Where the parties have agreed that there is to be a chairman, they are free to agree what the functions of the chairman are to be in relation to the making of decisions, orders and awards.

(2) If or to the extent that there is no such agreement, the following provisions apply.

(3) Decisions, orders and awards shall be made by all or a majority of the arbitrators (including the chairman).

(4) The view of the chairman shall prevail in relation to a decision, order or award in respect of which there is neither unanimity nor a majority under subsection (3).

NOTES

Statutory recognition of the office of chairman of an arbitral panel was new in 1996. Earlier law simply provided for majority decision-making. Section 20, by contrast, gives particular default powers to the chairman of the tribunal. The manner in which the chairman is selected is not convincingly dealt with by the Act. Section 15(2) provides that, if the parties have agreed to a tribunal consisting of an even number of members, an additional member is to be appointed (subject to clear contrary agreement) and that that additional member is to be regarded as chairman. Equally, section 16(1) permits the parties to choose the chairman or the procedure for appointing the chairman. By contrast, the Act does not deal with the situation in which the tribunal is to consist of three arbitrators and there is no express provision for the nomination of the chairman. It is possible that the matter is one which can be referred to the court under the catch-all provision, section 16(7), if either the parties or tribunal cannot reach agreement, though this is likely to be rare, since in most cases, even if not expressly provided for in the arbitration agreement, the mechanism of choice of the third arbitrator (by the first two selected or agreed upon by the parties) is such that the third arbitrator is almost always regarded as chairman. However, there is no need as such for a chairman to be appointed at all, as section 22 provides that, if the parties have agreed that there is to be no chairman, the arbitrators may act by a majority.

Section 20(1) deals with the case in which the parties have agreed that there is to be a chairman. Section 20(1) merely declares that the parties are free to fix his powers in the arbitration and over the award. It is apparent from section 20(1) that the chairman may be given the power to act on

1. DAC Report, para. 90.
2. *Virdee* v. *Virdi* [2003] EWCA Civ 41.

behalf of the tribunal in matters of procedure and substance. It is to be presumed, however, that the chairman cannot have the power to issue the final award in all cases, as this in effect converts him into an umpire.

Section 20(2) deals with two cases: (a) there is no agreement for a chairman but the appointment of a chairman is required under section 15(2) (even number of arbitrators) in the absence of any contrary agreement; (b) there is an agreement for a chairman but there is no agreement as to his powers. In either case, the default powers in section 20(3)–(4) are applicable. If the parties have agreed that there is not to be a chairman, section 22 simply provides that the arbitrators operate by majority.

Section 20(3) confirms the principle that the panel must act by a majority in all matters. However, in the event that there is no majority in relation to any decision (perhaps because one arbitrator has refused to reach a conclusion on a particular matter or is otherwise unable to do so), section 20(4) requires the matter to be determined by the chairman.

Umpire

21.—(1) Where the parties have agreed that there is to be an umpire, they are free to agree what the functions of the umpire are to be, and in particular—

(a) whether he is to attend the proceedings, and
(b) when he is to replace the other arbitrators as the tribunal with power to make decisions, orders and awards.

(2) If or to the extent that there is no such agreement, the following provisions apply.

(3) The umpire shall attend the proceedings and be supplied with the same documents and other materials as are supplied to the other arbitrators.

(4) Decisions, orders and awards shall be made by the other arbitrators unless and until they cannot agree on a matter relating to the arbitration.

In that event they shall forthwith give notice in writing to the parties and the umpire, whereupon the umpire shall replace them as the tribunal with power to make decisions, orders and awards as if he were sole arbitrator.

(5) If the arbitrators cannot agree but fail to give notice of that fact, or if any of them fails to join in the giving of notice, any party to the arbitral proceedings may (upon notice to the other parties and to the tribunal) apply to the court which may order that the umpire shall replace the other arbitrators as the tribunal with power to make decisions, orders and awards as if he were sole arbitrator.

(6) The leave of the court is required for any appeal from a decision of the court under this section.

NOTES

The use of umpires is very much an English practice, and a dying one: even though umpires do operate in other jurisdictions, particularly the US, the word is there used as meaning chairman of arbitrators.

Major conceptual problems arise with the very notion of two arbitrators disagreeing and then renouncing their authority in favour of an umpire, as at this point the arbitrators become advocates for the respective appointing parties and the principle of impartiality of arbitrators disappears. In other jurisdictions the office of umpire is not recognised, and the DAC Report, paragraph 94, indicates that the DAC seriously considered the abolition of the umpired tribunal and its replacement with chaired tribunals. However, the previously widespread use of the umpire in certain classes of reinsurance arbitrations steered the DAC away from this approach. Section 15(2) ensures that where the parties agree that the tribunal should consist of two arbitrators, there is a deeming provision that the tribunal shall have three members, although the third is a chairman and not an umpire. For that reason, it was almost inevitable that the passing of the 1996 would accelerate the decline in the use of umpires, and that has indeed proved to be the position.

The time at which an umpire is to be appointed is governed by section 16(6), and the procedure for appointment if the agreed procedure fails is set out in section 18. Section 21 is concerned with the rights and duties of the umpire. The DAC Report, paragraph 91, stated that the section was merely declaratory of existing law.

Section 21(1) contains the usual proposition for non-mandatory provisions that the parties themselves are free to agree on the role of the umpire once he has been appointed. The section also sets out the general role of the umpire, namely, to take over the decision-making role where the arbitrators cannot agree, and—where the parties so specify—to attend the proceedings prior to such disagreement, but not to participate in those proceedings: it might be noted that the July 1995 Bill erroneously contemplated that the umpire might have a formal role in the proceedings prior to any disagreement between the arbitrators, an assumption which is inconsistent with the settled role of umpires.

Section 21(2) introduces the default provisions.

Section 21(3) requires the umpire to attend the proceedings and to be given the same documents and materials as the arbitrators, but he is not to participate in the deliberations (such a power had been included in the July 1995 Bill, but was, quite properly, deleted by the December 1995 Bill). It is to be emphasised that at this stage the umpire has no jurisdiction to determine the dispute, as that is still a matter for the arbitrators. His attendance is required to ensure that in the event of disagreement between the arbitrators, at which point the umpire takes over the reference, there does not have to be a rehearing of the evidence and presentations made to the arbitrators. Under section 8(1) of the Arbitration Act 1950, there was no obligation on the parties to appoint an umpire with the right to attend the hearing prior to their disagreement on the issues in the reference,[1] and if they failed to do so a rehearing would be required in the event of their disagreement. The position of the umpire under section 21(3), reflecting the position under the 1950 Act, is that, prior to any disagreement between the arbitrators, the umpire may not become involved in any decision-making,[2] but is entitled to any fees for this period as agreed between him and the arbitrators.[3] An umpire is, under the 1996 Act, given a statutory right either to agreed fees or, in the absence of agreement, to reasonable fees, for the period during which he has attended hearings but has not entered onto the reference. This is achieved by section 28(6).[4] If the umpire's fees and expenses are unpaid, the arbitrators have the right under section 56 to withhold the award until payment is made.

Section 21(4) specifies the point at which the umpire enters onto the reference, namely, when the arbitrators are unable to agree on one or more issues arising in the arbitration, the Bill being amended to make it clear, in accordance with the DAC's February 1996 Report, paragraph 360, that disagreement on any single issue—rather than on all issues—is the trigger for the application of this provision.[5] At that point, the arbitrators are replaced and the umpire becomes the arbitral panel. Section 21(4) requires formal notice to be given to the parties and to the umpire. Section 21(4) permits the arbitrators to continue to make decisions pending disagreement, a statement which the DAC Report, paragraph 93, regarded merely as declaratory of existing law.

Section 21(5) contains the procedure to ensure that the umpire can enter onto the reference in the event of disagreement between the arbitrators: a party may make an application to the court for an order. Application is by means of an arbitration claim form. Notice, in the form of a copy of the arbitration claim form and any supporting evidence, must be given to the other parties to the arbitration, and they are to be made parties to the application.[6] There is the familiar provision in

1. They were nevertheless impliedly empowered (but not obliged) to do so, despite any objection by either party: *Fletamentos Maritimos SA* v. *Effjohn International BV* [1995] 1 Lloyd's Rep 311.

2. *Potter* v. *Newman* (1835) 4 Dowl 504; *Fletamentos Maritimos SA* v. *Effjohn International BV (No 3)* [1997] 2 Lloyd's Rep 302.

3. *Tackaberry* v. *Phaidon Navegacion SA* [1992] ADRLJ 112.

4. See below.

5. Noted in the DAC Supplementary Report, para. 22.

6. CPR r. 62.6(2)–(3).

section 21(6) whereby there is no appeal against the court's decision other than with the permission of the court itself.

Decision-making where no chairman or umpire

22.—(1) Where the parties agree that there shall be two or more arbitrators with no chairman or umpire, the parties are free to agree how the tribunal is to make decisions, orders and awards.

(2) If there is no such agreement, decisions, orders and awards shall be made by all or a majority of the arbitrators.

NOTES

In most situations involving a three-member arbitral tribunal, there will be a chairman or umpire. Section 15(2) provides that an agreement for two arbitrators is, subject to contrary provision, to be taken as requiring the appointment of a third, chairman, arbitrator. In other cases, the parties will generally make provision for the appointment of a chairman or umpire. In those rare cases in which the parties have agreed that there are to be two or more arbitrators, but no chairman or umpire, section 22 of the Act (added by the December 1995 Bill) provides that the parties are to decide how decisions, orders and awards are to be agreed and that in the absence of agreement the principle of majority voting prevails. The DAC Report, paragraph 95, recognised that an arbitration probably could not work in these circumstances, and that the provision indicating that it is up to the parties to reach agreement was included merely for the sake of completeness.

Revocation of arbitrator's authority

23.—(1) The parties are free to agree in what circumstances the authority of an arbitrator may be revoked.

(2) If or to the extent that there is no such agreement the following provisions apply.

(3) The authority of an arbitrator may not be revoked except—

(a) by the parties acting jointly, or
(b) by an arbitral or other institution or person vested by the parties with powers in that regard.

(4) Revocation of the authority of an arbitrator by the parties acting jointly must be agreed in writing unless the parties also agree (whether or not in writing) to terminate the arbitration agreement.

(5) Nothing in this section affects the power of the court—

(a) to revoke an appointment under section 18 (powers exercisable in case of failure of appointment procedure), or
(b) to remove an arbitrator on the grounds specified in section 24.

NOTES

Under section 1 of the Arbitration Act 1950 (a section which in a different form dates back to 1833), the authority of an arbitrator was irrevocable except by the agreement of the parties or the permission of the High Court. The purpose of section 1 was apparently purely negative, that is, to prevent a party revoking the authority of an arbitrator appointed by him, rather than to give the court a wide-ranging discretion to revoke the authority of an arbitrator on the application of the appointee when the court thought fit. The superimposition of the court was thus a check on the appointor's freedom of action. Section 23 removes any residual jurisdiction which may have existed for the revocation of the authority of an arbitrator by the courts. It is clear from section 23 that the only situations in which the authority of an arbitrator can be revoked are those expressly agreed by the parties or, in default of agreement, by the parties acting jointly and in writing (writing being dispensed with where they have agreed to terminate the arbitration agreement, by way of exception to section 5, section 23(4) or by the action of the arbitral body vested with the relevant powers (section 23(3)). The irrevocability of an arbitrator's authority other than on the ground of lack of qualifications is also provided for by Article 12(2) of the Model Law. The DAC, in its February 1996 Report, paragraph 97, rejected the argument that the court's approval should be necessary for revocation, as the DAC regarded such intrusion into the parties' autonomy as unwarranted.

For the sake of completeness, attention should be drawn to the comment in the DAC Report, paragraph 98, that the difference between "revoke" and "remove" is of no legal significance, and that the ultimate effect is the same.

Section 23 provides useful clarification. The 1950 Act empowered the court to remove an arbitrator in a number of situations, and these are reproduced in sharper form in section 24 of the Act. Nevertheless, it was argued under the 1950 Act that the general power to revoke authority conferred upon the court by section 1 of the 1950 Act allowed the court to dispose of an arbitration in appropriate circumstances by combining its powers to revoke the authority of the arbitrators under section 1, and to set aside the arbitration agreement itself under section 25(2)(b). The courts regularly refused to exercise their powers in this way, on the ground that the powers were not an end in themselves, and on this basis section 1 was not pressed into use to dispose of an arbitration where the claimant had been guilty of delay.[1] The only illustration of section 1 being used to dispose of an arbitration was *NPB Developments* v. *Buildco Ltd*,[2] where the arbitration proceedings had effectively come to an end by reason of assignment.

The effect of the 1996 Act is that an arbitrator's services may be dispensed with by the court only by his removal, such power being expressly preserved by section 23(5), and there no longer exists the possibility of the revocation of his authority other than by the agreement of the parties or the responsible arbitral authority. In short, revocation of authority is a matter for the parties acting together, whereas removal is a matter for the court alone.

Where an arbitrator's authority is terminated, the arbitrator remains able to claim any agreed fees and expenses, plus fees and expenses which would otherwise have been recoverable by him but for the withdrawal of authority, and the parties cannot bring proceedings against the arbitrator unless he has been guilty of some action involving bad faith, in accordance with section 29. Accordingly, it may be necessary for the parties to request the court, acting under sections 23(5) and 24, to remove an arbitrator whose authority has been revoked, thereby bringing into play the financial consequences set out in that section. If the arbitrator pre-empts matters and resigns voluntarily under section 25, he may apply to the court under section 25(3) for orders as to his liability to the parties and theirs to him.

Power of court to remove arbitrator

24.—(1) A party to arbitral proceedings may (upon notice to the other parties, to the arbitrator concerned and to any other arbitrator) apply to the court to remove an arbitrator on any of the following grounds—

(a) that circumstances exist that give rise to justifiable doubts as to his impartiality;

(b) that he does not possess the qualifications required by the arbitration agreement;

(c) that he is physically or mentally incapable of conducting the proceedings or there are justifiable doubts as to his capacity to do so;

(d) that he has refused or failed—

1. *Tankrederei Ahrenkeil GmbH* v. *Frahuil SA, The Multitank Holsatia* [1988] 2 Lloyd's Rep 486. The problem of delay is now resolved by s. 40 of the Act.

2. 1992, unreported.

(i) properly to conduct the proceedings, or
(ii) to use all reasonable despatch in conducting the proceedings or making an award, and that substantial injustice has been or will be caused to the applicant.

(2) If there is an arbitral or other institution or person vested by the parties with power to remove an arbitrator, the court shall not exercise its power of removal unless satisfied that the applicant has first exhausted any available recourse to that institution or person.

(3) The arbitral tribunal may continue the arbitral proceedings and make an award while an application to the court under this section is pending.

(4) Where the court removes an arbitrator, it may make such order as it thinks fit with respect to his entitlement (if any) to fees or expenses, or the repayment of any fees or expenses already paid.

(5) The arbitrator concerned is entitled to appear and be heard by the court before it makes any order under this section.

(6) The leave of the court is required for any appeal from a decision of the court under this section.

NOTES

Section 24 sets out in more detail the grounds upon which an arbitrator may be removed, for the first time distinguishing between consensual removal (by revocation of authority under section 23), and non-consensual removal (by court order under section 24), and notes the role of arbitration institutions responsible for supervising the conduct of arbitrations. Section 24 brings together the various grounds for removal and subjects them to the same procedural rules. The Act is silent on the question of whether an application to remove an arbitrator can be made at any time during the proceedings, or only after the award is made and has been challenged, but there is nothing in section 24 which restricts the applicant's rights in a temporal sense. It was equally the case under section 23(1) of the 1950 Act that in exceptional circumstances an arbitrator could be removed during the course of the proceedings.[1]

Section 24(1) modifies and expands the various grounds for removal set out in earlier legislation. Article 4 of the Model Law, which provides that the right of a party to object to a procedural error will be lost if he is aware of his right but does not seek remedial action in relation to it, has been incorporated into section 73 of the Act. A party who is aware that he has the right to apply for the removal of an arbitrator but who continues to take part in the arbitration may be taken to have waived his right, in accordance with section 73, in what the DAC in its February 1996 Report, paragraph 105, described as the "put up or shut up" provision. However, a party who has failed to honour a partial award even though permission to enforce it has been given by the court is not necessarily precluded from bringing proceedings to remove the arbitrators under section 24.[2]

A party seeking the removal of an arbitrator must make an arbitration application to the court. Application is by means of an arbitration claim form. The arbitrator in question must be made a party to the application (along with any other party to the arbitration)[3] and must be given notice of allegations against him.[4] If the application is successful, a costs order may be made against the arbitrator personally.[5] The application must be made as soon as the applicant becomes aware of

1. *Pratt* v. *Swanmore Builders Ltd* [1980] 2 Lloyd's Rep 504; *Modern Engineering (Bristol) Ltd* v. *C Miskin & Sons Ltd* [1981] 1 Lloyd's Rep 135.
2. *ASM Shipping Ltd of India* v. *TTMI Ltd (No 2)* [2007] 2 Lloyd's Rep 155.
3. CPR, r. 62.6(1). Any other arbitrator is required by s. 24 of the 1996 Act to be given notice of the application and is thereby entitled to make themselves a defendant to the application or (probably more likely in practice) to make written representations to the court: CPR PD 62, para. 4.1.
4. *Miller Construction* v. *James Moore Earthmoving* [2001] 1 All ER (Comm) 598.
5. *Wicketts and Sterndale* v. *Brine Builders* [2001] CILL 1805.

grounds for doing so: failure to act immediately may give rise to a finding of waiver under the general provisions of section 73 of the 1996 Act.[1]

The various grounds for the removal of an arbitrator by the court are as follows.

Section 24(1)(a): *Justifiable doubts as to impartiality.* Impartiality is, indeed, one of the general principles relating to arbitration set out in section 1(1)(a) of the Act. The Model Law is strict on impartiality, and provides for full disclosure by the arbitrator, followed, in the case of justifiable doubts as to impartiality or independence, by a challenge procedure to be resolved by the arbitral tribunal itself.[2] The Departmental Advisory Committee chose not to follow the Model Law in regarding lack of independence as a ground for removal, and preferred to retain the old rule that lack of independence is significant only where it leads to a justifiable doubt about the arbitrator's impartiality: were it otherwise, the Committee feared that there might be complex and unnecessary arguments about exactly how independent the arbitrator has to be, and the parties might be precluded from appointing an arbitrator with expertise in the field in question (see the February 1996 Report, paragraphs 101–103). Lord Donaldson also pointed out on Second Reading that any requirement of independence would run counter to the long-established procedure in England whereby each party appoints his own arbitrator: in such a case, the only issue is whether the arbitrators have acted impartially irrespective of whether or not they are "independent" in the full sense of the word.[3] The authorities on impartiality—which make it clear that all arbitrators have to be impartial, including party-appointed arbitrators, and that there has to be a real likelihood of bias or grounds for reasonable suspicion[4]—remain good law. The old approach has been continued under the 1996 Act. The cases may be classified under several heads.

(a) There is the potential for bias where there is a commercial relationship between the arbitrator and one of the parties, although this depends upon the nature and continuing nature of that relationship.[5] In *Laker Airways Inc* v. *FLS Aerospace Ltd*[6] it was held that there was no objection to a barrister acting as arbitrator even though he was in the same chambers as a barrister acting for one of the parties. The question was whether there were circumstances which raised justifiable doubts as to the arbitrator's impartiality, but as barristers were not partners or fellow employees and had their own interests and reputations to further, no such doubts could be demonstrated.[7]

(b) The arbitrator and one of the parties have in the past been involved in a dispute or have competing commercial interests: there is normally a need for a clear link between the dispute and the arbitration for this ground to be of significance.[8] It is not enough to show bias against arbitrators A and B that the applicant party has previously sought the removal of arbitrator C on the ground of bias and arbitrators A and B had given their support to arbitrator C remaining a member of the panel.[9]

(c) The arbitrator has a personal interest in the outcome of the arbitration.[10]

1. *Wicketts and Sterndale* v. *Brine Builders* [2001] CILL 1805.
2. Model Law, Arts 12–13.
3. *A T & T Corporation* v. *Saudi Cable Co* [2000] 2 Lloyd's Rep 127.
4. *R* v. *Gough* [1993] AC 646; *R* v. *Bow Street Magistrate, ex parte Pinochet (No 2)* [1999] 2 WLR 272; *Director General of Fair Trading* v. *Proprietary Association of Great Britain* [2001] 1 WLR 700; *Porter* v. *Magill* [2002] 2 AC 357; *AMEC Capital Projects Ltd* v. *Whitefriars City Estates* [2005] BLR 1. See also *Locabail (UK)* v. *Bayfield Properties Ltd* [2000] 1 All ER 65, in which the Court of Appeal discussed a number of situations in which a judge or other person with judicial functions was to be regarded either as automatically disqualified (direct pecuniary or personal interest) or capable of being removed (risk or appearance of bias).
5. *Cook International Inc* v. *Handelsmaatschappij Jean Delvaux BV* [1985] 2 Lloyd's Rep 225; *Save and Prosper Pensions Ltd* v. *Homebase Ltd* [2001] L & TR 11.
6. [1999] 2 Lloyd's Rep 45.
7. The DAC Report, para. 102, had anticipated this result on these very facts.
8. *Fletamentos Maritimos SA* v. *Effjohn International BV (No 3)* [1997] 2 Lloyd's Rep 302; *Rustal Trading SA* v. *Gill Duffus SA* [2000] 1 Lloyd's Rep 14; *A T & T Corporation* v. *Saudi Cable Co* [2000] 2 Lloyd's Rep 127.
9. *ASM Shipping Ltd* v. *Harris* [2008] 1 Lloyd's Rep 61.
10. *Blanchard* v. *Sun Fire Office* (1890) 6 TLR 365; *Watson* v. *Prager* [1991] 3 All ER 487.

(d) The arbitrator has indicated that his mind is closed as to the outcome or on particular issues or evidence in the arbitration.[1]

If the arbitrator is not precluded from acting as such by reason of potential bias, then his award may nevertheless be challenged if actual bias is shown in the conduct of the proceedings: actual bias in the conduct of the arbitration leading to a tainted award amounts to a serious irregularity and can be challenged under section 68 of the 1996 Act.[2]

Section 24(1)(b): *Lack of qualifications*. There were not in the 1950 Act any stated qualifications for arbitrators, and this remains the position under the 1996 Act. The qualifications referred to in this clause are thus qualifications specified in the arbitration agreement itself or otherwise separately agreed. The mere fact that one party intended an arbitrator to possess particular qualifications is not a ground for removal, as a unilateral mistake of this type does not vitiate what has actually been agreed as opposed to what one party might have intended.[3] Where qualifications are required, in practice they tend to relate to the experience of the arbitrator in the industry in question. Lack of contractual qualifications did not appear in the 1950 Act as a ground of removal, but the court was able to remove an arbitrator who did not possess the necessary contractual qualifications as a matter of pure contract.[4] The challenge procedure set out in the Model Law for impartiality is also applicable to qualifications, but has not been adopted by the Act. The Act does, however, recognise, in section 30(1)(b), that the panel has the initial right to determine whether its members are properly qualified: the procedure for challenge to such a determination is set out in sections 30 to 32.

Section 24(1)(c): *Physical or mental incapacity*. The common law is unclear as to whether an arbitrator who lacks the relevant physical or mental capacity to do the job can be appointed as arbitrator. The Act in effect provides that such a person can be appointed, but may be removed.

Section 24(1)(d): *Failure to conduct the proceedings properly or speedily*. This is really a catch-all provision, potentially extending to matters such as refusal by an arbitrator to sign the award[5] in circumstances in which the validity of the award depends upon his signature. Under the July 1995 version of the Bill, excess of jurisdiction was treated as a distinct ground for removal, adopting the principle developed under the Arbitration Act 1950 by which an arbitrator who acted in excess of his jurisdiction was guilty of misconduct and was liable to be removed as well as having his award set aside. It is to be presumed that excess of jurisdiction is treated as subsumed into the general heading of failure to conduct the proceedings properly. The DAC in its February 1996 Report, paragraphs 105–106, set out the limits of section 24(1)(d), and its views contain useful guidelines for the courts:

> We trust that the Courts will not allow [the arbitrators' failure properly to conduct the proceedings] to be abused by those intent on disrupting the arbitral process . . . We have every confidence that the Courts will carry through the intent of this part of the [Act], which is that it should only be available where the conduct of the arbitrator is such as to go so beyond anything that could reasonably be defended that substantial injustice has resulted or will result. The provision is not intended to allow the Court to substitute its own view as to how the arbitral proceedings should be conducted. Thus the choice by an arbitrator of a particular procedure, unless it breaches the duty laid on arbitrators by [section] 33, should on no view justify the removal of an arbitrator, even if the Court would not itself have adopted that procedure.

1. *Re Steamship Catalina and Motor Vessel Norma NV* (1938) 61 Ll L Rep 360; *Tracomin SA* v. *Gibbs* [1985] 1 Lloyd's Rep 586; It was held in *Amec Capital Projects Ltd* v. *Whitefriars City Estates Ltd* [2005] BLR 1 that an arbitrator is not biased simply because he has previously heard the matter and is required to hear it afresh.

2. Actual bias is required, as a challenge to the award itself is predicated on the notion that the complainant has suffered substantial injustice: see, on this point, *Hussmann (Europe) Ltd* v. *Pharaon* [2003] 1 All ER (Comm) 879. See the notes to s. 68, below.

3. *Continental Grain Co* v. *China Petroleum Technology Development Corporation* 1998, unreported.

4. See *Pando Compania Naviera SA* v. *Filmo SAS* [1975] QB 742: *Pan Atlantic Group Inc* v. *Hassneh Insurance Co of Israel Ltd* [1992] 2 Lloyd's Rep 120.

5. *Cargill International SA Antigua* v. *Sociedad Iberica de Molturacion SA* [1998] 1 Lloyd's Rep 489 (dissenting arbitrator refused to sign unless allowed to give reasons for dissent).

This approach has been one adopted by the courts in relation to applications for the removal of allegedly dilatory[1] or incompetent[2] arbitrators.

The purpose of the expansion of the grounds of removal into specific heads is that of clarity, so that a specific allegation can be made rather than a general statement that the arbitrator has been guilty of misconduct. The entire concept of misconduct in any event disappears under the 1996 Act and is replaced with that of "serious irregularity".[3]

The July 1995 Bill laid down criteria which the court had to take into account in determining whether an arbitrator was to be removed under section 24. These were:

- — any agreement by the parties as to the arbitrator's qualifications;
- — any failure by the applicant to apply with reasonable diligence; and
- — the need to ensure a fair determination of the result with minimal cost and delay.

These criteria were removed by the December 1995 Bill, and as a result the court appears to have a complete discretion on this matter.

Section 24(2) places a restriction on the right of a party to apply to the court under section 24(1) where there is an arbitration body empowered to remove an arbitrator: the procedure involving recourse to that body has to be exhausted before an application may be made. As the DAC noted in its February 1996 Report, paragraph 107, "it will be a very rare case indeed where the Court will remove an arbitrator notwithstanding that that process has reached a different conclusion".

Section 24(3) was inserted in the December 1995 Bill as a result of consultation. Its effect is to allow the arbitration to continue even though there is a pending application for removal. In the event that the application is dismissed, the arbitration will not have been delayed: the existence of this provision removes the ability of a party to seek removal for purely tactical reasons, thereby delaying the arbitration.

Section 24(4) provides that the question of fees and expenses is a general one, relevant to all cases of removal, and adopts the rule that the court may make an order in respect of this matter. Removal by the court does not, therefore, operate as an automatic disentitlement to fees. It should be noted that section 24(4) does not apply to revocation of an arbitrator's authority by the parties or by an arbitration body under section 23, and that whether or not the arbitrator receives any fees is a matter of his contract with the parties. Doubtless, in taking into account its discretion under section 24(4), the contract and the reason for removal will be crucial to the court, and the DAC Report indicated that an arbitrator's fees should be lost only where his behaviour was "inexcusable" (paragraph 108). Such a case was *Wicketts and Sterndale* v. *Brine Builders*,[4] where the arbitrator's main concern appears to have been to secure his own payment and his conduct was described by the court as "quite the most outrageous that I have ever seen". It will also be noted that section 24(4) does not permit a general action for damages against an arbitrator, as any such action may be brought only where the arbitrator has acted in bad faith, in accordance with section 29, and equally it does not authorise the court to make an order relieving the arbitrator from, or capping, any liability which he may have incurred. The DAC Report, paragraph 361, suggested that it was anomalous that the court had no power to lift the arbitrator's immunity in a case in which the court chose to remove him, but no change was made. In its Supplementary Report, paragraphs 23–24, the DAC accepted that the problem was more apparent than real, and that if a power to limit or remove an arbitrator's immunity existed the parties might apply to the court for the removal of an arbitrator in the hope that his immunity would be denied or restricted, rather than agreeing to remove him directly.

1. *Home of Homes Ltd* v. *Hammersmith and Fulham London Borough Council* (2003) 92 Con LR 48.
2. *Kelsey Housing Association Ltd* v. *Ruddy Developments Ltd* [1998] ADRLN 6; *Conder Structures* v. *Kvaerner Construction Ltd* [1999] ADRLJ 305; *Dredging and Construction Co Ltd* v. *Delta Civil Engineering Ltd* (2000) 68 Con LR 87; *Petroships Pte of Singapore* v. *Petec Trading and Investment Corporation of Vietnam* [2001] 2 Lloyd's Rep 348; *Miller Construction* v. *James Moore Earthmoving* [2001] 2 All ER (Comm) 598; *Groundshire* v. *VHE Construction* [2001] BLR 395; *AOOT Kalmneft* v. *Glencore International AG* [2002] 1 Lloyd's Rep 128; *Sinclair* v. *Woods of Winchester* (2006) 109 Con LR 14. Contrast: *Damond Lock Grabowski* v. *Laing Investments (Bracknell) Ltd* (1993) 60 BLR 112; *Wicketts and Sterndale* v. *Brine Builders* [2001] CILL 1805; *Norbrook Laboratories Ltd* v. *Tank* [2006] 2 Lloyd's Rep 485.
3. Arbitration Act 1996, s. 68.
4. [2001] CILL 1805.

Section 24(5), in the interests of justice,[1] entitles an arbitrator to be heard by the court in an application against him for his removal. This is given effect by CPR 62.6(1), by virtue of which the arbitrator sought to be removed must be made a defendant, thereby entitling him to the usual right to be heard afforded to any party to English civil court proceedings.

Section 24(6) is the familiar prevention of the proliferation of legal proceedings on non-substantive issues, by requiring the permission of the court for any appeal from its ruling. The "court" means the trial judge and not the Court of Appeal.[2]

Resignation of arbitrator

25.—(1) The parties are free to agree with an arbitrator as to the consequences of his resignation as regards—

(a) his entitlement (if any) to fees or expenses, and
(b) any liability thereby incurred by him.

(2) If or to the extent that there is no such agreement the following provisions apply.

(3) An arbitrator who resigns his appointment may (upon notice to the parties) apply to the court—

(a) to grant him relief from any liability thereby incurred by him, and
(b) to make such order as it thinks fit with respect to his entitlement (if any) to fees or expenses or the repayment of any fees or expenses already paid.

(4) If the court is satisfied that in all the circumstances it was reasonable for the arbitrator to resign, it may grant such relief as is mentioned in subsection (3)(a) on such terms as it thinks fit.

(5) The leave of the court is required for any appeal from a decision of the court under this section.

NOTES

This is a section which had no predecessor in earlier legislation and which is explained by the Departmental Advisory Committee's July 1995 Report as follows:

> An arbitrator who resigns may be in breach of his contract with the person or institution who appointed him. Since the thrust of the Bill is to promote party autonomy an arbitrator may find after his appointment and unexpectedly that the parties have agreed a procedure with which he is unfamiliar or for other reasons cannot agree. In these circumstances it may be fair and proper for the arbitrator to be allowed to resign without incurring liability for breach of contract. The clause confers power on the court to grant relief in these circumstances on such terms as it thinks fit.

Section 25(1) provides that the parties are free to reach agreement in writing with an arbitrator as to the consequences of his resignation on his fees and on any liabilities faced by him. The subsection does not apply to any other form of agreement, for example, an agreement not to resign at all, or to resign in specified circumstances (DAC Report, paragraph 113). An agreement within the subsection can presumably be made either when the arbitration is appointed, or when the problems have arisen. The 1996 Act does not confer upon the court any power to reopen or adjust an agreement falling within section 25(1): a provision to this effect in the July 1995 Bill was dropped following consultation.

1. DAC Report, para. 109.
2. *Henry Boot Construction (UK) Ltd* v. *Malmaison Hotel (Manchester) Ltd* [2001] 1 QB 388; *Athletic Union of Constantinople* v. *National Basketball Association* [2002] 1 Lloyd's Rep 305; *Virdee* v. *Virdi* [2003] EWCA Civ 41.

In the absence of any such agreement, section 25(2) introduces default provisions in the remainder of the section.

Section 25(3) sets out the basic right of an arbitrator to apply to the court for relief from liability for breach of contract and for an order as to his fees and expenses, following his resignation. The application is to be made to the court by way of arbitration claim. It is unclear from the CPR whether notice, in the form of a copy of the arbitration claim form and any supporting evidence, must be given to all the parties to the arbitration, or whether they are to be made defendants to the application.[1] It will be seen that section 25(3) goes further than the DAC, in recognising that an arbitrator in breach of contract may be unable to recover any expenses or fees unless he has substantially performed his obligations (unlikely if the matter has progressed to an award), and, conversely, that if the arbitrator has been paid he will as matter of common law be entitled to retain all of his fees on the basis that consideration has not totally failed. An arbitrator who has acted in bad faith additionally faces liability under section 29 of the Act, but the extent of any immunity from this liability will form part of the arbitrator's application to the court under section 25(3)(a).

The right of resignation conferred by the section is not restricted to the situation identified by the DAC, namely, the adoption of a procedure with which the arbitrator is not comfortable, although it is clear from the wording of section 25(4) that relief will be granted only where reasonable. The situation identified by the DAC is that which most readily springs to mind as constituting reasonable justification for resignation,[2] although it is less likely to arise under the 1996 Act than under the 1950 Act, in the light of section 34(1), which confers upon the arbitrators the right to determine the procedure in the majority of cases. The problem is most likely to surface where the parties have adopted a procedure which the arbitrators regard as contravening their general and mandatory obligations to act in accordance with the rules of natural justice and in proportion to the dispute, and it is clear that in such circumstances relief from any possible liability incurred by resignation would be almost automatic.[3] Arbitrators might, however, resign for other reasons, for example, because their authority has been revoked by the parties under section 23: in such a case, the arbitrators are equally entitled to resign and to seek financial adjustment under section 25(3). Again, resignation may be prompted by the length of time that the proceedings are taking (see the DAC Report, paragraph 115).

The permission of the court is required for any appeal. The "court" means the trial judge and not the Court of Appeal.[4]

Death of arbitrator or person appointing him

26.—(1) The authority of an arbitrator is personal and ceases on his death.

(2) Unless otherwise agreed by the parties, the death of the person by whom an arbitrator was appointed does not revoke the arbitrator's authority.

1. CPR r. 62.6(2) provides that where notice must be given "to an arbitrator or any other person" it may be given by sending him a copy of the arbitration claim form and supporting evidence. It is not clear whether a party is to be regarded as "any other person", but the safest course is probably to treat them as such. CPR r. 62.2(3) states that where the 1996 Act requires an application to the court to be made on notice "to any other party to the arbitration", that notice must be given by making that party a defendant. The wording here clearly envisages an application being made by a party and not by an arbitrator. Nevertheless, the sensible course would be to make the parties defendants to the application (since no doubt the application has been necessitated by their disagreeing with the arbitrator concerned as to the consequences of his resignation).

2. Illness, whether short-term or long-term, is likely to be a frustrating event. The arbitrator is not, therefore, in breach of contract, and will not need to rely upon s. 24 for relief. Whether the arbitrator is entitled to be paid is quite another matter: see s. 28.

3. DAC Report, para. 160.

4. *Henry Boot Construction (UK) Ltd* v. *Malmaison Hotel (Manchester) Ltd* [2001] 1 QB 388; *Athletic Union of Constantinople* v. *National Basketball Association* [2002] 1 Lloyd's Rep 305; *Virdee* v. *Virdi* [2003] EWCA Civ 41.

NOTES

Section 26(1) makes the obvious[1] point, not previously found in English legislation, that the services of an arbitrator are personal and that death brings an end to his authority. He may be replaced in accordance with the provisions of section 27.

Section 26(2) deals with the case in which a party to an arbitration agreement has died after he has appointed an arbitrator. His death has no effect on the arbitration agreement itself, unless there is some contrary agreement,[2] and likewise the appointment of the arbitrator is not invalidated. Section 26(2) is not mandatory, and is subject to contrary agreement, so that the parties can agree that death is to determine the agreement, or to leave the agreement intact but revoke the authority of the arbitrator appointed by him.

Filling of vacancy, &c

27.—(1) Where an arbitrator ceases to hold office, the parties are free to agree—

(a) whether and if so how the vacancy is to be filled,
(b) whether and if so to what extent the previous proceedings should stand, and
(c) what effect (if any) his ceasing to hold office has on any appointment made by him (alone or jointly).

(2) If or to the extent that there is no such agreement, the following provisions apply.

(3) The provisions of sections 16 (procedure for appointment of arbitrators) and 18 (failure of appointment procedure) apply in relation to the filling of the vacancy as in relation to an original appointment.

(4) The tribunal (when reconstituted) shall determine whether and if so to what extent the previous proceedings should stand.

This does not affect any right of a party to challenge those proceedings on any ground which had arisen before the arbitrator ceased to hold office.

(5) His ceasing to hold office does not affect any appointment by him (alone or jointly) of another arbitrator, in particular any appointment of a chairman or umpire.

NOTES

Section 27(1) reflects Article 15 of the Model Law. In the case of a casual vacancy or judicial removal of an arbitrator the parties were free to set out a procedure for replacement, or to agree on non-replacement: this right is preserved by section 27(1). In the case of a revocation of authority, the principle of party autonomy is adopted: the position under the 1950 Act where an appointment was made by the court was thought to raise the spectre of unfairness as against the party whose chosen arbitrator had been removed (DAC Report, paragraph 117). It is relatively unusual for arbitration clauses to deal with the appointment of replacement arbitrators, and in *Federal Insurance Co* v. *Transamerica Occidental Life Insurance Co Ltd*[3] Rix J held that wherever possible it was necessary to extend the agreement between the parties for the appointment of the first arbitrators to the appointment of replacement arbitrators even if that meant some manipulation of the wording of the arbitration clause. In the absence of express agreement, section 27(2) introduces fallback provisions.

1. "[Section] 26(1) is mandatory—it is difficult to see how parties could agree otherwise" (DAC Report, para. 116.).
2. Section 8(1), re-enacts s. 2(1) of the Arbitration Act 1950. See the Notes to s. 8, where it was pointed out that s. 2 of the 1950 Act was included to confirm the reversal, by the Law Reform (Miscellaneous Provisions) Act 1934, of the common law rule that a cause of action died with the claimant.
3. [1999] 2 Lloyd's Rep 286.

Section 27(3) refers back to sections 16 and 18 for the appointment of replacement arbitrators and for the default procedure in the event that no appointment is made. Those procedures have been explained earlier in this work.[1] As mentioned above, the original procedures apply even where an arbitrator has been removed by the court under section 24. In *Federal Insurance Co* v. *Transamerica Occidental Life Insurance Co Ltd* Rix J construed section 27(3) as requiring the court to look at the agreement between the parties for the appointment of the original arbitrators, and that it was legitimate to import whatever aspects of the default provisions in section 16 as were necessary to render the arbitration clause applicable to the appointment of a replacement. It was there decided that a clause which required each party to make an appointment within 30 days of the other requesting arbitration could be given effect by importing section 16(5)(a)—a request for an appointment to be made—as the trigger for the running of the 30-day appointment period for a replacement.

Section 27(4) is a logical statement of the position where the tribunal has been reconstituted. Presumably a decision to rehear, or not to rehear, evidence is one which is capable of challenge for "serious irregularity" under section 68. The purpose of the proviso to section 27(4) is explained by the DAC Report, paragraph 118, as preserving the right of a party to challenge those aspects of the arbitration which the newly constituted panel has allowed to stand. Accordingly, the fact that the arbitrators have been replaced does not prevent the applicant from challenging the final award under sections 56 to 58.

Section 27(5) is a saving provision, protecting the validity of the appointment of any arbitrator or umpire made by the arbitrator in question prior to his ceasing to hold office unless the parties have agreed to the contrary.[2]

Joint and several liability of parties to arbitrators for fees and expenses

28.—(1) The parties are jointly and severally liable to pay to the arbitrators such reasonable fees and expenses (if any) as are appropriate in the circumstances.

(2) Any party may apply to the court (upon notice to the other parties and to the arbitrators) which may order that the amount of the arbitrators' fees and expenses shall be considered and adjusted by such means and upon such terms as it may direct.

(3) If the application is made after any amount has been paid to the arbitrators by way of fees or expenses, the court may order the repayment of such amount (if any) as is shown to be excessive but shall not do so unless it is shown that it is reasonable in the circumstances to order repayment.

(4) The above provisions have effect subject to any order of the court under section 24(4) or 25(3)(b) (order as to entitlement to fees or expenses in case of removal or resignation of arbitrator).

(5) Nothing in this section affects any liability of a party to any other party to pay all or any of the costs of the arbitration (see sections 59 to 65) or any contractual right of an arbitrator to payment of his fees and expenses.

(6) In this section references to arbitrators include an arbitrator who has ceased to act and an umpire who has not replaced the other arbitrators.

NOTES

Section 28 replaced some unnecessarily complex corresponding provisions in the 1950 Act by rather simpler statements of principle and a streamlined enforcement mechanism. The section applies to arbitrators' fees and expenses which are deemed to include the fees and expenses of experts appointed by the arbitrators (section 37(2)).

1. See the notes to ss. 16 and 18, above.
2. DAC Report, para. 119.

The starting point is section 28(5), which recognises that the arbitrators are entitled to be paid, by way of fees and expenses, the amount (or on the basis) agreed by them with the parties. The section does not refer expressly to fees as determined by an arbitral body, but it must be assumed that acceptance of the terms of such a body amounts to an agreement to pay fees and expenses in accordance with those terms.[1] The right to enforce any agreement as to fees and expenses is subject to the principles in sections 24(4) and 25(3)(b), which empower the court to deprive the arbitrators of some or all of their remuneration on removal or resignation unless—in the case of resignation under section 25—the consequences of resignation have been agreed between the parties (section 28(4)).[2] In apparent contrast to the case under the 1950 Act, any agreement with the arbitrator under section 28 need not be made with both parties. If one party alone accepts the arbitrator's terms and conditions, that party must remain liable contractually regardless of the liability of the other party. It should be noted that section 28(5) is not at all concerned with the issue as to where the burden of the costs of the arbitration should lie as between the parties. The allocation of any agreed sums between the parties is a matter for the award as to costs, governed by sections 59 to 65, which lay down rules both as to allocation and as to what proportion of accrued costs is recoverable under an award for costs made by the arbitrators. Section 28(5) accordingly provides that section 28 does not affect the liability of any party to pay the overall costs of the arbitration.

In the absence of any agreement on amount of the arbitrators' fees and expenses, section 28(1) provides that the parties are liable to pay the arbitrators "such reasonable fees and expenses (if any) as are appropriate in the circumstances". Section 28(1) will apply to any determination of fees in the award itself, and to any *quantum meruit* claim where the proceedings do not lead to an award by reason of early settlement or other termination of the proceedings by the parties. It is unclear whether section 28(1) is impliedly subject to any written agreement between the parties and the arbitrator(s). In principle, it ought to be, although section 28 is a mandatory provision and therefore to apply notwithstanding any agreement to the contrary (see section 4 and Schedule 1). It is suggested that this can be reconciled only by interpreting the section as providing that regardless of any agreement, the parties are jointly and severally liable for the tribunal's *reasonable* fees and expenses, though any party who has contractually obligated itself to pay what may be regarded as *excessive* or unreasonable fees (e.g., based on an unreasonably high hourly rate) will be liable in contract to pay to the arbitrator(s) (or to its appointed member of the tribunal if for example, a three-arbitrator panel is appointed) such excess fees. However, in order to protect the position whereby one party agrees an unreasonably high level of fees and expenses with its appointed arbitrator, the other party's liability is to pay only the arbitrator's *reasonable* fees and expenses, but not the surplus sum.[3]

Other arrangements on this matter may legitimately be made, for example, that the parties are each to pay one half of the fees.[4] Any agreement as to how the arbitrators are to be paid is necessarily without prejudice to the rights of the parties between themselves. Thus, if the parties have agreed that the fees are to be distributed between them in a particular way (permitted under section 60 provided that the agreement is made after the dispute has arisen), or if the allocation of the costs of the arbitration has been included in the award (as required by section 61), and the party making payment to the arbitrators is not liable for the full amount as between the parties, that party may make a claim against the other for reimbursement of any sums paid by him in excess of the agreement or award, as the case may be.

Section 28(2) addresses the difficult question as to how the reasonableness of the arbitrators' fees and expenses is to be determined in the absence of any express agreement. This provision may be relevant either before or after the arbitrators exercise their power in section 63(3) to determine their

1. This was so held in *Hussmann (Europe) Ltd* v. *Al Ameen Development & Trade Co* [2000] 2 Lloyd's Rep 83, a rare case in which the expenses (though not the fees) of the arbitrators were reduced on an application under s. 28(2).

2. Note that s. 28(4), which renders s. 8 subject to ss. 24(4) and 25(3), applies only to the preceding provisions of s. 28, and s. 28(5) is expressly stated not to be affected by anything else in s. 28, which would seem to include s. 28(4): if this is right, the result is that an express agreement for fees and costs cannot be overturned by the court when it removes or accepts the resignation of an arbitrator. This would appear to be the intention underlying s. 25(1) in any event: see the Notes to that section, above.

3. This problem was foreshadowed in the DAC Report, para. 123 (see Appendix 8).

4. *Carter* v. *Simpson Associates (Architects) Ltd* [2004] 2 Lloyd's Rep 512.

own costs and expenses as part of the award.[1] Section 28(2) provides that, where there is no express agreement as to fees and expenses (this position being saved by section 28(5)), any party may apply to the court for an order adjusting the amount of fees and expenses on such basis as the court may direct. This power is available whether or not the arbitrators have asserted their lien over the award (now made statutory by section 56), and whether or not the fees and expenses have been paid in order to secure the release of the award. The result is, therefore, a general power in the court to determine the arbitrators' fees and expenses where a party objects to the determination by the arbitrators themselves.[2]

By virtue of section 28(3), the court's power of adjustment may be exercised even after fees and expenses have been paid to the arbitrators. The DAC Report, paragraph 124, highlighted the situation in which the arbitrators have been paid in advance of the hearing, and the hearing turns out to be of far shorter duration than was originally assumed. However, the DAC emphasises that repayment will not be ordered automatically even in those circumstances, and that in particular repayment should not be ordered where there has been a delay in making application for adjustment[3] or where "the arbitrator has in good faith acted in such a way that it would be unjust to order repayment". The latter situation would seem to correspond to the defence of change of position available in restitutionary actions, and may mean no more than that the arbitrator has spent the money in question.

The application is to be made to the court by way of arbitration claim. Notice, in the form of a copy of the arbitration claim form and any supporting evidence, must be given to the other parties to the arbitration, and they are to be made defendants to the application.[4] The arbitrators themselves must be made parties to the application.[5]

It is necessary to distinguish the section 28(2) procedure from that contained in section 64. The purpose of section 28(2) is to determine whether or not the arbitrators have charged an unreasonable amount in respect of their fees and expenses. Section 64 is concerned with the distinct question of what proportion of the arbitrators' fees and expenses is to form part of the award of costs. The principle of section 64 is that it is not always the case that all the fees and expenses that the arbitrators are entitled to receive from the parties can be included in the award of costs. Section 64 thus provides a mechanism for determining what proportion of the fees and expenses are to be included in the costs award, without challenging arbitrators' own entitlement.

Section 28(6) has two effects. The first part of the clause extends the rights in section 28 to an arbitrator who has ceased to act for any reason, although this is necessarily subject to section 24(4) in respect of an arbitrator who has ceased to act. The second part of the clause is concerned with umpires. Under section 21 of the 1996 Act an umpire is required to attend hearings but does not have any formal status until he enters upon the reference following disagreement between the arbitrators. Section 28(6) confers upon the umpire, prior to disagreement between the arbitrators, a right to agree fees and, in the absence of agreement, the right to be paid a reasonable sum for his efforts. The right of the arbitrators to withhold the award under section 56 pending the payment of unpaid fees and expenses extends to the fees and expenses of the umpire under section 56(5).

The manner in which the arbitrators' fees and expenses are to be allocated as between the parties is governed by sections 59 to 65. Those sections are also based on the notion that, in the absence of any agreement between the parties and the arbitrators, the arbitrators can include in their award only a reasonable level of fees and expenses.

1. Note that an application to the court may be made to determine the tribunal's fees and expenses contained in an award under either s. 63(4) or s. 64(2): see the Notes to those sections.

2. See *Agrimex Ltd* v. *Tradigrain SA* [2003] 2 Lloyd's Rep 537, where there was a successful challenge to the level of fees charged by the arbitrators for their use of a legally-qualified draftsman employed to prepare the award.

3. But see *United Tyre Company* v. *Born* [2004] EWCA Civ 1236, where the Court of Appeal endorsed the decision of the judge at first instance that an investigation into an arbitrator's fees could proceed under s. 28(3) even after the arbitrator had been paid and notwithstanding a lengthy delay in bringing the claim.

4. CPR r. 62.6(2)–(3).

5. CPR r. 62.6(1).

There is no express right of appeal against a court decision under section 28(2), but it was held by the House of Lords in *Inco Europe Ltd* v. *First Choice Distribution*[1] that a right of appeal exists. Permission to appeal may presumably be given by either the trial judge or the Court of Appeal.

Immunity of arbitrator

29.—(1) An arbitrator is not liable for anything done or omitted in the discharge or purported discharge of his functions as arbitrator unless the act or omission is shown to have been in bad faith.

(2) Subsection (1) applies to an employee or agent of an arbitrator as it applies to the arbitrator himself.

(3) This section does not affect any liability incurred by an arbitrator by reason of his resigning (but see section 25).

NOTES

The immunity of arbitrators under section 29 is derived from the immunity of judges from negligent liability to the parties. Judicial immunity is based upon three considerations: the need for the independence of the judiciary; the need to avoid threats to judicial decision-making; and the avoidance of the rehearing of actions, which follows inevitably from an allegation of negligence. The extension of immunity to arbitrators, confirmed long before the 1996 Act with some reservations by the House of Lords in *Sutcliffe* v. *Thackrah*[2] and *Arenson* v. *Casson Beckman Rutley Co*,[3] is based on more or less the same considerations. The bad faith restriction on immunity also appears from the pre-Act authorities.

Section 29 is another mandatory provision and, therefore, applies notwithstanding any agreement between the parties to the contrary. Nevertheless, if, for example, the parties have agreed to make any arbitration subject to the rules of any of the major arbitral institutions, each one provides in terms for a fairly unqualified immunity from suit on the part of the arbitrators and the institution itself.[4] An arbitral institution (e.g., the American Arbitration Association or London Court of International Arbitration or International Chamber of Commerce) which, for example, is accused of having acted negligently in its appointment of the arbitrators or otherwise failing to exercise its supervisory or other powers with reasonable care also has a similar immunity conferred upon it, though curiously this is set out in a separate section of the Act (section 74).

Section 29 is concerned only with immunity in respect of matters done or omitted by the arbitrator in the discharge or purported discharge of his functions. An arbitrator who fails to act at all is likely to be guilty of breach of contract and can be sued accordingly (subject to the terms of the contract) whether or not he had acted in bad faith. Equally, an arbitrator may be stripped of his entitlement to fees if he is removed for a cause under section 24 of the Act and he may also face liability and the loss of fees if he resigns under section 25 of the Act, in both cases irrespective of bad faith (see section 29(3), which expressly preserves liability under section 25 in the absence of bad faith, subject to any ruling of the court under section 25(2)(a), following the recommendation of the DAC Report, paragraph 135). Curiously, the Act creates the anomaly—pointed out by the DAC Report, paragraph 361—that an arbitrator who is removed by the court under section 24 does not lose immunity from suit (other than in terms of loss of fees and expenses) unless he has acted in bad faith. Attempts at the Bill stage to impose liability on an arbitrator whose actions resulted in wasted costs—for example, by withdrawing from the arbitration at short notice or failing to attend the hearing on a particular day thereby causing the parties to incur a range of wasted legal, attendance and room-hiring costs—were rejected by the Government. Lord Donaldson, speaking against this

1. [2000] 1 Lloyd's Rep 467.
2. [1974] 1 All ER 859.
3. [1975] 3 All ER 901.
4. See, e.g.: ICC Rules of Arbitration, Art. 34; LCIA Rules of Arbitration, Art. 31; and the AAA Rules of Arbitration, Art. 35. The UNCITRAL Rules of Arbitration are silent on the issue of an arbitrator's immunity from suit.

proposal, pointed out that dilatory parties might use such a provision to cast blame on the arbitrators for failing to force them to get on with the arbitration by the use of their powers to make peremptory orders under section 41 of the Act. The DAC itself reversed its position in the January 1997 Report, paragraph 24, noting that the parties would have an incentive to apply to the court to have an arbitrator removed—thereby paving the way for removal of immunity—rather than simply agreeing to remove him.

The section also reflects the common use of exclusion clauses in agreements between an arbitrator and the parties, whereby such arbitrator seeks to exclude liability for errors. Presumably such an agreement will be subject to any applicable provisions of the Unfair Contract Terms Act if expressly or impliedly subject to English law.

The section seemingly does not operate to give the arbitrator immunity from a costs order made against him in successful proceedings brought by one party for his removal.[1]

Jurisdiction of the Arbitral Tribunal

Competence of tribunal to rule on its own jurisdiction

30.—(1) Unless otherwise agreed by the parties, the arbitral tribunal may rule on its own substantive jurisdiction, that is, as to—

(a) whether there is a valid arbitration agreement,
(b) whether the tribunal is properly constituted, and
(c) what matters have been submitted to arbitration in accordance with the arbitration agreement.

(2) Any such ruling may be challenged by any available arbitral process of appeal or review or in accordance with the provisions of this Part.

NOTES

Arbitration is peculiarly affected by the fact that it is a creature of contract. Prior to the decision of the Court of Appeal in *Harbour Assurance Co Ltd* v. *Kansa General International Insurance Co Ltd*,[2] there had been a long-standing issue as to whether an arbitration could proceed in terms of a dispute resolution procedure if the underlying contract was struck down in some way as being legally invalid. *Harbour Assurance* decided that the main contract and the obligation to arbitrate were distinct agreements, and that, provided that the arbitration clause was sufficiently widely worded, the arbitrators in principle would have the jurisdiction to determine whether the main agreement was valid. In many cases both before and since *Harbour Assurance*, the courts have grappled with arbitration clauses of varying width and language in order to determine the extent to which the clause permits the arbitrators to determine their jurisdiction. Since the decision in *Fiona Trust* v. *Privalov & Ors*,[3] cases that would otherwise have turned on the scope of the arbitration clause ought now to be rare: whereas formerly arbitration clauses limited to disputes "under" an agreement were considered as excluding, for example, misrepresentation or rescission claims, the principle of one-stop shopping has been deemed to have supremacy, so that an arbitration clause will, in the absence of clear words to the contrary, be taken to include all claims arising in connection with a contract. This will include claims, for example, that the agreement is void, illegal or voidable. The conceptual problem of an arbitral tribunal considering questions which go to the heart of their own jurisdiction has been dealt with by section 7 of the Act (see the Notes to that section). In summary, section 7 sets out the principle of the separability of the arbitration clause from

1. *Wicketts and Sterndale* v. *Brine Builders* [2001] CILL 1805, although the point was not there argued.
2. [1993] 1 Lloyd's Rep 455, applied in *Fletamentos Maritimos SA* v. *Effjohn International BV (No 2)* [1996] 2 Lloyd's Rep 304.
3. [2008] 1 Lloyd's Rep 254.

the underlying contract, and section 30 confers upon the arbitrators the ability, subject to contrary agreement,[1] to determine their own jurisdiction (recognised on the Continent as the principle of *Kompetenz-Kompetenz*).[2] In so providing the section has adopted in a modified form the principles contained in Article 16 of the Model Law, with the difference that section 30 is not mandatory and can be contracted out of by the parties.[3] The provisions of section 30 were new, but reflected the common law principle of waiver of rights by submission. The advantage of *Kompetenz-Kompetenz* is that the scope for one party to delay the proceedings by claiming want of jurisdiction and taking the matter to the courts is considerably reduced.

Section 30 sets out the basic principle that, subject to the precise wording of the arbitration clause itself and to any other agreement between the parties, the arbitral tribunal may determine its own substantive jurisdiction. Regardless as to whether or not the arbitration clause does itself authorise a determination of jurisdiction, it is open to the parties to enter into an *ad hoc* agreement which does confer such jurisdiction.[4] Section 30 extends to the validity of the arbitration agreement (including its existence and legality),[5] whether the tribunal has been properly constituted[6] and whether the issues referred to the tribunal fall within the arbitration agreement.[7] This differs from the Model Law, Article 16(1), which permits a ruling on jurisdiction irrespective of what has been agreed between the parties. It is uncertain whether the list of jurisdictional issues is exhaustive, and it has been suggested that section 30 applies also to the question of whether a reference to arbitration was, in the light of other agreed dispute resolution mechanisms which had not been exhausted, premature.[8] It was held in *Azov Shipping Co* v. *Baltic Shipping Co (No 1)*[9] that the justiciability of an issue was a question which went to jurisdiction. In other cases, the identity of the correct claimant and/or respondent may also be an issue which goes to jurisdiction.[10]

The distinction between jurisdictional and non-jurisdictional issues is normally clear enough. An arbitrator who exceeds his powers in conducting an arbitration is not to be regarded as having exceeded his jurisdiction: the former relates only to procedure, and the rules on jurisdiction are inapplicable.[11] One of the areas of difficulty in this context is where the respondent alleges that there is no valid agreement between the parties. If the allegation relates solely to the arbitration agreement, then any ruling by the tribunal on the validity or otherwise of the arbitration agreement is a matter of jurisdiction and falls within section 30. By contrast, where the allegation is that there is no main agreement between the parties and thus nothing to go to arbitration, then the severability principle in section 7 allows the tribunal to deal with that allegation under the independent

1. In practice, cases where the parties have agreed to deprive the arbitrators of the right to investigate their own jurisdiction are likely to be rare.

2. As indicated above, as a matter of English law, for arbitrations proceedings in England and Wales, any determination on jurisdiction made by the arbitral tribunal is also subject to the overriding and non-excludable right of any party to have such determination reviewed by the court under s. 67.

3. DAC Report, para. 139.

4. *Christiani and Nielsen Ltd* v. *The Lowry Development Co Ltd*, 2000, unreported (no agreement on the facts); *LG Caltex Gas Co Ltd* v. *China National Petroleum Co* [2001] BLR 325 (no agreement on the facts). It was assumed in *LG Caltex* that a ruling reached under an *ad hoc* agreement could not be challenged under s. 67 of the 1996 Act. This, however, would seem to depend upon whether the ruling of the arbitrators goes to the substantive agreement itself or to the jurisdiction of the arbitrators. A ruling under an *ad hoc* agreement that there is no substantive agreement between the parties plainly falls outside s. 67, whereas a ruling under an *ad hoc* agreement that there is or is not jurisdiction to determine a particular issue under the *ad hoc* agreement, is one which goes to jurisdiction. See, for this distinction, *Vee Networks Ltd* v. *Econet Wireless International Ltd* [2004] EWHC 2909 (Comm).

5. *ABB Lummus Global Ltd* v. *Keppel Fels Ltd* [1999] 2 Lloyd's Rep 24; *XL Insurance Ltd* v. *Owens Corning* [2000] 2 Lloyd's Rep 500.

6. *Minermet SpA Milan* v. *Luckyfield Shipping Corporation SA* [2004] 2 Lloyd's Rep 348.

7. *Al-Naimi* v. *Islamic Press Agency Inc* [2000] 1 Lloyd's Rep 522; *Fleming and Wendeln GmbH* v. *Sanoi SA/AG* [2003] 2 Lloyd's Rep 473; *Ronly Holdings* v. *JSC Zestafoni G Nikoladze Ferroalloy Plant* [2004] 2 Lloyd's Rep 335; *Westland Helicopters Ltd* v. *Sheikh Salah Al-Hejailan* [2004] 2 Lloyd's Rep 523.

8. *Mackley & Co Ltd* v. *Gosport Marina Ltd* [2002] BLR 367.

9. [1999] 1 Lloyd's Rep 68.

10. See, e.g., *Peterson Farms Inc* v. *C & M Farming* [2004] 1 Lloyd's Rep 603; *Primetrade AG* v. *Ythan Ltd, The Ythan* [2006] 1 Lloyd's Rep 457.

11. *Petroships Pte Ltd of Singapore* v. *Petec Trading & Investment Corporation* [2001] 2 Lloyd's Rep 348; *Lesotho Highlands Development Authority* v. *Impregilo SpA* [2005] 2 Lloyd's Rep 310.

arbitration clause and may thereafter issue an award on the consequences of finding an agreement (e.g., an action for breach) or of not finding an agreement (e.g., a restitutionary or tortious claim), as the case may be: no jurisdictional issue under section 30 is at stake in such a case.[1] There is an intermediate possibility, namely an allegation that there is no main agreement and no arbitration clause: in such a case the severability principle allows the tribunal to rule on the validity of the main issue, but any preliminary ruling made by it in respect of the arbitration clause itself is one which goes to jurisdiction under section 30.

Section 30(2) refers to the review procedures in the remainder of the Act. These are important, since the arbitral tribunal cannot be allowed to have the final say as to whether or not it possesses jurisdiction over a particular matter and thus whether it can alter the rights of a person under a procedure to which he has not agreed. Any ruling on jurisdiction given by the tribunal is provisional only, in the sense that it is always challengeable by the disaffected party. The manner of the challenge depends upon the respondent's attitude to the arbitration. The respondent may simply refuse to have anything to do with the arbitration, in which case he may bring an immediate action for injunctive or declaratory relief (section 72), or he may await the award itself and then challenge it under section 67. Using the mechanism in section 31, the respondent may participate in the arbitration, but if the award or ruling is subsequently to be challenged the participation must be under protest, in the form of an objection to jurisdiction made at the first available opportunity: the tribunal, having received the objection, may then deal with the matter themselves either by a partial award confined to jurisdiction or by a final award which encompasses both jurisdictional and substantive issues.[2] That award may then be challenged by the respondent under section 67. As an alternative to these procedures, section 32 sets out a mechanism for the court to rule on any jurisdictional issue if all the other parties to the arbitration or the arbitrators agree to a preliminary reference.

Any appeal under section 67 against the award on jurisdictional grounds must be brought within 28 days of the making of the award, or, if there has been any arbitral process of appeal or review, of the date when the applicant or appellant was notified of the result of that process in accordance with section 70(3) (though the appellant may apply to the court to extend the 28-day limit under the CPR). A final determination on jurisdiction may be regarded by the courts as an award even if not stated to be so by the arbitrators,[3] although if the fact that an award has been made is not appreciated by the party seeking to challenge it, the courts have a discretion to extend time under section 80(5).[4]

Objection to substantive jurisdiction of tribunal

31.—(1) An objection that the arbitral tribunal lacks substantive jurisdiction at the outset of the proceedings must be raised by a party not later than the time he takes the first step in the proceedings to contest the merits of any matter in relation to which he challenges the tribunal's jurisdiction.

A party is not precluded from raising such an objection by the fact that he has appointed or participated in the appointment of an arbitrator.

(2) Any objection during the course of the arbitral proceedings that the arbitral tribunal is exceeding its substantive jurisdiction must be made as soon as possible after the matter alleged to be beyond its jurisdiction is raised.

1. *Vee Networks Ltd* v. *Econet Wireless International Ltd* [2005] 1 Lloyd's Rep 192. See also *Albon* v. *Naza Motor Trading (No 3)* [2007] 2 Lloyd's Rep 1, where the issue was the validity of a joint venture agreement, but in reality the existence of that agreement had been alleged only because it was said to contain an arbitration clause: *Albon* was thus about jurisdiction and not about the existence of a contract.

2. See s. 31(4).

3. As in *Ranko Group* v. *Antarctic Maritime SA, The Robin* [1998] ADRLN 35 and *Hussmann (Europe) Ltd* v. *Al Ameen Development and Trade Co* [2000] 2 Lloyd's Rep 83.

4. *The Robin* [1998] ADRLN 35, in which the court declined to exercise this discretion in the appellant's favour.

(3) The arbitral tribunal may admit an objection later than the time specified in subsection (1) or (2) if it considers the delay justified.

(4) Where an objection is duly taken to the tribunal's substantive jurisdiction and the tribunal has power to rule on its own jurisdiction, it may—

(a) rule on the matter in an award as to jurisdiction, or
(b) deal with the objection in its award on the merits.

If the parties agree which of these courses the tribunal should take, the tribunal shall proceed accordingly.

(5) The tribunal may in any case, and shall if the parties so agree, stay proceedings whilst an application is made to the court under section 32 (determination of preliminary point of jurisdiction).

NOTES

Section 31, taken with section 32, establishes the procedure whereby a party may object to the arbitrators' assertion of jurisdiction. This is taken from Article 16 of the Model Law. Section 31(1) lays down the stringent requirements that any objection to jurisdiction must be raised by the complainant party no later than the time at which he takes the first step in the proceedings to contest the merits of the issue to which the jurisdictional point relates,[1] although the arbitrators are free to extend time in accordance with section 31(3) in the event of a justifiable delay (reflecting Article 16(2) of the Model Law). The section by its wording provides for a separability of issues: the mere fact that the complainant has submitted to the jurisdiction of the arbitrators on some matters does not mean that he has done so in respect of those matters for which jurisdiction is contested. Making an objection preserves his right to challenge the substantive award on the jurisdictional point at some later stage (provided that the question of jurisdiction has not earlier been resolved by preliminary ruling under section 32), either by a challenge to the award on jurisdictional grounds under section 67 or by contesting enforcement proceedings in accordance with section 66(3) (refusal of enforcement where the arbitrators acted without jurisdiction). If, by contrast, no objection is taken at the time specified by section 31(1), then there are two independent but overlapping reasons to prevent a subsequent challenge: there is no jurisdictional issue before the arbitrators against which an appeal can be made,[2] and the party contesting jurisdiction will be taken to have waived any irregularity by a virtue of section 73, which provides that failure to raise an objection at the stated time amounts to a waiver of the right to object at a later stage.[3] The result is that, if a party has not objected to the arbitrators' assertion of jurisdiction but has proceeded with the hearing on the merits, the award cannot be challenged on jurisdictional grounds under section 67, nor can enforcement of the award be contested, as the proviso to section 66(3) makes it clear that the right to contest enforcement may be lost. Equally, the right of a party to seek a preliminary ruling as to jurisdiction from the court, under section 32, will be lost. It is likely that the common law would have reached the same conclusion as to waiver independently of these provisions of the Act. It should be noted that section 31 is a mandatory provision, not capable of being ousted by express contrary agreement.

Section 31(2) deals with the situation in which a jurisdictional issue arises during the course of (as opposed to at the outset of) the proceedings, that is, after the complainant has submitted to the jurisdiction of the arbitrators: this might be, for example, that one of the arbitrators has ceased to be qualified or a party attempts to include in, for example, the arbitrators' terms of reference a matter that the other party argues lies outside their jurisdiction. In such a case, the complainant must

1. Art. 16(2) of the Model Law refers to "the submission of the statement of defence". This formulation was rejected in the DAC Report, as there may not be anything which constitutes a "statement of defence". A step in the proceedings is something more than asserting in an initial response to the proceedings, possibly in the form of negotiations with the arbitrators, that the arbitration clause is not binding: *Athletic Union of Constantinople* v. *National Basketball Association* [2002] 1 Lloyd's Rep 305; *Caparo Group Ltd* v. *Fagor Arrasate Sociedad Cooperative* [2000] ADRLJ 254.
2. *Vee Networks Ltd* v. *Econet Wireless International Ltd* [2004] EWHC 2909 (Comm).
3. *Ibid.*

register his objection as soon as possible after the matter has been raised.[1] Once again, this section, taken in conjunction with section 73, means that a failure to object at the stated time amounts to a waiver of the right to object by way of direct challenge under section 67 or by contesting enforcement under section 66(3), subject to the power of the arbitrators in section 31(3) to extend the time for making an objection in the case of a justifiable delay (as provided for in Article 16(2) of the Model Law).

Section 31(3), as mentioned above, permits the arbitrators to extend time for the registering of objections under sections 31(1) and 31(2). It is unclear whether, in the absence of any extension, the aggrieved party would be permitted to apply to the court under section 79 of the Act (court powers to extend "time limits"), as that section appears to be more concerned with specific deadlines for particular acts.

Section 31(4) of the Act echoes (with an important modification) Article 16(3) of the Model Law and, when read in combination with section 31(5), contemplates that the jurisdictional issue may be dealt with in one of three ways:

(a) by a preliminary award confined to the jurisdictional issue, challengeable under section 67;
(b) by an award on the merits of the dispute, also challengeable under section 67 insofar as it relates to jurisdiction; or
(c) by reference to the court under section 32 (see below).[2]

The parties' agreement as to how the arbitrators are to proceed must be honoured by them, but in the absence of agreement they can determine the matter for themselves and their decision as to how to proceed cannot be challenged on the grounds of excess of jurisdiction.[3] Either party affected by the outcome of a preliminary award on jurisdiction may challenge it before the court. In other words, a positive or negative ruling on jurisdiction is challengeable. The DAC Report, paragraph 146, rejected the argument that either party ought to have the right to insist upon a preliminary award as to jurisdiction being made: the DAC's view was that this decision should remain with the arbitrators if the parties are not agreed, and that in some cases it may be impractical to distinguish jurisdiction from merits. The modification from the Model Law is the failure by the 1996 Act to adopt the concept of the "preliminary reference", whereby the tribunal can rule on its jurisdiction by a preliminary decision which does not take effect as an award. The DAC Report, paragraph 412, saw no justification for the introduction of a hybrid form of ruling which did not amount to a full award, and this view is echoed in the Act.

An award on jurisdiction by the arbitrators is a full award in every sense, and is subject to the provisions of the Act on the making of awards and on challenges to them. Consequently, the jurisdictional aspect of any award may be challenged under section 67, and enforcement (if it is coupled with a dispositive award on the merits) resisted under section 66, provided of course that the party seeking to make the challenge has complied with the procedural requirements as to objections in section 31. If the arbitrators choose to make an award on jurisdiction only, it will be necessary for the party wishing to contest that award to do so in accordance with the 28-day time limit laid down by section 70 for such challenges, even though the remaining aspects of the arbitration are unresolved. For this reason, section 67(2) allows the arbitrators to continue the substantive proceedings even though an appeal against their award on jurisdiction is outstanding. It is here important to emphasise that the rejection of the hybrid preliminary ruling means that any binding decision by the arbitrators as to their jurisdiction will take effect as an award even though it is not classified as such by them: the significance of this is of course the fact that the time limits for challenging the decision as an award under section 67 of the 1996 Act will begin to run immediately the arbitrators have made their decision. This was so held by Toulson J in *Ranko Group* v. *Antarctic Maritime SA, The Robin*,[4] in which the arbitrator wrote to the parties stating that he had made "rulings" on the validity of his own appointment, on the existence of an arbitration agreement

1. See *Hussmann (Europe) Ltd* v. *Al Ameen Development and Trade Co* [2000] 2 Lloyd's Rep 83, where the objection was held to be timely.
2. DAC Report, para. 140.
3. *AOOT Kalmneft* v. *Glencore International AG* [2002] 1 Lloyd's Rep 128.
4. [1998] ADRLN 35.

and on the validity of the submission of disputes to him. Toulson J decided that the "rulings" in favour of jurisdiction constituted an award on jurisdiction, and as there had been no challenge within the statutory 28 days (allowed by section 70(3)), the award was binding on the parties.

The common law principle that a jurisdictional point which has not been waived can be resolved by the court by declaration or injunction up to the making of an award[1] is left unaffected by section 72, which permits a person who has refused to participate in the arbitration proceedings, on the basis of want of jurisdiction, to contest jurisdiction at any time.

Determination of preliminary point of jurisdiction

32.—(1) The court may, on the application of a party to arbitral proceedings (upon notice to the other parties), determine any question as to the substantive jurisdiction of the tribunal.

A party may lose the right to object (see section 73).

(2) An application under this section shall not be considered unless—

- (a) it is made with the agreement in writing of all the other parties to the proceedings, or
- (b) it is made with the permission of the tribunal and the court is satisfied—
    - (i) that the determination of the question is likely to produce substantial savings in costs,
    - (ii) that the application was made without delay, and
    - (iii) that there is good reason why the matter should be decided by the court.

(3) An application under this section, unless made with the agreement of all the other parties to the proceedings, shall state the grounds on which it is said that the matter should be decided by the court.

(4) Unless otherwise agreed by the parties, the arbitral tribunal may continue the arbitral proceedings and make an award while an application to the court under this section is pending.

(5) Unless the court gives leave, no appeal lies from a decision of the court whether the conditions specified in subsection (2) are met.

(6) The decision of the court on the question of jurisdiction shall be treated as a judgment of the court for the purposes of an appeal.

But no appeal lies without the leave of the court which shall not be given unless the court considers that the question involves a point of law which is one of general importance or is one which for some other special reason should be considered by the Court of Appeal.

NOTES

The original draft Bill laid down a procedure (based on Article 16 of the Model Law) in respect of a preliminary ruling by the arbitral tribunal as to jurisdiction, and which had to be complied with if the preliminary ruling was to be contested at any point in the future. It involved an application to the court for the arbitrators' preliminary ruling to be considered, with the arbitrators having the power to continue with the substantive hearing pending the application to the court, thereby preventing a plea of want of jurisdiction resolved by preliminary ruling being used as a device to hold up the proceedings.

1. As in *Metal Scrap Trade Corporation Ltd* v. *Kate Shipping Co Ltd, The Gladys* [1990] 1 All ER 397, a case which illustrates the problems that may be raised if a declaration is sought in the English courts by a party who does not wish to submit to the substantive jurisdiction of the English courts.

The section as drafted rejected the arbitrators' preliminary ruling approach. Accordingly, the jurisdiction issue must be dealt with by award, whether devoted to the jurisdiction question alone or as part of an overall award on the merits. Section 32 lays down a procedure under which the jurisdiction of the arbitrators can be determined by the court by way of preliminary ruling, that is, during the course of the arbitration. This procedure is based closely on the preliminary ruling on point of law procedure originally contained in section 2 of the Arbitration Act 1979 and re-enacted as section 45 of the 1996 Act. Its use was intended by the DAC to be the exception rather than the rule, and accordingly it is narrowly drawn (DAC Report, paragraphs 141 and 147): the DAC Report indeed exhorts the courts to ensure that the section 32 procedure is exceptional and does not become the ordinary method for challenging jurisdiction.[1] In particular, an application under section 32 is not regarded as appropriate (even where brought by agreement between the parties) where the challenge being made is not a complete challenge to the tribunal's jurisdiction, but only a partial challenge, for example, in respect of certain claims.[2] In general terms, an application to the court under section 32 does not amount to an appeal from the arbitrators' award on jurisdiction, but either is a substitute for such an award[3] or may be used where the arbitrators themselves have no power under the terms of the arbitration clause to rule on their own jurisdiction.[4] The court has no power other than to give a ruling on jurisdiction: the court may not under this section grant an anti-suit injunction in support of the arbitration.[5]

A party is entitled, under section 32(1), to apply to the court for a preliminary ruling, providing that he has objected in accordance with section 31 and, thus, has not lost the right to object under the waiver rule in section 73. The application, in the form of an arbitration claim,[6] must under section 32(2), either be agreed by all of the parties, or made with the permission of the arbitrators.[7] In the latter case: (i) the arbitration claim must set out the evidence upon which the application is based;[8] and (ii) the court has no jurisdiction to make a preliminary ruling unless the three conditions in section 32(2)(b) are met,[9] there being no appeal from the court's decision as to its jurisdiction unless the court itself gives permission to appeal (section 32(5)).[10] Section 32(3) also provides that the grounds on which the application is made are to be stated (i.e., in the arbitration claim form). In order to avoid delay, the arbitrators are, under section 32(4), permitted to continue the arbitration unless the parties agree that the proceedings should be stayed. The ultimate ruling by the court is to be treated as a judgment under section 32(6),[11] but no appeal may be made against it unless the twin cumulative conditions are met that: (i) the court considers that a point of law of general importance is raised or that there is some other reason for an appeal; and (ii) the court gives

1. Confirmed by *ABB Lummus Global Ltd* v. *Keppel Fels Ltd* [1999] 2 Lloyd's Rep 24 and *Vale do Rio Doce Navegaçao SA* v. *Shanghai Bao Steel Ocean Shipping Co Ltd* [2000] 2 Lloyd's Rep 1. Nevertheless, if the application is one made with the consent of the parties (as opposed to one made with the permission of the tribunal where one party declines to agree), it is difficult to envisage circumstances in which the court would refuse to entertain the application, e.g., on the basis of delay.

2. See *Peterson Farms* v. *C&M Farming Inc* [2004] 1 Lloyd's Rep 614, *per* Langley J.

3. *National Boat Shows Ltd* v. *Tameside Marine*, July 2001, unreported.

4. *Esso Exploration & Production UK Ltd* v. *Electricity Supply Board* [2004] 1 All ER (Comm) 926.

5. *Welex AG* v. *Rosa Maritime Ltd* [2003] 2 Lloyd's Rep 509.

6. Curiously, the section only requires notice to be given to the other party or parties to the arbitration, i.e. not to the tribunal, though in practice it would be extremely odd if the tribunal were not made aware of the application itself, or at least the intention to make it, particularly if (as would have to be the case) it were agreed by both or all parties.

7. These are jurisdictional requirements, so the absence of consent of the other parties or the permission of the arbitrators precludes an application: *Mackley & Co Ltd* v. *Gosport Marina Ltd* [2002] BLR 367. In terms of permission by an arbitral tribunal consisting of three arbitrators, permission need only be granted by a majority (provided that it is in writing, e.g., in the form of a procedural order made during the reference): see ss. 20(3) and 22(2).

8. CPR PD 62, para. 9.2.

9. The question whether the court is satisfied as to the matters set out in s. 32(2)(b) may be decided without a hearing: see CPR PD 62, para. 10.1.

10. See DAC Supplementary Report, para. 27, emphasising that there is no appeal to the Court of Appeal against a refusal of leave to appeal.

11. This is probably the case so as to ensure that the decision on jurisdiction is binding on the parties, i.e. that it will make the jurisdictional question *res judicata*.

permission to appeal. The "court" for this purpose means the trial judge and not the Court of Appeal.[1] Identical tests apply to preliminary rulings on points of law under section 45, as discussed below.

The parties are under a duty, imposed by section 40(2), to take without delay any necessary steps to obtain a decision of the court on the preliminary question of jurisdiction. (In practice, however, such an obligation is unlikely to be relevant once either the tribunal gives permission or both parties agree that a preliminary reference on jurisdiction is required, provided that there has been no waiver under section 73.)

As section 32 is mandatory (see section 4(1) and Schedule 1), it will apply to any arbitration with its seat in England even if the parties have chosen some other law as the curial law of the arbitration.[2]

The Arbitral Proceedings

General duty of the tribunal

33.—(1) The tribunal shall—

(a) act fairly and impartially as between the parties, giving each party a reasonable opportunity of putting his case and dealing with that of his opponent, and
(b) adopt procedures suitable to the circumstances of the particular case, avoiding unnecessary delay or expense, so as to provide a fair means for the resolution of the matters falling to be determined.

(2) The tribunal shall comply with that general duty in conducting the arbitral proceedings, in its decisions on matters of procedure and evidence and in the exercise of all other powers conferred on it.

NOTES

Section 33(1) lays down two overriding obligations imposed on the arbitrators in their handling of the dispute: (a) acting fairly and impartially as between the parties, giving each party a reasonable opportunity of putting his case and dealing with that of the opponent; and (b) adopting procedures suitable to the circumstances of the case, avoiding unnecessary delay or expense and providing a fair means for the resolution of the matters falling to be determined. The DAC Report, paragraph 150, points out that the section is drafted in the widest possible terms, so as to give maximum flexibility to arbitrators in their handling of the dispute, but that the requirements of section 33(1) are the minimum conditions consistent with an arbitration procedure: for this reason, section 33(1) is a mandatory provision. Any agreement by the parties as to the procedure to be adopted by the arbitrators which falls short of the principles set out in section 33(1) is void.[3] Voidness is unlikely, however, to be significant where the parties have agreed a procedure which the arbitrators—reluctantly or otherwise—adopt, for if either party subsequently chose to challenge the award by objecting to the procedure on the grounds of unfairness it would be difficult to anticipate the court granting relief under section 68:[4] this result could be reached either by the court refusing to find that

1. *Henry Boot Construction (UK) Ltd* v. *Malmaison Hotel (Manchester) Ltd* [2001] 1 QB 388; *Athletic Union of Constantinople* v. *National Basketball Association* [2002] 1 Lloyd's Rep 305; *Virdee* v. *Virdi* [2003] EWCA Civ 41.
2. *ABB Lummus Global Ltd* v. *Keppel Fels Ltd* [1999] 2 Lloyd's Rep 24.
3. For these propositions, see DAC Report, paras 155–158.
4. DAC Report, para. 161.

there exists the necessary substantial injustice to the applicant (under section 68(2)) or on the basis of the waiver principle, even if an objection is raised during the conduct of the proceedings.[1]

The Act heralds an unequivocal attempt to move away from arbitrations which resemble court proceedings, and was intended to remove the possibility that arbitrators without legal qualifications can be bullied or baffled by lawyers appearing before them. The DAC was indeed of the view that making arbitrations less legalistic and instead subject to broad principles of fairness would encourage the use of lay (in terms of legal qualifications) arbitrators (see paragraphs 152 to 153 of the February 1996 Report). In particular, the section was intended to "explode the theory that an arbitration has always to follow Court procedures".[2]

Obligation (a) is a basic statement of the rules of natural justice which have always been applied to arbitrations by the common law, and encompasses the concepts previously referred to as "misconduct" (which under the 1950 Act could lead to the remission or setting aside of the award and the removal of the arbitrators) and "procedural mishap" (which, although not recognised by the 1950 Act, could lead to remission of the award). However, it should be commented that the concept of "procedural mishap" is wider than the concept set out in section 33, and in particular applied to cases in which the failure of the arbitrators to provide a fair hearing resulted from the failure by one or both of the parties to present their case properly. Procedural mishap in that very broad sense does not survive the 1996 Act.[3] The formulation in section 33(1) is based on Article 18 of the Model Law, the main difference being that the Model Law refers to "full opportunity" to present the case, whereas section 33(1) refers to "reasonable opportunity": the DAC Report, paragraph 165, makes the point that the formulation "full opportunity" may lead to unreasonable delays, contrary to the interests of justice. The section even extends to the arbitrators' decisions on costs. Where an arbitrator felt influenced in the exercise of his discretion on costs by factors which had not been drawn to the attention of the parties (who had therefore not had the opportunity to deal with them), he did not act fairly and impartially if no such opportunity was given to the parties.[4]

Obligation (a) does not imply that arbitrators may never proceed in the absence of one party. The duty under section 33 is not violated by their doing so, as indicated by section 41, under which the arbitrators are permitted to proceed in the absence of a party if that party fails without good cause to attend a hearing of which it had notice, or to submit written evidence or make written submissions.

Obligation (b) requires the arbitrators to adopt suitable procedures matching the circumstances of the case. This provision is vital in the light of section 34(1), which confers upon the arbitrators the power to decide all procedural and evidential matters, and which is a change from the principle enshrined in the July 1995 Bill that determination of the procedure is a matter for the parties. If arbitrators, faced with a commodity claim in which the only issue is quality and which can be disposed of on a "look and sniff" basis, choose to adopt an elaborate procedure involving unnecessary expense and delay, the general obligation in section 33(1)(b) will presumably have been broken. The parties may of course agree upon an arbitration procedure which the arbitrators regard as disproportionate in that the costs[5] and time incurred are likely to be far greater than necessary. Once again, the mandatory nature of section 33 means that such an agreement is probably void, and the arbitrators can legitimately refuse to adopt it and, if the parties refuse to see what the arbitrators regard as sense, resign.[6] For the reasons stated above in relation to principle (a), the voidness of the parties' agreement is unlikely to render the arbitration a nullity and instead will produce an award which is all but immune from challenge under section 68.

If there is a failure by the arbitrators to comply with section 33 of the Act which in the opinion of the court will cause substantial injustice unless the court acts, there is deemed to be "serious irregularity" (section 68(1) and (2)(a)), and the court has the power to remit the award to the

1. The waiver principle is partially codified by s. 74, although only in the situation in which no objection is taken at the time. However, it might be thought that waiver would by analogy apply if the parties had agreed at the outset that a particular procedure would be adopted, and an objection was subsequently taken: the voidness of the agreement under s. 33 would, it is thought, not prevent waiver from becoming operative.
2. DAC Report, para. 153.
3. *Bandwidth Shipping Corporation* v. *Intaari* [2008] 1 Lloyd's Rep 7.
4. *Gbangbola* v. *Smith Sherriff Ltd* [1998] 3 All ER 730.
5. The arbitrators do have the power to cap costs under s. 65, but this can be overridden by agreement.
6. DAC Report, February 1996, para. 162.

arbitrators, to set the award aside or to declare it to be of no effect where the arbitrators have acted without jurisdiction (section 68(3). If the award is not remitted, the court has the discretion to hear the matter itself by refusing to stay its own proceedings, provided that the arbitration agreement is domestic, although the court must stay its proceedings for a fresh hearing in the case of a non-domestic arbitration agreement unless both parties wish the matter to be resolved in the courts.[1] If the award is remitted or the matter falls again to be resolved by arbitration, the court retains its power under section 23(1) of the Arbitration Act 1950 to remove the arbitrators: this is contained in the general provisions of section 24.

There are numerous authorities on the meaning of misconduct under the 1950 Act, and the factual situations in those cases remain important illustrations of the scope of section 33 of the 1996 Act. The most important categories of misconduct and, these days, substantial irregularity, include: treating the parties in a discriminatory fashion;[2] failing to hear one of the parties, for example, by refusing to hear his primary evidence;[3] denying one of the parties a right to reply, for example, by accepting evidence in his absence;[4] and giving weight to evidence not presented by the parties and not disclosed to them.[5] The cases are fully discussed in the notes to section 68.

Section 33(2) as originally drafted in the July 1995 Bill stated that the principle in section 33(1) overrode all other considerations. The version of section 33(2) in the final version of the 1996 Act does not so provide in terms, but it may be assumed that this remains its general effect.

Procedural and evidential matters

34.—(1) It shall be for the tribunal to decide all procedural and evidential matters, subject to the right of the parties to agree any matter.

(2) Procedural and evidential matters include—

(a) when and where any part of the proceedings is to be held;

(b) the language or languages to be used in the proceedings and whether translations of any relevant documents are to be supplied;

(c) whether any and if so what form of written statements of claim and defence are to be used, when these should be supplied and the extent to which such statements can be later amended;

(d) whether any and if so which documents or classes of documents should be disclosed between and produced by the parties and at what stage;

(e) whether any and if so what questions should be put to and answered by the respective parties and when and in what form this should be done;

(f) whether to apply strict rules of evidence (or any other rules) as to the admissibility, relevance or weight of any material (oral, written or other) sought to be tendered on any matters of fact or opinion, and the time, manner and form in which such material should be exchanged and presented;

(g) whether and to what extent the tribunal should itself take the initiative in ascertaining the facts and the law;

(h) whether and to what extent there should be oral or written evidence or submissions.

1. This follows from the general principles relating to stay, in s. 9.
2. *Stockport Metropolitan Borough Council* v. *O'Reilly* [1983] 2 Lloyd's Rep 70.
3. *Re Enoch and Zaretsky, Bock Co* [1910] 1 KB 327; *Modern Engineering (Bristol) Ltd* v. *C Miskin & Sons Ltd* [1981] 1 Lloyd's Rep 135.
4. *Re Fuerst Brothers Co Ltd and Stephenson* [1951] 1 Lloyd's Rep 429.
5. *Interbulk Ltd* v. *Aiden Shipping Co Ltd, The Vimeira* [1984] 2 Lloyd's Rep 66; *Pacol Ltd* v. *Joint Stock Co Rossakhar* [2000] 1 Lloyd's Rep 109.

(3) The tribunal may fix the time within which any directions given by it are to be complied with, and may if it thinks fit extend the time so fixed (whether or not it has expired).

NOTES

The Arbitration Act 1950 operated on the presumption that the arbitrators were to act in accordance with the ordinary rules of evidence.[1] This presumption could be ousted by the express agreement of the parties authorising the reception of otherwise inadmissible evidence, but such agreements were comparatively rare and the procedure fell to be determined by the arbitrators themselves. As arbitrators were unwilling to depart from traditional approaches and procedures, arbitrations tended to resemble court proceedings. The original version of section 34 in the July 1995 Bill freed the arbitrators from the rules of evidence previously applicable to them and, in the absence of the agreement of the parties as to procedure, to determine their own procedure. In so doing, section 34 followed the specific points made in the Model Law. Consultation on the July 1995 Bill demonstrated a general view that arbitrators are better equipped than the parties to decide what procedure to use, and that arbitrators appointed because of their expertise and experience should not be forced to conduct an arbitration based on unfamiliar procedures agreed by the parties. Accordingly, section 34(1) was revised to make it clear that all issues of evidence and procedure are to be determined by the arbitrators, subject to the right of the parties "to agree any matter": this wording indicates that the parties may agree on specific issues, but not on the entire range of matters which might arise. In the event that the parties do opt for a particular procedure which the arbitrators feel unable to comply with, or if the parties' agreements on procedure become intrusive or operate to extend the arbitration beyond tolerable limits, the Act contemplates resignation by the arbitrators coupled with release from what would otherwise be liability for breach of contract: this is the effect of section 25. Indeed, as commented in the Notes to section 33, resignation may be the only option open to the arbitrators where the parties insist upon a procedure which the arbitrators view as contravening the mandatory natural justice and proportionality requirements established by section 33,[2] and in such circumstances they would almost certainly be relieved by the court of any possible liability for breach of contract.[3]

Section 34(1) sets out the principle that all procedural and evidential questions are matters for the arbitrators. In so doing, it adopts the principle found in Article 19(2) of the Model Law. Failure by the arbitrators, in reaching decisions under section 34, to adhere to the basic principles of fairness as set out in section 33 may be challenged by an application to remove the arbitrators under section 24 or, once the award has been issued, by a challenge to the award for serious irregularity under section 68: in both situations the courts have proved reluctant in the utmost to intervene.[4] The principle that the arbitrators are masters of their own procedure means that they may vary the procedure during the course of the arbitration, and in particular may reverse any of their own previous procedural rulings provided that in doing so they adhere to the general fairness principle set out in section 33 of the 1996 Act: issue estoppel does not apply to procedural rulings.[5] The right of the parties to agree these matters—provided for in Article 19(1) of the Model Law—is relegated to the status of subsidiary possibility: this contrasts with the Model Law, which envisages that the arbitrators' power to determine the evidential and procedural aspects of the arbitration are default powers only, operating where the parties themselves have failed to reach agreement. Where the parties do determine any aspect of the procedure themselves, their agreement must be in writing in accordance with the general rule in section 5, and the DAC noted in its July 1995 commentary on the clauses that such agreement might be independent of the arbitration agreement itself. Once the various matters governed by section 34 are fixed, either by the determination of the arbitrators or the express agreement of the parties on one or more of those matters, the parties are under a duty to do

1. *Cf. Land Securities plc* v. *Westminster City Council* [1994] 44 EG 153.
2. DAC Report, para. 159.
3. DAC Report, para. 160.
4. See the notes to ss. 24 and 68, and in particular the views of the DAC cited in the notes to s. 24.
5. *Charles M Willie Co (Shipping) Ltd* v. *Ocean Laser Shipping Ltd, The Smaro* [1999] 1 Lloyd's Rep 225.

all things necessary for the proper and expeditious conduct of the arbitration proceedings (section 40).[1]

Where there is a procedure agreed by the parties, which is accepted by the arbitrators, failure by the arbitrators to adhere to that procedure constitutes serious irregularity within section 68(2)(c) of the Act and attracts the remedial powers of the court conferred by that section.[2] However, as section 33 is mandatory, it follows that any agreement between the parties must conform to the basic standards set out in section 33(1). The arbitrators are not given any power to depart from any such agreement, and their option in such a case is either to resign (in accordance with section 25, with the likelihood in such circumstances of preserving immunity from suit for breach of contract under section 25(3)) or to adhere to the agreement despite their own views of it. If they do choose to adhere to an agreement which contravenes the basic principles in section 33, it seems unlikely that they could subsequently be accused of having been guilty of serious misconduct. All of these propositions are put forward by the DAC Report, paragraphs 157–161.

The basic effect of section 34 is that it is not possible to attack arbitration awards on the basis that judicial rules of evidence and procedure have not been followed. This is, however, subject to the general principles in section 33 that the arbitrators are to act impartially, to allow each party to put his case and to adopt a procedure suitable to the circumstances of the case. Whatever procedure is agreed upon must, therefore, be impartial, fair and appropriate. Subject to that, the arbitrators are, in default of agreement between the parties, given almost total autonomy.

Section 34(2) sets out an inclusive list of the matters which can be determined by the arbitrators. This list is deliberately framed in non-technical language, to emphasise the point that arbitrators need not in their proceedings seek to emulate judges. The list was intended to be a checklist of possible powers, it being left to the parties to determine which of them—and, indeed, which other powers—are appropriate to the arbitration in question. For this reason the DAC saw no need to make different provision for small arbitrations and for international commercial arbitrations: what is relevant can be left to the good sense of the parties (DAC Report, paragraphs 166–167). The list is also intended to be of assistance to arbitration institutions in fixing their own rules of procedure.

Section 34(2)(a) follows Article 20 of the Model Law in allowing the arbitrators to fix the place at which any part of the proceedings is to be held if the parties have failed to do so: an agreement by the parties as to the physical location of the arbitration which is disregarded by the arbitrators will only give rise to a challenge under section 68 if the breach has caused serious injustice to the parties, as opposed to some inconvenience.[3] The Model Law, unlike section 34(2)(a), refers to the convenience of the parties, although the DAC Report, paragraph 169, pointed out that this was subsumed in the arbitrators' general obligations under section 33. The section also allows the arbitrators to determine the time as well as the place of proceedings. Article 20(2) of the Model Law further empowers the arbitrators to meet at any place for consultation and to hear experts and inspect property, and this power is presumed to fall within the general provisions of section 34(2)(a). There is a distinction between the seat of the arbitration, which is the focus of the arbitration and determines which courts have curial power over the arbitration,[4] and the various places at which the arbitrators may choose to hold hearings or carry out their deliberations. The mere fact that arbitrators choose to meet in a different place for the purposes of receiving evidence or inspecting property does not affect the seat of the arbitration, neither does it have any necessary effect upon the law which is to apply to the arbitration proceedings.[5]

Section 34(2)(b) follows Article 22 of the Model Law in allowing the arbitrators to determine the language of the proceedings and whether any documents are to be translated into some other language.

1. See DAC Report, February 1996, para. 175, where it is pointed out that there is no conflict between the proviso to s. 34(1) and s. 40, as the duty of the parties under s. 40 relates only to what has been validly laid down by the arbitrators or the parties themselves under s. 34.
2. See the notes to s. 68.
3. *Tongyuan (USA) International Trading Group* v. *Uni-Clan Ltd* 2001, unreported.
4. See s. 2 and the notes thereto.
5. See generally: *James Miller & Partners Ltd* v. *Whitworth Street Estates (Manchester) Ltd* [1970] AC 583; *Naviera Amazonica Peruana SA* v. *Compania Internacional de Seguros del Peru* [1988] 1 Lloyd's Rep 116; *Bay Hotel and Resort Ltd* v. *Cavalier Construction Ltd* [2001] UKPC 34.

Section 34(2)(c) is loosely based on Article 23 of the Model Law. It indicates that the accepted procedure of the service and exchange of points of claim and defences, with latitude to make amendments, is one which can be dispensed with if the arbitrators think fit, provided (in accordance with section 33) that the parties are given an opportunity to put forward the issues and rebuttals. If the procedure is retained to any extent, its operation is in the hands of the arbitrators.

Section 34(2)(d) empowers the arbitrators to make disclosure and production orders. As is the case with litigation,[1] disclosure of documents is not automatic and the appropriate orders have to be made. Once disclosure has been ordered, the subsection indicates that the arbitrators can go on to require the relevant documents to be produced by way of evidence. The subsection appears to confer very wide powers on the arbitrators as to disclosure and production of documents,[2] and it is of course open to the parties to agree that disclosure is not available at all or is limited to specific matters. The power is presumably to be read subject to rules of privilege, preventing disclosure of documents which are privileged as between lawyer and client or documents which are confidential, for example, because they have been prepared for the purposes of some other set of arbitration proceedings. The arbitrators are entitled to accept at face value an undertaking given by counsel in the arbitration that full disclosure has been made in compliance with the arbitrators' order.[3]

Section 34(2)(e) is not provided for in terms by the Model Law; but is a necessary corollary to the general discretion of the arbitrators. It refers to questions by the parties to each other and to questions put by the arbitrators.

Section 34(2)(f) follows Article 19(2) of the Model Law, which confers upon the arbitrators the power "to determine the admissibility relevance, materiality and weight of any evidence". It is clear from this that arbitrators are no longer bound by the strict rules of evidence, so that they can rely on evidence that would otherwise be inadmissible. This would seem to represent a change in the law; as under the 1950 Act, absent any agreement between the parties, the arbitrators were required to follow rules on admissibility,[4] although there was little authority on the wider question of whether rules of evidence in general were mandatory in arbitrations.[5] It should be noted in this regard that the rule against the admission of hearsay evidence has for all relevant purposes been abolished by the Civil Evidence Act 1995. The subsection also gives the arbitrator the right to determine the time at which evidence is presented, and it is therefore perfectly proper for the arbitrators to give the last word to the respondent rather than the claimant, contrary to the procedure adopted in litigation in England.[6]

The statement that the arbitrators can determine the weight to be given to any evidence taken at its widest is also new in legislative terms, as there was a good deal of authority under the 1950 Act for the proposition that any demonstrable failure by the arbitrators to give weight to what the court regarded as material evidence amounted to misconduct.[7] It remains to be seen whether section 34(2)(f) does amount to a substantial change in the law in this respect, for it is possible to argue that ignoring material evidence amounts to a breach of the overriding duty under section 33 of allowing the parties a reasonable opportunity to put their cases, and it may be that there is a distinction to be drawn between receiving evidence with an open mind and disregarding it, and not receiving evidence with anything approaching an open mind. If this is right, it may be that section 34(2)(f) does no more than confirm the old principle that the weighing of evidence is a matter for the arbitrators provided that they have put their mind to the issue of weight,[8] although it should be said

1. CPR Part 31.

2. The implementation of this section was anticipated by Longmore J in *GEC Alsthom Metro Cammell Ltd* v. *Firema Consortium*, 1997, unreported (exercise of discretion as to disclosure not reviewable).

3. *Lincoln National Life Insurance Co* v. *Sun Life Assurance Co of Canada, American Phoenix Life and Reassurance Co and Phoenix Home Life Mutual Insurance Co* [2004] 1 Lloyd's Rep 737, reversed on other grounds [2005] 1 Lloyd's Rep 606.

4. See, e.g., *Brown* v. *CBS Contractors* [1987] 1 Lloyd's Rep 279. But see *Living Waters Christian Centres Ltd* v. *Fetherstonaugh* [2000] 2 EGLR 1.

5. DAC Report, February 1996, para. 170.

6. *Margulead Ltd* v. *Exide Technologies* [2004] 2 All ER (Comm) 727.

7. E.g., *Trayfoot* v. *Lock* [1957] 1 All ER 423.

8. *Lewis Emanuel & Son Ltd* v. *Sammut* [1959] 2 Lloyd's Rep 629; *Marklands Ltd* v. *Virgin Retail Ltd* [2004] 2 EGLR 43.

that the intention behind the section—as explained in the DAC Report, paragraph 17—was to put an end to any argument that whether the evidence supported a finding of fact could amount to a question of law. However, it is now extremely doubtful whether factual findings in the reasons for an award which are unsupported by the evidence are to be regarded as challengeable as errors of law.[1]

Section 34(2)(g) is one of the most significant provisions of the 1996 Act, and states that the arbitrators may dispense with the adversarial process and adopt instead an inquisitorial approach whereby the initiative is taken by the arbitrators. The general assumption is that the Arbitration Act 1950 did not permit such a radical departure from accepted procedures without the agreement of the parties. It is of course unlikely that many arbitrators trained under earlier legislation will opt for the inquisitorial approach, as it remains an unfamiliar procedure in England. Fears were expressed to the DAC in response to the July 1995 Bill that the unfamiliarity of such a power means that it might be abused—albeit in good faith—by arbitrators, although the DAC was happy that the overriding fairness requirement in section 33 of the Act would operate to prevent this contingency.[2] Moreover, if the parties are not comfortable with this method of proceeding, they can always agree to remove the power so to act from the arbitrators.[3]

Section 34(2)(h) follows Article 24(1) of the Model Law and restates a principle familiar to certain forms of English arbitration which are conducted on a documents-only basis.[4] The Act does not expressly authorise, but by implication permits, "look and sniff" arbitrations in which the only issue is the quality of the subject matter supplied under the main contract. Documents-only arbitrations are also contemplated so there is no assumed automatic entitlement to a hearing if requested.[5] Although under Article 24 of the Model Law, a hearing must be held if required by even one party, there is no similar provision in section 34. Nevertheless, arbitrators who refuse a hearing in the face of a request by one party should be careful to ensure that they are satisfied in so refusing that they are not acting in breach of their duty under section 33 to allow all parties a reasonable opportunity of putting their cases. In some cases, perhaps something less than a full hearing (including lengthy oral opening and closing statements) is appropriate. This is commonly the practice in arbitrations taking place in civil law jurisdictions, where hearings are permitted (and are indeed the norm) but are limited to the receipt of witness evidence.

Section 34(3) confers upon the arbitrators the power to fix time limits to their orders, and to vary them on application before or after their expiry. This power applies only to the arbitrators' own directions, and cannot affect contractual or statutory time limits. Subject to any variation agreed by the arbitrators, the parties are under an express obligation to comply with any directions of the arbitrators as to procedural or evidential matters, as part of their overall duty to do all things necessary for the proper and expeditious conduct of the arbitral proceedings: section 40(2)(a).

1. Although the presumption that findings of fact unsupported by evidence could be challenged as an error of law under s. 69 was assumed to be correct in *Fence Gate Ltd* v. *NEL Construction Ltd* (2001) 82 Con LR 41 and (albeit *obiter* by Etherton J) in *Guardcliffe Properties Ltd* v. *City & St James* [2003] 2 EGLR 16, after reviewing these cases, Cooke J in *Demco Investments and Commercial SA* v. *SE Banken Forsakring Holding Aktiebolag* [2005] 2 Lloyd's Rep 250 considered *Fence Gate* was wrongly decided and that the *obiter* statement in *Guardcliffe* was incorrect. If the award is unreasoned, and reasons cannot be ordered by the court under s.70(4), there is in any event no basis on which a challenge can be made.

2. DAC Report, para. 172.

3. DAC Report, para. 173. The DAC here rejected the argument that the arbitrators should have the ability to conduct proceedings on an inquisitorial basis whatever the parties may wish: this would be contrary to the Model Law, Art. 19 as well as an indefensible inroad into party autonomy; in practice an overriding power would be unenforceable as the parties could simply disregard directions; and in any event there is in practice most unlikely to be an agreement between the parties which sought to reject the arbitrators' method of proceeding.

4. See *General Construction Ltd* v. *Aegon Insurance Co (UK) Ltd*, 1999, unreported; *Paul* v. *Royal and Sun Alliance Insurance Group plc*, 1999, unreported.

5. But see *Ocean Marine Navigation Ltd* v. *Koch Carbon Inc, The Dynamic* [2003] 2 Lloyd's Rep 693, where Simon J warned that arbitrators should be flexible and should consider holding a hearing where appropriate. See also: *Pacol Ltd* v. *Joint Stock Co Rossakhar* [2000] 1 Lloyd's Rep 109; *Boulos Gad Tourism & Hotels Ltd* v. *Uniground Shipping Co Ltd*, November 2001, unreported; *O'Donoghue* v. *Enterprise Inns plc* [2008] EWHC B15 (Ch).

Consolidation of proceedings and concurrent hearings

35.—(1) The parties are free to agree—

(a) that the arbitral proceedings shall be consolidated with other arbitral proceedings, or

(b) that concurrent hearings shall be held, on such terms as may be agreed.

(2) Unless the parties agree to confer such power on the tribunal, the tribunal has no power to order consolidation of proceedings or concurrent hearings.

NOTES

One of the major weaknesses of the use of arbitration as opposed to the courts is that, as arbitral proceedings are consensual, it is not possible for a series of distinct but identical or related claims between different parties to be disposed of in the same proceedings. Moreover, an award and the evidence adduced in one arbitration is private and may not be used in later arbitrations if a different party is involved, so that the same questions have to be determined and the same evidence adduced in a series of separate hearings.[1] It is also the case that an arbitration award is determinative only of the rights of the parties as against each other, and will not bind either of the parties in respect of third party claims arising out of the same facts.[2] Thus, if A brings an action against B, and B is found to be liable to A by reason of a default of C for which B is responsible, then B must bring separate proceedings against C in order to recover an indemnity from C and cannot rely upon the arbitration award.[3] Again, if A brings an action against B and B is found not to be liable because the defaulting party was C, A must bring a separate action against C and cannot rely upon the arbitration award.[4] Further, if A and B have a contract under which C is liable to A if B does not face any liability,[5] then an arbitration award which finds that B is not liable to A cannot be relied upon by A in his proceedings against C: it remains necessary for A to show, in the arbitration proceedings against C, that B did not face liability.[6] There are, however, exceptions to this general principle. An arbitration award which finds that B is liable to A is binding upon C if C has agreed to indemnify B,[7] and an arbitration award which finds that B has committed a wrongful act against A may be relied upon by C in proceedings against B where the issue is whether B committed that act.[8] It has even been suggested that a person who is not a party to the arbitration, but is "privy" to it by reason of his interest in it, may be bound by the award, although there is no clear authority on the circumstances in which the necessary privity can be established.[9]

There may be many situations in which consolidation makes good sense: one is where there is a chain of contracts (particularly sales) involving the same subject matter, where the point in issue is quality; another is where the question is the construction of a contract which has been used in a related transaction (reinsurance being a good illustration of the point). The position under the 1950 Act was that, unless the parties agreed, the arbitrators themselves could not order concurrent

1. See the authorities cited in the Notes to s. 1.

2. *Samsun Logix Corporation* v. *Oceantrade Corporation* [2008] 1 Lloyd's Rep 450.

3. *Sacor Maritima SA* v. *Repsol Petroleo SA* [1998] 1 Lloyd's Rep 518.

4. *Aneco Reinsurance Underwriting Ltd* v. *Johnson Higgins Ltd* [1998] 1 Lloyd's Rep 565; *Aquator Shipping Ltd* v. *Kleimar NV, The Capricorn* [1998] 2 Lloyd's Rep 379.

5. E.g., a default insurance/reinsurance policy.

6. *Drake Insurance Co* v. *Provident Insurance Co* [2004] 1 Lloyd's Rep 268; *Sun Life Assurance Company of Canada* v. *The Lincoln National Life Insurance Co* [2005] 1 Lloyd's Rep 606.

7. Under a contract of indemnity, insurance or reinsurance: *Stargas SpA* v. *Petredec Ltd, The Sargasso* [1994] 1 Lloyd's Rep 412; *King* v. *Brandywine Reinsurance Co (UK) Ltd* [2004] 2 Lloyd's Rep 670, affirmed on other grounds [2005] 1 Lloyd's Rep 655. The position may be different in relation to guarantees: *Re Kitchin* (1881) 17 Ch D 668; *Bruns v Colocotronis, The Vasso* [1979] 2 Lloyd's Rep 412; *Sabah Shipyard (Pakistan) Ltd* v. *Government of Pakistan* [2008] 1 Lloyd's Rep 210.

8. *George Moundreas & Co SA* v. *Navimpex Central Navala* [1985] 2 Lloyd's Rep 515; *Co-Operative Wholesale Society* v. *Birse Construction Ltd* (1997) 84 BLR 58.

9. See *Dadourian Group International Inc* v. *Simms* May 2004, unreported, a decision of Dyson LJ.

hearings, even if the same arbitrators had been appointed to resolve each individual dispute.[1] This remains the case under the 1996 Act. The removal of the power of the courts to refuse a stay of judicial proceedings, by section 9 of the 1996 Act, means that closely related disputes between different parties may have to be heard in parallel in judicial proceedings and in arbitration, the courts having no power to consolidate the two actions into one set of judicial proceedings.[2]

Section 35(1) of the 1996 Act merely codifies the common law by allowing consolidation or concurrent hearings if all the parties agree to it. The adoption of standard form arbitration rules which do provide for consolidation or concurrent hearings is sufficient to amount to an agreement for the purposes of section 35(1). The further option would have been to confer upon the arbitrators the power to consolidate arbitrations in certain circumstances unless the parties had agreed to the contrary, but the DAC noted in its July 1995 Report that any such approach—however sensible in terms of speed and efficiency—would have undermined the principle of party autonomy, a view affirmed by it in the February 1996 Report, paragraphs 177–182, and the possibility is expressly excluded by section 35(2). The effect of the section is, therefore, to act as a prompt to the parties to investigate the possibility of consolidation.

The DAC Report, paragraphs 263–264, rejected a further clarification in the form of a provision to the effect that, irrespective of what the parties might agree, the award is not binding on third parties. The DAC felt that this was difficult to draft, unnecessarily potentially contrary to the laws of other countries (giving rise to a problem if the contract was governed by some other law), and not strictly accurate.

The parties' freedom to agree to consolidate proceedings is encoded in the ICE Arbitration Procedure and in the Construction Industry Model Arbitration Rules (CIMAR). The Rules of Arbitration of the Chartered Institute of Arbitrators go further, in providing the arbitrators with the power to order consolidated proceedings and/or concurrent hearings, to give any necessary consequential directions and deliver a consolidated award (or awards) in respect of any consolidated proceedings (but separate awards where only the hearings are concurrent).[3] By contrast, the LCIA Rules of Arbitration provide that arbitrators may allow third parties to be joined to the proceedings on the application of one party, provided those third parties consent in writing.[4] Cases considering the JCT Rules, which provide that if any dispute between the employer and the project manager is connected with any claims against a contractor, then the former dispute could be referred to the arbitrator appointed to resolve the latter dispute, have decided that the use of a common arbitrator is appropriate even though the two sets of proceedings are not identical and that it is sufficient if there is a material overlap in the issues in the two arbitrations.[5]

Legal or other representation

36. Unless otherwise agreed by the parties, a party to arbitral proceedings may be represented in the proceedings by a lawyer or other person chosen by him.

NOTES

The Arbitration Act 1950 was silent on the rights to legal representation, but it was generally assumed that such a right existed[6] unless it was removed by contract[7] (commonly the situation in commodity arbitrations). Section 36 of the Act is a codifying provision. The DAC Report, paragraph

1. *Oxford Shipping Co* v. *Nippon Yusen Kaisha, The Eastern Saga* [1984] 3 All ER 835; *Abu Dhabi Gas Liquefaction Co* v. *Eastern Bechel Corporation* [1982] 2 Lloyd's Rep 425; *Aquator Shipping Ltd* v. *Kleimar NV, The Capricorn I* [1998] 2 Lloyd's Rep 379.
2. *Wealands* v. *CLC Contractors Ltd* [1999] 2 Lloyd's Rep 739.
3. CIArb Rules (2002), Arts 7.1 to 7.7.
4. LCIA Rules (1998), Art. 22.1(h). There is no equivalent provision in either the ICC or UNCITRAL Rules of Arbitration.
5. *Trafalgar House Construction (Regions) Ltd* v. *Railtrack plc* (1995) 75 BLR 55; *City & General (Holborn) Ltd* v. *AYH plc* [2005] EWHC 2494 (Comm).
6. *Hookway Co Ltd* v. *Alfred Isaacs Sons* [1954] 1 Lloyd's Rep 491.
7. An agreement that the parties are to make verbal representations "personally" has been held to exclude legal representation: *Virdee* v. *Virdi* [2003] EWCA Civ 41.

184, makes it clear that the phrase "other person chosen by him"—in contradistinction to the phrase "other person of his choice" in the July 1995 Bill—does not allow a party to insist upon a particular individual as his representative and to refuse to participate until that individual is available, thereby delaying the proceedings. In the event of unavailability, the implication is that some other person may be chosen.

The DAC Report, paragraph 185, also rejected the suggestion that a party wishing to be represented by another person should be required to give some form of advance notice to the other parties of his intention. While the DAC accepted the desirability of such notice being given, it could not see an easy method of legislating for all possibilities and indeed of providing sanctions in the event that notice was not given.

If a representative who is not legally qualified is chosen, issues as to privilege may arise. The DAC Report, paragraph 186, took the view that the existence or otherwise of privilege in these circumstances was a question of general significance which it would not be appropriate to address in the limited context of arbitration.

The right to be represented does not necessarily extend to every aspect of the proceedings. In *How Engineering Services Ltd* v. *Lindner Ceilings Floors Partitions plc*[1] an arbitrator was held not to have acted unfairly by excluding lawyers from a meeting between experts.

Power to appoint experts, legal advisers or assessors

37.—(1) Unless otherwise agreed by the parties—

(a) the tribunal may—

(i) appoint experts or legal advisers to report to it and the parties, or

(ii) appoint assessors to assist it on technical matters,

and may allow any such expert, legal adviser or assessor to attend the proceedings; and

(b) the parties shall be given a reasonable opportunity to comment on any information, opinion or advice offered by any such person.

(2) The fees and expenses of an expert, legal adviser or assessor appointed by the tribunal for which the arbitrators are liable are expenses of the arbitrators for the purposes of this Part.

NOTES

Section 37(1) confers upon the arbitrators the right to appoint experts, whether legal[2] or technical, following Articles 24(3) and 26 of the Model Law. An expert falling within this section must be one who can give the arbitrators substantive assistance: a draftsman who is appointed by the arbitrators to prepare the award according to their instructions is not an "expert" for these purposes.[3] The right to appoint an expert is necessarily subject to contrary agreement by the parties. The Model Law goes on to require the parties to submit evidence to the experts, and further allows the parties to examine and cross-examine the expert. The former point is not covered by the Act, but follows from the arbitrators' right under section 34 to determine the procedure of the arbitration. The latter point is covered by the express provision in section 37(1)(b). The arbitrators are, under section 37(1)(a), given the right to allow experts to attend the proceedings, an issue not previously dealt with by the English courts. The English authorities on experts do nevertheless indicate that the arbitrators cannot delegate their decision-making powers to an expert without the consent of the parties:[4] this principle doubtless holds good under the Act. The DAC Report, paragraph 187, regarded the power as a

1. 1999, unreported.
2. *Hussmann (Europe) Ltd* v. *Al Ameen Development & Trade Co* [2000] 2 Lloyd's Rep 83.
3. *Agrimex Ltd* v. *Tradigrain SA* [2003] 2 Lloyd's Rep 537.
4. See, e.g., *Eastern Counties Railway Co* v. *Eastern Union Railway Co* (1863) De G J Sm 610.

useful one, but its exercise by arbitrators must be proportionate in accordance with their general duty under section 33 of the 1996 Act.

The parties are therefore prevented from agreeing otherwise and thereby depriving the experts of their remuneration.[1] Section 37(2) deems the expense of the experts engaged by the tribunal to be recoverable as part of the costs of the arbitration under section 64(2): see the Notes to section 64.

General powers exercisable by the tribunal

38.—(1) The parties are free to agree on the powers exercisable by the arbitral tribunal for the purposes of and in relation to the proceedings.

(2) Unless otherwise agreed by the parties the tribunal has the following powers.

(3) The tribunal may order a claimant to provide security for the costs of the arbitration.

This power shall not be exercised on the ground that the claimant is—

(a) an individual ordinarily resident outside the United Kingdom, or
(b) a corporation or association incorporated or formed under the law of a country outside the United Kingdom, or whose central management and control is exercised outside the United Kingdom.

(4) The tribunal may give directions in relation to any property which is the subject of the proceedings or as to which any question arises in the proceedings, and which is owned by or is in the possession of a party to the proceedings—

(a) for the inspection, photographing, preservation, custody or detention of the property by the tribunal, an expert or a party, or
(b) ordering that samples be taken from, or any observation be made of or experiment conducted upon, the property.

(5) The tribunal may direct that a party or witness shall be examined on oath or affirmation, and may for that purpose administer any necessary oath or take any necessary affirmation.

(6) The tribunal may give directions to a party for the preservation for the purposes of the proceedings of any evidence in his custody or control.

NOTES

The effect of the 1996 Act is to transfer from the court to the arbitrators the interim and procedural powers necessary to the conduct of an arbitration, albeit subject to contrary agreement between the parties. The Act retains fall-back judicial powers over these matters, in sections 42 to 44, but in general resort may be had to the court only if the arbitrators do not themselves have the necessary authority or are for some other reason unable to exercise their powers. The overall effect is that the court has a restricted role at the interlocutory stage of an arbitration, and that role is relevant only where the arbitrators themselves are unable to act or where their orders are disobeyed. The right of the arbitrators to exercise interlocutory powers, insofar as these relate to the taking of security, is based on Article 17 of the Model Law.

Section 38(1) confers upon the parties the right to define the interlocutory powers of the arbitrators. In default of agreement, section 38(2) introduces the various powers that the arbitrators may exercise. There is nothing in the Act which permits the court to interfere with the exercise of

1. DAC Report, para. 188.

the arbitrators' substantive interlocutory powers, as the court may intervene only following the making of an award.[1] If the arbitrators refuse to exercise their powers, it would seem that their decision cannot be attacked. By contrast, if they decide to exercise their powers, that exercise can be challenged indirectly by disobedience to the order made by the arbitrators: it is then open to the party adversely affected by the order to challenge its validity where an application is made to the court for the enforcement of the order under section 42.

Section 38(2) introduces the default powers open to the arbitrators in the absence of any agreement by the parties. It follows from the range of default powers that the parties must be free under section 38(1) to confer upon the arbitrators powers which are beyond those in the default list, most importantly the power to grant a freezing injunction over the defendant's assets as security for any future award. The Court of Appeal in *Kastner* v. *Jason*[2] nevertheless declined to comment on whether the parties could agree to confer the power to grant freezing injunctions on arbitrators, and it may be noted that in the consultation on the 1996 Bill it was generally thought that this power should not be open to them as it could be exercised oppressively. In *Kastner* Rix LJ noted that if it was the case that arbitrators were empowered to grant freezing injunctions, then English law would strive to give effect to their order so that the order would be binding on third parties.[3]

Section 38(3) empowers the arbitrators to order the claimant or counterclaimant to provide security for the costs of the arbitration (which, as defined by section 59, include both the costs of the arbitrators and the parties' own costs). The previous law required resort to the courts, and was based on the notion that arbitrators were under a duty to resolve the dispute and accordingly could not be permitted to refuse to do so on the basis of a procedural requirement. The existence or otherwise of any power to order security for costs in an arbitration, nevertheless, proved to be one of the more controversial aspects of the legislation. It was more or less common ground that, if the power did exist, it should not be exercisable by the courts, as fear of the judicial exercise of this power might have the effect of driving foreign arbitrations away from London: for that reason, the decision of the House of Lords shortly before the passing of the Act, *Coppee-Lavalin SA/NV* v. *Ken-Ren Chemicals and Fertilizers*,[4] in which security was ordered in respect of an arbitration the parties to which had no connection with this jurisdiction, was greeted with widespread dismay. Beyond this, there was disagreement. One view was that the power should be excluded completely; the other, which ultimately prevailed, was that the power should be available, but that it should be exercisable only by the arbitrators themselves although the parties would have the right to agree that there should be no order for security by the arbitrators. The DAC Report, paragraph 192, rejected the common law theory which prevented arbitrators from ordering security for costs, as in the DAC's view an agreement to go to arbitration encompasses agreement to adhere to the procedural requirements of the process as well as to the ultimate result. The DAC also rejected the argument that an application for security might involve disclosure of the fact that an offer of settlement had been or was about to be made: the DAC's response was that arbitrators who properly performed their duty should not be influenced by such disclosure.[5]

As far as the courts are concerned, security for costs may be ordered by them only in respect of specified judicial proceedings under the 1996 Act, that is, on applications and appeals under sections 67 to 69 (want of jurisdiction, serious irregularity and error of law: see section 70). The 1996 Act adopted the DAC's view that it would be wrong to give the courts any residual power to order security for costs in respect of the arbitration, even in respect of the period before the appointment of the arbitrators.[6]

As will be appreciated, from section 38(3), the view that the power to order security for costs should be exercisable only by the arbitrators prevailed. It remains to consider the grounds upon which arbitrators with the power to order security for costs should exercise that power. There are set

1. This was also the position under the Arbitration Act 1950: *Three Valleys Water Committee* v. *Binnie* [1990] 52 BLR 47; *Fletamentos Maritimos SA* v. *Effjohn International BV (No 3)* [1997] 2 Lloyd's Rep 302.
2. [2005] 1 Lloyd's Rep 397.
3. The point did not arise in *Kastner*, as the law governing the arbitral procedure did not permit the grant of freezing injunctions which prevailed over the rights of third parties, and the position could be no different under English law.
4. [1994] 2 WLR 631.
5. DAC Report, paras 195–196.
6. DAC Report, para. 194.

grounds on which the High Court has jurisdiction to order security for costs, in CPR r. 25.13. The most important situation is that in which the claimant is ordinarily resident out of the jurisdiction and not resident within the EU or EFTA, the others being where the claimant is a nominal claimant representing other parties; where the claimant has given a false address; or where the claimant has changed his address with intent to evade his obligations. The original version of clause 38(3) in the December 1995 Bill provided that the power was available, and was to be exercised, as for judicial proceedings. The DAC in its February 1996 Report, paragraphs 364–370, expressed unhappiness with this approach, for three reasons: (i) it was not user-friendly in that it would be necessary for those wishing to ascertain the law to consult the numerous cases decided under the Rules of Court; (ii) permitting an order for security for costs to be made purely on the ground of residence, in accordance with what is now CPR r. 25.13, would simply have the effect of driving away overseas undertakings from the London arbitration market; and (iii) laying down an obligation on the arbitrators to comply with legal principles ran counter to the general theme of the Act that the wide-ranging powers conferred upon arbitrators were challengeable under section 68 for serious irregularity, by reference only to general principles of fairness as stated in section 33. Accordingly, section 38(3) was redrafted to remove any restriction on the basis upon which the power to order security for costs may be ordered, and in any event to oust—in accordance with consideration (ii) above—the possibility that an order might be made on the basis of residence.[1] It would seem from the drafting that residence must be excluded as a factor completely: it was suggested in the debates by Lord Donaldson, Lord Mustill being sympathetic, that the word "only" might be added after the phrase "on the ground" so that residence could be taken into account if other reasons for ordering security for costs existed. The Government remained unmoved. It might be added that it is any event clear that Article 6 of the EC Treaty prohibits any national procedural rule which discriminates against litigants from other EU member states, and the residence ground in the predecessor to CPR r. 25.13, RSC, Ord. 23, r. 1, was itself successfully challenged on this basis in the Court of Appeal in *Fitzgerald* v. *Williams*.[2] This led to an amendment to the Rules of Court, and CPR r. 25.13 specifically states (as noted above) that it is not a ground for making an order that the defendant is resident within the EU or EFTA: such a power is in any event unnecessary, given that English judgments are readily enforceable within the EU and EFTA under Council Regulation 44/2001 and the Lugano Convention. For this reason, as was pointed out by Lord Lester, any possible use of residence as a reason to order security for costs, even as a makeweight for other reasons, could have been included in the Act only if it did not apply to EU residents.

The result, then, is a very broad discretion, (subject always to the right of the parties to agree otherwise) and while it is the case that a decision whether or not to make an order can be challenged only if it gives rise to serious irregularity in the shape of unfairness, it would be most surprising if arbitrators did not in practice have regard to the provisions of CPR r. 25.13 by way of guidance. It might be thought that the alternative danger of open-endedness in discretion, expressed by Lord Wilberforce, that arbitrators might have the power as a "wonderful new toy" to be played with on every possible occasion, is less of a likelihood. In practice an order should be made only if there is a strong likelihood that the claimant will not be able to meet any costs order or if the claimant's assets are located in a jurisdiction in which the enforcement of an award against him might be problematic. It is wholly illegitimate for arbitrators to use the power to order security for costs in a fashion designed purely to ensure that they are paid.[3]

The power to order security for costs may be ordered against counterclaimants as well as claimants, as under section 82(1) of the Act the word "claimant" includes, unless the context otherwise requires (which is not the case here), "counterclaimant": this is confirmed by paragraph 370 of the DAC Report. The power to order security for costs cannot, however, be used as against

1. DAC Supplementary Report, para. 28.
2. [1996] 2 All ER 171, based upon the European Court of Justice's rulings in *Mund & Fester* v. *Hatrex Internationaal Transport* [1994] ECR I–467 and *Hubbard* v. *Hamburger* [1993] ECR I–3777 and upholding doubts as to the validity of the rule expressed by the Court of Appeal in *Porzelack KG* v. *Porzelack (UK) Ltd* [1987] 1 All ER 1074 and *De Brie* v. *Fitzgerald* [1990] 1 All ER 560. The ruling of the Court of Appeal in *Berkeley Administration Inc* v. *McClelland* [1990] 2 QB 407, upholding the use of the predecessor to CPR r. 25.13 against EU litigants on the ground that any discrimination is on the grounds of domicile and not nationality, is no longer good law.
3. *Wicketts and Sterndale* v. *Brine Builders* [2001] CILL 1805.

the respondent, hence the use of the word "claimant" in distinction to "party":[1] as was noted by Lord Fraser on Report in the House of Lords, "it would be unjust to enable a tribunal to order security for costs against a respondent as the price for being allowed to defend himself". The same principle applies to litigation.

If an order for security is made, the sanction open to arbitrators is to make a peremptory order for security, which (if not complied with) will lead to an award dismissing the claim, in accordance with section 41(6). There was no sensible alternative to this approach: the judicial remedy, of staying proceedings pending compliance, was thought not to be appropriate in the context of arbitration.[2] Nevertheless, certain standard rules still permit the arbitrators to stay the proceedings rather than dismiss them.[3]

As noted above, the Act does not confer upon arbitrators the default power to secure the sum in dispute by an order taking effect as an injunction, although it is possible to seek a freezing injunction from the High Court under section 44(2)(e) of the Act. As also noted earlier, the High Court does not have any general residual power to order security for costs[4] in respect of the arbitration itself where the arbitrators themselves have no power to do so, even in relation to the period up to the date at which the arbitrators were appointed: this was a deliberate policy decision, based on the view of the House of Lords in *Coppee-Lavalin SA/NV* v. *Ken-Ren Chemicals and Fertilizers Ltd*[5] to the effect that the court should not grant security for costs where the parties' arbitration agreement has contemplated that there is no power to do so. If the arbitrators have made a peremptory order for security for costs against the claimant or counterclaimant, any failure by him to comply may lead to the arbitrators making an award dismissing the claim under section 41(6).

Section 38(4) confers upon arbitrators the power to make orders in respect of the property which is the subject matter of the proceedings. The power is equivalent to that of the court in judicial proceedings under the Civil Procedure Rules, Part 25. The orders set out in section 38(4) relate to the use of the property as evidence, and permit the arbitrators to require its inspection, photographing, preservation, custody or detention, or to require samples to be taken from it. These powers are exercisable by the court under section 44(2)(c) of the Act where the arbitrators have no power themselves to act in this regard.

Section 38(5) sets out the power of the arbitrators to require evidence on oath or affirmation from any party or witness, and to administer the oath or take the affirmation. The attendance of witnesses can be compelled by a party to the proceedings, by application to the court, under the powers conferred on him by section 43.

Section 38(6) confers upon the arbitrators the right to make an order for the preservation of evidence. The High Court can act under section 44(2)(b) if the arbitrators are not empowered to do so or are unable for the time being to act effectively (e.g., because the tribunal has not been constituted).

Power to make provisional awards

39.—(1) The parties are free to agree that the tribunal shall have power to order on a provisional basis any relief which it would have power to grant in a final award.

(2) This includes, for instance, making—

(a) a provisional order for the payment of money or the disposition of property as between the parties, or

1. DAC Supplementary Report, para. 29.
2. DAC Report, para. 198.
3. See e.g. Art. 25.2 of the LCIA Rules (1998) permits the arbitrators to "stay or dismiss" the claim.
4. But see the Notes to s. 44.
5. [1994] 2 All ER 449. The House of Lords by a majority did make an order for security for costs, but on the limited basis that the facts of that case were exceptional, in that the claimant was in reality a fronting company for a state, the state being willing to take the benefit of any award but not to stand behind the claimant in case of failure. The decision nevertheless attracted a good deal of criticism for making an order in respect of a foreign arbitration even in those exceptional circumstances.

(b) an order to make an interim payment on account of the costs of the arbitration.

(3) Any such order shall be subject to the tribunal's final adjudication; and the tribunal's final award, on the merits or as to costs, shall take account of any such order.

(4) Unless the parties agree to confer such power on the tribunal, the tribunal has no such power.

This does not affect its powers under section 47 (awards on different issues, &c.).

NOTES

Section 39 was new to the 1996 Act[1] and empowers the arbitrators to grant interim relief, including provisional orders for payment of money representing anticipated liability or costs. Under the July 1995 Bill, the power to make an interim order was exercisable in all cases. As a result of consultation, the provision was amended so that the power becomes exercisable only where it has been conferred upon the arbitrators by the agreement of the parties. This is spelt out by section 39(4).

Section 39(3) specifies that the final award must take into account the sums awarded under any provisional order, so that payment is not duplicated. The section is not intended to empower arbitrators to make orders the equivalent of freezing injunctions or search orders and they fall—if at all—within section 38 only. It was held at first instance in *Kastner* v. *Jason*[2] that section 39 could be used by the arbitrators to grant a freezing injunction where the parties had agreed that such a power was open to them,[3] but on appeal[4] the Court of Appeal reserved its position on the point and noted that the weight of commentary on section 39 was contrary to the judge's conclusion. The purpose of section 39(2) is rather more limited and it would typically be used to grant interim financial relief on the same basis that interim damages can be awarded by a court, thereby preserving the claimant's cash flow (see the DAC Report, paragraph 201) in proceedings which he is bound to win but for an—at the time—unascertained amount.

The power of the arbitrators to make a provisional award or order is to be distinguished from their power to make an award on a limited aspect of the dispute[5]—referred to misleadingly under the 1950 Act as an interim award, and since the passing of the 1996 Act known as a partial award[6]—finally disposing of a severable matter. Such partial awards are full awards in their own right, and are so treated by section 47 of the 1996 Act. Although the heading of the section refers to "provisional awards", the section in essence deals only with provisional *orders*. A careful distinction should be made so as not to confuse the two. A provisional order is not an award for the purposes of, for example, requiring the formalities of section 52 to be complied with.

A provisional award, being an award in its own right, may be challenged on jurisdictional or procedural grounds (sections 67 and 68, respectively) or on the basis of an error of (English) law (section 69).

However, if the matter complained of has been held over by the arbitrators for later consideration, the challenge will be regarded as misconceived.[7]

Of the standard arbitration rules, the arbitrators' power to order provisional relief under section 39 is expressly accorded to them. For example, Article 25.1(c) of the LCIA Rules (1998) provides that the arbitrators may order on a provisional basis "subject to final determination in an award" any relief which they would have power to grant in an award, including a provisional order for the

1. The courts had previously held that no such power existed: *The Kostas Melas* [1981] 1 Lloyd's Rep 18.

2. [2004] 2 Lloyd's Rep 233.

3. In that case by the adoption of procedural rules which contained such a power.

4. [2004] EWCA Civ 1599.

5. Section 47 of the 1996 Act.

6. See the Notes to s. 47, below.

7. *BMBF (No 12) Ltd* v. *Harland and Wolff Shipbuilding and Heavy Industries Ltd* [2001] 2 Lloyd's Rep 227.

payment of money or the disposition of property as between any parties. Similarly, Article 23 of the ICC Rules (1998) gives arbitrators the power to "order any interim or conservatory measure" they deem appropriate. However, it is unclear whether this provision in the ICC Rules gives the arbitrators power to make provisional orders under this section. The better view (given the language) is that the provision does give the arbitrators such power, particularly in view of the widely drafted wording, and since this is not a reference to interim or partial awards. Article 7.1 of the CIArb Rules (2000) expressly assigns to arbitrators the power to make provisional orders under section 39. By contrast there is no such power in the LMAA Rules.[1]

General duty of parties

40.—(1) The parties shall do all things necessary for the proper and expeditious conduct of the arbitral proceedings.

(2) This includes—

(a) complying without delay with any determination of the tribunal as to procedural or evidential matters, or with any order or directions of the tribunal, and

(b) where appropriate, taking without delay any necessary steps to obtain a decision of the court on a preliminary question of jurisdiction or law (see sections 32 and 45).

NOTES

Section 40(1) requires the parties to do all things necessary for the proper and expeditious conduct of the arbitration. The most important specific aspects of that duty are set out in section 40(2), namely to comply with the arbitrators' orders and, where appropriate, to make any necessary steps to resolve jurisdictional issues or preliminary points of law in accordance with the procedures in sections 32 and 45.

It is not possible to contract out of this provision, as it is deemed to be mandatory, but the duty is nevertheless subject to the consideration that the arbitrators may exercise only those powers open to them either by default under section 34 (procedure and evidence) or conferred upon them by the parties under sections 35 (consolidation) and 37 to 39 (substantive interlocutory powers). Any attempt by the arbitrators to go beyond their express authority in issuing orders and imposing obligations can, therefore, be ignored—section 40 is plainly to be construed as extended only to those matters which the arbitrators are entitled to decide in the absence of contrary agreement[2]—and may well amount to serious irregularity. The DAC in its February 1996 Report, paragraph 175, could see no conflict between the right of the parties to determine the procedure, and the obligation of the parties not to frustrate the arbitration.

Section 40, unlike its predecessor in the July 1995 Bill, does not draw attention to the remedies which are available to the arbitrators where one party fails to do all things necessary for the proper conduct of the arbitration or disobeys an interlocutory order. The problem can be dealt with by the arbitrators themselves, under section 41, or, in the case of a peremptory order which cannot be enforced by the arbitrators themselves, by the court under section 42. Each of these powers can be removed by agreement, and if they are it follows that there is little that anyone can do to ensure that the arbitration can proceed effectively. Where there is no available remedy, the aggrieved party may simply commence judicial proceedings.

1. *Starlight Shipping Co* v. *Tai Ping Insurance Co* [2008] 1 Lloyd's Rep 230.

2. DAC Report, para. 175, where it is pointed out that the right of the parties to agree any matter for themselves, under the proviso to s. 34(1), necessarily qualifies their duty to adhere to the procedure fixed by the arbitrators.

Powers of tribunal in case of party's default

41.—(1) The parties are free to agree on the powers of the tribunal in case of a party's failure to do something necessary for the proper and expeditious conduct of the arbitration.

(2) Unless otherwise agreed by the parties, the following provisions apply.

(3) If the tribunal is satisfied that there has been inordinate and inexcusable delay on the part of the claimant in pursuing his claim and that the delay—

(a) gives rise, or is likely to give rise, to a substantial risk that it is not possible to have a fair resolution of the issues in that claim, or

(b) has caused, or is likely to cause, serious prejudice to the respondent, the tribunal may make an award dismissing the claim.

(4) If without showing sufficient cause a party—

(a) fails to attend or be represented at an oral hearing of which due notice was given, or

(b) where matters are to be dealt with in writing, fails after due notice to submit written evidence or make written submissions,

the tribunal may continue the proceedings in the absence of that party or, as the case may be, without any written evidence or submissions on his behalf, and may make an award on the basis of the evidence before it.

(5) If without showing sufficient cause a party fails to comply with any order or directions of the tribunal, the tribunal may make a peremptory order to the same effect, prescribing such time for compliance with it as the tribunal considers appropriate.

(6) If a claimant fails to comply with a peremptory order of the tribunal to provide security for costs, the tribunal may make an award dismissing his claim.

(7) If a party fails to comply with any other kind of peremptory order, then, without prejudice to section 42 (enforcement by court of tribunal's peremptory orders), the tribunal may do any of the following—

(a) direct that the party in default shall not be entitled to rely upon any allegation or material which was the subject matter of the order;

(b) draw such adverse inferences from the act of non-compliance as the circumstances justify;

(c) proceed to an award on the basis of such materials as have been properly provided to it;

(d) make such order as it thinks fit as to the payment of costs of the arbitration incurred in consequence of the non-compliance.

NOTES

Section 41(1) allows the parties to agree the powers of the arbitrators in the event that one of the parties fails to do something necessary for the proper conduct of the arbitration. In the absence of agreement, section 41(2) introduces the default powers contained in section 41(3)–(7). Whether or not these powers are exercised is a matter for the arbitrators: the Government's intention was to avoid the prospect of arbitrators being sued for negligence in failing to expedite the arbitration proceedings in the face of default by one or both of the parties. This intention was manifested by its refusal to accept proposed amendments to section 29 to that effect.

Section 41(3) re-enacts section 13A of the Arbitration Act 1950, which was itself inserted by section 102 of the Courts and Legal Services Act 1990. Section 13A proved to be necessary following a series of cases in which it was held that severe delay by the claimant could not be remedied by a striking out for want of prosecution, as there was no statutory basis for the arbitrators' exercise of that power. Moreover, various alternative attempts to confer the necessary jurisdiction, for example, by construing failure to proceed as an offer to terminate the arbitration agreement which was accepted by the respondent's inactivity also proved to be abortive other than in exceptional circumstances.[1] Section 41(3) reflects the power of the court to strike out an action for want of prosecution. Article 25(a) of the Model Law contains a similar approach, allowing the arbitrators to terminate the proceedings if the claimant fails to communicate his statement of claim. It is to be noted that the power under section 41(3) is not a striking out, as is the case in judicial proceedings,[2] but rather is a power to make an award dismissing the action. There are detailed judicial guidelines laid down by the House of Lords on the meaning of inordinate and excusable delay and on the exercise of the striking out power for court proceedings,[3] and these provide that the courts may take into account the cumulative effect of a number of small delays and the existence of any justifications for delay. Further, it is rarely appropriate for an award to be made within the limitation period applicable to the claim, as it is always open to the claimant to commence fresh arbitration proceedings. A disregard of these guidelines may amount to an error of law challengeable under section 69,[4] as delay will rarely be inordinate of it is still within the limitation period.[5]

The effect of an award is uncertain, although the view of Rix J in *James Lazenby & Co* v. *McNicholas Construction Co Ltd*[6] was that an award under section 41(3), even though it is not on the merits, is to be treated as precluding, by virtue of some form of estoppel, a further action by the claimant either in arbitration or in the courts. This principle is irrelevant where the award is (exceptionally) made within the limitation period because the claimant can restart, and is likely only to be of significance where the award is made after the contractual limitation period for commencing an arbitration has expired but the ordinary statutory limitation period for judicial proceedings is unaffected.[7]

Section 41(4) is based on Article 25(c) of the Model Law and authorises the arbitrators to proceed notwithstanding that one party fails to attend a hearing of which due notice has been given or if he fails after due notice to provide written evidence or submissions. This has been described as a regular occurrence.[8] Before the passing of the 1996 Act this approach was recognised as permissible to counter delaying tactics adopted by one party: the arbitrators were generally held to be justified, after having given proper notice of their intention, to proceed where one party persistently failed to co-operate with the arbitrators.[9] It may be that some arbitrators will prefer the safety of the

1. *The Bremer Vulkan* [1981] 1 All ER 289; *The Antclizo* [1988] 2 All ER 513; *Thai-Europe Tapioca Service Ltd* v. *Seine Navigation Co Inc, The Maritime Winner* [1989] 2 Lloyd's Rep 506. For more modern authority, see *Downing* v. *Al Tameer Establishment* [2002] 2 All ER (Comm) 545; *Indescon Ltd* v. *Ogden* [2005] 1 Lloyd's Rep 31.

2. See CPR r. 3.4, although there is no express provision in the CPR for striking out for want of prosecution.

3. See, in particular: *Birkett* v. *James* [1978] AC 297; *Department of Transport* v. *Chris Smaller (Transport) Ltd* [1989] 1 All ER 897; *Roebuck* v. *Mungovin* [1994] 1 All ER 568; *Grovit* v. *Doctor* [1997] 2 All ER 417.

4. *TAG Wealth Management* v. *West* [2008] EWHC 1466 (Comm), although the arbitrator was found not to have erred. It is also clear from this case that factual findings are not challengeable.

5. *Birkett* v. *James* [1978] AC 297; *James Lazenby & Co* v. *McNicholas Construction Co Ltd* [1995] 2 Lloyd's Rep 30; *Scanports Shipping* v. *Sienna Marine* September 2001; *TAG Wealth Management* v. *West* [2008] EWHC 1466 (Comm).

6. [1995] 2 Lloyd's Rep 30.

7. In fact, most arbitration clauses which impose time limits are construed as barring the claim itself, and not simply barring a claim in arbitration, so the point is likely to be academic.

8. *Entico Corporation Ltd* v. *United Nations Educational Scientific and Cultural Association* [2008] 1 Lloyd's Rep 673.

9. E.g., *Golodetz* v. *Schrier* (1947) 80 Ll L Rep 647. Of the standard rules of arbitration, the ICC Rules of Arbitration (1998) provide (in Art. 21.2) that if any party fails to appear without valid excuse at a hearing to which he has been duly summoned, the arbitrators may proceed with the hearing. Art. 6.3 also provides that if any party refuses or fails to take part in the arbitration or any stage thereof, the arbitration shall proceed notwithstanding such refusal or failure. Similarly, Art. 15.8 of the LCIA Rules provides that if at any point any party "fails to avail itself of the opportunity to present its case", the arbitrators may proceed with the arbitration and make an award.

peremptory order procedure before proceeding in the absence of the defaulting party, as there is less likelihood of a successful challenge on procedural grounds where the arbitrators can show that they have issued a peremptory order which has been disobeyed. It is to be noted that section 33 of the 1996 Act requires the arbitrators to allow both sides a reasonable opportunity to present their case, so that proceeding in the absence of the defaulting party is very much an approach of last resort.[1]

In the context of international arbitrations in particular, arbitrators should consider carefully offering a recalcitrant party every opportunity to participate before in effect allowing the arbitration to proceed in the absence of one party. To do otherwise may render nugatory any award made on enforcement.

Section 41(5) empowers the arbitrators to make a peremptory order against a party who fails to comply with any earlier order or direction of the arbitrators. The word "peremptory" merely implies the inclusion of a sanction for non-compliance (most commonly in the form that unless the party does some act within the time specified, a particular sanction will follow). The issue of a peremptory order is a preliminary step which the arbitrators may—and indeed are probably advised to—take where a party has failed to comply within the time originally prescribed for complying with a previous order or direction, as this triggers the enforcement powers of the arbitrators under section 41(6)–(7) and the default powers of the court under section 42 (assuming that those clauses have not been excluded by contract). A peremptory order can be issued only as an enforcement measure in respect of existing directions or orders.[2] The Act does not contemplate that a failure by one party to comply with a peremptory order should as a matter of course lead to an award against him, and the Act deliberately provides a range of alternative sanctions against non-compliance to prevent this from happening.[3] The fact that an order is made definite and that a further opportunity has been given for compliance may negative any challenge that a defaulting party may make to the arbitrators' ultimate decision to treat him as being in default. The imposition of a time limit is also significant if under the agreement between the parties the arbitrators themselves have no enforcement powers and it is necessary to have recourse to the court under section 42. Under section 42(4) the court may intervene only where the time for obeying a peremptory order has passed or, if no time is specified, when a reasonable time has elapsed: making the order peremptory confers jurisdiction on the court, and specifying a time limit removes arguments as to whether a reasonable time for compliance has elapsed. It should be noted that in all situations the arbitrators are required to adhere to the overriding fair treatment principle in section 33 of the Act, so that the imposition of a time limit which is unreasonably short would infringe section 33 and might lead to a challenge to the award under section 68 (serious irregularity). Too short a time limit may also cause a court to refuse in its discretion to exercise enforcement powers in relation to a peremptory order, under section 42. It should perhaps also be stressed that a peremptory order must be to the "same effect" as the earlier order or directions to which it relates: as the DAC Report, paragraph 209, states, "it could be quite unfair for an arbitrator to be able to make any type of peremptory order, on any matter, regardless of its connection with the default in question".

Section 41(6) is confined to the specific case in which the arbitrators have made an order for security for costs under express powers or under powers implied under section 38(3) of the Act. Their ability to make an award dismissing the claim is the equivalent remedy to that available in the High Court—generally a stay of the proceedings—where a court order for security for costs has not been obeyed. If the arbitrators are not empowered to dismiss the action, the court may be requested to do so under its default powers in section 42.

Section 41(7) is based on Article 25(b)–(c) of the Model Law, and is concerned with failure to obey a peremptory order other than one for security for costs. The arbitrators themselves may exercise any of the powers specified in section 41(7), which may include a decision to proceed *ex parte* or to refuse to hear any argument which is based on documents or other evidence not produced despite the arbitrators' order for production. The Act deliberately holds back from empowering the arbitrators to make an award dismissing the claim in the event of failure to comply with a peremptory order, as this was regarded by the DAC as too draconian (DAC Report, paragraph 211).

1. *Cf.* DAC Report, para. 208.
2. *Wicketts and Sterndale* v. *Brine Builders* [2001] CILL 1805.
3. DAC Report, para. 212.

If the arbitrators do not possess the powers necessary to enforce a peremptory order, the court may be requested to enforce the order under its default powers in section 42.

Powers of Court in Relation to Arbitral Proceedings

Enforcement of peremptory orders of tribunal

42.—(1) Unless otherwise agreed by the parties, the court may make an order requiring a party to comply with a peremptory order made by the tribunal.

(2) An application for an order under this section may be made—

(a) by the tribunal (upon notice to the parties),
(b) by a party to the arbitral proceedings with the permission of the tribunal (and upon notice to the other parties), or
(c) where the parties have agreed that the powers of the court under this section shall be available.

(3) The court shall not act unless it is satisfied that the applicant has exhausted any available arbitral process in respect of failure to comply with the tribunal's order.

(4) No order shall be made under this section unless the court is satisfied that the person to whom the tribunal's order was directed has failed to comply with it within the time prescribed in the order of, if no time was prescribed within a reasonable time.

(5) The leave of the court is required for any appeal from a decision of the court under this section.

NOTES

Section 42(1) permits the enforcement of any peremptory order of the arbitrators by the Court. Non-peremptory orders may not be enforced under this section. This procedure differs slightly from that originally contained in the July 1995 Bill, under which the arbitrators could apply to the court seeking an order authorising them to enforce their peremptory orders as if the peremptory order had been one of the court. Subject to contrary agreement, the arbitrators are free to convert any of their requests or orders into peremptory orders by exercising their powers under section 41(5), thereby bringing section 42 into play. The section is not mandatory, and the parties are free to contract out of resort to the courts in this fashion. The section applies only to peremptory orders: it is not possible to enforce the obligation of a party in section 40(1) "to do all things necessary for the proper . . . conduct of the arbitral proceedings" by means of section 42(1) unless the party has been put under a specific obligation by a peremptory order of the arbitrators. To prevent proliferation of litigation on procedural matters, section 42(5) contains the usual rule that an appeal against the court's decision either way can be made only with the permission of the court itself, and for this purpose the "court" means the trial judge and not the Court of Appeal.[1]

The enforcement mechanism can, in accordance with section 42(2), be initiated by either the arbitrators; or by any party with the permission of the arbitrators. One party acting without the agreement of the arbitrators is powerless to seek assistance from the court, as the section is devised to assist the arbitrators themselves. The application is to be made to the court by way of an arbitration claim form. If the claim is made by the arbitrators, notice, in the form of a copy of the arbitration claim form and any supporting evidence, must be given to the parties to the arbitration (section 42(2)(a)), and they are to be made parties to the application.[2] If the claim is made by a party,

1. *Henry Boot Construction (UK) Ltd* v. *Malmaison Hotel (Manchester) Ltd* [2001] 1 QB 388; *Athletic Union of Constantinople* v. *National Basketball Association* [2002] 1 Lloyd's Rep 305; *Virdee* v. *Virdi* [2003] EWCA Civ 41.
2. CPR r. 62.6(2)–(3).

he must obtain the consent of the arbitrators (which is to be exhibited in the arbitration claim form) and give notice to the other parties (section 42(2)(b)) by serving the claim on them and making them parties to the claim.[1]

Section 42(3)–(4) is concerned to keep the matter within the arbitration as far as is possible, and imposes two preconditions to the granting of relief by the court. It will be noted that these conditions go to jurisdiction and not to discretion, so that unless they are met the court cannot act. The two conditions are as follows:

(a) The time for compliance with the peremptory order must have expired, or if no time was given a reasonable time for compliance must have expired. The arbitrators are free to impose a time limit, under section 41(5) of the Act, subject to that time limit not being too short and thereby infringing the fair treatment principle in section 33 of the Act. In such a case, the DAC noted in its July 1995 Report that the court's discretion to assist under section 42 would almost certainly be refused.

(b) The applicant must have exhausted any available arbitral process. In most cases any failure to obey a peremptory order can lead to the arbitrators proceeding to an award in the absence of the defaulting party, or at least drawing the necessary inferences from the deliberate non-production of evidence. This will normally be sufficient to overcome disobedience of a peremptory order, and it follows that the most important situation in which it will be necessary to seek the court's assistance is where the arbitration agreement precludes awards made following proceedings held in the absence of a defaulting party.

The section does not indicate exactly what type of remedial measures may be put into place by the court, although the DAC Report, paragraph 212, gave as an example the imprisonment of a party for contempt.

Securing the attendance of witnesses

43.—(1) A party to arbitral proceedings may use the same court procedures as are available in relation to legal proceedings to secure the attendance before the tribunal of a witness in order to give oral testimony or to produce documents or other material evidence.

(2) This may only be done with the permission of the tribunal or the agreement of the other parties.

(3) The court procedures may only be used if—

(a) the witness is in the United Kingdom, and

(b) the arbitral proceedings are being conducted in England and Wales or, as the case may be, Northern Ireland.

(4) A person shall not be compelled by virtue of this section to produce any document or other material evidence which he could not be compelled to produce in legal proceedings.

NOTES

Section 43 permits a party to secure the attendance of witnesses. It is based on Article 27 of the Model Law, which similarly requires the assistance of the curial court.

Arbitrators have jurisdiction only over the parties themselves: the assistance of the court has to be invoked where evidence from a third party is necessary to the arbitration. Section 43(1) contains the basic right of a party to use court procedures under the CPR to secure the attendance of witnesses and the production of documents or other evidence by that witness. The relevant procedures for witness summonses are set out in CPR Part 34, as applied by CPR PD 62 paragraphs 7.1 to 7.3. In

1. CPR r. 62.6(2)–(3).

court proceedings, a witness summons may be used to secure the attendance of the witness at the trial, or for examination at a hearing prior to trial (where the evidence is known as a "deposition"), or to require the witness to produce documents to the court at the trial or at a hearing prior to trial (e.g., a "Khanna" hearing, where the witness summons is used merely to obtain documents and prove their authenticity), the witness producing them not being relied on to give any other evidence. In the latter case, the practice is to specify a date for production of the documents which is earlier than the date fixed for the rest of the trial.[1] A witness summons is used not just to secure the attendance of a witness who is reluctant to come to court but also, for example, to enable the witness to produce evidence (e.g., to an employer) of the requirement to attend court or to secure priority so that the witness is not summonsed to appear elsewhere on the same day. In deposition hearings, the witness is examined and cross-examined as if he or she were in the trial proper, with all parties present. In court proceedings, the examination may take place in court (before a judge), or elsewhere before an examiner appointed by the court (if not agreed by the parties). If an examiner is required, the most usual choice is a neutral barrister (often a QC) and the evidence is taken in chambers and transcribed. In arbitrations whose seat is in England and Wales or Northern Ireland, the witness may be examined before the arbitrators, before a court (e.g., in the locality of the witness's residence) or by an examiner. If the examination is before a judge or examiner, the transcribed evidence will generally be produced to the arbitrators at or before the final hearing.[2]

It is not clear whether the reference in CPR PD 62 paragraph 7.1 to CPR Part 34 should be taken to exclude the possibility of the court making an order under this section for a witness to be examined by video-conference (VCF). Taking evidence by VCF is becoming more and more common in the context of making orders for examination of witnesses in support of foreign proceedings. However, the limitation in section 43 suggests that any order for examination by VCF is not within the court's powers under this section: the "same" court procedures are those either (a) to secure the attendance before the tribunal of a witness or (b) to produce documents or other evidence. The better view is that the court's power to order a witness to be examined by VCF is available under section 44(2)(a).[3]

CPR PD 62, paragraph 7.2 requires an applicant for an order under this section to file written evidence of either the arbitrators' or the other parties' consent to the order.

Section 43(2) requires that an application under this section may be made only if the arbitrators consent, or if the agreement of the other parties can be obtained:[4] these safeguards prevent extraneous and irrelevant evidence being sought, and also prevent a party from overriding the arbitrators' decision to hold a documents-only arbitration (see the DAC Report, paragraph 213). An order will be made only if the evidence is necessary for a fair disposal of the issues in the arbitration, so that if equivalent evidence is available from one of the parties there is no basis for the making of an order.[5] Any order must also be confined to requiring the witness to produce specific documents, fishing expeditions not being permitted.[6] In any event the court has no jurisdiction in support of an arbitration to order general disclosure by a third party,[7] even though such a power does exist in relation to judicial proceedings.[8] Documents must be "described in some compendious manner that enabled the individual documents falling within the scope of the [order] to be identified".[9]

1. See *Khanna* v. *Lovell White Durrant* [1995] 1 WLR 121 and CPR r. 34.
2. *Cf.* CPR r. 34.8.
3. See the notes to s. 44.
4. CPR PD 62 para. 7.3 provides that the witness summons will not be issued until the applicant files written evidence showing that the application is made with the permission of the arbitrators or the agreement of the other parties.
5. *South Tyneside Borough Council* v. *Wickes Building Supplies Ltd* [2004] EWHC 2428 (Comm).
6. *Sunderland Steamship P&I Association* v. *Gatoil International Inc, The Lorenzo Halcoussi* [1998] 1 Lloyd's Rep 180; *South Tyneside Borough Council* v. *Wickes Building Supplies Ltd* [2004] EWHC 2428 (Comm); *Assimina Maritime Ltd* v. *Pakistan Shipping Corporation* [2005] 1 Lloyd's Rep 525; *Tajik Aluminium Plant* v. *Hydro Aluminium AS* [2006] 1 Lloyd's Rep 155.
7. *BNP Paribas* v. *Deloitte and Touche LLP* [2004] 1 Lloyd's Rep 233 (Comm); *Assimina Maritime Ltd* v. *Pakistan Shipping Corporation* [2005] 1 Lloyd's Rep 525.
8. In CPR r. 31.17.
9. *Tajik Aluminium Plant* v. *Hydro Aluminium AS* [2006] 1 Lloyd's Rep 155.

Section 43(3) restricts the power in section 43(1) to witnesses within the jurisdiction: evidence can be obtained from a witness outside the jurisdiction by means of application to the court under section 44(2)(a), although if the witness is a party the matter can probably be dealt with by the arbitrators themselves under section 41 by the making of a peremptory order requiring evidence to be given. The proceedings must also be conducted in England, Wales or Northern Ireland under section 43(3)(b), but it is specifically stated by section 2(3) that section 43 can be used whether or not the seat of the arbitration is in England. The phrase "conducted in" in section 43(3)(b) must, therefore, necessarily mean something different from the proposition that the arbitration has its seat in England, and it may be that it simply refers to a transitory phase of the arbitration which happens to have been held in England. It would seem, therefore, that an arbitration with its seat abroad but requiring the attendance of a witness who happens to be in the United Kingdom, can reconvene in England and Wales or Northern Ireland—so that the arbitration is at that point being conducted within the jurisdiction—and a party is thereby empowered to seek the court's assistance for the attendance of that witness. The court does, however, have the discretion under section 2(3) to refuse its assistance where granting assistance would not be appropriate, and it may be that in the circumstances outlined above the court would take the view that, while it possesses the necessary jurisdiction, there is not sufficient connection between the arbitration and England and Wales or Northern Ireland to make such an order. On the other hand, there may be no reason in principle why the arbitrators in an arbitration with its seat abroad should not be able to convene a hearing within the jurisdiction in order to take advantage of the powers available under this section, if one party requests this. However, whereas a witness in respect of whom an order is sought under CPR r. 34.8 for examination before the hearing in court proceedings may be examined either before a judge or an examiner, the requirement for the arbitral proceedings to be "conducted" within the jurisdiction clearly suggests that, at the very least, the parties will be required to hold a hearing within the jurisdiction (at what might be a considerable cost) for the purposes of receiving the evidence from the witness in respect of whom an order is sought, even if the seat is abroad.

Section 43(4) preserves any rights that a witness may have to withhold evidence, based on privilege or any duty of confidentiality.[1]

Section 43, unlike the equivalent provision in the July 1995 Bill, does not make specific provision for witnesses in prison to be called to give evidence. It was doubtless thought unnecessary to deal with this point, as it is apparently subsumed within the general provisions of section 43(3).

Court powers exercisable in support of arbitral proceedings

44.—(1) Unless otherwise agreed by the parties, the court has for the purposes of and in relation to arbitral proceedings the same power of making orders about the matters listed below as it has for the purposes of and in relation to legal proceedings.

(2) Those matters are—

(a) the taking of the evidence of witnesses;

(b) the preservation of evidence;

(c) making orders relating to property which is the subject of the proceedings or as to which any question arises in the proceedings—

  (i) for the inspection, photographing, preservation, custody or detention of the property or

  (ii) ordering that samples be taken from, or any observation be made of or experiment conducted upon, the property;

  and for that purpose authorising any person to enter any premises in the possession or control of a party to the arbitration;

(d) the sale of any goods the subject of the proceedings;

(e) the granting of an interim injunction or the appointment of a receiver.

1. *Cf.* CPR r. 34.2(5).

(3) If the case is one of urgency, the court may, on the application of a party or proposed party to the arbitral proceedings, make such orders as it thinks necessary for the purpose of preserving evidence or assets.

(4) If the case is not one of urgency, the court shall act only on the application of a party to the arbitral proceedings (upon notice to the other parties and to the tribunal) made with the permission of the tribunal or the agreement in writing of the other parties.

(5) In any case the court shall act only if or to the extent that the arbitral tribunal, and any arbitral or other institution or person vested by the parties with power in that regard, has no power or is unable for the time being to act effectively.

(6) If the court so orders, an order made by it under this section shall cease to have effect in whole or in part on the order of the tribunal or of any such arbitral or other institution or person having power to act in relation to the subject-matter of the order.

(7) The leave of the court is required for any appeal from a decision of the court under this section.

NOTES

The general scheme of the 1996 Act is to transfer to the parties the right by agreement to determine the powers of the arbitrators to conduct the arbitration and to adopt interim protective measures. There are also statutory default powers. In the absence of contrary agreement, the arbitrators have the power to: order security for costs (section 38(3)); examine witnesses on oath (section 38(5)); preserve evidence for the purposes of the proceedings (section 38(6)); and order the inspection, preservation or detention of the subject matter (section 38(4)). It is thus necessary to have resort to the court only in respect of those powers which the arbitrators under the arbitration agreement are precluded from exercising, or, in respect of powers outside section 38, which the arbitrators cannot exercise either in default of agreement or at all.

Section 44 lists the support powers exercisable by the court. These are all of an interim nature. The only other statutory provision under which support powers may be exercised is section 37 of the Supreme Court Act 1981, which empowers the court to grant both temporary and permanent injunctions: the relationship between the two sections is discussed in the context of injunctions, below. Section 44(5) makes it clear that the statutory powers are available only to the extent to which the arbitrators either do not possess the necessary powers themselves or are unable to act. In all cases, therefore, where the exercise of a power is required, the sequence of questions will be:

(a) do the arbitrators have the particular power expressly conferred upon them by the parties (section 38(1));
(b) if not, do the arbitrators have default powers under section 38(3)–(6);
(c) if not, is the court empowered to provide support under section 44?

The powers listed in section 44 are, under section 2(3) of the 1996 Act, available whether or not the arbitration has its seat in England and whether or not the person against whom they are sought is domiciled in England,[1] provided that it is appropriate for them to be exercised in such a case. If the seat of the arbitration is outside England, it may well be appropriate to exercise section 44 powers in two cases:

(a) where English law has been chosen as the relevant procedural law;[2] and the only hope of assistance is provided by the English courts; or

1. Service of an arbitration claim form seeking relief under s. 44 can be effected outside the jurisdiction—see CPR r. 62.5(1)(b).

2. Or in cases where there is sufficient unity between the exercise of the court's powers and the content of the curial law: *Commerce and Industry Insurance Co of Canada* v. *Lloyd's Underwriters* [2002] 1 Lloyd's Rep 219.

(b) where the arbitration has no connection with England as such, but there is evidence in England which needs to be obtained or preserved,[1] or one of the parties has assets within the jurisdiction which can be preserved by means of an English freezing injunction, or there is some overriding reason for intervention, for example, the need to prevent fraud.[2]

In other cases relief will be refused.[3] The powers in section 44 will be exercised in favour of an arbitration with its seat elsewhere only where the procedures of the law of the seat are similar to those of England, thereby ensuring that the powers are exercised in England for the purpose for which they were designed: in *Commerce and Industry Insurance Co of Canada* v. *Lloyd's Underwriters*,[4] an attempt to use section 44 in support of a US arbitration was rejected once it became clear that the object was not to obtain specific evidence but rather to order US-style depositions which was regarded as akin to a fishing expedition to determine what evidence might be in existence, a procedure not recognised in England.

The power of the court to grant interim measures in support of foreign proceedings, set out in section 25 of the Civil Jurisdiction and Judgments Act 1982, has no application to foreign arbitrations,[5] so measures are available only under section 44 or, in the case of injunctive relief, under section 37 of the 1981 Act. One important exception relates to arbitrations conducted by the International Centre for the Settlement of Investment Disputes (ICSID), the Convention establishing ICSID having been given legal force in the UK by the Arbitration (International Investment Disputes) Act 1966. The 1996 Act applies to ICSID arbitrations only to the extent that it has been extended to such arbitrations by Order in Council, and no relevant Order in Council has been made in respect of section 44.[6]

The court does not have the power to order security for costs. The Act takes the view that this is a matter for the arbitrators alone (using the power available—if not excluded—under section 38(3)), and that if they have no power to order security for costs under the terms of the arbitration agreement, the court should not overturn that agreement by making an order of its own.[7]

The court's powers under section 44 are available only in support of arbitration proceedings. If an application is made to the court for interim relief in support of judicial proceedings, for example, for some form of injunction (which the court has the power to grant under its general powers in relation to litigation under section 37 of the Supreme Court Act 1981), the court may exercise those powers even though there is an arbitration agreement between the parties and it is possible that the defendant may seek a stay of the judicial proceedings. The fact that a stay is subsequently obtained does not retrospectively invalidate the court's order.[8]

Section 44(1) sets out the basic proposition that the court may intervene in the same way as if the proceedings were brought in a court. The equivalent powers of the court in judicial proceedings are set out in CPR r. 25.1. Relief may be granted against a person who is not himself a party to the

1. See *Copsa Enterprises Ltd* v. *Technomarine SpA*, 1998, unreported. Contrast: *Econet Wireless Ltd* v. *Vee Networks Ltd* [2006] 2 Lloyd's Rep 428, where the arbitration was taking place in Nigeria and there were no relevant assets in England; *Mobil Cerro Negro Ltd* v. *Petroleos de Venezuela SA* [2008] 1 Lloyd's Rep 684, where again there were no English assets.

2. *Mobil Cerro Negro Ltd* v. *Petroleos de Venezuela SA* [2008] 1 Lloyd's Rep 684, although there was no evidence of fraud on the facts.

3. *Econet Wireless Ltd* v. *Vee Networks Ltd* [2006] 2 Lloyd's Rep 428.

4. [2002] 1 Lloyd's Rep 219.

5. *ETI Euro Telecom International NV* v. *Republic of Bolivia* [2008] 2 Lloyd's Rep 421.

6. *ETI Euro Telecom International NV* v. *Republic of Bolivia* [2008] 2 Lloyd's Rep 421. It follows that the English courts have no power to grant relief in respect of an ICSID arbitration if the defendant is domiciled outside the jurisdiction and there is no connecting factor with England within CPR 6.20: the English court simply has no jurisdiction to give permission for service outside the jurisdiction.

7. See the notes to s. 38(3), citing the House of Lords decision in *Coppee-Lavalin SA/NV* v. *Ken-Ren Chemicals and Fertilizers Ltd* [1994] 2 Lloyd's Rep 109. The House of Lords by a 3-2 majority decided to award security for costs despite the fact that the parties had not conferred the necessary power on the arbitrators. That decision is reversed by the omission of security for costs from the list of powers in s. 44(2). The position now is that this may be done, if at all, only by the arbitrators under s. 38(3). However, the court may order security for costs in respect of its own proceedings involving challenges to the award on the grounds of excess of jurisdiction, serious irregularity or error of law (ss. 67–69).

8. *Gildepath Holdings BV* v. *Thompson* [2004] EWHC 2234 (QB).

arbitration agreement: thus, an order against property may be made even though the person in possession of it is a third party who has purchased that property.[1]

The court's ability to intervene is not available where the parties have contracted out of the exercise of all or some of the listed powers. The mere fact that the arbitration agreement provides that any dispute is to be submitted to the "exclusive jurisdiction" of arbitrators does not operate to exclude the court's powers under section 44, as a distinction is to be drawn between substantive and procedural matters, and that an exclusive agreement refers to the former but not to the latter.[2] However, an arbitration clause which confers exclusivity on the arbitrators not only in relation to the substantive issues but also as regards "other legal proceedings" may be construed as excluding recourse to curial courts.[3]

Assuming no express contrary agreement, the powers listed in section 44(2) are available on the application of any party, provided that (in non-urgent cases) the application is made with the permission of the arbitrators or the written agreement of the other parties—see section 44(4). The LCIA arbitration rules (1998 edition, Article 25.3), the ICC Rules of Arbitration (1998 edition, Article 23.2), the UNCITRAL Rules of Arbitration (Article 26.3) and the AAA Arbitration Rules (2008 edition, Article 21.2) all provide in terms that applications to the courts for interim or injunctive relief in support of an arbitration shall not be treated in any way as a waiver of the right to arbitrate or as being incompatible with the arbitration agreement.

Section 44(2) sets out the powers which a court may exercise. The subsection is based on Articles 9 and 27 of the Model Law, which respectively permit the curial court to grant interim measures of protection before or during arbitration proceedings and to give assistance in taking evidence.

Section 44(2)(a) is concerned with the taking of evidence. The July 1995 Bill subdivided this general power into that of taking evidence on oath and that of issuing the commission or request for the examination of a witness outside the jurisdiction. The revised version of section 44(2)(a) must be assumed to have regarded these two specific matters as within the general power of the court to obtain evidence. It is hardly likely, however, that an application would ever be made under this section purely for the court to order a witness to be examined on oath in the absence of the arbitrators' power to do so. Nevertheless, the power to take evidence exercisable on oath is apparently applicable only where the arbitrators do not themselves have the necessary power to order examination on oath (see section 38(5) of the Act). Plainly only the court can order the taking of evidence from a witness outside the jurisdiction. The equivalent powers of the court in respect of witnesses abroad is set out in CPR Part 34, although it should be noted that the Evidence (Proceedings in Other Jurisdictions) Act 1975 does not apply to foreign private arbitrations.[4] As is the case with section 43, this subsection does not confer upon the court a general power to order a third party to disclose documents.[5]

Section 44(2)(b) is concerned with the preservation of evidence. As this is a power which may be removed from the arbitrators under section 38(6) of the Act, the court may intervene only where the arbitrators do have the necessary power but for some reason are unable to exercise it effectively. The subsection may be used to obtain evidence in the hands of a third party and which had to be preserved for the purposes of the arbitration, so that an order can be made where it can be shown that a question has arisen in relation to documents[6] in the hands of a third party as long as those documents could be identified either specifically or by class.[7]

1. If the third party is abroad, permission must be sought for service on him under CPR Part 6.20 as a necessary and proper party to the proceedings, which in turn means that the other party to the arbitration must have been served at the date of application for service out against the third party, failing which there are no proceedings in respect of which the third party can be joined. See: *The Cienvik* [1996] 2 Lloyd's Rep 395; *Tate & Lyle Industries Ltd* v. *CIA Usina Bulhoes* [1997] 1 Lloyd's Rep 355; *Vale do Rio Doce Navegaçao SA* v. *Shanghai Bao Steel Ocean Shipping Co Ltd and Sea Partners Ltd* [2000] 2 Lloyd's Rep 1.

2. *Re Q's Estate* [1999] 1 Lloyd's Rep 931. *Cf. Macob Civil Engineering* v. *Morrison* [1999] BLR 93.

3. *Mantovani* v. *Carapelli SpA* [1980] 1 Lloyd's Rep 375, as explained in *Re Q's Estate* [1999] 1 Lloyd's Rep 931.

4. *Commerce and Industry Insurance Co of Canada* v. *Lloyd's Underwriters* [2002] 1 Lloyd's Rep. 219.

5. *Assimina Maritime Ltd* v. *Pakistan Shipping Corporation* [2005] 1 Lloyd's Rep 525.

6. Including computer material: *Assimina Maritime Ltd* v. *Pakistan Shipping Corporation* [2005] 1 Lloyd's Rep 525.

7. *Assimina Maritime Ltd* v. *Pakistan Shipping Corporation* [2005] 1 Lloyd's Rep 525.

Section 44(2)(c) is concerned with orders in respect of property. The arbitrators themselves may be empowered to take these steps,[1] so that the court may be asked to intervene only where those powers have not been conferred on the arbitrators. Contracts for the sale of goods—particularly items such as ships—often themselves contain inspection clauses whereby the decision to purchase rests upon the outcome of an inspection by the purchaser or an independent third party (e.g., a classification society). If such provisions do exist, they may render the need for an order under section 44(2)(c) superfluous. More significantly, if the inspection provisions are more limited, the courts will not permit the claimant to use section 44(2)(c) to obtain an inspection beyond that to which he was entitled under the contract.[2]

Section 44(2)(d) authorises ordering the sale of goods. The arbitrators cannot be empowered to order a sale of the property which is the subject matter of the dispute, so that the court's assistance will be required.

Section 44(2)(e)—interim injunctions and appointment of receivers,[3] provides authority, *inter alia*, for the issue of freezing injunctions and temporary anti-suit injunctions. The arbitrators themselves clearly do not possess any jurisdiction to grant a freezing injunction and appoint a receiver, and this is possibly the case even if the parties have agreed that they are to have those powers,[4] and so resort to the court will be necessary. A freezing injunction may be made by the court only where there is reason to believe that the respondent will seek to shift his assets into a jurisdiction where they cannot be reached, or otherwise dissipate them other than in a bona fide fashion, and even then the application must be made without delay and all material facts must be disclosed to the court on a without notice application (failing which the order can be set aside).[5] Section 44(2)(e) is not limited to freezing injunctions in respect of the preservation of evidence and assets, and can be used to prevent the respondent from frustrating the arbitration in ways other than by the disposal of his assets, for example, by pre-empting the outcome of the arbitration or by moving assets following an award.[6] In *Hiscox Underwriting* v. *Dickson Manchester & Co Ltd*[7] the court made an order requiring the respondent underwriting agents to hand over details of insurance policies which they had written on behalf of the claimant insurers, as the issue in the arbitration was whether the respondents were seeking to place renewal business with their own parent company rather than the claimants and it was a matter of urgency for the claimants to know how pending renewals were being treated. It was further decided in *Hiscox* that the power in section 44(2)(e) was not limited by reference to the purposes listed in section 44(3), and although that ruling was reversed by the Court of Appeal in *Cetelem SA* v. *Roust Holdings*[8] the outcome in *Hiscox* was nevertheless held to be the correct one. In *Cetelem* the Court of Appeal ruled that the word "assets" in section 44(2)(e) encompasses choses in action, including existing rights under a contract: accordingly, although section 44(2)(e) does not on its face authorise the grant of an injunction to restrain a breach of contract, as was held in *Hiscox*, that result can be effectively achieved under *Cetelem* by the classification of a contractual right as an "asset" and thus capable of preservation by interim

1. See *Copsa Enterprises Ltd* v. *Technomarine SpA* 1998, unreported.
2. *Tsako's Shipping Trading SA* v. *Orizon Tanker Co Ltd, The Centauras Mar* 1998, unreported.
3. The power to appoint a receiver extends to a foreign asset: *Masri* v. *Consolidated Contractors International Co SAL* [2008] EWCA Civ 303.
4. In *Kastner* v. *Jason* [2005] 1 Lloyd's Rep 397 the Court of Appeal left open the question whether the arbitrators could be given the power to grant freezing injunctions under either ss. 38 or 39 of the Act: see the Notes to those sections.
5. See, e.g., *Swift-Fortune Ltd* v. *Magnifica Marine SA, The Capaz Duckling* [2008] 1 Lloyd's Rep 54. For the established guidelines on the circumstances in which a freezing injunction should be enforced, see *Dadourian Group Int Inc* v. *Simms* [2006] 2 Lloyd's Rep 354.
6. *Tsavliris Salvage (International) Ltd* v. *The Grain Board of Iraq* [2008] EWHC 612 (Comm).
7. [2004] 2 Lloyd's Rep 438. See also *National Insurance and Guarantee Corporation Ltd* v. *M Young Legal Services Ltd* [2005] 2 Lloyd's Rep 46, where the court ordered the handing over of documents to the claimant in advance of the commencement of an arbitration by the defendant and any application by the defendant to stay judicial proceedings. The case must now be read, in the light of *Cetelem*, as one in which the order was for the preservation of assets.
8. [2005] 2 Lloyd's Rep 494. See also: *Mobil Cerro Negro Ltd* v. *Petroleos De Venezuela SA* [2008] 1 Lloyd's Rep 684.

injunction.[1] Thus, in *Permasteelisa Japan UK* v. *Bouygesstroi*[2] a temporary injunction was granted to prevent a call on a performance bond, as the disputed sums formed a part of the arbitration.

The court has no power to grant a permanent injunction under this provision, and thus cannot use it to grant a permanent anti-suit injunction against a person who has initiated proceedings in some other jurisdiction in contravention of an arbitration clause.[3] The power of the court to grant a permanent anti-suit injunction arises exclusively under the general provisions of section 37 of the Supreme Court Act 1981,[4] and is exercised by the court as a matter of course in order to hold the parties to their agreement to go to arbitration;[5] it may also be used to prevent a party who has lost the arbitration from reopening the issues resolved by the arbitrators in some other forum[6] and to prevent a party seeking to invoke curial jurisdiction in a place other than that of the seat of the arbitration.[7] It would seem, however, that the court has concurrent power under section 37 of the 1981 Act and section 44(3) of the 1996 Act to grant temporary relief:[8] the relationship between these two provisions has yet to be fully worked out,[9] although it has been held that it would not be appropriate to grant interim relief under section 37 of the 1981 Act in circumstances where the requirements of section 44 have not been satisfied.[10] It is not clear whether an anti-suit injunction can be granted where the judicial proceedings have been commenced in an EU or EFTA state. The European Court of Justice has held that a court may not issue an anti-suit injunction to restrain a defendant from continuing proceedings elsewhere in the EU or EFTA where the foreign court is first seised of the action, as jurisdiction is a matter for that court: this is so even if the foreign proceedings are in breach of an exclusive jurisdiction clause or otherwise oppressive.[11] However, the Court of Appeal subsequently ruled, in *Through Transport Mutual Insurance Association (Eurasia) Ltd* v. *New India Assurance Co Ltd*,[12] that the exclusion of "arbitration" from the Conventions and the

1. *Cf. Lauritzencool AB* v. *Lady Navigation Inc* [2006] 1 All ER 866.
2. [2007] All ER (D) 97 (TCC).
3. *Welex AG* v. *Rosa Maritime Ltd* [2003] 2 Lloyd's Rep 509.
4. *Welex AG* v. *Rosa Maritime Ltd* [2003] 2 Lloyd's Rep 509; *Ace Capital Ltd* v. *CMS Energy Corporation* [2008] 1 Lloyd's Rep 93; *Steamship Mutual Underwriting Association (Bermuda) Ltd* v. *Sulpicio Lines Inc* [2008] EWHC 914 (Comm); *Crusader (Nigeria) plc* v. *Aviation Development Co plc*, July 2008, unreported. The restrictions in s. 44 are, therefore, inapplicable to an application for a permanent injunction.
5. *Pena Copper Mines Ltd* v. *Rio Tinto Co Ltd* (1911) 105 LT 846; *Aggeliki Charis Compania Maritima SA* v. *Pagnan SA, The Angelic Grace* [1995] 2 Lloyd's Rep 87; *Shell International Petroleum Co Ltd* v. *Coral Oil Co Ltd* [1999] 1 Lloyd's Rep 72; *XL Insurance Ltd* v. *Owens Corning* [2000] 2 Lloyd's Rep 500; *Welex AG* v. *Rosa Maritime Ltd* [2003] 2 Lloyd's Rep 509; *American International Speciality Lines Insurance Co* v. *Abbott Laboratories* [2004] Lloyd's Rep IR 815; *Goshawk Dedicated Ltd* v. *ROP Inc* [2006] Lloyd's Rep IR 711; *Kallang Shipping SA* v. *AXA Assurances Senegal* [2007] 1 Lloyd's Rep 160; *West Tankers Inc* v. *Ras Riunione Adriatica di Sicurta SpA, The Front Comor* [2005] 2 Lloyd's Rep 257, not addressed on appeal [2007] 1 Lloyd's Rep 391 (where the claimant was in reality an insurer exercising subrogation rights). If the claim is brought by a third party in its own name under legislation which confers a direct action, the third party cannot be said to be in breach of the arbitration clause because he is not a party to the contract, so an anti-suit injunction is inappropriate. However, if the third party's claim is subject to the same conditions as by a contracting party, the English court may grant a declaration to the effect that the arbitration clause is binding on the third party, and that may be taken into account by the foreign court in question and certainly by an court which is asked to enforce any award in favour of the third party: see *Through Transport Mutual Insurance Association (Eurasia) Ltd* v. *New India Assurance Co Ltd* [2005] 1 Lloyd's Rep 67 where a subrogated claim was brought under Finnish legislation so that the claimant was not in breach of the arbitration clause, and *cf. Markel International Co Ltd* v. *Craft* [2007] Lloyd's Rep IR 403.
6. *Noble Assurance Co* v. *Gerling-Konzern General Insurance Co (UK)* [2008] Lloyd's Rep IR 1.
7. *C* v. *D* [2008] 1 Lloyd's Rep 239.
8. *XL Insurance* v. *Owens Corning* [2000] 2 Lloyd's Rep 500; *Hiscox Underwriting Ltd* v. *Dixon Manchester Holdings Ltd* [2004] 2 Lloyd's Rep 438.
9. *Cetelem SA* v. *Roust Holdings Ltd* [2005] 2 Lloyd's Rep 494; *ETI Euro Telecom International NV* v. *Republic of Bolivia* [2008] 2 Lloyd's Rep 421; *Emmott* v. *Michael Wilson & Partners Ltd* [2008] 1 Lloyd's Rep 616.
10. *Starlight Shipping Co* v. *Tai Ping Insurance Co* [2008] 1 Lloyd's Rep 230; *Mobil Cerro Negro Ltd* v. *Petroleos de Venezuela SA* [2008] 1 Lloyd's Rep 684.
11. Case C-116/20 *Erich Gasser GmbH* v. *MISAT Srl* [2004] 1 Lloyd's Rep 222; Case C-159/02 *Turner* v. *Grovit* [2004] 1 Lloyd's Rep 216.
12. [2005] I Lloyd's Rep 67. The same conclusion had earlier been reached in *Navigation Maritime Bulgare* v. *Rustal Trading Ltd* [2002] 2 Lloyd's Rep 106.

Regulation meant that an anti-suit injunction to restrain breach of an arbitration clause was permissible. This matter is presently pending before the European Court of Justice on a reference for a preliminary ruling by the House of Lords.[1]

If the defendant is not within the jurisdiction of the English courts, he may be served outside the jurisdiction under CPR r. 62.5. The power to grant injunctive relief is discretionary, although it will normally be exercised in favour of the grant of an injunction unless the foreign proceedings are at an advanced stage or if there is a risk of conflicting decisions.[2] If judicial proceedings are commenced in some other jurisdiction in breach of an arbitration clause, and those proceedings are successfully stayed by the applicant or he is awarded an anti-suit injunction, he is entitled to damages for breach of the arbitration clause, representing the legal costs incurred by him in bringing the proceedings to an end.[3]

Section 44(3) confers upon the court power to intervene in an urgent case[4] to make an order preserving evidence or property. The exercise of the power conferred by section 44(3) may be particularly important prior to the appointment of the arbitrators,[5] where the arbitrators have no power to act for themselves or where the evidence or property is in the hands of a third party over whom the arbitrators possess no jurisdiction.[6] One purpose of this provision is to make it clear that the court can make a search order to this effect in support of arbitral proceedings. Under that jurisdiction, the court may grant an order authorising the search of business or domestic premises for material evidence which, without early seizure, is likely to be disposed of by the person in possession of it. As noted above, it was held in *Cetelem SA* v. *Roust Holdings Ltd*,[7] overruling *Hiscox Underwriting* v. *Dickson Manchester & Co Ltd*,[8] that section 44(3) is not independent of the power to grant injunctive relief under section 44(2)(e), so that the latter provision does not authorise the grant of injunctions other than in respect of the preservation of assets and evidence. However, as also seen in the discussion of *Cetelem* above, the definition of "preservation of assets and evidence" is a wide one.

All applications must be commenced by means of an arbitration claim form.[9] In the absence of urgency, section 44 can be invoked on application by any party provided that notice has been given to the other parties and either the arbitrators or the other parties have consented (section 44(4)). The application must be made by way of arbitration claim form which must be served on the other parties

1. *West Tankers Inc* v. *RAS Reunione Adriatica di Sicurta SpA* [2007] 1 Lloyd's Rep 391: their Lordships were strongly supportive of the approach taken in *Through Transport*. See Case C-185/07 *Allianz SpA* v. *West Tankers Inc, The Front Comor*, where the Advocate-General ruled (on a reference from the House of Lords) that anti-suit relief is not available within the EU and EFTA in respect of arbitration clauses. This opinion has yet to be confirmed by the European Court of Justice.
2. *Aggeliki Charis Compania Maritima SA* v. *Pagnan SpA, The Angelic Grace* [1995] 2 Lloyd's Rep 87; *Schiffahrtsgesellschaft Detlev von Appen GmbH* v. *Voest Alpine Intertrading, The Jay Bola* [1997] 2 Lloyd's Rep 379; *Alfred C Toepfer International* v. *Société Cargill France* [1998] 1 Lloyd's Rep 379; *Shell International Petroleum Co Ltd* v. *Coral Oil Co Ltd* [1999] 1 Lloyd's Rep 72; *Bankers Trust Co* v. *P T Jakarta International* [1999] 1 Lloyd's Rep 910; *Verity Shipping SA* v. *Chartworld Shipping Corporation, The Skier Star* [2008] 1 Lloyd's Rep 652.
3. *Kyrgyz Mobil* v. *Fellowes International* [2005] EWHC 1314 (Comm); *A* v. *B (No 2)* [2007] 1 Lloyd's Rep 358; *National Westminster Bank plc* v. *Rabobank Netherland (No 3)* [2008] 1 Lloyd's Rep 16; *C* v. *D* [2008] 1 Lloyd's Rep 239.
4. If the case is not urgent the court may not intervene: *ETI Euro Telecom International NV* v. *Republic of Bolivia* [2008] 2 Lloyd's Rep 421.
5. See, however, *Decca Music Group Ltd* v. *Jagger* [2004] EWHC 2542 (Ch) (decided on a quite different point involving the scope of an arbitration clause) where it was held that a failure to disclose documents which were to form the basis of an audit could be adequately compensated in damages. In such a case it may be surmised that s. 44(3) would not be applicable.
6. *Pacific Maritime (Asia) Ltd* v. *Holystone Overseas Ltd* [2008] 1 Lloyd's Rep 371.
7. [2005] 2 Lloyd's Rep 494.
8. [2004] 2 Lloyd's Rep 438. *Cf. National Insurance and Guarantee Corporation Ltd* v. *M Young Legal Services Ltd* [2005] 2 Lloyd's Rep 46.
9. CPR PD para. 8.1.

and they must be made parties to the application:[1] the supporting evidence must also set out the necessary consent.[2] The need for consent is an important limitation, the DAC Report, paragraph 215, pointing out that it operates to prevent any suggestion that the court is usurping the functions of the arbitrators. Where there is urgency, the arbitration application may be made without notice to the other party, although the appended affidavit or witness statement must indicate why the application has been made without notice.[3] Urgent applications are regarded by the English courts as justified in exceptional circumstances only, so that without notice applications are to be granted only where "it would be likely to defeat the purpose of seeking the injunction if forewarning were given".[4]

Section 44(5)–(7) is largely jurisdictional and procedural.

Section 44(5) contains the important jurisdictional rule referred to above whereby a court may exercise its powers under section 44(2) if the arbitrators themselves either have no power to act (by virtue of the arbitration agreement between the parties[5]) or are unable to act (e.g., because the full panel has yet to be appointed and interlocutory relief pending the commencement of the proceedings is required). If the arbitrators are in place, there is no basis for judicial intervention[6] unless the court is satisfied that any order which they make will be of little or no value, for example, because it cannot be enforced or because third parties are involved.[7]

Section 44(6) is a novel power which allows the court to stipulate in any order made by it that the order may be varied or set aside by the arbitrators themselves. The typical scenario will be that the court will have made an order under section 44 at a time at which the arbitrators themselves were unable to act, for example, where some or all of the arbitrators were not appointed when the application for an order was made,[8] or where they have no power to act. Thereafter, if the court order so provides, it is left to the arbitrators to determine how long the order should remain in force. This approach is a further illustration of the Act's desire to achieve party autonomy.[9]

Any decision of the court as to whether or not to grant relief can be appealed only with the permission of the court (section 44(7)). The "court" for this purpose means the trial judge and not the Court of Appeal.[10]

Determination of preliminary point of law

45.—(1) Unless otherwise agreed by the parties, the court may on the application of a party to arbitral proceedings (upon notice to the other parties) determine any question of law arising in the course of the proceedings which the court is satisfied substantially affects the rights of one or more of the parties.

An agreement to dispense with reasons for the tribunal's award shall be considered an agreement to exclude the court's jurisdiction under this section.

(2) An application under this section shall not be considered unless—

(a) it is made with the agreement of all the other parties to the proceedings, or
(b) it is made with the permission of the tribunal and the court is satisfied—

1. CPR r. 62.6(2)–(3).
2. CPR r. 62.4(1)(c).
3. CPR r. 62.4(1)(f)(ii).
4. *Petroleum Investment Co Ltd* v. *Kantupan Holdings Co Ltd* [2002] 1 All ER (Comm) 124, *per* Toulson J.
5. *Starlight Shipping Co* v. *Tai Ping Insurance Co* [2008] 1 Lloyd's Rep 230.
6. *NB Three Shipping Ltd* v. *Harebell Shipping Ltd* [2005] 1 Lloyd's Rep 509.
7. *Pacific Maritime (Asia) Ltd* v. *Holystone Overseas Ltd* [2008] 1 Lloyd's Rep 371.
8. *PLD Telekom Inc* v. *Commerzbank AG* 2000, unreported.
9. DAC Report, para. 216.
10. *Henry Boot Construction (UK) Ltd* v. *Malmaison Hotel (Manchester) Ltd* [2001] 1 QB 388; *Athletic Union of Constantinople* v. *National Basketball Association* [2002] 1 Lloyd's Rep 305; *Virdee* v. *Virdi* [2003] EWCA Civ 41.

(i) that the determination of the question is likely to produce substantial savings in costs, and
(ii) that the application was made without delay.

(3) The application shall identify the question of law to be determined and unless made with the agreement of all the other parties to the proceedings, shall state the grounds on which it is said that the question should be decided by the court.

(4) Unless otherwise agreed by the parties, the arbitral tribunal may continue the arbitral proceedings and make an award while an application to the court under this section is pending.

(5) Unless the court gives leave, no appeal lies for a decision of the court whether the conditions specified in subsection (2) are met.

(6) The decision of the court on the question of law shall be treated as a judgment of the court for the purposes of an appeal.

But no appeal lies without the leave of the court which shall not be given unless the court considers that the question is one of general importance, or is one which for some other special reason should be considered by the Court of Appeal.

NOTES

Section 45 re-enacts, with minor changes, section 2 of the Arbitration Act 1979, which has no equivalent in the Model Law. Section 2 was itself a modification of the consultative case procedure latterly provided for by section 21 of the Arbitration Act 1950 and subsequently abolished by section 1 of the Arbitration Act 1979. The objective is to allow a point of law which arises in the course of the arbitration to be referred to the High Court for its determination, and the format of the section has been adopted by section 32, which permits the court to consider as a preliminary issue the question of the arbitrators' jurisdiction. The court's power to make a preliminary ruling may be excluded by agreement, in accordance with section 45(1), and in particular any agreement by the parties to dispense with reasons for the award is deemed to be an agreement excluding section 45(1). The right to contract out is absolute in the case of a non-domestic arbitration agreement, but in the case of a domestic arbitration agreement may be effected only after the dispute has arisen: this is the effect of section 87(1)(a) of the Act, although section 87 has not been brought into effect, so that the right to contract out is in practice absolute in all cases. The principles which govern the validity of agreements to exclude a court's entitlement to determine preliminary points of law are set out in detail in the commentary to section 69, where the identical issue arises.

It was suggested in authorities[1] decided under the earlier arbitration legislation that an alternative method of achieving judicial consideration of a preliminary point of law arose where the arbitrators made an award dealing with that point alone (under what is now section 47 of the 1996 Act) in advance of dealing with other aspects of the dispute. It would then be open to one party to appeal against that award on a point of law (under section 69). In this way, the requirement in section 45(2) that all of the parties, or one party and the arbitrators, agree to the reference, can be side-stepped. It would seem that this procedure remains available under the Act.

It was suggested to the DAC on consultation following the publication of the July 1995 Bill, that the power of the court to give preliminary rulings should be removed either entirely, or at least in the context of non-domestic agreements. The DAC (1996 Report, paragraphs 218 and 221 rejected such suggestions, on the basis that the power is a useful one both for the parties themselves and for the wider development of the law where the legal consequences of a particular matter have wider interest, for example, the effect of a particular act by a government (banning waterway access or prohibiting imports of a common commodity). That said, the section has scarcely been used.[2]

1. *The Vasso* [1983] 3 All ER 211.

2. The only instances appear to be *Beegas Nominees* v. *Decco Ltd* [2003] EWHC 1891 (Ch) and *Taylor Woodrow Holdings Ltd* v. *Barnes & Elliott Ltd* [2006] BLR 377.

Section 45(1) sets out the basic right of a party to apply to the High Court for a preliminary determination. The use of the word "may" means that the court has a discretion whether or not to hear an application, and cases decided under the 1979 Act indicate that it will be exercised sparingly even if the parties have agreed that there should be a reference.[1]

Under section 45(2), the application must be consensual, in that it must be with the approval of the arbitrators or with the written consent of the other parties to the arbitration. The term "question of law" is defined in section 82(1) of the Act as referring to the law of England, Wales or Northern Ireland, so that if the law governing the substance of the dispute is the law of some other jurisdiction no application can be made to the English courts.[2] Procedural matters cannot be the subject of preliminary rulings.[3]

The right of the parties to seek a preliminary ruling under section 45 is confined to the case in which the arbitration has its seat in England. If the law applicable to the agreement is English law, it may well be appropriate for the parties to seek a ruling from the English courts, and while this is specifically permissible under the 1996 Act itself, there is no reason why the matter cannot be heard by the English courts under the general discretion conferred by section 2(4) of the Act provided that it has jurisdiction over the defendant in the proceedings, either because the respondent is domiciled here, or the provisions of CPR r. 62.5 are satisfied (which they inevitably will be in cases of applications under section 45).

For the court to have jurisdiction to hear an application under section 45(1), it must be satisfied that the question of law raised "substantially affects the rights of one or more of the parties".

There is a distinction drawn in section 45(2) between applications with the consent of all parties (section 45(2)(a)), and applications with the consent of the arbitrators (section 45(2)(b), where, presumably, one party objects). In the latter case the conditions set out in section 45(2) have to be satisfied in order for the court to have jurisdiction to deal with the issue. In addition, an application under section 45(2)(b) must satisfy the procedural requirements in section 43(3). First, under section 45(2)(b)(i), the savings in costs must be "likely".[4] The threshold for applications has thus been raised. Secondly, section 45(2)(b)(ii) requires that the application has been made without delay.

The procedure for applying under this section is set out in CPR Part 62 and CPR PD 62, paragraph 9. If the application is made with the consent of the other parties, the supporting affidavit or witness statement must set out the evidence by which it is asserted that the court should consider the claim and identify the question of law to be determined by the court. The substantive issues raised by application will generally be heard in open court.[5]

In the requirement of the permission of the court itself for an appeal against its decision whether or not to entertain an application, in section 45(5), the "court" means the trial judge and not the Court of Appeal.[6]

Section 45(6) deems the court's decision on the point of law referred to it to be an enforceable judgment, and goes on to deal with the possibility of an appeal on the substantive issue. Such an appeal is available when the court itself gives permission[7] in circumstances[8] where it is satisfied that

1. *Babanaft International Co SA* v. *Avant Petroleum Inc, The Oltenia* [1982] 3 All ER 244; *Taylor Woodrow Holdings Ltd* v. *Barnes & Elliott Ltd* [2006] BLR 377.

2. If the contract is governed by a foreign law but the content of that law is the same as English law, it is nevertheless the case that any point of law cannot be one of English law: see the Notes to s. 69.

3. But see: *How Engineering Services Ltd* v. *Lindner Ceilings Floors Partitions plc* [1996] ADRLN 2 and *Attorney General for the Falkland Islands* v. *Gordon Forbes Construction (Falklands) Ltd (No 2)* 2003, unreported, where apparently procedural issues were held to fall within s. 45.

4. Under the 1979 Act it was enough that savings in costs "might" have resulted from the application: *The Vasso* [1983] 3 All ER 211.

5. CPR r. 62.10.

6. *Henry Boot Construction (UK) Ltd* v. *Malmaison Hotel (Manchester) Ltd* [2001] 1 QB 388; *Athletic Union of Constantinople* v. *National Basketball Association* [2002] 1 Lloyd's Rep 305; *Virdee* v. *Virdi* [2003] EWCA Civ 41.

7. See DAC Supplementary Report, para. 27, emphasising that there is no appeal to the Court of Appeal against a refusal of leave to appeal.

8. The drafting was amended in Committee to make it clear that leave may be given only where the point is of general importance etc, as was the case in *DST* v. *Rakoil* [1987] 1 All ER 769, decided under the 1979 Act.

the point is one either of general importance or which should for some other special reason be considered by the Court of Appeal.[1]

The parties are under a duty, imposed by section 40(2) of the Act, to take without delay any necessary steps to obtain a decision of the court on a preliminary question of law. In any event, the jurisdiction of the court depends upon a timeous application (section 45(2)(b)(ii)), and section 45(4)—a provision introduced for the first time in the December 1995 Bill—states that the arbitrators are free (subject to contrary agreement by the parties) to continue the proceedings and, if appropriate, to proceed to an award, pending the outcome of the application under section 45.

The Award

Rules applicable to substance of dispute

46.—(1) The arbitral tribunal shall decide the dispute—

(a) in accordance with the law chosen by the parties as applicable to the substance of the dispute, or

(b) if the parties so agree, in accordance with such other considerations as are agreed by them or determined by the tribunal.

(2) For this purpose the choice of the laws of a country shall be understood to refer to the substantive laws of that country and not its conflict of laws rules.

(3) If or to the extent that there is no such choice or agreement, the tribunal shall apply the law determined by the conflict of laws rules which it considers applicable.

NOTES

Section 46 closely follows Article 28 of the Model Law. As will be seen, it potentially introduces at least one far-reaching change into the law, but as a whole the section is open to the criticism that it raises more questions than it actually answers.

Section 46 is concerned only with the law applicable to the substance of the dispute. It is not concerned with the law applicable to the arbitration agreement or the law applicable to the arbitral procedure. The law applicable to the arbitration agreement is a matter which falls within the jurisdiction of the arbitrators and governs all substantive issues arising under the arbitration clause.[2] As far as the law applicable to the arbitration clause itself is concerned, the position is governed by the common law: the Rome Convention 1980, implemented into English law by the Contracts (Applicable Law) Act 1990,[3] expressly excludes "arbitration agreements". The general common law principles are that: (a) the parties are free to choose the applicable law, more or less without restraint, although it must be the law of a country,[4] and an express choice of a governing law for the

1. Leave will be given in exceptional circumstances only, and in particular where the resolution of the issue would resolve the dispute: *The Oltenia* [1982] 3 All ER 244.

2. Including the validity of the clause. If there is a dispute as to whether the arbitration clause is valid, the approach adopted by the English courts is to apply the "putative" applicable law, i.e., to determine which law would apply if the clause was valid and then to apply the rules of that law to determine whether or not it is valid: *The Parouth* [1982] 2 Lloyd's Rep 351; *Marc Rich & Co AG* v. *Societa Italiana Impianti PA, The Atlantic Emperor* [1989] 1 Lloyd's Rep 548; *Egon Oldendorff* v. *Libra Corporation* [1995] 2 Lloyd's Rep 64; *The Heidberg* [1994] 2 Lloyd's Rep 287; *Continental Enterprises Ltd* v. *Shandong Zhucheng Foreign Trade Group Co* [2005] EWHC 92 (Comm).

3. The Rome Convention will cease to operate on 17 December 2009, and will be replaced by the Rome Regulation, European Parliament and Council Regulation 593/2008/EC. The provision does not make any substantive change to the principles set out in the text.

4. *Al Midani* v. *Al Midani* [1999] 1 Lloyd's Rep 923 holds that an arbitration agreement may be governed by religious law rather than the law of a country, but this decision cannot stand with *Shamil Bank of Bahrain* v. *Beximco Pharmaceuticals Ltd* [2004] 2 Lloyd's Rep 1; *Musawi* v. *R E International (UK) Ltd* [2008] 1 Lloyd's Rep 326.

main contract will generally operate as an express or at the very least implied choice of the law of the arbitration agreement despite the severability principle;[1] (b) in the absence of an express choice, the courts will look for a necessary implication based on the provisions of the contract, for example, the language in which it is written[2] or any express choice of the seat of the arbitration;[3] and (c) in the absence of any express or implied choice, all surrounding circumstances.

The law applicable to the procedure of the arbitration is governed by the 1996 Act itself: if the seat is in England and Wales then the mandatory provisions of the 1996 Act will apply, and the non-mandatory default provisions will apply unless the parties agree to the contrary.[4]

Section 46 is, by contrast, concerned with the law applicable to the main agreement, and that law is relevant to all matters relating to the substance of the dispute between the parties, including validity, interpretation,[5] performance,[6] nullity,[7] termination,[8] the identity of the parties,[9] and the validity of any assignment of contractual rights.[10]

Section 46(1)(a) requires the arbitrators to decide the dispute in accordance with the law chosen by the parties as applicable to the substance of the dispute. Under Article 3 of the Rome Convention 1980, a choice of law is valid if it is expressed with reasonable certainty, a concept which encompasses express and implied choice of law as recognised by the common law. An express choice of seat operates as a choice of applicable law for this purpose.[11] It is the duty of the arbitrators to comply with any such choice, and their failure to do so goes to their jurisdiction so that a challenge may be made under section 67 of the 1996 Act.[12] It should be noted that the Rome Convention does impose some restrictions upon the application of the chosen law: there are, for example, modifications for insurance contracts[13] and consumer contracts, and the Convention permits disregard of certain rules of the applicable law on public policy grounds. It is unclear whether the wording of section 46(1)(a) is sufficient justification for arbitrators to disregard these variations.

1. *XL Insurance Ltd* v. *Owens Corning* [2000] 2 Lloyd's Rep 500; *Tonicstar Ltd* v. *American Home Assurance Co* [2005] Lloyd's Rep IR 32; *Peterson Farms Inc* v. *C & M Farming Ltd* [2004] 2 Lloyd's Rep 603. Contrast *Tamil Nadu Electricity Board* v. *ST-CMS Electric Co Private Ltd* [2008] 1 Lloyd's Rep 93 where different laws for the substantive agreement and for the arbitration clause had been chosen expressly.

2. *Al Midani* v. *Al Midani* [2000] 1 Lloyd's Rep 923.

3. *DST* v. *Rakoil* [1987] 1 All ER 769; *King* v. *Brandywine Reinsurance Co (UK) Ltd* [2005] 1 Lloyd's Rep 655. The cases indicate that the law applicable to the arbitration clause will generally follow the law of the seat of the arbitration rather than the law applicable to the substantive agreement if they are different: *Compagnie Tunisienne de Navigation SA* v. *Compagnie d'Armement Maritime SA* [1971] AC 572; *Black-Clawson* v. *Papierwerke* [1981] 2 Lloyd's Rep 446; *C* v. *D* [2008] 1 Lloyd's Rep 239. *Cf. Miller & Partners Ltd* v. *Whitworth Street Estates (Manchester) Ltd* [1970] AC 583.

4. See the notes to s. 2, above.

5. Rome Convention, Art. 10.1(a).

6. Rome Convention, Art. 10.1(b).

7. Rome Convention, Art. 10.1(e). See: *Egon Oldendorff* v. *Libra Corporation* [1995] 2 Lloyd's Rep 64; *Welex AG* v. *Rosa Ltd, The Epsilon Rosa (No 2)* [2003] 2 Lloyd's Rep 509; *Continental Enterprises Ltd* v. *Shandong Zhucheng Foreign Trade Group Co* [2005] EWHC 92 (Comm).

8. Rome Convention, Art. 10.1(d).

9. *Peterson Farms Inc* v. *C & M Farming Ltd* [2004] 2 Lloyd's Rep 603.

10. *Hussmann (Europe) Ltd* v. *Al Ameen Development and Trading Establishment of Saudi Arabia* [2000] 2 Lloyd's Rep 83; *Raiffeisen Zentralbank Osterreich AG* v. *Five Star General Trading LLC* [2001] Lloyd's Rep IR 460.

11. *Compagnie d'Armement Maritime SA* v. *Compagnie Tunisienne de Navigation SA* [1971] 2 AC 572. Contrast: *Mitsubishi Corporation* v. *Castletown Navigation Ltd, The Castle Alpha* [1989] 2 Lloyd's Rep 383; *King* v. *Brandywine Reinsurance Co (UK) Ltd* [2004] 2 Lloyd's Rep 670, affirmed on other grounds [2005] 1 Lloyd's Rep 655; *Travelers Casualty and Surety Co of Europe Ltd* v. *Sun Life Assurance Co of Canada (UK) Ltd* [2004] Lloyd's Rep IR 846.

12. *Peterson Farms Inc* v. *C & M Farming Ltd* [2004] 2 Lloyd's Rep 603.

13. Choice of law rules for insurance agreements where the risk or commitment is situated within the EU are contained in the Financial Services and Markets Act 2000 (Law Applicable to Contracts of Insurance) Regulations 2001, SI 2001 No 2635. Risks situated elsewhere, and reinsurance contracts, are regulated by the Rome Convention. These Regulations will cease to operate when the Rome Regulation comes into force, as they are incorporated into it.

The purpose of section 46(2) is to make it clear that an express choice of law incorporates the substantive rules of the system of law chosen and not its conflict of laws rules. Were the latter the case, the conflict of laws rules of the chosen country might provide that the applicable law is to be some other law. This process, known as *renvoi*, is excluded by section 46(2).

Section 46(1)(b) is expressed in very general terms, and deals with the situation in which there is a choice of law which is not recognised by ordinary conflict rules. This may arise because the parties have chosen *lex mercatoria*, religious law or some other system of law other than that of a country, or because the arbitrators have been relieved from applying strict rules of law. While it is the case that the Rome Convention requires a chosen law to be that of a country,[1] that principle does not apply to arbitrations, and section 46(1)(b) permits a choice which would not be permitted in other cases. As regards *lex mercatoria*, it was recognised before the passing of the Arbitration Act 1996 that such a choice was valid,[2] and this is confirmed by section 46(1)(b). A choice of religious law is also valid.[3] As regards contracting out of strict rules of law is concerned, a choice of that type is variously known as arbitration "*ex aequo et bono*", "amiable composition" or "equitable arbitration". This form of arbitration, which in England is at present encountered at best rarely, although it has in the past been used in certain reinsurance agreements, authorises the arbitrators to disregard express contract wordings or rules of construction, and to reach equitable results. There is no standard wording in use, and other clauses go even further and permit the arbitrators to ignore substantive rules of law. Equity clauses have come before the English courts on a number of occasions, and their validity has been held to rest upon their width. Thus, while it is permissible to oust strict construction wordings,[4] any attempt to oust substantive rules of law threatens the validity of the clause itself for want of certainty,[5] and possibly even the entire contract for ousting the jurisdiction of the courts.[6] The problem is that section 46(1)(b) does not really indicate whether there has been a codification of existing principles or a substantive change. It merely authorises the dispute to be resolved in accordance with "other considerations" provided that the parties have so agreed in writing. It is certainly arguable that the phrase "other considerations" is broad enough to encompass principles not recognised by any legal system, and the objection to that sort of approach is largely removed by the ability of the parties, under section 69 of the Act, to contract out of judicial review. Indeed, the DAC Report, paragraph 223, noted that the effect of an equity clause is to exclude any right of appeal as there is no point of law involved; accordingly, the assumption is that section 46(1)(b) authorises equity clauses of all types and however widely cast. It may be that the main protection provided here is the overriding obligation of the arbitrators under section 33 to act impartially and to allow each party to present his case. The provisions relating to equitable arbitration were not brought into force along with the rest of the legislation. It will be recalled that the Act was brought into force on the basis that it would apply to all proceedings commenced on or after 31 January 1997 irrespective of when the arbitration agreement was made, thereby conferring a limited retroactivity. That retroactivity was removed in the case of equity clauses, and section 46(1)(b) applies only to those agreements made on or after 31 January 1997 so as to prevent a different reading of equity clauses agreed prior to that date.

Section 46(3) is concerned with the situation in which there is no express choice of law. Under Article 4 of the Rome Convention the general default rule is that the agreement is governed by the law with which the contract is most closely connected, and there is a strong presumption in favour of the law of the place where the party whose performance characterises the contract is located: typically, in a contract of supply, the law of the supplier's home state will be adopted. Under section 46(3) the arbitrators are empowered to determine the conflict of laws rules which should apply, and

1. *Shamil Bank of Bahrain* v. *Beximco Pharmaceuticals Ltd* [2004] 2 Lloyd's Rep 1.
2. *DST v. Rakoil* [1987] 1 All ER 769.
3. *Halpern* v. *Halpern* [2006] 2 Lloyd's Rep 83, affirmed [2007] 2 Lloyd's Rep 56; *Musawi* v. *R E International (UK) Ltd* [2008] 1 Lloyd's Rep 326.
4. *Eagle Star Insurance Co* v. *Yuval Insurance Co Ltd* [1978] 1 Lloyd's Rep 357; *Kansa General Insurance Co Ltd* v. *Bishopsgate Insurance plc* [1988] 1 Lloyd's Rep 503, [1988] 1 FTLR 190; *Overseas Union Inc* v. *AA Mutual International Ltd* [1988] 1 FTLR 421; *Home and Overseas Insurance Co Ltd* v. *Mentor Insurance Co (UK) Ltd* [1989] 3 All ER 74; *Hiscox* v. *Outhwaite (No 3)* [1991] 2 Lloyd's Rep 524.
5. *Orion Compania Espanola de Seguros* v. *Belfort Maatschappij Voor Algemene Verzekringeen* [1962] 2 Lloyd's Rep 257; *Home Insurance* v. *ADAS* [1983] 2 Lloyd's Rep 674.
6. *Marine Insurance Co* v. *Assecuranz-Union-von 1865* (1935) 52 Ll L Rep 16.

then to apply those conflict of laws rules to decide which law should apply to the contract: such authorisation is in any event commonly found in arbitration agreements. The wording of section 46(3) is taken from the Model Law, and the DAC sought not to amplify or alter it, on the ground of the complexities involved (February 1996 Report, paragraph 225). Two issues of law nevertheless arise here: is the arbitrators' choice of the relevant conflict of laws rules correct; and is their application of those rules to determine the law applicable to the contract correct?

The first question would, under the wording of the Act, appear not to be problematic, as the arbitrators are given a completely free hand in this regard. The second question, which will arise when the arbitrators decide that English conflict of laws rules apply,[1] is whether the arbitrators' decision as to the applicable law indicated by English law is correct. As noted earlier, as a matter of English law the default rules in the absence of choice are set out in Article 4 of the Rome Convention. If the arbitrators choose an applicable law which has no relationship to the contract or to the parties, this is presumably an error of law only, and may be attacked—if at all—under the error of law provisions in section 69 of the Act.

Awards on different issues, &c

47.—(1) Unless otherwise agreed by the parties, the tribunal may make more than one award at different times on different aspects of the matters to be determined.

(2) The tribunal may, in particular make an award relating—

(a) to an issue affecting the whole claim, or
(b) to a part only of the claims or cross-claims submitted to it for decision.

(3) If the tribunal does so, it shall specify in its award the issue, or the claim or part of a claim, which is the subject matter of the award.

NOTES

Section 47 re-enacts sections 13(1) and 14 of the Arbitration Act 1950, under which arbitrators could make an award at any time, and could also make an interim award, that is, a final award on a discrete issue between the parties. The combined effect of these sections was that arbitrators could make a series of awards as they went along, dealing with severable parts of the dispute. Section 47(1) re-enacts that right. It will be noted that the phrase "interim award" has been dropped from the legislation. This is to avoid the common misunderstanding of the phrase which had justifiably grown up and which took an interim award to be some form of temporary or interlocutory determination or order by the arbitrators. Nevertheless, the term "interim award" remains in widespread use even though there is no reference to it in the 1996 Act. The appropriate terminology for an award which disposes of all of the issues in dispute[2] is a final award (section 47(2)(a)), whereas an award which is confined to particular matters is a partial award (section 47(2)(b)). The power to make awards on different issues should be contrasted with the power conferred on arbitrators by section 39 to make provisional awards, that is, to grant provisional relief pending the making of a final award. The awards contemplated by section 47 are all determinative, albeit that some may be limited to specific issues. Of the major institutional rules, Article 26.7 of the LCIA Rules (1998 edition) enables the arbitrators to make separate awards on different issues at different times, and Article 2 of the ICC Rules of Arbitration (1998 edition) defines "award" as including a

1. If the arbitrators decide that some other law is applicable, the courts have no power to review the arbitrators' decisions on points of law under s. 69 of the 1996 Act, so that the arbitrators' final award applying any law other than English law is effectively immune from challenge on substantive grounds.

2. Or at least all issues in dispute which fall within the jurisdiction of the arbitrators. It is, nevertheless, not permitted for an arbitrator to refuse to award a final remedy on the basis that there are matters falling outside his jurisdiction which will have to be resolved in some other forum and accordingly that a full award of damages is inappropriate: see *JSC Zestafoni G Nikoladze Ferroalloy Plant* v. *Ronly Holdings* [2004] 2 Lloyd's Rep 355, where Gross J held that the arbitrator must not attempt to anticipate the outcome of proceedings falling outside his jurisdiction.

partial award. Article 32.1 of the UNCITRAL Rules of Arbitration permits the making of "interim, interlocutory or partial" awards.

All awards, whenever made, are treated in the same way by the Act, so that an award may be enforceable or subject to challenge even though issues remain outstanding between the parties.[1] However, it is plainly not appropriate to challenge a partial award on the basis that it has left open matters in dispute between the parties.[2]

Section 47 does no more than confer a discretion upon the arbitrators, and they may refuse to make more than one award despite a request by one of the parties for an award to be made in advance of the resolution of all issues. Authority under the earlier legislation indicated that the arbitrators' decision not to make an award was not an award in its own right and thus could not be challenged, and even if the decision not to make an award was itself described as an award and amounted to an award it was not a decision of law and could not be challenged as an error of law.[3] Nevertheless, the hope was expressed in the DAC Report, paragraph 230, that arbitrators would make much use of their power, which is to be regarded as an aspect of their general duty in section 33(1)(b) to adopt suitable procedures for the speedy and effective disposal of the matter before them, provided that this is consistent with allowing each party the opportunity to present their case. Arbitrators should perhaps note that the courts, particularly since the adoption of the Civil Procedure Rules 1998, seek the most expeditious method of resolving a dispute, so that there is no longer any right for a party to demand that all issues be resolved in a single hearing,[4] and the DAC also emphasised that it regarded the power to make awards on different issues as "very important".[5] Thus, although section 47 does not change the law, its inclusion is intended to emphasise that the power is there to be exercised.

As might be expected, the parties may by agreement remove the right of the arbitrators to treat the dispute in this way and they may require a single award or a small number of awards. The parties may also impose time limits upon the making of an award, in which case there is a mechanism under which application to the court may be made for the enlargement of time (under section 50 of the 1996 Act, which may be excluded by agreement). An agreement which does impose time limits for the making of an award is not, unless the wording is compelling, to be construed as confining the jurisdiction of the arbitrators only to those disputes which are capable of being arbitrated within the agreed time period.[6]

Section 47(2) gives illustrations of the type of matters that may be dealt with by a final award pending the resolution of the entire dispute between the parties, and section 47(3) requires arbitrators to indicate the issue disposed of in their award. It is common for costs to be reserved for a separate award after the main dispute has been resolved, and the argument that the arbitrators, by issuing a final award without costs, no longer have jurisdiction to make a costs order, has been rejected by the courts.[7]

Whether or not an award, final or otherwise, has been made is a matter of crucial importance, for two main reasons. First, the making of an award triggers the time limits for applications to the arbitrators for modification of the award under the slip rule in section 57 of the 1996 Act, and for applications and appeals to the court under sections 67 to 69, whereas a procedural decision short of an award can be challenged only once the award itself has been made, provided that an objection is raised at the time in order to avoid the operation of the waiver principle in section 73 of the 1996 Act. Secondly, once an award has been made, the tribunal becomes *functus officio* in relation to the matter dealt with by the award and it cannot be revisited; by contrast, any procedural decision short

1. *Marine Contractors Inc* v. *Shell Petroleum Co of Nigeria Ltd* [1984] 2 Lloyd's Rep 77; *Overseas Fortune Shipping Pte Ltd* v. *Great Eastern Shipping Co Ltd, The Singapore Fortune* [1987] 1 Lloyd's Rep 270.
2. *BMBF (No 12) Ltd* v. *Harland and Wolff Shipbuilding and Heavy Industries Ltd* [2001] 2 Lloyd's Rep 227.
3. *Japan Line Ltd* v. *Aggeliki Charis Compania Maritima SA, The Angelic Grace* [1980] 1 Lloyd's Rep 288; *The Trade Fortitude* [1992] 1 Lloyd's Rep 169.
4. DAC Report, para. 228.
5. DAC Report, para. 226.
6. *John Mowlem Construction plc* v. *Secretary of State for Defence* (2001) 82 Con LR 140.
7. *Sea Trade Maritime Corporation* v. *Hellenic Mutual War Risks Association (Bermuda) Ltd, The Athena* [2006] 2 Lloyd's Rep 147.

of an award can be revised as the arbitrators think fit.[1] Accordingly, it is necessary to determine whether what the arbitrators have done is to make an award, or simply made a procedural decision. The key test is whether the arbitrators have disposed of the issue: if so, they have made an award no matter how their document is phrased.[2] In *Charles M Willie Co (Shipping) Ltd* v. *Ocean Laser Shipping Ltd, The Smaro*,[3] Rix J held that a letter to which the arbitrator allowed amendments to be made was held not to be an award as it was not dispositive of any issue nor did it relate to the merits of the case. By contrast, in *Ranko Group* v. *Antarctic Maritime SA, The Robin*,[4] a letter by the arbitrator in which he stated that he had made "rulings" as to his jurisdiction was held to be a partial award which had to be challenged under section 67 of the 1996 Act within the permitted 28 days.

Remedies

48.—(1) The parties are free to agree on the powers exercisable by the arbitral tribunal as regards remedies.

(2) Unless otherwise agreed by the parties, the tribunal has the following powers.

(3) The tribunal may make a declaration as to any matter to be determined in the proceedings.

(4) The tribunal may order the payment of a sum of money, in any currency.

(5) The tribunal has the same powers as the court

(a) to order a party to do or refrain from doing anything;

(b) to order specific performance of a contract (other than a contract relating to land);

(c) to order the rectification, setting aside or cancellation of a deed or other document.

NOTES

Section 48 of the Act allows the parties to agree what remedies are available, and which provide default powers in the absence of agreement. The section is concerned purely with remedies awarded by arbitrators in their substantive awards, and does not authorise the grant of security during the course of the arbitration.[5]

Section 48(1) is drafted in wide terms, and permits the parties to reach agreement as to what remedies are to be available to the arbitrators provided that the agreement is in writing. The DAC intended this clause to be of wide ambit. As stated by the DAC in its commentary on the July 1995 Bill:

> The clause . . . contemplates the possibility that the parties may in the arbitration agreement confer upon the tribunal different, and possibly greater, powers than those available to the court. Parties may wish to confer the power on a tribunal to order a particular composite remedy, or a remedy on different grounds from those used by the High Court, or a different remedy that is ordinarily available in another jurisdiction.

Obvious illustrations of the type of remedy which arbitrators may be empowered to grant, which are unavailable in the general law, include punitive damages and (in misrepresentation and non-disclosure cases) apportionment as an alternative to avoidance. A clause which removes from the

1. *Charles M Willie Co (Shipping) Ltd* v. *Ocean Laser Shipping Ltd, The Smaro* [1999] 1 Lloyd's Rep 225.
2. *Cargill* v. *Kadinopoulos* [1992] 1 Lloyd's Rep 1; *The Trade Fortitude* [1992] 1 Lloyd's Rep 169.
3. [1999] 1 Lloyd's Rep 225. See also: *National Boat Shows Ltd* v. *Tameside Marine* July 2001, unreported.
4. [1998] ADRLN 35.
5. *Kastner* v. *Jason* [2005] 1 Lloyd's Rep 397.

arbitrators the power to grant injunctive relief also has the effect of limiting the jurisdiction of the arbitrators to disputes which can be resolved other than by an injunction.[1]

Section 48(2) introduces the default powers which are available to arbitrators in the absence of contrary agreement. These powers may supplement those actually conferred upon the arbitrators by express agreement. In addition to those specifically mentioned, arbitrators have all powers open to the courts unless the parties provide otherwise: such powers include, for example, that of apportionment under the Civil Liability (Contribution) Act 1978.[2]

Section 48(3) empowers the arbitrators to give declaratory judgments. This power was open to them under earlier legislation, although not expressly so. The main problem with a declaration is that it is not enforceable directly, and judicial assistance will generally be required to give it any real meaning. Lord Donaldson, speaking in the Second Reading debate in the House of Lords, expressed the view that the power to grant declaratory relief could not extend to issues of status, for example, whether the parties were or were not married, as a declaration of that type could not be enforced by the courts.[3] Where a declaration is granted, the arbitrators may also declare that interest is payable.[4]

Section 48(4) is concerned with what is undoubtedly the primary remedy, namely, an order for the payment of money. There is also express statutory authority for the award of money in any currency. This power was originally denied to the English courts by the old principle confirmed by the House of Lords in *Re United Railways of the Havana and Regla Warehouses Ltd*,[5] although that ruling was overturned by their Lordships in *Miliangos* v. *George Frank (Textiles) Ltd.*[6] In the meantime, the Court of Appeal ruled in *Jugoslavenska Oceanska Plovidba* v. *Castle Investments Co Inc*[7] that arbitrators, unlike the courts, did have the power to make awards in foreign currencies. The effect of section 48(4) is to codify the *Jugoslavenska* and *Miliangos* decisions.[8] Where such an award is made, and is to be enforced in England, it will be converted into sterling at the rate prevailing at the date of the enforcement action. Guidelines as to when a claim may be made in a foreign currency have been laid down by the courts.[9] The power of the arbitrators to express an award in any currency is one which derives from the 1996 Act and does not depend upon the law applicable to the contract in question,[10] so that it rests on the fact that England is the seat of the arbitration: a failure by the arbitrators to apply the law applicable to the agreement, or the rules laid down by the parties, as to the currency of the award, is an error of law under section 69 rather than serious irregularity under section 68.[11] Of the major institutional rules, only the LCIA Rules (1998 edition, Article 26.6) permit an award to be expressed in any currency.

Section 48(5) states that the arbitrators have the same power as the court to grant various types of relief. The word "court" is defined in section 105 of the 1996 Act as the High Court or a county court, so that a power which is open to some but not all courts is excluded from section 48(5). On this basis it was held in *Kastner* v. *Jason*[12] that arbitrators have no power to grant freezing injunctions as that power is confined to the High Court and specific county courts.

1. *Vertex Data Science Ltd* v. *Powergen Retail Ltd* [2006] 2 Lloyd's Rep 591.
2. *Wealands* v. *CLC Contractors Ltd* [1999] 2 Lloyd's Rep 739.
3. A declaratory award may also give rise to conceptual difficulties with the running of the limitation period, as if it is merely declared that one party has a particular right it is probably the case that the limitation period for the enforcement of such a right runs from the date of its infringement rather than from the date of the declaration. See generally *Hayter* v. *Nelson (No 1)* 1989, unreported.
4. Arbitration Act 1996, s. 49(5).
5. [1961] AC 1007.
6. [1976] AC 443.
7. [1974] QB 292.
8. *Lesotho Highlands Development Authority* v. *Impregilo SpA* [2005] 2 Lloyd's Rep 310. Lord Steyn, dissenting, was of the view that s. 48(4) gave the court a wide discretion unrestricted by previous authority.
9. Most recently in *Virani Ltd* v. *Manuel Revert y CIA SA* [2004] 2 Lloyd's Rep 14, applying *Services Europe Atlantique Sud* v. *Stockholms Rederiaktiebolag Svea, The Folias* [1979] AC 685. See also: *The Texaco Melbourne* [1994] 1 Lloyd's Rep 473.
10. *Lesotho Highlands Authority* v. *Impregilo SpA* [2005] 2 Lloyd's Rep 310.
11. *Lesotho Highlands Authority* v. *Impregilo SpA* [2005] 2 Lloyd's Rep 310 (Lord Phillips dissenting).That means that if the right of appeal has been excluded by agreement, there can be no challenge to a decision on currency.
12. [2004] 2 Lloyd's Rep 233. The point did not arise on appeal.

Section 48(5)(a) empowers arbitrators to grant injunctive relief (other than freezing injunctions and other injunctive relief, confined to the High Court and specified county courts). There are various illustrations of the courts enforcing awards which impose obligations on one of the parties,[1] including anti-suit injunctions.[2]

Section 48(5)(b) re-enacts section 15 of the Arbitration Act 1950 in allowing the arbitrators to grant specific performance of contracts other than those involving land.[3] The restriction relating to land was introduced originally as it was felt that express authorisation by the parties was required for the grant of a drastic remedy of this type. The 1994 Bill proposed the removal of the restriction. The 1996 Act has, however, retained the land restriction, presumably on the basis that the parties are perfectly free to agree to the grant of this remedy in line with their general autonomy under section 45(1).

Section 48(5)(c), conferring the power on the arbitrators to rectify, set aside or cancel a document or deed, is consistent with the common law's recognition of such powers where the contract contemplates their exercise.[4] Lord Donaldson at Second Reading saw, by a combination of this section and sections 51 (agreed awards) and 66 (judgment in terms of the award), "intriguing possibilities for tax evasion using the machinery of an agreed award of rectification of contractual documents coupled with a judgment to the like effect", thereby creating "an amended and backdated document which was more taxpayer friendly than the original", this being achieved without the arbitrators and the court being aware of the abuse. The DAC Report, paragraph 242, saw no problem here. It was most unlikely that a tribunal would knowingly associate itself with such a scheme and it could refuse to make an award of the type requested; and whether or not there was any connivance by the arbitrators, an award is binding only as between the parties and cannot affect their position *vis-à-vis* third parties such as tax authorities.

Interest

49.—(1) The parties are free to agree on the powers of the tribunal as regards the award of interest.

(2) Unless otherwise agreed by the parties the following provisions apply.

(3) The tribunal may award simple or compound interest from such dates, at such rates and with such rests as it considers meets the justice of the case—

- (a) on the whole or part of any amount awarded by the tribunal, in respect of any period up to the date of the award;
- (b) on the whole or part of any amount claimed in the arbitration and outstanding at the commencement of the arbitral proceedings but paid before the award was made, in respect of any period up to the date of payment.

(4) The tribunal may award simple or compound interest from the date of the award (or any later date) until payment, at such rates and with such rests as it considers meets the justice of the case, on the outstanding amount of any award (including any award of interest under subsection (3) and any award as to costs).

(5) References in this section to an amount awarded by the tribunal include an amount payable in consequence of a declaratory award by the tribunal.

(6) The above provisions do not affect any other power of the tribunal to award interest.

1. See, e.g., *Ethiopian Oilseeds and Pulses Export Corporation* v. *Rio del Mar Foods Inc* [1990] 1 Lloyd's Rep 86.
2. *Welex AG* v. *Rosa Maritime Ltd* [2003] 2 Lloyd's Rep 509.
3. E.g., a construction contract: *Telia Sonera AB* v. *Hilcourt (Docklands) Ltd*, August 2003, unreported.
4. See, e.g., *Winter* v. *Lethbridge* (1824) 13 Price 533.

NOTES

The powers of the arbitrators to award interest under the Arbitration Act 1950 were not complete. Section 20 of the 1950 Act authorised the arbitrators to award interest on the award as from the date of their award and, indeed, it was presumed that this was the case unless the award provided otherwise. The rate of interest was, however, strictly confined to the judgment debt rate prevailing at the date of the award, although this principle was relaxed in the case of awards made in a foreign currency; section 20 was amended by the Private International Law (Miscellaneous Provisions) Act 1995, section 3 to allow the award of interest in this situation at such rate as the arbitrators deemed appropriate. That section is superseded by the 1996 Act, and accordingly is repealed by Schedule 4 to the 1996 Act.

More difficult was the award of interest for late payment of sums due to the successful party. At the time of the passing of the 1996 Act it was generally believed that the courts had no power to award interest for wrongful detention of sums due unless the contract provided for such interest,[1] although that principle was subsequently modified by the House of Lords in *Sempra Metals Ltd* v. *Inland Revenue Commissioners*[2] to the effect that interest can be recovered at common law if the claimant can prove his loss in accordance with the usual rules of remoteness. Before that decision, however, there had been unsatisfactory attempts at piecemeal statutory reform, and as far as arbitrations were concerned the old principle was sidestepped by the Administration of Justice Act 1982, which inserted section 19A into the Arbitration Act 1950. Section 19A authorised arbitrators, subject to contract, to award simple interest on unpaid sums but not on sums paid late but before the commencement of the arbitration proceedings. The 1996 Act extended the earlier provision by authorising the award of compound interest on a compensatory basis[3] (and not on a punitive basis: see the DAC Report, paragraph 237), but some problems of the previous law remain.

Section 49(1), which covers both interest on the award and interest for late payment of sums owing, reflects the common law[4] and allows the parties to make any agreement that they think fit for the award of interest. The parties may thus agree that interest is not to be awardable.[5] If the claimant does not make any claim for interest, the arbitrators are not empowered to award interest as it does not form a part of the reference, although if a claim for interest is subsequently added and the respondent does not object then the arbitrator's jurisdiction may be regarded as having been extended accordingly.[6]

In the absence of any agreement to the contrary, default powers are introduced by section 49(2). As interest is not a matter of substance governed by the law applicable to the main contract, but is rather a matter of procedure governed by the law applicable to the arbitral procedure, the default rules are applicable irrespective of the law applicable to the main contract and not merely where the main contract is governed by English law unless there is an agreement in writing between the parties that the statutory default powers are inapplicable.[7]

1. A rule confirmed by the House of Lords in *La Pintada Compania Navegacion SA* v. *President of India, The La Pintada* [1984] 2 Lloyd's Rep 9.
2. [2007] UKHL 34.
3. When the 1996 Act was passed English law did not permit the award of compound interest: *Westdeutsche Landesbank Girozentrale* v. *Islington London Borough Council* [1996] 2 All ER 961. That position has to some extent now been relaxed by the House of Lords in *Sempra Metals Ltd* v. *Inland Revenue Commissioners* [2007] UKHL 34.
4. *Cf. Minter Ltd* v. *Welsh Health Technical Services Organisation* (1980) 13 BLR 1.
5. This is the apparent effect of the Motor Insurers Bureau Agreement on Untraced Drivers 1996, although it was accepted by the Court of Appeal in *Evans* v. *Motor Insurers Bureau* [1999] Lloyd's Rep IR 30 that the provision is potentially in conflict with the EU's motor insurance Directives, as confirmed by the European Court of Justice in its ruling on a preliminary reference in subsequent proceedings against the UK Government for failure to implement the Directives properly, Case C-63/01 *Evans* v. *Secretary of State for the Environment, Transport and the Regions* [2004] Lloyd's Rep IR 391. The revised MIB Agreement on Untraced Drivers 2003, which applies to accidents occurring on or after 14 February 2003, remedies this omission and allows the arbitrator to award interest "in an appropriate case".
6. *Westland Helicopters Ltd* v. *Sheikh Salah Al-Hejailan* [2004] 2 Lloyd's Rep 523.
7. *Lesotho Highlands Development Authority* v. *Impregilo SpA* [2005] 2 Lloyd's Rep 310.

Section 49(3) requires the arbitrators to award interest on the basis of "the interests of justice", and it is unlikely that their discretion will lightly be interfered with by the courts.[1]

Section 49(3)(a) is concerned with the situation in which the tribunal has awarded a sum which has not been paid at the date of the award. The arbitrators may award simple or compound interest and are not confined to simple interest. The rate of interest payable, and the periods in respect of which it is payable, are matters for the arbitrators, although there is judicial guidance as to the running of interest which may be of significance in consideration of the matter.[2]

Section 49(3)(b) is concerned with sums outstanding when the proceedings were commenced but paid during the course of the proceedings and prior to the award. Section 49(3) authorises the arbitrators to award compound interest. The gap in section 19A of the 1950 Act—interest on sums paid late but prior to the commencement of the arbitration—is not filled by section 49(3), and it remains the case that in the absence of any agreement no interest can be awarded on such sums.

Section 49(4) governs the award of interest on the sum awarded, from the date of the award until the date of payment. It is made clear that the arbitrators can award compound interest as well as simple interest, and that interest can be awarded on costs as well as the sum awarded in the substantive part of the award. The DAC regarded the ability of arbitrators to award compound interest as an important extension to the effectiveness of arbitration, as the award of compound interest provides a strong incentive for the defeated party to honour the award rapidly rather than—as was the case in the past—to hold on to the money in the hope of exceeding the amount of simple interest by some other investment of the money (DAC Report, paragraph 237). Compound interest aside, section 49(4) of the 1996 Act removes the link with the judgment debt rate,[3] so that the arbitrators can award interest at any rate which they think fit in all cases and not just in cases where the award is made in a foreign currency.[4] If post-award interest is not awarded by the arbitrators the court itself cannot, when giving permission to enforce the award under section 66(1) of the 1996 Act, award interest under its usual powers in the Supreme Court Act 1981, section 35A: that is because the order under section 66(1) is confined to the enforcement of obligation of the parties to honour the award.[5] However, it appears that the court can order interest under section 17 of the Judgments Act 1838 if the court enters judgment in the terms of the award under section 66(2).[6]

Section 49(5), inserted by the December 1995 Bill, clarifies the position where a declaration is made by the arbitrators: such a declaration (e.g., that a sum is owed by one party to another) may include an element for interest, as if it were an award ordering the payment of a sum. However, this is possible only if the sum is found to be owing from a date prior to the award: if the award itself gives rise to the liability for a sum to be paid, a declaration that interest is to run from any date prior to the award is beyond the jurisdiction of the arbitrators.[7]

Section 49(6) renders section 49 without prejudice to any other power of the arbitrators to award interest. It is to be presumed that the draftsman had in mind interest which may be awarded under various statutes which provide for arbitration governed by arbitration legislation.

The Late Payment of Commercial Debts (Interest) Act 1998 appears to apply to arbitrations. Under this Act a supplier of goods or services is entitled to a lump sum and interest in the event of late payment of a debt incurred under a contract between businesses. The rate of interest is the

1. See, the pre-1996 Act decision in *Amec Building Ltd* v. *Cadmus Investment Co Ltd* [1997] 5 CL 33.

2. Interest will normally run from the date of the breach of duty complained of, although the courts will refuse to award interest, or may vary the rate of interest, for any period in respect of which the claimant has been the architect of his own loss, e.g., by dilatory conduct in pursuing the legal proceedings: *Derby Resources AG* v. *Blue Corinth Marine Co Ltd, The Athenian Harmony (No 2)* [1998] 2 Lloyd's Rep 425; *Quorum AS* v. *Schramm (No 2)* [2003] Lloyd's Rep IR 315. One particular rule of note here is that arbitrators may not award interest for any period prior to the date on which the cause of action arose: *Durham County Council* v. *Darlington Borough Council* [2003] EWHC 2598 (Admin).

3. Confirmed by the House of Lords in *London and Overseas Freighters Ltd* v. *Timber Shipping Co SA* [1972] AC 1. The rate is currently 8%.

4. Thereby answering the plea of Donaldson J in *Fratelli Moretti SpA* v. *Nidera Handelscompagnie BV* [1980] 1 Lloyd's Rep 534.

5. *Walker* v. *Rowe* [2000] 1 Lloyd's Rep 116; *Pirtek* v. *Deanswood* [2005] 2 Lloyd's Rep 728.

6. *Pirtek* v. *Deanswood* [2005] 2 Lloyd's Rep 728; *Gater Assets Ltd* v. *NAK Naftogaz Ukrainiy (No 2)* [2008] EWHC 1108 (Comm).

7. *Durham County Council* v. *Darlington Borough Council* [2003] EWHC 2598 (Admin).

official dealing rate of the Bank of England plus 8%. There are no reported illustrations of the use of the legislation in arbitration.

Extension of time for making award

50.—(1) Where the time for making an award is limited by or in pursuance of the arbitration agreement, then, unless otherwise agreed by the parties, the court may in accordance with the following provisions by order extend that time.

(2) An application for an order under this section may be made—

(a) by the tribunal (upon notice to the parties), or
(b) by any party to the proceedings (upon notice to the tribunal and the other parties),

but only after exhausting any available arbitral process for obtaining an extension of time.

(3) The court shall only make an order if satisfied that a substantial injustice would otherwise be done.

(4) The court may extend the time for such period and on such terms as it thinks fit, and may do so whether or not the time previously fixed (by or under the agreement or by a previous order) has expired.

(5) The leave of the court is required for any appeal from a decision of the court under this section.

NOTES

Section 50 confers upon the court the power to enlarge the time for making an award where the arbitrators are under some time limit. The section takes account of the wishes of the parties.

Section 50(1) confers upon the court the basic power to extend time. It is non-mandatory, and the parties are free to contract out of its provisions. A provision in the arbitration agreement whereby the parties or the arbitrators may extend time does not operate as an exclusion of the fallback power of the court to do so.[1]

Section 50(2) allows the application to be made by the arbitrators themselves, or by any party on giving notice to the arbitrators and the other parties. Section 50(2) of the 1996 Act is no more than a statement of the obvious, although it does contain the important procedural point that an application by a party must have been notified to the other party and the arbitrators.

If the parties have agreed on their own procedure for extending time (e.g., by conferring an express power on the arbitrators in this respect), it is necessary under the proviso to section 50(2) for that procedure to have been exhausted before application may be made to the court. This provision also implies that the mere existence of an express contractual procedure for extending time is not to be taken as ousting the power of the court to extend time (as is allowed by section 50(1)).[2] However, the DAC Report, paragraph 239, noted that "it would be a rare case indeed where the Court extended the time notwithstanding that this had not been done through an available arbitral process".

An arbitration application under section 50 may be made by the arbitrators, who must serve the parties and make them parties to the application, or by a party, who must serve the other parties and make them parties to the application.[3]

Section 50(3) for the first time lays down the governing criterion for the enlargement of time. The test of substantial injustice is the same as that contained in section 79, which sets out the power of the court to extend any time limit specified in Part I of the Act. It is unclear what the test involves

1. *John Mowlem Construction plc* v. *Secretary of State for Defence* (2001) 82 Con LR 140.
2. *Cf.* the analysis of the same provision in s. 12: see the Notes to s. 12, above.
3. CPR r. 62.6(2)–(3).

in the present context. It might be speculated that if the time has expired due to the successful delaying tactics of one party, or for other reasons beyond the control of the arbitrators, time will be extended. By contrast, if the delay is that of the arbitrators themselves, it might be thought that requiring the parties to bring breach of contract proceedings against the arbitrators in lieu of obtaining their award would amount to "substantial injustice".

Section 50(4) gives the court the power to extend time for such period and on such terms as it thinks fit. Time may be extended whether or not it has expired. While it would make sense for an application to be made prior to the expiry of time, so that the award when finally made is known to be valid, it is possible that time has expired and an award has been made without any attempt to extend time having been made. This occurred in *Oakland Metal Co Ltd* v. *Benaim Co Ltd*,[1] where it was held that the court retained power to extend time retrospectively in proceedings to enforce the award. Section 50(4) preserves this position.

Section 50(5) is the usual provision requiring the permission of the court for any appeal from its decision whether or not to extend time. The "court" means the trial judge and not the Court of Appeal.[2]

Settlement

51.—(1) If during arbitral proceedings the parties settle the dispute, the following provisions apply unless otherwise agreed by the parties.

(2) The tribunal shall terminate the substantive proceedings and, if so requested by the parties and not objected to by the tribunal, shall record the settlement in the form of an agreed award.

(3) An agreed award shall state that it is an award of the tribunal and shall have the same status and effect as any other award on the merits of the case.

(4) The following provisions of this Part relating to awards (sections 52 to 58) apply to an agreed award.

(5) Unless the parties have also settled the matter of the payment of the costs of the arbitration, the provisions of this Part relating to costs (sections 59 to 65) continue to apply.

NOTES

Section 51, which reproduces the effect of Article 30 of the Model Law, gives a statutory basis to the long-established procedure of the parties requesting the arbitrators to make a consent award recording any settlement of the dispute reached by the parties without the need for a full award by the arbitrators. The Bill of July 1995 referred to such an award as an "agreed award"; terminology which has been retained by the 1996 Act.

Section 51(1) lays down the overriding principle that the parties themselves are free to determine the effect of a settlement reached by them during the course of the proceedings. If they neglect to do so, the remaining provisions of section 51 apply by default.

Section 51(2) states that on settlement during the proceedings, the arbitrators are to terminate the proceedings and, if requested by the parties, must record the settlement in the form of an agreed award. The arbitrators are not, by the wording of section 51(2), given any right to object, but if they do refuse to make an award there is no obvious method of overcoming their objection under the legislation: the issue for the parties is, it would seem, one of procedural inconvenience rather than substance within section 67 of the 1996 Act. In the DAC Report, paragraph 242, the view was expressed that the arbitrators could legitimately refuse to make an agreed award if there was some intent by the parties to deceive third parties, for example, the tax authorities (see the comments on

1. [1953] 2 QB 261.

2. *Henry Boot Construction (UK) Ltd* v. *Malmaison Hotel (Manchester) Ltd* [2001] 1 QB 388; *Athletic Union of Constantinople* v. *National Basketball Association* [2002] 1 Lloyd's Rep 305; *Virdee* v. *Virdi* [2003] EWCA Civ 41.

section 48(5)(c)), and it may be that there are other public policy reasons which would justify such refusal.

If an award is made, it can be enforced in summary fashion under section 66(1), whereas if no award is made it will be necessary for a party wishing to enforce the agreed settlement to bring an action on it.

The arbitrators have no right, unless invited by the parties, to become involved in any settlement negotiations. In particular they have no right to give directions to the parties as to how the settlement negotiations are conducted and what the scope of the negotiations should be. An attempt by the arbitrator, in *Wicketts and Sterndale* v. *Brine Builders*,[1] to control the settlement negotiations by directions in order to secure payment of his own fee, was described by HHJ Seymour QC as "outrageous" and merited the removal of the arbitrator under section 24 of the 1996 Act.

Section 51(3) provides that where an award reflecting the settlement is made, it is to be treated as any other award on its merits. This is significant for enforcement purposes, and also—by virtue of section 51(4)—insofar as the formalities attaching to all awards (in sections 52 to 58) are applicable. An agreed award is also, under section 51(5), to settle the allocation of costs, unless the parties have reached their own agreement on costs.

An agreed award is not to contain reasons, by virtue of section 52(4), thereby effectively rendering it immune from challenge on the ground of error of law. This provision probably adds little, as it is highly unlikely that the court would in its absence give permission for an appeal on point of law in the case of an agreed award.

There is no requirement for the award to state that it is an agreed award: the view was expressed in the DAC Report, paragraphs 244 and 378, that there was no justification for this, although it was accepted by the DAC that the court ought to be informed that the award was agreed in the event of proceedings having to be brought to enforce it under section 66 of the 1996 Act. The point is considered further in the Notes to section 66.

Form of award

52.—(1) The parties are free to agree on the form of an award.

(2) If or to the extent that there is no such agreement, the following provisions apply.

(3) The award shall be in writing signed by all the arbitrators or all those assenting to the award.

(4) The award shall contain the reasons for the award unless it is an agreed award or the parties have agreed to dispense with reasons.

(5) The award shall state the seat of the arbitration and the date when the award is made.

NOTES

Section 52(1) restates an implicit rule of the common law that the parties are free to determine the form and content of an award. In many cases coming before the courts, no such agreement was reached and the law had to consider whether what the arbitrators had done was sufficient to discharge their obligation to make an award. Contrary to the implication given by the heading, there is little in section 52, or indeed the Act itself, as to the substantive requirements of an award, although there is much authority for the propositions that an award must:

(a) resolve all issues referred to the arbitrators;
(b) disregard extraneous issues going beyond the jurisdiction of the arbitrators;
(c) be final and unconditional;
(d) be certain and capable of performance by the parties; and
(e) be capable of enforcement by the courts.

1. [2001] CILL 1805.

If an award does not meet these criteria, or if it otherwise fails to meet any of the requirements of section 52, there is deemed to be "serious irregularity" (replacing the old concept of misconduct) under section 68(2), and the court is—as before—empowered to remit the award to the arbitrators, to set the award aside or to declare the award to be a nullity, although substantial injustice will have to be shown before the court so acts. It is the duty of the arbitrators to draft their own award. In *Agrimex Ltd* v. *Tradigrain SA*[1] Thomas J held that a legally-qualified draftsman appointed by the arbitrators to attend the proceedings and thereafter to draft the award in accordance with their instructions did not qualify as an "expert" within section 37, as his functions were purely administrative, so that his appointment—in the absence of exceptional circumstances, for example, where there were language difficulties—was probably not authorised by the legislation. On the facts of that case the sole issue was whether the fees charged by the draftsman were excessive (no point being taken as to the validity of the appointment); Thomas J concluding that this was the case.

Section 52(2) introduces the minimum default provisions for the form and content of an award in the absence of any agreement.

Section 52(3) is based on Article 31(1) of the Model Law, and requires the award to be in writing and signed by or on behalf of all arbitrators or all those assenting to the award. The July 1995 Bill, following the Model Law, by contrast, required signature by a majority of the arbitrators only. The DAC Report, paragraph 252, noted that in some circumstances dissenting arbitrators might not wish to be identified as such, and ought to be allowed to sign the award. Accordingly, the apparent intention of section 52(3) is to permit a dissenting arbitrator to sign the award if he so wishes, but to allow him the right to refuse to sign it. The drafting is far from happy, and there is at least an argument that an award signed by the majority only is not enforceable if the dissenting arbitrator wishes to sign it but has not been given the opportunity to do so. Doubtless such a situation could be corrected by the arbitrators themselves under section 57 insofar as the omission was accidental.

The agreement may require all arbitrators to sign the award, in which case the award is not valid unless each arbitrator signs. A dissenting arbitrator who refuses to sign the award is in breach of his contract with the parties, and accordingly can be removed by the court for refusing to act.[2]

Section 52(3) also reverses the common law position whereby an oral award was valid,[3] although it is rare for oral awards to be made these days. Nevertheless, if at the conclusion of the hearing the arbitrator informs the parties of his award, and reasons are not required, there is nothing to prevent such a statement taking effect as an award if the parties agree to accept it as such.

Section 52(4) imposes a *prima facie* obligation on the arbitrators to give reasons for their award. This follows Article 31(2) of the Model Law, and the DAC stated in its July 1995 and February 1996 commentaries on the Arbitration Bill 1995 that requiring reasons is in line with the principle accepted by English law that persons whose legal rights have been affected are entitled to be told why this is the case. The DAC rejected the argument that a requirement to give reasons could lengthen the arbitral process and could make appeals more likely: the DAC's response was that the giving of reasons had nothing to do with appeals as such, and that in any event the 1996 Act makes it less easy for permission to appeal to be obtained and makes it easier for agreements to be made excluding the right of appeal. It is open to the parties to contract out of the obligation of the arbitrators to give reasons, or to restrict the obligation to one which merely explains the award.[4]

Under the Arbitration Acts 1950 to 1979 there was no obligation on the arbitrators to give reasons for their award, and the practice had developed up to 1979 for many awards to be made either without any reasons at all, or with reasons given in a separate document not forming part of the award and being classified as confidential. The object of avoiding the giving of reasons was to render inapplicable section 21 of the Arbitration Act 1950, which allowed the court to review, under the case stated procedure, any award which was defective on its face: by keeping the reasons off the face of the award there could be no conclusion capable of being corrected. Section 21 of the 1950 Act was repealed by the Arbitration Act 1979, section 1(1), and was replaced with the far more

1. [2003] 2 Lloyd's Rep 537.
2. *Cargill International SA Antigua* v. *Sociedad Iberica de Molturacion SA* [1998] 1 Lloyd's Rep 489.
3. *Thompson* v. *Miller* (1867) 15 WR 353.
4. As in *Bay Hotel and Resort Ltd* v. *Cavalier Construction Co Ltd* [2001] UKPC 34, where it was held that the explanation did not satisfy the requirements of a reasoned award but was nevertheless sufficient to comply with the terms of the arbitration clause.

restrictive procedure in section 1 of the 1979 Act under which an error of law in an award could be challenged. The giving of reasons, nevertheless, remained a crucial element of judicial review for if there were no reasons then there was nothing which could be reviewed. Accordingly, section 1(5) of the Arbitration Act 1979 empowered the court to demand reasons from the arbitrators where none had been given, in order to facilitate judicial review. Reasons could not, however, be obtained where the parties had agreed that the award should be made without reasons or where, absent special circumstances, neither party had requested reasons prior to the award being made.

The 1996 Act operates in the following way:

(a) the arbitrators are, subject to contrary agreement, required to give reasons for their award (section 52);
(b) if reasons are given, but are inadequate to allow the court to determine whether an error of law has been made, the court has jurisdiction under section 70(4) to order further and better reasons, and an agreement between the parties that reasons are not to be given, but which is disregarded by the arbitrators, will preclude judicial review or the ordering of further reasons in respect of an application under section 69 based on error of law in the award;
(c) the power of the court under section 70(4) to order further and better reasons is also available where there has been an application to the court challenging the award for want of jurisdiction under section 67[1] or serious irregularity under section 68—reasons can be demanded even if they are to form a part of a separate confidential document[2] and, possibly, even if the parties have agreed to oust the obligation of the arbitrators to give reasons;[3]
(d) as there is an obligation on the arbitrators to give reasons in the absence of contrary agreement, the power of the court to require them to do so has been removed from the legislation—an agreement that reasons shall not be given is expressly stated to amount to an exclusion of judicial review by section 69(1) of the Act;
(e) if the arbitrators are obliged to give reasons but do not do so, the proper remedy is an application to the court under section 68 on the ground of serious irregularity; and
(f) if the parties have by agreement excluded judicial review for errors of law under section 69(1), the court has no jurisdiction under the Act to order reasons or better reasons.

Section 52(4) does not attempt to define exactly what is meant by "reasons", although the cases demonstrate that a reasoned award should set out the arbitrators' findings and their conclusions based upon those findings with sufficient clarity for a court to determine what those conclusions actually were.[4] It has been emphasised that it is not necessarily helpful for an award to contain a great deal of detail as to the conflicting assertions of the parties which have no real relevance to the ultimate conclusion.[5] It is not expected that reasons given by arbitrators, particularly trade arbitrators, are to display "the accuracy of wording or the cogency of expression that is required of a judgment".[6] In particular, there is no justification for the arbitrators to appoint a legally qualified draftsman to produce a formal detailed award akin to a work of literature,[7] and if legal advice has been taken there is no need for that advice to be appended to the award if the reasons for the award are otherwise clear.[8]

1. Reasons are of less significance here, as a challenge under s. 67 is not by way of judicial review of the award but by way of substantive rehearing.
2. *Tame Shipping Ltd* v. *Easy Navigation Ltd, The Easy Rider* [2004] 2 Lloyd's Rep 626.
3. The *obiter* view of Moore-Bick J in *Tame Shipping Ltd* v. *Easy Navigation Ltd, The Easy Rider* [2004] 2 Lloyd's Rep 626.
4. *Trave Schiffahrtsgesellschaft mbH Co KG* v. *Ninemia Maritime Corporation, The Niedersachsen (No 2)* [1986] 1 Lloyd's Rep 393.
5. *Transcatalana de Commercio SA* v. *Incobrasa Industrial e Commercial Brazileira SA* [1995] 1 Lloyd's Rep 215.
6. *Per* Colman J in *General Feeds Inc Panama* v. *Slobodna Plovidba Yugoslavia* [1999] 1 Lloyd's Rep 688, 695. See also *Zermalt Holdings SA* v. *Nu-Life Upholstery Repairs Ltd* [1985] 2 EGLR 14.
7. *Agrimex Ltd* v. *Tradigrain SA* [2003] 2 Lloyd's Rep 537.
8. *Home of Homes Ltd* v. *Hammersmith and Fulham London Borough Council* (2003) 92 Con LR 48.

Section 52(4) excludes the obligation to give reasons where the award is an agreed award made under section 51. In the absence of reasons, the award is not challengeable on a point of law under section 69 of the Act, so that the effect of this provision is to prevent one party from seeking to overturn an agreed award by challenging the legal basis on which it was made. Section 52(4) also excludes reasons where the parties have agreed that no reasons are required. As previously mentioned, by virtue of section 69(1), such an agreement is effective to oust any judicial review on the basis of error of law.

Section 52(5), following Article 31(3) of the Model Law, requires the award to state the seat of the arbitration. The seat of the arbitration is defined in section 3, and, as was commented on in the Notes to that section, the seat is the arbitration's centre of gravity rather than the particular places in which the arbitrators have from time to time conducted their proceedings. The significance of the seat has been considered earlier,[1] but it is worthy of emphasis that the seat of the arbitration determines the place of the award (under section 53) and, thus, whether the award can be challenged. If the seat is England, the English courts have jurisdiction over the award and may respond to challenges to it, whereas if the seat is a country which is party to the New York Convention the award must be enforced in England more or less without question. Failure by the arbitrators to state the seat would not, however, be likely to render the award liable to be set aside as such failure can rarely give rise to "substantial injustice" as required by section 68 of the 1996 Act.[2]

Section 52(5) also requires the award to be dated. It is to be assumed that the intention of the subsection is to render the date on the award presumptively correct, and this may be relevant in respect of time limits for challenges to it under sections 67 to 69 of the Act, and in respect of alterations to the award or the making of additional awards in the event of error or omission, under section 57 of the Act. The use of the date is a helpful clarification of the law, as previously the date on which an award was made was regarded as the date at which it was signed by the arbitrators or at least subjected to an "expression of final determination",[3] giving rise to problems where the award was signed at different times and where dissenting arbitrators were involved.

Place where award treated as made

53. Unless otherwise agreed by the parties, where the seat of the arbitration is in England and Wales or Northern Ireland, any award in the proceedings shall be treated as made there, regardless of where it was signed, despatched or delivered to any of the parties.

NOTES

Section 53, following Article 31(3) of the Model Law, provides that, subject to contrary agreement, where the seat of the arbitration is England, Wales or Northern Ireland, the seat is to be treated as the place at which the award was made.[4] This would appear to be a deeming provision rather than a mere presumption, and the section goes on to require considerations such as the place of the award's signature or delivery to be disregarded. The same principle is extended to the enforcement of New York Convention awards by section 100(2)(b).

Sections 53 and 100(2)(b) represent a significant change in the law. In *Hiscox* v. *Outhwaite (No 1)*[5] the House of Lords held that an award is made where it is signed. That gave rise to the curious situation in which an arbitration between English parties concerning English liabilities and held in London was held to be a French award merely because the arbitrator signed the award while on a short visit to France. By opting for the seat of the arbitration as the place at which the award is to be regarded as having been made, the curial powers of the English courts over what is in essence

1. See the notes to s. 3, above. See also s. 53, below.
2. DAC Report, para. 250.
3. *Hiscox* v. *Outhwaite (No 1)* [1991] 3 All ER 641.
4. See *Dubai Islamic Bank PJSC* v. *Paymentech Merchant Services* [2001] 1 Lloyd's Rep 65.
5. [1991] 13 All ER 641.

an English arbitration are preserved wherever the award happens to be signed.[1] The section is, of course, of much greater relevance in the context of international arbitrations, where enforcement under the New York Convention may require confirmation of the seat.

Date of award

54.—(1) Unless otherwise agreed by the parties, the tribunal may decide what is to be taken to be the date on which the award was made.

(2) In the absence of any such decision, the date of the award shall be taken to be the date on which it is signed by the arbitrator or, where more than one arbitrator signs the award, by the last of them.

NOTES

The date on which an award is made is probably of greatest significance in determining the running of the limitation period for its enforcement, which is six years from its making,[2] and for the lodging of a challenge to the award, which must be effected within 28 days from its making.[3] It may also be relevant as regards the time fixed by the parties for the making of the award[4] and as regards the correction of the award by the arbitrators.[5] The award may also give the losing party a given period in which to honour the award, running from the date on which the award was made.

The Act provides that the arbitrators, unless prohibited by the parties, may decide the date of the award. In the absence of any such decision, the award is deemed to be made when it is signed by the sole arbitrator, or, if there is more than one arbitrator, by the last of them. It would seem to be irrelevant that the last arbitrator proves to be a dissenting arbitrator, although if such arbitrator declines to sign the award, it is no doubt open to the other two arbitrators subsequently to decide that the date on which the award is made is not related to the signature of the dissenting arbitrator.

Notification of award

55.—(1) The parties are free to agree on the requirements as to notification of the award to the parties.

(2) If there is no such agreement, the award shall be notified to the parties by service on them of copies of the award, which shall be done without delay after the award is made.

(3) Nothing in this section affects section 56 (power to withhold award in case of non-payment).

NOTES

Section 55(1) allows the parties to fix by agreement the method by which the award is to be notified to them. In the absence of agreement, section 55(2), following Article 31(4) of the Model Law,

1. In *Hiscox* v. *Outhwaite* it had been possible to argue that, given that the award was a French award, it had to be enforced in England as a New York Convention award, rather than an English award, thereby precluding any judicial review of the award. The House of Lords, by a construction of the Arbitration Act 1975 which was little short of judicial sleight of hand, rejected this argument and held that the English courts did not lose curial jurisdiction despite the fact that the award was not made in England. The need for such artificiality has now been circumvented.

2. Or, at the outside, six years from the expiry of any period set out in the award for compliance: see the Notes to s. 13.

3. Section 70(3).

4. Section 50 permits the time to be extended.

5. Section 57 permits correction or the making of an additional award.

requires the arbitrators to serve a copy of the award on all of the parties without delay. This duty is, however, by virtue of section 55(3), subject to the right of the arbitrators—under section 56 of the Act—to withhold the award as security for the payment of their fees.

The section provides that the award must be notified to both parties. This prevents the situation in which the award has been notified to the successful party only, and they have sat on it until the time limits for appeal have passed before disclosing its existence to the losing party (DAC Report, paragraph 255). If there has been a delay in notifying the award, and this has prejudiced the losing party in respect of any appeal or application in respect of the award, the court is able to extend time under its general power in section 79 of the Act.

Power to withhold award in case of non-payment

56.—(1) The tribunal may refuse to deliver an award to the parties except upon full payment of the fees and expenses of the arbitrators.

(2) If the tribunal refuses on that ground to deliver an award, a party to the arbitral proceedings may (upon notice to the other parties and the tribunal) apply to the court, which may order that—

- (a) the tribunal shall deliver the award on the payment into court by the applicant of the fees and expenses demanded, or such lesser amount as the court may specify,
- (b) the amount of the fees and expenses properly payable shall be determined by such means and upon such terms as the court may direct, and
- (c) out of the money paid into court there shall be paid out such fees and expenses as may be found to be properly payable and the balance of the money (if any) shall be paid out to the applicant.

(3) For this purpose the amount of fees and expenses properly payable is the amount the applicant is liable to pay under section 28 or any agreement relating to the payment of the arbitrators.

(4) No application to the court may be made where there is any available arbitral process for appeal or review of the amount of the fees or expenses demanded.

(5) References in this section to arbitration include an arbitrator who has ceased to act and an umpire who has not replaced the other arbitrators.

(6) The above provisions of this section also apply in relation to any arbitral or other institution or person vested by the parties with powers in relation to the delivery of the tribunal's award.

As they so apply, the references to the fees and expenses of the arbitrators shall be construed as including the fees and expenses of that institution or person.

(7) The leave of the court is required for any appeal from a decision of the court under this section.

(8) Nothing in this section shall be construed as excluding an application under section 28 where payment has been made to the arbitrators in order to obtain the award.

NOTES

The heading to this section is perhaps somewhat misleading, as it is concerned not just with the arbitrators' right to withhold the award but also the right of the parties, in certain circumstances, to challenge the amount of fees charged in it. The section is a codification of the common law and of section 19(1) of the Arbitration Act 1950, and should be read in conjunction with sections 28 (right of arbitrators to be remunerated) and 59 to 65 (award of costs and fees in the award as between the parties to the arbitration). The section is of necessity mandatory.

Section 56(1) codifies the common law right of arbitrators to retain the award, by way of lien, as security for payment of outstanding fees and expenses.[1] This provision takes priority over the normal duty of the arbitrators to release copies of the award to the parties as soon as it is made, under section 55.

Section 56(2), re-enacting with a significant modification section 19(1) of the Arbitration Act 1950, deals with the situation in which the arbitrators have exercised their right of lien under section 56(1) and the party seeking the release of the award wishes to contest the level of fees or expenses. In such a case, an application may be made to the court, following which the award is to be released on condition that the fees or expenses demanded are paid into court. The application is to be by way of arbitration claim form, which must be served on the other parties and they must be made parties to the claim,[2] and the arbitrators themselves are to be served and made parties.[3] The court must direct a review and adjustment of the fees or expenses, and depending upon the outcome order payment of such fees as it regards as reasonable (under the assessment formula in section 28 of the Act, as applied by section 56(3)):[4] this constitutes a form of assessment under a different name. The right of a party to challenge the amount of the arbitrators' fees and expenses is, however, ousted in three cases:

(a) section 56(2) does not apply where there is a written agreement fixing the amount of fees under section 55(3)—section 56(2) is a default provision preventing overcharging by arbitrators where there has been no previous agreement;
(b) section 56(2) does not protect the applicant where the arbitrators have been willing to release the award prior to payment, relying on action to enforce their right to fees rather than the statutory lien. Nevertheless, section 28(2) permits an application to the court for the arbitrators' fees and expenses to be considered and adjusted even though the award has been released without any insistence on payment; and
(c) section 56(2) can be used only where the party seeking release of the award refuses to pay—once payment is made, the right to challenge under section 56(2) is lost, although an independent right to apply to the court for the arbitrators' fees and expenses to be considered and adjusted—under section 28(2)—can be pressed into use. This is confirmed by section 56(8).

In addition, section 56(4) precludes any application to the court if there is some other agreed method for assessing the arbitrators' fees and expenses: although this might be thought to be where the arbitration has taken place under the auspices of an arbitral institution, none of the main bodies (ICC, LCIA, AAA, UNCITRAL or CIArb) has any formal process for reviewing the tribunal's fees. In the case of the ICC Rules, the tribunal's fees will have been set according to the scale of fees and it is, therefore, difficult to see in such a case on what basis the court would interfere with the tribunal's fees providing that they were in line with the applicable ICC scale.[5]

The main change introduced by section 56(2) is the power of the court in section 56(2)(a) to order that a sum less than that claimed by the arbitrators for fees and expenses is to be paid into court, rather than—as under section 19 of the 1950 Act—the full amount claimed. The DAC Report, paragraph 259, noted that this discretion was a safeguard against the possibility that an arbitrator might demand an extortionately large sum which cannot be afforded, and by this means defeat the possible use of the mechanism in section 56.

Section 56(3) confirms that a written agreement fixing the arbitrators' fees cannot be reopened, and the arbitrators have an absolute right to withhold the award pending the honouring of the agreement and the payment of the fees in this situation.

1. *R* v. *South Devon Railway Co* (1850) 15 QB 1043.
2. CPR r. 62.6(2)–(3).
3. CPR r. 62.6(1).
4. See above.
5. See ICC Rules of Arbitration, Arts 30 and 31 and Appendix III.

Section 56(5) extends the benefit of the lien to arbitrators who have ceased to act by the time of the making of the award (assuming that they remain entitled to their fees)[1] and to an umpire who has not been required to enter on the reference.[2]

Section 56(6) extends the benefit of the lien to the arbitration institution responsible for supervising the arbitration and whose costs and fees have not been met.

Section 56(7) contains the familiar provision preventing an appeal from any decision of the court under section 53(2) without the permission of the court. The "court" means the trial judge and not the Court of Appeal.[3]

Section 56(8) provides that the section does not affect the right of a party to challenge the fees and expenses by means of an application under section 28. A party who wishes to make a challenge under section 28 is, by reason of section 56(8), not estopped from doing so by having made payment in order to release the award from the lien.

As a practical matter, if the tribunal seeks further costs as a condition of releasing the award, it will have given no indication as to which party has won and which has lost. It will, therefore, usually ask each party to contribute a half share of the remaining amount. In such circumstances, it is always open to one party to pay the full amount (i.e., to pay its own share and that of the other party or parties), and (if successful) to seek to recover those costs as part of the award from the losing party. In any event, a party seeking an order of the court under section 56 should consider carefully whether it wishes to pursue that right, rather than pay and challenge under section 64(2) (see the Notes to section 64), particularly if it is considering appealing against or challenging the award in some way. This is because the 28-day period from the date of the award for challenges or appeals against awards under section 70(3) is not extended automatically merely because an application has been made under section 56. Accordingly, since an application under section 56 is unlikely to be completed in anywhere near enough time to mount any subsequent challenge, once the award is released, a party may risk losing the right of challenge or appeal (subject to a separate application after the 28-day period has elapsed to extend time under section 80(5)).[4] However, the circumstances in which both parties refuse to pay will be rare, unless neither party is confident enough to consider it has won and, therefore, pay the whole amount sought, then seek reimbursement from the other (if correct!).

Correction of award or additional award

57.—(1) The parties are free to agree on the powers of the tribunal to correct an award or make an additional award.

(2) If or to the extent there is no such agreement, the following provisions apply.

(3) The tribunal may on its own initiative or on the application of a party—

(a) correct an award so as to remove any clerical mistake or error arising from an accidental slip or omission or clarify or remove any ambiguity in the award, or

(b) make an additional award in respect of any claim (including a claim for interest or costs) which was presented to the tribunal but was not dealt with in the award.

1. See s. 24(4), which empowers a court to reduce or wipe out the arbitrators' entitlement to fees if they have been removed under that section.

2. See ss. 21 and 28(6) and the notes thereto.

3. *Henry Boot Construction (UK) Ltd* v. *Malmaison Hotel (Manchester) Ltd* [2001] 1 QB 388; *Athletic Union of Constantinople* v. *National Basketball Association* [2002] 1 Lloyd's Rep 305; *Virdee* v. *Virdi* [2003] EWCA Civ 41.

4. This issue was foreshadowed by the DAC in the February 1996 report at para 294. The DAC preferred to leave the question to be decided by the court on an application for extension of time under what became s. 80(5): see the Notes to that section.

These powers shall not be exercised without first affording to the other parties a reasonable opportunity to make representations to the tribunal.

(4) Any application for the exercise of those powers must be made within 28 days of the date of the award or such longer period as the parties may agree.

(5) Any correction of an award shall be made within 28 days of the date the application was received by the tribunal or, where the correction is made by the tribunal on its own initiative, within 28 days of the date of the award or, in either case, such longer period as the parties may agree.

(6) Any additional award shall be made within 56 days of the date of the original award or such longer period as the parties may agree.

(7) Any correction of an award shall form part of the award.

NOTES

Section 57, which is based on Article 33 of the Model Law, is concerned to allow the arbitrators themselves to correct errors in their award.

The effect of section 57 is to extend the provisions of the 1950 Act and to reduce the number of cases in which recourse to the courts for an order remitting the award will be necessary. Indeed, the concluding words of section 68(1) do not permit matters of serious irregularity (including errors and omissions of various types) to be considered by the court until the corrective powers of the arbitrators themselves have been exhausted. This is a crucial aspect of the operation of section 57, and goes to the jurisdiction of the court.[1] For this reason the scope of section 57 is a matter of major significance where an application under section 68 is being contemplated. It should here be noted that under section 70(3) any application to the court under section 68 must be brought within 28 days from the date of the award, or from the date when the party applying for the relief under section 68 was notified of the result of any arbitral process of appeal or "review". The earlier time limit may be impossible to meet where there has been an initial application to the arbitrators to correct their award under section 57: the balance of authority is in favour of the proposition that the running of the 28-day period laid down for a section 68 application is triggered by the issue of the corrected award or the refusal to issue a corrected award, and not from the date of the original award.[2]

Section 57(1) allows the parties to set down the powers of the arbitrators to correct their awards. In the absence of any express agreement, the default powers of the arbitrators to correct errors, introduced by section 57(2), are contained in section 57(3), and these may be exercised by the arbitrators either on their own initiative or on application by a party.

Section 57(3)(a) allows the arbitrators to correct clerical errors and also to "clarify or remove any ambiguity in the award". The correction of clerical errors deals with the situation in which the arbitrators have failed to write what was intended by them.[3] The power also extends to errors in computation, where the figures have either been incorrectly transcribed or incorrectly calculated.[4] It also covers the accidental omission of a part of the award,[5] including a deficiency in, or a total

1. See the notes to s. 68, below.

2. *Blackdale Ltd* v. *McLean Homes South East Ltd* 2001, unreported; *Al Hadha Trading Co* v. *Tradigrain SA* [2002] 2 Lloyd's Rep 512. The earlier decision in *R C Pillar & Sons* v. *Edwards* [2001] CILL 1799, which requires an application to the court to be made within 28 days of the original award, complies with the strict wording of the legislation but is unworkable and probably no longer good law. The difficulty is brought about by the fact that while s. 70(2) forbids any challenge or review unless any right to either an "arbitral process of appeal or review" or to any recourse under s. 57 has been exhausted, s. 70(3) refers to the former and not the latter, so that a corrected award under s. 57 cannot be considered as an "arbitral process of appeal or review" for the purposes of s. 70(3).

3. A "slip of the pen". See, under the 1996 Act, *Gannet Shipping Ltd* v. *Eastrade Commodities Inc* [2001] 1 Lloyd's Rep 713.

4. *Omnibridge Consulting Ltd* v. *Clearsprings (Management) Ltd*, 2004, unreported.

5. *Pancommerce SA* v. *Veecheema BV* [1983] 2 Lloyd's Rep 304; *The Montan* [1985] 1 All ER 520. This is now specifically covered by s. 57(3)(b).

absence of, the reasons for the award.[1] By this means section 57(3)(a) can thus be used to require the arbitrators to show whether issues put to them were, in fact, considered by them.[2] The slip rule does not, however, entitle the arbitrators to review their award on its merits in order to decide whether their original views were right or to review the evidence;[3] a point confirmed by cases decided under the 1996 Act.[4] On the same basis, the slip rule cannot be used by a party to seek to overturn the arbitrators' reasoning.[5] The relevant distinction here is between an award the reasons for which are opaque so that the evidential route cannot be traced (within the slip rule), and an award the reasons for which are clear but unfavourable to the applicant (outside the slip rule). The addition to the slip rule of the power to correct ambiguities probably adds little to the previous law, although it puts beyond doubt the point that, short of altering the analysis and outcome of the award, wide powers are intended. It should further be noted that ambiguities can be corrected by the arbitrators on their own motion, whereas under the Model Law an application to the arbitrators by one of the parties is required.

Section 57(3)(b) allows the arbitrators to make a further award on any "claim", including interest and costs, which was presented to the tribunal but was omitted from the original award: as noted above, it was likely that this falls within the scope of the basic slip rule, but the position is put beyond doubt by section 57(3)(b). Failure to make an award on a particular matter should be distinguished from the situation in which the arbitrators have made a final substantive award but have reserved costs for a further award: in that situation the arbitrators retain power to make that award under section 47 and there is no need to invoke section 57.[6] Again, the arbitrators can act in response to an application from one of the parties or (unlike the Model Law) on their own initiative. The word "claim" for this purpose refers to a claim in respect of which a remedy is sought, and not a particular feature of a claim. Thus, if the arbitrators have failed to decide whether a contract can be avoided for misrepresentation a claim has been left unresolved, but if they have decided that the contract cannot be avoided then section 57(2)(b) does not empower them to reconsider the evidence on the question whether there was sufficient inducement[7] as inducement is not a "claim" in its own right.[8] Section 57(3)(b) has no application to the case in which the arbitrators have held over a particular matter for consideration in the event that the parties have failed to reach agreement themselves.[9] It should be emphasised that section 57(3)(b) applies only if the claim is one presented to the arbitrators: it is not available if the claim is one which was not originally presented to arbitrators.[10]

The proviso to section 57(3) sets out the procedural obligation on the arbitrators to allow the parties to make representations on any intended change.

If the tribunal has ruled that it has no jurisdiction and thus has become *functus officio*, it has no power to hear an application under the slip rule to reverse that initial award.[11]

Section 57(4)–(6) sets out the time limits for the operation of section 57. In all cases, references to the date of the making of the award are to the date on which it was signed,[12] and the time limits

1. *Groundshire* v. *VHE Construction* [2001] BLR 395; *Al Hadha Trading Co* v. *Tradigrain SA* [2002] 2 Lloyd's Rep 512; *Torch Offshore LLC* v. *Cable Shipping Inc* [2004] 2 Lloyd's Rep 446.

2. *Torch Offshore LLC* v. *Cable Shipping Inc* [2004] 2 Lloyd's Rep 446.

3. *Sutherland Co* v. *Hannevig Brothers Ltd* [1921] 90 LJKB 225; *Fuga AG* v. *Bunge AG* [1975] 2 Lloyd's Rep 192; *King* v. *Thomas McKenna Ltd* [1991] 2 QB 480.

4. *Bloor Construction (UK) Ltd* v. *Bowner & Kirkland (London) Ltd* [2000] BLR 314; *Al Hadha Trading Co* v. *Tradigrain SA* [2002] 2 Lloyd's Rep 512; *Hawk Shipping Ltd* v. *Cron Navigation Ltd* [2003] EWHC 1828 (Comm); *Torch Offshore LLC* v. *Cable Shipping Inc* [2004] 2 Lloyd's Rep 446.

5. *World Trade Corporation Ltd* v. *Czarnikow Sugar Ltd* [2004] 2 All ER (Comm) 813.

6. *Sea Trade Maritime Corporation* v. *Hellenic Mutual War Risks Association (Bermuda) Ltd, The Athena* [2007] 1 Lloyd's Rep 280.

7. *Torch Offshore LLC* v. *Cable Shipping Inc* [2004] 2 Lloyd's Rep 446.

8. See also: *World Trade Corporation Ltd* v. *Czarnikow Sugar Ltd* [2004] 2 All ER (Comm) 813.

9. *Cf. M/S Alghanim Industries Inc* v. *Skandia International Insurance Corporation* [2001] 2 All ER (Comm) 30.

10. *Pirtek* v. *Deanswood* [2005] 2 Lloyd's Rep 728 (no claim made for interest—not awardable under s. 57(3)(b)).

11. *Dredging and Construction Co Ltd* v. *Delta Civil Engineering Ltd* (1999) 68 Con LR 87.

12. By virtue of s. 54.

laid down may be extended by the parties' agreement.[1] There are no formal requirements for an application to the arbitrators under section 57: a request for the award to be reviewed will suffice.[2] The time limits are as follows.

(a) Any application to the arbitrators for the correction of the award or for the making of an additional award must be made within 28 days of the date on which the award was made (section 57(4), reduced from 30 days in the July 1995 Bill to avoid time expiring on a weekend). The arbitrators must make the correction within a further 28 days running from the receipt of the application (section 57(5)). An application is treated as having been received when it is served within the meaning of the default rules on service in section 76 of the 1996 Act: this means that if an application is sent but not seen (e.g., because the arbitrator is away at the time), the date of the application is the date on which it would in the ordinary course of events have arrived.[3]

(b) If the arbitrators make an additional award rather than merely correct their original award, that award must in any event be made within 56 days (reduced from 60 days in the July 1995 Bill), running from the date on which the first award was made (which may be more or less than 28 days from the date on which they receive the application—section 57(5)).

(c) If the arbitrators act on their own initiative, they must correct the award within 28 days of its making, or issue an additional award within 56 days of the making of the original award.

(d) The above time limits may not be extended by the arbitrators—this contrasts with the July 1995 Bill, which allowed an enlargement of time by them to such extent as the justice of the case requires; it is nevertheless open to the court on application to enlarge time under its general powers in section 79.

Time may be extended by the court under the general provisions in section 79 of the 1996 Act.[4]

Section 57(7) treats any correction of an award to form part of the original award. In the event that an award is varied or reissued as a result of the operation of the section 57 process, the arbitrators have the power to make a consequential adjustment to any award of costs made by them: accordingly, there is no need for an application to be made to the court under section 68 for a costs award to be varied in these circumstances.[5]

Effect of award

58.—(1) Unless otherwise agreed by the parties, an award made by the tribunal pursuant to an arbitration agreement is final and binding both on the parties and on any persons claiming through or under them.

(2) This does not affect the right of a person to challenge the award by any available arbitral process of appeal or review or in accordance with the provisions of this Part.

NOTES

This section, which was inserted by the December 1995 Bill, states that the award is binding on the parties to it and on any parties claiming through or under them, subject to any review or appeal which may be sought under the Act. The common law regarded the obligation to enforce an arbitration award as arising out of an implied term in the arbitration agreement itself rather than the

1. *Home of Homes Ltd* v. *Hammersmith and Fulham London Borough Council* (2003) 92 Con LR 48.
2. *R C Pillar & Sons* v. *Edwards* [2001] CILL 1799.
3. *R C Pillar & Sons* v. *Edwards* [2001] CILL 1799.
4. *Pirtek* v. *Deanswood* [2005] 2 Lloyd's Rep 728, where no application was made but the court was satisfied that it would have been refused by reason of the 17-month delay before the applicant had sought to have the award corrected. Guidelines were laid down in *Gold Coast Ltd* v. *Naval Gijon SA* [2006] 2 Lloyd's Rep 400, where time was extended by reason of the applicant's oversight in spotting the error in the award and its immediate application under s. 79 for retrospective relief.
5. *Gannet Shipping Ltd* v. *Eastrade Commodities Inc* [2002] 1 Lloyd's Rep 713.

agreement to which the arbitration clause applied. It is for this reason that the limitation period for the enforcement of an award runs from the date on which the award should have been honoured rather than from the date on which the underlying contract was broken,[1] and that a vessel cannot be arrested to enforce an arbitration award arising out of a charterparty as the jurisdiction of the Admiralty Court to arrest a vessel is to enforce the charterparty rather than the award under the entirely separate arbitration agreement.[2] A party who seeks to challenge the award in a place other than that of the seat is in breach of his statutory duty under section 58[3] and is liable in damages.[4]

As at common law, an award remains a private matter between the parties, and cannot directly affect the rights of third parties. This matter was discussed in the Notes to section 35.

For the distinction between an award and an interim or procedural decision, see the Notes to section 47.

Costs of the Arbitration

Costs of the arbitration

59.—(1) References in this Part to the costs of the arbitration are to—

(a) the arbitrators' fees and expenses,

(b) the fees and expenses of any arbitral institution concerned, and

(c) the legal or other costs of the parties.

(2) Any such reference includes the costs of or incidental to any proceedings to determine the amount of the recoverable costs of the arbitration (see section 63).

NOTES

In the modern world of arbitration, costs have become an extremely important issue for the parties. Many arbitrations involving, for example, large corporations represented by major law firms and long hearings, particularly if large sums of money are at stake, can involve costs running into millions of pounds. In some very large disputes, the tribunal's fees alone may reach seven figures.[5]

For arbitrations proceeding in England, the Act provides (in sections 59 to 65) a fairly comprehensive code dealing with costs. It should be borne in mind that the sections are non-mandatory (with the exception of section 60), so the parties are free to agree how costs are dealt with. Most major arbitral bodies contain within their rules provisions concerning costs.[6] In the absence of any agreement, the Act will apply.

The 1996 Act replaced the concepts of "costs of the reference" and "costs of the award" with the single term "costs of the arbitration" which is defined in this section, and the allocation of which as between the parties is dealt with by sections 61 to 65. The costs of the arbitration are now generally understood to include:

1. *Argomet Motoimport Ltd* v. *Maulden Engineering Co (Beds) Ltd* [1985] 2 All ER 436.

2. *SC Rolinay Sea Star Srl* v. *Owners and Charterers of the Ship "Bumbesti", The Bumbesti* [1999] 2 Lloyd's Rep 481, not following *The Saint Anna* [1983] 1 Lloyd's Rep 637.

3. *Associated Electric and Gas Insurance Services Ltd* v. *European Reinsurance Co of Zurich* [2003] 1 WLR 1041; *A* v. *B* [2007] 1 Lloyd's Rep 237.

4. *C* v. *D* [2008] 1 Lloyd's Rep 239.

5. Arbitrations proceeding under the auspices of the ICC are subject to a "costs calculator", in which the amount in dispute and the number of arbitrators can be inputted into the online version of the calculator, which then produces the minima and maxima for the tribunal's fees. E.g., in the case of an arbitration where the sum in dispute is $1 billion, the maximum sum payable in respect of the tribunal's fees and administrative expenses exceeds $2.5 million. See www.iccwbo.org/court/arbitration/id4097/index.html.

6. See, e.g.: LCIA Rules of Arbitration, Arts 24 and 28; ICC Rules of Arbitration, Arts 30 and 31; AAA Rules of Arbitration, Arts 31 to 33; UNCITRAL Rules, Arts 40 and 41.

(a) the costs of the tribunal, that is, the arbitrators' fees and expenses, the costs of experts, legal advisers or assessors appointed by the arbitrators, and the administrative costs of any arbitral institution involved;
(b) the necessarily incidental costs of the arbitration, for example, hiring accommodation for the hearing and arranging for recording and transcription of hearings (such costs are very often contributed to jointly by the parties before the hearing, that is, in the case of two parties, each side agrees to contribute a half share of such costs in advance directly to the body concerned); and
(c) the legal and other costs of the parties incurred in presenting their case, including the lawyers' fees, witness expenses, experts engaged by a party, translation fees, accommodation costs of the party and/or their legal representatives, etc.

As will be seen, the following sections of the 1996 Act are concerned with the principle of allocating liability for the costs of the arbitration as between the parties, as well as with determining the amount of recoverable costs. Four matters arise in relation to the allocation of costs:

(a) *The determination of the amount of the fees and expenses of the arbitrators and other costs incurred by the tribunal related to the arbitration which are to be included in an award of costs for allocation between the parties.* The amount of the tribunal's fees and expenses is very rarely agreed in advance with the parties. Nevertheless, the almost universal practice in England is for the tribunal to provide an estimate in advance of any hearing or important stage of the arbitration of the likely fees, and require each party to deposit the requisite share of costs with the tribunal or with the arbitral institution, if any, some time before any award is made. Upon making any award dealing with costs as between the parties, the tribunal will probably confirm the amount of its fees and expenses, and confirm who, as between the parties, is to bear responsibility for them. In the event that the tribunal has already been paid in advance, any party may challenge the amount of the tribunal's fees or expenses by applying under either section 28 or section 64 (see the Notes to those sections). If the tribunal has not been paid in advance, and seeks a further sum from the parties as a condition of releasing its award, the procedure for challenging the amount is set out in section 56 (see the Notes to section 56). Under either section, the overriding principle is that (absent any agreement) only a reasonable sum representing the arbitrators' fees and expenses may be included in the award of costs as between the parties. It should be emphasised that the amount which may be included in the award may differ from the amount in respect of which the parties owe joint and several liability to the arbitrators under section 28. The effect of section 28 is to make the parties jointly and severally liable either for the agreed figure, or for a reasonable figure, determined in the case of dispute by the court on application under section 28(2).[1]
(b) *The allocation of the arbitrators' fees and expenses, determined under (a) above, as between the parties.* The allocation is to be made by the arbitrators under section 61. Any challenge to the allocation may only take effect as a challenge to the award itself on the ground of serious irregularity, under section 68 (i.e., failure to act impartially between the parties when allocating costs). However, challenges to awards under section 68 based on the allocation of costs are naturally rare, and successful ones probably rarer still.
(c) *The amount of the costs of the parties.* These are to be determined by the arbitrators under section 63(3) or left to the determination of the court under section 63(4). See the notes to section 63.
(d) *The allocation of party costs as between the parties.* Party costs (which will almost always include the costs of, for example, hiring accommodation etc) will form part of the costs of the arbitration, and will usually be allocated as between the parties by the arbitrators in the award of costs under section 61.[2] That allocation is subject to challenge but only by means

1. For a rare instance in which the fees of the tribunal were adjusted under s. 28, see: *Hussmann (Europe)* v. *Al Ameen Development & Trade Co* [2000] 2 Lloyd's Rep 83.

2. The tribunal may make an award dealing with the substantive issues and costs together, or, as is more common in larger arbitrations, make an award dealing with costs once the substantive issues have been disposed of.

of an attack on the award itself under section 68, based on serious irregularity or under section 69 as an error of law.[1] As above, successful challenges to awards in relation to allocation of costs are rarely likely to be brought, let alone succeed.

Agreement to pay costs in any event

60. An agreement which has the effect that a party is to pay the whole or part of the costs of the arbitration in any event is only valid if made after the dispute in question has arisen.

NOTES

Section 60 is a mandatory provision which negatives any pre-dispute agreement between the parties allocating costs between them by requiring one or more of the parties to pay all or part of their own costs. The purpose of the section is to prevent the situation in which a party who wishes to pursue his claim in arbitration finds that he is unable to do so because, whatever the result, he has agreed to bear some or all of his own costs. These provisions were at one time common in insurance policies. Although clauses of this type have necessarily fallen into disuse, the DAC Report, paragraph 267, thought it unwise to repeal the provision lest such clauses re-emerged. The section is concerned with agreement as to the ultimate liability for costs only: an agreement that the parties are to pay the fees of the arbitrators equally does not contravene section 60, as such an agreement is concerned with the act of payment of fees only, rather than the manner in which liability for them is ultimately to be allocated between the parties.[2]

Section 60 does, however, permit such an agreement to be made where the decision to go to arbitration is taken after the dispute has arisen, as it is to be assumed that in such a case there can be no pressure or obligation to arbitrate and the costs agreement can be at arm's length.[3]

Award of costs

61.—(1) The tribunal may make an award allocating the costs of the arbitration as between the parties, subject to any agreement of the parties.

(2) Unless the parties otherwise agree, the tribunal shall award costs on the general principle that costs should follow the event except where it appears to the tribunal that in the circumstances this is not appropriate in relation to the whole or part of the costs.

NOTES

The allocation of the recoverable costs of the arbitration between the parties is, subject to the contrary agreement of the parties, within the jurisdiction of the arbitrators as part of their award by virtue of section 61(1).

Prior to the Act, there was a long-standing common law principle that, exceptional circumstances aside, costs were to follow the event,[4] and this principle was given statutory force by section 61(2).[5]

1. An appeal under s. 69 against a costs award was successfully brought in *Fence Gate Ltd* v. *NEL Construction Ltd* [2001] Con LR 41, though the correctness of the decision in that case was doubted by Cooke J in *Demco Investments and Commercial SA* v. *SE Banken Forsakring Holding Aktiebolag* [2005] 2 Lloyd's Rep 250.

2. *Carter* v. *Simpson Associates (Architects) Ltd* [2004] 2 Lloyd's Rep 512. Such an agreement overrides the basic rule in s. 28 that the parties are jointly and severally liable to the arbitrators for their fees.

3. See *Virdee* v. *Virdi* [2003] EWCA (Civ) 41, in which the trial judge ruled that the parties had entered into a post-dispute agreement each to bear the costs of their legal representation. The Court of Appeal disagreed, holding that the effect of the agreement was to exclude legal representation entirely so that no question of costs arose.

4. The root case is *Smeaton, Hanscomb & Co Ltd* v. *Sassoon I Setty, Son & Co (No 2)* [1953] 2 All ER 1588.

5. See *Newfield* v. *Tomlinson* [2004] EWHC 3051 (TCC).

The parties are free to contract out of the general rule,[1] and the arbitrators themselves may depart from it where they consider that the general rule is inappropriate.

Some guidance may be afforded to arbitrators acting within what may be regarded as a purely domestic arbitration by reference to the approach to costs adopted in civil proceedings under the Civil Procedure Rules (CPR). Under CPR Part 44 the allowing or disallowing of costs is very much a part of a court's case management functions; and it is apparent that a party who fails to prepare properly, delays or does not take advantage of settlement possibilities will be punished by costs. The rule that costs follow the event remains intact, but much will turn on the manner in which the parties have conducted the proceedings. The relevant part of CPR Part 44 is as follows:

> 44.3(1) The court has discretion as to—
> (a) whether costs are payable by one party to another;
> (b) the amount of those costs; and
> (c) when they are to be paid.
> (2) If the court decides to make an order about costs—
> (a) the general rule is that the unsuccessful party will be ordered to pay the costs of the successful party; but
> (b) the court may make a different order.
>
> . . .
>
> (4) In deciding what order (if any) to make about costs, the court must have regard to all the circumstances, including—
> (a) the conduct of all the parties;
> (b) whether a party has succeeded on part of his case, even if he has not been wholly successful; and
> (c) any . . . admissible offer to settle made by a party which is drawn to the court's attention.
> (5) The conduct of the parties includes—
> (a) conduct before, as well as during, the proceedings, and in particular the extent to which the parties follow any relevant pre-action protocol;
> (b) whether it was reasonable for a party to raise, pursue or contest a particular allegation or issue;
> (c) the manner in which a party has pursued or defended his case or a particular allegation or issue;
> (d) whether a claimant who has succeeded in his claim, in whole or in part, exaggerated his claim.
> (6) The orders which the court may make under this rule include an order that a party must pay—
> (a) a proportion of another party's costs;
> (b) a stated amount in respect of another party's costs;
> (c) costs from or until a certain date only;
> (d) costs incurred before proceedings have begun;
> (e) costs relating to particular steps taken in the proceedings;
> (f) costs relating only to a distinct part of the proceedings; and
> (g) interest on costs from or until a certain date, including a date before judgment.
> (7) Where the court would otherwise consider making an order under paragraph (6)(e), it must instead, if practicable, make an order under paragraph (6)(a) or (c).

Arbitrators would be well advised to take note of these guiding principles, given that their duty is to act judicially, and that if they allow the determination of costs to be undertaken by the court under section 63(4), the court will certainly follow the CPR guidelines set out above. Any failure to act judicially, by taking into account irrelevant considerations in the award of costs, has been classified

1. If they do depart from the rule, the parties have the right to be heard: *Gbangbola* v. *Smith & Sherriff Ltd* [1998] 3 All ER 730; *Fence Gate Ltd* v. *NEL Construction Ltd* (2001) 82 Con LR 41; *Linpave Building Ltd* v. *Gillingham FC Ltd* 2002, unreported (John Tackaberry, QC) (which also held that any departure from the usual rule should be accompanied by reasons for so doing).

as an error of law challengeable under section 69 of the 1996 Act[1] assuming, of course, that the other conditions for the grant of permission to appeal are satisfied.

In practice, it may be difficult to determine whether a party has "won", that is, to determine what the "event" is that should be followed. In some cases, a party will have brought several discrete claims, and succeeded in some and failed in others. In those circumstances, if the tribunal has not already made individual issue-based costs orders, it may consider it appropriate either to reduce the successful claimant's costs as proportionately as it can to reflect the measure of success, or in fact order that there should be no order as to costs, so that each side will end up bearing its own costs. Even where the "event" is clear, in that a party can easily be said to have "won", arbitrators may deem it appropriate to order that costs should not follow the event. In particular, where it considers that one party has behaved unreasonably during the reference, particularly in a way in which costs have been incurred by the other party unnecessarily, for example, by raising frivolous issues, or pursuing a number of hopeless claims or defences to the end. In those circumstances, the tribunal may regard itself as entirely justified in penalising the badly behaving party with an appropriate order, usually by discounting the amount of costs that would otherwise be payable to that party. If the badly behaving party has lost the arbitration, the tribunal may regard itself as entitled to award costs against that party on an indemnity basis (see the Notes to section 63). In every case, the tribunal ought to have regard to the overall result, and to all the surrounding circumstances, in determining the appropriate and ultimate costs result, and ought to express in clear terms why it has reached the result it has. If it does so, the award (at least insofar as regards costs) is likely to be unimpeachable.

Subject to the above, costs will ordinarily "follow the event" provided that a party has been at least partially successful. A respondent to a monetary sum should, therefore, be concerned about the risk of having an award made against them for at least some of the amount claimed, with a consequent adverse costs penalty. Since the removal in civil proceedings in April 2007 of payments into court,[2] the methods by which parties faced with claims in civil proceedings and arbitration are not broadly dissimilar. In arbitration proceedings, a party may still protect itself to some extent (so far as costs are concerned) in two ways. The first method is by making a sealed offer (sealed in the sense that an offer is made to the other party, communicated in writing and a copy of the offer, contained in a sealed envelope, is passed to the arbitrators). The envelope may not then be opened until the arbitrators have made all their findings on the merits and before the decision as to costs is made, so as to see whether the offer has been "beaten" by the claimant or not (i.e., whether the claimant has been awarded a higher sum than that offered, when interest is taken into account). If the offer has not been beaten, the arbitrators may take the view that the claiming party should bear the whole of the costs of the arbitration: see *Cadmus Investment Ltd* v. *Amec Building Ltd*[3] and *Lindner Ceilings Floors Partitions plc* v. *How Engineering Services Ltd.*[4] However, a better approach may be to adopt that under the CPR. Part 36 of the CPR deals with offers and payments into court. The general rule under that provision is that an offer which is not beaten at trial will result in the offeror being awarded his costs (on an enhanced recovery basis and with interest) from the latest time the offer could be accepted (usually offers must be open for acceptance for at least 21 days). The offeree would still in principle be entitled to his costs up to the latest time for acceptance, so there will inevitably be a "netting out" between the two. (For this reason, there is an added incentive on offerors to make their offers as early as possible in the proceedings, or even before they have commenced, in order to gain the maximum advantage in terms of costs.)

A much more common alternative to a sealed offer is the making of an offer "without prejudice save as to costs" (known as a "Calderbank" offer). Calderbank offers are not copied to the arbitrators who are, therefore, unaware of any such offer having been made until after their findings on the merits, when the existence of the offer will be drawn to their attention (though only if the maker has beaten the claim against him, that is, offered more than the award provided by way of

1. *Fence Gate Ltd* v. *NEL Construction Ltd* (2001) 82 Con LR 41.

2. Payments into court have now been dispensed with in all cases: see CPR Part 36. Defendants to monetary claims now protect themselves by offering to pay a particular sum, and if accepted, such an offer creates a binding contract on which the claimant may obtain judgment if the sum is not paid within 14 days of acceptance (or such longer period as is agreed): see CPR r. 36.11(6)–(7).

3. [1998] ADRLJ 72.

4. [2001] BLR 90.

damages, etc.). In those circumstances, the better view is that the arbitrators should treat the Calderbank offer in the same way as a sealed offer, so that costs should not follow the event if the offer is better than the amount awarded.

In relation to either sealed offers or Calderbank offers, there seems no reason in principle why arbitrators should not adopt an approach that mirrors that of the CPR. For that reason, a party to an arbitration proceeding in England seeking to make a sealed or Calderbank offer should consider carefully following as closely as possible the strict requirements of the CPR in terms of the period for acceptance, and clarifying and ensuring that the offer is clear (e.g., as to whether and to what extent it comprises any interest) and capable of acceptance without the offeree requiring further information or clarification. If an offer is made and revealed to the arbitrators after making their findings, and betters the amount they have awarded, there appears to be no objection in principle to arbitrators awarding costs to the offeror from the latest time of acceptance on an indemnity basis,[1] although it is unclear whether arbitrators have the equivalent power in terms of awarding enhanced rates of interest on any sum awarded or on costs.[2]

There is some debate as to whether section 61 permits awards of costs on discrete issues (e.g., costs awarded in relation to partial awards). The majority view appears to be that although not expressly permitted by the 1996 Act, there is no objection to arbitrators making separate awards on costs on discrete issues, provided that such costs are in the form of awards containing reasons. There is greater doubt as to whether costs may be ordered to be paid following, for example, an unsuccessful interlocutory application, as is common in court proceedings. There may be no objection to a tribunal determining that the costs of any such interlocutory hearing are payable by one party "in any event", but such costs are usually not determined (and are therefore not payable) until either the conclusion of the arbitration (or until, for example, a partial award is made encompassing the matters in respect of which costs were left in abeyance), at which time a final "reckoning" will take account of any interlocutory costs orders. What may be more problematic are interlocutory costs orders that are "summarily assessed" (the method routinely adopted by the courts) and ordered to be paid immediately or within a short time following the interlocutory hearing or disposal of the application. Such orders may constitute an order to make an interim payment on account of the costs of the arbitration and, therefore, fall foul of the prohibition on such orders in section 39(4) of the Act (unless the parties have agreed to confer such power on the arbitrators). In the absence of the parties agreeing to allow the arbitrators to make any such interlocutory costs orders, the safer course for arbitrators to adopt is to confine any costs orders to those contained in final reasoned awards (including partial awards, where appropriate).

Effect of agreement or award about costs

62. Unless the parties otherwise agree, any obligation under an agreement between them as to how the costs of the arbitration are to be borne, or under an award allocating the costs of the arbitration, extends only to such costs as are recoverable.

NOTES

This non-mandatory section introduces sections 63 to 65 and the concept of "recoverable costs". The effect of this section and the following provisions is to limit any award of the costs of the arbitration to recoverable costs, which are (in the absence of agreement between the parties) those costs determined by the arbitrators as being reasonable. The provision is, however, curious, in that as per section 63, the parties are free to agree what costs are recoverable. If they do so agree, and

1. Costs in arbitration are awarded on the indemnity basis by resolving the doubt as to whether the costs are reasonable in favour of the receiving party (i.e., reversing the presumption under s. 63(5)(b) that any doubt should be resolved in favour of the paying party)—see the Notes to s. 63.

2. There certainly does not seem to be an objection in principle to arbitrators awarding interest on costs already paid, if claimed by the successful party, regardless as to whether this is in the context of offers to settle or generally.

agree how the costs are to be borne, section 62 will be irrelevant.[1] What is clear is that, if there is no agreement between the parties, the recoverable costs will be determined in accordance with sections 63 and 64.

The recoverable costs of the arbitration

63.—(1) The parties are free to agree what costs of the arbitration are recoverable.

(2) If or to the extent there is no such agreement, the following provisions apply.

(3) The tribunal may determine by award the recoverable costs of the arbitration on such basis as it thinks fit. If it does so, it shall specify—

(a) the basis on which it has acted, and
(b) the items of recoverable costs and the amount referable to each.

(4) If the tribunal does not determine the recoverable costs of the arbitration, any party to the arbitral proceedings may apply to the court (upon notice to the other parties) which may—

(a) determine the recoverable costs of the arbitration on such basis as it thinks fit, or
(b) order that they shall be determined by such means and upon such terms as it may specify.

(5) Unless the tribunal or the court determines otherwise—

(a) the recoverable costs of the arbitration shall be determined on the basis that there shall be allowed a reasonable amount in respect of all costs reasonably incurred, and
(b) any doubt as to whether costs were reasonably incurred or were reasonable in amount shall be resolved in favour of the paying party.

(6) The above provisions have effect subject to section 64 (recoverable fees and expenses of arbitrators).

(7) Nothing in this section affects any right of the arbitrators, any expert, legal adviser or assessor appointed by the tribunal, or any arbitral institution, to payment of their fees and expenses.

NOTES

Section 63(1) sets out the basic rule that the parties are free to agree what costs of the arbitration are to be recoverable[2] in the award. In the absence of any agreement as to the powers of the arbitrators, section 63(2) introduces the default powers in section 63(3)–(7).

The basic provision is contained in section 63(3), which provides that the determination of the recoverable costs of the arbitration, consisting of the arbitrators' fees and expenses and the parties' costs, is a matter for the arbitrators.

1. The DAC Report of February 1996 (see Appendix 8) does not contain any specific comment on what was cl. 62. Although para. 268 refers to cl. 62, this is clearly an error and should be read as a reference to cl. 61.
2. Older clauses use the now superseded word "taxed".

Section 63(3) is a modified re-enactment of section 18(1) of the Arbitration Act 1950, although the arbitrators are now under a duty to set out the basis on which they have defined the recoverable costs and to itemise the recoverable costs.[1]

If the arbitrators have no jurisdiction (which is very unlikely), or choose not to perform this task, it may be carried out by or under the authority of the court under section 63(4), on the application of any party to the proceedings. Any application to the court must be by way of arbitration claim form, and the applicant must give notice to the other parties by making them parties and serving on them the arbitration claim form and any supporting written evidence.[2] Whether the arbitrators have the power to determine recoverable costs but have failed to do so in their award, it is a matter of the construction of the award whether they have finally declined or whether they have reserved the right to revisit the issue in the event that the parties cannot agree. An award might typically provide "costs to be agreed or determined in default of agreement" or "costs determined if not agreed": both forms of wording have been held to mean that the arbitrators had reserved the right to determine recoverable costs if the parties themselves could not reach agreement.[3] It would seem sensible in principle for arbitrators to make clear in any award that they are reserving the right to determine costs, for example, in the absence of agreement by the parties.

Section 63(5) lays down guidelines as to how the recoverable costs are to be ascertained. The guiding principle is that recoverable costs are the reasonable amount of costs reasonably incurred, any doubt being resolved in favour of the party required by the award to pay the costs. This is the equivalent to the standard basis for recovering costs in civil proceedings. However, the arbitrators (or, under section 63(4), the court) may depart from the reasonableness principle. No guidance is contained in section 63(5) as to when it might be appropriate to award costs on an indemnity rather than the standard basis,[4] and it should be noted that if there is a departure from the usual principle without good reasons, those reasons being articulated in the award itself, the arbitrators' award as to costs may be challenged on the basis of serious irregularity under section 68. As far as civil proceedings are concerned, the relevant principles are contained in the CPR, Parts 43 to 48 and the Costs Practice Direction. If costs fall to be ascertained by the court, these provisions will be applied.[5] By way of guidance to arbitrators, the courts will take into account under the CPR whether the costs were proportionately and reasonably incurred and reasonable in amount, and more specifically will take into account, *inter alia*, the conduct of the parties before and during the proceedings, attempts by the parties to settle the dispute, the value and importance of the dispute and the complexity of the issues involved.[6]

In an arbitral context, certain situations are likely to give rise to an order in which costs are either diminished (for the successful party) or the basis enhanced to that of indemnity costs (against an unsuccessful party, and quite apart from the question of pre-award offers, which is dealt with in the notes to section 61). For example, a recalcitrant and ultimately unsuccessful respondent, who raises frivolous defences, or who is obstructive in disclosure, or repeatedly fails without good reason to adhere to the procedural timetable, thereby incurring unnecessary costs, may find that it is penalised with an order for costs on an indemnity basis. Likewise, an ultimately unsuccessful claimant bringing a hopeless claim, or bringing endless applications for disclosure of irrelevant material, or

1. In this sense, the reference to individual items of recoverable costs in s. 63(3)(b) is unclear. In the authors' experience, costs are assessed by arbitrators much more commonly (i.e., assessments by the court are relatively uncommon). In making their determinations, tribunals more often than not adopt a "broad brush" approach to costs, and will reach global figures quite often, though these will usually break down between: (a) the tribunal's fees and expenses; (b) a party's legal fees; and (c) a party's other incidental expenses.

2. CPR r. 62.6(2)–(3). As indicated in the above footnote, such applications to the court are comparatively rare and there are no known reported decisions.

3. *M/S Alghanim Industries Inc* v. *Skandia International Insurance Corporation* [2001] 2 All ER (Comm) 30.

4. The principles on which costs might be awarded on an indemnity basis rather than the standard basis are not set out in the CPR itself, but guidance from the cases in which such costs have been ordered or considered may be found in para. 44.4.3 of the White book. There is an additional difference introduced by the CPR between standard and indemnity costs, in that the principle of proportionality applies only to the former. There would seem to be no objection in principle to arbitrators adopting a similar approach, though in terms of limiting costs, the costs-capping provisions in s. 65 should be adhered to closely (see the Notes to s. 65).

5. CPR r. 43.2(2).

6. CPR r. 44.5(3).

engaging in "bullying tactics", may find itself at the receiving end of an award ordering it to pay the respondent's costs on an indemnity basis, particularly if the tribunal has not already made interim decisions on costs of failed applications. (As discussed in the notes to section 61, while it is unclear whether arbitrators have jurisdiction to order costs of interim applications, there seems to be an increasing tendency to do so, even if such orders are not formally enforceable under section 66 as awards.) Arbitrators have a wide discretion overall, at least as wide as judges, in determining the final burden and allocation of costs as between the parties.

Section 63(6) renders section 63 subject to section 64. Section 64 provides that a costs award may include only a reasonable level of the arbitrators' fees and expenses, and in the event of disagreement over the appropriate figure that matter may be determined by the court (see the Notes to section 64).

Contingency fees are permissible in arbitrations[1] and thus may be allowed by arbitrators. The costs of lay representatives[2] and lawyers not qualified within the jurisdiction[3] may also be allowed.

Section 63(7) confirms that the provisions of section 63 do not in any way restrict the right of arbitrators and, indeed, experts or arbitral bodies to recover either their agreed fees and expenses or a reasonable sum: the sole purpose of section 63 is to prevent a party from facing an unreasonable level of costs awarded against him. Any challenge to the arbitrators' determination of their own costs and expenses may be made under either section 28(2) or section 64(2) if the costs award has been made. One good practical example of how section 64(2) may operate is in the context of a three-arbitrator panel, where the winning party appointed and paid for an extremely expensive arbitrator, whose fees were included in the award made against the losing party (along with the fees of the other two arbitrators). In such a case, the losing party would use the mechanism under section 64(2) to apply to the court for an order determining the winning party's arbitrator's fees at a lower amount, on the grounds that such fees were not agreed by the losing party and were unreasonable and excessive. However, there is no reported decision on section 64(2), so presumably such applications are extremely rare.

Recoverable fees and expenses of arbitrators

64.—(1) Unless otherwise agreed by the parties, the recoverable costs of the arbitration shall include in respect of the fees and expenses of the arbitrators only such reasonable fees and expenses as are appropriate in the circumstances.

(2) If there is any question as to what reasonable fees and expenses are appropriate in the circumstances, and the matter is not already before the court on an application under section 63(4), the court may on the application of any party (upon notice to the other parties)

(a) determine the matter, or
(b) order that it be determined by such means and upon such terms as the court may specify.

(3) Subsection (1) has effect subject to any order of the court under section 24(4) or 25(3)(b) (order as to entitlement to fees or expenses in case of removal or resignation of arbitrator).

(4) Nothing in this section affects any right of the arbitrator to payment of his fees and expenses.

1. *Bevan Ashford* v. *Geoff Yeandle (Contractors) Ltd* [1998] 3 All ER 238, confirmed by the Courts and Legal Services Act 1990, s. 58A (inserted by the Access to Justice Act 1999, s. 27).
2. *Piper Double Glazing Ltd* v. *DC Contracts (1992) Ltd* [1994] 1 All ER 177.
3. Such costs are not, however, permitted in judicial proceedings, including proceedings to challenge an arbitration award: *Westland Helicopters Ltd* v. *Sheikh Sala Al-Hejailan (No 2)* [2004] 2 Lloyd's Rep 535.

NOTES

Where an arbitrator has reached an agreement with the parties as to his fees and expenses, he is entitled to be paid the agreed sum in all circumstances. In the absence of such agreement, the arbitrators are entitled to recover the sum which they have awarded themselves, subject to a challenge in the court under section 28(2), section 56 (if the tribunal is withholding the award pending payment of its fees) or section 64(2). These principles are left untouched by section 64, which is concerned solely with the amount of arbitrators' fees and expenses that may be included in any costs award allocating liability between the parties. Section 64(4) preserves any contractual rights which the arbitrators may have to fees and expenses: section 64 does not permit the court to rewrite contracts between the arbitrators and the parties.[1]

Section 64(1) permits the parties to agree that the full amount of the arbitrators' costs are to be included in the award, or they may make some other agreement as to allocation. In the absence of any such agreement, section 64(1) provides that only those fees and expenses that are reasonable in the circumstances are to be included in the costs award, disregarding costs and expenses which the arbitrators are unable to retain by reason of removal or resignation (section 64(3)). In the event of any dispute, the matter may be resolved by application to the court under section 64(2). The application must be by way of arbitration claim form which is served on the other parties and they are to be made parties to the application.[2] Since there is no reported decision on section 64, it is presumed (unsurprisingly) that applications under that section are fairly rare.

Power to limit recoverable costs

65.—(1) Unless otherwise agreed by the parties, the tribunal may direct that the recoverable costs of the arbitration, or of any part of the arbitral proceedings, shall be limited to a specified amount.

(2) Any direction may be made or varied at any stage, but this must be done sufficiently in advance of the incurring of costs to which it relates, or the taking of any steps in the proceedings which may be affected by it, for the limit to be taken into account.

NOTES

The purpose of this section, which has no counterpart in earlier legislation or in the Model Law, is, subject to contrary agreement by the parties, to empower the arbitrators to limit the recoverable costs of the proceedings to a specified amount. The stated objective of the provision is to make arbitration more cost-effective than might otherwise be the case. It is thought that this power is aimed at the legal and other costs of the ultimately successful party, which the arbitrators fear may prove to be excessive. Section 65 permits the arbitrators to issue a direction at any stage in the proceedings limiting the recoverable party costs (of the whole arbitration or for any part of the proceedings, for example, disclosure) to a given amount, provided that the parties are made aware of the limit and are thereby able to adjust their affairs accordingly. The most obvious stage at which this power might be exercised is at the outset of the arbitration, once the arbitrator has been able to assess the issues involved and what evidence might be needed, although doubtless an order can be made at any later stage if the costs of one or both parties look as though they might be getting out of hand.[3] The operation of this provision was explained in the DAC Report, paragraph 272:

> [S]uch a power, properly used, could prove to be extremely valuable as an aid to reducing unnecessary expenditure . . . [It] enables the tribunal to put a ceiling on costs, so that while a

1. DAC Report, para. 271.
2. CPR r. 62.6(2)–(3). Extraordinarily, and unlike applications under s. 28 or s. 56, there is no requirement to add the arbitrator in question as defendant, though it would be sensible at least to notify the arbitrator formally that an application is being made.
3. Care must here be exercised not to prejudice the right of the parties to present their case, if they were basing themselves on the assumption that costs would not be capped. *Cf.* the comments of the Court of Appeal in *King* v. *Telegraph Group Ltd* [2004] EMLR 23.

party can continue to spend as much as it likes on an arbitration it will not be able to recover more than the ceiling limit from the other party. This will have the added virtue of discouraging those who wish to use their financial muscle to intimidate their opponents into giving up through fear that by going on they might be subject to a costs order which they could not sustain.

Subsection (2) authorises the arbitrators to vary any order on the capping of costs.[1] The parties must, on general fairness grounds, be heard where a variation is intended.

Powers of the Court in Relation to Award

Enforcement of the award

66.—(1) An award made by the tribunal pursuant to an arbitration agreement may, by leave of the court, be enforced in the same manner as a judgment or order of the court to the same effect.

(2) Where leave is so given, judgment may be entered in terms of the award.

(3) Leave to enforce an award shall not be given where, or to the extent that, the person against whom it is sought to be enforced shows that the tribunal lacked substantive jurisdiction to make the award.

The right to raise such an objection may have been lost (see section 73).

(4) Nothing in this section affects the recognition or enforcement of an award under any other enactment or rule of law, in particular under Part II of the Arbitration Act 1950 (enforcement of awards under Geneva Convention) or the provisions of Part III of this Act relating to the recognition and enforcement of awards under the New York Convention or by an action on the award.

NOTES

Section 66 encompasses two separate procedures.

Section 66(1) entails the permission of the court for the enforcement of the award in the same way as a judgment. This is so irrespective of the location of the seat of the arbitration (section 2(2)(b)). The DAC Report, paragraph 378, was of the view that the court before which enforcement of the award was sought ought to be informed that the award was an agreed award made under section 51 of the 1996 Act, and that the court in its enforcement order should so state. This would put third parties on notice of the nature of the award (a point which might be of particular interest to liability insurers and reinsurers, who are bound by awards but not always by settlements). This amendment was not, however, made in the Act itself but appears in the Civil Procedure Rules CPR r. 62.18(5).[2] An application for the enforcement of an award as a judgment may be made in the Royal Courts of Justice or any district registry, by way of arbitration claim form.[3]

The application for permission may be made without notice to the other parties, although if this is the case the applicant must disclose all material facts to the court,[4] and in any event the court may

1. See: *Home of Homes Ltd* v. *Hammersmith and Fulham London Borough Council* (2003) 92 Con LR 48, where an arbitrator who took legal advice on a variation was held not to have acted in a dilatory or indecisive fashion justifying removal under s. 24 of the 1996 Act, given that he had been pressurised by the parties.

2. The DAC Supplementary Report, para. 34, recognised that such a provision was more appropriately included in rules of court rather than the main legislation.

3. CPR r. 62.18(1). Curiously, there is no Appendix A to the Practice Direction to Part 62 (containing the arbitration claim form). However, the form is available online at: www.hmcourts-service.gov.uk/courtfinder/forms/n8.pdf.

4. *Curacao Trading BV* v. *Harkisandas & Co* [2002] 2 Lloyd's Rep 186; *Socadec SA* v. *Pan Africa Impex Co Ltd* [2003] EWHC 2086 (QB).

require that the application be served on the other parties.[1] If necessary, service may be ordered to be effected outside the jurisdiction.[2] The applicant must supply written evidence exhibiting the arbitration agreement and the award and must state that it has not been honoured (or the extent to which it has not been honoured).[3] The claim form and witness statement submitted by the claimant must be signed, although if they are not the court has the power to correct the defect under its general powers in CPR 3.10,[4] although there is no need for the applicant to show that he has complied with any contract terms imposing conditions on the invoking of the arbitration clause.[5] If the applicant wishes to enforce an award of interest any part of which relates to a period after the award, he must file a certificate stating whether the interest was simple or compound, the date from which interest was awarded, the rate, whether any rests were provided for, and a calculation showing the total sum.[6] The order itself must be drawn up by the applicant and served on the respondent.[7]

The enforcement order is purely in respect of the award itself: the court cannot correct deficiencies in the award, for example, by awarding interest if this was not included in the award itself.[8] Further, permission under section 66(1) does not amount to a court order in its own right,[9] so that if there is a subsequent failure to honour the award the defaulting party cannot be said to be in contempt of court.[10] Permission may, however, be given in respect of a part of the award only.[11] The power to enforce the award is discretionary, although it is to be used in all but exceptional cases where there is real doubt as to the validity of the award.[12] The fact that a foreign court has refused enforcement does not create a judgment estoppel against the claimant in the English enforcement proceedings,[13] although if the foreign court's refusal of enforcement is based on a particular finding of fact or law, there will be an issue estoppel which prevents that point being relitigated in England.[14] The execution of an enforcement order may be stayed by the court under its general powers, if enforcement would be "inexpedient":[15] this power may be exercised where there are outstanding proceedings between the parties involving a counterclaim or a challenge to the award.[16]

1. CPR r. 62.18(2).
2. CPR r. 62.18(4). It is not clear whether permission is required to serve the arbitration claim form out of the jurisdiction on defendants situated in an EU or Lugano Convention country, since ordinarily no such permission is required under CPR r. 6.19. It is presumed that permission under CPR r. 62.18(4) is required only in cases where CPR r. 6.19 does not apply, i.e., where CPR r. 6.20 would otherwise apply. In such cases, an application may be made simultaneously for an extension of time for service of the arbitration claim form.
3. CPR r. 62.18(6).
4. *Colliers International Property Consultants* v. *Colliers Jordan Lee Jafaar Sdn Bhd* [2008] EWHC 1524 (Comm), which also decides that the arbitration clause itself need not be signed.
5. *Colliers International Property Consultants* v. *Colliers Jordan Lee Jafaar Sdn Bhd* [2008] EWHC 1524 (Comm).
6. CPR r. 62.19.
7. CPR r. 62.18(7).
8. *Walker* v. *Rowe* [2000] 1 Lloyd's Rep 116; *Pirtek* v. *Deanswood* [2005] 2 Lloyd's Rep 728.
9. *ED & F Man Sugar Ltd* v. *Lendoudis* [2007] 2 Lloyd's Rep 579.
10. *ASM Shipping Ltd of India* v. *TTMI Ltd (No 2)* [2007] 2 Lloyd's Rep 155.
11. *ASM Shipping Ltd of India* v. *TTMI Ltd* [2006] 1 Lloyd's Rep 401; *IPCO (Nigeria) Ltd* v. *Nigerian National Petroleum Corporation (No 2)* [2008] EWCA Civ 1157.
12. *Middlemiss* v. *Hartlepool Corporation* [1973] 1 All ER 172; *Hall & Wodehouse Ltd* v. *Panorama Hotel Properties Ltd* [1974] 2 Lloyd's Rep 413; *Kohn* v. *Wagschal* [2006] EWHC 3356, affirmed on other grounds [2007] EWCA Civ 1022; *Tsavliris Salvage (International) Ltd* v. *The Grain Board of Iraq* [2008] EWHC 612 (Comm).
13. *Good Challenger Nevegante SA* v. *Metalimportexport SA* [2004] 1 Lloyd's Rep 67.
14. See: *Good Challenger Nevegante SA* v. *Metalimportexport SA* [2004] 1 Lloyd's Rep 67, where a Romanian court refused to enforce an award on the basis that the application was time-barred under Romanian law. The suggestion by the Romanian court that the application was time-barred under English law as well was held not to be the basis of that court's decision and therefore not binding on the English court.
15. *Far Eastern Shipping Co* v. *AKP Sovcomflot* [1995] 1 Lloyd's Rep 520.
16. *Apis AS* v. *Fantazia Kereskedelmi KFT* [2001] 1 All ER (Comm) 348; *Socadec SA* v. *Pan Afric Impex Co Ltd* [2003] EWHC 2086 (QB).

It appears from the judgment of Aikens J in *SC Rolinay Sea Star Srl* v. *Owners and Charterers of the Ship "Bumbesti", The Bumbesti*,[1] that the court has no jurisdiction to arrest a vessel as security for the enforcement of an arbitration award on a charterparty, as the obligation of the parties to honour the award arose not out of charterparty but out of an implied obligation in the award itself. Accordingly, the obligation broken by failure to honour an award was not a maritime obligation falling within the court's admiralty jurisdiction[2] but rather an obligation arising from the arbitration agreement itself.

Section 66(2) additionally empowers the court to give a judgment in the terms of the award, thereby allowing the judgment rather than the award to be enforced. Because the court itself is giving a judgment, it is empowered to make an order for the payment of interest from the date of the award until payment, in accordance with section 17 of the Judgments Act 1838.[3] A judgment entered on the award must be in the terms of the award, one consequence of which is that if the award specifies payment within a fixed period and the judgment is given after that period has expired, the judgment will still specify payment on the date required by the award.[4]

Section 66(3) prevents the enforcement of an award which was made outside the jurisdiction of the arbitrators, provided that the party taking the jurisdiction point has not lost the right to do so.[5] Where the tribunal is acting without jurisdiction, and a party nevertheless participates in the proceedings without objection, the combined effect of sections 30 and 73 is to regard that party as having waived the jurisdictional point. Consequently, the right of a party to rely upon want of jurisdiction at enforcement stage will be dependent upon his not having participated in the arbitration proceedings (which is his right under section 72) or upon his having participated after having registered an objection. Moreover, if he has objected, and the matter has been resolved by a preliminary ruling by the court under the procedure set out in section 32 rather than in the ultimate award, the jurisdiction point cannot be reopened at the stage where the award is to be enforced.

Earlier drafts of the Bill stated that permission to enforce an award was not to be given in respect of an award so defective in form or substance that it is incapable of enforcement, or whose enforcement would be contrary to public policy. This list was omitted from the final version of the Act, on the basis that it was not exhaustive and the inclusion of a non-exhaustive list might have been misleading. Nevertheless, these two grounds remain important illustrations of situations in which awards will not be enforced.

The DAC in its February 1996 Report, paragraphs 371 to 376, was relatively happy that the provisions of section 66(3) were sufficiently wide to justify refusal of enforcement in all cases where such refusal was appropriate. Moreover, it was of the view that section 66(3) was not an exhaustive statement of the court's powers, and that refusal might be justified on other grounds (paragraph 374). However, consultation on the July 1995 Bill threw up two situations which might fall outside section 66(3) and in respect of which the DAC thought it appropriate to make express provision:

(i) where the award purports to decide matters not capable of resolution by arbitration (e.g., the custody of children); and
(ii) where the award grants relief which would improperly affect the rights of third parties (the condition of improper effect being intended to recognise that arbitration awards do properly affect the rights of certain third parties, such as liability insurers).

The DAC proposed a draft clause to bring these exceptions into effect, but this was not ultimately incorporated into the 1996 Act. Instead, it was made clear in section 81 of the Act that any public policy rule relating to recognition, and any common law rule affecting the arbitrability of a particular matter, was unaffected by the legislation. Those amendments make it clear that an award is not

1. [1999] 2 Lloyd's Rep 481, not following the decision of Sheen J in *The Saint Anna* [1983] 1 Lloyd's Rep 637.
2. Supreme Court Act 1981, s. 20(2).
3. *Pirtek* v. *Deanswood* [2005] 2 Lloyd's Rep 728; *Gater Assets Ltd* v. *NAK Naftogaz Ukrainiy (No 2)* [2008] EWHC 1108 (Comm).
4. *Colliers International Property Consultants* v. *Colliers Jordan Lee Jafaar Sdn Bhd* [2008] EWHC 1524 (Comm).
5. *Peoples' Insurance Co of China* v. *Vysanthi Shipping Co Ltd* [2003] 2 Lloyd's Rep 617.

enforceable under the 1996 Act if it would not have been enforceable under the pre-existing law.[1] Public policy issues are discussed in the Notes to section 103.

Section 66(4) creates a saving for awards which are to be recognised and enforced under other regimes, most importantly, foreign awards governed by the Geneva and New York Conventions. The enforcement of such awards is governed by sections 99 to 104 of the Act. An action may also be brought upon such awards: this was added to the Act specifically to make it clear that the action on the award had been preserved by the 1996 Act.[2] Awards are not enforceable under Council Regulation 44/2001, as that Regulation is confined to judgments.[3]

The section is silent on any right of appeal, but it was held by the House of Lords in *Inco Europe Ltd* v. *First Choice Distribution*[4] that a right of appeal exists. Permission to appeal may presumably be given by either the trial judge or the Court of Appeal.

Challenging the award: substantive jurisdiction

67.—(1) A party to arbitral proceedings may (upon notice to the other parties and to the tribunal) apply to the court—

(a) challenging any award of the arbitral tribunal as to its substantive jurisdiction; or

(b) for an order declaring an award made by the tribunal on the merits to be of no effect, in whole or in part, because the tribunal did not have substantive jurisdiction.

A party may lose the right to object (see section 73) and the right to apply is subject to the restrictions in section 70(2) and (3).

(2) The arbitral tribunal may continue the arbitral proceedings and make a further award while an application to the court under this section is pending in relation to an award as to jurisdiction.

(3) On an application under this section challenging an award of the arbitral tribunal as to its substantive jurisdiction, the court may by order—

(a) confirm the award,

(b) vary the award, or

(c) set aside the award in whole or in part.

(4) The leave of the court is required for any appeal from a decision of the court under this section.

NOTES

Section 67 is derived from Article 34(2) of the Model Law. It permits a challenge to an award which is allegedly made without jurisdiction. The phrase "substantive jurisdiction" is defined in section 30 of the 1996 Act to mean: "(a) whether there is a valid arbitration agreement, (b) whether the tribunal is properly constituted,[5] and (c) what matters have been submitted to arbitration in accordance with the arbitration agreement".[6] Section 67 is mandatory (see section 4 and Schedule 1), and it is not

1. DAC Supplementary Report, para. 32.
2. DAC Supplementary Report, para. 33.
3. *Arab Business Consortium International Finance and Investment Co* v. *Banque Franco-Tunisienne* [1997] 1 Lloyd's Rep 531. The same rule applies to the EC Council Regulation 44/2001.
4. [2000] 1 Lloyd's Rep 467.
5. For two recent examples of jurisdictional challenges based on the alleged defective appointment of the tribunal, see *Sumukan* v. *Commonwealth Secretariat* [2008] 1 Lloyd's Rep 40 (CA) and *Crest Nicholson (Eastern) Ltd* v. *Western* [2008] EWHC 1325 (TCC).
6. The definition is repeated in s. 82(1).

possible to contract out of the right to challenge an award on the basis of lack of substantive jurisdiction.[1] Although it is unclear whether the categories are completely closed, it is established that there are certain matters that are *not* matters of substantive jurisdiction. For example, the arbitrator's jurisdiction is not deprived by virtue of an allegation that a compromise agreement had been entered into which removed any right to compensation under another agreement containing an arbitration clause.[2] Nor is the arbitrator deprived of jurisdiction by virtue of an allegation that an issue formerly in dispute between the parties had been conceded by one party during the arbitration.[3]

It is clear that both questions of fact and questions of law which affect jurisdiction are within the right of appeal under section 67 (DAC Report, paragraph 143). For this reason, the hearing under section 67 is a full one, and the court has to rehear all the arguments and evidence put to the arbitrators in the situation in which the objecting party has participated in a hearing as to jurisdiction before the arbitrators but does not accept the outcome. The process is not, therefore, a mere judicial review but a complete retrial. As was said by Rix J in *Azov Shipping Co* v. *Baltic Shipping Co (No 1)*,[4] where a party seeks to challenge an award as to jurisdiction, the court should not be placed in a worse position than the arbitrators for the purpose of determining that challenge. The court's function under section 67 is to decide whether the arbitrators reached the correct result, not whether they were entitled to reach the decision they did.[5] There may, nevertheless, be a limitation on whether new evidence can be submitted to the court relating to jurisdiction if this was not put before the tribunal. Although there is no express restriction on admitting new evidence in the course of a challenge under section 67, the parties should not be encouraged "to seek two evidential bites of the cherry".[6] It has been recently held that a party challenging an award under section 67 who wishes to rely on new evidence in support of a new or different argument within an existing ground of objection must give notice to the other side. If the new evidence is opposed, permission must be obtained from the court (at an appropriate interlocutory hearing). Permission to admit the new evidence could be refused if it would result in substantial prejudice to the other side which could not fairly be dealt with in costs or by an adjournment.[7]

Sections 30 to 32 are concerned with jurisdictional matters and how they are dealt with during the currency of the arbitration. The notes to those sections should be consulted for a fuller explanation, but in summary:

(a) Unless otherwise agreed, the arbitrators are entitled to proceed to determine their own substantive jurisdiction over a dispute by means of an award (section 30).
(b) If they choose to do so, and no objection is taken to this approach by either party, the parties are deemed to have waived their right to object to the proposed course of action on the grounds of any alleged serious irregularity by virtue of section 73.
(c) At that point, if one party wishes to contest the tribunal's jurisdiction, he may either:
    (i) refuse to participate in the arbitration proceedings, in which case he retains the right to challenge the award on jurisdictional grounds under section 67, to contest the

1. It was assumed at first instance in *LG Caltex Gas Co Ltd* v. *China National Petroleum Co* [2001] BLR 325 that a ruling by the arbitrators pursuant to an *ad hoc* agreement made between the parties that the arbitrators should determine an issue going to their jurisdiction could not be challenged under s. 67 of the 1996 Act. It is difficult, however, to reconcile this idea with the mandatory nature of the section.
2. *DDT Trucks of North America* v. *DDT Holdings Ltd* [2007] 2 Lloyd's Rep 213.
3. *Claire & Co* v. *Thames Water Utilities Ltd* [2005] BLR 366.
4. [1999] 1 Lloyd's Rep 68. See also: *Astra SA Insurance and Reinsurance Co* v. *Sphere Drake Insurance Ltd* [2000] 2 Lloyd's Rep 550; *AOOT Kalmneft* v. *Glencore* [2002] 1 Lloyd's Rep 128; *Zaporozhye Production Aluminium Plan Open Shareholders Society* v. *Ashly Ltd* [2002] EWHC 1410 (Comm); *Electrosteel Castings Ltd* v. *Scan-Trans Shipping & Chartering Sdn Bhd* [2003] 1 Lloyd's Rep 190; *Peoples' Insurance Co of China* v. *Vysanthi Shipping Co Ltd* [2003] 2 Lloyd's Rep 617; *Peterson Farms Inc* v. *C & M Farming Ltd* [2004] 2 Lloyd's Rep 603; *Amec Civil Engineering Ltd* v. *Secretary of State for Transport* [2004] EWHC 2339 (TCC); *Metal Distributors (UK) Ltd* v. *ZCCM Investment Holdings plc* [2005] EWHC 156 (Comm); *Oceanografia SA de CV* v. *DSND Subsea AS* [2007] 1 Lloyd's Rep 37.
5. *Peterson Farms* v. *C & M Farming Ltd* [2004] 1 Lloyd's Rep 603.
6. *Per* Gross J in *Electrosteel Castings Ltd* v. *Scan-Trans Shipping & Chartering Sdn Bhd* [2003] 1 Lloyd's Rep 190.
7. *Primetrade AG* v. *Ythan Ltd* [2006] 1 Lloyd's Rep 457.

enforcement of the award under section 66 or to seek injunctive or declaratory relief at any stage under section 72:[1] or

(ii) participate in the arbitration proceedings, having raised an objection to the asserted jurisdiction of the arbitrators—such objection must be made before he has taken a step in the substantive proceedings or as soon as he is aware of a jurisdictional issue (section 31). If the objection is not made at the proper time, and the tribunal refuses to enlarge time under its power to do so in section 31(3), the objection is invalid and it may be said that no jurisdictional issue has been put to the arbitrators. Accordingly, there is nothing against which an appeal can be made. Alternatively, he will be taken to have waived any right to challenge on jurisdictional grounds under section 73.[2]

(d) Where there has been an objection in due time, the arbitrators may, under section 31(4), deal with the matter in one of two ways (and if the parties agree which alternative course the arbitrators should adopt, they have no choice but to follow that route):

(i) they may make a preliminary award. If they do so, there can be an appeal against the award on the basis of want of jurisdiction, under section 67, and a failure to appeal against the award within the time limits laid down in respect of section 67 by section 70(3) (as extendable under section 80(5)) will deprive the applicant of any right of challenge; or

(ii) they may proceed with the arbitration and deal with the issue by means of an award on the entire dispute, including the jurisdictional issue. Here, a party may use section 67 to challenge the validity of the award on jurisdictional grounds.

(e) Alternatively, the parties, or the arbitrators, may agree to allow an application to the court for a preliminary ruling on jurisdiction under section 32.

The right to challenge an award under section 67 is confined to the situations in which the arbitrators have determined their own jurisdiction and: (1) the party has not appeared in the arbitration; or (2) the party has appeared in the arbitration and has registered a timely objection which has not been resolved by a preliminary ruling. It might be commented that the distinction between want of jurisdiction, on the one hand, and serious irregularity, on the other hand, might at the margins be hard to distinguish, and it is probably sensible for a party to err on the side of caution and to treat any possible excess of jurisdiction precisely as that, and to register an objection under section 31. If this is not done, there might be some argument that the right to challenge the award under section 67 has been lost, even though the right to challenge the award under section 68 might not have been lost. The two sections probably operate identically in terms of what constitutes waiver under section 73, and share common time limits under section 70(3), but there is a small risk that failure to protest about an excess of jurisdiction in reliance on the fact that the problem may be one relating to the conduct of the proceedings under section 68 might deprive the applicant of his rights. Assuming that a protest has been made, it might also be sensible for the applicant to apply under sections 67 and 68 as alternatives, so that the claim is not defeated by lapse of time (or at least subject to the discretion of the court to extend time under section 80(5)) if the wrong basis for application has been chosen first.

Section 67(1) sets out the right of a party to challenge an award on the basis of want of substantive jurisdiction, including the scope or validity of the arbitration agreement, the constitution of the tribunal and what claims are properly submitted to arbitration. As commented in the Notes to section 30, it is not clear whether the categories of substantive jurisdiction set out in that section are closed. The award must purport to determine substantive jurisdiction, and must not merely relate to the validity of the main contract (which is not a jurisdictional issue)[3] or to a procedural decision by the arbitrators as to how a jurisdictional issue is to be resolved.[4]

1. It is likely that having agreed to the arbitrators proceeding to consider their jurisdiction, the complainant will have thereby lost the right to make any application under s. 72, since he will be held to have taken a part in the proceedings. See the notes to s. 72.

2. *Vee Networks Ltd* v. *Econet Wireless International Ltd* [2005] 1 Lloyd's Rep 192.

3. *Vee Networks Ltd* v. *Econet Wireless International Ltd* [2005] 1 Lloyd's Rep 192; *Continental Enterprises Limited* v. *Shandong Zhucheng Foreign Trade Group Co* [2005] EWHC 92 (Comm).

4. *AOOT Kalmneft* v. *Glencore International AG* [2002] 1 Lloyd's Rep 128.

Section 67(1) has two provisos. The first recognises that the right to apply will be lost under section 73 where the applicant has participated in the arbitration proceedings without objecting to a doubtful assertion of jurisdiction (section 73(1)), or where the applicant has not challenged an award made by the arbitrators on the jurisdiction issue prior to the main award (section 73(2)). For further details as to the effect of section 73, see the Notes to that section.

The second proviso introduces the conditions in section 70(2)–(3): an application may not be brought until any internal appeal procedure has been exhausted, and must be brought within 28 days from the date of the award (or when the applicant was notified of the result of any internal appeal procedure). This period can be extended by the court under its general power in section 80(5). The proviso does not apply where the party bringing the challenge has exercised his right in section 72(1) not to participate in the proceedings at all (section 72(2)).

It was held in *Westland Helicopters Ltd* v. *Sheikh Salah Al-Hejailan*[1] that the claim must refer to all heads of jurisdictional challenge which are to be relied upon and that no amendment may be made after the 28-day period has expired if the claimant was aware of that additional ground within the 28-day period. By the same token, if new material for a challenge has come to light and could not reasonably have been discovered prior to the expiry of the 28-day period, and the applicant is not taken to have waived any right of appeal, an extension of time may be granted. On the other hand, it is clear that each ground of objection must previously have been raised before the arbitrator before it could be relied upon under section 67.[2]

Section 67(2) recognises that the jurisdiction issue may have been dealt with, on a preliminary basis, by the arbitrators by means of an award devoted to that issue alone. In such a case, it will be necessary for the applicant to challenge the award within the permitted 28 days, while in the meantime the arbitration proceedings may still continue: section 67(2) confers upon the arbitrators the power to continue the arbitration while the appeal against the award as to jurisdiction is resolved.

Section 67(3) sets out the order-making powers of the court in a section 67 application, and section 71(2) adds that if the award is varied under section 67(3)(b) the variation imposed by the court takes effect as part of the award itself. It might also be noted that, where the arbitration clause is in *Scott* v. *Avery* form, rendering arbitration a condition precedent to a legal action, and the court makes a ruling in favour of the applicant, it may also—under section 71(4)—nullify the clause insofar as it relates to the issue resolved by the court. There appears to be no significant difference between an order declaring the award to be of no effect (section 67(1)(b)) and an order setting aside an award (section 67(3)(c)).[3]

Finally, section 67(4) sets out the usual condition that the permission of the court is required for any appeal from a decision of the court. The "court" means the trial judge and not the Court of Appeal.[4] Unlike the position under section 69 (appeal on error of law, discussed below) there are no statutory constraints on the circumstances in which the judge may give permission to appeal under section 67(4). This is necessarily the case, given that the nature of section 67 proceedings is an assertion that there should never have been an award, as opposed to an appeal under section 69 where the challenge is based on alleged errors of law in an agreed arbitral procedure.[5]

Section 70(6)–(7) confers upon the court the power to protect the respondent to a section 67 challenge, by requiring the applicant to provide security for the costs of the application and to pay the sum owing under the award into court or otherwise to secure that sum as a condition of the application (see the Notes to section 70).

The doctrine of non-justiciability does not prevent an English court entertaining an application under this section to review the substantive jurisdiction of a tribunal appointed under a bilateral investment treaty (BIT), where London is chosen by the parties (or determined by the arbitral

1. [2004] 2 Lloyd's Rep 523.

2. *JSC Zestafoni G Nikoladze Ferroalloy Plant* v. *Ronly Holdings* [2004] 2 Lloyd's Rep 335 at [64]. See also: *Athletic Union of Constantinople* v. *National Basketball Association* [2002] 1 Lloyd's Rep 305 at 311.

3. *Hussmann (Europe) Ltd* v. *Pharaon* [2003] 1 All ER (Comm) 879.

4. *Henry Boot Construction (UK) Ltd* v. *Malmaison Hotel (Manchester) Ltd* [2001] 1 QB 388; *Athletic Union of Constantinople* v. *National Basketball Association* [2002] 1 Lloyd's Rep 305; *Virdee* v. *Virdi* [2003] EWCA Civ 41.

5. *Macepark (Whittlebury) Ltd* v. *Sargeant*, 2002, unreported.

tribunal) as the seat of arbitration.[1] Nor does the doctrine operate to deprive a tribunal hearing a claim based on a BIT from considering words and phrases in the BIT itself.[2]

As regards the practicalities of commencing an application under section 67, the detail is set out in CPR Part 62.[3] Within the 28 days allowed, the arbitration claim form must have been issued, although the court is empowered to extend this time limit.[4] The arbitration claim form and any supporting evidence must be served on the other parties (who will be defendants to the application) within one month of its issue.[5] The same material must also be served on the arbitrators,[6] who have the right to apply to become a defendant (which will obviously be rare) or to make written representations.[7] The subsequent case management directions are set out in the Practice Direction to CPR Part 62.

Challenging the award: serious irregularity

68.—(1) A party to arbitral proceedings may (upon notice to the other parties and to the tribunal) apply to the court challenging an award in the proceedings on the ground of serious irregularity affecting the tribunal, the proceedings or the award.

A party may lose the right to object (see section 73) and the right to apply is subject to the restrictions in section 70(2) and (3).

(2) Serious irregularity means an irregularity of one or more of the following kinds which the court considers has caused or will cause substantial injustice to the applicant—

- (a) failure by the tribunal to comply with section 33 (general duty of tribunal);
- (b) the tribunal exceeding its powers (otherwise than by exceeding its substantive jurisdiction: see section 67);
- (c) failure by the tribunal to conduct the proceedings in accordance with the procedure agreed by the parties;
- (d) failure by the tribunal to deal with all the issues that were put to it;
- (e) any arbitral or other institution or person vested by the parties with powers in relation to the proceedings or the award exceeding its powers;
- (f) uncertainty or ambiguity as to the effect of the award;
- (g) the award being obtained by fraud or the award or the way in which it was procured being contrary to public policy;
- (h) failure to comply with the requirements as to the form of the award; or
- (i) any irregularity in the conduct of the proceedings or in the award which is admitted by the tribunal or by any arbitral or other institution or person vested by the parties with powers in relation to the proceedings or the award.

(3) If there is shown to be serious irregularity affecting the tribunal, the proceedings or the award, the court may—

1. *Republic of Ecuador* v. *Occidental Exploration and Production Co* [2005] 2 Lloyd's Rep 707 (CA).
2. *Czech Republic* v. *European Media Ventures SA* [2008] 1 Lloyd's Rep 186.
3. See Part 1 of this work for a general summary of arbitration claims.
4. CPR r. 62.9.
5. Unless the court orders otherwise: CPR r. 62.4(2). Service of evidence with the claim form is implied from CPR r. 62.6(2), where the reference to "any other person" is probably deemed to include any other party to the arbitration.
6. CPR r. 62.6(2).
7. CPR PD 62 paras 4.1–4.2. Written representations were made in *Claire & Company* v. *Thames Water Utilities Ltd* [2005] BLR 366 and *Sumakan* v. *Commonwealth Secretariat* [2007] 2 Lloyd's Rep 87 (CA).

(a) remit the award to the tribunal, in whole or in part, for reconsideration,
(b) set the award aside in whole or in part, or
(c) declare the award to be of no effect, in whole or in part.

The court shall not exercise its power to set aside or to declare an award to be of no effect, in whole or in part, unless it is satisfied that it would be inappropriate to remit the matters in question to the tribunal for reconsideration.

(4) The leave of the court is required for any appeal from a decision of the court under this section.

NOTES

The heads of serious irregularity contained in section 68 are based on former English case law and on Article 34 of the Model Law (which lists the situations in which an award need not be enforced). There is probably little novel in section 68 in terms of principle when compared with the Model Law, but the terminology and codification are different. The list is, however, exhaustive, and there is no room for the courts to develop new grounds of serious irregularity in a manner that might lead to a general supervisory jurisdiction.[1]

Section 68(1) provides that a party, on notice to the other parties and to the tribunal, may apply to the court for an exercise of its powers under section 68(3) in the case of serious irregularity as defined by section 68(2). The section is mandatory, so it is not possible to contract out of the right to challenge an award on the basis of serious irregularity. The right to apply is subject to the waiver principle in section 73(1), and to the procedural requirements of section 70, as discussed below.

First, an application must be brought within 28 days of the date of the award[2] or the termination of any appeal process which the applicant must first exhaust (section 70(3)). The court has power to extend time under section 80(5) of the Act: extension of time is discussed in the notes to section 80. The detail of the application to the court is set out in CPR Part 62. Notice is given to the other parties by making them parties to the claim and serving on them the arbitration claim form and any supporting written evidence.[3] As noted above, if it is uncertain whether the complaint relates to jurisdiction under section 67 or serious irregularity under section 68, it would seem sensible to apply in the alternative to prevent the running of time in the event that the wrong ground is first chosen. The procedures in each case are identical. One particular difficulty has arisen where party A has succeeded in the arbitration despite a procedural error that has worked against him, but fears a challenge to the award by party B on the grounds of error of law under section 69. If party B appeals and is successful in having the award overturned, party A will have lost the right to challenge the initial arbitral proceedings under section 68. The solution adopted in *Icon Navigation Corporation* v. *Sinochem International Petroleum (Bahamas) Co Ltd*[4] is for party A to contest the section 69 application under section 69(3) on the basis that a successful appeal would give rise to serious injustice to him.

Secondly, an application may not be made before any available or agreed procedure has been exhausted by the applicant (section 70(2)). In the absence of any express contractual powers conferred on the arbitrators, the effect of section 57 should here be borne in mind. That section confers upon the arbitrators the power to correct errors, to clarify ambiguities and to make additional awards to deal with matters omitted from the original award. The 28-day time limit imposed for the making of an application to the court under section 68 runs from the date of the completion of the process under section 57 (by the issue of a new or revised award or of a decision not to amend the award) and not from the date of the original award, albeit time may run from the date of the original

1. DAC Report, para. 282.
2. Or the date the applicant is notified of the outcome of any arbitral process of review (s. 70(3)). Note that in the case of the award, the key date is not when the parties were notified of the award, or when it was delivered if, e.g., there was a delay in paying the tribunal's fees before the award was released, but when it was made, i.e., signed.
3. CPR r. 62.6(2)–(3).
4. [2004] 1 All ER (Comm) 405.

award in relation to any challenge based on substantive dispositive parts of the award that are unamended.[1]

The court's power to order security for costs or for the sum owing under the award to be brought into court as condition of hearing the application are available under section 68 (section 70(6)–(7)).

Section 68(2), which defines serious irregularity, is concerned with procedural, as opposed to substantive or jurisdictional, irregularity, and maintains the strict division between error of law and failure of procedure as drawn by the Arbitration Act 1979. There is serious irregularity if any of the grounds set out in section 68(2) is met, provided that the applicant has suffered or will suffer substantial injustice from the irregularity. The preliminary requirement of substantial injustice emphasises that the court does not have a general supervisory role over arbitrations but can be called upon to intervene only if there is clear and substantial injustice. The point is explained in the DAC Report, paragraph 280:

> The test [of substantial injustice] is not what would have happened had the matter been litigated. To apply such a test would be to ignore the fact that the parties have agreed to arbitrate, not litigate. Having chosen arbitration, the parties cannot validly complain of substantial injustice unless what has happened simply cannot on any view be defended as an acceptable consequence of that choice. In short [section 68] is really designed as a long stop, only available in extreme cases where the tribunal has gone so wrong in its conduct of the arbitration that justice calls out for it to be corrected.

This narrow approach has been recognised and applied by the courts, and most recently by the House of Lords in *Lesotho Highlands Development Authority* v. *Impregilo SpA*.[2] The decision in that case affirmed many previous judicial pronouncements to the effect that the section 68 threshold is a very high one, that being consonant with the philosophy behind the Act of minimal judicial intervention. In other words, only the most extreme cases will succeed under section 68.[3] This appears to be borne out by the statistics, in that the vast majority of section 68 challenges fail. Accordingly, a mere failure by the arbitrators to act as efficiently as they might,[4] or a minor divergence from the procedural rules established by the parties themselves,[5] is not of itself sufficient to justify a remedy under section 68. Again, if the parties have agreed that a given procedure is to be adopted, there can scarcely be substantial injustice to the claimant if that procedure is followed even if it is not one which complied with the mandatory requirements of section 33 (see the Notes to section 33 where this view is expanded). What has to be shown is that, by reason of the serious irregularity, the applicant has not been given an adequate opportunity to present his case and as a result it is possible that a different decision had thereby been reached.[6] However, even if a different result might arguably have been reached, there is not necessarily serious irregularity, as it may still

1. *Blackdale Ltd* v. *McLean Homes South East Ltd*, 2001, unreported, disapproving the contrary view expressed in *R C Pillar & Sons* v. *Edwards* [2001] CILL 1799; *Al Hadha Trading Co* v. *Tradigrain SA* [2002] 2 Lloyd's Rep 512. See further the notes to s. 57.

2. [2005] 2 Lloyd's Rep 310.

3. For a recent reaffirmation of this principle by the Court of Appeal, see *Bandwidth Shipping Corp* v. *Intaari* [2008] EWCA Civ 998.

4. *Conder Structures* v. *Kvaerner Construction Ltd* [1999] ADRLJ 305; *Andrews* v. *Bradshaw* [2000] BLR 6.

5. *Tongyuan (USA) International Trading Group* v. *Uni-Clan Ltd* 2001, unreported (Moore-Bick J) but a full summary is available at (2001) 26 Yearbook of Commercial Arbitration 886 (physical location of arbitration).

6. See: *Aquator Shipping Ltd* v. *Kleimar NV, The Capricorn I* [1998] 2 Lloyd's Rep 379; *Sanghi Polyesters Ltd* v. *The International Investor KCSC* [2000] 1 Lloyd's Rep 480; *Canadian Forest Navigation Co Ltd* v. *Minerals Transportation Ltd* 2001, unreported; *Apis AS* v. *Fantazia Kereskedelini KFT (No 2)* 2001, unreported; *Profilati Italia Srl* v. *Paine Webber Inc* [2001] 1 All ER (Comm) 1065; *Ascot Commodities NV* v. *Olam International* [2002] CLC 277; *Warborough Investments Ltd* v. *S Robinson & Sons (Holding) Ltd* [2003] 2 EGLR 149; *Checkpoint Ltd* v. *Strathclyde Pension Fund* [2003] 1 EGLR 1; *Icon Navigation Corporation* v. *Sinochem International Petroleum (Bahamas) Ltd* [2004] 1 All ER (Comm) 405; *St George's Investment Co* v. *Gemini Consulting Ltd* [2005] 1 EG 96; *Newfield* v. *Tomlinson* [2004] EWHC 3051 (TCC); *Vee Networks Ltd* v. *Econet Wireless International Ltd* [2005] 1 Lloyd's Rep 192; *Thyssen Canada Ltd* v. *Mariana Maritime SA* [2005] 1 Lloyd's Rep 640.

be the case that the costs of seeking to correct the error are disproportionate to the loss suffered by the applicant.[1]

The grounds upon which an award may be challenged as set out in section 68(2)(a)–(i) are not mutually exclusive. As will be discussed, the categories of serious irregularity may be divided into those which affect the arbitral procedure and those which affect the award.[2]

Section 68(2)(a) (breach by tribunal of principle of fairness) is perhaps the most significant provision in this list, and requires the arbitrators to adhere to the fair treatment requirement in section 33. As noted earlier, section 33 is an overriding provision.[3] Nevertheless, the tribunal has an absolute discretion in so many matters, and it would seem that such discretion is challengeable only in cases of bad faith or where there had been a complete failure by the tribunal to exercise its discretion on any identifiable basis.

There are numerous cases decided under this provision. The general principle which underlies the cases, as stated by Cresswell J in *Petroships Pte Ltd* v. *Petec Trading and Investment Corporation, The Petro Ranger*,[4] is that there can be intervention only "where it can be said that what has happened is so far removed from what can reasonably be expected of the arbitral process".[5] It is not enough, therefore, that one party asserts that he has lost confidence in the arbitrator.[6] What is required is that the complainant has been denied the opportunity to present his case fairly, for example, because the arbitrators have decided the case by reference to evidence or considerations not before them so that representations on the relevant material have not been possible,[7] or, for example, because the arbitrators have reached conclusions following direct contact with witnesses without the parties or their representatives being present,[8] or have discussed one side's expert evidence with the expert in question.[9] The Court's task on this type of application is not to second-guess the tribunal's views on any additional submissions which one side might have made if called upon to do so. It may be sufficient if that party has been deprived of the opportunity to advance submissions which were "at least reasonably arguable", or even simply something better than "hopeless".[10] That said, the arbitrators are perfectly entitled to limit the amount of evidence put to them on particular issues,[11] to assess the evidence for themselves without being forced to hear evidence on every possible inference that they might draw from it when further representations would add nothing,[12] to take account of their own expertise (in many cases the reason for their

1. *Egmatra AG* v. *Marco Trading Corporation* [1999] 1 Lloyd's Rep 862; *Weldon Plant Ltd* v. *Commission for the New Towns* [2000] BLR 496; *Pacol Ltd* v. *Joint Stock Co Rossakhar* [2000] 1 Lloyd's Rep 109; *Groundshire Ltd* v. *VHE Construction plc* [2001] BLR 395; *Mohsin* v. *Commonwealth Secretariat* [2002] EWHC 377 (Comm).

2. See the judgment of Lord Steyn in *Lesotho Highlands* at [29].

3. See the notes to s. 34 for authorities under earlier legislation.

4. [2001] 2 Lloyd's Rep 348.

5. For very similar formulations, see: *Hussmann (Europe) Ltd* v. *Pharaon* [2003] 1 All ER (Comm) 879; *Warborough Investments Ltd* v. *S Robinson & Son (Holdings) Ltd* [2003] 2 EGLR 149.

6. *Hussmann (Europe) Ltd* v. *Pharaon* [2003] 1 All ER (Comm) 879; *Conder Structures* v. *Kvaerner Construction Ltd* [1999] ADRLJ 305; *Hussmann (Europe) Ltd* v. *Al-Ameen Development & Trade Co* [2000] 2 Lloyd's Rep 83.

7. *Gbangbola* v. *Smith & Sheriff Ltd* [1998] 3 All ER 730; *Pacol Ltd* v. *Joint Stock Co Rossakhar* [2000] 1 Lloyd's Rep 109; *Apis AS* v. *Fantazia Kerskedelmi KFT (No 2)*, 2001, unreported; *Groundshire Ltd* v. *VHF Construction plc* [2001] BLR 395; *Guardcliffe Properties Ltd* v. *City & St James* [2003] 2 EGLR 16; *Vee Networks Ltd* v. *Econet Wireless International Ltd* [2005] 1 Lloyd's Rep 192; *Omnibridge Consulting Ltd* v. *Clearsprings (Management) Ltd*, October 2004, unreported.

8. *Norbrook Laboratories Co* v. *Tank* [2006] EWHC 1055 (Comm).

9. *Hussmann (Europe) Ltd* v. *Al Ameen Development & Trade Co and Ors* [2000] 2 Lloyd's Rep 83.

10. *OAO Northern Shipping Co* v. *Remolcadores de Marin SL* [2007] EWHC 1821 (Comm), *per* Gloster J at [26].

11. *Ranko Group* v. *Antarctic Maritime SA, The Robin* [1998] ADRLN 35; *Egmatra AG* v. *Marco Trading Corporation* [1999] 1 Lloyd's Rep 862; *Canadian Forest Navigation Co Ltd* v. *Minerals Transportation Ltd*, 2001, unreported.

12. *Hussmann (Europe)* v. *Al Ameen Development & Trade Co* [2000] 2 Lloyd's Rep 83; *BMBF (No 12) Ltd* v. *Harland and Wolff Shipbuilding and Heavy Industries Ltd* [2001] 2 Lloyd's Rep 227; *Balfour Beatty Construction Ltd* v. *Kelston Sparkes Contractors Ltd*, June 2001, unreported; *Bulfracht (Cyprus) Ltd* v. *Boneset Shipping Co, The MV Pamphilos* [2002] 2 Lloyd's Rep 681; *Al Hadha Trading* v. *Tradigrain SA* [2002] 2 Lloyd's Rep 512; *Miller Construction* v. *James Moore Earthmoving* [2001] 2 All ER (Comm) 598; *Tame Shipping Ltd* v. *Easy Rider Navigation Ltd, The Easy Rider* [2004] 2 Lloyd's Rep 626; *Shuttari* v. *Solicitors*

appointment) to analyse the evidence put to them[1] as long as fresh material is not introduced without giving the parties the opportunity to comment on it[2] and to adhere to procedural rules agreed to by the parties or adopted by the arbitrators within their powers under section 34.[3] If an arbitrator has failed to act impartially, the award may be challenged under this provision: the test for setting aside the award is the same as that for the removal of an arbitrator on the ground of bias under section 24 of the 1996 Act.[4] Equally, if an arbitrator has delegated his judicial functions to a third party, any decision by the third party that is adopted by the arbitrators in their award is to be treated as obtained by way of serious irregularity,[5] although there is a distinction between delegating decision-making power and relying upon the advice of an independent expert appointed by them as is their entitlement under section 37 of the 1996 Act.[6] In a recent case, the approach adopted by the majority of the tribunal members, as to the way the case was presented through the evidence and submissions without warning or giving the complainant an opportunity to address the way the majority were thinking or came to think, was held to be sufficiently unfair to warrant the award being remitted back to the arbitrators.[7] A tribunal that dismisses a claim for want of prosecution under section 41(3) does not thereby commit a serious irregularity for the purpose of section 68.[8] Likewise, there will be no serious irregularity where one party's attorney was not given the last opportunity to be heard.[9]

Section 68(2)(b) (excess of procedural powers) may be made out where, for example, the arbitrators have applied the wrong system of law to particular issues[10] or refused to grant a final remedy despite finding for the claimant,[11] but not where the procedure adopted by the arbitrator has been requested by one party and concurred in by the other.[12] As the section makes clear, the ground does not apply to cases where the tribunal has exceeded its substantive jurisdiction.[13]

Section 68(2)(c) (failure by tribunal to conduct proceedings in accordance with agreed procedure) may overlap to some extent with section 68(2)(b). In practice this head will be of little significance, as the arbitrators are free to determine the procedure in the absence of any agreement to the contrary and there is rarely any such agreement. In those cases where there is agreement, the arbitrators are entitled to adhere to what has been agreed[14] or accepted by way of variation.[15] A statement by the arbitrators as to how the arbitration is to be conducted must be adhered to by them.[16]

Section 68(2)(d) (tribunal's failure to deal with all issues) reflects the previous common law position that an award which does not deal with all the issues may be remitted back to the arbitrators

Indemnity Fund Ltd [2004] EWHC 1537 (Ch); *Alphapoint Shipping Ltd* v. *Rotem Amfert Negev Ltd, The Agios Dimitros* [2005] 1 Lloyd's Rep 23; *Icon Navigation Corporation* v. *Sinochem International Petroleum (Bahamas) Co Ltd* [2004] 1 All ER (Comm) 405; *O'Donoghue* v. *Enterprise Inns Plc* [2008] EWHC B15 (Ch).

1. *Thomas Borthwick (Glasgow) Ltd* v. *Faure Fairclough Ltd* [1968] 1 Lloyd's Rep 16; *Sanghi Polyesters Ltd* v. *The International Investor KCFC (Kuwait)* [2000] 1 Lloyd's Rep 480; *Checkpoint Ltd* v. *Strathclyde Pension Fund* [2003] 1 EGLR 1; *Warborough Investments Ltd* v. *S Robinson & Sons (Holding) Ltd* [2003] 2 EGLR 149; *Hawk Shipping Ltd* v. *Cron Navigation Ltd* [2003] EWHC 1828 (Comm); *Alphapoint Shipping Ltd* v. *Rotem Amfert Negev Ltd, The Agios Dimitrios* [2005] 1 Lloyd's Rep 23; *Bottiglieri di Navigatzione SpA* v. *Cosco Qingdao Ocean Shipping Co, The Bunga Saga Lima*, 2005, unreported.

2. *Fox* v. *P G Wellfair* [1982] 2 Lloyd's Rep 514; *St George's Investment Co* v. *Gemini Consulting Ltd* [2005] 1 EG 96.

3. *Brandeis (Brokers) Ltd* v. *Black* [2001] 2 Lloyd's Rep 359; *AOOT Kalmneft* v. *Glencore International AG* [2002] 1 Lloyd's Rep 128; *Westland Helicopters Ltd* v. *Sheikh Salah Al-Hejailan* [2004] 2 Lloyd's Rep 523; *Margulead Ltd* v. *Exide Technologies* [2004] 2 All ER (Comm) 727.

4. *Rustal Trading SA* v. *Gill & Duffus SA* [2000] 1 Lloyd's Rep 14.

5. *Al Midani* v. *Al Midani* [2000] 1 Lloyd's Rep 923.

6. *Hussmann (Europe) Ltd* v. *Al Ameen Development & Trade Co* [2000] 2 Lloyd's Rep 83.

7. *Cameroon Airlines* v. *Transnet Ltd* [2004] EWHC 1829 (Comm), *per* Langley J.

8. *TAG Wealth Management* v. *West* [2008] All ER (D) 386 (Jun).

9. *Margulead Ltd* v. *Exide Technologies* [2005] 1 Lloyd's Rep 324.

10. *Lesotho Highlands Authority* v. *Impregilo SpA* [2003] 2 Lloyd's Rep 497 (interest).

11. *Ronly Holdings* v. *JSC Zestafoni G Nikoladze Ferroalloy Plant* [2004] EWHC 1354 (Comm).

12. *Westland Helicopters Ltd* v. *Sheikh Salah Al-Hejailan* [2004] 2 Lloyd's Rep 523.

13. A challenge under s. 68(2)(b) was held to be one more properly falling under s. 67 in *Bernuth Lines Ltd* v. *High Seas Shipping Ltd, The Eastern Navigator* [2006] 1 Lloyd's Rep 537.

14. *Minermet SpA Milan* v. *Luckyfield Shipping Corporation SA* [2004] 2 Lloyd's Rep 348.

15. *Westland Helicopters Ltd* v. *Sheikh Salah Al-Hejailan* [2004] 2 Lloyd's Rep 523.

16. *Checkpoint Ltd* v. *Strathclyde Pension Fund* [2003] 1 EGLR 1 (no promise of the type alleged, on the facts).

with a direction to remedy the deficiency.[1] There is nevertheless a distinction between failing to deal with major issues[2] and failing to deal in the award with every argument in detail that was put to the arbitrators: the latter allegation will fail unless the claimant can show that, on a fair reading of the award, key issues were not considered at all.[3] Further, an "issue" for these purposes is one which is of decisive effect on the outcome, and not an incidental or peripheral matter whose resolution was largely immaterial to the overall result or which fell away in the light of other holdings.[4] Section 68(2)(d) cannot be used where the reality of the allegation is that the issue was resolved, but not to the satisfaction of the claimant,[5] for example, because the findings were expressed briefly or even unclearly.[6] Furthermore, there is no serious irregularity if a tribunal decides a case on the basis of a point not argued before it, so long as the issue in question was "in play" in the arbitration.[7] Section 68 is not available for use as a backdoor attempt to challenge findings of fact.[8]

As noted above, section 68(1) itself states it is possible to bring proceedings for serious irregularity only where the requirements of section 70(2) have been complied with. That subsection provides that it is necessary for the claimant to exhaust "any available recourse under section 57". Section 57 is available where a claim submitted to the arbitrator has not been dealt with in the award, and the aggrieved party may then apply to the arbitrators for the award to be corrected. It is apparent from section 68(1) that any failure to make an application to the arbitrators under section 57(1) within the statutory time limits set out in that section will mean that the claimant will have failed to avail himself of "any available recourse", and will thus be barred from appealing against the award under section 68. This is of particular significance in relation to section 68(2)(d), any complaint under which will almost inevitably fall within section 57. Accordingly, an application to the arbitrator under section 57 is a jurisdictional pre-requisite to an application based on section 68(2)(d).[9]

Section 68(2)(e) (excess of power by arbitral body or similar). This would apply to, for example, errors in an appeal procedure conducted under the auspices of an arbitral body. There are no reported decisions on this ground, which is probably as a result of the circumstances in which it could be invoked being extremely rare.[10]

Section 68(2)(f) (award uncertain or ambiguous) codifies the common law principle that an award must be clear and capable of performance and enforcement in order to be valid.[11] Minor ambiguity

1. This point is illustrated by numerous cases. For a recent restatement of the principle by the Court of Appeal, see *Checkpoint Ltd* v. *Strathclyde Pension Fund* [2003] EWCA Civ 84.

2. *Petroships Pte Ltd of Singapore* v. *Petec Trading and Investment Corporation of Vietnam* [2001] 2 Lloyd's Rep 348; *Ascot Commodities NV* v. *Olam International Ltd* [2002] CLC 277; *Ronly Holdings* v. *JSC Zestafoni G Nikoladze Ferroalloy Plant* [2004] EWHC 1354 (Comm).

3. Allegations of this type, based on the reasoning in the award, were made and rejected in: *Hussmann (Europe)* v. *Al Ameen Development & Trade Co* [2000] 2 Lloyd's Rep 83; *Al Hadha Trading Co* v. *Tradigrain SA* [2002] 2 Lloyd's Rep 512; *CR Sugar Trading Ltd* v. *China National Sugar and Alcohol Group* [2003] 1 Lloyd's Rep 279; *Torch Offshore LLC* v. *Cable Shipping Inc* [2004] 2 Lloyd's Rep 446; *Margulead Ltd* v. *Exide Technologies* [2004] 2 All ER (Comm) 727; *Benaim (UK) Ltd* v. *Davies Middleton & Davies* [2005] EWHC 1370 (TCC); *Fidelity Management SA* v. *Myriad International Holdings* [2005] 2 Lloyd's Rep 508; *Protech Projects Construction* v. *Al-Kharafi & Sons* [2005] 2 Lloyd's Rep 779.

4. *Weldon Plant Ltd* v. *Commission for the New Towns* [2000] BLR 496; *Checkpoint Ltd* v. *Strathclyde Pension Fund* [2003] 1 EGLR 1. See also: *Fidelity Management SA* v. *Myriad International Holdings* [2005] 2 Lloyd's Rep. 508.

5. *World Trade Corporation Ltd* v. *Czarnikow Sugar Ltd* [2004] 2 All ER (Comm) 813, cited with approval by HHJ Peter Coulson QC in *Benaim (UK) Ltd* v. *Davies Middleton & Davies* [2005] EWHC 1370 (TCC).

6. *ABB AG* v. *Hochtief Airport GmbH* [2006] 2 Lloyd's Rep 1.

7. *ABB AG* v. *Hochtief Airport GmbH* [2006] 2 Lloyd's Rep 1.

8. *Warborough Investments Ltd* v. *S Robinson and Sons Holdings Limited* [2003] EWCA Civ 751; *JD Wetherspoon plc* v. *Jay Mar Estates* [2007] EWHC 856 (TCC).

9. *Groundshire* v. *VHE Construction* [2001] BLR 395; *Al Hadha Trading Co* v. *Tradigrain SA* [2002] 2 Lloyd's Rep 512; *Torch Offshore LLC* v. Cable Shipping Inc [2004] 2 Lloyd's Rep 446; *World Trade Corporation Ltd* v. *Czarnikow Sugar Ltd* [2004] 2 All ER (Comm) 813.

10. There is no equivalent ground in the Model Law.

11. See the notes to s. 52. The leading authorities under earlier legislation are: *Lee* v. *Elkins* (1701) 12 Mod Rep 585; *Lawrence* v. *Hodgson* (1826) 1 YJ 16; *Fenton* v. *Dimes* (1840) 9 LJQB 297; *Montrose Canned Foods Ltd* v. *Eric Wells (Merchants) Ltd* [1965] 1 Lloyd's Rep 597; *River Plate Products Netherlands BV* v. *Etablissement Coargrain* [1982] 1 Lloyd's Rep 628.

not affecting the substance of the award is excluded from challenge. The wording of this provision is intended to reflect the fact that ambiguities in the reasoning or other aspects of the award are not of themselves serious irregularities: the Act is concerned only with the ability of the winning party to enforce the award, and what is required is that the obligations of the parties under the award are free from ambiguity.[1] It is essential that application is first made to the arbitrators under section 57, failing which section 68(1) precludes any appeal.

Section 68(2)(g) (award obtained by fraud, etc) states a series of obvious principles relating to fraud and public policy. What is required to trigger this head of appeal is fraud on the part of the successful party in the arbitration, for example, the deliberate withholding of material evidence or abuse of the arbitral process.[2] A negligent or innocent failure to produce evidence,[3] or the absence of unconscionable behaviour in the conduct of the arbitration,[4] will not suffice. To be contrary to public policy, the impugned conduct had to involve more than inadvertence and generally had to involve something which could readily be described as unconscionable or reprehensible.[5] A dishonest intention to mislead the tribunal would suffice, or conduct that could be "comfortably described" as fraud.[6] The test to be applied to show serious irregularity, where the award was alleged to have been obtained by fraud in the shape of perjury, was that the claimant had to produce evidence newly discovered since the trial which could not have been produced at the trial with reasonable diligence and which was so material that its production at the trial would probably have affected the result and (when the fraud consists of perjury) was so strong that it would reasonably be expected to be decisive at the re-hearing.[7] A failure in memory on the part of the lawyers or the party applying under this head of section 68 and/or a failure to obtain a document which could otherwise have been obtained before the arbitration hearing was a lack of due diligence.[8] An allegation of perjury against another party to the arbitration would not itself be sufficient, particularly if the credibility of the witnesses was in issue before the arbitrators.[9]

Section 68(2)(h) (failure to comply with formal requirements of award) refers back to section 52, which sets out the minimum requirements for the form of an award: the parties are free to agree these, but if they fail to do so section 52 provides minimum default requirements.[10] A failure to provide a reasoned award will, therefore, justify an appeal under this subsection, although it is essential that application is first made to the arbitrators under section 57, failing which section 68(1) precludes any appeal.[11]

Section 68(2)(i) (admitted irregularity) deals with a specific ground upon which remission was available under the 1950 Act. It had long been recognised that, if the award contained an error not capable of correction under the "slip" rule now contained in (and expanded by) section 57, the arbitrators, or the parties themselves, could apply to the court for the award to be remitted to them for correction.[12] In its origins the power of the court to remit was confined to admitted mistakes, but in later cases the power was exercised if a mistake was subsequently discovered whether or not it

1. DAC Supplementary Report, para. 35. See *Tongyuan (USA) International Trading Group* v. *Uni-Clan Ltd* January 2001, unreported (Moore-Bick J) but a full summary is available at (2001) 26 Yearbook of Commercial Arbitration 886.

2. An allegation of this type was made in *Thyssen Canada Ltd* v. *Mariana Maritime SA* in [2005] 1 Lloyd's Rep 640 and *DDT Trucks of North America* v. *DDT Holdings Ltd* [2007] 2 Lloyd's Rep 213. The provision is not concerned with public policy considerations which might affect the substance of the award: *R* v. *V* [2008] EWHC 1531 (Comm).

3. *Profilati Italia Srl* v. *Paine Webber Inc* [2001] 1 Lloyd's Rep 715.

4. *Cuflet Chartering* v. *Carousel Shipping Co Ltd, The Marie H* [2001] 1 Lloyd's Rep 707.

5. *Protech Projects Construction* v. *Al-Kharafi & Sons* [2005] 2 Lloyd's Rep 779.

6. *Gater Assets* v. *Nak Naftogaz Ukrainy (No 2)* [2008] 1 Lloyd's Rep 479.

7. *Thyssen Canada Ltd* v. *Mariana Maritime SA* in [2005] 1 Lloyd's Rep 640. See also: *DDT Trucks of North America Ltd* v. *DDT Holdings Ltd* [2007] 2 Lloyd's Rep 213.

8. *DDT Trucks of North America Ltd* v. *DDT Holdings Ltd* [2007] 2 Lloyd's Rep 213.

9. *Thyssen Canada Ltd* v. *Mariana Maritime SA* [2005] 1 Lloyd's Rep 640. See also: *L Brown & Sons Ltd* v. *Crosby Homes (North West) Ltd* [2008] EWHC 817 (TCC).

10. See the notes to s. 52.

11. *Groundshire* v. *VHE Construction* [2001] BLR 395; *Al Hadha Trading Co* v. *Tradigrain SA* [2002] 2 Lloyd's Rep 512; *Torch Offshore LLC* v. *Cable Shipping Inc* [2004] 2 Lloyd's Rep 446.

12. *Anderson* v. *Darcy* (1812) 18 Ves Jr 447; *Flynn* v. *Robertson* (1869) LR 4 CP 324.

was admitted by the arbitrators.[1] Section 68(2)(i) confines application for relief to admitted mistakes,[2] although it is likely that a number of both admitted and non-admitted mistakes previously curable only by remission can be dealt with by the arbitrators acting on their own initiative under the expanded slip rule in section 57. If the arbitrators fail to admit that they have made a mistake and thus refuse to exercise their powers to review their award under the slip rule, there is no obvious remedy as none of the grounds under section 68(2) appear to be applicable.[3]

Section 68(3) sets out the powers of the court following a finding by the court that the award is affected by serious irregularity. In short, the court may remit, set aside or declare the award to be of no effect.[4]

In each case the court's order may apply to part of an award rather than to all of it.[5] Prior to the passing of the 1996 Act the entire award had to be remitted, although the arbitrators were permitted to reconsider only those aspects of the award identified by the court. The distinction between remitting the entire award but directing parts of it for reconsideration, and partial remission, was significant where, for example, there was an attempt to enforce those issues in the award not remitted. The effect of the pre-1996 law was that a remitted award was suspended in its entirety.[6]

If the award is remitted, it is likely that the same arbitrators will be retained, for although an arbitrator becomes *functus officio* once the award is made, his jurisdiction is revived by remission, albeit only to the extent of the remission so that no new matters can be argued.[7] Indeed, those parts of the award not remitted remain valid and enforceable.[8] If, by contrast, the award is set aside or nullified but the dispute remains in arbitration, the court has the power (if requested by a party) to remove the arbitrators under section 24 of the Act, and (if so removed) they are to be replaced in accordance with the procedure for appointment of the original arbitrators, under section 27 of the Act.

The proviso to section 68(3) codifies the principle developed under the 1950 Act that, faced with a choice of remitting or setting aside the award, the court is to remit wherever it can and to set aside only where remission would not be appropriate.[9] The cases demonstrate that setting aside the award is appropriate where irregularity is so severe that there has to be a full rehearing,[10] or where it is otherwise inappropriate to allow the original arbitrators to reconsider their award due, for example, to incompetence or bias.[11] It may also be appropriate to order a new hearing if there has been considerable delay between the award and the order for remission and there is room for dispute as to exactly what transpired at the initial arbitration.[12]

1. *Mutual Shipping Corporation* v. *Bayshore Shipping Co, The Montan* [1985] 1 Lloyd's Rep 189; *Food Corporation of India* v. *Marastro Compania Naviera SA, The Trade Fortitude* [1985] 2 Lloyd's Rep 579; *Danae Air Transport Société Anonyme* v. *Air Canada* [1999] 2 Lloyd's Rep 547.

2. E.g., failure to adjust an award on costs following variation of the main award: *Gannet Shipping Ltd* v. *Eastrade Commodities Inc* [2002] 1 Lloyd's Rep 713.

3. In *Danae Air Transport Société Anonyme* v. *Air Canada* [1999] 2 Lloyd's Rep 547 the Court of Appeal held that there could be remission under the 1950 Act in this situation, but did not comment on the position under the 1996 Act, although the court appears to have been of the view that the same result was somehow obtainable: it is not easy to see the basis for this view. Contrast *Costain Civil Engineering Ltd* v. *Zanen Dredging and Contracting Co Ltd* (1998) 14 Const LJ 44, in which HHJ Humphrey Lloyd, QC, ruled that an error of fact or law was not misconduct or otherwise a ground for remission under the 1950 Act.

4. It was held in *Hussmann (Europe) Ltd* v. *Pharaon* [2003] 1 All ER (Comm) 879 that in the context of an order made under s. 67, there was no material difference between an order setting an award aside and an order declaring the award to be of no effect. There is no reason in principle why the same reasoning ought not to apply to s. 68.

5. See: *Petroships Pte Ltd of Singapore* v. *Petec Trading and Investment Corporation of Vietnam* [2001] 2 Lloyd's Rep 348.

6. *Huyton SA* v. *Jakil SpA* [1999] 2 Lloyd's Rep 83, a point not established until after the passing of the 1996 Act.

7. *Glencore International AG* v. *Beogradska Plovidba, The Avala* [1996] 2 Lloyd's Rep 311.

8. *Carter* v. *Simpson Associates (Architects) Ltd* [2004] 2 Lloyd's Rep 512.

9. *Miller's Timber Trust Co* v. *Plywood Factory Julius Potempa* (1939) 63 Ll L Rep 184.

10. *Pacol Ltd* v. *Joint Stock Co Rossakhar* [2000] 1 Lloyd's Rep 109.

11. Representative authorities include: *Eastcheap Dried Fruit Co* v. *NV Gebroeders Catz Handelsvereeniging* [1962] 1 Lloyd's Rep 283; *Hagop Ardahalian* v. *Unifruit International SA, The Elissar* [1984] 1 Lloyd's Rep 206; *Bremer Handelsgesellschaft mbH* v. *Ets Soules et Cie* [1985] 1 Lloyd's Rep 160; *Miller Construction Ltd* v. *James Moore Earthmoving* [2001] BLR 322.

12. *Ascot Commodities NV* v. *Olam International Ltd* [2002] CLC 277.

Section 68(4) contains the usual provision that any appeal from the court's decision is possible only where the court itself has given permission: for this purpose the "court" means the trial judge and not the Court of Appeal.[1] For this reason, a refusal by the trial judge of permission to appeal is a decision under the section and cannot be challenged by way of appeal to the Court of Appeal even if the decision was wrong or obviously wrong.[2]

Appeal on point of law

69.—(1) Unless otherwise agreed by the parties, a party to arbitral proceedings may (upon notice to the other parties and to the tribunal) appeal to the court on a question of law arising out of an award made in the proceedings.

An agreement to dispense with reasons for the tribunal's award shall be considered an agreement to exclude the court's jurisdiction under this section.

(2) An appeal shall not be brought under this section except—

(a) with the agreement of all the other parties to the proceedings, or
(b) with the leave of the court.

The right to appeal is also subject to the restrictions in section 70(2) and (3).

(3) Leave to appeal shall be given only if the court is satisfied—

(a) that the determination of the question will substantially affect the rights of one or more of the parties,
(b) that the question is one which the tribunal was asked to determine,
(c) that, on the basis of the findings of fact in the award—
 (i) the decision of the tribunal on the question is obviously wrong, or
 (ii) the question is one of general public importance and the decision of the tribunal is at least open to serious doubt, and
(d) that, despite the agreement of the parties to resolve the matter by arbitration, it is just and proper in all the circumstances for the court to determine the question.

(4) An application for leave to appeal under this section shall identify the question of law to be determined and state the grounds on which it is alleged that leave to appeal should be granted.

(5) The court shall determine an application for leave to appeal under the section without a hearing unless it appears to the court that a hearing is required.

(6) The leave of the court is required for any appeal from a decision of the court under this section to grant or refuse leave to appeal.

(7) On an appeal under this section the court may by order—

(a) confirm the award,
(b) vary the award,
(c) remit the award to the tribunal, in whole or in part, for reconsideration in the light of the court's determination, or
(d) set aside the award in whole or in part.

1. *Henry Boot Construction (UK) Ltd* v. *Malmaison Hotel (Manchester) Ltd* [2001] 1 QB 388; *Athletic Union of Constantinople* v. *National Basketball Association* [2002] 1 Lloyd's Rep 305; *Virdee* v. *Virdi* [2003] EWCA Civ 41.
2. *ASM Shipping* v. *TTMI Ltd* [2007] 1 Lloyd's Rep 136.

The court shall not exercise its power to set aside an award, in whole or in part, unless it is satisfied that it would be inappropriate to remit the matters in question to the tribunal for reconsideration.

(8) The decision of the court on an appeal under this section shall be treated as a judgment of the court for the purposes of a further appeal.

But no such appeal lies without the leave of the court which shall not be given unless the court considers that the question is one of general importance or is one which for some other special reason should be considered by the Court of Appeal.

NOTES

Section 69 broadly re-enacts earlier legislation. The former provisions (as clarified by case law) were left more or less intact under the 1996 Act, although the right of appeal was restricted in a number of respects. The main changes were that the criteria which have to be met before permission for a non-consensual appeal will be given were adopted in a modified form by section 69, and that it has become easier for the parties to exclude review by agreeing that no reasons are to be given in the award. The other changes were largely technical.

It was put to the DAC during consultation on the July 1995 Bill that the right of appeal on a point of law should be abolished in its entirety, as by going to arbitration the parties had agreed to abide by the ruling of the arbitrators and not to treat it as a preliminary step to judicial proceedings. The DAC rejected this approach, even though it is adopted in other jurisdictions, on the ground that a limited right of appeal is not inconsistent with an agreement to arbitrate, and the parties may well have intended that the result is to comply with established legal principle, for example, where they have specifically chosen the law applicable to their substantive agreement (DAC Report, paragraph 285).

Section 69(1) sets out the basic right of any party to apply to the court for permission to appeal against the award on a point of law. The section applies to any award, including a provisional or partial award, although an application based on the incompleteness of such an award is almost doomed to fail given that the arbitrators have the opportunity to deal with further issues in their final award.[1] The alleged error of law must arise "out of the award", and it has been held that an error which became apparent in post-award correspondence between the parties and the arbitrator falls within the section.[2] Directions given by the arbitrators are not awards and are not within section 69.[3]

Many of the cases decided under the 1979 Act involved the issue whether the point of error was one of fact (unreviewable) or law (reviewable). In general, and at risk of over-simplification, questions concerning the scope or meaning of a contract,[4] or the meaning of an earlier arbitration award[5] are questions of law, whereas questions concerning the performance of the parties to a contract or the application of the contract are questions of fact.[6] It has been held under the 1996 Act that factual findings made by the arbitrators which have no basis whatsoever in the evidence amount to errors of law,[7] although this approach seems to be inconsistent with the principle that arbitrators

1. *BMBF (No 12) Ltd* v. *Harland and Wolff Shipbuilding and Heavy Industries Ltd* [2001] 2 Lloyd's Rep 227.

2. *Checkpoint Ltd* v. *Strathclyde Pension Fund* [2002] EWHC 432 (Ch); the point did not arise on appeal, [2003] 1 EGLR 1.

3. *Urban Small Space Ltd* v. *Burford Investment* (1990) 28 EG 116. Such an issue cannot in any event satisfy the requirement in s. 69(3)(a).

4. *Islamic Republic of Iran Shipping Lines* v. *The Royal Bank of Scotland, The Anna Ch* [1987] 1 Lloyd's Rep 266; *Islamic Republic of Iran Shipping Lines* v. *Ierax Shipping Co of Panama, The Forum Craftsman* [1991] 1 Lloyd's Rep 81.

5. *Sun Life Assurance Company of Canada* v. *The Lincoln National Life Insurance Co* [2004] EWCA Civ 1660.

6. *Moran* v. *Lloyd's* [1983] 1 Lloyd's Rep 51; *Marc Rich Co AG* v. *Beogradska Plovidba, The Avala* [1994] 2 Lloyd's Rep 363; *Cadmus Investment Co* v. *Amec Building Ltd* [1998] ADRLJ 72.

7. *Fence Gate Ltd* v. *NEL Construction Ltd* (2001) 82 Con LR 41; *Guardcliffe Properties Ltd* v. *City & St James* [2003] 2 EGLR 16; *Newfield* v. *Tomlinson* [2004] EWHC 3051 (TCC).

alone are entitled to find the facts.[1] The courts have deprecated attempts to dress up factual findings[2] or procedural errors[3] as errors of law for the purpose of an application to the courts. In any event, the term "question of law", under section 82(1), refers to domestic law, so that the English courts will not seek to deal with issues of foreign law,[4] and this is the case even if the foreign law is the same as (or treated as identical to) English law.[5]

As indicated by the opening words of section 69(1), the right to appeal can be excluded by agreement. The concluding words of section 69(1) deal with the situation in which the parties have agreed that reasons for the award are not to be given. If reasons are excluded, but are nevertheless given, section 69(2) continues to prevent review of the award for error of law.

An agreement to exclude judicial review, as is the case with all agreements under the Act (see section 5), must be in writing. Although the 1996 Act does not say so, it may be presumed that the exclusion agreement need not form part of the arbitration clause, as it is valid only if entered into after the commencement of arbitration proceedings. It remains under the 1996 Act possible for the arbitration clause to refer to standard institutional rules which contain exclusion provisions.[6]

It would seem from the unqualified wording of section 69(2)(a) that an agreement to appeal can be included in the arbitration clause itself[7] or made at any stage in the arbitration proceedings, and not just made after the award has been issued. This interpretation was confirmed in the DAC Report, paragraph 292, and the same approach has been adopted in subsequent judicial decisions,[8] although the DAC pointed out that an agreement to permit an appeal does not necessarily give any right to appeal as far as the courts are concerned, as the remaining conditions of sections 69 and 70 still have to be met.[9] An agreement will operate as one excluding the right of appeal if it purports to waive all rights of appeal insofar as this is permissible,[10] and it was held in *Al Hadha Trading Co* v. *Tradigrain SA*[11] that a statement that the award is to be "final, conclusive and binding" also operates

1. See s. 34(2)(f). The root case, *Fence Gate*, draws a distinction between insufficient evidence (no error of law) and an absence of evidence (potentially an error of law). The problem, however, is that there has to be a review of the award and of the evidence in order to discover which category is involved.

2. *Torch Offshore LLC* v. *Cable Shipping Inc* [2004] 2 Lloyd's Rep 446; *Mowlem plc* v. *PHI Group Ltd* [2004] BLR 421.

3. *Petroships Pte Ltd of Singapore* v. *Petec Trading & Investment Corporation* [2001] 2 Lloyd's Rep 348; *Lesotho Highlands Development Authority* v. *Impregilo SpA* [2003] 2 Lloyd's Rep 497; *Marklands Ltd* v. *Virgin Retail Ltd* [2004] 2 EGLR 43.

4. *Egmatra AG* v. *Marco Trading Corporation* [1999] 1 Lloyd's Rep 862; *Hussmann (Europe) Ltd* v. *Al Ameen Development & Trade Co* [2000] 2 Lloyd's Rep 83; *Sanghi Polyesters Ltd* v. *The International Investor KCFC (Kuwait)* [2000] 1 Lloyd's Rep 480; *Athletic Union of Constantinople* v. *National Basketball Association* [2001] 1 Lloyd's Rep 305.

5. *Reliance Industries Ltd* v. *Enron Oil and Gas Ltd* [2002] 1 Lloyd's Rep 645.

6. Such as under the LCIA and ICC Rules of Arbitration.

7. Or incorporated from some other document: *Arab African Energy Corporation Ltd* v. *Olieprodukten Nederland BV* [1983] 2 Lloyd's Rep 419; *Marine Contractors Inc* v. *Shell Petroleum Development Co of Nigeria Ltd* [1984] 2 Lloyd's Rep 77. There are some standard word building contracts that have been judicially confirmed as including the requisite agreement under s. 69(2)(a): see *Taylor Woodrow Civil Engineering Ltd* v. *Hutchinson Development Ltd* [1999] ADLRJ 83 and *Fence Gate Ltd* v. *NEL Construction Ltd* [2001] 82 Con LR 41.

8. *Vascroft (Contractors) Ltd* v. *Seeboard plc* (1996) 78 BLR 132; *Poseidon Schiffahrt GmbH* v. *Nomadic Navigation Co Ltd, The Trade Nomad* [1998] 1 Lloyd's Rep 57; *Ballast Wilshier* v. *Thomas Barnes & Sons*, 1998, unreported; *Taylor Woodrow Civil Engineering Ltd* v. *Hutchinson IDH Development Ltd* (1998) 75 Con LR 1.

9. See *Royal & Sun Alliance Insurance plc* v. *BAe Systems* [2008] EWHC 743 (Comm) at [8].

10. *Arab African Energy Corporation Ltd* v. *Olieprodukten Nederland BV* [1983] 2 Lloyd's Rep 419; *Sanghi Polyesters Ltd* v. *The International Investor KCFC (Kuwait)* [2000] 1 Lloyd's Rep 480. There is a valid agreement to this effect contained in the ICC Rules of Arbitration (1998 edition, Art. 28.6) and the LCIA Rules (1998 edition, Art. 26.9), as these each contain an express waiver of the right of appeal.

11. [2002] 2 Lloyd's Rep 512. It is nevertheless unclear whether the formula by which the parties agree to treat the award as "final and binding" (found in both the UNCITRAL Rules of Arbitration (Art. 32.2) and the AAA Arbitration Rules (2008 edition, Art. 27.1) is sufficient to amount to an exclusion of the right of appeal on a point of law under this section, although there is authority from New Zealand to suggest that the inclusion of similar wording in the arbitration agreement is a matter the court is likely to take into account in deciding whether to exercise its discretion to permit an appeal to be made: *Gold and Resource Developments (NZ) Ltd* v. *Doug Hood Ltd* [2000] NZCA 131. In *DDT Trucks of North America* v. *DDT Holdings Ltd* [2007] 2 Lloyd's Rep 213, permission would have been granted for an appeal on a point of law notwithstanding the fact that the arbitration was subject to the AAA Rules (but was refused on other grounds).

as an exclusion agreement. One type of wording which is clearly intended to exclude any judicial review is the adoption by the parties of an "equity" arbitration clause, whereby the arbitrators are free to disregard strict rules of law or construction. The validity of such clauses was in doubt prior to the passing of 1996 Act, but they now appear to be validated by section 46(1)(b), and the DAC has expressed the view that such a clause effectively excludes judicial review as there can be no point of law involved. It is also the case that there can be no appeal against an agreed award made under section 51, representing a settlement between the parties, by virtue of section 52(4), as no reasons for the award can be given (for by definition in most cases there will be no reasons).

Section 69(2) re-enacts the 1979 Act in providing that an appeal may be brought only if either all the parties agree or if the court gives permission. The proviso incorporating the requirements of section 70(2) and (3) is new to the 1996 Act, but familiar as regards applications under sections 67 and 68 based on excess of jurisdiction and substantial irregularity. Section 69(2) requires the applicant to exhaust any internal appeal or other arbitral procedure before applying to the court. In the case of a commodity arbitration, for example, any procedure involving a Board of Appeal must be conducted prior to the application, and any ambiguity must first be resolved by an application to the arbitrators under section 57.[1] Section 70(3) imposes a 28-day time limit for the application to the court, running from the date of the award or of the outcome of any internal appeal. The period is extendable by the court under its general discretion in section 80(5). The detail of the application to the court is set out in CPR Part 62. An arbitration claim form must be issued within 28 days, and must be served on the other parties along with any written evidence, and they must be made parties to the application.[2] The statutory formalities are exhaustive, so that the applicant is not allowed to submit further documents, in particular the pleadings or evidence used in the arbitration: it was decided in *Foleys Ltd* v. *City and East London Family and Community Services*[3] and confirmed in *HOK Sport Ltd* v. *Aintree Racecourse Co Ltd*[4] that, as the only question is whether the arbitrators have erred in law, such material is irrelevant. Indeed, in *The Northern Pioneer*[5] the Court of Appeal warned against excessive paperwork, and stated that

> any written submissions placed before the Court in support of an application for permission to appeal from findings in an arbitral award should normally be capable of being read and digested by the Judge within the half-hour that, under the old regime, used to be allotted for such applications.

If the appeal is not consensual, the arbitration application must, under section 69(4), identify the question of law and state the ground on which the claimant alleges that permission should be granted,[6] and there must be supplementary written evidence showing that the statutory criteria for an appeal have been satisfied and that permission should be given.[7] If the respondent wishes to oppose the application, the written evidence must state the grounds of opposition, set out any evidence relating to the statutory criteria and specify the grounds upon which the award should be upheld.[8]

Where the application is made with the written consent of all of the parties (the writing requirement being new), the appeal may go ahead without more: it is permissible for that consent to be contained in the arbitration clause itself or in an agreement made at any other time prior to the award.[9] If, by contrast, as is nearly always the case, the application is made by one party without

1. *Gbangbola* v. *Smith & Sheriff Ltd* [1998] 3 All ER 730.
2. CPR r. 62.6(2)–(3).
3. [1997] ADRLJ 401.
4. [2003] BLR 156.
5. [2003] 1 All ER (Comm) 204.
6. Arbitration Act 1996, s. 69(4) and CPR PD 62, para. 12.1.
7. CPR PD 62, para. 12.2.
8. CPR PD 62, para. 12.3.
9. *Vinava Shipping Co Ltd* v. *Finelvet AG, The Chrysalis* [1983] 1 Lloyd's Rep 503; *Taylor Woodrow Civil Engineering Ltd* v. *Hutchinson IDH Development Ltd* (1998) 75 Con LR 1; *Fence Gate Ltd* v. *NEL Construction Ltd* (2001) 82 Con LR 41. See also Royal *& Sun Alliance Insurance plc* v. *BAe Systems* [2008] EWHC 743 (Comm), where an express contractual term permitting an appeal was held to override the exclusion of any right of appeal under the LCIA Rules.

the consent of the other, section 69(3) imposes a series of conditions precedent to the giving of permission by the court.

Section 69(3)(a) requires that the determination of the question of law will substantially affect the rights of the parties. This may go to the jurisdiction of the court.[1] However, in a case where an appeal was brought under section 69 against an arbitral award in conjunction with a challenge under section 68, permission was refused on the basis that the rights of the parties would not be substantially affected in the light of the section 68 application failing.[2] This particular jurisdictional condition precedent applies only to applications for permission made without the consent of one or more of the parties. The requirement will not be satisfied if the issue is purely hypothetical, because the award was determined by reference to other issues,[3] or if the disputed matter is one of procedure only which does not affect the substantive outcome.[4] The word "rights" refers to the rights of the parties in respect of the dispute, and not to any extraneous considerations: the applicant for permission to appeal cannot, therefore, pray in aid considerations which have nothing to do with the dispute, for example, its financial position.[5]

Section 69(3)(b) requires the point of law which has been appealed to be one which not only was dealt with in the award, but also one which has been raised in the proceedings. The effect of section 69(3)(b) is to impose an estoppel on the parties from seeking permission to appeal a point which they did not argue before the arbitrators.[6] If a point of law has not been raised before the arbitrators but they have nevertheless chosen to deal with it, section 69(3)(b) does seemingly not—despite its express wording—preclude a challenge under section 69 where they have erred in their conclusions in relation to that point of law and it has a significant impact on the outcome.[7]

Section 69(3)(c) appears on its face to purport to codify guidelines laid down in *The Nema*[8] as to appeals on a question of law under the 1979 Act in a simpler form. However, it is clear from the decision of the Court of Appeal in *The Northern Pioneer*[9] that this is not the case and that there is potentially greater scope for the grant of permission to appeal under the 1996 Act than was the case under the 1979 Act. The initial distinction to be drawn is between a point of law of general public importance, where the test is whether the conclusion is "open to serious doubt", and other (one-off) cases, where the test is whether the tribunal is "obviously wrong".[10] A point of law is of general public importance where it raises the construction of a standard form contract or where the facts are commonly encountered. By contrast, a case is "one off" if the contract is individually negotiated, or contains unusual provisions, or has arisen for construction in the light of unique facts.

The principles established by *The Nema* hold good in most circumstances,[11] so that the mere fact that the court might have reached a different conclusion does not render an award open to serious

1. The point of law must affect the outcome of the arbitration, and must not merely affect one small and severable part of the award: *Stinnes Interoil GmbH* v. *Halcoussis Co, The Yanxilas* [1982] 2 Lloyd's Rep 445; *President of India* v. *Jadranska Slobodna Plovidba* [1992] 2 Lloyd's Rep 274.

2. *DDT Trucks of North America* v. *DDT Holdings Ltd* [2007] 2 Lloyd's Rep 213.

3. *Torch Offshore LLC* v. *Cable Shipping Inc* [2004] 2 Lloyd's Rep 446.

4. *Urban Small Space Ltd* v. *Burford Investment* (1990) 28 EG 116.

5. *CMA CGM SA* v. *Beteiligungs-Kommanditsgesellschaft MS "Northern Pioneer" Schiffartgesellschaft mbH & Co, The Northern Pioneer* [2003] 1 Lloyd's Rep 212.

6. Thereby reversing the decision in *Petraco (Bermuda) Ltd* v. *Petromed International SA* [1988] 2 Lloyd's Rep 357, where it was held that this point went to discretion rather than jurisdiction. See, for the position under the 1996 Act: *CMA CGM SA* v. *Beteiligungs-Kommanditsgesellschaft MS "Northern Pioneer" Schiffartgesellschaft mbH & Co, The Northern Pioneer* [2003] 1 Lloyd's Rep 212; *Durham County Council* v. *Darlington Borough Council* [2003] EWHC 2598 (Admin); *Marklands Ltd* v. *Virgin Retail Ltd* [2004] 2 EGLR 43.

7. *Omnibridge Consulting Ltd* v. *Clearsprings (Management) Ltd*, 2004, unreported.

8. *Pioneer Shipping Ltd* v. *BTP Tioxide Ltd, The Nema* [1981] 2 All ER 1030.

9. [2003] 1 Lloyd's Rep 212.

10. Lord Noel-Buxton in the Second Reading on the Bill commented that the alternative formulation contained in the July 1995 Bill had been rightly disregarded as it widened the scope for seeking permission and thus ran contrary to the need for finality and certainty in arbitration. However, the wording finally adopted as subsequently construed has indeed operated to widen the scope of permission to appeal.

11. As the post-Act cases show. See, e.g.: *Egmatra AG* v. *Marco Trading Corporation* [1999] 1 Lloyd's Rep 862.

doubt.[1] However, in *The Northern Pioneer*[2] the Court of Appeal held that section 69(3)(c)(ii) was not a straight codification of the earlier law, and that permission to appeal could appropriately be granted where the question of law was not covered by any previous judicial decision or was subject to differing opinions which had not been resolved by judicial decision. The test was summarised by Lord Phillips MR:

> The guideline of Lord Diplock which has been superseded by section 69(3)(c)(ii) was calculated to place a particularly severe restraint on the role of the Commercial and higher courts in resolving issues of commercial law of general public importance. This is because the likelihood of conflicting decisions in relation to such issues, where they related to standard clauses in widely used charterparties containing arbitration clauses, was greatly reduced by the guideline itself. We consider that the facts of this case demonstrate that changing circumstances can raise issues of general public importance in relation to such clauses that are not covered by judicial decision.

One of the most difficult and recurring questions concerns the construction of documents. In *Trustees of Edmond Stern Settlement* v. *Levy*,[3] HHJ Peter Coulson QC stated:

> Questions of construction are often a matter of impression. Whilst I can see how and why the arbitrator could have come to a different view, I am unable to say that he was obviously wrong in reaching the conclusion he did. It seems to me that either interpretation was available to him and, as he was bound to do, he chose one over the other. I do not consider that he was obviously wrong in the choice he made. Furthermore, given that this is a question of construction that had to be answered against the background of the relevant factual material in accordance with the well-known principles in *Investors Compensation Scheme* v. *West Bromwich Building Society*,[4] it should only be in the clearest cases that a judge considering a section 69 application, who has not heard such evidence, should substitute his own construction for that of the arbitrator, who has.

It is fairly well accepted that the construction of a document is a question of law (or at least a mixed question of fact and law). Ordinarily, in non one-off cases where documents are being construed, that is, the "obviously wrong" test, the threshold should be high and permission rarely granted. This is consistent with the principle that an error of law does not arise if the tribunal, having identified the correct legal principle, goes on to apply it incorrectly.[5]

Section 69(3)(d) adds a "just and proper" criterion. This was not express under the 1979 Act, but the courts nevertheless developed the view that even if the guidelines in *The Nema* were satisfied, the question of whether permission should or should not be given was subject to a general discretion. Section 69(3)(d) has been described as an overall "catch-all" provision "albeit an important one".[6] Thus, if it was clear from the arbitration agreement that a quick resolution of disputes was required, permission would not be given.[7] If the parties had selected an experienced Queen's Counsel as arbitrator, permission is less likely to be given.[8] The purpose of section 69(3)(d) is to permit the court to take into account such matters, although its inclusion was criticised in the debates in the House of Lords as conferring too wide a discretion for intervention on the courts. The

1. See generally *Ipswich Borough Council* v. *Fisons plc* [1990] 1 All ER 730; *British Railways Board* v. *Ringbest Ltd* [1996] 30 EG 94.
2. [2003] 1 Lloyd's Rep 212.
3. [2007] EWHC 1187 (TCC).
4. [1998] 1 WLR 896.
5. *Northern Elevator Manufacturing* v. *United Engineers (Singapore)* [2004] 2 SLR 494, approved in *Benaim* v. *Davies Middleton & Davies* [2005] EWHC 1370 (TCC). It is difficult to reconcile this decision with the result in *Covington Marine Corp* v. *Xiamen Shipbuilding Industry Co Ltd* [2005] EWHC 291, where the arbitrator's decision that no binding agreement had been reached, based on the construction of an exchange of letters, was overturned.
6. *Per* Akenhead J in *Braes of Doune Wind Farm (Scotland) Ltd* v. *Alfred McAlpine Business Services Ltd* [2008] 1 Lloyd's Rep 608 at [31].
7. *National Rumour Co SA* v. *Lloyd-Libra Navegacao SA* [1982] 1 Lloyd's Rep 472.
8. See *Keydon Estates Ltd* v. *Western Power Distribution (South Wales) Ltd* [2004] EWHC 996 (Ch); *Braes of Doune Wind Farm (Scotland) Ltd* v. *Alfred McAlpine Business Services Ltd* [2008] 1 Lloyd's Rep 608.

DAC Report, paragraphs 289 to 290, pointed out that it was entirely proper for the court to consider whether the fact that the parties had agreed to go to arbitration was in the circumstances a sufficient reason to refuse permission to appeal.[1] Cases decided under the 1996 Act show that the key consideration will be that if the parties have agreed to submit their dispute to an expert arbitrator there is good reason not to grant permission for an appeal, given the underlying desire of the parties for speedy resolution and finality.[2] If it is the case that the grant of permission to appeal would of itself cause serious injustice to the successful party in the arbitration, by depriving him of the right to challenge the award for serious irregularity under section 68 in the event that the award is varied under section 69 in favour of the losing party, there may be some basis for contesting the application for permission to appeal.[3] More generally, if an application falls within both sections 68 and 69, the court will wherever possible deal with the matter under section 68 so that the award can more readily be remitted to the arbitrators as opposed to being overturned for error of law.[4]

Permission may be given subject to a condition as to security for costs (section 70(6)), the payment into court of sums due under the award (section 70(7)) and any other conditions which the court in its discretion determines to impose (section 70(8)).

Section 69(4) confirms that the application must identify the question of law to be determined and state the grounds on which it is alleged that leave to appeal should be granted.

Section 69(5) lays down the general rule, which may be waived by the court in appropriate circumstances, that application for permission to appeal is to be considered without a hearing. The DAC Report, paragraph 291, commented that such a procedure was consistent with the need for speed in dealing with an appeal, and that in most cases it would be possible for a court to ascertain on written material alone whether an award was obviously wrong or open to serious doubt. The adoption of a documents-only policy for section 69 applications was challenged before the Court of Appeal in *BLCT (13096) Ltd* v. *J Sainsbury plc*,[5] but the application was rejected on the grounds that appeals were governed exclusively by section 69(5) and CPR Part 62 rather than by CPR r. 52.3(4) which confers a general right to oral hearings, and that there was no objection on human rights grounds[6] to a documents-only application given that the parties had in the first place opted to go to arbitration. The Court of Appeal did nevertheless accept that there may be exceptional circumstances justifying an oral hearing, and in practice there will be an oral hearing where an appeal under section 67 or section 68 is combined with an application for permission to appeal under section 69. Combining proceedings may well be advantageous, as it provides a mechanism whereby the determinative question can be considered first,[7] although the courts have been wary of abuse whereby an oral hearing is obtained for an application for permission to appeal by the device of adding a makeweight appeal under section 67 or 68.[8] Detailed reasons for a decision to dismiss an application for permission to appeal are not required, but Article 6 of the European Convention on Human Rights requires the applicant to be told which of the threshold tests has not been satisfied.[9] The substantive hearing itself may be dealt with by the same judge who gave permission to appeal

1. See *Icon Navigation Corporation* v. *Sinochem International Petroleum (Bahamas) Co Ltd* [2004] 1 All ER (Comm) 405.
2. *India Steamship Co Ltd* v. *Arab Potash Co Ltd*, 1997, unreported; *Reliance Industries Ltd* v. *Enron Oil and Gas India Ltd* [2002] 1 Lloyd's Rep 645; *Keydon Estates Ltd* v. *Western Power Distribution (South Wales) Ltd* [2004] EWHC 996 (Ch).
3. *Icon Navigation Corporation* v. *Sinochem International Petroleum (Bahamas) Co Ltd* [2004] 1 All ER (Comm) 405.
4. *Omnibridge Consulting Ltd* v. *Clearsprings (Management) Ltd*, 2004, unreported.
5. [2003] EWCA Civ 884.
6. Article 6 of the European Convention on Human Rights entitles every person to a full and fair hearing.
7. *Bulfracht (Cyprus) Ltd* v. *Boneset Shipping Co Ltd, The MV Pamphilos* [2002] 2 Lloyd's Rep 681; *HOK Sport Ltd* v. *Aintree Racecourse Co Ltd* [2003] BLR 156; *Newfield* v. *Tomlinson* [2004] EWHC 3051 (TCC); *Alphapoint Shipping Ltd* v. *Rotem Amfert Negev Ltd, The Agios Dimitros* [2005] 1 Lloyd's Rep 23.
8. *Miller Construction* v. *James Moore Earthmoving* [2001] BLR 10 (not considered on appeal, [2001] 2 All ER (Comm) 598); *London Borough of Lewisham* v. *Shepherd Hill*, 2001, unreported.
9. *North Range Shipping Ltd* v. *Seatrans Shipping Corporation* [2002] 2 Lloyd's Rep 1, accepting (with minor modification) the view of David Steel J in *Mousaka Inc* v. *Golden Seagull Maritime Inc* [2001] 2 Lloyd's Rep 657 that the implementation of the Convention in England overrode the previous principle, laid down in *The Nema* [1984] 3 All ER 229, that no reasons at all were to be given.

(the practice in the TCC, but not in the Commercial Court), and in some cases it may be appropriate to combine the application for permission to appeal with the substantive hearing itself.[1]

Section 69(6) provides, in line with the rest of the Act, that any appeal from the decision of the court to give or refuse permission has to have the permission of the court: for this purpose the "court" means the trial judge and not the Court of Appeal.[2] The provision re-enacts earlier legislation that was brought into force in order to prevent any possible rash of appeals from permission, thereby further undermining the finality of the arbitral process. Authorities under the 1979 Act reached the position that the Court of Appeal had no jurisdiction to challenge the judge's refusal to give permission,[3] and that permission was not to be given unless some elucidation of the guidelines in *The Nema* was required.[4] In *The Northern Pioneer*[5] the Court of Appeal confirmed that the position remains the same under the 1996 Act: the Court of Appeal had no jurisdiction to grant permission to appeal where this has been refused by the trial judge;[6] and given that the criteria for permission to appeal are now statutory, there was no basis for the grant of permission to appeal based on the need for the elucidation of the criteria.

Section 69(7) sets out the options open to the court following its determination of the substantive appeal (confirm, vary, remit, set aside). All those options were available to the court under the 1979 Act. The change is contained in section 69(7)(c) and (d), which allow the award to be remitted or set aside in part as opposed to as a whole, as was previously the case. If the court remits the award, section 71(3) empowers the court to require the arbitrators to make a fresh award within three months of the date of the order (or such shorter or longer period as the court may direct). Even if the court finds that the appellant has demonstrated an error of law in the award, the court is not required to provide a remedy, as section 69(7) specifically uses the word "may". The effect is that the court can refuse relief if it takes the view that the arbitrator would have come to the same conclusion or that the error was insignificant.[7] However, the court cannot take account of matters falling outside the scope of the appeal in deciding which remedy should be granted: the court cannot, therefore, refuse a remedy on the ground that the winning party in the arbitration would be prejudiced by the overturning of the award and the loss of his ability to assert serious irregularity under section 68 in that the point of law in question should never have been admitted in the first place. Extraneous matters are to be considered at the stage of application for permission to appeal, under section 69(3)(d).[8]

Section 69(8) is new and states that a judgment of the court on the substantive appeal is to be treated as any other judgment and is enforceable as such. An important change is, however, made in relation to appeals from the substantive determination. Under section 1(7) of the 1979 Act, an appeal was possible if two conditions were satisfied:

(a) permission to appeal was given either by the court or, on appeal, to the Court of Appeal; and
(b) the judge had certified that the question of law involved in its decision was one of general importance or for some other special reason should be considered by the Court of Appeal.

1. *HOK Sport Ltd* v. *Aintree Racecourse Co Ltd* [2003] BLR 156.
2. *Henry Boot Construction (UK) Ltd* v. *Malmaison Hotel (Manchester) Ltd* [2001] 1 QB 388; *Athletic Union of Constantinople* v. *National Basketball Association* [2002] 1 Lloyd's Rep 305; *Virdee* v. *Virdi* [2003] EWCA Civ 41.
3. *Aden Refinery Co Ltd* v. *Ugland Management Co Ltd* [1986] 2 Lloyd's Rep 336.
4. *The Antaios* [1984] 3 All ER 229.
5. [2003] 1 Lloyd's Rep 212.
6. Other than in the wholly exceptional situation where the trial judge had failed to act judicially in considering whether or not permission to appeal should be granted: see *North Range Shipping Ltd* v. *Seatrans Shipping Corporation* [2002] 2 Lloyd's Rep 1 and *BLCT (13096) Ltd* v. *J Sainsbury plc* [2003] EWCA Civ 884 in each of which the issue was the procedures to be adopted in the handling of applications for permission to appeal against the award and permissions to appeal against a judgment given under s. 69.
7. *Ballast Wiltshier plc* v. *Thomas Barnes & Sons Ltd*, 1998, unreported.
8. *Icon Navigation Corporation* v. *Sinochem International Petroleum (Bahamas) Co Ltd* [2004] 1 All ER (Comm) 405.

Under section 69(8), the Court of Appeal can no longer give permission to appeal,[1] so that the entire matter is in the hands of the judge to give permission if he considers that the relevant criteria are met. A point of law will qualify for permission to appeal if it is of general importance,[2] or if there is some other special reason for allowing the matter to go to the Court of Appeal, for example, because a point of law of wider interest is raised[3] or because a large amount of money is at stake in the case itself.[4] However, permission was given only if there was some doubt as to the court's ruling.[5]

Challenge or appeal: supplementary provisions

70.—(1) The following provisions apply to an application or appeal under section 67, 68 or 69.

(2) An application or appeal may not be brought if the applicant or appellant has not first exhausted—

- (a) any available arbitral process of appeal or review, and
- (b) any available recourse under section 57 (correction of award or additional award).

(3) Any application or appeal must be brought within 28 days of the date of the award or, if there has been any arbitral process of appeal or review, of the date when the applicant or appellant was notified of the result of that process.

(4) If on an application or appeal it appears to the court that the award—

- (a) does not contain the tribunal's reasons, or
- (b) does not set out the tribunal's reasons in sufficient detail to enable the court properly to consider the application or appeal,

the court may order the tribunal to state the reasons for its award in sufficient detail for that purpose.

(5) Where the court makes an order under subsection (4), it may make such further order as it thinks fit with respect to any additional costs of the arbitration resulting from its order.

(6) The court may order the applicant or appellant to provide security for the costs of the application or appeal, and may direct that the application or appeal be dismissed if the order is not complied with.

The power to order security for costs shall not be exercised on the ground that the applicant or appellant is—

- (a) an individual ordinarily resident outside the United Kingdom, or
- (b) a corporation or association incorporated or formed under the law of a country outside the United Kingdom, or whose central management and control is exercised outside the United Kingdom.

1. See DAC Supplementary Report, para. 27, emphasising that there is no appeal to the Court of Appeal against a refusal of leave to appeal.
2. See generally, *Geogas SA* v. *Trammo Gas Ltd, The Baleares* [1991] 1 Lloyd's Rep 349 where the Court of Appeal indicated that a certificate was appropriate in cases which would not be regarded as "one-off" under the guidelines in *The Nema*.
3. *Sealace Shipping Co Ltd* v. *Ocean Voice Ltd, The Alecos M* [1990] 1 Lloyd's Rep 82.
4. *British Gas plc* v. *Dollar Land Holdings plc* [1992] 12 EG 141.
5. It remains to be determined what degree of uncertainty is required. In *The Baleares* [1991] 1 Lloyd's Rep 349 differing views were expressed about the degree of doubt necessary to justify the giving of leave.

(7) The court may order that any money payable under the award shall be brought into court or otherwise secured pending the determination of the application or appeal, and may direct that the application or appeal be dismissed if the order is not complied with.

(8) The court may grant leave to appeal subject to conditions to the same or similar effect as an order under subsection (6) or (7).

This does not affect the general discretion of the court to grant leave subject to conditions.

NOTES

This section applies to applications and appeals in respect of jurisdiction, serious irregularity and errors of law, and brings together various rules which, under earlier legislation, applied—if at all—individually to each.

Section 70(2) lays down the principle that application for appeal may be made only where all internal procedures have been exhausted. The operation of this provision in each of the three contexts to which it applies has been discussed in those contexts. It should be noted that the obligation to exhaust internal procedures does not apply to a party who contests jurisdiction and exercises his right not to appear in the proceedings (section 72(2)). In *Gbangbola* v. *Smith Sherriff Ltd*[1] it was decided that an application to the arbitrators under section 57 of the 1996 Act for clarification or correction of their award does not fall within section 70(2) and, thus, does not affect the running of time under section 70(3). Were it otherwise, a dilatory party could apply to the arbitrators under section 57, and only after their decision had been reached would it be necessary for him to initiate an application or appeal to the court under sections 67 to 69. An award is, therefore, severable so that nothing prevents an application or appeal being made even though other parts of the award are concurrently being reconsidered by the arbitrators: should the same issues arise before the court and the arbitrators, the court is free to postpone its hearing until the arbitrators have made their own ruling.

Section 70(3) lays down a unified time limit for applications and appeals, namely, 28 days from the date of the award—as to which see section 54—or from the date the parties are notified of the outcome of any appeal process under section 57. Time can, however, be extended by the court under its general power in section 80(5) of the Act (see the Notes to section 80). A problem might arise where the arbitrators withhold the award under section 56 as security for payment of their fees and expenses, as by the time the award is released the 28-day period may have expired. The DAC in its February 1996 Report, paragraph 294, decided that such a case should be dealt with not by altering the rule that time runs from the date of the award—which has the distinct merit of certainty over concepts such as the release of the award, which are on the grounds of uncertainty unsuited to be triggers for time limits—but by an extension of time by the court under what became section 80. It is also to be noted that there may be a fine line between an award and an interlocutory decision, and what may appear to be the latter (e.g., by virtue of its description) may prove to be the former if it deals with the merits of an issue and disposes of that issue.[2] Where an award has been reconsidered by the arbitrators under the slip rule in section 57, the 28-day time limit runs from the date on which the arbitrators have amended, or refused to amend, the award, and not from the date of the original award.[3]

Section 70(4) is concerned with reasons. Clearly it is not possible for the court to review an award if the reasons for the award are not given or are inadequate. The 1996 Act imposes a general obligation on the arbitrators to give reasons, in section 52(4), enforceable by an initial application

1. [1998] 3 All ER 730.

2. *Charles M Willie Co (Shipping) Ltd* v. *Ocean Laser Shipping Ltd, The Smaro* [1999] 1 Lloyd's Rep 225; *Ranko Group* v. *Antarctic Maritime SA, The Robin* [1998] ADRLN 35.

3. *Blackdale Ltd* v. *McLean Homes South East Ltd* 2001, unreported; *Al Hadha Trading Co* v. *Tradigrain SA* [2002] 2 Lloyd's Rep 512. *R C Pillar & Sons* v. *Edwards* 2001, unreported, is to the contrary, but was rejected in *Blackdale* and not referred to in *Al Hadha*.

to the arbitrators under section 57[1] and then by an application to the court under section 68 on the ground of serious irregularity in the award should they fail to do so. Consequently, there is no longer any need for the judicial review provisions to deal with the situation in which, by wrongful omission, no reasons have been given. Nevertheless, the court may still require reasons, or adequate reasons where the reasons given are inadequate, for the purposes of exercising its various jurisdictions under sections 67 to 69, and section 70(4)–(5) so provides.[2] The novel feature of section 70(4) is to extend the court's ability to order reasons beyond appeal on a point of law under section 69, to applications under sections 67 and 68.

At this point a serious ambiguity arises. If the parties have contracted out of the arbitrators' obligation to give reasons, as they are entitled to do under section 52(4), such an agreement operates as agreement to exclude the right of the court to review an award on point of law, by virtue of section 69(1). It is unclear, however, whether the arbitrators may still be required to give reasons for the purposes of an application under section 67 (jurisdiction) or section 68 (serious irregularity). Where there is a challenge to jurisdiction under section 67, the issue is not whether the arbitrators had made an error of law in their reasoning, but whether as a matter of law—to be determined by the court—the arbitrators had jurisdiction, so that reasons are not relevant. The main difficulty concerns section 68, and in *Tame Shipping Ltd* v. *Easy Navigation Ltd, The Easy Rider*,[3] it was held that the court could insist upon reasons being given for the purpose of determining whether there had been a serious irregularity even though the parties had agreed that there were to be no reasons for the award itself and that reasons were to be contained in a separate document not forming part of the award. It must be doubtful whether the same reasoning can extend to the case where no reasons at all were required, although in *Tame* Moore-Bick J was of the view that even in that situation the arbitrators could be ordered to provide reasons. It is nevertheless suggested, therefore, that section 70(4) will be relevant only where the arbitrators were obliged to give reasons in some or other form: section 70(4) can then be used to order better reasons from arbitrators for the purpose of an appeal under sections 68 or 69, where the reasons given by them are inadequate to allow the court to determine whether there has been an error of law or serious irregularity. If no reasons have been given at all, the matter can be dealt with under section 68 whether or not an appeal is to be lodged.

Section 70(5) is a new power, allowing the court to make an order for costs in the arbitration given the consequences of the request for more reasons.

Section 70(6) permits the court to make an order for security for costs in the event of an application or appeal under any of sections 67 to 69. The grounds upon which the court may order security for costs generally are set out in CPR r. 25.13, and these include, most importantly, that the claimant is resident outside the jurisdiction but not within the EU or EFTA or the claimant is a company which may not be able to pay its debts. As is the case with ordinary judicial proceedings, there is no basis for making an order as to costs if the applicant or appellant has sufficient assets to meet the costs and those assets are readily available to pay costs in the event that the respondent is successful.[4]

Section 70(7) authorises the court to order that, in the event of a challenge to an award, any money payable under the award is to be brought into court or otherwise secured. The purpose of the provision is that, in the words of the DAC in its February 1996 Report, "it helps avoid the risk that, while the appeal is pending, the ability of the losing party to honour the award may, by design or otherwise, be diminished". The power is nevertheless to be exercised sparingly and may be based on the risk of the sum being dissipated. That said, in a section 69 case the appeal can go ahead only if there is a strong likelihood of success in the first place, and in a section 67 case the applicant's

1. See: *Groundshire* v. *VHE Construction* [2001] 1 Lloyd's Rep 395; *Al Hadha Trading Co* v. *Tradigrain* [2002] 2 Lloyd's Rep 512; *Torch Offshore LLC* v. *Cable Shipping Inc* [2004] 2 Lloyd's Rep 446.

2. See: *Petroships Pte Ltd of Singapore* v. *Petec Trading and Investment Corporation of Vietnam* [2001] 2 Lloyd's Rep 348.

3. [2004] 2 Lloyd's Rep 626.

4. See *Azov Shipping Co* v. *Baltic Shipping Co (No 2)* [1999] 2 Lloyd's Rep 39, where the applicant's assets were thought not to be readily accessible as they were located in a jurisdiction from which they could not easily be extricated.

argument is that he should never have been involved in the arbitration. The power to order security would, therefore, in practice seem to be largely confined to section 68 applications.[1]

Under section 70(8) the permission of the court is required for an appeal. The "court" means the trial judge and not the Court of Appeal.[2]

Challenge or appeal: effect of order of court

71.—(1) The following provisions have effect where the court makes an order under section 67, 68 or 69 with respect to an award.

(2) Where the award is varied, the variation has effect as part of the tribunal's award.

(3) Where the award is remitted to the tribunal, in whole or in part, for reconsideration, the tribunal shall make a fresh award in respect of the matters remitted within three months of the date of the order for remission or such longer or shorter period as the court may direct.

(4) Where the award is set aside or declared to be of no effect, in whole or in part, the court may also order that any provision that an award is a condition precedent to the bringing of legal proceedings in respect of a matter to which the arbitration agreement applies, is of no effect as regards the subject matter of the award or, as the case may be, the relevant part of the award.

NOTES

Section 71 applies to application and appeals under sections 67 to 69.

Section 71(2) makes an obvious point as regards the variation of the award by the court, and re-enacts earlier legislation.

Section 71(3), giving the arbitrators three months or such other period as the court may direct to produce a new award on remission, also re-enacts earlier legislation. It is unclear whether section 79 would apply in case the arbitrators required a longer period, so that one party would have to come back with an application to the court for more time. However, it is difficult to see what consequences would befall the tribunal if it took longer than the assigned period. There are no known reported cases on the issue.

Section 71(4) allows the court to override a *Scott* v. *Avery* arbitration clause where an award is questioned on the ground of substantive jurisdiction, serious irregularity or error of law. Under a *Scott* v. *Avery* arbitration clause, arbitration is a condition precedent to the bringing of judicial proceedings, and the parties may sue each other only on the award itself. If the award is set aside, the clause prevents any further legal proceedings: for this reason, the court has a discretion to set aside the clause itself in order to allow the entire issue to be resolved in court by refusing a stay of its own proceedings if judicial proceedings are commenced.

Miscellaneous

Saving for rights of person who takes no part in proceedings

72.—(1) A person alleged to be a party to arbitral proceedings but who takes no part in the proceedings may question—

1. *Peterson Farms* v. *C & M Farming Ltd* [2004] 2 Lloyd's Rep 603; *Peterson Farms* v. *C & M Farming Ltd (No 2)* [2004] 2 Lloyd's Rep 614.

2. *Henry Boot Construction (UK) Ltd* v. *Malmaison Hotel (Manchester) Ltd* [2001] 1 QB 388; *Athletic Union of Constantinople* v. *National Basketball Association* [2002] 1 Lloyd's Rep 305; *Virdee* v. *Virdi* [2003] EWCA Civ 41.

(a) whether there is a valid arbitration agreement,
(b) whether the tribunal is properly constituted, or
(c) what matters have been submitted to arbitration in accordance with the arbitration agreement,

by proceedings in the court for a declaration or injunction or other appropriate relief.

(2) He also has the same right as a party to the arbitral proceedings to challenge an award—

(a) by an application under section 67 on the ground of lack of substantive jurisdiction in relation to him, or
(b) by an application under section 68 on the ground of serious irregularity (within the meaning of that section) affecting him;

and section 70(2) (duty to exhaust arbitral procedures) does not apply in his case.

NOTES

This mandatory section has no counterpart in the Model Law. It is designed to protect a person who refuses to participate in the arbitration proceedings[1] on the basis that the arbitrators have no jurisdiction over him. In these circumstances, that person retains, under section 72(1), the right formerly granted to him at common law to contest the jurisdiction of the arbitrators, by seeking injunctive or declaratory[2] relief at any stage during the proceedings or thereafter. This right is available only where the seat of the arbitration is in England, Wales or Northern Ireland.[3] Under section 72(2) he may, in the alternative, challenge the award itself on the ground of lack of substantive jurisdiction (section 67) or serious irregularity (section 68—serious irregularity including acting without jurisdiction). He is also freed from the general obligation in section 70(2) to exhaust internal appeal procedures, though seemingly not free from the 28-day time limit set by section 70(3) in respect of any application under section 72(2).[4] The court's power is discretionary, and an application for injunctive or declaratory relief may be refused if, for example, the applicant has delayed in making the application until the last possible moment before the commencement of the arbitration.[5] In *Law Debenture Trust Corp* v. *Elektrim Finance BV*,[6] the court rejected the argument that an actual (as opposed to an alleged) party to an arbitration agreement could not avail itself of section 72. The overall purpose of the section is to permit an application by a party who has not yet participated in the proceedings:

> There are a number of reasons why he might not have that status. One is whether he is a legitimate party at all—for example, he might say that he is not a party to the agreement containing what is clearly on its face an arbitration agreement. Another is while accepting he was a party to the agreement, he might wish to say that for some reason he is not a proper party to what are alleged to be arbitral proceedings—for example, because the agreement does not cover the dispute in question and therefore the proceedings are not proper arbitral proceedings (see paragraph (c) of section 72(1)). A third is the situation where there is no dispute about the arbitration agreement or the fact that it covers the dispute in question, but there is a dispute as to the constitution of the tribunal in question (see para (b) of the subsection). In this situation

1. As to which, see *Caparo Group Ltd* v. *Fagor Arrasate Sociedad Cooperative* [2000] ADRLJ 254; *Athletic Union of Constantinople* v. *National Basketball Association* [2002] 1 Lloyd's Rep 305 (preliminary objection to jurisdiction not amounting to participation).
2. See *Mackley & Co Ltd* v. *Gosport Marina Ltd* [2002] BLR 367.
3. *Arab National Bank* v. *El Sharif Saoud Bin Masoud Bin Haza'a El-Abdali* [2004] EWHC 2381 (Comm).
4. *Bernuth Lines Ltd* v. *High Seas Shipping Ltd, The Eastern Navigator* [2006] 1 Lloyd's Rep 537.
5. *Industrie Chimiche Italia Centrale* v. *Alexander Tsavliris & Sons, The Choko Star* [1987] 1 Lloyd's Rep 508; *Zaporozhye Production Aluminium Plan Open Shareholders Society* v. *Ashly Ltd* [2002] EWHC 1410 (Comm).
6. [2005] 2 Lloyd's Rep 755.

the proceedings might be said to be only "alleged proceedings" so that the party can only be an "alleged" party.[1]

One possible basis for an application under section 72 is where the non-participating applicant establishes that the award has been procured by fraud: see *Arab National Bank* v. *El-Abdali*.[2]

In *Fiona Trust & Holding Corp* v. *Privalov*[3] the Court of Appeal stated that, although section 72 provides that a party who takes no part in arbitration proceedings should be entitled in court to "question whether there is a valid arbitration agreement", the arbitrators should, in general, be the first tribunal to consider whether there is a valid arbitration agreement and whether the arbitrators have jurisdiction to determine the dispute. Where a party who denied the existence of a valid arbitration agreement had himself instituted court proceedings, and the party who relied on the arbitration clause had applied for a stay under section 9, the application for a stay was the primary matter that needed to be decided. This should be contrasted with the solution adopted in *Law Debenture Trust*, where the court held that, if a section 72 application is met by a section 9 stay, once the court determines that the section 72 application gives rise to issues of the arbitrators' jurisdiction, it should proceed to determine those issues, so that the result one way or the other will mean that the section 9 stay application becomes unnecessary. It is submitted that the correct approach is that adopted in *Fiona Trust*, except perhaps in those cases where there is a direct attack on the integrity of the arbitration clause itself.

A party to an arbitration proceeding under the auspices of the ICC will not be held to have taken part in the proceedings merely by writing to the ICC to confirm that it was not a party to the contract.[4] Section 72 does not deal with the point in terms, but its use would also seem to be open to a person who does not participate in the arbitration proceedings not to take any positive steps against the award himself but rather to contest its enforcement against him under section 66(4). This is perhaps a high-risk strategy, particularly where the award is to be enforced in another jurisdiction where pleas of want of jurisdiction may as a matter of pure practicality be more difficult to sustain. A person who does participate in the arbitration may not sit back and then challenge the enforcement of the award, because section 73(3) provides that a participating party must challenge within the 28 days permitted by section 70(3).

The section is not designed to permit a person who wishes to pursue arbitration proceedings to apply to the court for a declaration that there is[5] or there is not[6] a binding arbitration agreement: the proper approach is for that person to participate in the arbitration in the usual way and to contest any jurisdictional challenge in the arbitration.[7]

There is no express right of appeal against a court decision on jurisdiction, but it was held by the House of Lords in *Inco Europe Ltd* v. *First Choice Distribution*[8] that a right of appeal exists, though, as is the case with appeals under sections 67 and 68, permission to appeal may presumably only be given by the trial judge.

Loss of right to object

73.—(1) If a party to arbitral proceedings takes part, or continues to take part, in the proceedings without making, either forthwith or within such time as is allowed by the arbitration agreement or the tribunal or by any provision of this Part, any objection—

1. [2005] 2 Lloyd's Rep 755 at [18] *per* Mann J.
2. [2005] 1 Lloyd's Rep 541.
3. [2007] 2 Lloyd's Rep 267 (CA), affirmed without reference to this point by the HL, [2008] 1 Lloyd's Rep 254.
4. *Caparo Group Ltd* v. *Fagor Arrasate Soc* [2000] ADRLJ 254. See also *Law Debenture Trust Corp* v. *Elektrim Finance BV* [2005] 2 Lloyd's Rep 755 (correspondence with LCIA seeking to persuade it not to appoint a tribunal pending application to the court held not to amount to participation).
5. *Vale do Rio Doce Navegaçao SA* v. *Shanghai Bao Steel Ocean Shipping Co Ltd and Sea Partners* [2000] 2 Lloyd's Rep 1.
6. *ABB Lummus Global Ltd* v. *Keppel Fels Ltd* [1999] 2 Lloyd's Rep 24.
7. This has since been confirmed as the correct approach by the House of Lords in *Fiona Trust & Holding Corp* v. *Privalov* [2008] 1 Lloyd's Rep 254.
8. [2000] 1 Lloyd's Rep 467.

(a) that the tribunal lacks substantive jurisdiction,
(b) that the proceedings have been improperly conducted,
(c) that there has been a failure to comply with the arbitration agreement or with any provision of this Part, or
(d) that there has been any other irregularity affecting the tribunal or the proceedings,

he may not raise that objection later, before the tribunal or the court, unless he shows that, at the time he took part or continued to take part in the proceedings, he did not know and could not with reasonable diligence have discovered the grounds for the objection.

(2) Where the arbitral tribunal rules that it has substantive jurisdiction and a party to arbitral proceedings who could have questioned that ruling—

(a) by any available arbitral process of appeal or review; or
(b) by challenging the award

does not do so, or does not do so within the time allowed by the arbitration agreement or any provisions of this Part he may not object later to the tribunal's substantive jurisdiction on any ground which was the subject of that ruling.

NOTES

Section 73 was new to English arbitration law in 1996, and is based on Article 4 of the Model Law. The broad effect of the provision is to prevent a party from relying upon his right to challenge any aspect of the proceedings or the award for want of jurisdiction or irregularity if he has participated in the proceedings with (actual or constructive) knowledge of the problem but without having registered an objection promptly (see below). It is important to stress that section 73 is relevant to all applications or appeals, whether to the courts or to the arbitrators themselves under an agreed or statutory procedure.

Section 73(1) differs from the Model Law, Article 4, in one important respect. The Model Law requires actual knowledge of the problem before there can be waiver. Section 73(1), by contrast, brings waiver into play unless the complainant can show that he did not know and could not with reasonable diligence have discovered the problem. The burden of proof is thus put squarely on the applicant (a point not dealt with specifically by the Model Law), and this is coupled with a "reasonable diligence" test. The objection taken by the applicant must be "forthwith", a word which has been held to mean "acting promptly" or "without unnecessary delay" given the circumstances.[1] The court will not permit an applicant to continue protesting, for example, against the apparent bias of an arbitrator both before and after a hearing, and after the award had been published. The threat of objection cannot be held over the head of the tribunal until after they have made their decision; to do so could otherwise be seen as an attempt to put unfair pressure upon them.[2] Unless a party makes it clear that he is withdrawing from the arbitral proceedings, he continues to take part in them until they reach their conclusion, normally in the publication of a final award, even if in, for example, the period between the hearing and the award nothing actually happens.[3]

Section 73(1)(a) reflects the right of the arbitrators, under section 30 of the Act, to determine their own substantive jurisdiction. Section 31 requires the complainant to register his objection to the arbitrators' assertion of jurisdiction before he has taken a step to contest the issue on its merits or, if the issue arises in the course of the arbitration, as soon as possible.[4] If he does not comply with these time limits, he is taken by section 73(1)(a) to have waived his right to object at a later stage,

1. *Wicketts and Sterndale* v. *Brine Builders* [2001] CILL 1805.
2. *ASM Shipping Ltd* v. *TTMI Ltd* [2006] 1 Lloyd's Rep 375.
3. *Rustal Trading SA* v. *Gill & Duffus SA* [2000] 1 Lloyd's Rep 14. See also: *Thyssen Canada Ltd* v. *Mariana Maritime* [2005] 1 Lloyd's Rep 640.
4. *Peoples' Insurance Co of China* v. *Vysanthi Shipping Co Pte* [2003] 2 Lloyd's Rep 617; *Peterson Farms Inc* v. *C & M Farming Ltd* [2004] 2 Lloyd's Rep 603.

for example, when he wishes to contest the validity of the award. The point here is that a jurisdictional objection cannot be raised for the first time before a court,[1] unless the applicant did not know and could not with reasonable diligence have discovered the jurisdictional problem during the course of the arbitration. A jurisdictional issue discovered during the course of the arbitration must be raised in the arbitration as soon as possible after discovery.[2] The words "any objection" in section 73(1) have been interpreted to mean that an applicant may not raise a new objection before the court that had not previously been raised before the tribunal.[3] Nevertheless, provided that what may be regarded as a new point is broadly based on the original objection, it may be argued before the court even if it had not been raised before the arbitrators.[4]

Section 73(2) deals with the situation in which the arbitrators have already ruled, by means of an award, that they do have substantive jurisdiction: section 73(2) prevents the applicant from reopening the question of the validity of that award—either at the stage when an award is made disposing of the remaining issues, or when an application is made for the enforcement of the award—unless he has sought to challenge it either under the agreed arbitral procedure or by a timely application under section 67. Section 73(1)(a) necessarily does not apply to cases in which the applicant has refused to participate in the proceedings, as is his right under section 72.

Section 73(1)(b) is concerned primarily with procedural irregularity normally falling within section 68 of the Act,[5] and applies also to an application to remove an arbitrator under section 24.[6]

Section 73(1)(c) is concerned with failure by the arbitrators to comply with the arbitration agreement or those provisions of the Arbitration Act 1996 which apply to the arbitration: these errors will also generally constitute serious irregularity which may be remedied by a challenge to the award under section 68. Section 73(1)(d) is a sweeping-up provision which applies to other irregularities.

Some arbitral institution rules contain waiver of objection provisions in similar terms to section 73, albeit based on actual knowledge of the grounds for objection, as opposed to constructive knowledge.[7]

Immunity of arbitral institutions, &c

74.—(1) An arbitral or other institution or person designated or requested by the parties to appoint or nominate an arbitrator is not liable for anything done or omitted in the discharge or purported discharge of that function unless the act or omission is shown to have been in bad faith.

(2) An arbitral or other institution or person by whom an arbitrator is appointed or nominated is not liable, by reason of having appointed or nominated him, for anything done or omitted by the arbitrator (or his employees or agents) in the discharge or purported discharge of his functions as arbitrator.

1. *Athletic Union of Constantinople* v. *National Basketball Association* [2002] 1 Lloyd's Rep 305; *JSC Zestafoni G Nicoladze Ferroalloy Plant* v. *Ronly Holdings Ltd* [2004] 2 Lloyd's Rep 335; *Westland Helicopters Ltd* v. *Sheikh Salah Al-Hejailan* [2004] 2 Lloyd's Rep 523; *Vee Networks Ltd* v. *Econet Wireless International Ltd* [2005] 1 Lloyd's Rep 192.

2. *Hussmann (Europe) Ltd* v. *Al Ameen Development and Trade Co* [2000] 2 Lloyd's Rep 83.

3. See, e.g.: *Margulead Ltd* v. *Exide Technologies* [2005] 1 Lloyd's Rep 324 (claimant's failure to object about tribunal's failure to permit an oral closing speech until after award).

4. *Primetrade AG* v. *Ythan Ltd* [2006] 1 Lloyd's Rep 457 (a case under s. 67).

5. See *Hussmann (Europe) Ltd* v. *Pharaon* [2003] 1 All ER (Comm) 879; *Rustal Trading SA* v. *Gill & Duffus SA* [2000] 1 Lloyd's Rep 14; *Mohsin* v. *Commonwealth Secretariat* [2002] EWHC 377 (Comm); *Lesotho Highlands Development Authority* v. *Impregilo SpA* [2003] 2 Lloyd's Rep 497; *JSC Zestafoni G Nikoladze Ferroalloy Plant* v. *Ronly Holdings* [2004] 2 Lloyd's Rep 335; *Thyssen Canada Ltd* v. *Mariana Maritime SA* [2005] 1 Lloyd's Rep 640.

6. *Wicketts and Sterndale* v. *Brine Builders*, 2001, unreported.

7. See, e.g.: LCIA Rules of Arbitration, Art. 32; ICC Rules of Arbitration, Art. 33; UNCITRAL Rules of Arbitration, Art. 30; American Arbitration Association Rules of Arbitration, Art. 25.

(3) The above provisions apply to an employee or agent of an arbitral or other institution or person as they apply to the institution or person himself.

NOTES

Section 29 codifies the common law principle that arbitrators are immune from suit in respect of matters done or not done in pursuit of their functions unless they have acted in bad faith.[1] The common law did not make any provision for arbitration institutions responsible for appointing arbitrators and otherwise exercising functions in relation to the arbitration. Section 74 of the Act was prepared by way of response to the market's general view that immunity should be extended to institutions, although in practice immunity can be achieved by means of an exclusion clause. As the DAC's February 1996 Report, paragraph 301, points out, many arbitral institutions do not have the funds to meet claims against them or to take out the requisite liability insurance, and the imposition of liability could thus hamper the undoubtedly beneficial operations of such institutions.

Section 74(1) excludes the personal liability of an arbitration institution for any failings in the discharge or purported discharge of its functions, for example, in the appointment of arbitrators and in providing subsequent assistance to the arbitration under the institution's rules. No immunity is conferred for failing to comply with contractual obligations, for example, for failing to appoint arbitrators at the required time or failing to supervise the proceedings: the immunity arises only for misguided attempts to adhere to the contract. If liability is to be excluded for other matters, this must be provided for in the contract between the institution and the parties.

Section 74(2) excludes any possible liability of an arbitration institution for the acts or omissions of the arbitrators in the discharge or purported discharge of their functions, where the liability arises purely from the appointment. The stated intention of section 74(2) is to limit the immunity to this particular form of liability: any other liabilities which might attach to the arbitration institution flowing from its conduct are expressly preserved.[2]

Section 74(3) extends the immunity of the institution to the institution's employees or agents, thereby preventing the side-stepping of immunity by the bringing of actions against culpable individuals.

Charge to secure payment of solicitors' costs

75. The powers of the court to make declarations and orders under section 73 of the Solicitors Act 1974 or Article 71H of the Solicitors (Northern Ireland) Order 1976 (power to charge property recovered in the proceedings with the payment of solicitors' costs) may be exercised in relation to arbitral proceedings as if those proceedings were proceedings in the court.

NOTES

Section 73 of the Solicitors Act 1974 (along with its Northern Ireland equivalent), empowers a court to declare that a solicitor (engaged in legal proceedings before it) is entitled to a charge on property recovered or preserved in the proceedings, by way of security for his taxed costs. This section extends that power to arbitration proceedings. No change in the law is effected.

1. See the Notes to s. 29, above.

2. See DAC Report, para. 381, where a proposal for tightening the clause to put this beyond all doubt was made. The suggestion put forward by the DAC was accepted in a different form. The section as drafted means that the institution is not liable simply because it has appointed the arbitrator, but that the institution remains liable for any other conduct of its own, e.g., collusion with the arbitrator. See DAC Supplementary Report, para. 38.

Supplementary

Service of notices, &c

76.—(1) The parties are free to agree on the manner of service of any notice or other document required or authorised to be given or served in pursuance of the arbitration agreement or for the purposes of the arbitral proceedings.

(2) If or to the extent that there is no such agreement the following provisions apply.

(3) A notice or other document may be served on a person by any effective means.

(4) If a notice or other document is addressed, pre-paid and delivered by post

(a) to the addressee's last known principal residence or, if he is or has been carrying on a trade, profession or business, his last known principal business address, or

(b) where the addressee is a body corporate, to the body's registered or principal office,

it shall be treated as effectively served.

(5) This section does not apply to the service of documents for the purposes of legal proceedings, for which provision is made by rules of court.

(6) References in this Part to a notice or other document include any form of communication in writing and references to giving or serving a notice or other document shall be construed accordingly.

NOTES

The Arbitration Act 1950 did not contain any provisions on the service of documents. The only applicable provision was to be found in section 34(4) of the Limitation Act 1980, which was relevant only to the question of whether a notice initiating arbitration proceedings had been validly served. The deficiency is remedied by section 76, which is of general application, although it is of the greatest significance in fixing the date of service and thus whether arbitration proceedings have been commenced within the limitation period.[1] The section reflects the provisions of Article 3 of the Model Law.

Section 76(1) allows the parties to agree on the method of service of any notice or other document, defined widely in section 76(6), other than documents relating to judicial proceedings which are covered by the Civil Procedure Rules 1998 (section 76(5)). The Civil Procedure Rules impose some limits on the service of documents electronically, but there are no such restrictions in section 76.[2] The Act provides also that the parties may agree that documents are to be given rather than "served", an amendment which serves to maximise flexibility. If there is no valid or sustainable[3] agreement on service, then there are default rules. Those rules may be utilised only if there is no agreement on service: where the procedure for service is laid down but not complied with, the court cannot apply the default rules.[4]

Assuming that the default rules are available, section 76(3) states that a document may be served by any effective means: this is a significant relaxation in the position laid down by the July 1995 Bill, which laid down a series of mandatory rules on service. The purpose of section 76(4) is to assist the person seeking to serve, by laying down methods of service which are deemed to be valid (provided that there is no agreement within section 76(1)), although this does not preclude the use

1. See s. 13.
2. *Bernuth Lines Ltd* v. *High Seas Shipping Ltd, The Eastern Navigator* [2006] 1 Lloyd's Rep 537
3. The July 1995 Bill provided that if the agreement did not allow for the ascertainment of the address of the recipient, the agreement was void. An express statement to this effect is probably unnecessary, for such an agreement would necessarily fall on the ground of uncertainty.
4. *Van Oord ACZ Ltd* v. *The Port of Mostyn*, 2003, unreported.

of section 76(3) to justify any other method which is effective. The two cases of deemed effective service are, in the case of a company its registered office, and in any case the addressee's last known residence or business address.

Powers of court in relation to service of documents

77.—(1) This section applies where service of a document on a person in the manner agreed by the parties, or in accordance with provisions of section 76 having effect in default of agreement, is not reasonably practicable.

(2) Unless otherwise agreed by the parties, the court may make such order as it thinks fit—

(a) for service in such manner as the court may direct, or
(b) dispensing with service of the document.

(3) Any party to the arbitration agreement may apply for an order, but only after exhausting any available arbitral process for resolving the matter.

(4) The leave of the court is required for any appeal from a decision of the court under this section.

NOTES

If it is not possible for service to be effected by the method agreed, if any, or by any other means, the court is given the power either to direct how service is to be effected or to waive it completely. The parties are, however, free to contract out of this provision, which means that if service cannot be effected under section 76, the arbitration may be halted in its tracks: the Act does not specify what is to happen if service cannot be effected for this reason. Section 77(3) contemplates that the parties may have conferred upon the arbitrators some form of power to deal with the situation in which service proves to be impossible, and states that there can be application to court until any such agreed procedure has been exhausted: the July 1995 Bill, by contrast, gave the arbitrators power to stipulate the form of service where the agreed method or any default method could not be used. Section 77 has no equivalent in the Model Law, and the DAC in its February 1996 Report, paragraph 306, noted, with regret, that it was needed in order to overcome the problems raised by a party who deliberately seeks to avoid being served.

The permission of the court is required for an appeal. The "court" means the trial judge and not the Court of Appeal.[1]

Reckoning periods of time

78.—(1) The parties are free to agree on the method of reckoning periods of time for the purposes of any provision agreed by them or any provision of this Part having effect in default of such agreement.

(2) If or to the extent there is no such agreement, periods of time shall be reckoned in accordance with the following provisions.

(3) Where the act is required to be done within a specified period after or from a specified date, the period begins immediately after that date.

1. *Henry Boot Construction (UK) Ltd* v. *Malmaison Hotel (Manchester) Ltd* [2001] 1 QB 388; *Athletic Union of Constantinople* v. *National Basketball Association* [2002] 1 Lloyd's Rep 305; *Virdee* v. *Virdi* [2003] EWCA Civ 41.

(4) Where the act is required to be done a specified number of clear days after a specified date, at least that number of days must intervene between the day on which the act is done and that date.

(5) Where the period is a period of seven days or less which would include a Saturday, Sunday or a public holiday in the place where anything which has to be done within the period falls to be done, that day shall be excluded.

In relation to England and Wales or Northern Ireland, a "public holiday" means Christmas Day, Good Friday or a day which under the Banking and Financial Dealings Act 1971 is a bank holiday.

NOTES

This section makes general provision for the reckoning of time under the Act, in the absence of any contrary agreement between the parties. The basic rules are that:

(a) working days only are to count (section 78(5));
(b) the term "clear days" as used at various points in the Act excludes the starting and finishing points between which the days must run (section 78(4)); and
(c) where a specified period is stated to run from a date, the period commences immediately after that date (section 78(3)).

This provision was included so as to assist with the aim of making the Arbitration Act 1996 a self-contained code.

Power of court to extend time limits relating to arbitral proceedings

79.—(1) Unless the parties otherwise agree, the court may by order extend any time limit agreed by them in relation to any matter relating to the arbitral proceedings or specified in any provision of this Part having effect in default of such agreement.

This section does not apply to a time limit to which section 12 applies (power of court to extend time for beginning arbitral proceedings).

(2) An application for an order may be made—

(a) by any party to the arbitral proceedings (upon notice to the other parties and to the tribunal), or
(b) by the arbitral tribunal (upon notice to the parties).

(3) The court shall not exercise its power to extend a time limit unless it is satisfied—

(a) that any available recourse to the tribunal, or to any arbitral or other institution or person vested by the parties with power in that regard, has first been exhausted, and
(b) that a substantial injustice would otherwise be done.

(4) The court's power under this section may be exercised whether or not the time has already expired.

(5) An order under this section may be made on such terms as the court thinks fit.

(6) The leave of the court is required for any appeal from a decision of the court under this section.

NOTES

Section 79(1) is intended to give the court a discretion to extend any time limit agreed by the parties or any provision of Part I of the Act which operates in default of agreement between the parties, subject to contrary agreement by the parties excluding the operation of section 79. A contractual provision which allows the parties or the arbitrators to extend time is not to be regarded as an exclusion of the court's power to do so.[1]

The power to extend time may be exercised on application by means of arbitration claim form, either before or after the time limit has expired. In practice, an application for the extension of time may be made in the actual proceedings in which substantive relief is sought. Section 79(1) does not apply to a time limit laid down by the Act which applies other than in default of agreement by the parties: perhaps the most important exclusion on this basis is the 28-day limit in section 70(3) for the bringing of applications and appeals against awards under sections 67 to 69 of the Act. Applications to extend time for applications and appeals to the court against arbitration awards fall only within section 80(5).[2] The DAC in its February 1996 Report, paragraph 382, recommended that the Bill be amended so that section 79 applied to any time limit applicable under the Bill: the wording proposed by the DAC was not accepted, but the point was covered by the amendment of section 80(5) to extend to this situation.[3] In *Ranko Group* v. *Antarctic Maritime SA, The Robin*,[4] Toulson J held that the power to extend time for applications and appeals to the court in section 80(5) is not limited by the restrictions imposed upon the extension of time under section 79.

Part I of the Act contains a number of time limits, of varying types, within which an application must be made or some other action must be taken, and others under which the arbitrators are themselves entitled to extend time, for example, under section 30 (objection to arbitrators' assertion of jurisdiction): it is clear that the court can further extend the time allowed by the arbitrators, but it is equally clear—as pointed out by the DAC in its February 1996 Report, paragraph 309—that it will rarely be appropriate for the court to do so if the arbitrators themselves have refused.

Section 79(3) sets out the two conditions for the extension of time. First, section 79(3)(a) requires the applicant to exhaust any procedure open to the arbitrators to extend time. Secondly, section 79(3)(b) lays down the "substantial injustice" test for determining whether or not time should be adopted. The authorities on the meaning of that phrase in this context authorise the court to take into account relative fault, the sum at stake and the consequences of failure to act.[5] The same phrase is used in section 50(3) (extension of agreed time limits for making awards) of the Act. The courts have also held that an application under section 79 must be made "as soon as reasonably possible after that party ought to appreciate that it is required".[6]

Section 79(6) contains the usual requirement that the permission of the court be obtained before any appeal can be made. The "court" means the trial judge and not the Court of Appeal.[7]

The arbitration claim form and the supporting written evidence must be served on the other parties, making them parties to the application, which must be served on the other parties and they must be made parties to the application.[8]

1. *John Mowlem Construction plc* v. *Secretary of State for Defence* (2001) 82 Con LR 140.
2. *Ranko Group* v. *Antarctic Maritime SA, The Robin* [1998] ADRLN 35; *RC Pillar & Sons* v. *Edwards*, 2001, unreported; *AOOT Kalmneft* v. *Glencore International AG* [2002] 1 Lloyd's Rep 128.
3. DAC Supplementary Report, paras 41 and 42.
4. [1998] ADRLN 35.
5. See *Minermet SpA Milan* v. *Luckyfield Shipping Corporation SA* [2004] 2 Lloyd's Rep 348 where these criteria were held to be relevant to an application for the extension of time for the appointment of a party arbitrator—extension of time was unnecessary, as the arbitrator could continue before a sole arbitrator in accordance with s. 17 of the 1996 Act. See also: *Pirtek* v. *Deanswood* [2005] 2 Lloyd's Rep 728; *Gold Coast Ltd* v. *Naval Gijon SA* [2006] 2 Lloyd's Rep 400.
6. *Equatorial Traders Ltd* v. *Louis Dreyfus Trading Ltd* [2002] 2 Lloyd's Rep 638. In *Pirtek* v. *Deanswood* [2005] 2 Lloyd's Rep 728 it was commented that a 17-month delay would have been fatal to any application to extend time an application to correct an award under the slip rule in s. 57.
7. *Henry Boot Construction (UK) Ltd* v. *Malmaison Hotel (Manchester) Ltd* [2001] 1 QB 388; *Athletic Union of Constantinople* v. *National Basketball Association* [2002] 1 Lloyd's Rep 305; *Virdee* v. *Virdi* [2003] EWCA Civ 41.
8. CPR r. 62.6(2)–(3).

Notice and other requirements in connection with legal proceedings

80.—(1) References in this Part to an application, appeal or other step in relation to legal proceedings being taken "upon notice" to the other parties to the arbitral proceedings, or to the tribunal, are to such notice of the originating process as is required by rules of court and do not impose any separate requirement.

(2) Rules of court shall be made—

(a) requiring such notice to be given as indicated by any provision of this Part, and
(b) as to the manner, form and content of any such notice.

(3) Subject to any provision made by rules of court, a requirement to give notice to the tribunal of legal proceedings shall be construed—

(a) if there is more than one arbitrator, as a requirement to give notice to each of them; and
(b) if the tribunal is not fully constituted, as a requirement to give notice to any arbitrator who has been appointed.

(4) References in this Part to making an application or appeal to the court within a specified period are to the issue within that period of the appropriate originating process in accordance with rules of court.

(5) Where any provision of this Part requires an application or appeal to be made to the court within a specified time, the rules of court relating to the reckoning of periods, the extending or abridging of periods, and the consequences of not taking a step within the period prescribed by the rules, apply in relation to that requirement.

(6) Provision may be made by rules of court amending the provisions of this Part—

(a) with respect to the time within which any application or appeal to the court must be made,
(b) so as to keep any provision made by this Part in relation to arbitral proceedings in step with the corresponding provision of rules of court applying in relation to proceedings in the court, or
(c) so as to keep any provision made by this Part in relation to legal proceedings in step with the corresponding provision of rules of court applying generally in relation to proceedings in this court.

(7) Nothing in this section affects the generality of the power to make rules of court.

NOTES

Under the Act, an application to the court by one party without the consent of the others requires notice to be given by the applicant to those other parties and the arbitrators, as the case may be. Section 80 is merely an enabling provision, the relevant principles being set out in the Civil Procedure Rules. An application to extend time made before the relevant period has expired is to be by means of application notice under CPR Part 23, as applied by CPR PD paragraph 11.1(1): under CPR r. 62.9(2) the application may be made without notice and need not be served on the other parties. An application made to extend time after the relevant period has expired is to be made by way of arbitration claim form[1] and the application must state the grounds on which the application is made. The claim form must be served on the other parties, and any such party may within seven

1. CPR PD 62, para. 11.1(2).

days of service file written evidence opposing the application.[1] The general discretion to extend time is contained in CPR r. 3.2(1)(a), and this is not—unlike section 79—limited by any requirement that the claimant would suffer prejudice without an extension of time. The discretion to extend time is thus a general one.

Section 80(5) allows the court to extend time in relation to any period specified by the Act for application to the court. The application to the court may be made during the 28-day period, in which case it must be in the form of an application notice,[2] although if it is made after that period has expired the application must be made in a separately identified part of the claim form which seeks the relief in question.[3] The most important period falling within section 80(5) is the 28-day period allowed for applications and appeals to the court against an award under sections 67 to 69 of the 1996 Act.[4] There is no provision for appeal, but it was held by the House of Lords in *Inco Europe Ltd* v. *First Choice Distribution*[5] that a right of appeal exists. Permission to appeal may presumably be given by either the trial judge or the Court of Appeal. There are no criteria laid down in the legislation against which a decision to extend time is to be judged. In *AOOT Kalmneft* v. *Glencore International AG*[6] Colman J held that it would, in a section 68 case, generally be appropriate to consider:

(i) the length of the delay;
(ii) whether, in permitting the time limit to expire and the subsequent delay to occur, the party was acting reasonably in all the circumstances;
(iii) whether the respondent to the application or the arbitrator caused or contributed to the delay;
(iv) whether the respondent to the application would by reason of the delay suffer irremediable prejudice in addition to the mere loss of time if the application were permitted to proceed;
(v) whether the arbitration has continued during the period of delay and, if so, what impact on the progress of the arbitration or the costs incurred the determination of the application by the court might have;
(vi) the strength of the application; and
(vii) whether in the broadest sense it would be unfair to the applicant for him to be denied the opportunity of having the application determined.

This judgment was approved by the Court of Appeal in *Nagusina Naviera* v. *Allied Maritime Inc*,[7] although it was there commented that the key factors were (i) to (iii), that (iv) was not an essential pre-condition, that (v) was a minor factor, that (vi) rested upon clear evidence only so was not a primary factor, and that (vii) was to be considered in the context of the legislation and the need for finality. It has been said that the criteria are to be more strictly applied in a section 67 case, given that section 67 is expressly stated to be subject to the time limits in section 70(3).[8]

Proceedings under section 80(5) are normally to be resolved on paper only, without a hearing.[9]

1. CPR r. 62.9(3).
2. CPR PD 62, para. 11.1.
3. CPR PD 62, para. 11.2.
4. As specified by s. 70(3). That s. 80(5) has this effect was confirmed by Toulson J in *Ranko Group* v. *Antarctic Maritime SA, The Robin* [1998] ADRLN 35. In this case the court refused to extend time as the appellants had failed to challenge the substantive decision on the merits of the case.
5. [2000] 1 Lloyd's Rep 467.
6. [2002] 1 Lloyd's Rep 128.
7. [2002] EWCA Civ 1147. See also: *Dubai Islamic Bank PJSC* v. *Paymentech Merchant Services Inc* [2001] 1 Lloyd's Rep 65; *AOOT Kalmneft* v. *Glencore International AG* [2002] 1 Lloyd's Rep 128; *Nagusina Naviera* v. *Allied Maritime Inc* [2002] EWCA Civ 1147; *Peoples' Insurance Co of China* v. *Vysanthi Shipping Co Ltd* [2003] 2 Lloyd's Rep 617; *Sinclair* v. *Woods of Winchester* (2006) 109 Con LR 14; *DDT Trucks of North America Ltd* v. *DDT Holdings Ltd* [2007] 2 Lloyd's Rep 213; *Colliers International Property Consultants* v. *Colliers Jordan Lee Jafaar Sdn Bhd* [2008] EWHC 1524 (Comm); *L Brown & Sons Ltd* v. *Crosby Homes (North West) Ltd* [2008] EWHC 817 (TCC).
8. *Peoples' Insurance Co of China* v. *Vysanthi Shipping Co Ltd* [2003] 2 Lloyd's Rep 617.
9. CPR PD 62, para. 10.2.

Saving for certain matters governed by common law

81.—(1) Nothing in this Part shall be construed as excluding the operation of any rule of law consistent with the provisions of this Part, in particular, any rule of law as to—

(a) matters which are not capable of settlement by arbitration;
(b) the effect of an oral arbitration agreement; or
(c) the refusal of recognition or enforcement of an arbitral award on grounds of public policy.

(2) Nothing in this Act shall be construed as reviving any jurisdiction of the court to set aside or remit an award on the ground of errors of fact or law on the face of the award.

NOTES

Section 81 preserves the ordinary rules of contract and other rules of law which are not inconsistent with the Act.

Section 81(1)(a) is concerned with a limited range of disputes which have been held not to be capable of resolution by arbitral proceedings. These include disputes under illegal or void contracts[1] and matters involving criminality.[2] This provision was added following the recommendation of the DAC's February 1996 Report, paragraph 385.[3]

Section 81(1)(b) is necessary in the light of the decision to retain the requirement for a written arbitration clause before the Act can apply. Section 81(1)(b) confirms that oral arbitration agreements remain valid at common law, but that the courts cannot exercise the powers set out in the Arbitration Act 1996 to assist the parties.

Section 81(1)(c) confirms common law rules of public policy which prevent the enforcement of awards. Those rules are not well developed, but the cases indicate that an award will not be enforced if it was obtained by fraud or by means of a procedure contrary to the rules of natural justice, or if there is some element of illegality involved which would lead to harm to the public good were the award to be enforced or recognised.[4] Public policy has most frequently been discussed in the context of foreign awards: see the Notes to section 103 of the 1996 Act. The principle is that the English courts will enforce an award which is not on its face contrary to public policy, and it is not permissible for the court to go behind the award to ascertain whether the underlying agreement was contrary to public policy.[5]

Minor definitions

82.—(1) In this Part—

"arbitrator", unless the context otherwise requires, includes an umpire;

"available arbitral process", in relation to any matter, includes any process of appeal to or review by an arbitral or other institution or person vested by the parties with powers in relation to that matter;

"claimant", unless the context otherwise requires, includes a counterclaimant, and related expressions shall be construed accordingly;

"dispute" includes any difference;

1. *O'Callaghan* v. *Coral Racing Ltd*, 1999, unreported, discussed in the notes to s. 7.
2. *Keir* v. *Leeman* (1846) 9 QB 371.
3. DAC Supplementary Report, para. 44.
4. This was so stated by Lord Donaldson MR in *DST* v. *Rakoil* [1987] 2 Lloyd's Rep 246.
5. *R v. V* [2008] EWHC 1531 (Comm), adopting the majority view in *Soleimany* v. *Soleimany* [1998] 3 WLR 811. See the notes to s. 103.

"enactment" includes an enactment contained in Northern Ireland legislation;

"legal proceedings" means civil proceedings in the High Court or a county court;

"peremptory order" means an order made under section 41(5) or made in exercise of any corresponding power conferred by the parties;

"premises" includes land, building, moveable structures, vehicles, vessels, aircraft and hovercraft;

"question of law" means—

(a) for a court in England and Wales, a question of the law of England and Wales, and

(b) for a court in Northern Ireland, a question of the law of Northern Ireland;

"substantive jurisdiction", in relation to an arbitral tribunal, refers to the matters specified in section 30(1)(a) to (c), and references to the tribunal exceeding its substantive jurisdiction shall be construed accordingly.

(2) References in this Part to a party to an arbitration agreement include any person claiming under or through a party to the agreement.

NOTES

Section 82 contains the basic definitions used in the Act. Of these, only one is noteworthy.

The term "dispute" has given rise to a good deal of difficulty. The authorities are considered in the Notes to section 9.

The term "question of law" is relevant to sections 45 and 69 to the Act, which, subject to various jurisdictional and procedural safeguards, respectively allow a question of law arising in an arbitration to be referred to the High Court for a preliminary determination and provide for an appeal against the award. The effect of the definition, confining a question of law to the law of England or Wales, is to confine section 43 to domestic law issues, and there cannot be any reference to the English courts in respect of a matter of foreign law. This is necessarily the case, as, under English law, the content of any foreign law has to be proved as a matter of fact, and it would be contrary to the spirit of the Act for questions of fact arising in an arbitration to be resolved by the English courts. Foreign law which is the same as English law is, nevertheless, to be treated as falling outside the 1996 Act: *Reliance Industries Ltd* v. *Enron Oil and Gas India Ltd*.[1]

Section 82(2) is a general provision, treating all references to a party to an arbitration agreement as including all persons claiming through or under a party. The cases on this wording, used also in section 4 of the 1950 Act, established that an assignee (whether consensual or by operation of law) was such a person,[2] provided that the agreement did not prohibit assignment.[3] More difficult were the cases of guarantors[4] and companies in the same group as the party.[5] Mere mortgagees were held to be excluded.[6] In accordance with the usual principles of agency, a principal is a party to an arbitration agreement entered into on his behalf by an agent acting within the course of his authority[7] or whose unauthorised conduct has been ratified.[8] It is also the case that if an agreement between

1. [2002] 1 All ER (Comm) 59.

2. *Rumput (Panama) SA* v. *Islamic Republic of Iran Shipping Lines, The League* [1984] 2 Lloyd's Rep 259.

3. *Yeandle* v. *Wynn Realisations Ltd* (1995) 47 Con LR 1; *Bawejem* v. *MC Fabrications Ltd* [1999] 1 All ER (Comm) 377.

4. A guarantor claimed through or under a party only if he had unconditionally agreed to honour the award: *Alfred McAlpine Construction* v. *Unex Corporation* [1994] NPC 16.

5. A subsidiary company has been held to claim through or under its parent for the purpose of seeking a stay: *Roussel-Uclaf* v. *Searle Co* [1978] 1 Lloyd's Rep 225.

6. *Bonnin* v. *Neame* [1910] 1 Ch 732.

7. *Internaut Shipping Ltd* v. *Fercometal SARL* [2003] 2 Lloyd's Rep 430. Contrast *Electrosteel Castings Ltd* v. *Scan-Trans Shipping & Chartering Sdn Bhd* [2003] 1 Lloyd's Rep 190.

8. *Anglia Oils Ltd* v. *Owners of the Marine Champion* [2002] EWHC 2407 (Adm).

A and B contains an arbitration clause, and the agreement either requires B to confer a benefit on a third party, C, or is stated to be enforceable by C against B, then C may enforce the benefits against B under the Contracts (Rights of Third Parties) Act 1999, but any dispute between B and C in respect of the benefit must be referred to arbitration.[1] An insurer exercising subrogation rights is a person claiming under or through the assured who has been indemnified, and is thus bound by any arbitration clause affecting the assured's cause of action against the third party.[2]

Index of defined expressions: Part I

83. In this Part the expressions listed below are defined or otherwise explained by the provisions indicated—

agreement, agree and agreed	section 5(1)
agreement in writing	section 5(2) to (5)
arbitration agreement	sections 6 and 5(1)
arbitrator	section 82(1)
available arbitral process	section 82(1)
claimant	section 82(1)
commencement (in relation to arbitral proceedings)	section 14
costs of the arbitration	section 59
the court	section 105
dispute	section 82(1)
enactment	section 82(1)
legal proceedings	section 82(1)
Limitation Acts	section 13(4)
notice (or other document)	section 76(6)
party—	
—in relation to an arbitration agreement	section 82(2)
—where section 106(2) or (3) applies	section 106(4)
peremptory order	section 82(1) (and see section 41(5))
premises	section 82(1)
question of law	section 82(1)
recoverable costs	sections 63 and 64
seat of the arbitration	section 3
serve and service (of notice or other document)	section 76(6)
substantive jurisdiction (in relation to an arbitral tribunal)	section 82(1) (and see section 30(1)(a) to (c))
upon notice (to the parties or the tribunal)	section 80
written and in writing	section 5(6)

1. This is the effect of s. 8 of the 1999 Act, as construed by Colman J in *Nisshin Shipping Co Ltd* v. *Cleaves & Co Ltd* [2004] 1 Lloyd's Rep 28.
2. *Through Transport Mutual Insurance Association (Eurasia) Ltd* v. *New India Assurance Co Ltd* [2005] 1 Lloyd's Rep 67; *West Tankers Inc* v. *Ras Riunione Adriatica di Sicurta SpA, The Front Comor* [2005] 2 Lloyd's Rep 257 (the appeal, [2007] 1 Lloyd's Rep 391 turned on other issues).

NOTES

Section 83 embodies the familiar legislative technique of providing a table of defined terms, as used in Part I of the Act.

Transitional provisions

84.—(1) The provisions of this Part do not apply to arbitral proceedings commenced before the date on which this Part comes into force.

(2) They apply to arbitral proceedings commenced on or after that date under an arbitration agreement whenever made.

(3) The above provisions have effect subject to any transitional provision made by an order under section 109(2) (power to include transitional provisions in commencement order).

NOTES

Part I of the Act applies only to those arbitration agreements made after the commencement date. The July 1995 Report of the Departmental Advisory Committee considered the possibility that parties could agree to apply the Act to their contract prior to the Act coming into force, but did not come to a firm decision on the point. Parliament clearly regarded such a provision as giving rise to undue complexity. The result of the transitional provision is that the Act will apply to arbitral proceedings begun after commencement irrespective of when the agreement was made. The result will be a clear cut-off point in which the old law ceases to apply and the new law comes into play, and the old law will remain relevant only for those arbitrations which have been started by the commencement date of the legislation. As noted earlier, the Act came into force on 31 January 1997.

PART II OTHER PROVISIONS RELATING TO ARBITRATION

Domestic Arbitration Agreements

Modification of Part I in relation to domestic arbitration agreement

85.—(1) In the case of a domestic arbitration agreement the provisions of Part I are modified in accordance with the following sections.

(2) For this purpose a "domestic arbitration agreement" means an arbitration agreement to which none of the parties is—

(a) as individual who is a national of or habitually resident in, a state other than the United Kingdom, or

(b) a body corporate which is incorporated in, or whose central control and management is exercised in, a state other than the United Kingdom.

and under which the seat of the arbitration (if the seat has been designated or determined) is in the United Kingdom.

(3) In subsection (2) "arbitration agreement" and "seat of the arbitration" have the same meaning as in Part I (see sections 3, 5(1) and 6).

NOTES

Sections 85 to 87 of the Act have not been brought into force and it is unlikely that they will ever be. Conversely, it is highly unlikely that the sections will ever be formally repealed. Although several foreign jurisdictions retain the distinction between domestic and non-domestic arbitrations (including Canada, New Zealand and Australia), such as existed in English law prior to the coming into force of the Arbitration Act 1996, English law has effectively abolished the distinction by holding back these three sections from the statute as enacted.

Staying of legal proceedings

86.—(1) In section 9 (stay of legal proceedings), subsection (4) (stay unless the arbitration agreement is null and void, inoperative, or incapable of being performed) does not apply to a domestic arbitration agreement.

(2) On an application under that section in relation to a domestic arbitration agreement the court shall grant a stay unless satisfied—

(a) that the arbitration agreement is null and void, inoperative, or incapable of being performed, or

(b) that there are other sufficient grounds for not requiring the parties to abide by the arbitration agreement.

(3) The court may treat as a sufficient ground under subsection (2)(b) the fact that the applicant is or was at any material time not ready and willing to do all things necessary for the proper conduct of the arbitration or of any other dispute resolution procedures required to be exhausted before resorting to arbitration.

(4) For the purposes of this section the question whether an arbitration agreement is a domestic arbitration agreement shall be determined by reference to the facts at the time the legal proceedings are concerned.

NOTES

This section (along with sections 85 and 87) has not been brought into force, and though scheduled for repeal, it is likely to remain included in the statute but ignored for all purposes—see the Notes to section 85.

Effectiveness of agreement to exclude court's jurisdiction

87.—(1) In the case of a domestic arbitration agreement any agreement to exclude the jurisdiction of the court under

(a) section 45 (determination of preliminary point of law), or

(b) section 69 (challenging the award: appeal on point of law),

is not effective unless entered into after the commencement of the arbitral proceedings in which the question arises or the award is made.

(2) For this purpose the commencement of the arbitral proceedings has the same meaning as in Part I (see section 14).

(3) For the purposes of this section the question whether an arbitration agreement is a domestic arbitration agreement shall be determined by reference to the facts at the time the agreement is entered into.

NOTES

This section (along with sections 85 and 86) has not been brought into force—see the Notes to section 85.

Power to repeal or amend sections 85 to 87

88.—(1) The Secretary of State may by order repeal or amend the provisions of sections 85 to 87.

(2) An order under this section may contain such supplementary, incidental and transitional provisions as appear to the Secretary of State to be appropriate.

(3) An order under this section shall be made by statutory instrument and no such order shall be made unless a draft of it has been laid before and approved by a resolution of each House of Parliament.

NOTES

The purpose of this provision was explained in the Notes to section 85. Its provisions have yet to be exercised, as sections 85 to 87 have not been (and will not be) brought into force.

Consumer Arbitration Agreements

Application of unfair terms regulations to consumer arbitration agreements

89.—(1) The following sections extend the application of the Unfair Terms in Consumer Contracts Regulations 199[9] in relation to a term which constitutes an arbitration agreement.

For this purpose "arbitration agreement" means an agreement to submit to arbitration present or future disputes or differences (whether or not contractual).

(2) In those sections "the Regulations" mean those regulations and include any regulations amending or replacing those regulations.

(3) Those sections apply whatever the law applicable to the arbitration agreement.

NOTES

Sections 89 to 91 lay down a scheme for the regulation of consumer arbitration agreements, replacing the Consumer Arbitration Agreements Act 1988. The 1988 Act invalidated an arbitration agreement to which a consumer was a party and which fell within county court limits, provided that the agreement had been entered into prior to the dispute arising. The 1988 Act was all but rendered redundant[1] with effect from 1 July 1995 by the Unfair Terms in Consumer Contracts Regulations 1994,[2] re-enacted with minor amendments by the Unfair Terms in Consumer Contracts Regulations 1999,[3] and was duly repealed by the Arbitration Act 1996. The Regulations implement the EC's Unfair Terms in Consumer Contracts Directive 1993.[4] The 1999 Regulations apply to any contract between a consumer (i.e., a natural person making a contract for purposes outside his business) and a commercial concern (i.e., a person who supplies goods or services, for purposes relating to his

1. DAC Supplementary Report, para. 54.
2. SI 1994 No 3159.
3. SI 1999 No 2083.
4. 93/13/EC.

business, and including a profession, government department or local authority). Under the Regulations, a term in a contract with a consumer[1] is unfair, and is rendered unenforceable, if three conditions are met:[2]

(a) the term has not been individually negotiated—this refers to a term which has been drafted in advance and the consumer has not been able to influence its substance;
(b) the term is contrary to the requirement of good faith, a concept which is not defined by the 1999 Regulations, although there had been a detailed definition in the 1994 Regulations; and
(c) the term causes a significant imbalance in the parties' rights and obligations to the detriment of the consumer.

It is apparent that the Regulations apply to all manner of contract terms, most importantly, exclusion clauses. However, the Regulations are not so limited, and the Schedule to the Regulations sets out an illustrative list of potentially unfair terms. Item (q) in the schedule refers to any term which excludes or hinders the consumer's right to legal redress, in particular by the imposition of an obligation to go to arbitration. It is thought to be relatively unlikely that the presumption of unfairness can be rebutted in relation to arbitration clauses in consumer contracts, and accordingly the effect of the Regulations was to supersede the 1988 Act by providing more extensive protection to consumers.

The purpose of section 89 is to apply the 1999 Regulations to consumer arbitration agreements, and to repeal the 1988 Act so that consumer arbitration agreements are governed by a single set of rules. Section 89 is a curious provision, in that the Regulations independently of it apply to consumer arbitration agreements, and the main effect of section 89 is to declare the existing state of the law. However, section 89 does have some independent purpose, in that it confirms that the Regulations apply to arbitration clauses and in some respects extends the ambit of the Regulations. No distinction is drawn between pre- and post-dispute arbitration clauses, and any clause, whenever agreed to, is within the Regulations provided that it is drafted in advance by the supplier. It is, however, far more likely that an arbitration agreement freely entered into by a consumer after a dispute has arisen will be regarded as fair. Fairness is to be determined at the time the agreement was made and not in relation to what has happened subsequently, so the fact that the consumer has participated in the arbitration does not remove his right to allege that the clause was unfair by challenging the award.[3] A consumer who is sophisticated or who has had the benefit of legal advice when entering into the arbitration agreement is unlikely to benefit from the Regulations.[4]

Regulations apply where consumer is a legal person

90. The Regulations apply where the consumer is a legal person as they apply where the consumer is a natural person.

NOTES

This section operates to extend the Unfair Terms in Consumer Contracts Regulations 1999 to arbitration agreements between a commercial supplier and a consumer who is a company or partnership: this goes further than the Regulations themselves, which are confined to consumers who are natural persons. A company which obtains goods or services other than for the purposes of its business is, therefore, protected by the Regulations.

1. See: *Heifer International Inc* v. *Christiansen* [2007] EWHC 3015 (TCC).
2. See: *Zealander* v. *Laing Homes Ltd* [1999] CILL 1510, decided under the 1994 Regulations. Contrast *Mylcrist Builders Ltd* v. *Buck* [2008] EWHC 2172 (TCC).
3. *Case* C-168/05 *Claro* v. *Centro Movil Milenium SA*, 2006.
4. *Heifer International Inc* v. *Christiansen* [2007] EWHC 3015 (TCC).

Arbitration agreement unfair where modest amount sought

91.—(1) A term which constitutes an arbitration agreement is unfair for the purposes of the Regulations so far as it relates to a claim for a pecuniary remedy which does not exceed the amount specified by order for the purposes of this section.

(2) Orders under this section may make different provision for different cases and for different purposes.

(3) The power to make orders under this section is exercisable—

(a) for England and Wales, by the Secretary of State with the concurrence of the Lord Chancellor,
(b) for Scotland, by the Secretary of State [. . .], and
(c) for Northern Ireland, by the Department of Economic Development for Northern Ireland with the concurrence of the Lord Chancellor.

(4) Any such order for England and Wales or Scotland shall be made by statutory instrument which shall be subject to annulment in pursuance of a resolution of either House of Parliament.

(5) Any such order for Northern Ireland shall be a statutory rule for the purposes of the Statutory Rules (Northern Ireland) Order 1979 and shall be subject to negative resolution, within the meaning of section 41(6) of the Interpretation Act (Northern Ireland) Order 1954.

NOTES

The effect of section 91 is to authorise the making of an Order which fixes a financial limit for a financial remedy so that an arbitration clause which relates to a lesser sum is automatically unfair. The power was exercised by the Unfair Arbitration Agreements (Specified Amount) Order 1996,[1] fixing the limit at £3,000. The figure was raised to £5,000 by the Unfair Arbitration Agreements (Specified Amount) Order 1999. If the sum sought is greater than £5,000, the consumer necessarily retains the right to rely directly upon the Unfair Terms in Consumer Contracts Regulations 1999, so the mere fact that a dispute involving a large sum is outside section 89 does not mean that the arbitration clause in it is automatically valid, as it still has to pass the tests in the Regulations themselves.

Subsection (3) was amended by the Transfer of Functions (Lord Advocate and Secretary of State) Order 1999, SI 1999 No 679, Article 6.

Small Claims Arbitration in the County Court

Exclusion of Part I in relation to small claims arbitration in the county court

92. Nothing in Part I of this Act applies to arbitration under section 64 of the County Courts Act 1984.

NOTES

This section was originally designed to make it clear that the Act did not apply to county court arbitrations. Such arbitrations were governed by the special rules laid down in the County Courts Act 1984. The concept of introducing separate legislation for the resolution of consumer disputes was considered, but rejected, by the DAC in its February 1996 Report. The Civil Procedure Rules

1. DAC Supplementary Report, para. 55.

replaced county court arbitrations with the small claims track for such claims. Section 92 no longer has any effect, although it has not yet been repealed.

Appointment of Judges as Arbitrators

Appointment of judges as arbitrators

93.—(1) A judge of the Commercial Court or an official referee may, if in all the circumstances he thinks fit, accept appointment as a sole arbitrator or as umpire by or by virtue of an arbitration agreement.

(2) A judge of the Commercial Court shall not do so unless the Lord Chief Justice has informed him that, having regard to the state of business in the High Court and the Crown Court, he can be made available.

(3) An official referee shall not do so unless the Lord Chief Justice has informed him that, having regard to the state of official referees' business, he can be made available.

(4) The fees payable for the services of a judge of the Commercial Court or official referee as arbitrator or umpire shall be taken in the High Court.

(5) In this section—

"arbitration agreement" has the same meaning as in Part I; and

"official referee" means a person nominated under section 68(1)(a) of the Supreme Court Act 1981 to deal with official referees' business.

(6) The provisions of Part I of this Act apply to arbitration before a person appointed under this section with the modifications specified in Schedule 2.

NOTES

This section permits a judge or official referee to act as an arbitrator. The Act applies to a judge-arbitrator subject to the modifications listed in Schedule 2 to the Act. The section re-enacts section 4 of the Administration of Justice Act 1970, but remains confined to judges of the Commercial Court and judges involved in official referee's business. The DAC's February 1996 Report, paragraphs 341 and 343 stated a desire to extend the section to all judges and not just the two classes presently referred to, but agreement with the relevant departments could not be reached in time to permit this extension to be included.[1] The Report highlighted a particular problem in disputes involving patents, where commonly the only acceptable arbitrators are judges.

Section 95(2)–(3) makes it clear that the parties do not have the right to appoint a judge, and that any appointment is subject to availability.

The modifications to the Arbitration Act 1996, listed in Schedule 2 to the 1996 Act, re-enact the Administration of Justice Act 1970, Schedule 3. The purpose is to disapply those provisions of the 1996 Act which are not required by judges in the light of their existing powers.

It should be noted that, although the phrase "official referee" has not actually been repealed by statute, the office does not formally exist as such, and business previously referred to as "official referees' business" has, since September 1998, been dealt with by the Technology and Construction Court. Those judges formerly dubbed "official referees" are now judges of the Technology and Construction Court.

1. DAC Supplementary Report, para. 55.

Statutory Arbitrations

Application of Part I to statutory arbitrations

94.—(1) The provisions of Part I apply to every arbitration under an enactment (a "statutory arbitration"), whether the enactment was passed or made before or after the commencement of this Act subject to the adaptations and exclusions specified in sections 95 to 98.

(2) The provisions of Part I do not apply to a statutory arbitration if or to the extent that their application—

(a) is inconsistent with the provisions of the enactment concerned, with any rules or procedure authorised or recognised by it, or

(b) is excluded by any other enactment.

(3) In this section and the following provisions of this Part "enactment"

(a) in England and Wales, includes an enactment contained in subordinate legislation within the meaning of the Interpretation Act 1978;

(b) in Northern Ireland, means a statutory provision within the meaning of section 1(f) of the Interpretation Act (Northern Ireland) 1954.

NOTES

This section re-enacts section 31(1) of the Arbitration Act 1950, in extending the Act to the various statutes which provide for arbitration, subject to contrary provisions in those statutes.

General adaptation of provisions in relation to statutory arbitrations

95.—(1) The provisions of Part I apply to a statutory arbitration—

(a) as if the arbitration were pursuant to an arbitration agreement and as if the enactment were that agreement, and

(b) as if the persons by and against whom a claim subject to arbitration in pursuance of the enactment may be or has been made were parties to that agreement.

(2) Every statutory arbitration shall be taken to have its seat in England and Wales or, as the case may be, in Northern Ireland.

NOTES

This section is merely a deeming provision, providing that statutory arbitrations are deemed to be consensual for the purposes of the application of the Act.

Specific adaptations of provisions in relation to statutory arbitrations

96.—(1) The following provisions of Part I apply to a statutory arbitration with the following adaptations.

(2) In section 30(1) (competence of tribunal to rule on its own jurisdiction), the reference to paragraph (a) to whether there is a valid arbitration agreement shall be construed as a reference to whether the enactment applies to the dispute or difference in question.

(3) Section 35 (consolidation of proceedings and concurrent hearings) applies only so as to authorise the consolidation of proceedings, or concurrent hearings in proceedings, under the same enactment.

(4) Section 46 (rules applicable to substance of dispute) applies with the omission of subsection (1)(b) (determination in accordance with considerations agreed by parties).

NOTES

This section modifies the Act in its application to statutory arbitrations. The principle is derived from section 31(2) of the Arbitration Act 1950. The fact that statutory arbitrations are compulsory rather than voluntary prompted Lord Lester to introduce an amendment whereby arbitrators were required to be independent as well as impartial, on the basis that the lack of independence contravened the European Convention on Human Rights. The Government's response was that, if it proved to be the case that any particular tribunal demonstrated that it was not independent, steps could be taken to remedy the problem under the general delegated powers contained in section 98. The DAC in its February 1996 Report, paragraph 391, saw no need for this, a view adopted by the legislation.[1]

Provisions excluded from applying to statutory arbitrations

97. The following provisions of Part I do not apply in relation to a statutory arbitration—

(a) section 8 (whether agreement discharged by death of a party);
(b) section 12 (power of court to extend agreed time limits);
(c) sections 9(5), 10(2) and 71(4) (restrictions on effect of provision that award condition precedent to right to bring legal proceedings).

Power to make further provisions by regulations

98.—(1) The Secretary of State may make provision by regulations for adapting or excluding any provision of Part I in relation to statutory arbitration in general or statutory arbitrations of any particular description.

(2) The power is exercisable whether the enactment concerned is passed or made before or after the commencement of this Act.

(3) Regulations under this section shall be made by statutory instrument which shall be subject to annulment in pursuance of a resolution of either House of Parliament.

NOTES

No regulations have been made under this section.

1. DAC Supplementary Report, para. 56.

PART III RECOGNITION AND ENFORCEMENT OF CERTAIN FOREIGN AWARDS

Enforcement of Geneva Convention Awards

Continuation of Part II of the Arbitration Act 1950

99. Part II of the Arbitration Act 1950 (enforcement of certain foreign awards) continues to apply in relation to foreign awards within the meaning of that Part which are not also New York Convention awards.

NOTES

This section maintains in force Part II of the Arbitration Act 1950, which sets out the enforcement regime applicable to Geneva Convention awards. This provision has in practice been all but superseded by enforcement under the subsequent New York Convention. It remains in force only as regards those countries which have not acceded to the New York Convention. The list of signatory states to the New York Convention is set out in the UNCITRAL website: www.uncitral.org. It would appear that the remaining non-New York Convention countries that are still parties to the Geneva Convention are mostly current or former Commonwealth countries, including Anguilla, Belize, British Virgin Islands, Falkland Islands, Grenada, Guyana, Montserrat, Saint Christopher and Nevis, Saint Lucia, Turks & Caicos Islands and Samoa. However, enforcement of awards in those countries may still be effected under section 66 as an alternative to enforcement under the 1950 Act.

Recognition and Enforcement of New York Convention Awards

New York Convention awards

100.—(1) In this Part a "New York Convention award" means an award made, in pursuance of an arbitration agreement, in the territory of a state (other than the United Kingdom) which is a party to the New York Convention.

(2) For the purposes of subsection (1) and of the provisions of this Part relating to such awards—

(a) "arbitration agreement" means an arbitration agreement in writing, and
(b) an award shall be treated as made at the seat of the arbitration, regardless of where it was signed, despatched or delivered to any of the parties.

In this subsection "agreement in writing" and "seat of the arbitration" have the same meaning as in Part I.

(3) If Her Majesty by Order in Council declares that a state specified in the Order is a party to the New York Convention, or is a party in respect of any territory so specified, the Order shall, while in force, be conclusive evidence of that fact.

(4) In this section "the New York Convention" means the Convention on the Recognition and Enforcement of Foreign Arbitral Awards adopted by the United Nations Conference on International Commercial Arbitration on 10 June 1958.

NOTES

This section and sections 101 to 104 re-enact the Arbitration Act 1975, which in turn implemented into English law the New York Convention 1958. The Convention lays down common principles for the enforcement of foreign arbitration awards. Section 103(1) re-enacts the definition in section 7(1) of the Arbitration Act 1975, although it is now the case that an award is deemed to be made in the place where the arbitration had its seat (sections 53 and 103(2)(b)). This reverses the decision of the House of Lords in *Hiscox* v. *Outhwaite*,[1] which treated the place in which an award was made as the place in which it was signed.[2] Section 103(2) follows the DAC report recommendation that there should be a cross-reference to the definition of writing in what was then Part I of the Bill,[3] by the express reference to the definition of "agreement in writing" (now contained in section 5). The New York Convention contains a slightly narrower definition of "agreement in writing" than that set out in section 5.[4] However, the DAC considered that the definition of agreement in writing was "consonant" with the Convention.[5] Section 103(3) re-enacts section 7(2) of the Arbitration Act 1975, permitting the Secretary of State to give conclusive confirmation of parties to the Convention: the relevant Order is SI 1989 No 1348, as amended. However, the provision merely states that the inclusion of a country in the list contained in the Order is conclusive evidence of that fact. A country may be a party to the Convention but not (or not yet) included in the Order, though this ought not to make any practical difference, provided that there is evidence of such fact, for example, by first checking on the UNCITRAL website (www.uncitral.org), and (if necessary) having the matter confirmed in writing by a lawyer from the jurisdiction in question.[6]

Recognition and enforcement of awards

101.—(1) A New York Convention award shall be recognised as binding on the persons as between whom it was made, and may accordingly be relied on by those persons by way of defence, set-off or otherwise in any legal proceedings in England and Wales or Northern Ireland.

(2) A New York Convention award may, by leave of the court, be enforced in the same manner as a judgment or order of the court to the same effect.

As to the meaning of "the court" see section 105.

(3) Where leave is so given, judgment may be entered in terms of the award.

NOTES

This section is a simplified version of section 3 of the Arbitration Act 1975, and provides that a Convention award is to be recognised[7] in English proceedings,[8] and may be enforced in the same way as a domestic or foreign award is enforced under section 66 of the Act. An application for the enforcement of an award as a judgment under section 101 may be made using an arbitration claim form as set out in CPR Part 62.[9] The application may be made without notice to the other party,

1. [1992] 1 AC 562.
2. For the implications of this discussion, see the Notes to s. 53.
3. As recommended by the DAC Report, para. 392, noted in DAC Supplementary Report, para. 58.
4. New York Convention, Art. II.2. In July 2006, the United Nations Commission on International Trade Law (UNCITRAL) adopted a "recommendation" that Art. II.2 be applied "recognizing that the circumstances described therein are not exhaustive". See the UNCITRAL website for more information (www.uncitral.org). Note that s. 5 extends only to the provisions in Part I of the Act, i.e., to ss. 1 to 84, so that the cross-reference in s. 100 was required.
5. See DAC February 1996 report, para 348.
6. The exact url for the current list of contracting states (142 parties at the time of going to press) is www.uncitral.org/uncitral/en/uncitraltexts/arbitration/NYConventionstatus.html. Note that the United Kingdom has extended the territorial application of the Convention to Bermuda, Cayman Islands, Gibraltar, Guernsey, Isle of Man and Jersey. Note that the UK is one of approximately half of the contracting states that insist that the award should itself be made in a New York Convention state (known as the reciprocity reservation).
7. See *Irvani* v. *Irvani* [2000] 1 Lloyd's Rep 412.
8. Note that although the expression "legal proceedings" is defined in s. 82(1), that definition (as with all definitions in s. 82) is for the purposes of Part I of the Act only, whereas s. 101 is in Part III.
9. CPR r. 62.18(1). The arbitration claim form may be issued in the High Court or in any county court: see para. 4 of the High Court and County Court (Allocation of Arbitration Proceedings) Order 1996, SI 1996 No 3215, as amended.

although if this is the case the applicant must disclose all material facts to the court,[1] and in any event the court may require that the application be served on the other parties;[2] if necessary, service may be ordered to be effected outside the jurisdiction.[3] The applicant must supply written evidence exhibiting the original arbitration agreement and the originally authenticated award (or duly certified copies of those documents[4]) and must state that it has not been honoured.[5] If the applicant wishes to enforce an award of interest any part of which relates to a period after the award, he must file a certificate stating whether the interest was simple or compound, the date from which interest was awarded, the rate, whether any rests were provided for and a calculation showing the total sum.[6] The order must contain a statement of the respondent's right to apply within 14 days of service of the order (or such longer period as prescribed if served out of the jurisdiction) to set it aside and of the restrictions on enforcing it before the end of the application to set it aside has been disposed of finally.[7] The order itself must be drawn up by the applicant and served on the respondent.[8]

Section 101(3) states that the judgment may be entered in terms of the award. The applicant cannot seek any wider order from the court. Thus, if the award is made against a named defendant, the award may be enforced only against that defendant and not against some third party who is alleged by the applicant to be the principal of the defendant.[9] However, the applicant may seek partial enforcement of the award, that is, in respect of separate heads of claim in the award which are either unchallenged or unchallengeable, where for example other parts of the award are being challenged either in the supervisory courts of the arbitral seat or as part of the defence to enforcement proceedings in the English courts.[10]

Evidence to be produced by party seeking recognition or enforcement

102.—(1) A party seeking the recognition or enforcement of a New York Convention award must produce—

(a) the duly authenticated original award or a duly certified copy of it, and
(b) the original arbitration agreement or a duly certified copy of it.

(2) If the award or agreement is in a foreign language, the party must also produce a translation of it certified by an official or sworn translator or by a diplomatic or consular agent.

NOTES

This section reproduces in simplified form section 4 of the Arbitration Act 1975, and lays down the formalities required for the enforcement of a New York Convention award. The original version of the Bill provided a definition of "duly authenticated", but this was subsequently dropped and subsection (1) was redrafted to correspond with the wording of the New York Convention. There is no mechanism in English procedural law for a copy of an award or arbitration agreement to be "duly certified", and it is enough that the applicant has deposed that it is authentic.[11] Once the applicant has satisfied these procedural requirements, he has fulfilled his duties under the Act and the burden

1. *Curacao Trading BV* v. *Harkisandas & Co* [2002] 2 Lloyd's Rep 186; *Socadec SA* v. *Pan Afric Impex Co Ltd* [2003] EWHC 2086 (QB).
2. CPR r 62.18(2).
3. The permission of the court under CPR r. 6.20 for service out is not required here: CPR r. 62.18(4).
4. See s. 102.
5. CPR r. 62.18(6).
6. CPR r. 62.19.
7. CPR r. 62.18(9)–(10).
8. CPR r. 62.18(7).
9. *Norsk Hydro ASA* v. *State Property Fund of Ukraine* [2002] EWHC (Comm) 2120.
10. See: *IPCO (Nigeria) Ltd* v. *Nigerian National Petroleum Corp (No 2)* [2008] EWCA Civ 1157.
11. *Dardana Ltd* v. *Yukos Oil Co* [2002] 2 Lloyd's Rep 326.

of proof then switches to the respondent to make out one or more of the defences set out in section 103.[1]

Refusal of recognition or enforcement

103.—(1) Recognition or enforcement of a New York Convention award shall not be refused except in the following cases.

(2) Recognition or enforcement of the award may be refused if the person against whom it is invoked proves—

(a) that a party to the arbitration agreement was (under the law applicable to him) under some incapacity;
(b) that the arbitration agreement was not valid under the law to which the parties subjected it or, failing any indication thereon, under the law of the country where the award was made;
(c) that he was not given proper notice of the appointment of the arbitrator or of the arbitration proceedings or was otherwise unable to present his case;
(d) that the award deals with a difference not contemplated by or not falling within the terms of the submission to arbitration or contains decisions on matters beyond the scope of the submission to arbitration (but see subsection (4));
(e) that the composition of the arbitral tribunal or the arbitral procedure was not in accordance with the agreement of the parties or, failing such agreement, with the law of the country in which the arbitration took place;
(f) that the award has not yet become binding on the parties, or has been set aside or suspended by a competent authority of the country in which, or under the law of which it was made.

(3) Recognition or enforcement of the award may also be refused if the award is in respect of a matter which is not capable of settlement by arbitration, or if it would be contrary to public policy to recognise or enforce the award.

(4) An award which contains decisions on matters not submitted to arbitration may be recognised or enforced to the extent that it contains decisions on matters submitted to arbitration which can be separated from those on matters not so submitted.

(5) Where an application for the setting aside or suspension of the award has been made to such a competent authority as is mentioned in subsection (2)(f), the court before which the award is sought to be relied upon may, if it considers it proper, adjourn the decision on the recognition or enforcement of the award.

It may also on the application of the party claiming recognition or enforcement of the award order the other party to give suitable security.

NOTES

This section re-enacts section 5 of the Arbitration Act 1975. Section 103(1) lays down the basic rule that an English court cannot refuse the enforcement of a Convention award unless one of the grounds in section 103(2) is made out.

The list of defences in section 103(2) is taken almost verbatim from the New York Convention itself. Even if a defence is made out, the court has a discretion to enforce an award provided that

1. *Dardana Ltd* v. *Yukos Oil Co* [2002] 2 Lloyd's Rep 326.

substantial injustice would not be done by preventing reliance on a defence.[1] It has, nevertheless, been suggested more recently that the discretion of the court to grant enforcement even though a defence has been made out is limited to the case in which the respondent has, by reason of waiver, lost the right to contest the award.[2]

Section 103(2)(a)—incapacity—has not been discussed, but would appear to refer to incapacity under the law of the place of the defendant's domicile. Although there is some debate as to whether the incapacity referred to is physical or legal, the preferable view is that it ought to be referable to some legal incapacity. Any physical incapacity (e.g., that would prevent the party from participating in the proceedings) would be covered by section 103(2)(c) below. There is also some doubt as to whether the incapacity must relate to the time of entering into the agreement, or the time of commencement of the proceedings. On balance it ought to refer to the former, but there are no reported English decisions on this ground.[3]

Section 103(2)(b)—invalid arbitration agreement[4]—provides a defence where the arbitration agreement was invalid under the law applicable to it (whether by express or implied agreement of the parties)[5] or, by way of fallback, under the law of the seat (the seat being the place where the award was "made" by virtue of section 100(2)(b)). The subsection covers an allegation that the arbitrators had no jurisdiction,[6] e.g. because the applicant was not a party to the arbitration agreement.[7] The subsection does not require the applicant to be put to proof that the arbitration agreement was valid: once the applicant has produced the arbitration agreement or a copy of it under section 102, the burden then switches to the respondent to show that the agreement was invalid.[8] However, if the issue of validity of the arbitration agreement has already been decided in favour of the applicant in proceedings between the parties in the courts of the seat, that decision is binding so that an issue estoppel will generally arise against the respondent.[9]

1. *China Agribusiness Development Corporation* v. *Balli Trading* [1998] 2 Lloyd's Rep 76; *Minmetals Germany GmbH* v. *Ferco Steel Ltd* [1999] 1 All ER (Comm) 315; *Tongyuan (US) International Trading Group* v. *Uni-Clan Ltd* 2001, unreported (Moore-Bick J) but a full summary is available at (2001) 26 Yearbook of Commercial Arbitration 886.

2. *Dardana Ltd* v. *Yukos Oil Co* [2002] 2 Lloyd's Rep 326. See also: *Svenska Petroleum Exploration AB* v. *Government of the Republic of Lithuania (No 1)* [2005] 1 Lloyd's Rep 515, where the court recognised an award even though there was a jurisdictional challenge to it, on the basis that the applicant had participated in the arbitration and would have been treated under s. 73 as having waived the right to challenge the award.

3. In *Kanoria* v. *Guinness* [2006] 1 Lloyd's Rep 701, the Court of Appeal referred to the decision of Gloster J at first instance (unreported) in which she accepted the fact that the English respondent in person to the arbitration was apparently suffering from severe cancer and, therefore, unable to attend hearings in India was sufficient to mean that he was under an incapacity for the purposes of s. 103(2)(a). However, this must be regarded as open to question, since the preferable basis for relying on physical incapacity in terms of participation in the arbitration would be s. 103(2)(c) (inability to present case).

4. The reference is to the arbitration agreement rather than to the submission to arbitration: *Dallah Real Estate and Tourism Holding Co* v. *Ministry of Religious Affairs, Government of Pakistan* [2008] EWHC 1901 (Comm). It sometimes occurs that parties make their arbitration agreements subject to a different governing law to that of the underlying contract, though there rarely appears to be any advantage in doing so. In the absence of any intention to the contrary, the law applicable to the arbitration agreement will usually be taken to be the same law as that applicable to the underlying contract (if any). Although there is some difficulty in this regard, in that the Rome Convention on the Law Applicable to Contractual Obligations excludes arbitration agreements from its scope (see Art. 1.2(d)), the fallback provisions of English private international law will still apply, so that the governing law of the underlying contract will usually determine (insofar as it is relevant) the law applicable to the arbitration agreement. This is to be distinguished from the law governing the arbitration proceedings, which will usually be governed by the law of the seat of arbitration. See the Notes to s. 46.

5. This means the substantive law of that country and not its conflict of laws rules: *Dallah Real Estate and Tourism Holding Co* v. *Ministry of Religious Affairs, Government of Pakistan* [2008] EWHC 1901 (Comm).

6. *Dardana Ltd* v. *Yukos Oil Co* [2002] 2 Lloyd's Rep 326. But see *Dallah Real Estate and Tourism Holding Co* v. *Ministry of Religious Affairs, Government of Pakistan* [2008] EWHC 1901 (Comm) where the view was expressed that the subsection is concerned with formal validity only.

7. *Svenska Petroleum Exploration AB* v. *Government of the Republic of Lithuania* [2005] 1 Lloyd's Rep 515.

8. *Dardana Ltd* v. *Yukos Oil Co* [2002] 2 Lloyd's Rep 326. A full rehearing is required, as is the case under s. 67: *Dallah Real Estate and Tourism Holding Co* v. *Ministry of Religious Affairs, Government of Pakistan* [2008] EWHC 1901 (Comm).

9. *Dardana Ltd* v. *Yukos Oil Co* [2002] 2 Lloyd's Rep 326 (CA).

Section 103(2)(c)—inability to present case—is concerned only with the situation in which the defendant has not been afforded a reasonable opportunity to present his case, so that if the defendant could have made submissions to the arbitrators but failed to do so, there is no basis for refusing enforcement.[1] By contrast, if he has not been afforded the opportunity to put his case, then the court may refuse enforcement.[2] Where allegations of fraud or dishonesty are put forward as the basis for a claim against a respondent apparently too ill to attend an arbitration, but not brought to his attention in any way, enforcement of the award may be refused.[3]

Section 103(2)(d)—jurisdictional issues—is concerned with substantive rather than procedural matters, so that an objection to procedure falls within section 103(2)(c) or the general public policy rules rather than this provision.[4] It has been suggested that this head applies only to a jurisdictional issue arising under a valid arbitration, as opposed to a jurisdictional issue which prevents the arbitration agreement from operating at all.[5]

Section 103(2)(e) deals with a breach in agreed composition or procedure. Such a breach may be disregarded if it is trivial[6] or if it has been waived by the defendant by failing to object at the appropriate time.[7]

Section 103(2)(f)—order to set aside/suspend award made by supervisory court—is concerned with an order which has already been made when enforcement is sought. It does not apply when an application before the supervisory court is merely pending.[8] In such a case the English court may, in accordance with section 103(5),[9] adjourn any decision on the recognition or enforcement of the award, although it may order the respondent to provide security for the award.[10] In cases where an application to set aside is pending before the supervisory court of the arbitral seat, enforcement may also be granted of those parts of the award that are either unchallenged or in respect of which there is no realistic prospect of challenge.[11] Relevant considerations in a decision on the adjournment of the proceedings and on the grant of security will include the likelihood of the award being overturned, the manner in which the respondent has pursued his application to challenge the award and the risk that the respondent may dissipate his assets in the absence of an order for security.[12] The applicant may also be ordered to provide security for the respondent's future costs, as there is a risk that the applicant may discontinue the enforcement proceedings if the award is successfully challenged.[13]

Section 103(3)—the public policy defence—has been considered in a number of cases many of which have been decided since the passing of the 1996 Act. The most important aspects of public policy[14] are:

(a) the award has been obtained by perjury or fraud;[15]

1. *Minmetals Germany GmbH* v. *Ferco Steel Ltd* [1999] 1 All ER (Comm) 315.
2. *Irvani* v. *Irvani* [2000] 1 Lloyd's Rep 412.
3. *Kanoria* v. *Guinness* [2006] 1 Lloyd's Rep 701.
4. *Minmetals Germany GmbH* v. *Ferco Steel Ltd* [1999] 1 All ER (Comm) 315.
5. *Dardana Ltd* v. *Yukos Oil Co* [2002] 1 Lloyd's Rep 225: the point did not arise on appeal.
6. *China Agribusiness Development Corporation* v. *Balli Trading* [1998] 2 Lloyd's Rep 76; *Tongyuan (US) International Trading Group* v. *Uni-Clan Ltd*, 2001, unreported (Moore-Bick J) but a full summary is available at (2001) 26 Yearbook of Commercial Arbitration 886.
7. *Minmetals Germany GmbH* v. *Ferco Steel Ltd* [1999] 1 All ER (Comm) 315.
8. *IPCO (Nigeria)* v. *Nigerian National Petroleum Corp* [2005] 2 Lloyd's Rep 326.
9. Section 103(5) is taken almost verbatim from Art. VI of the New York Convention.
10. See generally: *Soleh Boneh International* v. *Government of the Republic of Uganda* [1993] 2 Lloyd's Rep 208; *Minmetals Germany GmbH* v. *Ferco Steel Ltd* [1999] 1 All ER (Comm) 315 and *IPCO (Nigeria) Ltd* v. *Nigerian National Petroleum Corp* [2005] 2 Lloyd's Rep 326. The court has no jurisdiction under s. 103(5) to order security for any reason other than that the enforcement proceedings have been adjourned: *Dardana Ltd* v. *Yukos Oil Co* [2002] 2 Lloyd's Rep 326.
11. See: *IPCO (Nigeria) Ltd* v. *Nigerian National Petroleum Corp (No 2)* [2008] EWCA Civ 1157.
12. *Dardana Ltd* v. *Yukos Oil Co* [2002] 2 Lloyd's Rep 326.
13. *Ibid.*
14. The courts have suggested that in the context of enforcement, public policy means the public policy of the source country.
15. *Westacre Investments Inc* v. *Jugoimport-SDPR Holding Co Ltd* [1999] 2 Lloyd's Rep 65 (CA). *Tamil Nadu Electricity Board* v. *ST-CMS Electric Company Private Ltd* [2008] 1 Lloyd's Rep 93.

(b) the losing party is at risk of having to make payment in some other jurisdiction as well as in England;[1]

(c) the award is tainted by illegality.[2] If the arbitrators have jurisdiction under the arbitration clause to determine the legality of the underlying contract,[3] and have concluded that the contract is valid under its applicable law, the award is generally enforceable[4] even though the contract was illegal in the place of its performance, although in exceptional circumstances the court may go behind the award and apply overriding principles of public policy, for example, the prevention of corruption,[5] or to save the law of the place of performance from being flouted.[6] Equally, if the arbitrators have ignored "palpable and indisputable illegality" the award will not be enforced.[7] By contrast, if illegality under the applicable law has not been raised before the arbitrators, the English court may consider whether the underlying contract was illegal under its applicable law although the presumption is in favour of enforcement;[8]

(d) the underlying agreement is contrary to overriding principles of EU law, in particular the competition laws set out in Articles 81 and 82 of the Treaty on European Union;[9]

(e) the award was obtained in breach of the rules of natural justice. This is a limited defence, for the losing party will normally have a right to seek to have the award overturned by the courts of the jurisdiction in which the award was given, and if the losing party has sought but failed to obtain relief from the curial courts, or has unreasonably not invoked the jurisdiction of the curial courts, the award will generally be enforced by the English courts;[10] and

(f) the award is unclear as to the obligations imposed on the parties and is accordingly incapable of enforcement.[11]

The fact that circumstances have altered after the award, rendering enforcement potentially unfair, is not a valid public policy ground upon which enforcement can be refused.[12]

Prior to the passing of the 1996 Act it was held that the court had a general discretion to stay

1. *Deutsche Schachtbau-und Tiefbohrgesellschaft mbH* v. *Shell Petroleum Ltd* [1990] 1 AC 295; *Soinco SACI* v. *Novokuznetsk Aluminium Plant (No 2)* [1998] 2 Lloyd's Rep 346 (where enforcement was granted).

2. The applicable principles were set out by Colman J at first instance in *Westacre*, a judgment which was, with minor modifications suggested by Waller LJ, approved by the Court of Appeal in *Westacre* itself and also in *Soleimany* v. *Soleimany* [1998] 3 WLR 811.

3. English public policy does not object to such jurisdiction if there is some overriding principle of English law involved: *Westacre Investments*, principles (ii) and (iii).

4. *Westacre Investments*, principle (v): *Soinco SACI* v. *Novokuznetsk Aluminium Plant (No 1)* [1998] 2 Lloyd's Rep 337; *Omnium de Traitement et de Valorisation SA* v. *Hilmarton Ltd* [1999] 2 Lloyd's Rep 222.

5. *Westacre Investments*, principle (i), as modified by Waller LJ in *Westacre* and in *Soleimany*. In the Court of Appeal in *Westacre* Mantell LJ and Sir David Hirst were of the view that the decision of arbitrators as to legality under the applicable law was not to be reopened in the absence of negligence or collusion on the part of the arbitrators. That generous approach will not be relevant in the case of a foreign judgment: *Lemenda Trading* v. *AMEPC* [1998] 1 Lloyd's Rep 361; *Tekron Resources Ltd* v. *Guinea Investment Co Ltd* [2004] 2 Lloyd's Rep 26.

6. *Lemenda Trading* v. *AMEPC* [1998] 1 Lloyd's Rep 361.

7. *Westacre Investments*, principle (iv); *Soleimany* v. *Soleimany* [1998] 3 WLR 811.

8. *Westacre Investments*, principle (vi).

9. *Eco Swiss China Time Ltd* v. *Benetton International BV* Case C-126/97 [1999] 2 All ER (Comm) 44.

10. *Minmetals Germany GmbH* v. *Ferco Steel Ltd* [1999] 1 All ER (Comm) 315, in which the principles applicable to judgments—as set out in the judgment of the Court of Appeal in *Adams* v. *Cape Industries Ltd* [1991] 1 All ER 921—were applied by Colman J. See also: *Dalmia Dairy Industries Ltd* v. *National Bank of Pakistan* [1978] 2 Lloyd's Rep 223.

11. *Tonguyan (USA) International Trading Group* v. *Uni-Clan Ltd*, 2001, unreported (Moore-Bick J) but a full summary is available at (2001) 26 Yearbook of Commercial Arbitration 886.

12. *Ibid.*

execution of a judgment on the ground of expediency.[1] This discretion has apparently survived the 1996 Act,[2] but is exercisable in exceptional circumstances only.[3]

Saving for other bases of recognition or enforcement

104. Nothing in the preceding provisions of this Part affects any right to rely upon or enforce a New York Convention award at common law or under section 66.

NOTES

This section, which re-enacts section 6 of the Arbitration Act 1975, provides that any other forms of enforcement available in England are not precluded simply because the award is a Convention award. The possibility of bringing an action on the award at common law is thus retained.

PART IV GENERAL PROVISIONS

Meaning of "the court": jurisdiction of High Court and county court

105.—(1) In this Act "the court" means the High Court or a county court, subject to the following provisions.

(2) The Lord Chancellor may by order make provision—

(a) allocating proceedings under this Act to the High Court or to county courts; or

(b) specifying proceedings under this Act which may be commenced or taken only in the High Court or in a county court.

(3) The Lord Chancellor may by order make provision requiring proceedings of any specified description under this Act in relation to which a county court has jurisdiction to be commenced or taken in one or more specified county courts.

Any jurisdiction so exercisable by a specified county court is exercisable throughout England and Wales or, as the case may be, Northern Ireland.

(3A) The Lord Chancellor must consult the Lord Chief Justice of England and Wales or the Lord Chief Justice of Northern Ireland (as the case may be) before making an order under this section.

(3B) The Lord Chief Justice of England and Wales may nominate a judicial office holder (as defined in section 109(4) of the Constitutional Reform Act 2005) to exercise his functions under this section.

(3C) The Lord Chief Justice of Northern Ireland may nominate any of the following to exercise his functions under this section—

(a) the holder of one of the offices listed in Schedule 1 to the Justice (Northern Ireland) Act 2002;

(b) a Lord Justice of Appeal (as defined in section 88 of that Act).

1. *Far Eastern Shipping Co* v. *AKP Sovcomflot* [1995] 1 Lloyd's Rep 520.

2. See: *Arab Business Consortium International Finance and Investment Co* v. *Banque Franco-Tunisienne* [1996] 1 Lloyd's Rep 485, affirmed on other grounds [1997] 1 Lloyd's Rep 531, where doubts were expressed.

3. *Air India* v. *Caribjet Inc* [2002] 1 Lloyd's Rep 314.

(4) An order under this section

(a) may differentiate between categories of proceedings by reference to such criteria as the Lord Chancellor sees fit to specify, and
(b) may make such incidental or transitional provision as the Lord Chancellor considers necessary or expedient.

(5) An order under this section for England and Wales shall be made by statutory instrument which shall be subject to annulment in pursuance of a resolution of either House of Parliament.

(6) An order under this section for Northern Ireland shall be a statutory rule for the purposes of the Statutory Rules (Northern Ireland) Order 1979 which shall be subject to annulment in pursuance of a resolution of either House of Parliament in like manner as a statutory instrument and section 5 of the Statutory Instruments Act 1946 shall apply accordingly.

NOTES

Subsections (3A) to (3C) were inserted by the Constitutional Reform Act 2005, Schedule 4(1), paragraph 250. The relevant order made under this section is the High Court and County Court (Allocation of Arbitration Proceedings) Order 1996, SI 1996 No 3215, as amended by the High Court and County Courts (Allocation of Arbitration Proceedings) (Amendment) Order 1999, SI 1999 No 1010 to take account of the implementation of the Civil Procedure Rules 1998.

Crown application

106.—(1) Part I of this Act applies to any arbitration agreement to which Her Majesty either in right of the Crown or of the Duchy of Lancaster or otherwise, or the Duke of Cornwall, is a party.

(2) Where Her Majesty is party to an arbitration agreement otherwise than in right of the Crown, Her Majesty shall be represented for the purpose of any arbitral proceedings—

(a) where the agreement was entered into by Her Majesty in right of the Duchy of Lancaster, by the Chancellor of the Duchy or such person as he may appoint, and
(b) in any other case, by such person as Her Majesty may appoint in writing under the Royal Sign Manual.

(3) Where the Duke of Cornwall is party to an arbitration agreement, he shall be represented for the purposes of any arbitral proceedings by such person as he may appoint.

(4) References in Part I to a party or the parties to the arbitration agreement or to arbitral proceedings shall be construed, where subsection (2) or (3) applies, as references to the person representing Her Majesty or the Duke of Cornwall.

NOTES

This section re-enacts section 30 of the Arbitration Act 1950, in extending the 1996 Act to the Crown.

Consequential amendments and repeals

107.—(1) The enactments specified in Schedule 3 are amended in accordance with that Schedule, the amendments being consequential on the provisions of this Act.

(2) The enactments specified in Schedule 4 are repealed to the extent specified.

NOTES

Certain of the enactments specified in Schedule 3 have been repealed by subsequent legislation. The enactments affected have been deleted from Schedule 3 in the present text.

Schedule 3, paragraph 37, amends section 18(1) of the Supreme Court Act 1981 by stating that there is to be no appeal from a High Court decision "except as provided by Part I of the Arbitration Act 1996". Taken at face value, this amendment has the drastic effect of removing the ordinary right of appeal against the outcome of an arbitration application to the High Court unless the relevant section expressly provides a right of appeal. The House of Lords in *Inco Europe Ltd* v. *First Choice Distribution*[1] was of the view that it could not have been Parliament's intention to remove a right of appeal by means of a consequential amendment, and thus ruled that a right of appeal to the Court of Appeal remained in place even in respect of arbitration applications which did not specifically provide for a right of appeal. The affected sections are: 9, 10, 13, 28, 64 and 72. The point is noted in the annotations to each of those sections.

Extent

108.—(1) The provisions of this Act extend to England and Wales and, except as mentioned below: to Northern Ireland.

(2) The following provisions of Part II do not extend to Northern Ireland—

section 92 (exclusion of Part I in relation to small claims arbitration in the county court), and

section 93 and Schedule 2 (appointment of judges as arbitrators).

(3) Sections 89, 90 and 91 (consumer arbitration agreements), extend to Scotland and the provisions of Schedules 3 and 4 (consequential amendments and repeals) extend to Scotland as far as they relate to enactments which so extend subject as follows.

(4) The repeal of the Arbitration Act 1975 extends only to England and Wales and Northern Ireland.

Commencement

109.—(1) The provisions of this Act come into force on such a day as the Secretary of State may appoint by order made by statutory instrument, and different days may be appointed for different purposes.

(2) An order under subsection (1) may contain such transitional provisions as appear to the Secretary of State to be appropriate.

Short title

110. This Act may be cited as the Arbitration Act 1996.

1. [2000] 1 Lloyd's Rep 467.

SCHEDULES

SCHEDULE 1: MANDATORY PROVISIONS OF PART I

(SECTION 4(1))

sections 9 to 11 (stay of legal proceedings);
section 12 (power of court to extend agreed time limits);
section 13 (application of Limitation Acts);
section 24 (power of court to remove arbitrator);
section 26(1) (effect of death of arbitrator);
section 28 (liability of parties for fees and expenses of arbitrators);
section 29 (immunity of arbitrator);
section 31 (objection to substantive jurisdiction of tribunal);
section 32 (determination of preliminary point of jurisdiction);
section 33 (general duty of tribunal);
section 37(2) (items to be treated as expenses of arbitrators);
section 40 (general duty of parties);
section 43 (securing the attendance of witnesses);
section 56 (power to withhold award in case of non-payment);
section 60 (effectiveness of agreement for payment of costs in any event);
section 66 (enforcement of award);
sections 67 and 68 (challenging the award: substantive jurisdiction and serious irregularity), and sections 70 and 71 (supplementary provisions; effect of order of court) so far as relating to those sections;
section 72 (saving for rights of person who takes no part in proceedings);
section 73 (loss of right to object);
section 74 (immunity of arbitral institutions, &c.);
section 75 (charge to secure payment of solicitors' costs).

The provisions listed in this Schedule are mandatory and cannot be ousted by the agreement of the parties. The Schedule refers back to section 4 of the Act.

SCHEDULE 2: MODIFICATIONS OF PART I IN RELATION TO JUDGE-ARBITRATORS (SECTION 93(6))

Introductory

1. In this Schedule "judge-arbitrator" means a judge of the Commercial Court or official referee appointed as arbitrator or umpire under section 93.

General

2.—(1) Subject to the following provisions of this Schedule, references in Part I to the court shall be construed in relation to a judge-arbitrator, or in relation to the appointment of a judge-arbitrator, as references to the Court of Appeal.

(2) The references in sections 32(6), 45(6) and 69(8) to the Court of Appeal shall in such a case be construed as references to the House of Lords.

Arbitrator's fees

3.—(1) The power of the court in section 28(2) or other consideration and adjustment of the liability of a party for the fees of an arbitrator may be exercised by a judge-arbitrator.

(2) Any such exercise of the power is subject to the powers of the Court of Appeal under sections 24(4) and 25(3)(b) (directions as to entitlement to fees or expenses in case of removal or resignation).

Exercise of court powers in support of arbitration

4.—(1) Where the arbitral tribunal consists of or includes a judge-arbitrator the powers of the court under sections 42 to 44 (enforcement of peremptory orders, summoning witnesses, and other court powers) are exercisable by the High Court and also by the judge-arbitrator himself.

(2) Anything done by a judge-arbitrator in the exercise of those powers shall be regarded as done by him in his capacity as judge of the High Court and have effect as if done by that court.

Nothing in this sub-paragraph prejudices any power vested in him as arbitrator or umpire.

Extension of time for making award

5.—(1) The power conferred by section 50 (extension of time for making award) is exercisable by the judge-arbitrator himself.

(2) Any appeal from a decision of a judge-arbitrator under that section lies to the Court of Appeal with the leave of that court.

Withholding award in case of non-payment

6.—(1) The provisions of paragraph 7 apply in place of the provisions of section 56 (power to withhold award in the case of non-payment) in relation to the withholding of an award for non-payment of the fees and expenses of a judge-arbitrator.

(2) This does not affect the application of section 56 in relation to the delivery of such an award by an arbitral or other institution or person vested by the parties with powers in relation to the delivery of the award.

7.—(1) A judge-arbitrator may refuse to deliver an award except upon payment of the fees and expenses mentioned in section 56(1).

(2) The judge-arbitrator may, on an application by a party to the arbitral proceedings, order that if he pays into the High Court the fees and expenses demanded, or such lesser amount as the judge-arbitrator may specify—

(a) the award shall be delivered,
(b) the amount of the fees and expenses properly payable shall be determined by such means and upon such terms as he may direct, and
(c) out of the money paid into court there shall be paid out such fees and expenses as may be found to be properly payable and the balance of the money (if any) shall be paid out to the applicant.

(3) For this purpose the amount of fees and expenses properly payable is the amount the applicant is liable to pay under section 28 or any agreement relating to the payment of the arbitrator.

(4) No application to the judge-arbitrator under this paragraph may be made where there is any available arbitral process for appeal or review of the amount of the fees or expenses demanded.

(5) Any appeal from a decision of a judge-arbitrator under this paragraph lies to the Court of Appeal with the leave of that court.

(6) Where a party to arbitral proceedings appeals under sub-paragraph (5), an arbitrator is entitled to appear and be heard.

Correction of award or additional award

8. Subsections (4) to (6) of section 57 (correction of award or additional award: time limit for application or exercise of power) do not apply to a judge-arbitrator.

Costs

9. Where the arbitral tribunal consists of or includes a judge-arbitrator the powers of the court under section 63(4) (determination of recoverable costs) shall be exercised by the High Court.

10.—(1) The power of the court under section 64 to determine an arbitrator's reasonable fees and expenses may be exercised by a judge-arbitrator.

(2) Any such exercise of the power is subject to the powers of the Court of Appeal under sections 24(4) and 25(3)(b) (directions as to entitlement to fees or expenses in case of removal or resignation).

Enforcement of award

11. The leave of the court required by section 66 (enforcement of award) may in the case of an award of a judge-arbitrator be given by the judge-arbitrator himself.

Solicitor's costs

12. The powers of the court to make declarations and orders under the provisions applied by section 75 (power to charge property recovered in arbitral proceedings with the payment of solicitors' costs) may be exercised by the judge-arbitrator.

Powers of court in relation to service of documents

13.—(1) The power of the court under section 77(2) (powers of court in relation to service of documents) is exercisable by the judge-arbitrator.

(2) Any appeal from a decision of a judge-arbitrator under that section lies to the Court of Appeal with the leave of that court.

Powers of court to extend time limits relating to arbitral proceedings

14.—(1) The power conferred by section 79 (power of court to extend time limits relating to arbitral proceedings) is exercisable by the judge-arbitrator himself.

(2) Any appeal from a decision of a judge-arbitrator under that section lies to the Court of Appeal with the leave of that court.

This Schedule modifies the Arbitration Act 1996 insofar as it applies to judge-arbitrators and official referee-arbitrators. It refers back to section 93, and re-enacts the Administration of Justice Act 1970, Schedule 3.

SCHEDULE 3: CONSEQUENTIAL AMENDMENTS (SECTION 107(1))

Merchant Shipping Act 1894 (c. 60)

1. In section 496 of the Merchant Shipping Act 1894 (provisions as to deposits by owners of goods), after subsection (4) insert—

"(5) In subsection (3) the expression 'legal proceedings' includes arbitral proceedings and as respects England and Wales and Northern Ireland the provisions of section 14 of the Arbitration Act 1996 apply to determine when such proceedings are commenced.".

Stannaries Court (Abolition) Act 1896 (c. 45)

2. In section 4(1) of the Stannaries Court (Abolition) Act 1896 (references of certain disputes to arbitration), for the words from "tried before" to "any such reference" substitute "referred to arbitration before himself or before an arbitrator agreed on by the parties or an officer of the court".

. . .

Paragraph 3 was repealed by the Statute Law (Repeals) Act 2004, Schedule 1(6).

Paragraph 4 was repealed by the Education Act 1996, Schedule 38.

Commonwealth Telegraphs Act 1949 (c. 39)

5. Section 8(2) of the Commonwealth Telegraphs Act 1949 (proceedings of referees under the Act) for "the Arbitration Acts 1889 to 1934, or the Arbitration Act (Northern Ireland) 1937," substitute "Part I of the Arbitration Act 1996".

Lands Tribunal Act 1949 (c. 42)

6. In section 3 of the Lands Tribunal Act 1949 (proceedings before the Lands Tribunal)—

(a) in subsection (6)(c) (procedural rules: power to apply Arbitration Acts), and
(b) in subsection (8) (exclusion of Arbitration Acts except as applied by rules),

for "the Arbitration Acts 1889 to 1934" substitute "Part I of the Arbitration Act 1996".

. . .

Paragraph 7 was repealed by the Telecommunications Act 2003, Schedule 19.

Patents Act 1949 (c. 87)

8. In section 67 of the Patents Act 1949 (proceedings as to infringement of pre-1978 patents referred to comptroller), for "The Arbitration Acts 1889 to 1934" substitute "Part I of the Arbitration Act 1996".

National Health Service (Amendment) Act 1949 (c. 93)

9. In section 7(8) of the National Health Service (Amendment) Act 1949 (arbitration in relation to hardship arising from the National Health Service Act 1946 or the Act), for "the Arbitration Acts 1889 to 1934" substitute "Part I of the Arbitration Act 1996" and for "the said Acts" substitute "Part I of that Act".

Arbitration Act 1950 (c. 27)

10. In section 36(1) of the Arbitration Act 1950 (effect of foreign awards enforceable under Part II of that Act) for "section 26 of this Act" substitute "section 66 of the Arbitration Act 1996".

Interpretation Act (Northern Ireland) 1954 (c. 33 (N.I.))

11. In section 46(2) of the Interpretation Act (Northern Ireland) 1954 (miscellaneous definitions), for the definition of "arbitrator" substitute—

" 'arbitrator' has the same meaning as in Part I of the Arbitration Act 1996;".

Agricultural Marketing Act 1958 (c. 47)

12. In section 12(1) of the Agricultural Marketing Act 1958 (application of provisions of Arbitration Act 1950)—

(a) for the words from the beginning to "shall apply" substitute "Sections 45 and 69 of the Arbitration Act 1996 (which relate to the determination by the court of questions of law) and section 66 of that Act (enforcement of awards) apply"; and

(b) for "an arbitration" substitute "arbitral proceedings".

Carriage by Air Act 1961 (c. 27)

13.—(1) The Carriage by Air Act 1961 is amended as follows.

(2) In section 5(3) (time for bringing proceedings)—

(a) for "an arbitration" in the first place where it occurs substitute "arbitral proceedings"; and

(b) for the words from "and subsections (3) and (4)" to the end substitute "and the provisions of section 14 of the Arbitration Act 1996 apply to determine when such proceedings are commenced.".

(3) In section 11(c) (application of section 5 to Scotland)—

(a) for "subsections (3) and (4)" substitute "the provisions of section 14 of the Arbitration Act 1996"; and

(b) for "an arbitration" substitute "arbitral proceedings".

Factories Act 1961 (c. 34)

14. In the Factories Act 1961, for section 171 (application of Arbitration Act 1950), substitute—

"Application of the Arbitration Act 1996.

171. Part I of the Arbitration Act 1996 does not apply to proceedings under this Act except in so far as it may be applied by regulations made under this Act.".

Clergy Pensions Measure 1961 (No. 3)

15. In the Clergy Pensions Measure 1961, section 38(4) (determination of questions), for the words "The Arbitration Act 1950" substitute "Part I of the Arbitration Act 1996".

Transport Act 1962 (c. 46)

16.—(1) The Transport Act 1962 is amended as follows.

(2) In section 74(6)(f) (proceedings before referees in pension disputes), for the words "the Arbitration Act 1950" substitute "Part I of the Arbitration Act 1996".

(3) In section 81(7) (proceedings before referees in compensation disputes), for the words "the Arbitration Act 1950" substitute "Part I of the Arbitration Act 1996".

(4) In Schedule 7, Part IV (pensions), in paragraph 17(5) for the words "the Arbitration Act 1950" substitute "Part I of the Arbitration Act 1996".

Corn Rents Act 1963 (c. 14)

17. In the Corn Rents Act 1963, section 1(5) (schemes for apportioning corn rents, &c.), for the words "the Arbitration Act 1950" substitute "Part I of the Arbitration Act 1996".

. . .

Paragraph 18 was repealed by the Plant Varieties Act 1997, Schedule 4.

Lands Tribunal and Compensation Act (Northern Ireland) 1964 (c. 29 (N.I.))

19. In section 9 of the Lands Tribunal and Compensation Act (Northern Ireland) 1964 (proceedings of Lands Tribunal), in subsection (3) (where Tribunal acts as arbitrator) for "the Arbitration Act (Northern Ireland) 1937" substitute "Part I of the Arbitration Act 1996".

Industrial and Provident Societies Act 1965 (c. 12)

20.—(1) Section 60 of the Industrial and Provident Societies Act 1965 is amended as follows.

(2) In subsection (8) (procedure for hearing disputes between society and member, &c.)—

(a) in paragraph (a) for "the Arbitration Act 1950" substitute "Part I of the Arbitration Act 1996"; and

(b) in paragraph (b) omit "by virtue of section 12 of the said Act of 1950".

(3) For subsection (9) substitute—

"(9) the court or registrar to whom any dispute is referred under subsections (2) to (7) may at the request of either party state a case on any question of law arising in the dispute for the opinion of the High Court or, as the case may be, the Court of Session".

Carriage of Goods by Road Act 1965 (c. 37)

21. In section 7(2) of the Carriage of Goods by Road Act 1965 (arbitrations: time at which deemed to commence), for paragraphs (a) and (b) substitute—

"(a) as respects England and Wales and Northern Ireland, the provisions of section 14(3) to (5) of the Arbitration Act 1996 (which determine the time at which an arbitration is commenced) apply;".

Factories Act (Northern Ireland) 1965 (c. 20 (N.I.))

22. In section 171 of the Factories Act (Northern Ireland) 1965 (application of Arbitration Act), for "The Arbitration Act (Northern Ireland) 1937" substitute "Part I of the Arbitration Act 1996".

. . .

Paragraph 23 was repealed by the International Organisations Act 2005, Schedule 1.

Arbitration (International Investment Disputes) Act 1966 (c. 41)

24. In the Arbitration (International Investment Disputes) Act 1966, for section 3 (application of Arbitration Act 1950 and other enactments) substitute—

"Application of provisions of Arbitration Act 1996

3.—(1) The Lord Chancellor may by order direct that any of the provisions contained in sections 36 and 38 to 44 of the Arbitration Act 1996 (provisions concerning the conduct of arbitral proceedings, &c.) shall apply to such proceedings pursuant to the Convention as are specified in the order with or without any modifications or exceptions specified in the order.

(2) Subject to subsection (1), the Arbitration Act 1996 shall not apply to proceedings pursuant to the Convention, but this subsection shall not be taken as affecting section 9 of that Act (stay of legal proceedings in respect of matter subject to arbitration).

(3) An order made under this section—

(a) may be varied or revoked by a subsequent order so made, and

(b) shall be contained in a statutory instrument.".

Poultry Improvement Act (Northern Ireland) 1968 (c. 12 (N.I.))

25. In paragraph 10(4) of the Schedule to the Poultry Improvement Act (Northern Ireland) 1968 (reference of disputes), for "The Arbitration Act (Northern Ireland) 1937" substitute "Part I of the Arbitration Act 1996".

Industrial and Provident Societies Act (Northern Ireland) 1969 (c. 24 (N.I.))

26.—(1) Section 69 of the Industrial and Provident Societies Act (Northern Ireland) 1969 (decision of disputes) is amended as follows.

(2) In subsection (7) (decision of disputes)—

(a) in the opening words, omit the words from "and without prejudice" to "1937";

(b) at the beginning of paragraph (a) insert "without prejudice to any powers exercisable by virtue of Part I of the Arbitration Act 1996,"; and

(c) in paragraph (b) omit "the registrar or" and "registrar or" and for the words from "as might have been granted by the High Court" to the end substitute "as might be granted by the registrar".

(3) For subsections (8) substitute—

"(8) The court or registrar to whom any dispute is referred under subsections (2) to (6) may at the request of either party state a case on any question of law arising in the dispute for the opinion of the High Court.".

Health and Personal Social Services (Northern Ireland) Order 1972 (N.I. 14)

27. In Article 105(6) of the Health and Personal Social Services (Northern Ireland) Order 1972 (arbitrations under the Order), for "the Arbitration Act (Northern Ireland) 1937" substitute "Part I of the Arbitration Act 1996".

Consumer Credit Act 1974 (c. 39)

28.—(1) Section 146 of the Consumer Credit Act 1974 is amended as follows.

(2) In subsection (2) (solicitor engaged in contentious business), for "section 86(1) of the Solicitors Act 1957" substitute "section 87(1) of the Solicitors Act 1974".

(3) In subsection (4) (solicitor in Northern Ireland engaged in contentious business), for the words from "business done" to "Administration of Estates (Northern Ireland) Order 1979" substitute "contentious business (as defined in Article 3(2) of the Solicitors (Northern Ireland) Order 1976.".

Friendly Societies Act 1974 (c. 46)

29.—(1) The Friendly Societies Act 1974 is amended as follows.

(2) For section 78(1) (statement of case) substitute—

> "(1) any arbitrator, arbiter or umpire to whom a dispute falling within section 76 above is referred under the rules of a registered society or branch may at the request of either party state a case on any question of law arising in the dispute for the opinion of the High Court or, as the case may be, the Court of Session.".

(3) In section 83(3) (procedure on objections to amalgamations, &c. of friendly societies), for "the Arbitration Act 1950 or, in Northern Ireland, the Arbitration Act (Northern Ireland) 1937" substitute "Part I of the Arbitration Act 1996".

Industry Act 1975 (c. 68)

30. In Schedule 3 to the Industry Act (arbitration of disputes relating to vesting and compensation orders), in paragraph 14 (application of certain provisions of Arbitration Acts)—

(a) for "the Arbitration Act 1950 or, in Northern Ireland, the Arbitration Act (Northern Ireland) 1937" substitute "Part I of the Arbitration Act 1996", and

(b) for "that Act" substitute "that Part".

. . .

Aircraft and Shipbuilding Industries Act 1977 (c. 3)

32. In Schedule 7 to the Aircraft and Shipbuilding Industries Act 1977 (procedure of Arbitration Tribunal), in paragraph 2—

(a) for "the Arbitration Act 1950 or, in Northern Ireland, the Arbitration Act (Northern Ireland) 1937" substitute "Part I of the Arbitration Act 1996", and
(b) for "that Act" substitute "that Part".

Patents Act 1977 (c. 37)

33. In section 130 of the Patents Act 1977 (interpretation), in subsection (8) (exclusion of Arbitration Act) for "The Arbitration Act 1950" substitute "Part I of the Arbitration Act 1996".

Judicature (Northern Ireland) Act 1978 (c. 23)

34.—(1) The Judicature (Northern Ireland) Act 1978 is amended as follows.

(2) In section 35(2) (restrictions on appeals to the Court of Appeal), after paragraph (f) insert—

"(fa) except as provided by Part I of the Arbitration Act 1996, from any decision of the High Court under that Part;".

(3) In section 55(2) (rules of court), after paragraph (c) insert—

"(cc) providing for any prescribed part of the jurisdiction of the High Court in relation to the trial of any action involving matters of account to be exercised in the prescribed manner by a person agreed by the parties and for the remuneration of any such person;".

Health and Safety at Work (Northern Ireland) Order 1978 (N.I. 9)

35. In Schedule 4 to the Health and Safety at Work (Northern Ireland) Order 1978 (licensing provisions), in paragraph 3, for "the Arbitration Act (Northern Ireland) 1937" substitute "Part I of the Arbitration Act 1996".

County Courts (Northern Ireland) Order 1980 (N.I. 3)

36.—(1) The County Courts (Northern Ireland) Order 1980 is amended as follows.

(2) In Article 30 (civil jurisdiction exercisable by district judge)—

(a) for paragraph (2) substitute—

"(2) Any order, decision or determination made by a district judge under this Article (other than one made in dealing with a claim by way of arbitration under paragraph (3)) shall be embodied in a decree which for all purposes (including the right of appeal under Part VI) shall have the like effect as a decree pronounced by a county court judge.";

(b) for paragraphs (4) and (5) substitute—

"(4) Where in any action to which paragraph (1) applies the claim is dealt with by way of arbitration under paragraph (3)—

(a) any award made by the district judge in dealing with the claim shall be embodied in a decree which for all purposes (except the right of appeal under Part VI) shall have the like effect as a decree pronounced by a county court judge;

(b) the district judge may, and shall if so required by the High Court, state for the determination of the High Court any question of law arising out of an award so made;

(c) except as provided by sub-paragraph (b), any award so made shall be final; and

(d) except as otherwise provided by county court rules, no costs shall be awarded in connection with the action.

(5) Subject to paragraph (4), county court rules may—

(a) apply any of the provisions of Part I of the Arbitration Act 1996 to arbitrations under paragraph (3) with such modifications as may be prescribed;

(b) prescribe the rules of evidence to be followed on any arbitration under paragraph (3) and, in particular, make provision with respect to the manner of taking and questioning evidence.

(5A) Except as provided by virtue of paragraph (5)(a), Part I of the Arbitration Act 1996 shall not apply to an arbitration under paragraph (3).".

(3) After Article 61 insert—

"Appeals from decisions under Part I of Arbitration Act 1996.

61A.—(1) Article 61 does not apply to a decision of a county court judge made in the exercise of the jurisdiction conferred by Part I of the Arbitration Act 1996.

(2) Any party dissatisfied with a decision of the county court made in the exercise of the jurisdiction conferred by any of the following provisions of Part I of the Arbitration Act 1996, namely—

(a) section 32 (question as to substantive jurisdiction of arbitral tribunal);

(b) section 45 (question of law arising in course of arbitral proceedings);

(c) section 67 (challenging award of arbitral tribunal; substantive jurisdiction);

(d) section 68 (challenging award of arbitral tribunal; serious irregularity);

(e) section 69 (appeal on point of law),

may, subject to the provisions of that Part, appeal from that decision to the Court of Appeal.

(3) Any party dissatisfied with any decision of a county court made in the exercise of the jurisdiction conferred by any other provision of Part I of the Arbitration Act 1996 may, subject to the provisions of that Part, appeal from that decision to the High Court.

(4) The decision of the Court of Appeal on an appeal under paragraph (2) shall be final.".

Supreme Court Act 1981 (c. 54)

37.—(1) The Supreme Court Act 1981 is amended as follows.

(2) In section 18(1) (restrictions on appeals to the Court of Appeal), for paragraph (g) substitute—

"(g) except as provided by Part I of the Arbitration Act 1996, from any decision of the High Court under that Part;".

(3) In section 151 (interpretation, &c.), in the definition of "arbitration agreement", for "the Arbitration Act 1950 by virtue of section 32 of that Act;" substitute "Part I of the Arbitration Act 1996;".

Merchant Shipping (Liner Conferences) Act 1982 (c. 37)

38. In section 7(5) of the Merchant Shipping (Liner Conferences) Act 1982 (stay of legal proceedings), for the words from "section 4(1)" to the end substitute "section 9 of the Arbitration Act 1996 (which also provides for the staying of legal proceedings).".

Agricultural Marketing (Northern Ireland) Order 1982 (N.I. 12)

39. In Article 14 of the Agricultural Marketing (Northern Ireland) Order 1982 (application of provisions of Arbitration Act (Northern Ireland) 1937)—

(a) for the words from the beginning to "shall apply" substitute "Section 45 and 69 of the Arbitration Act 1996 (which relate to the determination by the court of questions of law) and section 66 of that Act (enforcement of awards)" apply; and

(b) for "an arbitration" substitute "arbitral proceedings".

Mental Health Act 1983 (c. 20)

40. In section 78 of the Mental Health Act 1983 (procedure of Mental Health Review Tribunals), in subsection (9) for "The Arbitration Act 1950" substitute "Part I of the Arbitration Act 1996".

. . .

Paragraph 41 was repealed by the Care Standards Act 2000, Schedule 6.

Housing Act 1985 (c. 68)

42. In section 47(3) of the Housing Act 1985 (agreement as to determination of matters relating to service charges) for "section 32 of the Arbitration Act 1950" substitute "Part I of the Arbitration Act 1996".

. . .

Paragraph 43 was repealed by the Housing Act 1996, Schedule 19.

Credit Unions (Northern Ireland) Order 1985 (N.I. 12)

44.—(1) Article 72 of the Credit Unions (Northern Ireland) Order 1985 (decision of disputes) is amended as follows.

(20 In paragraph (7)—

(a) in the opening words, omit the words from "and without prejudice" to "1937";

(b) at the beginning of sub-paragraph (a) insert "without prejudice to any powers exercisable by virtue of Part I of the Arbitration Act 1996,"; and

(c) in sub-paragraph (b) omit "the registrar or" and "registrar or" and for the words from "as might have been granted by the High Court" to the end substitute "as might be granted by the registrar".

(3) For paragraph (8) substitute—

"(8) The court or registrar to whom any dispute is referred under paragraphs (2) to (6) may at the request of either party state a case on any question of law arising in the dispute for the opinion of the High Court.".

. . .

Paragraph 45 was repealed by the Regulatory Reform (Agricultural Tenancies) (England and Wales) Order 2006, SI 2006 No 2805, Schedule 2.

Insolvency Act 1986 (c. 45)

46. In the Insolvency Act 1986, after section 349 insert—

"Arbitration agreements to which bankrupt is party.

349A.—(1) This section applies where a bankrupt had become party to a contract containing an arbitration agreement before the commencement of his bankruptcy.

(2) If the trustee in bankruptcy adopts the contract, the arbitration agreement is enforceable by or against the trustee in relation to matters arising from or connected with the contract.

(3) If the trustee in bankruptcy does not adopt the contract and a matter to which the arbitration agreement applies requires to be determined in connection with or for the purposes of the bankruptcy proceedings—

(a) the trustee with the consent of the creditors' committee, or

(b) any other party to the agreement,

may apply to the court which may, if it thinks fit in all the circumstances of the case, order that the matter be referred to arbitration in accordance with the arbitration agreement.

(4) In this section—

'arbitration agreement' has the same meaning as in Part I of the Arbitration Act 1996; and

'the court' means the court which has jurisdiction in the bankruptcy proceedings.".

Building Societies Act 1986 (c. 53)

47. In Part II of Schedule 14 to the Building Societies Act 1986 (settlement of disputes: arbitration), in paragraph 5(6) for "the Arbitration Act 1950 and the Arbitration Act 1979 or, in Northern Ireland, the Arbitration Act (Northern Ireland) 1937" substitute "Part I of the Arbitration Act 1996".

Mental Health (Northern Ireland) Order 1986 (N.I. 4)

48. In Article 83 of the Mental Health (Northern Ireland) Order 1986 (procedure of Mental Health Review Tribunal), in paragraph (8) for "The Arbitration Act (Northern Ireland) 1937" substitute "Part I of the Arbitration Act 1996".

Multilateral Investment Guarantee Agency Act 1988 (c. 8)

49. For section 6 of the Multilateral Investment Guarantee Agency Act 1988 (application of Arbitration Act) substitute—

"Application of Arbitration Act

6.—(1) The Lord Chancellor may by order made by statutory instrument direct that any of the provisions of sections 36 and 38 to 44 of the Arbitration Act 1996 (provisions in relation to the conduct of the arbitral proceedings, & c.) apply, with such modifications or exceptions as are specified in the order, to such arbitration proceedings pursuant to Annex II to the Convention as are specified in the order.

(2) Except as provided by an order under subsection (1) above, no provision of Part I of the Arbitration Act 1996 other than section 9 (stay of legal proceedings) applies to any such proceedings.".

Copyright, Designs and Patents Act 1988 (c. 48)

50. In section 150 of the Copyright, Designs and Patents Act 1988 (Lord Chancellor's power to make rules for Copyright Tribunal), for subsection (2) substitute—

"(2) The rules may apply in relation to the Tribunal, as respects proceedings in England and Wales or Northern Ireland, any of the provisions of Part I of the Arbitration Act 1996.".

Fair Employment (Northern Ireland) Act 1989 (c. 32)

51. In the Fair Employment (Northern Ireland) Act 1989 section 5(7) (procedure of Fair Employment Tribunal), for "The Arbitration Act (Northern Ireland) 1937" substitute "Part I of the Arbitration Act 1996".

Limitation (Northern Ireland) Order 1989 (N.I. 11)

52. In Article 2(2) of the Limitation (Northern Ireland) Order 1989 (interpretation), in the definition of "arbitration agreement", for "the Arbitration Act (Northern Ireland) 1937" substitute "Part I of the Arbitration Act 1996".

Insolvency (Northern Ireland) Order 1989 (N.I. 19)

53. In the Insolvency (Northern Ireland) Order 1989, after Article 320 insert—

"Arbitration agreements to which bankrupt is party

320A.—(1) This Article applies where a bankrupt had become party to a contract containing an arbitration agreement before the commencement of his bankruptcy.

(2) If the trustee in bankruptcy adopts the contract, the arbitration agreement is enforceable by or against the trustee in relation to matters arising from or connected with the contract.

(3) If the trustee in bankruptcy does not adopt the contract and a matter to which the arbitration agreement applies requires to be determined in connection with or for the purposes of the bankruptcy proceedings—

(a) the trustee with the consent of the creditors' committee, or

(b) any other party to the agreement,

may apply to the court which may, if it thinks fit in all the circumstances of the case, order that the matter be referred to arbitration in accordance with the arbitration agreement.

(4) In this Article—

"arbitration agreement" has the same meaning as in Part I of the Arbitration Act 1996; and

"the court" means the court which has jurisdiction in the bankruptcy proceedings.".

. . .

Paragraph 54 was repealed by the Social Security Act 1998, Schedule 8.

Social Security Administration (Northern Ireland) Act 1992 (c. 8)

55. In section 57 of the Social Security Administration (Northern Ireland) Act 1992 (procedure for inquiries, &c.), in subsection (6) for "the Arbitration Act (Northern Ireland) 1937" substitute "Part I of the Arbitration Act 1996".

Trade Union and Labour Relations (Consolidation) Act 1992 (c. 52)

56. In sections 212(5) and 263(6) of the Trade Union and Labour Relations (Consolidation) Act 1992 (application of Arbitration Act) for "the Arbitration Act 1950" substitute "Part I of the Arbitration Act 1996".

Industrial Relations (Northern Ireland) Order 1992 (N.I. 5)

57. In Articles 84(9) and 92(5) of the Industrial Relations (Northern Ireland) Order 1992 (application of Arbitration Act) for "The Arbitration Act (Northern Ireland) 1937" substitute "Part I of the Arbitration Act 1996".

Registered Homes (Northern Ireland) Order 1992 (N.I. 20)

58. In Article 33(3) of the Registered Homes (Northern Ireland) Order 1992 (procedure of Registered Homes Tribunal) for "The Arbitration Act (Northern Ireland) 1937" substitute "Part I of the Arbitration Act 1996".

. . .

Paragraph 59 was repealed by the Education Act 1996, Schedule 38.

Roads (Northern Ireland) Order 1993 (N.I. 15)

60.—(1) The Roads (Northern Ireland) Order 1993 is amended as follows.

(2) In Article 131 (application of Arbitration Act) for "the Arbitration Act (Northern Ireland) 1937" substitute "Part I of the Arbitration Act 1996".

(3) In Schedule 4 (disputes), in paragraph 3(2) for "the Arbitration Act (Northern Ireland) 1937" substitute "Part I of the Arbitration Act 1996".

Merchant Shipping Act 1995 (c. 21)

61. In Part II of Schedule 6 to the Merchant Shipping Act 1995 (provisions having effect in connection with Convention Relating to the Carriage of Passengers and Their Luggage by Sea), for paragraph 7 substitute—

> "7. Article 16 shall apply to arbitral proceedings as it applies to an action; and, as respects England and Wales and Northern Ireland, the provisions of section 14 of the Arbitration Act 1996 apply to determine for the purposes of that Article when an arbitration is commenced.".

Industrial Tribunals Act 1996 (c. 17)

62. In section 6(2) of the Industrial Tribunals Act 1996 (procedure of industrial tribunals), for "The Arbitration Act 1950" substitute "Part of the Arbitration Act 1996".

SCHEDULE 4: REPEALS (SECTION 107(2))

Chapter	Short title	Extent of repeal
1892 c. 43.	Military Lands Act 1892.	In section 21(b), the words "under the Arbitration Act 1889".
1922 c. 51.	Allotments Act 1922.	In section 21(3), the words "under the Arbitration Act 1889".
1937 c. 8 (N.I.).	Arbitration Act (Northern Ireland) 1937.	The whole Act.
1949 c. 54.	Wireless Telegraphy Act 1949.	In Schedule 2, paragraph 3(3).
1949 c. 97.	National Parks and Access to the Countryside Act 1949.	In section 18(4), the words from "Without prejudice" to "England or Wales".
1950 c. 27.	Arbitration Act 1950.	Part I. Section 42(3).
1958 c. 47.	Agricultural Marketing Act 1958.	Section 53(8).
1962 c. 46.	Transport Act 1962.	In Schedule 11, Part II, paragraph 7.
1964 c. 14.	Plant Varieties and Seeds Act 1964.	In section 10(4) the words from "or in section 9" to "three arbitrators)". Section 39(3)(b)(i).
1964 c. 29 (N.I.).	Lands Tribunal and Compensation Act (Northern Ireland) 1964.	In section 9(3) the words from "so, however, that" to the end.
1965 c. 12.	Industrial and Provident Societies Act 1965.	In section 60(8)(b), the words "by virtue of section 12 of the said Act of 1950".
1965 c. 37.	Carriage of Goods by Road Act 1965.	Section 7(2)(b).
1965 c. 13 (N.I.).	New Towns Act (Northern Ireland) 1965.	In section 27(2), the words from "under and in accordance with" to the end.
1969 c. 24 (N.I.).	Industrial and Provident Societies Act (Northern Ireland) 1969.	In section 69(7)— (a) in the opening words, the words from "and without prejudice" to "1937"; (b) in paragraph (b), the words "the registrar or" and "registrar or".
1970 c. 31.	Administration of Justice Act 1970.	Section 4. Schedule 3.
1973 c. 41.	Fair Trading Act 1973.	Section 33(2)(d).
1973 N.I. 1.	Drainage (Northern Ireland) Order 1973.	In Article 15(4), the words from "under and in accordance" to the end. Article 40(4). In Schedule 7, in paragraph 9(2), the words from "under and in accordance" to the end.
1974 c. 47.	Solicitors Act 1974.	In section 87(1), in the definition of "contentious business", the words "appointed under the Arbitration Act 1950".
1975 c. 3.	Arbitration Act 1975.	The whole Act.

Chapter	Short title	Extent of repeal
1975 c. 74.	Petroleum and Submarine Pipelines Act 1975.	In Part II of Schedule 2— (a) in model clause 40(2), the words "in accordance with the Arbitration Act 1950"; (b) in model clause 40(2B), the words "in accordance with the Arbitration Act (Northern Ireland) 1937". In Part II of Schedule 3, in model clause 38(2), the words "in accordance with the Arbitration Act 1950".
1976 N.I. 12.	Solicitors (Northern Ireland) Order 1976.	In Article 3(2), in the entry "contentious business", the words "appointed under the Arbitration Act (Northern Ireland) 1937". Article 71H(3).
1977 c. 37.	Patents Act 1977.	In section 52(4) the words "section 21 of the Arbitration Act 1950 or, as the case may be, section 22 of the Arbitration Act (Northern Ireland) 1937 (statement of cases by arbitrators); but". Section 131(e).
1977 c. 38.	Administration of Justice Act 1977.	Section 17(2).
1978 c. 23.	Judicature (Northern Ireland) Act 1978.	In section 35(2), paragraph (g)(v). In Schedule 5, the amendment to the Arbitration Act 1950.
1979 c. 42.	Arbitration Act 1979.	The whole Act.
1980 c. 58.	Limitation Act 1980.	Section 34.
1980 N.I. 3.	County Courts (Northern Ireland) Order 1980.	Article 31(3).
1981 c. 54.	Supreme Court Act 1981.	Section 148.
1982 c. 27.	Civil Jurisdiction and Judgments Act 1982.	Section 25(3)(c) and (5). In section 26— (a) in subsection (1), the words "to arbitration or"; (b) in subsection (1)(a)(i), the words "arbitration or"; (c) in subsection (2), the words "arbitration or".
1982 c. 53.	Administration of Justice Act 1982.	Section 15(6). In Schedule 1, Part IV.
1984 c. 5.	Merchant Shipping Act 1984.	Section 4(8).
1984 c. 12.	Telecommunications Act 1984.	Schedule 2, paragraph 13(8).
1984 c. 16.	Foreign Limitation Periods Act 1984.	Section 5.
1984 c. 28.	County Courts Act 1984.	In Schedule 2, paragraph 70.
1985 c. 61.	Administration of Justice Act 1985.	Section 58. In Schedule 9, paragraph 15.
1985 c. 68.	Housing Act 1985.	In Schedule 18, in paragraph 6(2) the words from "and the Arbitration Act 1950" to the end.
1985 N.I. 12.	Credit Unions (Northern Ireland) Order 1985.	In Article 72(7)— (a) in the opening words, the words from "and without prejudice" to "1937"; (b) in sub-paragraph (b), the words "the registrar of" and "registrar or".

Chapter	Short title	Extent of repeal
1986 c. 45.	Insolvency Act 1986.	In Schedule 14, the entry relating to the Arbitration Act 1950.
1988 c. 8.	Multilateral Investment Guarantee Agency Act 1988.	Section 8(3).
1988 c. 21.	Consumer Arbitration Agreements Act 1988.	The whole Act.
1989 N.I. 11.	Limitation (Northern Ireland) Order 1989.	Article 72. In Schedule 3, paragraph 1.
1989 N.I. 19.	Insolvency (Northern Ireland) Order 1989.	In Part II of Schedule 8, paragraph 66.
1990 c. 41.	Courts and Legal Services Act 1990.	Sections 99 and 101 to 103.
1991 N.I. 7.	Food Safety (Northern Ireland) Order 1991.	In Articles 8(8) and 11(10), the words from "and the provisions" to the end.
1992 c. 40	Friendly Societies Act 1992.	In Schedule 16, paragraph 30(1).
1995 c. 8.	Agricultural Tenancies Act 1995.	Section 28(4).
1995 c. 21.	Merchant Shipping Act 1995.	Section 96(10). Section 264(9).
1995 c. 42.	Private International Law (Miscellaneous Provisions) Act 1995.	Section 3.

APPENDIX 1

TABLE OF DERIVATIONS

1996 Act	*English Legislation*
s. 1	New
s. 2(1)	New
(2)	New
(3)	New
(4)	New
(5)	New
s. 3	New
s. 4(1)	New
(2)	New
(3)	New
(4)	New
(5)	New
s. 5(1)	AA 1950, s. 32; AA 1975, s. 7(1)
s. 5(2)	AA 1975, s. 7(1)
(3)	New
(4)	New
(5)	New
(6)	New
s. 6(1)	AA 1950, s. 32; AA 1975, s. 7(1)
(2)	New
s. 7	New
s. 8(1)	AA 1950, s. 2(1)
(2)	AA 1950, s. 2(3)
s. 9(1)	AA 1950, s. 4; AA 1975, s. 1(1)
(2)	New
(3)	AA 1950, s. 4; AA 1975, s. 1(1)
(4)	AA 1975, s. 1(1)
(5)	New
s. 10(1)	AA 1950, s. 5
(2)	New
s. 11(1)	CJJA 1982, s. 26(1)
(2)	CJJA 1982, s. 26(3)
s. 12(1)	AA 1950, s. 27
(2)	AA 1950, s. 27
(3)	New
(4)	AA 1950, s. 27
(5)	AA 1950, s. 27
(6)	New
s. 13(1)	LA 1980, s. 34(1)
s. 13(2)	LA 1980, s. 34(5)
(3)	LA 1980, s. 34(2)
(4)	LA 1980, s. 34(7)

1996 Act	*English Legislation*
s. 14(1)	New
(2)	New
(3)	LA 1980, s. 34(3)
(4)	LA 1980, s. 34(3)
(5)	LA 1980, s. 34(3)
s. 15(1)	AA 1950, s. 6
(2)	New
(3)	AA 1950, s. 6
s. 16(1)	New
(2)	New
(3)	New
(4)	New
(5)	New
(6)	New
(7)	New
s. 17(1)	AA 1950, s. 7(b)
(2)	AA 1950, s. 7(b)
(3)	AA 1950, s. 7 proviso
(4)	New
s. 18(1)	New
(2)	AA 1950, s. 10(1)
(3)	AA 1950, s. 10
(4)	AA 1950, s. 10(2)
(5)	New
s. 19	New
s. 20(1)	New
(2)	New
(3)	New
(4)	New
s. 21(1)	New
(2)	New
(3)	New
(4)	AA 1950, s. 8(2)
(5)	AA 1950, s. 8(3)
(6)	New
s. 22(1)	New
(2)	AA 1950, s. 9
s. 23(1)	New
s. 23(2)	New
(3)	AA 1950, s. 1
(4)	New
(5)	New
s. 24(1)	AA 1950, s. 13(3), 23(1), 24(1)
(2)	New
(3)	New
(4)	New

1996 Act	*English Legislation*
s. 24(5)	New
(6)	New
s. 25(1)	New
(2)	New
(3)	New
(4)	New
(5)	New
s. 26(1)	New
(2)	AA 1950, s. 2(2)
s. 27(1)	AA 1950, s. 7(a), 10(b)(d)
(2)	New
(3)	AA 1950, ss. 7, 10
(4)	New
(5)	New
s. 28(1)	New
(2)	AA 1950, s. 19(3)
(3)	New
(4)	New
(5)	AA 1950, s. 19(2)
(6)	New
s. 29(1)	New
(2)	New
s. 30(1)	New
(2)	New
s. 31(1)	New
(2)	New
(3)	New
(4)	New
(5)	New
s. 32(1)	New
(2)	New
(3)	New
(4)	New
(5)	New
(6)	New
s. 33(1)	New
(2)	New
s. 34(1)	New
(2)	New
(3)	New
s. 35(1)	New
(2)	New
s. 36	New
s. 37(1)	New
(2)	New
s. 38(1)	New
s. 38(2)	New
(3)	New
(4)	New
(5)	AA 1950, s. 12(2)–(3)
(6)	New
s. 39(1)	New
(2)	New
(3)	New
s. 39(4)	New
s. 40(1)	New
(2)	New
s. 41(1)	New
(2)	New
(3)	AA 1950, s. 13A
(4)	AA 1979, s. 5(1)–(2)

1996 Act	*English Legislation*
s. 41(5)	New
(6)	New
(7)	New
s. 42(1)	AA 1979, s. 5(1)
(2)	New
(3)	New
(4)	AA 1979, s. 5(1)
(5)	New
s. 43(1)	AA 1950, s. 12(1), (4)
(2)	New
(3)	AA 1950, s. 12(4)
(4)	New
s. 44(1)	AA 1950, s. 12(6)
(2)	AA 1950, s. 12(5)–(6)
(3)	New
(4)	New
(5)	New
(6)	New
(7)	New
s. 45(1)	AA 1979, s. 2(1)
(2)	AA 1979, s. 2(2)
(3)	New
(4)	New
(5)	AA 1979, s. 2(2A)
(6)	AA 1979, s. 2(3)
s. 46(1)	New
(2)	New
(3)	New
s. 47(1)	AA 1950, s. 13(1), 14
(2)	AA 1950, s. 14
(3)	New
s. 48(1)	New
(2)	New
(3)	New
(4)	New
(5)	AA 1950, s. 15
s. 49(1)	New
(2)	New
(3)	AA 1950, s. 19A(1)
(4)	AA 1950, s. 20
(5)	New
(6)	AA 1950, s. 19A(2)
s. 50(1)	AA 1950, s. 13(2)
(2)	New
(3)	New
(4)	AA 1950, s. 13(2)
(5)	New
s. 51(1)	New
(2)	New
(3)	New
(4)	New
(5)	New
s. 52(1)	New
(2)	New
(3)	New
(4)	New
(5)	New
s. 53	New
s. 54(1)	New
(2)	New
s. 55(1)	New

1996 Act	*English Legislation*
s. 55(2)	New
(3)	New
s. 56(1)	AA 1950, s. 19(1)
(2)	AA 1950, s. 19(1)
(3)	New
(4)	New
(5)	New
(6)	New
(7)	New
(8)	New
s. 57(1)	New
(2)	New
(3)	AA 1950, ss. 17, 18(4)
(4)	New
(5)	New
(6)	New
(7)	New
s. 58(1)	AA 1950, s. 16
(2)	New
s. 59(1)	New
(2)	New
s. 60	AA 1950, s. 18(3)
s. 61(1)	AA 1950, s. 18(1)
(2)	New
s. 62	New
s. 63(1)	New
(2)	New
(3)	New
(4)	New
(5)	New
(6)	New
(7)	New
s. 64(1)	New
(2)	AA 1950, s. 18(2)
(3)	New
(4)	New
s. 65(1)	New
(2)	New
s. 66(1)	AA 1950, s. 26(1)
(2)	AA 1950, s. 26(1)
(3)	New
(4)	New
s. 67(1)	New
(2)	New
(3)	AA 1950, s. 22(1)
(4)	New
s. 68(1)	AA 1950, s. 23(2)
(2)	New
(3)	AA 1950, s. 22(1), 23(2)
(4)	New
s. 69(1)	AA 1979, s. 1(2)–(3), 3(1)
(2)	AA 1979, s. 1(3)
(3)	AA 1979, s. 1(4)
(4)	New
(5)	New
(6)	AA 1979, s. 1(7)
(7)	AA 1950, s. 21(2); AA 1979, s. 1(2)
(8)	AA 1979, s. 1(6A)
s. 70(1)	New
s. 70(2)	New
(3)	New
(4)	AA 1979, s. 1(5)
(5)	AA 1950, s. 28
(6)	AA 1950, s. 23(3)
s. 71(1)	New
(2)	AA 1979, s. 1(8)
(3)	AA 1950, s. 22(2); AA 1979, s. 1(2)
(4)	New
s. 72(1)	New
(2)	New
s. 73(1)	New
(2)	New
s. 74(1)	New
(2)	New
(3)	New
s. 75	AA 1950, s. 18(5)
s. 76(1)	LA 1980, s. 34(4)
(2)	New
(3)	New
(4)	LA 1980, s. 34(4)
(5)	New
(6)	New
s. 77(1)	New
(2)	New
(3)	New
(4)	New
(5)	New
s. 78(1)	New
(2)	New
(3)	New
(4)	New
(5)	New
s. 79(1)	New
(2)	New
(3)	New
(4)	New
(5)	New
(6)	New
s. 80(1)	New
(2)	New
(3)	New
(4)	New
(5)	New
(6)	New
(7)	New
s. 81(1)	New
(2)	AA 1979, s. 1(1)
s. 82(1)	New
(2)	New
s. 83	New
s. 84(1)	New
(2)	New
(3)	New
s. 85(1)	New
(2)	AA 1975, s. 1(4); AA 1979, s. 3(7)
(3)	New
s. 86(1)	New
(2)	AA 1950, s. 4

1996 Act	*English Legislation*
s. 86(3)	AA 1950, s. 4
(4)	New
s. 87(1)	AA 1950, s. 3
(2)	New
(3)	New
s. 88(1)	New
(2)	New
(3)	New
(4)	New
s. 89(1)	New
(2)	New
(3)	New
s. 90	New
s. 91(1)	CAAA 1988, s. 2
(2)	New
(3)	New
(4)	New
(5)	New
s. 92	New
s. 93(1)	AA 1950, s. 11(1); AJA 1970, s. 4(1)
(2)	AJA 1970, s. 4(2)
(3)	AA 1950, s. 11(2)
(4)	AA 1950, s. 11(3); AJA 1970, s. 4(3)
(5)	AA 1950, s. 11(6)
(6)	AA 1950, s. 11(4); AJA 1970, s. 3(4)
s. 94(1)	AA 1950, s. 31(1)
(2)	AA 1950, s. 31(1)
(3)	New
s. 95(1)	New
(2)	New
s. 96(1)	New
(2)	New
(3)	New
(4)	New
s. 97	New
s. 98(1)	New
(2)	New
(3)	New
s. 99	New
s. 100(1)	AA 1975, s. 7(1)
(2)	AA 1975, s. 7(1)
(3)	AA 1975, s. 7(2)
(4)	AA 1975, s. 7(1)
s. 101(1)	AA 1975, s. 3(1)–(2)
(2)	AA 1975, s. 3(1)
(3)	New
s. 102(1)	AA 1975, s. 4
(2)	AA 1975, s. 4
s. 103(1)	AA 1975, s. 5(1)
(2)	AA 1975, s. 5(2)
(3)	AA 1975, s. 5(3)
(4)	AA 1975, s. 5(4)
(5)	AA 1975, s. 5(5)
s. 104	AA 1975, s. 6
s. 105(1)	AA 1950, s. 30
(2)	AA 1950, s. 30
(3)	AA 1950, s. 30
(4)	AA 1950, s. 30
s. 106(1)	New
(2)	New
s. 107(1)	AA 1950, s. 34
(2)	New
(3)	New
(4)	New
s. 108(1)	New
(2)	New
s. 109	New
Sched. 1	New
2	AJA 1970, Sched. 3
3	New
4	New

APPENDIX 2

TABLE OF DESTINATIONS

Arbitration Act 1950	*1996 Act*
s. 1	23(3)
s. 2(1)	8(1)
(2)	26(2)
(3)	8(2)
s. 3(1)	87(1)
(2)	87(1)
s. 4(1)	9, 86(2)–(3)
s. 5	10(1)
s. 6	15
s. 7	17, 27(1), (3)
s. 8(1)	Repealed
(2)	21(4)
(3)	21(5)
s. 9	22(2)
s. 10(1)	18(2), 27(1), (3)
(2)	18(4)
(3)	Repealed
(3A)	Repealed
(3B)	Repealed
(3C)	Repealed
(3D)	Repealed
(4)	Repealed
s. 11(1)	93(1)
(2)	93(3)
(3)	93(4)
(4)	93(6)
(5)	Repealed
(6)	93(5)
(7)	Repealed
s. 12(1)	43(1)
(2)	38(5)
(3)	38(5)
(4)	43(1)
(5)	44(2)
(6)	44(1)–(2)
s. 13(1)	47(1)–(3)
(2)	50(1), (4)
(3)	24(1)
s. 13A(1)	41(3)
(2)	41(3)
(3)	Repealed
(4)	Repealed
(5)	Repealed
s. 14	47(1)–(2)
s. 15	48(5)
s. 16	55(1)

Arbitration Act 1950	*1996 Act*
s. 17	57(3)
s. 18(1)	61(1)
(2)	64(2)
(3)	60
(4)	57(3)
(5)	75
s. 19(1)	56(1)–(2)
(2)	28(5)
(3)	28(2)
(4)	Repealed
s. 19A(1)	49(3)
(2)	49(6)
s. 20	49(4)
s. 22(1)	67(3), 68(3), 69(7)
(2)	71(3)
s. 23(1)	24(1)
(2)	68(1), (3)
(3)	70(6)
s. 24(1)	24(1)
(2)	Repealed
(3)	Repealed
s. 25(1)	Repealed
(2)	Repealed
(3)	Repealed
(4)	Repealed
s. 26(1)	66(1)–(2)
(2)	Repealed
(3)	Repealed
s. 27	12
s. 28	70(5)
s. 29(1)	Repealed
(2)	Repealed
(3)	Repealed
s. 30	105(1)–(4)
s. 31(1)	94(1)–(2)
(2)	Repealed
s. 32	5(1), 6(1)
s. 33	Repealed
s. 34	107(1)
s. 35(1)	In force
(2)	In force
(3)	In force
s. 36(1)	In force
(2)	In force
s. 37(1)	In force
(2)	In force

Arbitration Act 1950	*1996 Act*
s. 37(3)	In force
s. 38(1)	In force
s. 38(2)	In force
(3)	In force
s. 39	In force
s. 40	81(1)–(2)
s. 41(1)	In force
(2)	In force
(3)	In force
(4)	In force
s. 42(1)	In force
(2)	In force
(3)	In force
(4)	In force
s. 43	In force
s. 44(1)	Repealed
(2)	Repealed
(3)	Repealed
Sched. 1	In force
Sched. 2	In force
Administration of Justice Act 1970	
s. 4(1)	93(1)
(2)	93(2)
(3)	93(4)
(4)	93(6)
(5)	Repealed
Sched. 3	Sched. 2
Arbitration Act 1975	
s. 1(1)	9(1), (3), (4)
(2)	Repealed
(3)	Repealed
(4)	85(2)
s. 2	Repealed
s. 3(1)	101(1)–(2)
(2)	101(1)
s. 4	102
s. 5(1)	103(1)
(2)	103(2)
(3)	103(3)
(4)	103(4)
(5)	103(5)
s. 6	104
s. 7(1)	5(1)–(2), 100(1), (2), (4)
(2)	100(3)
(3)	100(3)
s. 8(1)	Repealed
(2)	Repealed
(3)	Repealed
(4)	Repealed
Arbitration Act 1979	
s. 1(1)	81(3)
s. 1(2)	69(1), (7), 71(2)
(3)	69(1), (2)
(4)	69(3)

Arbitration Act 1979	*1996 Act*
s. 1(5)	70(4)
(6)	Repealed
(6A)	69(8)
(7)	69(6)
(8)	71(8)
s. 2(1)	45(1)
(2)	45(2)
(2A)	45(5)
(3)	45(6)
s. 3(1)	69(1)
(2)	Repealed
(3)	Repealed
(4)	Repealed
(5)	Repealed
(6)	87(1)
(7)	85(2)
s. 4(1)	Repealed
(2)	Repealed
(3)	Repealed
(4)	Repealed
(5)	Repealed
s. 5(1)	41(4), 42(1), (4)
(2)	41(4)
(3)	Repealed
(4)	Repealed
(5)	Repealed
(6)	Repealed
s. 6(1)	Repealed
(2)	Repealed
(3)	Repealed
(4)	Repealed
s. 7(1)	Repealed
(2)	Repealed
(3)	Repealed
s. 8(1)	Repealed
(2)	Repealed
(3)	Repealed
(4)	Repealed
Limitation Act 1980	
s. 34(1)	13(1)
(2)	13(3)
(3)	14(3)–(5)
(4)	76(1), (4)
(5)	13(2)
(6)	Repealed
(7)	13(4)
Civil Jurisdiction and Judgments Act 1982	
s. 26(1)	11(1)
(2)	N/A
(3)	11(3)
Consumer Arbitration Agreements Act 1988	Repealed *in toto*

APPENDIX 3

CONVENTION ON THE RECOGNITION AND ENFORCEMENT OF FOREIGN ARBITRAL AWARDS

Done at New York on 10 June 1958

Article I

1. This Convention shall apply to the recognition and enforcement of arbitral awards made in the territory of a State other than the State where the recognition and enforcement of such awards are sought, and arising out of differences between persons, whether physical or legal. It shall also apply to arbitral awards not considered as domestic awards in the State where their recognition and enforcement are sought.

2. The term "arbitral awards" shall include not only awards made by arbitrators appointed for each case but also those made by permanent arbitral bodies to which the parties have submitted.

3. When signing, ratifying or acceding to this Convention, or notifying extension under article X hereof, any State may on the basis of reciprocity declare that it will apply the Convention to the recognition and enforcement of awards made only in the territory of another Contracting State. It may also declare that it will apply the Convention only to differences arising out of legal relationships, whether contractual or not, which are considered as commercial under the national law of the State making such declaration.

Article II

1. Each Contracting State shall recognize an agreement in writing under which the parties undertake to submit to arbitration all or any differences which have arisen or which may arise between them in respect of a defined legal relationship, whether contractual or not, concerning a subject matter capable of settlement by arbitration.

2. The term "agreement in writing" shall include an arbitral clause in a contract or an arbitration agreement, signed by the parties or contained in an exchange of letters or telegrams.

3. The court of a Contracting State, when seized of an action in a matter in respect of which the parties have made an agreement within the meaning of this article, shall, at the request of one of the parties, refer the parties to arbitration, unless it finds that the said agreement is null and void, inoperative or incapable of being performed.

Article III

Each Contracting State shall recognize arbitral awards as binding and enforce them in accordance with the rules of procedure of the territory where the award is relied upon, under the conditions laid down in the following articles. There shall not be imposed substantially more onerous conditions or higher fees or charges on the recognition or enforcement of arbitral awards to which this Convention applies than are imposed on the recognition or enforcement of domestic arbitral awards.

Article IV

1. To obtain the recognition and enforcement mentioned in the preceding article, the party applying for recognition and enforcement shall, at the time of the application, supply:

(a) The duly authenticated original award or a duly certified copy thereof;
(b) The original agreement referred to in article II or a duly certified copy thereof.

2. If the said award or agreement is not made in an official language of the country in which the award is relied upon, the party applying for recognition and enforcement of the award shall produce a translation of these documents into such language. The translation shall be certified by an official or sworn translator or by a diplomatic or consular agent.

Article V

1. Recognition and enforcement of the award may be refused, at the request of the party against whom it is invoked, only if that party furnishes to the competent authority where the recognition and enforcement is sought, proof that:

(a) The parties to the agreement referred to in article II were, under the law applicable to them, under some incapacity, or the said agreement is not valid under the law to which the parties have subjected it or, failing any indication thereon, under the law of the country where the award was made; or
(b) The party against whom the award is invoked was not given proper notice of the appointment of the arbitrator or of the arbitration proceedings or was otherwise unable to present his case; or
(c) The award deals with a difference not contemplated by or not falling within the terms of the submission to arbitration, or it contains decisions on matters beyond the scope of the submission to arbitration, provided that, if the decisions on matters submitted to arbitration can be separated from those not so submitted, that part of the award which contains decisions on matters submitted to arbitration may be recognized and enforced; or
(d) The composition of the arbitral authority or the arbitral procedure was not in accordance with the agreement of the parties, or, failing such agreement, was not in accordance with the law of the country where the arbitration took place; or
(e) The award has not yet become binding on the parties, or has been set aside or suspended by a competent authority of the country in which, or under the law of which, that award was made.

2. Recognition and enforcement of an arbitral award may also be refused if the competent authority in the country where recognition and enforcement is sought finds that:

(a) The subject matter of the difference is not capable of settlement by arbitration under the law of that country; or
(b) The recognition or enforcement of the award would be contrary to the public policy of that country.

Article VI

If an application for the setting aside or suspension of the award has been made to a competent authority referred to in article V(1)(e), the authority before which the award is sought to be relied upon may, if it considers it proper, adjourn the decision on the enforcement of the award and may also, on the application of the party claiming enforcement of the award, order the other party to give suitable security.

Article VII

1. The provisions of the present Convention shall not affect the validity of multilateral or bilateral agreements concerning the recognition and enforcement of arbitral awards entered into by the Contracting States nor deprive any interested party of any right he may have to avail himself of an arbitral award in the manner and to the extent allowed by the law or the treaties of the country where such award is sought to be relied upon.

2. The Geneva Protocol on Arbitration Clauses of 1923 and the Geneva Convention on the Execution of Foreign Arbitral Awards of 1927 shall cease to have effect between Contracting States on their becoming bound and to the extent that they become bound, by this Convention.

Article VIII

1. This Convention shall be open until 31 December 1958 for signature on behalf of any Member of the United Nations and also on behalf of any other State which is or hereafter becomes a member of any specialized agency of the United Nations, or which is or hereafter becomes a party to the Statute of the International Court of Justice, or any other State to which an invitation has been addressed by the General Assembly of the United Nations.

2. This Convention shall be ratified and the instrument of ratification shall be deposited with the Secretary-General of the United Nations.

Article IX

1. This Convention shall be open for accession to all States referred to in article VIII.

2. Accession shall be effected by the deposit of an instrument of accession with the Secretary-General of the United Nations.

Article X

1. Any State may, at the time of signature, ratification or accession, declare that this Convention shall extend to all or any of the territories for the international relations of which it is responsible. Such a declaration shall take effect when the Convention enters into force for the State concerned.

2. At any time thereafter any such extension shall be made by notification addressed to the Secretary-General of the United Nations and shall take effect as from the ninetieth day after the day of receipt by the Secretary-General of the United Nations of this notification, or as from the date of entry into force of the Convention for the State concerned, whichever is the later.

3. With respect to those territories to which this Convention is not extended at the time of signature, ratification or accession, each State concerned shall consider the possibility of taking the necessary steps in order to extend the application of this Convention to such territories, subject, where necessary for constitutional reasons, to the consent of the Governments of such territories.

Article XI

In the case of a federal or non-unitary State, the following provisions shall apply:

(a) With respect to those articles of this Convention that come within the legislative jurisdiction of the federal authority, the obligations of the federal Government shall to this extent be the same as those of Contracting States which are not federal States;

(b) With respect to those articles of this Convention that come within the legislative jurisdiction of constituent states or provinces which are not, under the constitutional system of the federation, bound to take legislative action, the federal Government shall bring such articles with a favourable recommendation to the notice of the appropriate authorities of constituent states or provinces at the earliest possible moment;

(c) A federal State Party to this Convention shall, at the request of any other Contracting State transmitted through the Secretary-General of the United Nations, supply a statement of the law and practice of the federation and its constituent units in regard to any particular provision of this Convention, showing the extent to which effect has been given to that provision by legislative or other action.

Article XII

1. This Convention shall come into force on the ninetieth day following the date of deposit of the third instrument of ratification or accession.

2. For each State ratifying or acceding to this Convention after the deposit of the third instrument of ratification or accession, this Convention shall enter into force on the ninetieth day after deposit by such State of its instrument of ratification or accession.

Article XIII

1. Any Contracting State may denounce this Convention by a written notification to the Secretary-General of the United Nations. Denunciation shall take effect one year after the date of receipt of the notification by the Secretary-General.

2. Any State which has made a declaration or notification under article X may, at any time thereafter, by notification to the Secretary-General of the United Nations, declare that this Convention shall cease to extend to the territory concerned one year after the date of the receipt of the notification by the Secretary-General.

3. This Convention shall continue to be applicable to arbitral awards in respect of which recognition or enforcement proceedings have been instituted before the denunciation takes effect.

Article XIV

A Contracting State shall not be entitled to avail itself of the present Convention against other Contracting States except to the extent that it is itself bound to apply the Convention.

Article XV

The Secretary-General of the United Nations shall notify the States contemplated in article VIII of the following:

(a) Signatures and ratifications in accordance with article VIII;
(b) Accessions in accordance with article IX;
(c) Declarations and notifications under articles I, X and XI;
(d) The date upon which this Convention enters into force in accordance with article XII;
(e) Denunciations and notifications in accordance with article XIII.

Article XVI

1. This Convention, of which the Chinese, English, French, Russian and Spanish texts shall be equally authentic, shall be deposited in the archives of the United Nations.

2. The Secretary-General of the United Nations shall transmit a certified copy of this Convention to the States contemplated in article VIII.

[We gratefully acknowledge the assistance of the United Nations Commission on International Trade Law (UNCITRAL) and their kind permission to reproduce their copy material.]

APPENDIX 4

THE UNFAIR ARBITRATION AGREEMENTS (SPECIFIED AMOUNT) ORDER 1999

(S.I. 1999 No. 2167)

Made	*28th July 1999*
Laid before Parliament	*2nd August 1999*
Coming into force	*1st January 2000*

The Secretary of State, in exercise of the power conferred on him by section 91(1) and (3)(a) and (b) of the Arbitration Act 1996, with the concurrence (as respects England and Wales) of the Lord Chancellor, hereby makes the following Order:

1. This Order may be cited as the Unfair Arbitration Agreements (Specified Amount) Order 1999 and shall come into force on 1st January 2000.

2. The Unfair Arbitration Agreements (Specified Amount) Order 1996 is hereby revoked.

3. The amount of £5,000 is hereby specified for the purposes of section 91 of the Arbitration Act 1996 (arbitration agreement unfair where modest amount sought).

Kim Howells

Parliamentary Under-Secretary of State for Competition and Consumer Affairs, Department of Trade and Industry

27th July 1999

I concur

Irvine of Lairg, C.

28th July 1999

EXPLANATORY NOTE

(This note is not part of the Order)

This Order specifies the amount of £5,000 for the purposes of section 91 of the Arbitration Act 1996 for England and Wales and Scotland. It replaces the Unfair Arbitration Agreements (Specified Amount) Order 1996 which specified the amount of £3,000.

Section 9(1) of the 1996 Act provides that a term which constitutes an arbitration agreement is unfair for the purposes of the Unfair Terms in Consumer Contracts Regulations 1994 (S.I. 1994/3159) so far as it relates to a claim for a pecuniary remedy which does not exceed the amount specified by order for the purposes of that section. The 1994 Regulations implement Council Directive 93/13/EEC on unfair terms in consumer contracts (O.J. No. L95, 21.4.93, P. 29). The Unfair Terms in Consumer Contracts Regulations 1999 (S.I. 1999/2083) revoke and replace the 1994 Regulations with effect from 1st October 1999.

Section 89(1) of the 1996 Act defines "arbitration agreement" as an agreement to submit to arbitration present or future disputes or differences (whether or not contractual).

A Regulatory Impact Assessment of the costs and benefits which will result from this Order has been prepared by the Department of Trade and Industry and is available from Consumer Affairs Directorate, Department of Trade and Industry, Room 407, 1 Victoria Street, London SW1H 0ET (telephone 0171 215 0342). Copies have been placed in the libraries of both Houses of Parliament.

APPENDIX 5

THE HIGH COURT AND COUNTY COURT (ALLOCATION OF ARBITRATION PROCEEDINGS) ORDER 1996

(S.I. 1996 No. 3215)

Made	*19th December 1996*
Laid before Parliament	*20th December 1996*
Coming into force	*31st January 1997*

The Lord Chancellor, in exercise of the powers conferred on him by section 105 of the Arbitration Act 1996, hereby makes the following Order:

1.—(1) This Order may be cited as the High Court and County Courts (Allocation of Arbitration Proceedings) Order 1996 and shall come into force on 31st January 1997.

(2) In this Order, "the Act" means the Arbitration Act 1996.

2. Subject to articles 3 to 5, proceedings under the Act shall be commenced and taken in the High Court.

3. Proceedings under section 9 of the Act (stay of legal proceedings) shall be commenced in the court in which the legal proceedings are pending.

4. Proceedings under sections 66 and 101(2) (enforcement of awards) of the Act may be commenced in any county court.

5.—(1) Proceedings under the Act may be commenced and taken in the Central London County Court Business List.

(2) Where, in exercise of the powers conferred by sections 41 and 42 of the County Courts Act 1984 the High Court or the judge in charge of the Central London County Court Business List orders the transfer of proceedings under the Act which were commenced in the Central London County Court Business List to the High Court, those proceedings shall be taken in the High Court.

(3) Where, in exercise of its powers under section 40(2) of the County Courts Act 1984(c) the High Court orders the transfer of proceedings under the Act which were commenced in the High Court to the Central London County Court Business List, those proceedings shall be taken in the Central London County Court Business List.

(4) In exercising the powers referred to in paragraphs (2) and (3) regard shall be had to the following criteria—

(a) the financial substance of the dispute referred to arbitration, including the value of any claim or counterclaim;

(b) the nature of the dispute referred to arbitration (for example, whether it arises out of a commercial or business transaction or relates to engineering, building or other construction work);

(c) whether the proceedings are otherwise important and, in particular, whether they raise questions of importance to persons who are not parties, and

(d) the balance of convenience points to having the proceedings taken in the Central London County Court Business List,

and, where the financial substance of the dispute exceeds £200,000, the proceedings shall be taken in the High Court unless the proceedings do not raise questions of general importance to persons who are not parties.

(5) In this article—

"the Central London County Court Business List" means the business list established at the Central London County Court by Order 48C of the County Court Rules 1981;

"value" shall be construed in accordance with articles 9 and 10 of the High Court and County Courts Jurisdiction Order 1991.

(6) In this article "the Central London County Court Mercantile List" means the Mercantile Court established at the Central London County Court pursuant to Part 59 of the Civil Procedure Rules 1998.

6. Nothing in this Order shall prevent the judge in charge of the commercial list (within the meaning of section 62(3) of the Supreme Court Act 1981 (c)) from transferring proceedings under the Act to another list, court or Division of the High Court to which he has power to transfer proceedings and, where such an order is made, the proceedings may be taken in that list, court or Division as the case may be.

Mackay of Clashfern, C.

Dated 19th December 1996

EXPLANATORY NOTE

(This note is not part of the Order)

This Order specifies the courts in which proceedings under the Arbitration Act 1996 may be commenced and allocates proceedings between the High Court and the Central London County Court.

NOTES

Sub-paragraph (6) was added by the Civil Procedure (Modification of Enactments) Order 2002, SI 2002 No 439.

APPENDIX 6

CIVIL PROCEDURE RULES PART 62 AND PRACTICE DIRECTION TO PART 62

Scope of this Part and interpretation

62.1 (1) This Part contains rules about arbitration claims.

(2) In this Part—

(a) "the 1950 Act" means the Arbitration Act 1950([1]);
(b) "the 1975 Act" means the Arbitration Act 1975([2]);
(c) "the 1979 Act" means the Arbitration Act 1979([3]);
(d) "the 1996 Act" means the Arbitration Act 1996([4]);
(e) references to—
  (i) the 1996 Act; or
  (ii) any particular section of that Act
  include references to that Act or to the particular section of that Act as applied with modifications by the ACAS Arbitration Scheme (England and Wales) Order 2001([5]); and
(f) "arbitration claim form" means a claim form in the form set out in the practice direction.

(3) Part 58 (Commercial Court) applies to arbitration claims in the Commercial Court, Part 59 (Mercantile Court) applies to arbitration claims in the Mercantile Court and Part 60 (Technology and Construction Court claims) applies to arbitration claims in the Technology and Construction Court, except where this Part provides otherwise.

I CLAIMS UNDER THE 1996 ACT

Interpretation

62.2 (1) In this Section of this Part "arbitration claim" means—

(a) any application to the court under the 1996 Act;
(b) a claim to determine—
  (i) whether there is a valid arbitration agreement;
  (ii) whether an arbitration tribunal is properly constituted; or
  what matters have been submitted to arbitration in accordance with an arbitration agreement;

1. 1950 c. 27.
2. 1975 c. 3; repealed by the Arbitration Act 1996 (c. 23), section 107(2) and Schedule 4 but continues to apply to claims commenced before 31st January 1997 by virtue of the Arbitration Act 1996 (Commencement No. 1) Order 1996 (S.I. 1996/3146), article 4 and Schedule 2.
3. 1979 c. 42; repealed by the Arbitration Act 1996 (c. 23), section 107(2) and Schedule 4 but continues to apply to claims commenced before 31st January 1997 by virtue of the Arbitration Act 1996 (Commencement No. 1) Order 1996 (S.I. 1996/3146), article 4 and Schedule 2.
4. 1996 c. 23.
5. S.I. 2001/1185.

- (c) a claim to declare that an award by an arbitral tribunal is not binding on a party; and
- (d) any other application affecting—
  - (i) arbitration proceedings (whether started or not); or
  - (ii) an arbitration agreement.

(2) This Section of this Part does not apply to an arbitration claim to which Sections II or III of this Part apply.

Starting the claim

62.3 (1) Except where paragraph (2) applies an arbitration claim must be started by the issue of an arbitration claim form in accordance with the Part 8 procedure.

(2) An application under section 9 of the 1996 Act to stay legal proceedings must be made by application notice to the court dealing with those proceedings.

(3) The courts in which an arbitration claim may be started are set out in the practice direction.

(4) Rule 30.5(3) applies with the modification that a judge of the Technology and Construction Court may transfer the claim to any other court or specialist list.

Arbitration claim form

62.4 (1) An arbitration claim form must—

- (a) include a concise statement of—
  - (i) the remedy claimed; and
  - (ii) any questions on which the claimant seeks the decision of the court;
- (b) give details of any arbitration award challenged by the claimant, identifying which part or parts of the award are challenged and specifying the grounds for the challenge;
- (c) show that any statutory requirements have been met;
- (d) specify under which section of the 1996 Act the claim is made;
- (e) identify against which (if any) defendants a costs order is sought; and
- (f) specify either—
  - (i) the persons on whom the arbitration claim form is to be served, stating their role in the arbitration and whether they are defendants; or
  - (ii) that the claim is made without notice under section 44(3) of the 1996 Act and the grounds relied on.

(2) Unless the court orders otherwise an arbitration claim form must be served on the defendant within 1 month from the date of issue and rules 7.5 and 7.6 are modified accordingly.

(3) Where the claimant applies for an order under section 12 of the 1996 Act (extension of time for beginning arbitral proceedings or other dispute resolution procedures), he may include in his arbitration claim form an alternative application for a declaration that such an order is not needed.

Service out of the jurisdiction

62.5 (1) The court may give permission to serve an arbitration claim form out of the jurisdiction if—

- (a) the claimant seeks to—
  - (i) challenge; or
  - (ii) appeal on a question of law arising out of,

  an arbitration award made within the jurisdiction;

  (The place where an award is treated as made is determined by section 53 of the 1996 Act.)
- (b) the claim is for an order under section 44 of the 1996 Act; or
- (c) the claimant—

(i) seeks some other remedy or requires a question to be decided by the court affecting an arbitration (whether started or not), an arbitration agreement or an arbitration award; and
(ii) the seat of the arbitration is or will be within the jurisdiction or the conditions in section 2(4) of the 1996 Act are satisfied.

(2) An application for permission under paragraph (1) must be supported by written evidence—

(a) stating the grounds on which the application is made; and
(b) showing in what place or country the person to be served is, or probably may be found.

(3) Rules 6.24 to 6.29 apply to the service of an arbitration claim form under paragraph (1).
(4) An order giving permission to serve an arbitration claim form out of the jurisdiction must specify the period within which the defendant may file an acknowledgement of service.

Notice

62.6 (1) Where an arbitration claim is made under section 24, 28 or 56 of the 1996 Act, each arbitrator must be a defendant.
(2) Where notice must be given to an arbitrator or any other person it may be given by sending him a copy of—

(a) the arbitration claim form; and
(b) any written evidence in support.

(3) Where the 1996 Act requires an application to the court to be made on notice to any other party to the arbitration, that notice must be given by making that party a defendant.

Case management

62.7 (1) Part 26 and any other rule that requires a party to file an allocation questionnaire does not apply.
(2) Arbitration claims are allocated to the multi-track.
(3) Part 29 does not apply.
(4) The automatic directions set out in the practice direction apply unless the court orders otherwise.

Stay of legal proceedings

62.8 (1) An application notice seeking a stay of legal proceedings under section 9 of the 1996 Act([1]) must be served on all parties to those proceedings who have given an address for service.
(2) A copy of an application notice under paragraph (1) must be served on any other party to the legal proceedings (whether or not he is within the jurisdiction) who has not given an address for service, at—

(a) his last known address; or
(b) a place where it is likely to come to his attention.

(3) Where a question arises as to whether—

(a) an arbitration agreement has been concluded; or
(b) the dispute which is the subject-matter of the proceedings falls within the terms of such an agreement,

the court may decide that question or give directions to enable it to be decided and may order the proceedings to be stayed pending its decision.

1. 1996 c. 23.

Variation of time

62.9 (1) The court may vary the period of 28 days fixed by section 70(3) of the 1996 Act for—

(a) challenging the award under section 67 or 68 of the Act; and
(b) appealing against an award under section 69 of the Act.

(2) An application for an order under paragraph (1) may be made without notice being served on any other party before the period of 28 days expires.
(3) After the period of 28 days has expired—

(a) an application for an order extending time under paragraph (1) must—
  (i) be made in the arbitration claim form; and
  (ii) state the grounds on which the application is made;
(b) any defendant may file written evidence opposing the extension of time within 7 days after service of the arbitration claim form; and
(c) if the court extends the period of 28 days, each defendant's time for acknowledging service and serving evidence shall start to run as if the arbitration claim form had been served on the date when the court's order is served on that defendant.

Hearings

62.10 (1) The court may order that an arbitration claim be heard either in public or in private.
(2) Rule 39.2 does not apply.
(3) Subject to any order made under paragraph (1)—

(a) the determination of—
  (i) a preliminary point of law under section 45 of the 1996 Act; or
  (ii) an appeal under section 69 of the 1996 Act on a question of law arising out of an award,
will be heard in public; and
(b) all other arbitration claims will be heard in private.

(4) Paragraph (3)(a) does not apply to—

(a) the preliminary question of whether the court is satisfied of the matters set out in section 45(2)(b); or
(b) an application for permission to appeal under section 69(2)(b).

II OTHER ARBITRATION CLAIMS

Scope of this Section

62.11 (1) This Section of this Part contains rules about arbitration claims to which the old law applies.
(2) In this Section

(a) "the old law" means the enactments specified in Schedules 3 and 4 of the 1996 Act as they were in force before their amendment or repeal by that Act; and
(b) "arbitration claim" means any application to the court under the old law and includes an appeal (or application for permission to appeal) to the High Court under section 1(2) of the 1979 Act[1].

(3) This Section does not apply to—

(a) a claim to which Section III of this Part applies;

1. 1979 c. 42; repealed by the Arbitration Act 1996 (c. 23), section 107(2) and Schedule 4 but continues to apply to claims commenced before 31st January 1997 by virtue of the Arbitration Act 1996 (Commencement No. 1) Order 1996 (S.I. 1996/3146), article 4 and Schedule 2.

(b) a claim on the award.

Applications to Judge

62.12 A claim—

(a) seeking permission to appeal under section 1(2) of the 1979 Act;
(b) under section 1(5) of that Act (including any claim seeking permission); or
(c) under section 5 of that Act,

must be made in the High Court and will be heard by a judge of the Commercial Court unless any such judge directs otherwise.

Starting the claim

62.13 (1) Except where paragraph (2) applies an arbitration claim must be started by the issue of an arbitration claim form in accordance with the Part 8 procedure.

(2) Where an arbitration claim is to be made in existing proceedings—

(a) it must be made by way of application notice; and
(b) any reference in this Section of this Part to an arbitration claim form includes a reference to an application notice.

(3) The arbitration claim form in an arbitration claim under section 1(5) of the 1979 Act (including any claim seeking permission) must be served on—

(a) the arbitrator or umpire; and
(b) any other party to the reference.

Claims in District Registries

62.14 If—

(a) a claim is to be made under section 12(4) of the 1950 Act[1] for an order for the issue of a witness summons to compel the attendance of the witness before an arbitrator or umpire; and
(b) the attendance of the witness is required within the district of a District Registry,

the claim may be started in that Registry.

Time limits and other special provisions about arbitration claims

62.15 (1) An arbitration claim to

(a) remit an award under section 22 of the 1950 Act[2];
(b) set aside an award under section 23(2) of that Act[3] or otherwise; or
(c) direct an arbitrator or umpire to state the reasons for an award under section 1(5) of the 1979 Act,

must be made, and the arbitration claim form served, within 21 days after the award has been made and published to the parties.

1. 1950 c. 27; section 12(4) was repealed by the Arbitration Act 1996 (c. 23), section 107(2) and Schedule 4 but continues to apply to claims commenced before 31st January 1997 by virtue of the Arbitration Act 1996 (Commencement No. 1) Order 1996 (S.I. 1996/3146), article 4 and Schedule 2.

2. 1950 c. 27; section 22 was repealed by the Arbitration Act 1996 (c. 23), section 107(2) and Schedule 4 but continues to apply to claims commenced before 31st January 1997 by virtue of the Arbitration Act 1996 (Commencement No. 1) Order 1996 (S.I. 1996/3146), article 4 and Schedule 2.

3. 1950 c. 27; section 23(2) was repealed by the Arbitration Act 1996 (c. 23), section 107(2) and Schedule 4 but continues to apply to claims commenced before 31st January 1997 by virtue of the Arbitration Act 1996 (Commencement No. 1) Order 1996 (S.I. 1996/3146), article 4 and Schedule 2.

(2) An arbitration claim to determine any question of law arising in the course of a reference under section 2(1) of the Arbitration Act 1979 must be made, and the arbitration claim form served, within 14 days after—

(a) the arbitrator or umpire gave his consent in writing to the claim being made; or
(b) the other parties so consented.

(3) An appeal under section 1(2) of the 1979 Act must be filed, and the arbitration claim form served, within 21 days after the award has been made and published to the parties.

(4) Where reasons material to an appeal under section 1(2) of the 1979 Act are given on a date subsequent to the publication of the award, the period of 21 days referred to in paragraph (3) will run from the date on which reasons are given.

(5) In every arbitration claim to which this rule applies—

(a) the arbitration claim form must state the grounds of the claim or appeal;
(b) where the claim or appeal is based on written evidence, a copy of that evidence must be served with the arbitration claim form; and
(c) where the claim or appeal is made with the consent of the arbitrator, the umpire or the other parties, a copy of every written consent must be served with the arbitration claim form.

(6) In an appeal under section 1(2) of the 1979 Act—

(a) a statement of the grounds for the appeal specifying the relevant parts of the award and reasons; and
(b) where permission is required, any written evidence in support of the contention that the question of law concerns—
  (i) a term of a contract; or
  (ii) an event,
  which is not a "one-off" term or event,

must be filed and served with the arbitration claim form.

(7) Any written evidence in reply to written evidence under paragraph (6)(b) must be filed and served on the claimant not less than 2 days before the hearing.

(8) A party to a claim seeking permission to appeal under section 1(2) of the 1979 Act who wishes to contend that the award should be upheld for reasons not expressed or fully expressed in the award and reasons must file and serve on the claimant, a notice specifying the grounds of his contention not less than 2 days before the hearing.

Service out of the jurisdiction

62.16 (1) Subject to paragraph (2)—

(a) any arbitration claim form in an arbitration claim under the 1950 Act or the 1979 Act; or
(b) any order made in such a claim,
  may be served out of the jurisdiction with the permission of the court if the arbtiration to which the claim relates—
  (i) is governed by the law of England and Wales; or
  (ii) has been, is being, or will be, held within the jurisdiction.

(2) An arbitration claim form seeking permission to enforce an award may be served out of the jurisdiction with the permission of the court whether or not the arbitration is governed by the law of England and Wales.

(3) An application for permission to serve an arbitration claim form out of the jurisdiction must be supported by written evidence—

(a) stating the grounds on which the application is made; and
(b) showing in what place or country the person to be served is, or probably may be found.

Rules 6.24 to 6.29 apply to the service of an arbitration claim form under paragraph (1).

(4) Omitted

(5) An order giving permission to serve an arbitration claim form out of the jurisdiction must specify the period within which the defendant may file an acknowledgment of service.

III ENFORCEMENT

Scope of this Section

62.17 This Section of this Part applies to all arbitration enforcement proceedings other than by a claim on the award.

Enforcement of awards

62.18 (1) An application for permission under—

(a) section 66 of the 1996 Act[1];
(b) section 101 of the 1996 Act;
(c) section 26 of the 1950 Act;[2]; or
(d) section 3(1)(a) of the 1975 Act,;[3]

to enforce an award in the same manner as a judgment or order may be made without notice in an arbitration claim form.

(2) The court may specify parties to the arbitration on whom the arbitration claim form must be served.

(3) The parties on whom the arbitration claim form is served must acknowledge service and the enforcement proceedings will continue as if they were an arbitration claim under Section I of this Part.

(4) With the permission of the court the arbtiration claim form may be served out of the jurisdiction irrespective of where the award is, or is treated as, made

(5) Where the applicant applies to enforce an agreed award within the meaning of section 51(2) of the 1996 Act—

(a) the arbitration claim form must state that the award is an agreed award; and
(b) any order made by the court must also contain such a statement.

(6) An application for permission must be supported by written evidence—

(a) exhibiting—
  (i) where the application is made under section 66 of the 1996 Act or under section 26 of the 1950 Act, the arbitration agreement and the original award (or copies);
  (ii) where the application is under section 101 of the 1996 Act, the documents required to be produced by section 102 of that Act; or
  (iii) where the application is under section 3(1)(a) of the 1975 Act, the documents required to be produced by section 4 of that Act;
(b) stating the name and the usual or last known place or residence of business of the claimant and of the person against whom it is sought to enforce the award; and
(c) stating either—
  (i) that the award has not been complied with, or
  (ii) the extent to which it has not been complied with at the date of the application.

(7) An order giving permission must—

1. 1996 c. 23.

2. 1950 c. 27; section 26 was repealed by the Arbitration Act 1996 (c. 23), section 107(2) and Schedule 4 but continues to apply to claims commenced before 31st January 1997 by virtue of the Arbitration Act 1996 (Commencement No. 1) Order 1996 (S.I. 1996/3146), article 4 and Schedule 2.

3. 1975 c. 3; repealed by the Arbitration Act 1996 (c. 23), section 107(2) and Schedule 4 but continues to apply to claims commenced before 31st January 1997 by virtue of the Arbitration Act 1996 (Commencement No. 1) Order 1996 (S.I. 1996/3146), article 4 and Schedule 2.

(a) be drawn up by the claimant; and
(b) be served on the defendant by—
  (i) delivering a copy to him personally; or
  (ii) sending a copy to him at his usual or last known place of residence or business.

(8) An order giving permission may be served out of the jurisdiction—

(a) without permission; and
(b) in accordance with rules 6.24 to 6.29 as if the order were an arbitration claim form.

(9) Within 14 days after service of the order or, if the order is to be served out of the jurisdiction, within such other period as the court may set—

(a) the defendant may apply to set aside the order; and
(b) the award must not be enforced until after—
  (i) the end of that period; or
  (ii) any application made by the defendant within that period has been finally disposed of.

(10) The order must contain a statement of—

(a) the right to make an application to set the order aside; and
(b) the restrictions on enforcement under rule 62.18(9)(b).

(11) Where a body corporate is a party any reference in this rule to place of residence or business shall have effect as if the reference were to the registered or principal address of the body corporate.

Interest on awards

62.19 (1) Where an applicant seeks to enforce an award of interest the whole or any part of which relates to a period after the date of the award, he must file a statement giving the following particulars—

(a) whether simple or compound interest was awarded;
(b) the date from which interest was awarded;
(c) where rests were provided for, specifying them;
(d) the rate of interest awarded; and
(e) a calculation showing—
  (i) the total amount claimed up to the date of the statement; and
  (ii) any sum which will become due on a daily basis.

(2) A statement under paragraph (1) must be filed whenever the amount of interest has to be quantified for the purpose of—

(a) obtaining a judgment or order under section 66 of the 1996 Act (enforcement of the award); or
(b) enforcing such a judgment or order.

Registration in High Court of foreign awards

62.20 (1) Where—

(a) an award is made in proceedings on an arbitration in any part of a United Kingdom Overseas Territory (within the meaning of rule 6.18 (f)) or other territory to which Part I of the Foreign Judgments (Reciprocal Enforcement) Act 1933[1] ("the 1933 Act") extends;

1. 1933 c. 13 (23 & 24 Geo. 5).

(b) Part II of the Administration of Justice Act 1920[1] extended to that part immediately before Part I of the 1933 Act was extended to that part; and
(c) an award has, under the law in force in the place where it was made, become enforceable in the same manner as a judgment given by a court in that place,

rules 74.1 to 74.7 and 74.9 apply in relation to the award as they apply in relation to a judgment given by the court subject to the modifications in paragraph (2).

(2) The modifications referred to in paragraph (1) are as follows—

(a) for references to the State of origin are substituted references to the place where the award was made; and
(b) the written evidence required by rule 74.4 must state (in addition to the matters required by that rule) that to the best of the information or belief of the maker of the statement the award has, under the law in force in the place where it was made, become enforceable in the same manner as a judgment given by a court in that place.

Registration of awards under the Arbitration (International Investment Disputes) Act 1966

62.21 (1) In this rule—

(a) "the 1966 Act" means the Arbitration (International Investment Disputes) Act 1966[2];
(b) "award" means an award under the Convention;
(c) "the Convention" means the Convention on the settlement of investment disputes between States and nationals of other States which was opened for signature in Washington on 18th March 1965[3];
(d) "judgment creditor" means the person seeking recognition or enforcement of an award; and
(e) "judgment debtor" means the other party to the award.

(2) Subject to the provisions of this rule, the following provisions of Part 74 apply with such modifications as may be necessary in relation to an award as they apply in relation to a judgment to which Part I of the Foreign Judgments (Reciprocal Enforcement) Act 1933[4] applies—

(a) rule 74.1;
(b) rule 74.3;
(c) rule 74.4(1), (2)(a) to (d), and (4);
(d) rule 74.6 (except paragraph (3)(c) to (e)); and
(e) rule 74.9(2).

(3) An application to have an award registered in the High Court under section 1 of the 1966 Act[5] must be made in accordance with the Part 8 procedure.

(4) The written evidence required by rule 74.4 in support of an application for registration must—

(a) exhibit the award certified under the Convention instead of the judgment (or a copy of it); and
(b) in addition to stating the matters referred to in rule 74.4(2)(a) to (d) state whether—
   (i) at the date of the application the enforcement of the award has been stayed (provisionally or otherwise) under the Convention; and

1. 1920 c. 81 (10 & 11 Geo. 5); section 10 of Part II was substituted by the Civil Jurisdiction and Judgments Act 1982 (c. 27), section 35(2) and section 14 of Part II was amended by the Civil Jurisdiction and Judgments Act 1982 (c. 27), section 35(3).
2. 1966 c. 41.
3. The text of the Convention is set out in the Schedule to the Arbitration (International Investment Disputes) Act 1966 (c. 41).
4. 23 & 24 Geo. 5 c. 13.
5. 1966 c. 41; section 1 was amended by the Administration of Justice Act 1977 (c. 38), sections 4 and 32(4) and Schedule 5, Part I and by the Supreme Court Act 1981 (c. 54), section 152(1) and Schedule 5.

(ii) any, and if so what, application has been made under the Convention, which, if granted, might result in a stay of the enforcement of the award.

(5) Where, on granting permission to register an award or an application made by the judgment debtor after an award has been registered, the court considers—

(a) that the enforcement of the award has been stayed (whether provisionally or otherwise) under the Convention; or

(b) that an application has been made under the Convention which, if granted, might result in a stay of the enforcement of the award,

the court may stay the enforcement of the award for such time as it considers appropriate.

PRACTICE DIRECTION TO PART 62

SECTION I

1.1 This Section of this Practice Direction applies to arbitration claims to which Section I of Part 62 applies.

1.2 In this Section "the 1996 Act" means the Arbitration Act 1996.

1.3 Where a rule provides for a document to be sent, it may be sent—

(1) by first class post;
(2) through a document exchange; or
(3) by fax, electronic mail or other means of electronic communication.

62.3—Starting the claim

2.1 An arbitration claim under the 1996 Act (other than under section 9) must be started in accordance with the High Court and County Courts (Allocation of Arbitration Proceedings) Order 1996 by the issue of an arbitration claim form.

2.2 An arbitration claim form must be substantially in the form set out in Appendix A to this practice direction.

2.3 Subject to paragraph 2.1, an arbitration claim form—

(1) may be issued at the courts set out in column 1 of the table below and will be entered in the list set out against that court in column 2;
(2) relating to a landlord and tenant or partnership dispute must be issued in the Chancery Division of the High Court.

Court	*List*
Admiralty and Commercial Registry at the Royal Courts of Justice, London	Commercial list
Technology and Construction Court Registry, St. Dunstan's House, London	TCC list
District Registry of the High Court (where mercantile court established)	Mercantile list
District Registry of the High Court (where arbitration claim form marked "Technology and Construction Court" in top right hand corner)	TCC list
Central London County Court	Mercantile list

62.4—Arbitration claim form

Service

3.1 The court may exercise its powers under rule 6.8 to permit service of an arbitration claim form at the address of a party's solicitor or representative acting for him in the arbitration.

3.2 Where the arbitration claim form is served by the claimant he must file a certificate of service within 7 days of service of the arbitration claim form.

(Rule 6.10 specifies what a certificate of service must show).

Acknowledgement of service or making representations by arbitrator or ACAS

4.1 Where—

(1) an arbitrator; or
(2) ACAS (in a claim under the 1996 Act as applied with modifications by the ACAS Arbitration Scheme (England and Wales) Order 2001)

is sent a copy of an arbitration claim form (including an arbitration claim form sent under rule 62.6(2)), that arbitrator or ACAS (as the case may be) may—

(a) apply to be made a defendant; or
(b) make representations to the court under paragraph 4.3.

4.2 An application under paragraph 4.1(2)(a) to be made a defendant—

(1) must be served on the claimant; but
(2) need not be served on any other party.

4.3 An arbitrator or ACAS may make representations by filing written evidence or in writing to the court.

Supply of documents from court records

5.1 An arbitration claim form may only be inspected with the permission of the court.

62.7—Case management

6.1 The following directions apply unless the court orders otherwise.

6.2 A defendant who wishes to rely on evidence before the court must file and serve his written evidence—

(1) within 21 days after the date by which he was required to acknowledge service; or,
(2) where a defendant is not required to file an acknowledgement of service, within 21 days after service of the arbitration claim form.

6.3 A claimant who wishes to rely on evidence in reply to written evidence filed under paragraph 6.2 must file and serve his written evidence within 7 days after service of the defendant's evidence.

6.4 Agreed indexed and paginated bundles of all the evidence and other documents to be used at the hearing must be prepared by the claimant.

6.5 Not later than 5 days before the hearing date estimates for the length of the hearing must be filed together with a complete set of the documents to be used.

6.6 Not later than 2 days before the hearing date the claimant must file and serve—

(1) a chronology of the relevant events cross-referenced to the bundle of documents;
(2) (where necessary) a list of the persons involved; and
(3) a skeleton argument which lists succinctly—
    (a) the issues which arise for decision;
    (b) the grounds of relief (or opposing relief) to be relied upon;
    (c) the submissions of fact to be made with the references to the evidence; and
    (d) the submissions of law with references to the relevant authorities.

6.7 Not later than the day before the hearing date the defendant must file and serve a skeleton argument which lists succinctly—

(1) the issues which arise for decision;

(2) the grounds of relief (or opposing relief) to be relied upon;
(3) the submissions of fact to be made with the references to the evidence; and
(4) the submissions of law with references to the relevant authorities.

Securing the attendance of witnesses

7.1 A party to arbitral proceedings being conducted in England or Wales who wishes to rely on section 43 of the 1996 Act to secure the attendance of a witness must apply for a witness summons in accordance with Part 34.

7.2 If the attendance of the witness is required within the district of a district registry, the application may be made at that registry.

7.3 A witness summons will not be issued until the applicant files written evidence showing that the application is made with—

(1) the permission of the tribunal; or
(2) the agreement of the other parties.

Interim remedies

8.1 An application for an interim remedy under section 44 of the 1996 Act must be made in an arbitration claim form.

Applications under sections 32 and 45 of the 1996 Act

9.1 This paragraph applies to arbitration claims for the determination of—

(1) a question as to the substantive jurisdiction of the arbitral tribunal under section 32 of the 1996 Act; and
(2) a preliminary point of law under section 45 of the 1996 Act.

9.2 Where an arbitration claim is made without the agreement in writing of all the other parties to the arbitral proceedings but with the permission of the arbitral tribunal, the written evidence or witness statements filed by the parties must set out any evidence relied on by the parties in support of their contention that the court should, or should not, consider the claim.

9.3 As soon as practicable after the written evidence is filed, the court will decide whether or not it should consider the claim and, unless the court otherwise directs, will so decide without a hearing.

Decisions without a hearing

10.1 Having regard to the overriding objective the court may decide particular issues without a hearing. For example, as set out in paragraph 9.3, the question whether the court is satisfied as to the matters set out in section 32(2)(b) or section 45(2)(b) of the 1996 Act.

10.2 The court will generally decide whether to extend the time limit under section 70(3) of the 1996 Act without a hearing. Where the court makes an order extending the time limit, the defendant must file his written evidence within 21 days from service of the order.

62.9—Variation of time

11.1 An application for an order under rule 62.9(1)—

(1) before the period of 28 days has expired, must be made in a Part 23 application notice; and
(2) after the period of 28 days has expired, must be set out in a separately identified part in the arbitration claim form.

Applications for permission to appeal

12.1 Where a party seeks permission to appeal to the court on a question of law arising out of an arbitration award, the arbitration claim form must—

(1) identify the question of law; and
(2) state the grounds

on which the party alleges that permission should be given.

12.2 The written evidence in support of the application must set out any evidence relied on by the party for the purpose of satisfying the court—

(1) of the matters referred to in section 69(3) of the 1996 Act; and
(2) that permission should be given.

12.3 The written evidence filed by the respondent to the application must—

(1) state the grounds on which the respondent opposes the grant of permission;
(2) set out any evidence relied on by him relating to the matters mentioned in section 69(3) of the 1996 Act; and
(3) specify whether the respondent wishes to contend that the award should be upheld for reasons not expressed (or not fully expressed) in the award and, if so, state those reasons.

12.4 The court will normally determine applications for permission to appeal without an oral hearing.

12.5 Where the court refuses an application for permission to appeal without an oral hearing, it must provide brief reasons.

12.6 Where the court considers that an oral hearing is required, it may give such further directions as are necessary.

SECTION II

13.1 This Section of this Practice Direction applies to arbitration claims to which Section II of Part 62 applies.

62.13—Starting the claim

14.1 An arbitration claim must be started in the Commercial Court and, where required to be heard by a judge, be heard by a judge of that court unless he otherwise directs.

SECTION III

15.1 This Section of this Practice Direction applies to enforcement proceedings to which Section III of Part 62 applies.

62.21—Registration of awards under the Arbitration (International Investment Disputes) Act 1966

16.1 Awards ordered to be registered under the 1966 Act and particulars will be entered in the Register kept for that purpose at the Admiralty and Commercial Registry.

APPENDIX 7

UNCITRAL MODEL LAW ON INTERNATIONAL COMMERCIAL ARBITRATION

(As adopted by the United Nations Commission on International Trade Law on 21 June 1985, and as amended by the United Nations Commission on International Trade Law on 7 July 2006)

CHAPTER I. GENERAL PROVISIONS

Article 1. Scope of application

(1) This Law applies to international commercial arbitration, subject to any agreement in force between this State and any other State or States.

(2) The provisions of this Law, except articles 8, 9, 17H, 17I, 17J, 35 and 36, apply only if the place of arbitration is in the territory of this State.

(3) An arbitration is international if:

- (a) the parties to an arbitration agreement have, at the time of the conclusion of that agreement, their places of business in different States; or
- (b) one of the following places is situated outside the State in which the parties have their places of business:
  - (i) the place of arbitration if determined in, or pursuant to, the arbitration agreement;
  - (ii) any place where a substantial part of the obligations of the commercial relationship is to be performed or the place with which the subject-matter of the dispute is most closely connected; or
- (c) the parties have expressly agreed that the subject-matter of the arbitration relates to more than one country:
  - (i) in the interpretation of this Law, regard is to be had to its international origin and to the need to promote uniformity in its application and the observance of good faith;
  - (ii) questions concerning matters governed by this Law the arbitration agreement relates to more than one country.

(4) For the purposes of paragraph (3) of this article:

- (a) if a party has more than one place of business, the place of business is that which has the closest relationship to the arbitration agreement;
- (b) if a party does not have a place of business, reference is to be made to his habitual residence.

(5) This Law shall not affect any other law of this State by virtue of which certain disputes may not be submitted to arbitration or may be submitted to arbitration only according to provisions other than those of this Law.

Article 2. Definitions and rules of interpretation

For the purposes of this Law:

- (a) "arbitration" means any arbitration whether or not administered by a permanent arbitral institution;
- (b) "arbitral tribunal" means a sole arbitrator or a panel of arbitrators;
- (c) "court" means a body or organ of the judicial system of a State;
- (d) where a provision of this Law, except article 28, leaves the parties free to determine a certain issue, such freedom includes the right of the parties to authorize a third party, including an institution, to make that determination;

(e) where a provision of this Law refers to the fact that the parties have agreed or that they may agree or in any other way refers to an agreement of the parties, such agreement includes any arbitration rules referred to in that agreement;

(f) where a provision of this Law, other than in articles 25(a) and 32(2)(a), refers to a claim, it also applies to a counter-claim, and where it refers to a defence, it also applies to a defence to such counter-claim.

Article 2A. International origin and general principles

(1) In the interpretation of this Law, regard is to be had to its international origin and to the need to promote uniformity in its application and the observance of good faith.

(2) Questions concerning matters governed by this Law which are not expressly settled in it are to be settled in conformity with the general principles on which this Law is based.

Article 3. Receipt of written communications

(1) Unless otherwise agreed by the parties:

(a) any written communication is deemed to have been received if it is delivered to the addressee personally or if it is delivered at his place of business, habitual residence or mailing address; if none of these can be found after making a reasonable inquiry, a written communication is deemed to have been received if it is sent to the addressee's last-known place of business, habitual residence or mailing address by registered letter or any other means which provides a record of the attempt to deliver it;

(b) the communication is deemed to have been received on the day it is so delivered.

(2) The provisions of this article do not apply to communications in court proceedings.

Article 4. Waiver of right to object

A party who knows that any provision of this Law from which the parties may derogate or any requirement under the arbitration agreement has not been complied with and yet proceeds with the arbitration without stating his objection to such non-compliance without undue delay or, if a time-limit is provided therefor, within such period of time, shall be deemed to have waived his right to object.

Article 5. Extent of court intervention

In matters governed by this Law, no court shall intervene except where so provided in this Law.

Article 6. Court or other authority for certain functions of arbitration assistance and supervision

The functions referred to in articles 11(3), 11(4), 13(3), 14, 16(3) and 34(2) shall be performed by . . . [Each State enacting this model law specifies the court, courts or, where referred to therein, other authority competent to perform these functions.]

CHAPTER II. ARBITRATION AGREEMENT

Option I

Article 7. Definition and form of arbitration agreement

(1) "Arbitration agreement" is an agreement by the parties to submit to arbitration all or certain disputes which have arisen or which may arise between them in respect of a defined legal relationship, whether contractual or not. An arbitration agreement may be in the form of an arbitration clause in a contract or in the form of a separate agreement.

(2) The arbitration agreement shall be in writing.

(3) An arbitration agreement is in writing if its content is recorded in any form, whether or not the arbitration agreement or contract has been concluded orally, by conduct, or by other means.

(4) The requirement that an arbitration agreement be in writing is met by an electronic communication if the information contained therein is accessible so as to be useable for subsequent reference; "electronic communication" means any communication that the parties make by means of data messages; "data message" means information generated, sent, received or stored by electronic, magnetic, optical or similar means, including, but not limited to, electronic data interchange (EDI), electronic mail, telegram, telex or telecopy.

(5) Furthermore, an arbitration agreement is in writing if it is contained in an exchange of statements of claim and defence in which the existence of an agreement is alleged by one party and not denied by the other.

(6) The reference in a contract to any document containing an arbitration clause constitutes an arbitration agreement in writing, provided that the reference is such as to make that clause part of the contract.

Option II

Article 7. Definition of arbitration agreement

"Arbitration agreement" is an agreement by the parties to submit to arbitration all or certain disputes which have arisen or which may arise between them in respect of a defined legal relationship, whether contractual or not.

Article 8. Arbitration agreement and substantive claim before court

(1) A court before which an action is brought in a matter which is the subject of an arbitration agreement shall, if a party so requests not later than when submitting his first statement on the substance of the dispute, refer the parties to arbitration unless it finds that the agreement is null and void, inoperative or incapable of being performed.

(2) Where an action referred to in paragraph (1) of this article has been brought, arbitral proceedings may nevertheless be commenced or continued, and an award may be made, while the issue is pending before the court.

Article 9. Arbitration agreement and interim measures by court

It is not incompatible with an arbitration agreement for a party to request, before or during arbitral proceedings, from a court an interim measure of protection and for a court to grant such measure.

CHAPTER III. COMPOSITION OF ARBITRAL TRIBUNAL

Article 10. Number of arbitrators

(1) The parties are free to determine the number of arbitrators.

(2) Failing such determination, the number of arbitrators shall be three.

Article 11. Appointment of arbitrators

(1) No person shall be precluded by reason of his nationality from acting as an arbitrator, unless otherwise agreed by the parties.

(2) The parties are free to agree on a procedure of appointing the arbitrator or arbitrators, subject to the provisions of paragraphs (4) and (5) of this article.

(3) Failing such agreement:

(a) in an arbitration with three arbitrators, each party shall appoint one arbitrator, and the two arbitrators thus appointed shall appoint the third arbitrator; if a party fails to appoint the arbitrator within thirty days of receipt of a request to do so from the other party, or if the two arbitrators fail to agree on the third arbitrator within thirty days of their appointment, the appointment shall be made, upon request of a party, by the court or other authority specified in article 6;

(b) in an arbitration with a sole arbitrator, if the parties are unable to agree on the arbitrator, he shall be appointed, upon request of a party, by the court or other authority specified in article 6.

(4) Where, under an appointment procedure agreed upon by the parties,

(a) a party fails to act as required under such procedure, or

(b) the parties, or two arbitrators, are unable to reach an agreement expected of them under such procedure, or

(c) a third party, including an institution, fails to perform any function entrusted to it under such procedure,

any party may request the court or other authority specified in article 6 to take the necessary measure, unless the agreement on the appointment procedure provides other means for securing the appointment.

(5) A decision on a matter entrusted by paragraph (3) or (4) of this article to the court or other authority specified in article 6 shall be subject to no appeal. The court or other authority, in appointing an arbitrator, shall have due regard to any qualifications required of the arbitrator by the agreement of the parties and to such considerations as are likely to secure the appointment of an independent and impartial arbitrator and, in the case of a sole or third arbitrator, shall take into account as well the advisability of appointing an arbitrator of a nationality other than those of the parties.

Article 12. Grounds for challenge

(1) When a person is approached in connection with his possible appointment as an arbitrator, he shall disclose any circumstances likely to give rise to justifiable doubts as to his impartiality or independence. An arbitrator, from the time of his appointment and throughout the arbitral proceedings, shall without delay disclose any such circumstances to the parties unless they have already been informed of them by him.

(2) An arbitrator may be challenged only if circumstances exist that give rise to justifiable doubts as to his impartiality or independence, or if he does not possess qualifications agreed to by the parties. A party may challenge an arbitrator appointed by him, or in whose appointment he has participated, only for reasons of which he becomes aware after the appointment has been made.

Article 13. Challenge procedure

(1) The parties are free to agree on a procedure for challenging an arbitrator, subject to the provisions of paragraph (3) of this article.

(2) Failing such agreement, a party who intends to challenge an arbitrator shall, within fifteen days after becoming aware of the constitution of the arbitral tribunal or after becoming aware of any circumstance referred to in article 12(2), send a written statement of the reasons for the challenge to the arbitral tribunal. Unless the challenged arbitrator withdraws from his office or the other party agrees to the challenge, the arbitral tribunal shall decide on the challenge.

(3) If a challenge under any procedure agreed upon by the parties or under the procedure of paragraph (2) of this article is not successful, the challenging party may request, within thirty days after having received notice of the decision rejecting the challenge, the court or other authority specified in article 6 to decide on the challenge, which decision shall be subject to no appeal; while such a request is pending, the arbitral tribunal, including the challenged arbitrator, may continue the arbitral proceedings and make an award.

Article 14. Failure or impossibility to act

(1) If an arbitrator becomes *de jure* or *de facto* unable to perform his functions or for other reasons fails to act without undue delay, his mandate terminates if he withdraws from his office or if the

parties agree on the termination. Otherwise, if a controversy remains concerning any of these grounds, any party may request the court or other authority specified in article 6 to decide on the termination of the mandate, which decision shall be subject to no appeal.

(2) If, under this article or article 13(2), an arbitrator withdraws from his office or a party agrees to the termination of the mandate of an arbitrator, this does not imply acceptance of the validity of any ground referred to in this article or article 12(2).

Article 15. Appointment of substitute arbitrator

Where the mandate of an arbitrator terminates under article 13 or 14 or because of his withdrawal from office for any other reason or because of the revocation of his mandate by agreement of the parties or in any other case of termination of his mandate, a substitute arbitrator shall be appointed according to the rules that were applicable to the appointment of the arbitrator being replaced.

CHAPTER IV. JURISDICTION OF ARBITRAL TRIBUNAL

Article 16. Competence of arbitral tribunal to rule on its jurisdiction

(1) The arbitral tribunal may rule on its own jurisdiction, including any objections with respect to the existence or validity of the arbitration agreement. For that purpose, an arbitration clause which forms part of a contract shall be treated as an agreement independent of the other terms of the contract. A decision by the arbitral tribunal that the contract is null and void shall not entail *ipso jure* the invalidity of the arbitration clause.

(2) A plea that the arbitral tribunal does not have jurisdiction shall be raised not later than the submission of the statement of defence. A party is not precluded from raising such a plea by the fact that he has appointed, or participated in the appointment of, an arbitrator. A plea that the arbitral tribunal is exceeding the scope of its authority shall be raised as soon as the matter alleged to be beyond the scope of its authority is raised during the arbitral proceedings. The arbitral tribunal may, in either case, admit a later plea if it considers the delay justified.

(3) The arbitral tribunal may rule on a plea referred to in paragraph (2) of this article either as a preliminary question or in an award on the merits. If the arbitral tribunal rules as a preliminary question that it has jurisdiction, any party may request, within thirty days after having received notice of that ruling, the court specified in article 6 to decide the matter, which decision shall be subject to no appeal; while such a request is pending, the arbitral tribunal may continue the arbitral proceedings and make an award.

CHAPTER IV(A). INTERIM MEASURES AND PRELIMINARY ORDERS

Section 1. Interim measures

Article 17. Power of arbitral tribunal to order interim measures

(1) Unless otherwise agreed by the parties, the arbitral tribunal may, at the request of a party, grant interim measures.

(2) An interim measure is any temporary measure, whether in the form of an award or in another form, by which, at any time prior to the issuance of the award by which the dispute is finally decided, the arbitral tribunal orders a party to:

(a) Maintain or restore the status quo pending determination of the dispute;
(b) Take action that would prevent, or refrain from taking action that is likely to cause, current or imminent harm or prejudice to the arbitral process itself;
(c) Provide a means of preserving assets out of which a subsequent award may be satisfied; or
(d) Preserve evidence that may be relevant and material to the resolution of the dispute.

Article 17A. Conditions for granting interim measures

(1) The party requesting an interim measure under article 17(2)(a), (b) and (c) shall satisfy the arbitral tribunal that:

(a) Harm not adequately reparable by an award of damages is likely to result if the measure is not ordered, and such harm substantially outweighs the harm that is likely to result to the party against whom the measure is directed if the measure is granted; and
(b) There is a reasonable possibility that the requesting party will succeed on the merits of the claim. The determination on this possibility shall not affect the discretion of the arbitral tribunal in making any subsequent determination.

(2) With regard to a request for an interim measure under article 17(2)(d), the requirements in paragraphs (1)(a) and (b) of this article shall apply only to the extent the arbitral tribunal considers appropriate.

Section 2. Preliminary orders

Article 17B. Applications for preliminary orders and conditions for granting preliminary orders

(1) Unless otherwise agreed by the parties, a party may, without notice to any other party, make a request for an interim measure together with an application for a preliminary order directing a party not to frustrate the purpose of the interim measure requested.

(2) The arbitral tribunal may grant a preliminary order provided it considers that prior disclosure of the request for the interim measure to the party against whom it is directed risks frustrating the purpose of the measure.

(3) The conditions defined under article 17A apply to any preliminary order, provided that the harm to be assessed under article 17A(1)(a), is the harm likely to result from the order being granted or not.

Article 17C. Specific regime for preliminary orders

(1) Immediately after the arbitral tribunal has made a determination in respect of an application for a preliminary order, the arbitral tribunal shall give notice to all parties of the request for the interim measure, the application for the preliminary order, the preliminary order, if any, and all other communications, including by indicating the content of any oral communication, between any party and the arbitral tribunal in relation thereto.

(2) At the same time, the arbitral tribunal shall give an opportunity to any party against whom a preliminary order is directed to present its case at the earliest practicable time.

(3) The arbitral tribunal shall decide promptly on any objection to the preliminary order.

(4) A preliminary order shall expire after twenty days from the date on which it was issued by the arbitral tribunal. However, the arbitral tribunal may issue an interim measure adopting or modifying the preliminary order, after the party against whom the preliminary order is directed has been given notice and an opportunity to present its case.

(5) A preliminary order shall be binding on the parties but shall not be subject to enforcement by a court. Such a preliminary order does not constitute an award.

Section 3. Provisions applicable to interim measures and preliminary orders

Article 17D. Modification, suspension, termination

The arbitral tribunal may modify, suspend or terminate an interim measure or a preliminary order it has granted, upon application of any party or, in exceptional circumstances and upon prior notice to the parties, on the arbitral tribunal's own initiative.

Article 17E. Provision of security

(1) The arbitral tribunal may require the party requesting an interim measure to provide appropriate security in connection with the measure.

(2) The arbitral tribunal shall require the party applying for a preliminary order to provide security in connection with the order unless the arbitral tribunal considers it inappropriate or unnecessary to do so.

Article 17F. Disclosure

(1) The arbitral tribunal may require any party promptly to disclose any material change in the circumstances on the basis of which the measure was requested or granted.

(2) The party applying for a preliminary order shall disclose to the arbitral tribunal all circumstances that are likely to be relevant to the arbitral tribunal's determination whether to grant or maintain the order, and such obligation shall continue until the party against whom the order has been requested has had an opportunity to present its case. Thereafter, paragraph (1) of this article shall apply.

Article 17G. Costs and damages

The party requesting an interim measure or applying for a preliminary order shall be liable for any costs and damages caused by the measure or the order to any party if the arbitral tribunal later determines that, in the circumstances, the measure or the order should not have been granted. The arbitral tribunal may award such costs and damages at any point during the proceedings.

Section 4. Recognition and enforcement of interim measures

Article 17H. Recognition and enforcement

(1) An interim measure issued by an arbitral tribunal shall be recognized as binding and, unless otherwise provided by the arbitral tribunal, enforced upon application to the competent court, irrespective of the country in which it was issued, subject to the provisions of article 17I.

(2) The party who is seeking or has obtained recognition or enforcement of an interim measure shall promptly inform the court of any termination, suspension or modification of that interim measure.

(3) The court of the State where recognition or enforcement is sought may, if it considers it proper, order the requesting party to provide appropriate security if the arbitral tribunal has not already made a determination with respect to security or where such a decision is necessary to protect the rights of third parties.

Article 17I. Grounds for refusing recognition or enforcement

(1) Recognition or enforcement of an interim measure may be refused only:

(a) At the request of the party against whom it is invoked if the court is satisfied that:

- (i) such refusal is warranted on the grounds set forth in article 36(1)(a)(i), (ii), (iii) or (iv); or
- (ii) the arbitral tribunal's decision with respect to the provision of security in connection with the interim measure issued by the arbitral tribunal has not been complied with; or
- (iii) the interim measure has been terminated or suspended by the arbitral tribunal or, where so empowered, by the court of the State in which the arbitration takes place or under the law of which that interim measure was granted; or

(b) If the court finds that:

- (i) the interim measure is incompatible with the powers conferred upon the court unless the court decides to reformulate the interim measure to the extent necessary to adapt it to its own powers and procedures for the purposes of enforcing that interim measure and without modifying its substance; or

(ii) any of the grounds set forth in article 36(1)(b)(i) or (ii), apply to the recognition and enforcement of the interim measure.

(2) Any determination made by the court on any ground in paragraph (1) of this article shall be effective only for the purposes of the application to recognize and enforce the interim measure. The court where recognition or enforcement is sought shall not, in making that determination, undertake a review of the substance of the interim measure.

Section 5. Court-ordered interim measures

Article 17J. Court-ordered interim measures

A court shall have the same power of issuing an interim measure in relation to arbitration proceedings, irrespective of whether their place is in the territory of this State, as it has in relation to proceedings in courts. The court shall exercise such power in accordance with its own procedures in consideration of the specific features of international arbitration.

CHAPTER V. CONDUCT OF ARBITRAL PROCEEDINGS

Article 18. Equal treatment of parties

The parties shall be treated with equality and each party shall be given a full opportunity of presenting his case.

Article 19. Determination of rules of procedure

(1) Subject to the provisions of this Law, the parties are free to agree on the procedure to be followed by the arbitral tribunal in conducting the proceedings.

(2) Failing such agreement, the arbitral tribunal may, subject to the provisions of this Law, conduct the arbitration in such manner as it considers appropriate. The power conferred upon the arbitral tribunal includes the power to determine the admissibility, relevance, materiality and weight of any evidence.

Article 20. Place of arbitration

(1) The parties are free to agree on the place of arbitration. Failing such agreement, the place of arbitration shall be determined by the arbitral tribunal having regard to the circumstances of the case, including the convenience of the parties.

(2) Notwithstanding the provisions of paragraph (1) of this article, the arbitral tribunal may, unless otherwise agreed by the parties, meet at any place it considers appropriate for consultation among its members, for hearing witnesses, experts or the parties, or for inspection of goods, other property or documents.

Article 21. Commencement of arbitral proceedings

Unless otherwise agreed by the parties, the arbitral proceedings in respect of a particular dispute commence on the date on which a request for that dispute to be referred to arbitration is received by the respondent.

Article 22. Language

(1) The parties are free to agree on the language or languages to be used in the arbitral proceedings. Failing such agreement, the arbitral tribunal shall determine the language or languages to be used in the proceedings. This agreement or determination, unless otherwise specified therein, shall apply to any written statement by a party, any hearing and any award, decision or other communication by the arbitral tribunal.

(2) The arbitral tribunal may order that any documentary evidence shall be accompanied by a translation into the language or languages agreed upon by the parties or determined by the arbitral tribunal.

Article 23. Statements of claim and defence

(1) Within the period of time agreed by the parties or determined by the arbitral tribunal, the claimant shall state the facts supporting his claim, the points at issue and the relief or remedy sought, and the respondent shall state his defence in respect of these particulars, unless the parties have otherwise agreed as to the required elements of such statements. The parties may submit with their statements all documents they consider to be relevant or may add a reference to the documents or other evidence they will submit.

(2) Unless otherwise agreed by the parties, either party may amend or supplement his claim or defence during the course of the arbitral proceedings, unless the arbitral tribunal considers it inappropriate to allow such amendment having regard to the delay in making it.

Article 24. Hearings and written proceedings

(1) Subject to any contrary agreement by the parties, the arbitral tribunal shall decide whether to hold oral hearings for the presentation of evidence or for oral argument, or whether the proceedings shall be conducted on the basis of documents and other materials. However, unless the parties have agreed that no hearings shall be held, the arbitral tribunal shall hold such hearings at an appropriate stage of the proceedings, if so requested by a party.

(2) The parties shall be given sufficient advance notice of any hearing and of any meeting of the arbitral tribunal for the purposes of inspection of goods, other property or documents.

(3) All statements, documents or other information supplied to the arbitral tribunal by one party shall be communicated to the other party. Also any expert report or evidentiary document on which the arbitral tribunal may rely in making its decision shall be communicated to the parties.

Article 25. Default of a party

Unless otherwise agreed by the parties, if, without showing sufficient cause,

(a) the claimant fails to communicate his statement of claim in accordance with article 23(1), the arbitral tribunal shall terminate the proceedings;

(b) the respondent fails to communicate his statement of defence in accordance with article 23(1), the arbitral tribunal shall continue the proceedings without treating such failure in itself as an admission of the claimant's allegations;

(c) any party fails to appear at a hearing or to produce documentary evidence, the arbitral tribunal may continue the proceedings and make the award on the evidence before it.

Article 26. Expert appointed by arbitral tribunal

(1) Unless otherwise agreed by the parties, the arbitral tribunal

(a) may appoint one or more experts to report to it on specific issues to be determined by the arbitral tribunal;

(b) may require a party to give the expert any relevant information or to produce, or to provide access to, any relevant documents, goods or other property for his inspection.

(2) Unless otherwise agreed by the parties, if a party so requests or if the arbitral tribunal considers it necessary, the expert shall, after delivery of his written or oral report, participate in a hearing where the parties have the opportunity to put questions to him and to present expert witnesses in order to testify on the points at issue.

Article 27. Court assistance in taking evidence

The arbitral tribunal or a party with the approval of the arbitral tribunal may request from a competent court of this State assistance in taking evidence. The court may execute the request within its competence and according to its rules on taking evidence.

CHAPTER VI. MAKING OF AWARD AND TERMINATION OF PROCEEDINGS

Article 28. Rules applicable to substance of dispute

(1) The arbitral tribunal shall decide the dispute in accordance with such rules of law as are chosen by the parties as applicable to the substance of the dispute. Any designation of the law or legal system of a given State shall be construed, unless otherwise expressed, as directly referring to the substantive law of that State and not to its conflict of laws rules.

(2) Failing any designation by the parties, the arbitral tribunal shall apply the law determined by the conflict of laws rules which it considers applicable.

(3) The arbitral tribunal shall decide *ex aequo et bono* or as *amiable compositeur* only if the parties have expressly authorized it to do so.

(4) In all cases, the arbitral tribunal shall decide in accordance with the terms of the contract and shall take into account the usages of the trade applicable to the transaction.

Article 29. Decision making by panel of arbitrators

In arbitral proceedings with more than one arbitrator, any decision of the arbitral tribunal shall be made, unless otherwise agreed by the parties, by a majority of all its members. However, questions of procedure may be decided by a presiding arbitrator, if so authorized by the parties or all members of the arbitral tribunal.

Article 30. Settlement

(1) If, during arbitral proceedings, the parties settle the dispute, the arbitral tribunal shall terminate the proceedings and, if requested by the parties and not objected to by the arbitral tribunal, record the settlement in the form of an arbitral award on agreed terms.

(2) An award on agreed terms shall be made in accordance with the provisions of article 31 and shall state that it is an award. Such an award has the same status and effect as any other award on the merits of the case.

Article 31. Form and contents of award

(1) The award shall be made in writing and shall be signed by the arbitrator or arbitrators. In arbitral proceedings with more than one arbitrator, the signatures of the majority of all members of the arbitral tribunal shall suffice, provided that the reason for any omitted signature is stated.

(2) The award shall state the reasons upon which it is based, unless the parties have agreed that no reasons are to be given or the award is an award on agreed terms under article 30.

(3) The award shall state its date and the place of arbitration as determined in accordance with article 20(1). The award shall be deemed to have been made at that place.

(4) After the award is made, a copy signed by the arbitrators in accordance with paragraph (1) of this article shall be delivered to each party.

Article 32. Termination of proceedings

(1) The arbitral proceedings are terminated by the final award or by an order of the arbitral tribunal in accordance with paragraph (2) of this article.

(2) The arbitral tribunal shall issue an order for the termination of the arbitral proceedings when:

- (a) the claimant withdraws his claim, unless the respondent objects thereto and the arbitral tribunal recognizes a legitimate interest on his part in obtaining a final settlement of the dispute;
- (b) the parties agree on the termination of the proceedings;
- (c) the arbitral tribunal finds that the continuation of the proceedings has for any other reason become unnecessary or impossible.

(3) The mandate of the arbitral tribunal terminates with the termination of the arbitral proceedings, subject to the provisions of articles 33 and 34(4).

Article 33. Correction and interpretation of award; additional award

(1) Within thirty days of receipt of the award, unless another period of time has been agreed upon by the parties:

(a) a party, with notice to the other party, may request the arbitral tribunal to correct in the award any errors in computation, any clerical or typographical errors or any errors of similar nature;
(b) if so agreed by the parties, a party, with notice to the other party, may request the arbitral tribunal to give an interpretation of a specific point or part of the award.

If the arbitral tribunal considers the request to be justified, it shall make the correction or give the interpretation within thirty days of receipt of the request. The interpretation shall form part of the award.

(2) The arbitral tribunal may correct any error of the type referred to in paragraph (1)(a) of this article on its own initiative within thirty days of the date of the award.

(3) Unless otherwise agreed by the parties, a party, with notice to the other party, may request, within thirty days of receipt of the award, the arbitral tribunal to make an additional award as to claims presented in the arbitral proceedings but omitted from the award. If the arbitral tribunal considers the request to be justified, it shall make the additional award within sixty days.

(4) The arbitral tribunal may extend, if necessary, the period of time within which it shall make a correction, interpretation or an additional award under paragraph (1) or (3) of this article.

(5) The provisions of article 31 shall apply to a correction or interpretation of the award or to an additional award.

CHAPTER VII. RECOURSE AGAINST AWARD

Article 34. Application for setting aside as exclusive recourse against arbitral award

(1) Recourse to a court against an arbitral award may be made only by an application for setting aside in accordance with paragraphs (2) and (3) of this article.

(2) An arbitral award may be set aside by the court specified in article 6 only if:

(a) the party making the application furnishes proof that:
  (i) a party to the arbitration agreement referred to in article 7 was under some incapacity; or the said agreement is not valid under the law to which the parties have subjected it or, failing any indication thereon, under the law of this State; or
  (ii) the party making the application was not given proper notice of the appointment of an arbitrator or of the arbitral proceedings or was otherwise unable to present his case; or
  (iii) the award deals with a dispute not contemplated by or not falling within the terms of the submission to arbitration, or contains decisions on matters beyond the scope of the submission to arbitration, provided that, if the decisions on matters submitted to arbitration can be separated from those not so submitted, only that part of the award which contains decisions on matters not submitted to arbitration may be set aside; or
  (iv) the composition of the arbitral tribunal or the arbitral procedure was not in accordance with the agreement of the parties, unless such agreement was in conflict with a provision of this Law from which the parties cannot derogate, or, failing such agreement, was not in accordance with this Law; or
(b) the court finds that:
  (i) the subject-matter of the dispute is not capable of settlement by arbitration under the law of this State; or
  (ii) the award is in conflict with the public policy of this State.

(3) An application for setting aside may not be made after three months have elapsed from the date on which the party making that application had received the award or, if a request had been made under article 33, from the date on which that request had been disposed of by the arbitral tribunal.

(4) The court, when asked to set aside an award, may, where appropriate and so requested by a party, suspend the setting aside proceedings for a period of time determined by it in order to give the arbitral tribunal an opportunity to resume the arbitral proceedings or to take such other action as in the arbitral tribunal's opinion will eliminate the grounds for setting aside.

CHAPTER VIII. RECOGNITION AND ENFORCEMENT OF AWARDS

Article 35. Recognition and enforcement

(1) An arbitral award, irrespective of the country in which it was made, shall be recognized as binding and, upon application in writing to the competent court, shall be enforced subject to the provisions of this article and of article 36.

(2) The party relying on an award or applying for its enforcement shall supply the original award or a copy thereof. If the award is not made in an official language of this State, the court may request the party to supply a translation thereof into such language.

Article 36. Grounds for refusing recognition or enforcement

(1) Recognition or enforcement of an arbitral award, irrespective of the country in which it was made, may be refused only:

- (a) at the request of the party against whom it is invoked, if that party furnishes to the competent court where recognition or enforcement is sought proof that:
  - (i) a party to the arbitration agreement referred to in article 7 was under some incapacity; or the said agreement is not valid under the law to which the parties have subjected it or, failing any indication thereon, under the law of the country where the award was made; or
  - (ii) the party against whom the award is invoked was not given proper notice of the appointment of an arbitrator or of the arbitral proceedings or was otherwise unable to present his case; or
  - (iii) the award deals with a dispute not contemplated by or not falling within the terms of the submission to arbitration, or it contains decisions on matters beyond the scope of the submission to arbitration, provided that, if the decisions on matters submitted to arbitration can be separated from those not so submitted, that part of the award which contains decisions on matters submitted to arbitration may be recognized and enforced; or
  - (iv) the composition of the arbitral tribunal or the arbitral procedure was not in accordance with the agreement of the parties or, failing such agreement, was not in accordance with the law of the country where the arbitration took place; or
  - (v) the award has not yet become binding on the parties or has been set aside or suspended by a court of the country in which, or under the law of which, that award was made; or
- (b) if the court finds that:
  - (i) the subject-matter of the dispute is not capable of settlement by arbitration under the law of this State; or
  - (ii) the recognition or enforcement of the award would be contrary to the public policy of this State.

(2) If an application for setting aside or suspension of an award has been made to a court referred to in paragraph (1)(a)(v) of this article, the court where recognition or enforcement is sought may, if it considers it proper, adjourn its decision and may also, on the application of the party claiming recognition or enforcement of the award, order the other party to provide appropriate security.

[We gratefully acknowledge the assistance of the United Nations Commission on International Trade Law (UNCITRAL) and their kind permission to reproduce their copy material.]

APPENDIX 8

DEPARTMENTAL ADVISORY COMMITTEE
ON ARBITRATION LAW

REPORT ON THE ARBITRATION BILL*

February 1996

Chairman: The Rt Hon Lord Justice Saville QC
Members of the Committee: Professor J M Hunter (Deputy Chairman); Miss C R Allen (Secretary); Mr P Bovey; Mr A W S Bunch; Mrs S C Boyd QC; Dr K G Chrystie; Lord Dervaird; Mr J B Garrett; Professor R M Goode CBE, QC, FBA; Mr B Harris; Mrs J Howe; Mrs P Kirby-Johnson; Mr R A MacCrindle QC; Mr A L Marriott; Mr K S Rokison QC; Mr D Sarre; Mr J H M Sims; Professor D R Thomas; Professor J Uff QC; Mr V V Veeder QC.
The DAC has been greatly assisted by the invaluable work done by Mr T T Landau of counsel.

CONTENTS

CHAPTER 1—INTRODUCTION

1. In its Report of June 1989, the Departmental Advisory Committee on Arbitration Law (the DAC), under the chairmanship of Lord Justice Mustill (now Lord Mustill) recommended against England, Wales and Northern Ireland adopting the UNCITRAL Model Law on International Commercial Arbitration. Instead, the DAC recommended that there should be a new and improved Arbitration Act for England, Wales and Northern Ireland, with the following features (Paragraph 108):

"(1) It should comprise a statement in statutory form of the more important principles of the English law of arbitration, statutory and (to the extent practicable) common law.
(2) It should be limited to those principles whose existence and effect are uncontroversial.
(3) It should be set out in a logical order, and expressed in language which is sufficiently clear and free from technicalities to be readily comprehensible to the layman.
(4) It should in general apply to domestic and international arbitrations alike, although there may have to be exceptions to take account of treaty obligations.
(5) It should not be limited to the subject-matter of the Model Law.
(6) It should embody such of our proposals for legislation as have by then been enacted: see paragraph 100 [of the 1989 Report].
(7) Consideration should be given to ensuring that any such new statute should, so far as possible, have the same structure and language as the Model Law, so as to enhance its accessibility to those who are familiar with the Model Law."

2. In an Interim Report in April 1995, the DAC stated as follows:

> "The original interpretation of [paragraph 108 of the 1989 Report] led to the draft Bill which was circulated in February 1994. Although undoubtedly a highly skilful piece of work it now appears that this draft Bill did not carry into effect what most users in fact wanted. In the light of the responses, the view of the DAC is that a new Bill should still be grounded on the objectives set out in [paragraph 108 of the 1989 Report], but that, reinterpreted, what is called for is much more along the lines of a restatement of the law, in clear and 'user-friendly' language, following as far as possible, the structure and spirit of the Model Law, rather than simply a classic exercise in consolidation."

3. The DAC's proposals in the Interim Report led to a new draft Bill which was circulated for public consultation in July 1995. This draft was very much the product of a fresh start. Indeed, it will be noted that whereas the February 1994 draft had the following long-title:

> "To consolidate, with amendments, the Arbitration Act 1950, the Arbitration Act 1975, the Arbitration Act 1979 and related enactments"

this was altered for the July 1995 draft, and now begins:

> "An Act to restate and improve the law relating to arbitration pursuant to an arbitration agreement . . . "

4. The DAC remained of the view, for the reasons given in the Mustill Report, that the solution was not the wholesale adoption of the Model Law. However, at every stage in preparing a new draft Bill, very close regard was paid to the Model Law, and it will be seen that both the structure and the content of the July draft Bill, and the final draft, owe much to this model.

5. The task of the Committee has been made far easier by the extraordinary quantity and quality of responses we received both to the draft Bill published in February 1994 and to the draft Bill which was published in July 1995. A large number of people put substantial time and effort into responding to both drafts and putting forward suggestions, and we are very grateful to all of them. Indeed, both these consultation exercises have proved invaluable: the former showed that a new approach was required, while the latter showed that our April 1995 proposals seemed to be on the right track. Both sets of responses also contained carefully considered suggestions, many of which have been incorporated in the Bill. It should be emphasised that those suggestions which have not been adopted were only put on one side after lengthy consideration.

6. Among those who responded were a large number of institutions who offer arbitration services (such as the ICC) or who provide rules and administration for arbitrations concerning their members (such as the commodity associations). Both domestically and internationally institutions such as these play a very significant role in the field of arbitration. It seemed to us that the Bill should specifically recognise this, and that it should safeguard their spheres of operation. Consequently, there are many references to such institutions in the Bill, and, indeed, Clause 74 gives them what we believe to be a necessary degree of immunity from suit.

7. Given the extremely favourable response, the July 1995 draft was taken forward, with certain modifications, to form the basis of the final draft, which is explained in this Report.

8. As well as containing a guide to the provisions of the final draft, this Report also contains supplementary recommendations (in Chapter 6) on certain matters that have come to light since publication of the final draft, and since its second reading in the House of Lords.

CHAPTER 2—PART I OF THE BILL

9. The title to this Part is *Arbitration Pursuant to an Arbitration Agreement*. It is in this Part that we have attempted to restate within a logical structure the basic principles of our law of arbitration, as it relates to arbitration under an agreement to adopt this form of dispute resolution. The Bill does not purport to provide an exhaustive code on the subject of arbitration. It would simply not be practicable to attempt to codify the huge body of case law that has built up over the centuries, and there would be a risk of fossilising the common law (which has the great advantage of being able to adapt to changing circumstances) had we attempted to do so. Rather, we have sought to include what we consider to be the more important common law principles, whilst preserving all others, in so far as they are consistent with the provisions of the Bill (see Clause 81).

10. A small number of key areas, however, have not been included, precisely because they are unsettled, and because they are better left to the common law to evolve. One such example concerns privacy and confidentiality in arbitrations, which deserves special mention here.

11. Privacy and confidentiality have long been assumed as general principles in English commercial arbitration, subject to important exceptions. It is only recently that the English courts have been required to examine both the legal basis for such principles and the breadth of certain of these exceptions, without seriously questioning the existence of the general principles themselves (see e.g. *The Eastern Saga* [1988] 2 Lloyd's Rep. 373, 379 (Leggatt LJ); *Dolling-Baker* v. *Merrett* [1990] 1 WLR 1205, 1213 (Parker LJ); *Hassneh* v. *Mew* [1993] 2 Lloyd's Rep. 243 (Colman J); *Hyundai Engineering* v. *Active* (unreported, 9 March 1994, Phillips J); *Ins Company* v. *Lloyd's Syndicate* [1995] 2 Lloyd's Rep. 272 (Colman J); *London & Leeds Estates Limited* v. *Parisbas Limited (No. 2)* (1995) E.G. 134 (Mance J)).

12. In practice, there is also no doubt whatever that users of commercial arbitration in England place much importance on privacy and confidentiality as essential features of English arbitrations (e.g. see survey of users amongst the "Fortune 500" US corporations conducted for the LCIA by the London Business School in 1992). Indeed, as Sir Patrick Neill QC stated in his 1995 "Bernstein" Lecture, it would be difficult to conceive of any greater threat to the success of English arbitration than the removal of the general principles of confidentiality and privacy.

13. Last year's decision of the High Court of Australia in *Esso/BHP* v. *Plowman* (see [1995] 11 Arb. Int. 234) reinforced many people's interest in seeking to codify the relevant English legal principles in the draft Arbitration Bill. The implied term as the contractual basis for such principles was not in doubt under English law, and the English Courts were upholding these principles in strong and unequivocal terms. However, the Australian decision was to the effect that, as a matter of Australian law, this contractual approach was unsustainable as regards confidentiality. This has troubled users of commercial arbitration far outside Australia. The first response has been for arbitral institutions to amend their arbitration rules to provide expressly for confidentiality and privacy. The new WIPO Rules have sought to achieve this and we understand that both the ICC and the LCIA are currently amending their respective rules to similar effect.

14. In England, the second response was to consider placing these general principles on a firm statutory basis in the Arbitration Bill. This task was initially undertaken by the DAC mid-1995, and perhaps surprisingly, it soon proved controversial and difficult.

15. Whilst none could reasonably dispute the desirability of placing these general principles beyond all doubt on a firm statutory basis, applicable to all English arbitrations within the scope of the Bill (irrespective of the substantive law applicable to the arbitration agreement), grave difficulties arose over the myriad exceptions to these principles which are necessarily required for such a statutory provisions. There is of course no statutory guidance to confidentiality in the UNICTRAL Model Law whatever; and indeed, in a different context, Lord Mustill has recently warned against an attempt to give in the abstract an accurate exposition of confidentiality at large (see *In re D (Adoption Reports: Confidentiality)* [1995] 3 WLR 483, 496DL: "To give an accurate exposition of confidentiality at large would require a much more wide-ranging survey of the law and practice than has been necessary for a decision on the narrow issue raised by the appeal, and cannot in my opinion safely be attempted in the abstract.")

16. For English arbitration, the exceptions to confidentiality are manifestly legion and unsettled in part; and equally, there are important exceptions to privacy (e.g. in *The Lena Goldfields Case* (1930), the arbitration tribunal in London opened the hearing to the press (but not the public) in order to defend the proceedings against malicious charges made by one of the parties, the USSR). As to the former, the award may become public in legal proceedings under the Arbitration Acts 1950–1979 or abroad under the 1958 New York Convention; the conduct of the arbitration may also become public if subjected to judicial scrutiny within or without England; and most importantly, several non-parties have legitimate interests in being informed as to the content of a pending arbitration, even short of an award: e.g. parent company, insurer, P&I Club, guarantor, partner, beneficiary, licensor and licensee, debenture-holder, creditors' committee etc., and of course even the arbitral institution itself (such as the ICC Court members approving the draft award). Whilst non-parties to the arbitration agreement and proceedings, none of these are officious strangers to the arbitration. Further, any provisions as to privacy and confidentiality would have to deal with the duty of a company to make disclosure of, e.g., arbitration proceedings and actual or potential awards which have an effect on the company's financial position. The further Australian decision in *Commonwealth of Australia* v. *Cockatoo Dockyard Pty Ltd* (1995) 36 NSWLR 662 suggests that the public interest may also demand transparency as an exception to confidentiality: "Can it be seriously suggested that [the] parties private agreement can, endorsed by a procedural direction of an arbitrator, exclude from the public domain matters of legitimate concern . . . " per Kirby J. This decision raises fresh complications, particularly for statutory corporations. We are of the view that it would be extremely harmful to English arbitration if any statutory statement of general principles in this area impeded the commercial good-sense of current practices in English arbitration.

17. Given these exceptions and qualifications, the formulation of any statutory principles would be likely to create new impediments to the practice of English arbitration and, in particular, to add to English litigation on the issue. Far from solving a difficulty, the DAC was firmly of the view that it would create new ones. Indeed, even if acceptable statutory guidelines could be formulated, there would remain the difficulty of fixing and enforcing sanctions for non-compliance. The position is not wholly satisfactory. However, none doubt at English law the existence of the general principles of confidentiality and privacy (though there is not unanimity as to their desirability). Where desirable, institutional rules can stipulate for these general principles, even where the arbitration agreement is not governed by English law. As to English law itself, whilst the breadth and existence of certain exceptions remains disputed, these can be resolved by the English courts on a pragmatic case-by-case basis. In due course, if the whole matter were ever to become judicially resolved, it would remain possible to add a statutory provision by way of amendment to the Bill. For these reasons, the DAC is of the view that no attempt should be made to codify English law on the privacy and confidentiality of English arbitration in the Bill. We would, however, draw attention to our supplementary recommendations on this topic in Chapter 6 below.

Clause 1. General principles

18. The DAC was persuaded by the significant number of submissions which called for an introductory clause setting out basic principles. This Clause sets out three general principles. The first of these reflects what we believe to be the object of arbitration. We have not sought to define arbitration, since this poses difficulties that we discussed in our April 1995 Interim Report, and in the end we were not persuaded that an attempted definition would serve any useful purpose. We do,

however, see value in setting out the object of arbitration. Fairness, impartiality and the avoidance of unnecessary delay or expense are all aspects of justice, i.e. all requirements of a dispute resolution system based on obtaining a binding decision from a third party on the matters at issue. To our minds it is useful to stipulate that all the provisions of the Bill must be read with this object of arbitration in mind.

19. The second principle is that of party autonomy. This reflects the basis of the Model Law and indeed much of our own present law. An arbitration under an arbitration agreement is a consensual process. The parties have agreed to resolve their disputes by their own chosen means. Unless the public interest otherwise dictates, this has two main consequences. Firstly, the parties should be held to their agreement and secondly, it should in the first instance be for the parties to decide how their arbitration should be conducted. In some cases, of course, the public interest will make inroads on complete party autonomy, in much of the same way as there are limitations on freedom of contract. Some matters are simply not susceptible of this form of dispute resolution (e.g. certain cases concerning status or many family matters) while other considerations (such as consumer protection) may require the imposition of different rights and obligations. Again, as appears from the mandatory provisions of the Bill, there are some rules that cannot be overridden by parties who have agreed to use arbitration. In general the mandatory provisions are there in order to support and assist the arbitral process and the stated object of arbitration.

20. So far as the third principle is concerned this reflects Article 5 of the Model Law. This Article provides as follows:

> "In matters governed by this Law, no court shall intervene except where so provided in this Law."

21. As was pointed out in the Mustill Report (pp. 50–52) there would be difficulties in importing this Article as it stands. However, there is no doubt that our law has been subject to international criticism that the Courts intervene more than they should in the arbitral process, thereby tending to frustrate the choice the parties have made to use arbitration rather than litigation as the means for resolving their disputes.

22. Nowadays the Courts are much less inclined to intervene in the arbitral process than used to be the case. The limitation on the right of appeal to the Courts from awards brought into effect by the Arbitration Act 1979, and changing attitudes generally, have meant that the Courts nowadays generally only intervene in order to support rather than displace the arbitral process. We are very much in favour of this modern approach and it seems to us that it should be enshrined as a principle in the Bill.

Clause 2. Scope of application of provisions

23. International arbitrations can give rise to complex problems in the conflict of laws. A possible solution to some of these problems would have been to provide that all arbitrations conducted in England and Wales or in Northern Ireland should be subject to the provisions of the Bill, regardless of the parties' express or implied choice of some other system of law. We have not adopted this solution, which appears to us contrary to the basic principle that the parties should be free to agree how their disputes should be resolved. There appear to us to be no reasons of public policy to prevent the parties conducting an arbitration here under an agreement governed by foreign law or in accordance with a foreign procedural law. Clause 4(5) also follows the same basic principle. Of course, cases may well arise where considerations of our own concepts of public policy would lead to the refusal of the Court here to enforce an arbitration award. This, however, is covered by Clause 66(3).

24. The rules of the conflict of laws as they apply to arbitration are complex, and to some extent still in a state of development by the courts. It therefore seems to us inappropriate to attempt to codify the relevant principles, beyond the simple statements set out in clause 2(1). Thus, as clause 2(2) provides, matters referable to the arbitration agreement are governed by the law of England and Wales or of Northern Ireland, as the case may be, where that it the law applicable to the arbitration agreement, and matters of procedure are governed by that law where the seat of the arbitration is in England and Wales or in Northern Ireland: "seat" is defined in Clause 3. Beyond that we have not attempted to state the relevant rules of the conflict of laws, nor to embark on the issues of characterisation by which they are invoked.

25. Subsection (3) concerns the powers of the court to support the arbitration by staying proceedings brought in breach of an agreement to arbitrate, by compelling the attendance of witnesses, by granting those forms of interim relief which are set out in Clause 44, and by enforcing the award at common law by summary procedure. Such powers should obviously be available regardless of whether the seat of the arbitration is in England and Wales or in Northern Ireland, and regardless of what law is applicable to the arbitration agreement or the arbitral proceedings. Since we have used the expression "whatever the law applicable . . . ", it follows that Clause 2(3) is in no way restricted by Clause 2(1). It will be noted that in extending the power of the court to grant interim relief in support of arbitrations to arbitrations having a foreign seat we have given effect to our recommendation that section 25 of the Civil Jurisdiction and Judgments Act 1982 should be extended to arbitration proceedings. It should be appreciated that Rules of Court will have to be amended to give proper effect to the extension of the Court's jurisdiction in Clause 2(3) (i.e. so as to allow service out of the jurisdiction in cases where it is necessary). Subsection (4) enables the court to refuse to exercise its power in such cases, where the fact that the arbitration has a foreign seat makes it inappropriate to exercise that power.

Clause 3. The seat of the arbitration

26. The definition of "seat of the arbitration" is required by Clause 2, and as part of the definition of "domestic arbitration" in Clause 85. The concept of the "seat" as the juridical seat of the arbitration is known to English law but may be unfamiliar to some users of arbitration. Usually it will be the place where the arbitration is actually conducted: but this is not necessarily so, particularly if different parts of the proceedings are held in different countries.

27. In accordance with the principle of party autonomy, Clause 3 provides that the seat may be designated by the parties themselves or in some other manner authorised by them. Failing that it must be determined objectively having regard to the parties' agreement and all other relevant circumstances. English law does not at present recognise the concept of an arbitration which has no seat, and we do not recommend that it should do so. The powers of the court where the seat is in England and Wales or in Northern Ireland are limited to those necessary to carry into effect the principles enshrined in Clause 1. Where the seat is elsewhere, the court's powers are further limited by Clause 2(4). The process of consultation identified no need for an arbitration which was "delocalised" to a greater extent than this.

Clause 4. Mandatory and non-mandatory provisions

28. This provision is designed to make clear that the Bill has certain provisions that cannot be overridden by the parties; and for ease of reference these are listed in Schedule 1 to the Bill. The Clause also makes clear that the other provisions of this Part can be changed or substituted by the parties, and exist as "fall-back" rules that will apply if the parties do not make any such change or substitution, or do not provide for the particular matter in question. In this way, in the absence of any other contrary agreement, gaps in an arbitration agreement will be filled.

29. Subsection (5). Although we believe that the choice of a foreign law would anyway have the effect set out in this provision, it seemed for the sake of clarity to be useful to state this expressly, so as to remind all concerned that a choice of a foreign law does amount to an agreement of the parties to which due regard should be paid.

30. It should be made clear that the phrase "mandatory" is not used in either of the two senses that it is used, for example, in Articles 3 and 7 of the Rome Convention (see Goode, *Commercial Law*, 2nd Ed, at p. 1118); the mandatory provisions of Part I of the Bill are only mandatory in so far as the provisions of Part I apply (i.e. by virtue of Clause 2). The mandatory provisions would have no application if Part I does not apply.

Clause 5. Agreements to be in writing

(a) Arbitration agreements

31. Article 7 of the Model Law requires the arbitration agreement to be in writing. We have not followed the precise wording of this Article, for the reasons given in the Mustill Report (p. 52), though we have incorporated much of that Article in the Bill.

32. The requirement for the arbitration agreement to be in writing is the position at present under Section 32 of the Arbitration Act 1950 and Section 7 of the Arbitration Act 1975. If an arbitration agreement is not in writing then it is not completely ineffective, since the common law recognises such agreements and is saved by Clause 81(2)(a).

33. We remain of the view expressed in the Consultative Paper issued with the draft Clauses published in July 1995, that there should be a requirement of writing. An arbitration agreement has the important effect of contracting out of the right to go to the court, i.e. it deprives the parties of that basic right. To our minds an agreement of such importance should be in some written form. Furthermore the need for such form should help to reduce disputes as to whether or not an arbitration agreement was made and as to its terms.

34. We have, however, provided a very wide meaning to the words "in writing". Indeed this meaning is wider than that found in the Model Law, but in our view, is consonant with Article II.2 of the English text of the New York Convention. The non-exhaustive definition in the English text ("shall include") may differ in this respect from the French and Spanish texts, but the English text is equally authentic under Article XVI of the New York Convention itself, and also accords with the Russian authentic text ("КЛЮЧАЕТ"); see also the 1989 Report of the Swiss Institute of Comparative Law on Jurisdictional Problems in International Commercial Arbitration (by Adam Samuel), at pp. 81–85. It seems to us that English Law as it stands more than justifies this wide meaning; see, for example, *Zambia Steel* v. *James Clark* [1986] 2 Lloyd's Rep. 225. In view of rapidly evolving methods of recording we have made clear that "writing" includes recording by any means.

(b) Other agreements

35. These we have also made subject to a "writing" requirement. Had we not done so, we could envisage disputes over whether, for example, something the parties had agreed to during the conduct of the arbitration amounted to a variation of the arbitration agreement and required writing, or could be characterised as something else. By introducing some formality with respect to all agreements, the possibility of subsequent disputes (e.g. at the enforcement stage) is greatly diminished. Indeed it seemed to us that with the extremely broad definition we have given to writing, the advantages of requiring some record of what was agreed with regard to any aspect of an arbitration outweighed the disadvantages of requiring a specific form for an effective agreement.

(c) Further points

36. Subsection 5(3). This is designed to cover, amongst other things, extremely common situations such as salvage operations, where parties make an oral agreement which incorporates by reference the terms of a written form of agreement (e.g. Lloyd's Open Form), which contains an arbitration clause. Whilst greatly extending the definition of "writing", the DAC is of the view that given the frequency and importance of such activity, it was essential that it be provided for in the Bill. The reference could be to a written agreement containing an arbitration clause, or to a set of written arbitration rules, or to an individual written arbitration agreement. This provision would also cover agreement by conduct. For example, party A may agree to buy from party B a quantity of goods on certain terms and conditions (which include an arbitration clause) which are set out in writing and sent to party B, with a request that he sign and return the order form. If, which is by no means uncommon, party B fails to sign the order form, or send any document in response to the order, but manufactures and delivers the goods in accordance with the contract to party A, who pays for them in accordance with the contract, this could constitute an agreement "otherwise than in writing by reference to terms which are in writing . . . ", and could therefore include an effective arbitration agreement. The provision therefore seeks to meet the criticisms that have been made of Article 7(2) of the Model Law in this regard (see, e.g., the Sixth Goff Lecture, delivered by Neil Kaplan QC in Hong Kong in November 1995, (1996) 12 Arb.Int. 35). A written agreement made by reference to separate written terms would, of course, be caught by Clause 5(2).

37. Subsection 5(4). There has been some concern that a writing requirement with respect to every agreement might unduly constrain the parties' freedom and flexibility with respect to, for example, minor matters of procedure during a hearing. This subsection seeks to avoid this. An agreement will be evidenced in writing if recorded by, amongst others, a third party with the

authority of the parties to the agreement. Given that this third party could of course be the tribunal, the parties are free during a hearing to make whatever arrangements or changes to the agreed procedure they wish, as long as these are recorded by the tribunal. The DAC is of the view that this presents no serious hindrance to the parties' flexibility, and has the merit of reducing the risk of disputes later on as to what exactly was agreed. Clearly, this subsection also has a wider effect, allowing for the recording of an oral agreement at any stage.

38. Subsection 5(5). This provisions is based on Article 7(2) of the Model Law, but with certain important changes. The DAC has been careful to emphasise that for there to be an effective arbitration agreement for the purposes of this Part, it is not enough for one party to allege in a written submission that there is an arbitration agreement, in circumstances where the other party simply fails to respond at all. If this were enough, an unfair obligation would be placed on any party (including a stranger to the proceedings in question) to take the active step of serving a written submission in order to deny this allegation. Therefore, in order to satisfy this subsection, there must be a failure to deny an allegation by a party who has submitted a response submission.

39. It has been suggested that the term "written submissions" is too narrow, and that this should be replaced by "documents". The DAC does not agree with this, given that this would include the most informal of letters. It may well be unjust, for example, for one party to be able to point to one sentence in one letter in a long exchange with another party, in which there is an allegation that there exists an arbitration clause, and where this has not been denied.

40. Reference should also be made to subsection 23(4). Whilst any agreement as to an arbitration must be in writing, the DAC is of the view that it is impracticable to impose a writing requirement on an agreement to terminate an arbitration. Parties may well simply walk away from proceedings, or allow the proceedings to lapse, and it could be extremely unfair if one party were allowed to rely upon an absence of writing at some future stage. Where a claimant allows an arbitration to lapse, Clause 41(3) may be utilised.

THE ARBITRATION AGREEMENT

Clause 6. Definition of arbitration agreement

41. The first subsection reflects Article 7(1) of the Model Law and provides a more informative definition than that in Section 32 of the 1950 Act. We have used the word "disputes" but this is defined in Clause 82 as including "differences" since there is some authority for the proposition that the latter term is wider than the former; see *Sykes* v. *Fine Fare Ltd* [1967] 1 Lloyd's Rep. 53.

42. The second subsection reflects Article 7(2) of the Model Law. In English law there is at present some conflicting authority on the question as to what is required for the effective incorporation of an arbitration clause by reference. Some of those responding to the July 1995 draft Clauses made critical comments of the views of Sir John Megaw in *Aughton* v. *M F Kent Services* [1991] 57 BLR 1 (a construction contract case) and suggested that we should take the opportunity of making clear that the law was as stated in the charter party cases and as summarised by Ralph Gibson LJ in *Aughton*. (Similar disquiet has been expressed about decisions following *Aughton*, such as *Ben Barrett* v. *Henry Boot Management Ltd* [1995] Constr.Ind.Law Letter 1026.) It seemed to us, however, that although we are of the view that the approach of Ralph Gibson LJ should prevail in all cases, this was really a matter for the Court to decide. The wording we have used certainly leaves room for the adoption of the charter party rules in all cases, since it refers to references to a document containing an arbitration clause as well as a reference to the arbitration clause itself. Thus the wording is not confined to cases where there is specific reference to the arbitration clause, which Sir John Megaw (but not Ralph Gibson LJ) considered was a requirement for effective incorporation by reference.

Clause 7. Separability of arbitration agreement

43. This Clause sets out the principle of separability which is already part of English law (see *Harbour Assurance* v. *Kansa* [1993] QB 701), which is also to be found in Article 16(1) of the Model Law, and which is regarded internationally as highly desirable. However, it seems to us that the doctrine of separability is quite distinct from the questions of the degree to which the tribunal

is entitled to rule on its own jurisdiction, so that, unlike the Model Law, we have dealt with the latter elsewhere in the Bill (Clause 30).

44. In the draft Clauses published in July 1995 we inserted a provision to make clear that the doctrine of separability did not affect the question whether an assignment of rights under the substantive agreement carried with it the right or obligation to submit to arbitration in accordance with the arbitration agreement. This is now omitted as being unnecessary, since we have re-drafted subsection (1) in order to follow the relevant part of Article 16 of the Model Law more closely, and to make clear that the doctrine of separability is confined to the effect of invalidity etc of the main contract on the arbitration agreement, rather than being, as it was in the July 1995 draft, a free-standing principle. Similarly, in being so restricted, this Clause is not intended to have any impact on the incorporation of an arbitration clause from one document or contract into another (which is addressed in Clause 6(2)).

45. A number of those responding to our drafts expressed the wish for the Bill to lay down rules relating to assignment, e.g. that the assignment of rights under the substantive agreement should be subject to any right or obligation to submit to arbitration in accordance with the arbitration agreement unless either of these agreements provided otherwise. Indeed we included such a provision in the illustrative draft published in April 1995. However, on further consideration, we concluded that it would not be appropriate to seek to lay down any such rules.

46. There were two principal reasons for reaching this view.

(i) In the first place, under English law the assignability of a contractual right is governed by the proper law of that right, while the effectiveness of the assignment is governed by the proper law of the assignment. However, where the law governing the substantive agreement (or the arbitration agreement) is not English law, different rules may well apply and there is an added problem in that those rules (under the foreign law in question) may be categorised as either substantive or procedural in nature. The Bill would therefore have to address such problems whilst simultaneously not interfering with substantive rights and obligations. We were not persuaded that it would be either practicable or of any real use to attempt to devise general rules which would deal satisfactorily with this matter.

(ii) In the second place, English law distinguishes between legal and equitable assignments, so that any rules we devised would have to take this into account. In our view, an attempt to devise rules relating to assignments where no foreign law elements are involved is more the subject of reform of the law of assignment generally than of a Bill relating exclusively to arbitration.

47. Finally, it should be noted that the substantive agreement of which the arbitration agreement forms part need not itself be in writing for the Bill to apply, provided of course that the arbitration agreement itself is in writing. This should be clarified as we suggest in our supplementary recommendations in Chapter 6 below.

Clause 8. Whether agreement discharged by death of a party

48. This Clause sets out the present statutory position. The common law was that an arbitration agreement was discharged by the death of a party. That rule was altered by the Arbitration Act 1934 as re-enacted by Section 2 of the Arbitration Act 1950. We have avoided using the technical expression "right of action" which is to be found in Section 2(3) of the 1950 Act and which could perhaps give rise to problems for the reasons given in the consultative paper published with the draft Clauses in July 1995. In line with party autonomy, we have provided that the parties can agree that death shall have the effect of discharging the arbitration agreement.

49. This Clause deals only with the arbitration agreement. The effect of the death of a party on the appointment of an arbitrator (also to be found in Section 2 of the 1950 Act) is now dealt with in that part of the Bill concerned with the arbitral tribunal (see Clause 26(2)).

STAY OF LEGAL PROCEEDINGS

Clause 9. Stay of legal proceedings

50. We have proposed a number of changes to the present statutory position (section 4(1) of the 1950 Act and section 1 of the 1975 Act), having in mind Article 8 of the Model Law, our treaty obligations, and other considerations.

51. We have made it clear that a stay can be sought of a counterclaim as well as a claim. The existing legislation could be said not to cover counterclaims, since it required the party seeking a stay first to enter an "appearance", which a defendant to counterclaim could not do. Indeed, "appearance" is no longer the appropriate expression in the High Court in any event, and never was the appropriate expression in the county court. We have also made clear that an application can be made to stay part of legal proceedings, where other parts are not subject to an agreement to arbitrate.

52. Further, the Clause provides that an application is only to be made by a party against whom legal proceedings are brought (as opposed to any other party).

53. We have provided that an application may be made for a stay even where the matter cannot be referred to arbitration immediately, because the parties have agreed first to use other dispute resolution procedures. This reflects dicta of Lord Mustill in *Channel Tunnel* v. *Balfour Beatty* [1993] AC 334.

54. In this Clause we have made a stay mandatory unless the Court is satisfied that the arbitration agreement is null and void, inoperative, or incapable of being performed. This is the language of the Model Law and of course of the New York Convention on the Recognition and Enforcement of Foreign Arbitral Awards, presently to be found in the Arbitration Act 1975.

55. The Arbitration Act 1975 contained a further ground for refusing a stay, namely where the Court was satisfied that "there was not in fact any dispute between the parties with regard to the matter agreed to be referred". These words do not appear in the New York Convention and in our view are confusing and unnecessary, for the reasons given in *Hayter* v. *Nelson* [(*No. 2*)] [1990] 2 Lloyd's Rep. 265.

56. In Part II of the Bill these provisions are altered in cases of "domestic arbitration agreements" as there defined.

57. We have included a provision (subsection (5)) that where the Court refuses to stay the legal proceedings, any term making an award a condition precedent to the bringing of legal proceedings (known as a *Scott* v. *Avery* clause) will cease to have effect. This avoids a situation where the arbitration clause is unworkable, yet no legal proceedings can be successfully brought. Whilst one respondent suggested that this may go too far, it appears to be a matter of basic justice that a situation in which a party can neither arbitrate nor litigate must be avoided.

Clause 10. Reference of interpleader issue to arbitration

58. This Clause is based on Section 5 of the 1950 Act. We have however taken the opportunity of making a stay mandatory so as to comply with the New York Convention, as well as trying to express the provision in simpler, clearer terms. The Clause is required because "interpleader" arises where one party claiming no right himself in the subject matter, is facing conflicting claims from other parties and does not know to which of them he should account. English law allows such a party to bring those in contention before the Court which may order the latter to fight out the question between themselves. If they have agreed to arbitrate the matter then Clause 9 would not itself operate, since the party seeking interpleader relief would not be making a claim which he had agreed to arbitrate.

59. We have not defined "interpleader", although some suggested that we should, given that this is a legal term of art, which goes far beyond arbitration contexts.

Clause 11. Retention of security where Admiralty proceedings stayed

60. This Clause is not intended to do more than re-enact the present statutory position as found in section 26 of the Civil Jurisdiction and Judgments Act 1982.

61. Clauses 9 to 11 are, of course, mandatory.

COMMENCEMENT OF ARBITRAL PROCEEDINGS

Clause 12. Power of court to extend time for beginning arbitral proceedings, etc.

62. We have proposed a number of changes to the existing law.

63. The major change concerns the test that *the* Court must apply before extending the time.

64. The power of the Court to extend a contractual time limit which would otherwise bar the claim first appeared in our law in section 16(6) of the Arbitration Act 1934, which was re-enacted in section 27 of the Arbitration Act 1950.

65. From paragraph 33 of the Report of the MacKinnon Committee presented to Parliament in March 1927 it can be seen that the reason for suggesting that the Court should have power to extend the time was that the vast majority of submissions to arbitrations are contained in printed forms of contract, which cannot be carefully examined in the transaction of business and alteration of which it would be difficult for most people to secure. The Committee concluded that it might be sound policy to create a power to modify unconscionable provisions as regards common forms of submission in printed forms. It is also clear from paragraph 34 of the Report that the Committee had in mind cases where the time limit was very short, i.e. measured in days. The Committee suggested that the test should be whether the time limit created an "unreasonable hardship".

66. As can be seen from the Notes on Clauses to the 1934 Act, it was later felt that since the justification for giving the power was presumably either ignorance of the existence of the provision in the contract, or the acceptance of the provision through undue pressure by the other party, which could be the case whether or not the contract was in a common form, the power should not be limited to such forms.

67. Section 27 of the 1950 Act, with its test of undue hardship, seems to many to have been interpreted by the Courts in a way hardly envisaged by those who suggested the power in the first place. Indeed that interpretation seems to have changed over the years: see the discussion in Mustill and Boyd, *Commercial Arbitration*, 2nd Ed., pp. 201–215. Some responses indicated dissatisfaction with the way the Courts were using Clause 27 to interfere with the bargain that the parties had made. The present legal position would seem to owe much to a time, now some 20 years ago, when the Courts were flirting with the idea that they enjoyed some general power of supervisory jurisdiction over arbitrations.

68. The justification for time limits is that they enable commercial concerns (and indeed others) to draw a line beneath transactions at a much earlier stage than ordinary limitation provisions would allow. It should be mentioned, however, that other responses suggested that the position presently reached by the Courts should be maintained.

69. The present Committee re-examined section 27 in the light of the underlying philosophy of the Bill, namely that of party autonomy. This underlying philosophy seems to have been generally welcomed in this country and abroad and of course it fits with the general international understanding of arbitration. Party autonomy means, among other things, that any power given to the Court to override the bargain that the parties have made must be fully justified. The idea that the Court has some general supervisory jurisdiction over arbitrations has been abandoned.

70. It seemed to us in today's climate that there were three cases where the power could be justified in the context of agreed time limits to bring a claim. These are, firstly, where the circumstances are such as were outside the reasonable contemplation of the parties when they agreed the provision in question and that it would be fair to extend the time, secondly, where the conduct of one party made it unjust to hold the other to the time limit, and thirdly, where the respective bargaining position of the parties was such that it would again be unfair to hold one of them to the time limit.

71. The third of these cases seems to us to reflect the thinking of the MacKinnon Committee, while the other two have developed through the Courts' interpretation of section 27. However this third category is really an aspect of what nowadays would be called "consumer protection". This part of the Bill is not concerned with consumer protection, for which provision is made elsewhere and in respect of which there is a growing body of European law.

72. In these circumstances it seemed to us to be appropriate to set out in this part of the Bill the first and second of the cases we have described. Apart from anything else, this will give the Courts the opportunity to reconsider how to proceed in the light of the philosophy underlying the Bill as

a whole, namely that of party autonomy. As the MacKinnon Committee itself intimated, great care must be taken before interfering with the bargain that the parties have made.

73. It was suggested to the DAC that the principal matter to be taken into account by the court should be the length of the contractual period in question. The DAC is of the view that this is only one of several relevant matters, another factor being, for example, the contemplation of the parties. For this reason, the DAC concluded that a simple test of "substantial injustice", without more, would not suffice.

74. There are some other changes.

(i) Firstly, Clause 12(1)(b) contains a reference to other dispute resolution procedures. We understand that there is an increasing use of provisions which call for mediation and other alternative dispute resolution procedures to precede recourse to arbitration, so that we thought it proper to add this to the other step covered by the Clause, namely to begin arbitral proceedings. We do not intend to widen the scope of the Clause beyond this, so that unless the step in question is one of the two kinds described, the Clause will not operate. Thus this represents only a small but we think logical extension to the present law.

(ii) Secondly, it is made a pre-condition that the party concerned first exhausts any available arbitral process for obtaining an extension of time. In the view of the Committee it would be a rare case indeed where the Court extended the time in circumstances where there was such a process which had not resulted in an extension, for it would in the ordinary case be difficult if not impossible to persuade the Court that it would be just to extend the time or unjust not to do so, where by an arbitral process to which *ex hypothesi* the applying party had agreed, the opposite conclusion had been reached.

(iii) Thirdly, we have made any appeal from a decision of the Court under this Clause subject to the leave of that Court. It seems to us that there should be this limitation, and that in the absence of some important question of principle, leave should not generally be granted. We take the same view in respect of the other cases in the Bill where we propose that an appeal requires the leave of the Court.

(iv) Fourthly, whereas the existing statutory provision refers to terms of an agreement that provide that claims shall be "barred", this has been extended to read "barred, or the claimant's right extinguished".

75. For obvious reasons, this Clause is mandatory.

Clauses 13 and 14. Application of Limitation Acts and commencement of arbitral proceedings

76. The first of these provisions is designed to restate the present law. The reference to the Foreign Limitation Periods Act 1984 avoids (subject to the provisions of that Act) the imposition of an English limitation period where an applicable foreign law imposes a different period. The second provision reflects to a degree Article 21 of the Model Law, but sets out the various cases, including one not presently covered by the law. It will be noted that we have used the word "matter" rather than the word "disputes". This is to reflect the fact that a dispute is not the same as a claim; *cf.* Mustill and Boyd, *op. cit.* at p. 29 and *Commission for the New Towns* v. *Crudens* (1995) CILL 1035. The neutral word "matter" will cover both, so that an arbitration clause which refers to claims will be covered as well as one which refers to disputes.

77. Clause 13 is a mandatory provision.

THE ARBITRAL TRIBUNAL

Clause 15. The arbitral tribunal

78. Article 10(1) of the Model Law provides that the parties are free to determine the number of arbitrators. We have included a like provision.

79. Article 10(2) of the Model Law stipulates that failing such determination, the number of arbitrators shall be three. This we have not adopted, preferring the existing English rule that in the

absence of agreement the default number shall be one. The employment of three arbitrators is likely to be three times the cost of employing one, and it seems right that this extra burden should be available if the parties so choose, but not imposed on them. The provision for a sole arbitrator also accords but with common practice in this country, and the balance of responses the DAC received. The Model Law default does not, of course, cater for the situation where there are more than two parties to the arbitration.

Clause 16. Procedure for the appointment of arbitrators

80. Again we have had the Model Law (Article 11) very much in mind in drafting these provisions, though we have attempted to cater for more cases and also for the fact that under our law, there can be either an umpire or a chairman. We should note that this has caused some confusion abroad, particularly in the United States, where what we would describe as a "chairman" is called an "umpire". In Clauses 20 and 21 we set out the differences between these two which (in the absence of agreement between the parties) is the present position under English law.

81. The time limits we have imposed for appointments we consider to be fair and reasonable. They can be extended by the Court under Clause 79, but the power of the Court in this regard is limited as set out in that Clause. In the ordinary case we would not expect the Court to allow a departure from the Clause 16 time limits.

82. It might be noted that periods of 28 days, rather than 30 days (as in the Model Law) have been used throughout the Bill, in order to reduce the likelihood of a deadline expiring on a weekend.

Clause 17. Power in case of default to appoint sole arbitrator

83. This Clause is intended to replace the present rules concerning the appointment of a sole arbitrator where the other party is in default (section 7(b) of the 1950 Act). It only applies to a two party case. We have stipulated that the party in default must not only appoint his arbitrator within the specified period but also inform the other party that he has done so. This in our view is a significant improvement on the present law, where the defaulting party was under no obligation to say that he had made an appointment. This was calculated to cause unnecessary delay, confusion and expense.

84. Some of those responding objected to this Clause. The DAC, however, remains of the view that this provision is an example of the Court supporting the arbitral process, and reducing the opportunities available for a recalcitrant party. The DAC is advised that section 7(b) of the 1950 Act is used a great deal, and that its very existence constitutes a deterrent to those contemplating dilatory tactics. The alternative would be to simply provide for recourse to Court. This would be overly burdensome in most cases, and is available, in any event, under the provisions of the Bill.

85. It has been suggested that the Bill should set out grounds upon which the Court should exercise its discretion in Clause 17(3). The DAC is of the view, however, that this is best left for the Courts to develop, given the specific circumstances of each case, and in the light of the overall philosophy of the Bill.

86. One respondent queried the use of the word "refuses" in Clause 17(1). The advantage of this is that if a party does actually refuse to appoint an arbitrator, rather than simply failing to do so, the non-defaulting party need not wait for the expiration of the relevant time period within which the defaulting party may make such an appointment, but could use the mechanism in Clause 17 straight away.

Clause 18. Failure of appointment procedure

87. Again we have had the Model Law in mind when drafting this provision. The starting point is any agreement the parties may have made to deal with a failure of the appointment procedure. In the absence of any such agreement, the Court is given the power to make appointments. This is a classic case of the Court supporting and helping to carry through the arbitration process.

88. It will be noted that we have given the Court power to revoke any appointments already made. This is to cover the case where unless the Court took this step it might be suggested thereafter that the parties had not been fairly treated, since one had his own choice arbitrator while the other had an arbitrator imposed on him by the Court in circumstances that were no fault of his own. This

situation in fact arose in France in the *Dutco* case, where an award was invalidated for this reason.

89. The Model Law stipulates that there shall be no appeal from a decision of the Court. We have not gone as far as this, since there may well be questions of important general principle which would benefit from authoritative appellate guidance.

Clause 19. Court to have regard to agreed qualifications

90. This comes from Article 11(5) of the Model Law, which itself seeks to preserve as much of the parties' agreement as possible.

Clauses 20 and 21. Chairman and umpire

91. The parties are, of course, free to make what arrangements they like about the functions and powers of Chairmen or Umpires. We have set out what we believe to be the position under English law in the absence of any such agreement. As we understand the current position, in the absence of an agreement between the parties, an umpire can neither take part nor attend an arbitration until the arbitrators have disagreed.

92. A cause of delay and expense often exists under our umpire system where the umpire does not attend the proceedings and it is only at an advanced stage (when the arbitrators disagree) that he takes over, for much that has gone on may have to be repeated before him. Equally, the time and expense of an umpire may be wasted if he attends but the arbitrators are able to agree on everything. We have decided that it would be preferable to stipulate that (in the absence of agreement between the parties) the umpire should attend the proceedings (as opposed to taking part in the proceedings) and be supplied with the same documents and materials as the other arbitrators. We hope, however, that common sense will prevail and that the parties will make specific agreement over this question, tailored to the circumstances of the particular case.

93. Subsection 21(4) caused some concern amongst a few respondents, but this subsection simply reflects what is understood to be the current position.

94. We should record that we considered whether the peculiarly English concept of an umpire should be swept away in favour of the more generally used chaired tribunal. As we have pointed out above, in the United States what we would describe as a chairman is called an umpire. In the end we decided not to recommend this, and to continue to provide default provisions for those who wanted to continue to use this form of arbitral tribunal.

Clause 22. Decision-making where no chairman or umpire

95. We decided to include this situation for the sake of completeness, though the default provision can only work if there is unanimity or a majority. If there is neither, then it would appear that the arbitration agreement cannot operate, unless the parties can agree, or have agreed, what is to happen.

Clause 23. Revocation of arbitrator's authority

96. Statutory provisions making it impossible unilaterally to revoke the authority of an arbitrator have existed since 1833. The present Clause is designed to reflect the current position, save that we have imposed a writing requirement and thought it helpful to make express reference to arbitral institutions, etc. These of course only have such powers as the parties have agreed they shall have, so that strictly this provision is not necessary, but we consider that an express reference makes for clarity.

97. Some of those responding suggested that the parties' right to agree to revoke an arbitral appointment should be limited (e.g. that Court approval should be required in every case). The DAC has not adopted these suggestions since any tribunal is properly regarded as the parties' tribunal and to do so would derogate from the principle of party autonomy.

98. It will be seen that various terms are used in the Bill with respect to the termination of an arbitral appointment, such as "removal" and "revocation of authority". Different terms have been

adopted simply as a matter of correct English usage. The difference in terms is not intended to be of any legal significance.

99. Subsection 23(4). Whilst any agreement as to an arbitration must be in writing, as defined earlier, the DAC is of the view that it is impracticable to impose a writing requirement on an agreement to terminate an arbitration. Parties may well simply walk away from proceedings, or allow the proceedings to lapse, and it could be extremely unfair if one party were allowed to rely upon an absence of writing at some future stage. Where a Claimant allows an arbitration to lapse, Clause 41(3) may be utilised.

Clause 24. Power of court to remove arbitrator

100. We have set out the cases where the Court can remove an arbitrator.

101. The Model Law (Article 12) specifies justifiable doubts as to the independence (as well as impartiality) of an arbitrator as grounds for his removal. We have considered this carefully, but despite efforts to do so, no-one has persuaded us that, in consensual arbitrations, this is either required or desirable. It seems to us that lack of independence, unless it gives rise to justifiable doubts about the impartiality of the arbitrator, is of no significance. The latter is, of course, the first of our grounds for removal. If lack of independence were to be included, then this could only be justified if it covered cases where the lack of independence did not give rise to justifiable doubts about impartiality, for otherwise there would be no point including lack of independence as a separate ground.

102. We can see no good reason for including "non-partiality" lack of independence as a ground for removal and good reasons for not doing so. We do not follow what is meant to be covered by a lack of independence which does not lead to the appearance of partiality. Furthermore, the inclusion of independence would give rise to endless arguments, as it has, for example, in Sweden and the United State, where almost any connection (however remote) has been put forward to challenge the "independence" of an arbitrator. For example, it is often the case that one member of a barristers' Chambers appears as counsel before an arbitrator who comes from the same Chambers. Is that to be regarded, without more, as a lack of independence justifying the removal of the arbitrator? We are quite certain that this would not be the case in English law. Indeed the Chairman has so decided in a case in Chambers in the Commercial Court. We would also draw attention to the article "Barristers' Independence and Disclosure" by Kendall in (1992) 8 Arb. Int. 287. We would further note in passing that even the oath taken by those appointed to the International Court of Justice; and indeed to our own High Court, refers only to impartiality.

103. Further, there may well be situations in which parties desire their arbitrators to have familiarity with a specific field, rather than being entirely independent.

104. We should emphasise that we intend to lose nothing of significance by omitting reference to independence. Lack of this quality may well give rise to justifiable doubts about impartiality, which is covered, but if it does not then we cannot at present see anything of significance that we have omitted by not using this term.

105. We have included, as grounds for removal, the refusal or failure of an arbitrator properly to conduct the proceedings, as well as failing to use all reasonable despatch in conducting the proceedings or making an award, where the result has caused or will cause substantial injustice to the applicant. We trust that the Courts will not allow the first of these matters to be abused by those intent on disrupting the arbitral process. To this end we have included a provision allowing the tribunal to continue while an application is made. There is also Clause 73 which effectively requires a party to "put up or shut up" if a challenge is to be made.

106. We have every confidence that the Courts will carry through the intent of this part of the Bill, which is that it should only be available where the conduct of the arbitrator is such as to go so beyond anything that could reasonably be defended that substantial injustice has resulted or will result. The provision is not intended to allow the Court to substitute its own view as to how the arbitral proceedings should be conducted. Thus the choice by an arbitrator of a particular procedure, unless it breaches the duty laid on arbitrators by Clause 33, should on no view justify the removal of an arbitrator, even if the Court would not itself have adopted that procedure. In short, this ground only exists to cover what we hope will be the very rare case where an arbitrator so conducts the proceedings that it can fairly be said that instead of carrying through the object of arbitration as

stated in the Bill, he is in effect frustrating that object. Only if the Court confines itself in this way can this power of removal be justified as a measure supporting rather than subverting the arbitral process.

107. We have also made the exhaustion of any arbitral process for challenging an arbitrator a pre-condition to the right to apply to the Court. Again it will be a very rare case indeed where the Court will remove an arbitrator notwithstanding that that process has reached a different conclusion.

108. If an arbitrator is removed by the Court, we have given the Court power to make orders in respect of his remuneration. We would expect this power to be exercised where the behaviour of the arbitrator is inexcusable to the extent that this should be marked by depriving him of all or some of his fees and expenses. This subsection is also the subject of a supplementary recommendation in Chapter 6 below.

109. As a matter of justice, we have stipulated that an arbitrator is entitled to be heard on any application for his removal.

110. This is a mandatory provision. It seems to us that an agreement to contract out of the cases we specify would really be tantamount to an agreement to a dispute resolution procedure that is contrary to the basic principles set out in Clause 1.

Clause 25. Resignation of arbitrator

111. In theory it could be said that an arbitrator cannot unilaterally resign if this conflicts with the express or implied terms of his engagement. However, as a matter of practical politics an arbitrator who refuses to go on cannot be made to do so, though of course he may incur a liability for breach of his agreement to act.

112. In this Clause we have given an arbitrator who resigns the right to go to the Court to seek relief from any liability incurred through resigning and to make orders relating to his remuneration and expenses, unless the consequences of resignation have been agreed with the parties (e.g. by virtue of having adopted institutional rules).

113. We have chosen the words of subsection (1) with care so that the agreement referred to is confined to an agreement as to the consequences of resignation. A simple agreement not to resign (or only to resign in certain circumstances) with no agreement as to what will happen if this promise is broken is not within the subsection. This has to be so since otherwise (by virtue of subsection (2)), subsections (3) and (4) would never or hardly ever operate, for the arbitrator will not be under any liability or at risk as to his fees or expenses unless he is in breach by resigning.

114. In the July draft we suggested a provision which would have entitled the Court to grant relief in all circumstances including those where the arbitrator had made an agreement as to the consequences of his resignation. However, as the result of a response that we received we have concluded that where the parties have agreed with an arbitrator on the consequences it would be wrong to give the Court a power to adjust the position.

115. The reason we propose this is that circumstances may well arise in which it would be just to grant such relief to a resigning arbitrator. For example, the arbitrator may (reasonably) not be prepared to adopt a procedure agreed by the parties (i.e. under Clause 34) during the course of an arbitration, taking the view that his duty under Clause 33 conflicts with their suggestions (the relationship between the duty of arbitrators in Clause 33 and the freedom of the parties in Clause 34, is discussed in more detail below). Again, an arbitration may drag on for far longer than could reasonably have been expected when the appointment was accepted, resulting in an unfair burden on the arbitrator. In circumstances where the Court was persuaded that it was reasonable for the arbitrator to resign, it seems only right that the Court should be able to grant appropriate relief.

Clause 26. Death of arbitrator or person appointing him

116. This Clause complements Clause 8 and is included for the same reason. Clause 26(1) is mandatory—it is difficult to see how parties could agree otherwise.

Clause 27. Filling of vacancy, etc.

117. This Clause reflects Article 15 of the Model Law, but also deals with certain other important ancillary matters. It should be noted that we do not propose to re-enact the power given to the Court

under section 25 of the Arbitration Act 1950 to fill a vacancy created by its removal of an arbitrator. It seems to us that (in the absence of agreement between the parties) it is preferable for the original appointment procedure to be used, for otherwise (as in the *Dutco* case mentioned above) it might be argued that the parties were not being treated equally.

118. We have given the tribunal the right (when reconstituted) to determine to what extent the previous proceedings should stand, though we have also made clear that this does not affect any right a party may have to challenge what has happened.

119. Further, we have provided in Clause 27(5) that the fact of an arbitrator ceasing to hold office will not affect any appointment made by him (whether alone or jointly) of another arbitrator, unless the parties have otherwise agreed pursuant to Clause 27(1)(c).

Clause 28. Joint and several liability of parties to arbitrators for fees and expenses

120. Arbitration proceedings necessarily involve the incurring of expenditure. The arbitrators have to be paid, and the parties incur expense in presenting their cases to the tribunal. The issue of costs involves at least three quite discrete elements:

(i) As a matter of general contract law, arbitrators, experts, institutions and any other payees whatsoever are entitled to be paid what has been agreed with them by any of the parties. Therefore, for example, if a party appoints an arbitrator for an agreed fee, as a matter of general contract law (rather than anything in this Bill), that arbitrator is entitled to that fee.

(ii) It is generally accepted that all parties are jointly and severally liable for the fees of an arbitrator. This is an issue as to the entitlement of arbitrators, and as such is quite distinct from the third element.

(iii) As in court litigation, when one party is successful, that party should normally recover at least a proportion of his costs. This issue, being where the burden of costs should lie, is an issue as between the parties.

121. The Bill contains provisions as to costs and fees in two separate parts: the joint and several liability owed by the parties to the arbitrators (the second element) is addressed in this clause, whilst the third element (i.e. the responsibility for costs as between the parties) is addressed in Clauses 59–65. The first element, being a matter of general contract law, is not specifically addressed by either set of provisions, but is preserved in both. It is extremely important to distinguish between these provisions.

122. Clause 28 is concerned with the rights of the arbitrators in respect of fees and expenses. As subsection (5) makes clear, and as explained above, this provision is not concerned with which of the parties should (as between themselves) bear these costs as the result of the arbitration, which is dealt with later in the Bill, nor with any contractual right an arbitrator may have in respect of fees and expenses.

123. As we understand the present law, the parties are jointly and severally liable to the arbitrator for his fees and expenses. The present position seems to be that if these are agreed by one party, the other party becomes liable, even if he played no part in making that agreement; and circumstances may arise in which that party is unable to obtain a reduction of the amount by taxation. It seems to us that whilst arbitrators should be protected by this joint and several liability of the parties, a potentially unfair result must be avoided: a party who never agreed to the appointment by another party of an exceptionally expensive arbitrator should not be held jointly and severally liable for that arbitrator's exceptional fees. To this end, we have stipulated, in Clause 28(1), that a party's joint and several liability to an arbitrator only extends to "reasonable fees". Of course, if a party has agreed an exceptional fee with an arbitrator, that party may still be pursued by that arbitrator, under general contract law, which is preserved in Clause 28(5).

124. We have proposed a mechanism to allow a party to go to the Court if any question arises as to the reasonableness of the arbitrator's charges. The Court is empowered to adjust fees and expenses even after they have been paid, since circumstances may well arise in which a question about the level of fees and expenses only arises after payment has been made. For example, a large advance payment may be made at a time when it is considered that the arbitration will take a long time, but this does not turn out to be the case. However, the Court must be satisfied that it is

reasonable in the circumstances to order repayment. Thus an applicant who delays in making an application is likely to receive short shrift from the Court, nor is the Court likely to order repayment where the arbitrator has in good faith acted in such a way that it would be unjust to order repayment. It seems to us that it is necessary to set out expressly in the Bill that the power of the Court extends to dealing with fees and expenses yet to be paid.

125. These provisions are extended by subsection (6) to include an arbitrator who has ceased to act and an umpire who has not replaced the other arbitrators. An arbitrator may cease to act through the operation of Clauses 23 to 26, or if an umpire takes over following a disagreement.

126. The liability in Clause 28(1) is to "the parties". It seems to us to follow that a person who has not participated at all, and in respect of whom it is determined that the arbitral tribunal has no jurisdiction, would not be a "party" for the purposes of this clause (*cf.* Clause 72). More difficult questions may well arise in respect of persons who have participated, for there the doctrine of Kompetenz-Kompetenz (Clauses 30 and 31) may have to be weighed against the proposition that a party can hardly be under any liability in respect of the fees and expenses of the tribunal which he has successfully established should not have been acting at all on the merits of the dispute.

127. It is to be noted that arbitrators' fees and expenses include, by virtue of Clause 37(2), the fees and expenses of tribunal appointed experts, etc.

128. It seems that the present joint and several liability of the parties to an arbitrator for his fees may rest on some implied contract said to exist between them. Be this as it may, such an implied contract (in so far as it related to fees and expenses) would not survive by virtue of Clause 81 of this Bill, because this only saves rules of law which are consistent with Part I. Any implied contract imposing a liability for more than reasonable fees and expenses would clearly be inconsistent with Clause 28(1). Furthermore, since Clause 28(1) gives a statutory right there remains no good reason for any implied contractual right. As stated above, any specific contract would, however, of course be preserved by Clause 28(5).

129. Contrary to some suggestions made to us, it seems to us that rights of contribution between the parties in relation to their statutory liability under Clause 28(1) can best be left to the ordinary rules which relate to joint and several liability generally.

130. Clause 28 is made mandatory, since otherwise the parties could by agreement between themselves deprive the arbitrators of what seems to us to be a very necessary protection.

Clause 29. Immunity of arbitrators

131. Although the general view seems to be that arbitrators have some immunity under the present law, this is not entirely free from doubt. We were firmly of the view that arbitrators should have a degree of immunity, and most (though not all) the responses we received expressed the same view.

132. The reasons for providing immunity are the same as those that apply to Judges in our Courts. Arbitration and litigation share this in common, that both provide a means of dispute resolution which depends upon a binding decision by an impartial third party. It is generally considered that an immunity is necessary to enable that third party properly to perform an impartial decision making function. Furthermore, we feel strongly that unless a degree of immunity is afforded, the finality of the arbitral process could well be undermined. The prospect of a losing party attempting to re-arbitrate the issues on the basis that a competent arbitrator would have decided them in favour of that party is one that we would view with dismay. The Bill provides in our view adequate safeguards to deal with cases where the arbitral process has gone wrong.

133. This is a mandatory provision. Given the need and reason for immunity, it seems to us to follow that as a matter of public policy, this should be so.

134. The immunity does not, of course, extend to cases where it is shown that the arbitrator has acted in bad faith. Our law is well acquainted with this expression and although we considered other terms, we concluded that there were unlikely to be any difficulties in practice in using this test: see, for example, *Melton Medes Ltd* v. *Securities and Investment Board* [1995] 3 All ER 880.

135. Subsection 29(3). There was a concern that if a provision such as this was not included, Clause 25, when read together with Clause 29, could be said to preclude a claim against an arbitrator for resigning in breach of contract and similarly a defence (based on resignation) to a claim by an arbitrator for his fees, unless "bad faith" is proved.

136. Since the publication of the final draft of the Bill we have concluded that the Court should be given power to remove or modify the immunity as it sees fit when it removes an arbitrator. We consider this further in Chapter 6 below.

JURISDICTION OF THE ARBITRAL TRIBUNAL

Clause 30. Competence of tribunal to rule on its own jurisdiction

137. This Clause states what is called the doctrine of "Kompetenz-Kompetenz". This is an internationally recognised doctrine, which is also recognised by our own law (e.g. *Christopher Brown* v. *Genossenschaft Osterreichischer Waldbesitzer* [1954] 1 QB 8), though this has not always been the case.

138. The great advantage of this doctrine is that it avoids delays and difficulties when a question is raised as to the jurisdiction of the tribunal. Clearly the tribunal cannot be the final arbiter of a question of jurisdiction, for this would provide a classic case of pulling oneself up by one's own bootstraps, but to deprive a tribunal of a power (subject to Court review) to rule on jurisdiction would mean that a recalcitrant party could delay valid arbitration proceedings indefinitely by making spurious challenges to its jurisdiction.

139. The Clause and the following Clause are based on Article 16 of the Model Law, but unlike that model we have not made this provision mandatory so that the parties, if they wish, can agree that the tribunal shall not have this power. We have also spelt out what we mean by "substantive jurisdiction".

Clause 31. Objection to substantive jurisdiction of tribunal

140. In this Clause we set out how a challenge to the jurisdiction can be made, and the circumstances in which it must be made (following Article 16 of the Model Law). This reflects much of the Model Law but we have, for example, refrained from using expressions like "submission of the statement of defence" since this might give the impression, which we are anxious to dispel, that every arbitration requires some formal pleading or the like.

141. The Clause, in effect, sets out three ways in which the matter may proceed.

(i) The first is that the tribunal may make an award on the question of jurisdiction. If it does so then that award may be challenged by a party under Clause 67.

(ii) The second way is for the tribunal to deal with the question of jurisdiction in its award on the merits. Again on the jurisdiction aspect the award may be challenged under Clause 67.

We have provided these two methods because, depending on the circumstances, the one or the other may be the better course to take, bearing in mind the duty (in Clause 33) to adopt procedures suitable to the circumstances of the particular case, avoiding unnecessary delay or expense.

(iii) The third way of proceeding is for an application to be made to the Court before any award (pursuant to Clause 32). Again this third course is designed to achieve the same objective (albeit in limited circumstances). For example, cases arise where a party starts an arbitration but the other party, without taking part, raises an objection to the jurisdiction of the tribunal. In such circumstances, it might very well be cheaper and quicker for the party wishing to arbitrate to go directly to the Court to seek a favourable ruling on jurisdiction rather than seeking an award from the tribunal. Such an approach would be very much the exception, and, to this end, Clause 32 is narrowly drawn. In this connection it must be remembered that a party who chooses not to take any part in an arbitration cannot in justice be required to take any positive steps to challenge the jurisdiction, for to do otherwise would be to assume against that party (before the point has been decided) that the tribunal has jurisdiction. We return to this topic when considering Clause 72.

142. Article 16(3) of the Model Law provides that the arbitral tribunal may rule on a plea as to jurisdiction either as a preliminary question or in an award on the merits. The DAC is of the view that it is unnecessary to introduce a new concept of a "preliminary ruling", which is somehow

different from an award. Clause 31(4) therefore only refers to awards. This has the advantage that awards on jurisdiction will have the benefit of those provisions on awards generally (e.g. costs, lien, reasons, additional awards, etc), and, if appropriate, may be enforced in the same way as any other award.

143. A challenge to jurisdiction may well involve questions of fact as well as questions of law. Since the arbitral tribunal cannot rule finally on its own jurisdiction, it follows that both its findings of fact and its holdings of law may be challenged. The regime for challenging such awards is set out in Clause 67.

144. Clause 31(1) replaces the requirement set out in Article 16(2) of the Model Law (that a challenge to the overall jurisdiction of the tribunal must be raised no later than the submission of a statement of defence) with a requirement that such an objection be raised no later than the time a party takes the first step in the proceedings to contest the merits of any matter in relation to which he challenges the tribunal's jurisdiction. This allows for alternative procedures where there is no "statement of defence" as such.

145. Clause 31 is a mandatory provision. Under Clause 30, of course, the parties can agree that the tribunal shall not have power to rule on its own jurisdiction, but while this means (as subsection (4) points out) that the tribunal cannot then make an award on jurisdiction, the compulsory nature of Clause 31 means that the objection must be raised as there stipulated. It seems to us that this is highly desirable by way of support for the object of arbitration as set out in Clause 1.

146. It has been suggested to the DAC that there should be a mechanism whereby an objecting party, or even a non-objecting party, could require the tribunal forthwith to make an award as to jurisdiction, rather than merely incorporating a ruling in an award on the merits. The DAC disagrees with this. Unless the parties agree otherwise, the choice as to which course to take will be left with the tribunal, who will decide what is to be done consistent with their duty under Clause 33 (see below). Indeed, in some cases it may be simply impracticable to rule on jurisdiction, before determining merits. If, however, the parties agree which course is to be taken, and if, of course, their agreement is effective (i.e. it does not require the tribunal to breach its mandatory duty under Clause 33) then the provision under discussion requires the tribunal to take the course chosen by the parties.

Clause 32. Determination of preliminary point of jurisdiction

147. In this Clause we have set out the procedure for the third of the possible ways of dealing with a challenge to the jurisdiction. As stated above, this Clause provides for exceptional cases only: it is not intended to detract from the basic rule as set out in Clause 30. Hence the restrictions in Clause 32(2), and the procedure in Clause 32(3). It will be noted that we have required either the agreement of the parties, or that the Court is satisfied that this is, in effect, the proper course to take. It is anticipated that the Courts will take care to prevent this exceptional provision from becoming the normal route for challenging jurisdiction. Since this Clause concerns a power exercisable by the Court in relation to the jurisdiction of the tribunal, it is in our view important enough to be made mandatory.

148. Under this Clause the tribunal may continue the arbitral proceedings and make an award whilst the application to the Court is pending. Thus a recalcitrant party will not be able to mount spurious challenges as a means of delaying the arbitral process. Under subsection (5) of the preceding Clause the tribunal can, of course (and must if the parties agree) stay the arbitral proceedings whilst an application is made. Which course the tribunal takes (where it has power to choose) will of course depend once again on what it sees its Clause 33 duty to be.

149. The right of appeal from Court rulings is limited in the way set out in the Clause.

THE ARBITRAL PROCEEDINGS

Clause 33. General duty of the tribunal

150. This is one of the central proposals in our Bill (grounded on Article 18 of the Model Law). It is a mandatory provision, since, as is explained below, we fail to see how a proceeding which departed from the stipulated duties could properly be described as an arbitration. We endeavour to

set out, in the simplest, clearest terms we have been able to devise, how the tribunal should approach and deal with its task, which is to do full justice to the parties. In the following Clauses we set out in detail the powers available to the tribunal for this purpose.

151. It has been suggested that the generality of Clause 33 may be problematic: that it may be an invitation to recalcitrant parties to launch challenges, or that vagueness will give rise to arguments. The advantage of arbitration is that it offers a dispute resolution system which can be tailored to the particular dispute to an extent which litigation finds it difficult to do. Thus depending on the nature of the dispute, there will be numerous ways in which the arbitration can be conducted. It is quite impossible to list all the possible variants and to set out what may or may not be done. Indeed any attempt to do so would defeat one of the main purposes of the Bill, which is to encourage arbitral tribunals not slavishly to follow court or other set procedures. It follows that the only limits can be those set out in the present clause. It is to be hoped that the Courts will take a dim view of those who try to attack awards because of suggested breaches of this clause which have no real substance. At the same time, it can hardly be suggested that awards should not be open to attack when the tribunal has not acted in accordance with the principles stated.

152. It has further been suggested that this part of the Bill will cause the demise of the amateur arbitrator. If by this is meant the demise of people who purport to act as arbitrators but who are either unable or unwilling (or both) to conduct the proceedings in accordance with what most would regard as self-evident rules of justice, then we indeed hope that this will be one of the results. But since these rules of justice are generally accepted in our democratic society, and are not merely theoretical considerations that concern lawyers alone, we can see no reason why the Bill should discourage anyone who is ready willing and able to apply them. Indeed we consider that the Bill will encourage and support all such people.

153. Sometimes the parties to an arbitration employ lawyers who seek, in effect, to bully a non-legal arbitrator into taking a course of action which is against his better instincts, by seeking to blind him with legal "science" to get their way. Again, in some circles it is thought that somehow the procedures in an arbitration should be modelled on Court procedures, and that to adopt other methods would be "misconduct" (an expression that the Bill does not use) on the part of the arbitrator. This part of the Bill is designed to prevent such bullying and to explode the theory that an arbitration has always to follow Court procedures. If an arbitrator is satisfied that the way he wants to proceed fulfils his duty under this Clause and that the powers he wants to exercise are available to him under the following Clauses, then he should have the courage of his own convictions and proceed accordingly, unless the parties are agreed that he should adopt some other course.

The relationship between Clauses 1(b), 33 and 34(1)

154. It has been suggested to us there could be a conflict between:

(i) the mandatory duty cast on arbitrators by Clause 33 and
(ii) the principle of party autonomy in Clause 1(b) and the proviso in Clause 34(1). As we explain below, the DAC does not consider that there is any inconsistency between these two principles.

155. Under the principle of party autonomy, the parties are free to agree upon anything to do with the arbitration, subject only to such safeguards as are necessary in the public interest (Clause 1(b)). The mandatory provisions set out those matters which have effect notwithstanding any agreement to the contrary: see Clause 4. It seems to us that the public interest dictates that Clause 33 must be mandatory, i.e. that the parties cannot effectively agree to dispense with the duty laid on arbitrators under Clause 33. In other words, they cannot effectively agree that the arbitrators can act unfairly, or that the arbitrators can be partial, or that the arbitrators can decide that the parties (or one of them) should not have a reasonable opportunity of putting his case or answering that of his opponent, or indeed that the arbitrators can adopt procedures that are unsuitable for the particular circumstances of the case or are unnecessarily slow or expensive, so that the means for resolving the matters to be determined is unfair. It is, of course, extremely unlikely in the nature of things that the parties would wish deliberately to make such bizarre agreements, but were this to happen, then it seems to us that

such agreements should be ineffective for the purposes of this Bill, i.e. not binding on the parties or the tribunal.

156. However, a situation could well arise in practice in cases where the parties are agreed on a method of proceeding which they consider complies with the first of the general principles set out in Clause 1 (and which therefore the tribunal could adopt consistently with its duty under Clause 33) but the tribunal takes a different view, or where they are agreed in their opposition to a method of proceeding which the tribunal considers should be adopted in order to perform its Clause 33 duty.

157. In our view it is neither desirable nor practicable to stipulate that the tribunal can override the agreement of the parties. It is not desirable, because the type of arbitration we are discussing is a consensual process which depends on the agreements of the parties who are surely entitled (if they can agree) to have the final say on how they wish their dispute to be resolved. It is not practicable, since there is no way in which the parties can be forced to adopt a method of proceeding if they are agreed that this is not the way they wish to proceed. The latter is the case even if it could be established that their agreement was ineffective since it undermined or prevented performance of the duty made mandatory by Clause 33.

158. A party would be unable to enforce an ineffective agreement against the other parties, nor would such an agreement bind the tribunal, but the problem under discussion only exists while the parties are in fact at one, whether or not their agreement is legally effective.

159. In circumstances such as these, the tribunal (assuming it has failed to persuade the parties to take a different course) has the choice of adopting the course of preferred by the parties or of resigning. Indeed, resignation would be the only course if the parties were in agreement in rejecting the method preferred by the tribunal, and no other way of proceeding was agreed by them or considered suitable by the tribunal.

160. We have stipulated elsewhere in the Bill that the immunity we propose for arbitrators does not extend to any liability they may be under for resigning (Clause 29) though under Clause 25 they may seek relief in respect of such liability from the Court. The reason for the limitation on immunity is that cases may arise where the resignation of the arbitrator is wholly indefensible and has caused great delay and loss. In our view Clause 25 would suffice to protect arbitrators who resigned because they reasonably believed that the agreement of the parties prevented them from properly performing their Clause 33 duty. Furthermore, arbitrators could always stipulate for a right to resign in such circumstances as a term of their appointment.

161. If, on the other hand, the tribunal adopted a method of proceeding agreed by the parties, it seems to us that none of the parties could afterwards validly complain that the tribunal had failed in its Clause 33 duty, since the tribunal would only have done what the parties had asked it to do. Again, the fact that as between the parties such an agreement may have been ineffective as undermining or preventing performance of the Clause 33 duties seems to us to be wholly irrelevant. It could of course be said that the tribunal had breached its Clause 33 duty, but this would have no practical consequences since the parties themselves would have brought about this state of affairs, and would therefore be unable to seek any relief in respect of it.

162. Some people have expressed concern that there is a danger that lawyers will agree between themselves a method of proceeding which the tribunal consider to be unnecessarily long or expensive. However, if a tribunal considered, for example, that lawyers were trying either deliberately to "churn" the case for their own private advantage or were simply but misguidedly seeking to adopt unnecessary procedures etc, the obvious solution would be to ask them to confirm that their respective clients had been made aware of the views of the tribunal but were nevertheless in agreement that the course proposed by their lawyers should be adopted. At the end of the day, however, the fact remains that the only sanction the arbitrators have is to resign.

163. In summary, therefore, we consider that the duty of the arbitrators under Clause 33 and the right of the parties to agree how the arbitration should be conducted do fit together. Under Clause 33 the tribunal have the specified duties. Under Clause 34 therefore, the tribunal must decide all procedural and evidential matters, subject to the right of the parties to agree any matter. If the parties reach an agreement on how to proceed which clashes with the duty of the tribunal or which the tribunal reasonably considers does so, then the arbitrators can either resign and have the protection of Clause 25, or can adopt what the parties want and will not afterwards be liable to the parties for doing so.

Further points

164. In this Clause we have provided that the tribunal shall give each party a "reasonable opportunity" of putting his case and dealing with that of his opponent. Article 18 of the Model Law uses the expression "full opportunity".

165. We prefer the word "reasonable" because it removes any suggestion that a party is entitled to take as long as he likes, however objectively unreasonable this may be. We are sure that this was not intended by those who framed the Model Law, for it would entail that a party is entitled to an unreasonable time, which justice can hardly require. Indeed the contrary is the case, for an unreasonable time would *ex hypothesi* mean unnecessary delay and expense, things which produce injustice and which accordingly would offend the first principle of Clause 1, as well as Clauses 33 and 40.

Clause 34. Procedural and evidential matters

166. We trust that the matters we have listed in this Clause (which are partly drawn from Articles 19, 20, 22, 23 and 24 of the Model Law) are largely self-evident. We have produced a non-exhaustive check-list because we think it will be helpful both to arbitrating parties and to their arbitrators. We cannot emphasise too strongly that one of the strengths of the arbitral process is that it is able much more easily than any Court system to adapt its procedures to suit the particular case. Hence we have spelt this out as a duty under the preceding Clause. The list of powers helps the tribunal (and indeed the parties) to choose how best to proceed, untrammelled by technical or formalistic rules.

167. Some of those responding suggested that we should include a special code to deal with the arbitration of small claims. We have not adopted this suggestion for the very reason we have just stated. Any such code would have to have detailed rules, arbitrary monetary or other limits and other complicated provisions. In our view, proper adherence to the duties in Clause 33 will achieve the same result. A small claim will simply not need all the expensive procedural and other paraphernalia which might be required for the resolution of some huge and complicated international dispute.

168. Furthermore, we consider that associations and institutions concerned with specific areas of trade etc. can play a very significant part in formulating rules and procedures for arbitrating disputes concerning their members. Such bodies have the detailed knowledge and experience required to enable them properly to address this task, in relation both to small claims and otherwise. We feel strongly that it would be wrong for a Bill of the present kind to seek to lay down a rigid structure for any kind of case; and that different methods must be developed to suit different circumstances, by arbitral tribunals as well as those who have the necessary practical knowledge of those circumstances. Finally, of course, the Bill in no way impinges upon small claims procedures developed for use through the court system.

169. Subsection (a). Whilst Article 20(1) of the Model Law states that, in the absence of the agreement of the parties, "the place of arbitration shall be determined by the arbitral tribunal having regard to the circumstances of the case, including the convenience of the parties", subsection 34(2)(a) does not state that the tribunal should have the convenience of the parties in mind, given that this is a consideration that is really subsumed under the general duty of the Tribunal in Clause 33, and, further, because the DAC was of the view that like considerations apply to the other parts of Clause 34, such as subsection (b), even though the Model Law does not appear to reflect this. Unlike the Model Law, subsection (a) also refers to "when", as well as "where".

170. Subsection (f) makes it clear that arbitrators are not necessarily bound by the technical rules of evidence. In his 1993 Freshfields Lecture ((1994) 10 Arb. Int. 1), Lord Steyn questioned why the technical rules of evidence should apply to arbitration, even if (as he doubted) there was authority for this. This provision clarifies the position. It is to be noted that Clause 34(2)(f) helps to put an end to any arguments that it is a question of law whether there is material to support a finding of fact.

171. Subsection (g). Some anxiety was expressed at the power to act inquisitorially, to be found in subsection (g), on grounds that arbitrators are unused to such powers and might, albeit in good faith, abuse them.

172. We do not share this view. Once again it seems to us that provided the tribunal in exercising its powers follows its simple duty as set out in Clause 33 (and subsection (2) of this Clause tells the tribunal that this is what they must do) then in suitable cases an inquisitorial approach to all or some of the matters involved may well be the best way of proceeding. Clause 33, however, remains a control, such that, for example, if an arbitrator takes the initiative in procuring evidence, he must give all parties a reasonable opportunity of commenting on it.

173. A number of arbitrators who responded to our July 1995 draft suggested that the tribunal should be entitled to have the last word, i.e. should be given the power to override the agreement of the parties to follow a different course. The interrelationship of the tribunal's duties and party autonomy has already been discussed above. As is clear from that discussion, we disagree with this view for the following reasons:

(i) To give the tribunal such a power would be contrary to Article 19 of the Model Law. It would also be contrary to the present position under English law.
(ii) To allow the tribunal to override the agreement of the parties would to our minds constitute an indefensible inroad into the principle of party autonomy, upon which the Bill is based.
(iii) It is difficult to see how such a power could be backed by any effective sanction. If the parties agree not to adopt the course ordered by the tribunal, there is nothing the tribunal can do except resign.
(iv) It seems to us that the problem is more apparent than real. In most cases the parties rely on the tribunal to decide how to conduct the case and do not sit down and agree between themselves how it is to be done. In order to reflect what actually happens in practice we have accordingly reversed the way many of the other Clauses begin and stated that it is for the tribunal to decide all procedural and evidential matters, subject to the right of the parties to agree any matter. In our view, however, since arbitration is the parties' own chosen method of dispute resolution, we cannot see why they should be deprived of the right to decide what form the arbitration should take.

174. As we have made clear above, it is of course open to those who frame rules for arbitration which the parties incorporate into their agreement, to stipulate that the tribunal is to have the last word, and likewise arbitrators can stipulate this as a term of their agreement to act, though once again there would be no means, apart from persuasion or the threat of resignation, of enforcing such a stipulation if the parties later jointly took a different view.

175. It has been suggested that there could be a conflict between the proviso in Clause 34(1) and Clause 40. This is said to arise, for example, where the parties have agreed a procedural or evidential matter which they are entitled to do under Clause 34(1), but the tribunal are intent on taking a different course. Does the parties' agreement override their duty under Clause 40? The DAC considers that no such conflict exists:

(i) The parties are free to agree on all procedural and evidential matters, pursuant to Clause 34(1).
(ii) However, any such agreement will only be effective, if it is consistent with Clause 33, being a mandatory provision.
(iii) Any such agreement made pursuant to Clause 34(1), and consistent with Clause 33, will define the scope of Clause 40—i.e. the parties will have agreed on how the arbitration is to be conducted, or, in the words of Clause 40, what is to constitute the "proper and expeditious conduct of the arbitral proceedings". The determinations of the tribunal should follow that agreement (which would not be the case if such an agreement was inconsistent with Clause 33) and *ex hypothesi* the parties should be obliged to comply.
(iv) If there are matters on which the parties have not agreed, then the tribunal will fill the gap under Clause 34(1) and Clause 40(1) will again operate without conflict.

176. It has also been suggested that the Bill should include a provision that the arbitrator should encourage the parties to use other forms of ADR when this was considered appropriate. This suggestion has not been adopted, since the Bill is concerned with arbitration where the parties have chosen this rather than any other form of dispute resolution.

Clause 35. Consolidation of proceedings and concurrent hearings

177. This Clause makes clear that the parties may agree to consolidate their arbitration with other arbitral proceedings or to hold concurrent hearings.

178. During the consultation exercises, the DAC received submissions calling for a provision that would empower either a tribunal or the Court (or indeed both) to order consolidation or concurrent hearings. These were considered extremely carefully by the committee.

179. The problem arises in cases where a number of parties are involved. For example, in a construction project a main contractor may make a number of sub-contracts each of which contains an arbitration clause. A dispute arises in which a claim is made against one sub-contractor who seeks to blame another. In Court, of course, there is power to order consolidation or concurrent hearings, as well as procedures for allowing additional parties to be joined. In arbitrations, however, this power does not exist. The reason it does not exist is that this form of dispute resolution depends on the agreement of the contracting parties that their disputes will be arbitrated by a private tribunal, not litigated in the public courts. It follows that unless the parties otherwise agree, only their own disputes arising out of their own agreement can be referred to that agreed tribunal.

180. In our view it would amount to a negation of the principle of party autonomy to give the tribunal or the Court power to order consolidation or concurrent hearings. Indeed it would to our minds go far towards frustrating the agreement of the parties to have their own tribunal for their own disputes. Further difficulties could well arise, such as the disclosure of documents from one arbitration to another. Accordingly we would be opposed to giving the tribunal or the Court this power. However, if the parties agree to invest the tribunal with such a power, then we would have no objection.

181. Having said this, the DAC appreciates the common sense behind the suggestion. We are persuaded, however, that the problem is best solved by obtaining the agreement of the parties. Thus those who are in charge of drafting standard forms of contract, or who offer terms for arbitration services which the parties can incorporate into their agreements, (especially those institutions and associations which are concerned with situations in which there are likely to be numerous contracts and sub-contracts) could include suitable clauses permitting the tribunal to consolidate or order concurrent hearings in appropriate cases. For example, the London Maritime Arbitrators Association Rules have within them a provision along these lines. In order to encourage this, we have made clear in this Clause that with the agreement of the parties, there is nothing wrong with adopting such procedure.

182. It will be noted that whereas Clause 39 uses the expression "[t]he parties are free to agree that the tribunal shall have power to order . . . ", Clause 35 simple states that "[t]he parties are free to agree . . . ". This difference is easily explained. In both cases the parties are free to endow the tribunal with the power in question. This is implicit in Clause 35(1) by virtue of Clause 35(2). Under Clause 35(1), the parties may agree between themselves to consolidate two arbitrations, or to have concurrent hearings, before a tribunal has been appointed. This could, of course, have a bearing on how the tribunal is to be appointed in such a situation. Indeed the parties may agree on institutional rules that provide for this. However, an equivalent arrangement is difficult to imagine in the context of Clause 39. Overall, the difference in wording is not intended to impede the parties' freedom to agree what they like, when they like, in either case.

Clause 36. Legal or other representation

183. It seems to us that this reflects a basic right, though of course the parties are free to dispense with it if they wish.

184. In the draft produced in July we used the phrase "a lawyer or other person of his choice". We have changed this, because we felt that it might give the impression that a party could stubbornly insist on a particular lawyer or other person, in circumstances where that individual could not attend for a long time, thus giving a recalcitrant party a good means of delaying the arbitral process. This should not happen. "A lawyer or other person chosen by him" does not give this impression: if a party's first choice is not available, his second choice will still be "a lawyer or other person chosen by him". The right to be represented exists but must not be abused. Furthermore the right must be read with the first principle of Clause 1, as well as Clauses 33 and 40. If this is done then we trust that attempts to abuse the right will fail.

185. It has been suggested to the DAC that there should be some provision requiring a party to give advance notice to all other parties if he intends to be represented at a hearing. Whilst in some ways an attractive proposal, this would be difficult to stipulate as a statutory provision, given that it may be impossible in some circumstances, or simply unnecessary in others. Further, different sanctions may be appropriate depending on the particular case. It is clearly desirable that, as a general rule, such notice be given. If it is not, one sanction may be for the tribunal to adjourn a hearing at the defaulting party's cost. In the end, however, this must be a matter for the tribunal's discretion in each particular case.

186. It has been suggested that this Clause provides an opportunity of extending by statute the privilege enjoyed by legal advisers to non-legal advisers or representatives. We have not adopted this suggestion. It seems to us that it would be necessary to define with great precision which non-legal advisers or representatives are to be included (e.g. what relationship they must have to the arbitration and its conduct), and the precise classes of privilege which should be extended to them. Further, any such provision would necessarily have an impact on the position beyond arbitration. In short, it seems to us that this question cannot be confined to arbitrations and raises matters of general principle far beyond those of our remit.

Clause 37. Power to appoint experts, legal advisers or assessors

187. This to our minds would be a useful power in certain cases. We trust that the provisions we suggest are self-evident. Of course, the power can only be exercised if in the circumstances of the particular case its exercise falls within the scope of the duty of the tribunal set out in Clause 33.

188. Subsection (2) is made mandatory, to avoid the risk of the parties agreeing otherwise and thus disabling the tribunal from recovering from the parties expenses properly incurred.

Clause 38. General powers exercisable by the tribunal

189. These provisions represent a significant re-drawing of the relationship between arbitration and the Court. Wherever a power could properly be exercised by a tribunal rather than the Court, provision has been made for this, thereby reducing the need to incur the expense and inconvenience of making applications to Court during arbitral proceedings.

190. The first of the powers in this Clause is one which enables the tribunal to order security for costs. The power presently given to the Court to order security for costs in arbitrations is removed in its entirety.

191. This is a major change from the present position where only the Court can order security for costs. The theory which lay behind the present law is that it is the duty of an arbitral tribunal to decide the substantive merits of the dispute referred to it and that it would not be performing this duty if it stayed or struck out the proceedings pending the provision of security: see for example, *Re Unione Stearinerie Lanza and Weiner* [1917] 2 KB 558.

192. We do not subscribe to this theory, which Parliament has already abandoned in the context of striking out a claim for want of prosecution. In our view, when the parties agree to arbitrate, they are agreeing that their dispute will be resolved by this means. To our minds (in the absence of express stipulations to the contrary) this does not mean that the dispute is necessarily to be decided on its substantive merits. It is in truth an agreement that it will be resolved by the application of the agreed arbitral process. If one party then fails to comply with that process, then it seems to us that it is entirely within what the parties have agreed that the tribunal can resolve the dispute on this ground.

193. Apart from this, the proposition that the Court should involve itself in such matters as deciding whether a claimant in an arbitration should provide security for costs has received universal condemnation in the context of international arbitrations. It is no exaggeration to say that the recent decision of the House of Lords in *Coppee-Lavalin SA/NV* v. *Ken-Ren Chemicals and Fertilizers* [1994] 2 WLR 631 was greeted with dismay by those in the international arbitration community who have at heart the desire to promote our country as a world centre for arbitration. We share those concerns.

194. It has been suggested to the DAC that the court should retain a power to order security for costs that may be incurred up to the appointment of the tribunal. We have not been persuaded, however, that this is really necessary.

195. It has been pointed out that in some cases an application for security before an arbitral tribunal might involve disclosing to that tribunal the fact that an offer of settlement had been or was about to be made. Under the court system, such disclosure can be made to a court other than that which will try the merits of the case.

196. We are not disturbed by this. It seems to us that a tribunal, properly performing its duty under Clause 33, could and should not be influenced by such matters, if the case proceeds to a hearing on the merits, nor do we accept that the disclosure of such information could somehow disqualify the tribunal from acting.

197. Clause 38(3) has been the subject of significant criticism since the Bill was introduced. In the light of this, we have concluded that it must be redrawn. Chapter 6, to which reference should be made, contains a full discussion of the problems with this provision as currently drafted, and our recommendations for its amendment.

198. Whilst the sanction in court for a failure to provide security for costs is normally a stay of the action, this is inappropriate in arbitration: if an arbitrator stayed proceedings, the arbitration would come to a halt without there necessarily being an award which could be challenged (e.g. if a party seeks to continue the proceedings). We have therefore included a specific sanction with respect to a failure to provide security for costs, which is to be found in Clause 41(6). This provision also follows the practice of the English Commercial Court, which changed from the old practice of ordering a stay of proceedings if security was not provided. The disadvantage of the latter course was that it left the proceedings dormant but alive, so that years later they could be revived by the provision of security.

199. Clause 38 provides the tribunal with other powers in relation to the arbitration proceedings. We trust that these are self-explanatory.

Clause 39. Power to make provisional awards

200. In the July 1995 draft Clauses, this power did not require the agreement of the parties. As the result of responses, we have concluded on further consideration that this is necessary.

201. In *The Kostas Melas* [1981] 1 Lloyd's Rep. 18 at 26, Goff J, as he then was, made clear that it was no part of an arbitrator's function to make temporary or provisional financial arrangements between the parties. Furthermore, as can be demonstrated by the abundance of court cases dealing with this subject (in the context of applications for summary judgment, interim payments, *Mareva* injunctions and the like) enormous care has to be taken to avoid turning what can be a useful judicial tool into an instrument of injustice. We should add that we received responses from a number of practicing arbitrators to the effect that they would be unhappy with such powers, and saw no need for them. We should note in passing that the July 1995 draft would arguably (and inadvertently) have allowed arbitrators to order *ex parte Mareva* or even *Anton Piller* relief. These draconian powers are best left to be applied by the Courts, and the provisions of the Bill with respect to such powers have been adjusted accordingly.

202. There is a sharp distinction to be drawn between making provisional or temporary arrangements, which are subject to reversal when the underlying merits are finally decided by the tribunal; and dealing severally with different issues or questions at different times and in different awards, which we cover in Clauses 47. It is for this reason that in this provision we draw attention to that Clause.

203. These considerations have led us firmly to conclude that it would only be desirable to give arbitral tribunals power to make such provisional orders where the parties have so agreed. Such agreements, of course, will have to be drafted with some care for the reasons we have stated. Subject to the safeguards of the parties' agreement and the arbitrators' duties (Clause 33), we envisage that this enlargement of the traditional jurisdiction of arbitrators could serve a very useful purpose, for example in trades and industries where cash flow is of particular importance.

Clause 40. General duty of the parties

204. This is a mandatory provision, since it would seem that an ability to contract out of it would be a negation of the arbitral process.

205. We were asked what the sanction would be for non-compliance. The answer lies in other Clauses of the Bill. These not only give the tribunal powers in relation to recalcitrant parties (e.g.

Clause 41), but stipulate time limits for taking certain steps (e.g. applications to the Court, etc.) and (in Clause 73) making clear that undue delay will result in the loss of rights.

Clause 41. Powers of tribunal in case of party's default

206. The first part of this Clause sets out the present law (section 13A of the 1950 Act, which was inserted by section 102 of the Courts and Legal Services Act 1990) giving the arbitral tribunal power to strike out for want of prosecution.

207. The second part makes clear that in the circumstances stipulated, a tribunal may proceed *ex parte*, though we have forborne from using this expression (or indeed any other legal Latin words or phrases) in the Bill. The Clause has its roots in Article 25 of the Model Law.

208. It is a basic rule of justice that a court or tribunal should give all parties an opportunity to put their case and answer that of their opponents. That is why this appears in Clause 33 of the Bill. Equally, however, and for reasons already mentioned, that opportunity should, again for reasons of justice, be limited to a reasonable one. If for no good reason such an opportunity is not taken by a party then to our minds it is only fair to the other party that the tribunal should be able to proceed as we have set out in this Clause.

209. The last part of this Clause sets out a system of peremptory orders. It will be noted that a peremptory order must be "to the same effect" as the preceding order which was disobeyed (subsection (5)). It could be quite unfair for an arbitrator to be able to make any type of peremptory order, on any matter, regardless of its connection with the default in question.

210. For the reasons mentioned earlier, subsection (6) provides that where a party fails to comply with a peremptory order to provide security for costs, the tribunal may make an award dismissing the claim, thereby following the practice of the English Commercial Court, and avoiding the danger that the proceedings are halted indefinitely, without there being anything to challenge before the Court.

211. So far as failure to comply with other peremptory orders is concerned, we have provided a range of remedies. They do not include a power simply to make an award against the defaulting party. The reason for this is that (unlike a failure to comply with a peremptory order to provide security) it seems to us that this is too draconian a remedy, and that the alternatives we have provided very much better fit the justice of the matter.

POWERS OF COURT IN RELATION TO ARBITRAL PROCEEDINGS

Clause 42. Enforcement of peremptory orders of tribunal

212. Although in Clause 41 we have provided the tribunal with powers in relation to peremptory orders, it seemed to us that the Court should have power to order compliance with such orders, though (unless both parties have agreed) these can only be invoked with the permission of the tribunal. In our view there may well be circumstances where in the interests of justice, the fact the the Court has sanctions which in the nature of things cannot be given to arbitrators (e.g. committal to prison for contempt) will assist the proper functioning of the arbitral process. This Clause is a good example of the support the Court can give to that process. Subsection (3) requires that any other available recourse within the arbitral process be first exhausted.

Clause 43. Securing the attendance of witnesses

213. This Clause (which corresponds to Article 27 of the Model Law, and is derived from section 12(4) and (5) of the 1950 Act) is also designed to provide Court support for the arbitral process. It will be noted, in particular, that the agreement of the parties or the permission of the tribunal is required. The reason for this is to make sure that this procedure is not used to override any procedural method adopted by the tribunal, or agreed by the parties, for the arbitration. Thus, for

example, if the tribunal has decided that there shall be no oral evidence, then (unless all parties agree otherwise) this procedure cannot be used to get round that decision.

Clause 44. Court powers exercisable in support of arbitral proceedings

214. This provision corresponds in part to Article 9 of the Model Law. As part of the redefinition of the relationship between arbitration and the Court, which was mentioned above, the powers we have given the Court are intended to be used when the tribunal cannot act or act effectively, as subsection (5) makes clear. It is under this Clause that the Court has power to order *Mareva* or *Anton Piller* relief (i.e. urgent protective measures to preserve assets or evidence) so as to help the arbitral process to operate effectively. Equally, there may be instances where a party seeks an order that will have an effect on a third party, which only the Court could grant. For the same reason the Court is given the other powers listed.

215. In order to prevent any suggestion that the Court might be used to interfere with or usurp the arbitral process, or indeed any attempt to do so, we have stipulated that except in cases of urgency with regard to the preservation of assets or evidence, the Court can only act with the agreement of the parties or the permission of the tribunal. We have excepted cases of urgency, since these often arise before the tribunal has been properly constituted or when in the nature of things it cannot act quickly or effectively enough.

216. Furthermore, under subsection (6) the Court, after making an order, can in effect hand over to the tribunal the task of deciding whether or not that order should cease to have effect. This is a novel provision, but follows from the philosophy behind these provisions: if a given power could possibly be exercised by a tribunal, then it should be, and parties should not be allowed to make unilateral applications to the Court. If, however, a given power could be exercised by the tribunal, but not as effectively, in circumstances where, for example, speed is necessary, then the Court should be able to step in.

Clause 45. Determination of preliminary point of law

217. This Clause preserves what used to be the old Consultative Case procedure, though its availability is limited as we have set out, in order not to interfere with the arbitral process. The Clause is based on section 2 of the 1979 Act, with certain important changes.

218. It seems to us that with the limitations we have provided, this procedure can have its uses. For example, an important point of law may arise which is of great general interest and potentially the subject of a large number of arbitrations. This not infrequently happens when some major event occurs, as, for example, the closure of the Suez Canal or the United States embargo on the export of soya beans. It may well be considered by those concerned that in such special circumstances it would be cheaper and better for all to obtain a definitive answer from the Court at an early stage.

219. However, under subsection (1), unless the parties agree, the Court must now be satisfied that determination of the given question of law will substantially affect the rights of one or more of the parties. This last point is a departure from the 1979 Act, section 1 of which makes this precondition in relation to an appeal in respect of questions of law arising out of the award, but section 2 of which does not impose it in relation to the determination of a preliminary point of law.

220. Further, unless the parties agree, the Court will now have to be satisfied of the matters set out in subsection (2) before considering an application, so that the procedure can only be used (even with the permission of the tribunal) in cases where its adoption will produce a substantial saving in costs to the parties or one of them. The condition in section 2(2) of the 1979 Act, which requires that the question of law be one in respect of which leave to appeal would be likely to be given under section 1(3)(b) of that Act, is not repeated.

221. It has been suggested to the DAC that the right to refer to the Court under this Clause be removed from all non-domestic arbitrations, unless the parties otherwise agree. For the reasons given above as to the value of this provision, and for the reasons given below with respect to preserving the right of appeal in Clause 69, we were not persuaded by this.

THE AWARD

Clause 46. Rules applicable to substance of dispute

222. This Clause reflects much, though not all, of Article 28 of the Model Law. We have not, for example, directed the tribunal to "take into account the usages of the trade applicable to the transaction". If the applicable law allows this to be done, then the provision is not necessary; while if it does not, then it could be said that such a direction overrides that law, which to our minds would be incorrect.

223. Subsection (1)(b) recognises that the parties may agree that their dispute is not to be decided in accordance with a recognised system of law but under what in this country are often called "equity clauses", or arbitration "*ex aequo et bono*", or "*amiable composition*", i.e. general considerations of justice and fairness, etc. It will be noted that we have avoided using this description in the Bill just as we have avoided using the Latin and French expressions found in the Model Law. There appears to be no good reason to prevent parties from agreeing to equity clauses. However, it is to be noted that in agreeing that a dispute shall be resolved in this way, the parties are in effect excluding any right to appeal to the Court (there being no "question of law" to appeal).

224. Subsection (2) does, in effect, adopt the rule found in Article 28 of the Model Law, thereby avoiding the problems of *renvoi*.

225. Subsection (3) caters for the situation where there is no choice or agreement. This again is the language of the Model Law. In such circumstances the tribunal must decide what conflicts of law rules are applicable, and use those rules in order to determine the applicable law. It cannot simply make up rules for this purpose. It has been suggested to the DAC that more guidance be given as to the choice of a proper law, but it appears to us that flexibility is desirable, that it is not our remit to lay down principles in this highly complex area, and that to do so would necessitate a departure from the Model Law wording.

Clause 47. Awards on different issues, etc.

226. We regard this as a very important provision. Some disputes are very complex, raising a large number of complicated issues which, if they are all addressed and dealt with at one hearing, would necessarily take a very long time and be very expensive. Disputes concerning large scale construction contracts are a good example, though there are many other cases.

227. In recent years both the Commercial Court and the Official Referees Court in England (which deal with large cases) have adopted a different approach. The Judge plays much more of a managerial role, suggesting and indeed directing ways in which time and money can be saved. One of the ways is to select issues for early determination, not necessarily on the basis that they will be legally determinative of the entire litigation, but where they may well be commercially determinative, in the sense that a decision is likely to help the parties to resolve their other differences themselves without the need to spend time and money on using lawyers to fight them out. This has a further advantage. Cases fought to the bitter end often result in a permanent loss of goodwill between the warring factions, thus impeding or preventing future profitable relationships between them. The result is often in truth a loss to all the parties, whether or not they were the "winners" in the litigation.

228. In Court therefore, the old idea that a party is entitled to a full trial of everything at once has now largely disappeared: see, for example, the decision of the House of Lords in *Ashmore* v. *Corporation of Lloyd's* [1992] 2 Lloyd's Rep 1. Furthermore, this method of approach is reflected in the views expressed by Lord Woolf in his current consideration of how to improve our system of civil justice. The same reasoning, of course, applies to arbitrations.

229. As we have said earlier, arbitration enjoys an advantage over litigation, since the arbitral tribunal is appointed to deal with the particular dispute that has arisen, and is thus in a better position to tailor the procedure to suit the particular circumstances of that dispute. Furthermore, an arbitral tribunal is often able, for the same reason, to move much quicker than the Court.

230. For these reasons, we have tried to make clear in this Clause that the tribunal is empowered to proceed in this way. This is an aspect of the duty cast upon the tribunal to adopt procedures suitable to the circumstances of the particular case, which is set out in Clause 33(1)(a). We would

encourage arbitrators to adopt this approach in any case where it appears that time and money will be saved by doing so, and where such an approach would not be at the expense of any of the other requirements of justice.

231. In this connection we would draw attention to the decision of Goff J (now Lord Goff) in *The Kostas Melas, op. cit.* As we observed when considering Clause 39, the function of arbitrators is not to make temporary financial adjustments between the parties pending the resolution of the dispute, unless this is what they have agreed the arbitrators can do. As this case shows, there is a clear distinction between such arrangements and the right to make a permanent binding decision after considering the arguments, even though the later resolution of other issues (if this becomes necessary) may overall produce a different result.

232. We should emphasise that in this Clause we are not intending to give arbitral tribunals greater or different powers from those they presently have, but to emphasise how their powers should, in suitable cases, be exercised.

233. It might also be noted that we have been careful to avoid use of the term "interim award", which has become a confusing term, and in its most common use, arguably a misnomer.

Clause 48. Remedies

234. We trust that the matters addressed in this Clause are self-evident. We have excluded specific performance of land contracts, so as not to change the law in this regard, but clarified the power of arbitrators to award injunctive relief. Given that the parties are free to agree on the remedies that a tribunal may order, there is nothing to restrict such remedies to those available at Court.

Clause 49. Interest

235. The responses we received demonstrated to us that there was a general desire to give arbitral tribunals a general power to award compound interest.

236. There is no doubt that the absence of such a power adds to the delays (and thus the expense) of arbitrations and causes injustice, for it is often in a party's interest to delay the proceedings and the honouring of an award, since the interest eventually payable is less than can be made by holding on to funds which should be paid over to the other party, who of course is losing out by a like amount.

237. Some of those responding were fearful that arbitrators would abuse this power, and may, for example, award compound interest on a punitive rather than compensatory basis. We do not share those fears. To our minds any competent arbitrator seeking to fulfil the duties laid on him by the Bill will have no more difficulty in making decisions about compound interest than he will in deciding in any other context what fairness and justice require. Anyone who has such difficulties demonstrates, in our view, that he is really not fit to act as an arbitrator. In such a case, the award and the arbitrator will be susceptible of challenge.

238. Clauses 84 and 111 allow for transitional measures. In the context of this Clause, we understand that these may prove necessary in relation to the enforcement of awards through the country courts, who we are told are not presently equipped to calculate compound interest payable from the date of the award.

Clause 50. Extension of time for making award

239. This Clause re-enacts the existing law, though with two qualifications:

(i) arbitral procedures for obtaining an extension must be exhausted before recourse to the Court; and

(ii) the Court must be satisfied that substantial injustice would be done if the time were not extended. It seems to us that these qualifications are needed so as to ensure that the Court's power is supportive rather than disruptive of the arbitral process. For the same reason, it seems to us that it would be a rare case indeed where the Court extended the time notwithstanding that this had not been done through an available arbitral process.

Clause 51. Settlement

240. This Clause reflects Article 30 of the Model Law. It enables an agreed settlement of the dispute to be given the status of an arbitral award, which could then be enforced as such.

241. Concern has been expressed that this provision (taken from Article 30 of the Model Law) might be used by the parties either to obtain an award in respect of matters which are simply not arbitrable (e.g. matters which under our law cannot be settled by agreement between the parties), or to mislead third parties (e.g. the tax authorities). It was suggested that any agreed award should have to state on its face that it is such.

242. Dealing first with deception, in our view there is no material difference between Clause 51 and our present law: *cf.* p. 59 of the Mustill Report. As that Report observes, Article 30 and our present law recognise the right of the tribunal to refuse to make an award on agreed terms if it contains an objectionable feature, e.g. is structured to mislead third parties. Clause 51 preserves that right. Thus unless the tribunal is itself prepared to be a party to an attempted deception, we consider the risk that misleading awards will be made to be very small. If the tribunal is prepared to conspire with the parties, then nothing we could put in Clause 51 is likely to deter it. Furthermore, the whole of Clause 51 is based upon the assumption that there is a dispute between the parties which has been referred to arbitration and then settled. Nothing in the Clause would assist parties to mislead others where there was no genuine dispute or genuine reference or genuine settlement. The Clause would simply not apply to such a situation.

243. So far as arbitrability is concerned, this is a question that goes beyond agreed awards. We discuss this question when considering Clause 66 (see also the supplementary recommendations in Chapter 6 below).

244. We are not persuaded that we should require that any agreed award should state that it is such. Both under this Clause and Clause 52 the parties are free to agree on the form the award should take. In our view this is not only the position under the Model Law but also the position under our present law. A requirement that an agreed award should state that it is such would have to be made a mandatory provision to be effective. We are not aware of any problems arising under our present law and are reluctant to impose this formal requirement. Moreover, it would of course be open to the tribunal to record the agreement in the award if they thought it was appropriate to do so. However, at the enforcement stage we agree that the Court should be informed if the award is an agreed award, if this is not apparent from the award itself. We return to this point when considering Clause 66 below (see also Chapter 6).

Clause 52. Form of award

245. This Clause follows closely Article 31 of the Model Law. There are, however, two matters worthy of particular note.

246. In the first place, as in the Model Law, we have required the tribunal to give reasons, unless the award is an agreed award or the parties have agreed that reasons need not be given.

247. To our minds, it is a basic rule of justice that those charged with making a binding decision affecting the rights and obligations of others should (unless those others agree) explain the reasons for making that decision. This was also the view of the majority of those who commented on this.

248. It was suggested that having to give reasons would be likely to add to the cost of arbitrations and encourage applications for leave to appeal to the Court.

249. We do not agree. The need for reasons is that which we have explained above and has nothing to do with the question whether or not a Court should hear an appeal from an award. Further, we have introduced stricter conditions for the bringing of appeals in any event. As to cost, it is always open to the parties to agree to dispense with reasons if they wish to do so, though in the case of domestic arbitrations this can only be done after the dispute has arisen: see Clauses 69(1) and 87.

250. The second noteworthy point is that we have used the word "seat" instead of the Model Law phrase "place of arbitration". We consider that the Model Law uses this phrase to mean the seat (there being no obvious legal reason to stipulate the geographical place where the award was made), and since we have used this word earlier in the Bill (see Clauses 2 and 3) it would in our view only cause confusion not to use it here. Of course the seat is only of importance in international

arbitrations or where the question arises as to the enforcement of an award abroad. Therefore, in a purely domestic arbitration, if an arbitrator were to fail to state the "seat", or to state this incorrectly, it is extremely unlikely that the award could be challenged under Clause 68(2)(h), given that such a failure would be unlikely to result in "substantial injustice".

251. Subsection (3) provides that the award shall be in writing and signed by all the arbitrators or, alternatively, by all those assenting to the award. An earlier draft of this subsection had only stipulated that all arbitrators assenting to an award sign it. It was pointed out to the DAC, however, that (for whatever reason) some dissenting arbitrators may not wish to be identified as such, and that the provision should therefore be amended to provide for this.

252. It has been suggested to the DAC that there should be a provision allowing for somebody to sign on behalf of an arbitrator. This could invoke complicated principles of agency, and, overall, is better left to be resolved in each particular case.

Clause 53. Place where award is treated as made

253. This Clause is designed to avoid disputes over where an award is made and (in cases where Part I of the Bill applies to the arbitration in question) it reverses the decision (although not the result) of the House of Lords in *Hiscox* v. *Outhwaite* [1992] 1 AC 562.

Clause 54. Date of award

254. We trust this provision is self-explanatory.

Clause 55. Notification of award

255. This provision we also trust is self-explanatory. The obligations on the tribunal to notify the parties by service on them of copies of the award is important, given that certain time limits in the Bill for, e.g. challenging the award, run from the date of the award (which, under Clause 54, in the absence of any other agreement, is the date upon which it is signed). Time periods, of course, can be extended: see Clause 79. We have required the award to be notified to the "parties" so as to prevent one party from obtaining the award and sitting on it without informing the other party until the expiry of time limits for appeal etc, which we are aware has happened in practice.

256. Clause 55(3) provides that nothing in this section affects the power to withhold an award in the case of non-payment. However, it should be noted that the duty to notify all parties would of course revive once the tribunal's "lien" has been satisfied.

Clause 56. Power to withhold award in case of non-payment

257. These provisions enable a party to seek the assistance of the Court if he considers that the arbitrators are asking too much for the release of their award, though it is important to note from subsection (4) that there is already arbitral machinery for an appeal or review of the fees or expenses demanded.

258. Subsection (8) makes clear that this Clause does not affect the right to challenge fees and expenses under Clause 28, i.e. that paying them to get the award does not lose this right. The reason for this provision is that it may be important for a party to obtain the award quickly, rather than going to the Court for an order about fees and expenses before getting the award.

259. Unlike section 19 of the 1950 Act, this provision gives the Court a discretion to specify that a lesser amount than that claimed by the arbitration be paid into Court, in order to have the award released. If this were not so, an arbitrator could demand an extortionate amount, in effect preventing a party from taking advantage of the mechanism provided for here.

260. For obvious reasons, this provision is mandatory.

Clause 57. Correction of award or additional award

261. This Clause reflects Article 33 of the Model Law. In our view this is a useful provision, since it enables the arbitral process to correct itself, rather than requiring applications to the Court. In order to avoid delay, we have stipulated time limits for seeking corrections, etc.

Clause 58. Effect of award

262. This provision in effect simply restates the existing law.

263. It has been suggested that what is described as the other side of subsection (1) should be spelt out in the Bill, i.e. that whatever the parties may or may not agree, the award is of no substantive or evidential effect against any one who is neither a party nor claiming through or under a party.

264. Such a provision would, of course, have to be mandatory. It would have to confine itself to cases exclusively concerned with the laws of this country, for otherwise it could impinge on other applicable laws which have a different rule. Even where the situation was wholly domestic, it would also have to deal with all those cases (agreed or otherwise) in one way or another. In our view it would be very difficult to construct an acceptable provision and we are not persuaded that it is needed.

COSTS OF THE ARBITRATION

Clause 59. Costs of the arbitration

Clause 60. Agreement to pay costs in any event

Clause 61. Award of costs

Clause 62. Effect of agreement or award about costs

Clause 63. The recoverable costs of the arbitration

Clause 64. Recoverable fees and expenses of arbitrators

Clause 65. Power to limit recoverable costs

265. In these Clauses we have attempted to provide a code dealing with how the costs of an arbitration should be attributed between the parties. The question of the right of the arbitrators to fees and expenses is dealt with earlier in that part of the Bill concerned with the arbitral tribunal: see Clause 28.

266. Clause 59 defines costs.

267. Clause 60 is a mandatory provision preventing effective agreements to pay the whole or part of the costs in any event unless made after the dispute has arisen. The Clause is based on section 18(3) of the Arbitration Act 1950. The Committee are of the view that public policy continues to dictate that such a provision should remain.

268. Clause 62 empowers the arbitrators to make an award in relation to costs. Subsection (2) sets out the general principle to be applied, which is the same principle that is applicable in Court.

269. It has been suggested that arbitral tribunals should not be fettered in this way, but to our minds it is helpful to state the principle, especially for those who may not be lawyers and who otherwise might not know how to proceed. Furthermore, it seems to us that there is no reason why the general principle should not apply to arbitrations: it certainly does under the present law. The parties are, of course, free to agree on other principles, subject to Clause 60.

270. Clauses 63 and 64 are we hope more or less self-explanatory. Clearly there has to be a special regime for the fees and expense of the arbitrators, for otherwise they would be left with the power to decide for themselves whether or not they had overcharged!

271. Clause 64(4) presents any contractual right an arbitrator may have to payment of his fees and expenses. If a party has agreed these, then it would in our view be wrong to allow the Court to adjust the amount, i.e. to rewrite that agreement.

272. Clause 65 contains a new proposal. It gives the tribunal power to limit in advance the amount of recoverable costs. We consider that such a power, properly used, could prove to be extremely valuable as an aid to reducing unnecessary expenditure. It also represents a facet of the duty of the tribunal as set out in Clause 33. The Clause enables the tribunal to put a ceiling on the costs, so that while a party can continue to spend as much as it likes on an arbitration it will not be able to recover more than the ceiling limit from the other party. This will have the added virtue of discouraging those who wish to use their financial muscle to intimidate their opponents into giving

up through fear that by going on they might be subject to a costs order which they could not sustain.

POWERS OF THE COURT IN RELATION TO AWARD

Clause 66. Enforcement of the award

273. This reflects Article 35 of the Model Law. Enforcement through the Court provides the classic case of using the Court to support the arbitral process. Subsection (3)(a) is intended to state the present law: see Mustill & Boyd, *Commercial Arbitration*, 2nd Ed., at p. 546. Subsection (3)(b) is intended to cover cases where public policy would not recognise the validity of an award, for example awards purporting to decide matters which our law does not accept can be resolved by this means. For obvious reasons, this provision is mandatory.

274. Reference should be made to Chapter 6, where certain supplementary recommendations are made with respect to this Clause.

Clause 67. Challenging the award: substantive jurisdiction

275. Jurisdiction has already been considered in the context of that part of the Bill dealing with the jurisdiction of the arbitral tribunal: see Clauses 30 to 32.

276. Clause 31 allows the tribunal (where it has power to rule on its own jurisdiction) to make a "jurisdiction" award, either on its own, or as part of its award on the merits. Clause 67 provides the mechanisms for challenging the jurisdiction rulings in such awards, and is a mandatory provision. It also provides a mechanism for challenges to the jurisdiction by someone who has taken no part in the arbitral proceedings. We deal with such persons below, when considering Clause 72.

277. To avoid the possibility of challenges to the jurisdiction causing unnecessary delay, the rights given by this Clause are subject to qualifications, which explains the reference in subsection (1) to three other sections. In addition, subsection (2) means that a challenge to jurisdiction does not stop the tribunal from proceeding with other aspects of the arbitration while the application is pending.

Clause 68. Challenging the award: serious irregularity

278. We have drawn a distinction in the Bill between challenges in respect of substantive jurisdiction (i.e. those matters listed in Clause 30) and challenges in respect of what we have called "serious irregularity". We appreciate that cases may arise in which it might be difficult to decide into which category a particular set of circumstances should be placed, but since the time limits etc for both Clause 67 and Clause 68 are the same, this should cause no procedural difficulties. We are firmly of the view, however, that it is useful to have two categories.

279. The reason for this is that where jurisdiction is concerned, there can be no question of applying a test of "substantial injustice" or the like. An award of a tribunal purporting to decide the rights or obligations of a person who has not given that tribunal jurisdiction so to act simply cannot stand, though of course, if the party concerned has taken part in the arbitration, there is nothing wrong in requiring him to act without delay in challenging the award.

280. Irregularities stand on a different footing. Here we consider that it is appropriate, indeed essential, that these have to pass the test of causing "substantial injustice" before the Court can act. The Court does not have a general supervisory jurisdiction over arbitrations. We have listed the specific cases where a challenge can be made under this Clause. The test of "substantial injustice" is intended to be a applied by way of support for the arbitral process, not by way of interference with that process. Thus it is only in those cases where it can be said that what has happened is so far removed from what could reasonably be expected of the arbitral process that we would expect the Court to take action. The test is not what would have happened had the matter been litigated. To apply such a test would be to ignore the fact that the parties have agreed to arbitrate, not litigate. Having chosen arbitration, the parties cannot validly complain of substantial injustice unless what has happened simply cannot on any view be defended as an acceptable consequence of that choice.

In short, Clause 68 is really designed as a long stop, only available in extreme cases where the tribunal has gone so wrong in its conduct of the arbitration that justice calls out for it to be corrected.

281. By way of example, there have been cases under our present law where the Court has remitted awards to an arbitral tribunal because the lawyers acting for one party failed (or decided not to) put a particular point to the tribunal: see, for example, *Indian Oil Corporation* v. *Coastal (Bermuda) Ltd* [1990] 2 Lloyd's Rep. 407; *King* v. *Thomas McKenna* [1991] 2 QB 480; *Breakbulk Marine* v. *Dateline*, 19 March 1992, unreported (jurisdiction recognised but not exercised).

282. The responses we received were critical of such decisions, on the grounds that they really did amount to an interference in the arbitral process agreed by the parties. We agree. The Clause we propose is designed not to permit such interference, by setting out a closed list of irregularities (which it will not be open to the Court to extend), and instead reflecting the internationally accepted view that the Court should be able to correct serious failure to comply with the "due process" of arbitral proceedings: *cf.* Article 34 of the Model Law.

283. This Clause is, of course, mandatory.

Clause 69. Appeal on point of law

284. We received a number of responses calling for the abolition of any right of appeal on the substantive issues in the arbitration. These were based on the proposition that by agreeing to arbitrate their dispute, the parties were agreeing to abide by the decision of their chosen tribunal, not by the decision of the Court, so that whether or not a Court would reach the same conclusion was simply irrelevant. To substitute the decision of the Court on the substantive issues would be wholly to subvert the agreement the parties had made.

285. This proposition is accepted in many countries. We have considered it carefully, but we are not persuaded that we should recommend that the right of appeal should be abolished. It seems to us, that with the safeguards we propose, a limited right of appeal is consistent with the fact that the parties have chosen to arbitrate rather than litigate. For example, many arbitration agreements contain an express choice of the law to govern the rights and obligations arising out of the bargain made subject to that agreement. It can be said with force that in such circumstances, the parties have agreed that that law will be properly applied by the arbitral tribunal, with the consequence that if the tribunal fail to do this, it is not reaching the result contemplated by the arbitration agreement.

286. In these circumstances what we propose is a right to apply to the Court to decide a point of law arising out of an award. This right is limited, however, in several ways.

(i) The point of law must substantially affect the rights of one or more of the parties. This limitation exists, of course, in our present law.

(ii) The point of law must be one that was raised before the tribunal. The responses showed that in some cases applications for leave to appeal have been made and granted on the basis that an examination of the reasons for the award shows an error on a point of law that was not raised or debated in the arbitration. This method of proceeding has echoes of the old and long discarded common law rules relating to error of law on the face of award, and is in our view a retrograde step. In our view the right to appeal should be limited as we suggest.

(iii) There have been attempts, both before and after the enactment of the Arbitration Act 1979, to dress up questions of fact as questions of law and by that means to seek an appeal on the tribunal's decision on the facts. Generally these attempts have been resisted by the Courts, but to make the position clear, we propose to state expressly that consideration by the Court of the suggested question of law is made on the basis of the findings of fact in the award.

(iv) We have attempted to express in this Clause the limits put on the right to appeal by the House of Lords in *Pioneer Shipping Ltd* v. *BTP Tioxide Ltd (The Nema)* [1982] AC 724.

287. With respect to the last point, we think it is very important to do this. Many of those abroad who do not have ready access to our case law were unaware that the Arbitration Act 1979 had been construed by the House of Lords in a way that very much limited the right of appeal, and which was not evident from the words of the Act itself.

288. The test we propose is whether, in the ordinary case, the Court is satisfied that the decision of the tribunal is obviously wrong. The right of appeal is only available for such cases, for the reasons discussed above. Where the matter is one of general public importance, the test is less onerous, but the decision must still be open to serious doubt.

289. We propose a further test, namely whether, despite the agreement of the parties to resolve the matter by arbitration, it is just and proper in all the circumstances for the Court to determine the question.

290. We have been asked why we suggest this addition. The reason is that we think it desirable that this factor should be specifically addressed by the Court when it is considering an application. It seems to us to be the basis on which the House of Lords acted as it did in *The Nema, op. cit.* The Court should be satisfied that justice dictates that there should be an appeal; and in considering what justice requires, the fact that the parties have agreed to arbitrate rather than litigate is an important and powerful factor.

291. It will be noted that we have included a provision that the Court should determine an application without a hearing unless it appears to the Court that a hearing is required. This again reflects what was said in *The Nema op. cit.* about the tendency for applications for leave being turned into long and expensive court hearings. In our view, the tests for leave (i.e. obviously wrong or open to serious doubt) are such that in most cases the Court will be able to decide whether to allow or reject the application on written material alone.

292. Finally, a question has been raised as to whether an agreement in advance of the proceedings (i.e. contained in an arbitration clause more in the underlying contract) would satisfy Clause 69(2)(a). The Clause is intended to encompass such agreements, and in our view it plainly does so since the word agreement is not qualified. However, such an agreement will not automatically allow an appeal unless it complies with the other conditions set out in Clauses 69 and 70.

Clause 70. Challenge or appeal: supplementary provisions

Clause 71. Challenge or appeal: effect of order of the court

293. These provisions contain time-limits and other matters in relation to challenges to the award and applications and appeals. Some of these provisions are mandatory.

294. The time limit in Clause 70(3) runs from the date of the award, or, where applicable, the date when a party was notified of the result of any arbitral process of appeal or review. It has been suggested that difficulties might arise if an award is held back by the arbitrators, pending payment by the parties (i.e. under Clause 56). It is possible that the time limit in Clause 70(3) will have expired by the time an award is released. However, the DAC is of the view that the date of the award is the only incontrovertible date from which the time period should run. Any other starting point would result in great uncertainty (e.g. as to the exact point at which an award is "released" or "delivered"). Further, any difficulties arising from specific circumstances can be easily remedied by way of an extension of time under Clause 79.

MISCELLANEOUS

Clause 72. Saving for rights of persons who takes no part in proceedings

295. To our minds this is a vital provision. A person who disputes that an arbitral tribunal has jurisdiction cannot be required to take part in the arbitration proceedings or to take positive steps to defend his position, for any such requirement would beg the question whether or not his objection has any substance and thus be likely to lead to gross injustice. Such a person must be entitled, if he wishes, simply to ignore the arbitral process, though of course (if his objection is not well-founded) he runs the risk of an enforceable award being made against him. Those who do decide to take part in the arbitral proceedings in order to challenge the jurisdiction are, of course, in a different category, for then, having made that choice, such people can fairly and properly be required to abide by the time limits etc that we have proposed.

296. This is a mandatory provision.

Clause 73. Loss of right to object

297. Recalcitrant parties or those who have had an award made against them often seek to delay proceedings or to avoid honouring the award by raising points on jurisdiction etc which they have been saving up for this purpose or which they could and should have discovered and raised at an earlier stage. Article 4 of the Model Law contains some provisions designed to combat this sort of behaviour (which does the efficiency of arbitration as a form of dispute resolution no good) and we have attempted to address the same point in this Clause. In particular, unlike the Model Law, we have required a party to arbitration proceedings who has taken part or continued to take part without raising the objection in due time, to show that at that stage he neither knew nor could with reasonable diligence have discovered the grounds for his objection (the latter being an important modification to the Model Law, without which one would have to demonstrate actual knowledge, which may be virtually impossible to do). It seems to us that this is preferable to requiring the innocent party to prove the opposite, which for obvious reasons it might be difficult or impossible to do.

298. For the reasons explained when considering Clause 72, the provision under discussion cannot, of course, be applied to a party who has chosen to play no part at all in the arbitral proceedings.

Clause 74. Immunity of arbitral institutions, etc.

299. In this mandatory provision we have provided institutions and individuals who appoint arbitrators with a degree of immunity.

300. The reason for this proposal is that without such an immunity, there is in our view a real risk that attempts will be made to hold institutions or individuals responsible for the consequences of their exercise of the power they may be given to appoint or nominate arbitrators, or for what their appointed or nominate arbitrators then do or fail to do. This would provide a means of reopening matters that were referred to arbitration, something that might be encouraged if arbitrators were given immunity (as we have also proposed in Clause 29) but nothing was said about such institutions or individuals.

301. There is an additional point of great importance. Many organisations that provide arbitration services, including Trade Associations as well as bodies whose sole function it is to provide arbitration services, do not in the nature of things have deep pockets. Indeed much of the work is done by volunteers simply in order to promote and help this form of dispute resolution. Such organisations could find it difficult if not impossible to finance the cost of defending legal proceedings or even the cost of insurance against such cost. In our view the benefits which these organisations (and indeed individuals) have on arbitration generally fully justify giving them a measure of protection so that their good work can continue.

Clause 75. Charge to secure payment of solicitors' costs

302. This is a technical provision designed to maintain the present position.

SUPPLEMENTARY

Clause 76. Service of notices, etc.

303. The subject matter of this Clause was touched on the MacKinnon Report which led to the Arbitration Act 1934. In this Clause we have attempted to do three things.

(i) We have stipulated that the parties can agree on how service of notices and other documents can be done.

(ii) We have made clear that in the absence of agreement, service by any effective means will suffice.

(iii) We have provided in subsection (4) an option which can best be described as a "fail-safe" method, which a party may employ if he wishes, for example if he is not sure that other methods will be effective. We should emphasise that this fail safe method is not a compulsory or preferred method for service, but merely a means which, if employed, will be treated as effective.

305. These provisions do not apply in respect of service in Court proceedings, for the obvious reason that such service must comply with the rules of the Court concerned.

Clause 77. Powers of court in relation to service of documents

306. In this Clause we have given the Court powers to support the arbitral process so that it is not delayed or frustrated through difficulties over service. In the nature of human affairs, it is sadly the case that potential respondents to arbitration proceedings quite often go to considerable lengths to avoid service and thus to achieve this state of affairs, by making normal methods difficult or even impossible to use effectively. This Clause should, in appropriate cases, help to deal with such cases.

Clause 78. Reckoning periods of time

307. In our view it would be of great assistance to set out a code to deal with the reckoning of time, thus avoiding the need to refer to other sources. Hence this provision.

Clause 79. Power of court to extend time limits relating to arbitral proceedings

308. Here we propose that the Court should have a general right to extend time limits, except time limits for starting an arbitration, which is dealt with specifically in Clause 12. We propose that the wording of the Clause be clarified as set out in Chapter 6 below.

309. This power is limited in the ways set out in this Clause. In particular, no extension will be granted unless a substantial injustice would otherwise be done and any arbitral process for obtaining an extension must first be exhausted. As we have said in other contexts, it would be a rare case indeed where we would expect the Court to grant an extension where such has not been obtained through that process. With these limitations we take the view that this provision can properly be described as supporting the arbitral process.

Clause 80. Notice and other requirements in connection with legal proceedings

310. Legal proceedings must of course be subject to the rules of the Court concerned. We have made clear, therefore, that where the Bill provides for notice of legal proceedings to be given to others, this is a reference to such rules as the Court concerned may make; and is not a separate requirement over and above those rules.

Clause 81. Saving for certain matters governed by common law

311. As we have stated earlier, and as was stated in the Mustill Report, it would be neither practicable nor desirable to attempt to codify the whole of our arbitration law. Hence subsections (1) and (2) of this Clause.

312. It was suggested to us that a provision preserving the common law would enable arguments to be raised and accepted which were contrary to the spirit and intent of the Bill. We do not think that this will happen, in view of the opening words of the Clause and indeed the statements of principle in Clause 1. Equally, it seems to us to be necessary to make clear that the common law (so far as it is consistent with the Bill) will continue to make its great contribution to our arbitration law, a contribution that has done much to create and preserve the world wide popularity of arbitration in our country.

313. Subsection (3) is technically necessary to make clear that the repeal of the existing statutes does not have the effect of reviving the common law rules relating to errors on the face of the award.

Clause 82. Minor definitions

Clause 83. Index of defined expressions: Part I

314. The first of these Clauses provides the definition of words and phrases which are often repeated in the body of the Bill, so that repetition of the meaning is avoided, as well as providing a ready means of discovering the meaning of certain important words and phrases. The second of these Clauses is also designed to help the reader by identifying the place where other important words and phrases are defined or explained.

Clause 84. Transitional provisions

315. This Clause sets out the general proposition, namely that the Bill will apply to arbitral proceedings commenced after the legislation comes into force, whenever the arbitration agreement is made. There are respectable precedents for this, since the Arbitration Acts 1889, and 1934 contained a like provision. The 1950 Act, of course, was not a precedent, since this was a consolidating measure. We consider this to be a useful provision, since some arbitration agreements have a very long life indeed (for example, rent review arbitration agreements under leases) and it would be most unsatisfactory if the existing law and the proposed legislation were to run in parallel (if that is the right expression) indefinitely into the future.

316. Reference should also be made to Clause 111.

CHAPTER 3—PART II OF THE BILL
OTHER PROVISIONS RELATING TO ARBITRATION

DOMESTIC ARBITRATION AGREEMENTS

Clause 85. Modification of Part I in relation to domestic arbitration agreements

Clause 86. Staying of legal proceedings

Clause 87. Effectiveness of agreement to exclude court's jurisdiction

Clause 88. Power to repeal or amend ss. 85 to 87

317. Under our present law, a distinction is drawn between domestic and other arbitrations for two main purposes.

318. In the first place, the rules for obtaining a stay of legal proceedings differ. The reason for this is that under international Conventions, a stay in favour of an arbitration is mandatory except in certain specified circumstances. The current Convention is the New York Convention and the rules under that Convention we have now set out in Clause 9. With an exception that we have already discussed above, Clause 9 simply re-enacts the Arbitration Act 1975 so far as it concerns this matter.

319. Section 1 of the Arbitration Act 1975 does not apply to domestic arbitrations as there defined. These continue to be governed by section 4(1) of the Arbitration Act 1950, which makes the grant of a stay discretionary.

320. It is our view that consideration should be given to abolishing this distinction and applying the New York Convention rules to all cases. It seems to us that these rules fit much more happily with the concept of party autonomy than our domestic rules, which were framed at a time when attitudes to arbitrations were very different and the Courts were anxious to avoid what they described as usurpation of their process.

321. For example, there are cases justifying the refusal of a stay in cases where the Court considers that the party seeking to arbitrate has no defence to the claim and is merely seeking to delay the day of judgment. This has been explained on the basis that since there is no defence to the claim, there is no dispute that can be arbitrated. The difficulty with this argument is that it logically follows that only disputable matters can be arbitrated, or, in other words, that the arbitrators have no jurisdiction to deal with cases where there is no real defence. This in turn means that a claimant cannot refer a claim to arbitration where there is no real defence, since *ex hypothesi* the arbitrators

would have no jurisdiction. In short, this argument leads to consequences that in our view have only to be stated to be rejected. As to delaying tactics, it has been our intention throughout the Bill to provide the means whereby an agreement to arbitrate can produce (in suitable cases) a very quick answer indeed. Indeed, if in truth there is no defence to a claim, then it should not take more than a very short time for an arbitral tribunal to deal with the matter and produce an award.

322. For these reasons, which are those discussed in *Nelson* v. *Hayter* [1990] 2 Lloyd's Rep. 265, we consider that this ground for preserving the distinction between domestic and other arbitrations so far as stays are concerned is highly unconvincing.

323. The domestic rules have also have also been used to refuse stays where the disputes are likely to involve other parties, who could not be brought into the arbitration, since the agreement to arbitrate only binds those who were party to it. Here the justification for refusing to stay legal proceedings is that it would be much better for all the concerned parties to be brought into one proceeding, so that the whole matter can be sorted out between them all.

324. This reasoning of course is in one sense supported by common sense and justice, for in certain cases it would be better and fairer for all the disputes between all the parties involved to be dealt with by one tribunal, thereby avoiding delay and the possibility of inconsistent findings by different tribunals. However, as we observed in the context of considering whether there should be a power (without the agreement of the parties) to order consolidation or concurrent hearings in arbitrations (Clause 35), to refuse a stay because other parties are involved involves tearing up the arbitration agreement that the applicant for a stay has made. In other words, with the benefit of hindsight, the Court adjusts the rights and obligations of contracting parties.

325. We fully accept that for reasons of consumer protection, this on occasion can and should be done, but we are not persuaded that it should be a general rule in the context of stays of domestic arbitrations, for it sits uneasily with the principle of party autonomy and amounts to interference with rather than support for the arbitral process.

326. We should also note that the distinction drawn between domestic and other arbitrations produces odd results. An arbitration agreement between two English people is a domestic arbitration agreement, while an agreement between an English person and someone of a different nationality is not, even if that person has spent all his time in England. Furthermore, we are aware that it could be said that the distinction discriminates against European Community nationals who are not English, and is thus contrary to European law.

327. Notwithstanding the foregoing, we do not propose in this Bill to abolish the distinction. Some defend it and we have not had an opportunity to make all the soundings we would like on this subject. What we have done is to put the domestic arbitration rules in a separate part of the Bill, and provided in Clause 88 for a power of repeal through the mechanism of a positive joint resolution of each House of Parliament.

328. What we have felt able to do is to redraft the domestic rules on stays and to make two changes. Firstly we have removed the discretion and instead set out words which are wide enough to encompass the circumstances which the cases have developed as grounds for refusing a stay. Secondly and more importantly, we have reversed the existing burden of proof (and incidentally got rid of a double or perhaps treble negative in the previous legislation). It seemed to us that it was for the party seeking to litigate something which he had previously agreed to arbitrate to persuade the Court that he should be allowed to go back on his agreement.

329. The second purpose served by making a distinction between domestic and other arbitrations is to prevent the parties in a domestic case from effectively agreeing to exclude the jurisdiction of the Court to deal with preliminary points of law or with an appeal from an award on a point of law, until after the commencement of the arbitral proceedings. This necessarily means that until the arbitration starts such parties cannot make an effective agreement to dispense with reasons, for that is treated as an agreement to exclude the jurisdiction of the Court—see, now, Clause 69(1).

330. Again we are not persuaded of the value or the validity of this, but we have preserved the existing law for the same reason as we have preserved position on stays. Our own view is that this distinction should disappear.

331. It should be noted that we have not preserved the "special categories" dealt with in Section 4 of the Arbitration Act 1979. These were intended as a temporary measure, and the weight of the responses received persuaded us that they should now go.

CONSUMER ARBITRATION AGREEMENTS

Clauses 89 to 93

332. In these Clauses we have consolidated the provisions of the Consumer Arbitration Agreements Act 1988. We have suggested this in order to bring within the Bill all the current major enactments on arbitration, so as to provide as complete a code as possible.

333. We did not regard it as part of our remit to redraft this legislation, so we have not sought responses on it. However, we are aware that problems have arisen in construing this Act. For example, it has been suggested that what now appears as Clause 89 makes it far from clear whether a building contract made by a consumer falls outside the Act if the consumer has sought a number of quotes for the work.

334. We are also aware of a more fundamental problem. This country has recently implemented Council Directive 93/13 through the Unfair Terms in Consumer Contracts Regulations 1994 (S.I. 1994/3159). These Regulations came into force on 1 July 1995. Thus at the moment a situation exists where there are two parallel regimes for protecting consumer interests in the context of arbitration agreements.

335. To our minds this is an unsatisfactory state of affairs, likely to cause confusion and difficulties. Although we have not attempted to trespass into the field of consumer protection, it does seem to us that it would be unfortunate if the opportunity were not taken to clarify the position. On the face of it the solution would seem to be to maintain the suggested repeal of the 1988 Act and to omit Clauses 89 to 92 of the Bill. If this were to be done, then we would welcome at least a cross-reference in the Bill to the Regulations, so that anyone reading the Bill will be made aware of them. As we understand it, the Regulations would not affect our international obligations regarding arbitrations (for example, the New York Convention) though doubtless those charged with the question of consumer protection will consider this aspect of the matter.

336. We would, however, emphasise that the arbitration community is extremely anxious that the Bill should not be delayed. The fact is that this country has been very slow to modernise its arbitration law and this has done us no good in our endeavour to retain our pre-eminence in the field of international arbitration, a service which brings this country very substantial amounts indeed by way of invisible earnings.

337. It is for these reasons that we have included in Clause 88 a power to amend or repeal Clauses 89 to 93. If the situation cannot be clarified or settled without delaying the progress of the Bill, then this mechanism could allow the Bill to go forward with the Consumer Arbitration Agreements Act in it, and the matter dealt with later.

SMALL CLAIMS ARBITRATIONS IN THE COUNTRY COURT

Clause 94. Exclusion of Part I in relation to small claims in the county court

338. There is an entirely separate regime for the arbitration of small claims in the County Court. The Bill is not intended to affect this.

339. As we observed earlier in the Report, we considered the suggestion that we should incorporate in the Bill another system for the arbitration of small claims, but for the reasons given, we have not adopted this suggestion and do not recommend it.

APPOINTMENT OF JUDGES AS ARBITRATORS

Clause 95. Appointment of judges as arbitrators

340. In this Clause we have set out the existing provisions for the appointment of Commercial Judges and Official Referees as arbitrators.

341. We are firmly of the view that provision should be made for any Judge to be appointed as an arbitrator, rather than limiting the power to the two kinds of Judge presently included. It was not, however, possible to obtain agreement to this proposal from the concerned departments in time to put it in the Bill.

342. We appreciate that in view of the court commitments of Judges generally, it is not possible to allow Judges to act as arbitrators whenever they are asked and are willing to do so. Hence the present requirement now set out in subsections (2) and (3). We would suggest that the same or a similar provision is used for all other Judges.

343. We are told that the problem is particularly acute in the field of patents and the like, where the parties are anxious to arbitrate but where the only acceptable arbitrators are Judges.

STATUTORY ARBITRATIONS

Clauses 96 to 101

344. These provisions adapt Part I to statutory arbitrations. This exercise is not within our remit and we have played no part in it.

CHAPTER 4—PART III OF THE BILL

Clauses 102 to 107

345. The purpose of Part III is to re-enact the substance of the provisions relating to the recognition and enforcement of foreign arbitral awards contained in Part II of the Arbitration Act 1950 and the Arbitration Act 1975, which gave effect to the UK's treaty obligations under the Geneva and New York Conventions respectively.

346. The Geneva Convention only remains in force as between state parties to that Convention which have not subsequently become parties to the New York Convention. So far as the UK is concerned, it is believed that only a few states (e.g. Malta) remain in that category. Accordingly, in the interest of brevity, Clause 102 states simply that Part II of the Arbitration Act 1950 continues to apply to Geneva Convention awards which are not also New York Convention awards rather than restating or refraining the non-user friendly language of Part II of that Act.

347. The New York Convention on the Recognition and Enforcement of Foreign Arbitral Awards adopted by the UN Conference on International Arbitration on 10 June 1958 is not only the cornerstone of international dispute resolution; it is an essential ingredient more generally of world trade. If it did not exist, or even if it were not to have been widely adopted by the world's trading nations, contracting parties from different legal cultures might be reduced to resolving their disputes in the courts of a country which would be alien to either one or both of them (because of doubts as to the enforceability across national boundaries of arbitration awards made in a neutral country). Clauses 102 to 107 to the Bill restate the current implementing legislation (contained in the 1975 Act) in concise and simple language.

348. As we have indicated earlier in Chapter 2, we take the view that the definition of "in writing" is consistent with Article II.2 of the New York Convention. For clarity therefore, we consider that the Bill can be improved by including an express cross reference to this definition in Clause 103(2). This would have the added advantage of ensuring that the enforcement of foreign awards under Clause 66 and enforcement under the New York Convention are in this respect in line with each other.

349. One intriguing question was highlighted by the decision of the House of Lords in *Hiscox* v. *Outhwaite* [1992] 1 AC 562. This concerns the case of an arbitration with its "seat" in country A and an award that states expressly that it was "made" in country B. Country A might be a New York Convention country, and B not—or vice versa. (Article I.1 of the Convention provides that it shall apply to " . . . awards *made* in the territory of a State other than the State in which recognition and enforcement of such awards are sought . . . " (emphasis added).)

350. Distinguished authors (writing before the decision in *Hiscox*) are split on the question. Dr A. J. van den Berg in the first edition of his authoritative book on the Convention (at pp. 294/295) states: "The award must be deemed to be made in the country which is indicated in the award as [the] place where the award was made." (emphasis added) [*sic*].

351. But the late Dr F. A. Mann QC (in [1985] Arb. Int. 107/108) wrote, after recalling that little learning then existed on the question of where an award is made, "It is submitted that an award is 'made' at the place at which the arbitration is held, i.e. the arbitral seat . . . admittedly the view

suggested here attributes a somewhat strained meaning to the word 'made'. But for the reasons given the natural meaning of the word leads to such strange consequences that a less literal interpretation would seem to be justified".

352. In *Hiscox* the question arose as to whether, where the "seat" of arbitration was in England and for all practical purposes it was a domestic "English" arbitration, the award became a "foreign" award for the purposes of the Convention merely because it stated expressly on its face that it was signed in Paris? According to the House of Lords, applying a literal interpretation of Article I.1 of the Convention, the answer was "Yes".

353. So far as arbitrations held in England, Wales or Northern Ireland are concerned, the "strange consequences" of this result have been removed by Clause 53 of the Bill (see above).

354. The DAC is of the view that this question should be resolved by incorporating into Part III of the proposed new legislation an equivalent provision to that contained in Clause 53—to the effect that an award shall be treated as made at the seat of the arbitration, regardless of where it was signed, despatched or delivered to any of the parties. It seems to us that this is consonant with the UK's treaty obligations under the New York Convention.

CHAPTER 5—PART IV OF THE BILL

355. We have drawn attention to Clause 111 under Clause 84. The other Clauses in this Part we trust are self-evident, and were not within the remit of the DAC, although we do welcome the inclusion of Northern Ireland.

CHAPTER 6—SUPPLEMENTARY RECOMMENDATIONS

356. The foregoing discussion is based on the text of the Bill as it was introduced in December 1995. Since that date we have had the advantage of considering the speeches made in the House of Lords on the Second Reading and some comments and suggestions from others, as well as looking once again at the text of the Bill in the course of preparing this Report. In consequence, we make the following recommendations.

Clause 2. Scope of application

357. A number of foreign readers have expressed the view that Clause 2(2)(a) does not sufficiently make clear that the applicable law referred to is the law applicable to the arbitration agreement rather than the law applicable to the substantive agreement (which would have far reaching and wholly unintended consequences). For the sake of clarity, we would suggest an amendment along the following lines:

> " . . . where the applicable law *to that agreement* is the law of England and Wales or Northern Ireland; and . . . "

Clause 7. Separability of arbitration agreement

358. In view of the definition of "agreement" in Clause 5, we suggest that the words "(whether or not in writing)" be inserted after the words "another agreement" in Clause 7, since otherwise it could be said that this Clause is only effective in relation to such other agreements as are in writing. This is not the intention.

Clause 14(5). Commencement of arbitral proceedings

359. It has been suggested that the words "gives notice" should be replaced by "serves", in conformity with Clauses 14(3) and 14(4). This is a matter for Parliamentary Counsel to consider.

Clause 16(6)(b) and Clause 21(4)

360. The word "any" follows a negative and so could be read as meaning "all." This is not the intention. We therefore suggest that the words "one or more matters" follow the word "any" in these provisions.

Clause 24(4). Power of court to remove arbitrator

361. We have explained in Chapter 1 above the reasoning behind Clause 29(3). Upon further reflection, it appears to us that Clause 24(4) needs to be altered for the same reason. As currently drafted, if an arbitrator resigns and is sued for his fees, he is not protected from such a breach of contract action by the immunity in Clause 29. Rather, he can apply to the Court for protection under Clause 25(3), and the Court may see fit to grant this, if appropriate. However, if an arbitrator does not resign, but is removed by the Court under Clause 24, it would appear that he will have the benefit of the immunity in Clause 29, come what may. In such circumstances, the parties could not sue him for breach of contract, unless they could demonstrate "bad faith". This is anomalous. The DAC therefore recommends that Clause 24(4) be amended to provide that as well as making such order as it thinks fit with respect to an arbitrator's entitlement to fees, where the Court removes an arbitrator, it also be given a discretion to make such order as it thinks fit with respect to an arbitrator's immunity under Clause 29. Such wide words would enable the Court, for example, to remove the immunity but impose a ceiling on the amount of any liability.

362. Arbitrators may also be removed by agreement of the parties. However, the DAC does not consider that a similar provision be made with respect to this, given that it would be contrary to the whole basis of Clause 29 for parties to be able to agree on the removal of an arbitrator's immunity.

Clause 25(2). Resignation of arbitrator

363. There is a rogue "in writing" in this subsection, which should be deleted by virtue of Clause 5(1).

Clause 38(3). Security for costs

364. In the draft Clauses published in July 1995, the power to order security for costs was expressed in very general terms. This elicited a number of responses which expressed concern that there were no principles or guidelines for the exercise of this power. It is certainly the case that the power to order security for costs, unless exercised with great care, can all too easily work injustice rather than justice.

365. The rules and principles applied by the Courts with respect to security for costs have been carefully worked out over many years, and are contained in a large amount of case law that has developed alongside Order 23 of the Rules of the Supreme Court. Given the concerns referred to above, the DAC considered whether to set out these rules and principles in the Bill. In the end we decided that this would be simply impracticable: a codification of all the relevant case law would be extremely difficult, would result in very lengthy and complicated provisions, and may well have an unintended impact on how this area is approached by the Courts.

366. Clause 38(3) of the current draft of the Bill reflects what we initially concluded was the only solution to this difficulty: it provides that arbitrators are to have power to order a party to provide security for costs "wherever the court would have power . . . " and that this power is to be exercised: "on the same principles as the court." In the light of many comments received since the Bill was introduced (including a significant number of criticisms of this subsection from foreign arbitration specialists and institutions), we have had to reconsider this area, and, after much careful thought, we have concluded that Clause 38(3) requires amendment for the following reasons:

(i) As drafted, this subsection is very far from being "user-friendly". Without referring to the Rules of Supreme Court, and the case law referred to in the relevant part of the White Book, it would be impossible for any domestic or foreign user to determine what the nature and scope of the power conferred here is. Lay arbitrators may have difficulty locating or even, perhaps, understanding the relevant law (any error of law, of course, being a potential ground for appeal). In the case of a foreign arbitration that has its seat in this country for the sole reason that this is a neutral forum, it would be extremely undesirable for parties to have to instruct English lawyers in order to make sense of this provision. This alone could constitute a powerful disincentive to selecting this country as an arbitral seat. Indeed, throughout the Bill, we have been very careful to avoid any such express cross-references to other legal sources.

(ii) One of the grounds on which an order for security for costs may be made in Court is that the plaintiff is ordinarily resident out of the jurisdiction: see Order 23, Rule 1(1)(a) of the Rules of the Supreme Court. On further consideration of the matter, we have concluded that it would be very damaging to this country's position as the leading centre for international arbitrations to make this ground available to arbitral tribunals. It would reasonably appear to those abroad who are minded to arbitrate their claims here that foreigners were being singled out for special and undeserved treatment. (Of course if the parties agree to invest their tribunal with power to order security for costs on this ground, they are free to do so.)

(iii) On reflection, the concerns expressed above as to the potential scope of the power conferred by Clause 38(3) and the possibilities of injustice may be overstated. The other provisions of the Bill confer very far-reaching powers on arbitrators, and it has been made clear throughout that this is tempered, for example, by the mandatory duty in Clause 33. The same would be true of the power to order security for costs: in exercising the power, the tribunal would have to comply with Clause 33, and any serious irregularity could form the basis of a challenge. In agreeing to arbitration, parties in effect agree that their disputes could be decided differently from a Court, although in accordance with principles of justice. The fact that arbitrators may decide an issue as to security for costs differently from a judge appears to be no more than an aspect of this. It is true that if this power is improperly exercised, a claim could, for example, be stifled without justification. It is equally true, however, that the Bill contains mechanisms for parties to challenge any such injustice or improper conduct, and sufficient warnings to arbitrators as to their mandatory duties.

367. We remain of the view that the power to order security for costs is an important one, and should be given to arbitrators, and also that some basic restrictions should be set out in this Clause, in the light of the points made above. To this end, we recommend that Clause 38(3) be deleted, and replaced with a new provision along the following lines:

> "(3) The tribunal may order a claimant to provide security for the costs of the arbitration.
>
> Such power shall not be exercised on the grounds only that such party is
> (a) an individual ordinarily resident in a state other than the United Kingdom,
> (b) a body corporate which was incorporated in or has its central management and control exercised in a state other than the United Kingdom."

368. Such a provision would allow arbitrators a flexibility in exercising this power, within the confines of their strict duty in Clause 33. The risk of an order on the sole ground that a party is from abroad, would be removed. Similarly, there would be no need for an arbitrator, whether domestic or foreign, to discern the English or Northern Irish law in this area, or, indeed, to instruct local lawyers in this respect. An arbitrator may well exercise this power differently from a Court (as with many other powers conferred by the Bill), but any misuse could be corrected under the other provisions of the Bill.

369. It is of course the case that orders for security are not to be made automatically, but only when the justice of the case so requires. We appreciate that cases are likely to arise when deciding what is just may be very difficult. For example, a claimant may contend that he might be prevented from continuing if he has to put up security, whilst at the same time a respondent is contending that unless security is provided, he is likely to be ruined. However, to our minds, this is merely an example of the balancing of factors in order to achieve the most just result possible which is part of the essential function of arbitrators.

370. The power to award security for costs under the proposed provision could be exercised against counter-claimants as well as claimants. This we have covered in the definition Clause (see Clause 82(1)).

Clause 66. Enforcement of award

371. In the present Bill, we have provided that leave by a Court to enforce an award may not be given if the award was so defective in form or substance that it is incapable of enforcement, if its enforcement would be contrary to public policy or if the tribunal lacked substantive jurisdiction.

372. These are what are described as "passive" defences to the enforcement of an award. The "positive" steps that may be taken are those we have set out in Clause 67 to 69, together with the rights preserved in Clause 72 for someone who has taken no part in the arbitral proceedings.

373. In our view the way we have drafted Clause 66 sufficed to cover all the cases where enforcement should be refused. However, since the Bill was published it has been suggested to us that it would be advisable to spell out in more detail two particular cases, namely those where the arbitral tribunal has purported to decide matters which are simply not capable of resolution by arbitration, whatever the parties might have agreed (e.g. custody of a child) and those where the tribunal has made an award which (if enforced) would improperly affect the rights and obligations of those who were not parties to the arbitration agreement.

374. On the present wording, even if it could be said that either or both these cases fell outside the three categories where leave to enforce shall not be given, it does not follow that the Clause somehow sanctions enforcement in those cases. The reason for this is that the Clause does not require the Court to order enforcement, but only gives it a discretion to do so. That discretion is only fettered in a negative way, i.e. by setting out certain cases where enforcement shall not be ordered. To our minds there is nothing to prevent a Court from refusing to enforce an award in other appropriate cases. Unlike, for example, Clause 68, there is no closed list of cases where leave to enforce an award may be refused. However, on reflection we consider that it would be preferable to set out the two cases as further instances where the discretion of the Court is negatively fettered, and we would suggest that a further category is added to subsection (3) along the following lines:

> "it purports to decide matters which are not capable of resolution by arbitration or grants relief which (if enforced as a judgment or order of the court) would improperly affect the rights of persons other than the parties to the arbitration agreement."

375. Such a provision would best appear before the catch all case of public policy. It will be noted that this wording takes advantage of the definition of parties to an arbitration agreement to be found in Clause 82(2). Furthermore, to put the matter beyond any doubt, we would suggest that it is made clear that subsection (3) is not a closed list, by inserting suitable words.

376. It is vital to include some such word as "improperly" since there is no doubt that there are many cases where third party rights and obligations are perfectly properly affected, such as guarantors or insurers who have agreed to pay the amount of an award to which they are not a party. Furthermore, it must always be borne in mind that the parties' rights and obligations may well be governed by a law other than our own, under which, for example, matters are arbitrable which would not be the case under our own law. In such cases it would not automatically follow that the Court would refuse to enforce the award, unless of course public policy dictated that course.

377. Apart from the enforcement procedure set out in this clause, under our law it is possible to bring an action on an award, in much the same way as an action is brought on an agreement. This method is expressly saved in Clause 81(2)(b). There is also an oblique reference to this in Clause 66(5) in the reference to "rule of law". On reflection, it seems to us that it would make for greater clarity to add the words "or by an action on the award" at the end of this subsection.

378. There is one further point. It seems to us that there is much to be said for a suggestion that the Court must be informed on an application for enforcement if the award is an agreed award (see Clause 51) if this is not apparent from the award itself, and that any enforcement order or judgment of the Court should also state that it is made in respect of an agreed award, thus putting everyone concerned on notice of that fact and avoiding the risk that third parties might be misled into believing that the award was one made at arm's length. We suggest that these requirements be added to Clause 66.

Clause 69. Appeal on point of law

379. It has been pointed out that Clause 69(8) sets out the two pre-conditions to an appeal to the Court of Appeal as alternatives, whereas they should be cumulative (as with the similar pre-conditions in section 1(7) of the 1979 Act). We recommend that the Clause be amended accordingly.

Clause 70. Challenge or appeal: supplementary provisions

380. We note that the power to order security or bring the money payable under the award into court only extends at present to applications under Clauses 67 or 68. This should be extended so that the Court can impose these requirements as a condition of granting leave to appeal under Clause 69. This is a tool of great value, since it helps to avoid the risk that while the appeal is pending, the ability of the losing party to honour the award may (by design or otherwise) be diminished.

381. On reflection we consider that the wording of Clause 74(2) should be tightened so as to make clear that the institution or person concerned is not liable without more for anything done or omitted to be done by the arbitrator. Thus we suggest that the words "*by reason only of*" should be substituted for the word "*for*" in this subsection.

Clause 79. Powers of court to extend time limits relating to arbitral proceedings

382. It has been pointed out to us that Clause 79(1) as presently drafted could be said to be inapplicable to, for example, Clause 70(3) where the time stipulated is not one having effect in default of agreement between the parties. We agree with this comment and suggest that Clause 79(1) be amended along the following lines:

> " . . . the court may by order extend any time limit agreed by them in relation to any matter relating to the arbitral proceedings or *applicable by virtue of any provision of this Part.*"

Clause 81. Saving for certain matters governed by common law

383. We suggest that two additions should be made to the specific cases mentioned in sub-section (2).

384. The first of these relates to confidentiality. For reasons we have explained, we have not included specific provisions dealing with this matter. However, it seems to us that it would be valuable to highlight the fact that our law does deal with it. Thus we suggest a further category which could perhaps be in the following words:

> "confidentiality and privacy in relation to arbitrations."

385. The second addition we propose relates to arbitrability, which we have discussed in the context of Clause 66. Again there is a lot of important law on this topic. We suggest a further category which could perhaps be in the following words:

> "*whether a matter is capable of resolution by arbitration.*"

386. The title to this Clause is "*Saving for certain matters governed by common law*". We would prefer the expression "*other rules of law*" to the words "*common law*" as this would include legislation and be clearer to non-lawyers and those from abroad.

Clause 82. Minor definitions

387. The definition of "*question of law*" started life as part of the Clause dealing with appeals to the Court; now Clause 69. The objective was to make clear that there was no question of an appeal in respect of a matter of foreign law. Our law treats questions of foreign law as questions of fact. Furthermore, we can see no good reason for allowing an appeal on foreign law, since *ex hypothesi* the Court cannot give a definitive or authoritative ruling on such matters. The Courts have refused

to grant leave to appeal on questions of foreign law, but attempts are still made and it would be desirable to put the matter beyond doubt.

388. The definition was moved to this Clause. It had, of course, to accommodate the fact that the Bill is expressed to apply to Northern Ireland as well as England and Wales. However the present definition, while it does this, also seems to indicate that where the seat of the arbitration is in neither of these places, the meaning of "question of law" is not confined to questions of (respectively) English law or the law of Northern Ireland. We would suggest that the definition be amended, so that "question of law" means a question of law of England and Wales where the application for leave to appeal is made to a Court in England and Wales, and a question of the law of Northern Ireland, where an application for leave to appeal is made to a Court in Northern Ireland.

Clause 85. Domestic arbitration agreements

389. It has been pointed out to us that the way "domestic arbitration agreements" is defined (which is taken from the existing legislation) means that agreements made by sovereign states which incorporate an arbitration clause fall into this category. We are sure that this was not the intention, so that if the distinction between domestic and non-domestic arbitrations is to remain, the opportunity should be taken to correct this anomaly.

Clause 93. Appointment of judges as arbitrators

390. For the reasons set out in our discussion of this Clause in Chapter 1, we recommend that this provision be extended to judges generally.

Clauses 94–100. Statutory arbitrations

391. Although the application of Part I to statutory arbitrations is not part of our remit, we note that during the Second Reading Lord Lester suggested that it might be a requirement of European law in cases of compulsory arbitration that the arbitrators should be independent as well as impartial. We can offer no view on this point, but if it is felt appropriate to include any such requirement in the context of statutory arbitrations, great care should be taken to make clear that this requirement has no application to private or other consensual arbitrations, so as to avoid any risk of this concept being imported into other cases. This, for the reasons already given, would in our view be most damaging. We understand that Lord Lester shares our view that a requirement of independence for private or other consensual arbitrations is neither necessary nor desirable.

Clause 103. New York Convention awards

392. For the reasons set out in our discussion in Chapter 3, this Clause should be amended so as to cross-refer to the definition of writing to be found in Part I of the Bill, and should also incorporate the recommendation that an award should be treated as made at the seat of the arbitration, regardless of where it was signed, despatched or delivered to any of the parties.

Clause 107. Saving for other bases of recognition or enforcement

393. It has been pointed out that, as drafted, this Clause may not save enforcement under Part II of the 1950 Act. This is a matter for Parliamentary Counsel to consider.

CHAPTER 7—CONCLUSIONS

394. The Arbitration Bill and this Report are the result of a long and wide-ranging process of consultation with interested parties, probably the most comprehensive for any Bill of this kind. Our recommendations are based on the many responses that we have received as well as our own researches and discussions. In a number of cases, of course, we have had to make decisions on matters where more than one point of view has been expressed. What we should emphasise, however, is that all were agreed that it is high time we had new legislation, to the extent that many

people have stated to us that for this reason they were not disposed to delay progress by stubbornly insisting on their point of view on particular points; and have demonstrated that this is the case by being ready and willing to reach compromise solutions. We are convinced (as all are) that further delay will do grave and probably irretrievable damage to the cause of arbitration in this country, thus damaging our valuable international reputation as well as the promotion here of this form of dispute resolution.

395. We have attempted to produce a draft which can be read, understood and applied by everyone, not just lawyers learned in this branch of our law. Thus our aim has been to make the text "user-friendly" and the rules it contains clear and readily comprehensible, so that arbitration is available to all who wish to use it. This has not been an easy task, since in the nature of things this form of dispute resolution raises highly complex and sophisticated matters. We have attempted it, however, in the hope that our efforts will not only encourage and promote arbitration, but also help to achieve what we believe to be the true object of this form of dispute resolution, namely (in the words of Clause 1 of the Bill itself) to obtain the fair resolution of disputes by an impartial tribunal without unnecessary delay or expense.

APPENDIX 9

DEPARTMENTAL ADVISORY COMMITTEE ON ARBITRATION LAW

SUPPLEMENTARY REPORT ON THE ARBITRATION ACT 1996*

(January 1997: **Chairman**: The Rt Hon Lord Justice Saville)

SUPPLEMENT TO THE DAC REPORT ON THE ARBITRATION BILL, OF FEBRUARY 1996

CONTENTS

CHAPTER 1—INTRODUCTION

1. In our Report of February 1996 we discussed the provisions of the Arbitration Bill as introduced in the House of Lords in December 1995. In Chapter 6 of that Report we set out some recommendations for changes to some of the provisions of the Bill, having considered the speeches made in the House of Lords on the Second Reading and some comments and suggestions from others; and having also carried out our own re-examination of the Bill. This Report discusses the changes that were made to the Bill during its passage through Parliament and thus the differences between that Bill and the Arbitration Act 1996, which received the Royal Assent on 17 June 1996. All these changes were recommended by the Committee, though some differ from or are in addition to the suggestions originally made in Chapter 6. Not all the changes suggested in Chapter 6 were adopted, but again this met with the approval of the Committee, after yet further reflection and consideration of comments and suggestions made to us.

2. Certain decisions were also taken by the DAC after the Act received the Royal Assent, with respect to the commencement of its provisions. These are also discussed with respect to the particular sections affected, and in the context of the transitional provisions.

3. This Supplementary Report is to be read in conjunction with our Report of February 1996. The numbering of sections corresponds to the Act in its final form. As several sections were added to the Bill during its passage through Parliament, some of the references are slightly different from those in Chapter 6 of our February 1996 Report.

4. The new Order 73 of the Rules of the Supreme Court, together with the new Allocation Order (which stipulates the Courts to which arbitration applications may be made) have been included in

Appendix A to this Report, together with a short commentary. The new Order 73 has been completely recast in order to reflect the changes brought about by the Act and to simplify the procedure for Court applications concerning arbitration. Although drafted in consultation with some members of the DAC, the new rules were not within the latter's remit, and are therefore included here simply for ease of reference.

5. By the Arbitration Act (Commencement No. 1) Order 1996 (S.I. 1996 No. 3146), the Act (with the qualifications set out in that Order) comes into force on 31st January 1997. This Order also contains transitional provisions. The Order is reproduced in Appendix B, together with a short commentary.

CHAPTER 2—PART I OF THE ACT

Section 2. Scope of application

6. Clause 2 of the Bill as introduced in the House of Lords in December 1995, read as follows:

> "**2.**—(1) The provisions of this Part apply where the law of England and Wales or Northern Ireland is applicable, or the powers of the court are exercisable, in accordance with the rules of the conflict of laws.
>
> (2) They apply, in particular—
>
> (a) to matters relating to or governed by the arbitration agreement, where the applicable law is the law of England and Wales or Northern Ireland; and
> (b) to matters governed by the law applicable to the arbitral proceedings, where the seat of the arbitration is in England and Wales or Northern Ireland.
>
> (3) The following provisions apply whatever the law applicable to the arbitration agreement or the arbitral proceedings:
>
> (a) sections 9 to 11 (stay of legal proceedings);
> (b) section 43 (securing the attendance of witnesses) and section 44 (court powers exercisable in support of arbitral proceedings); and
> (c) section 66 (enforcement of arbitral awards).
>
> (4) The court may refuse to exercise any power conferred by this Part if, in the opinion of the court, the fact that the seat of the arbitration is outside England and Wales or Northern Ireland, or that when designated or determined the seat is likely to be outside England and Wales or Northern Ireland, makes it inappropriate to exercise that power."

7. This provision was explained at paragraphs 23 to 25 of our Report of February 1996. The intention was to set out a clear statement identifying the scope of application of the Act, without attempting to codify any rules of the conflict of laws. The basic elements of this clause, as originally drafted, may be summarised as follows:

(i) Clause 2(1) simply provided that the Act applies wherever English law is found to be applicable to an arbitration, or where the powers of the English Court are exercisable in relation to an arbitration. Whether or not English law is applicable, and whether or not the powers of the English Court are exercisable, are both matters to be determined by reference to appropriate rules of the conflict of laws, which are to be found elsewhere.

(ii) Clause 2(2), as originally drafted, further refined this basic principle by recognising that different elements in an arbitration may well be governed by different laws. The law governing the merits of the dispute (e.g. a choice of law clause in a contract) may not necessarily govern the arbitration clause itself, as the latter constitutes a separate agreement. Similarly, the law governing the procedure of the arbitration may well be a different law from that governing the merits of the dispute. Consequently, if the arbitration agreement was governed by English law, those provisions in the Act which concern arbitration agreements would apply (clause 2(2)(a)). Similarly, if the seat of the arbitration was in England and Wales or Northern Ireland, those parts of the Act which concern the arbitral procedure (as distinct from matters of substance) would apply (clause 2(2)(b)).

This further refinement was necessary in order to avoid the danger that all the provisions of Part I of the Act would be imported if English law is found to govern one particular aspect of an arbitration. For example, an arbitration may have a French seat, with French law governing the procedure, but English law governing the arbitration agreement. In such a situation, only those provisions of the Act which concern arbitration agreements should apply. It would be quite wrong to apply provisions of the Act which concern arbitral procedure, as this would be governed by French law. Indeed, if this were not the case, a choice of English law to govern an arbitration agreement would entitle a party to invoke the jurisdiction of the English Court wherever the seat of the arbitration might be, thereby endowing the English Court with an unacceptable extra-territorial jurisdiction.

(iii) The remaining parts of the original clause 2 made specific provision for the New York Convention (clause 2(3)(a) and (b)—stays of legal proceedings and the enforcement of awards) and enacted, section 25 of the Civil Jurisdiction and Judgments Act 1982 (clause 2(3)(b)—powers in support of foreign arbitrations).

8. In Chapter 6 of our February 1996 Report, at paragraph 357, we recommended that the original clause 2(2)(a) be slightly amended in order to make clear that the applicable law referred to there was the law applicable to the arbitration agreement, rather than the law applicable to the substantive agreement.

9. Following the introduction of the Bill into Parliament, we had the benefit of further detailed discussions with a number of leading arbitration experts from abroad, and took the opportunity of reconsidering this provision. It is fair to say that whilst there was unanimous support for the inclusion of such a provision identifying the scope of the Act, there was considerable disquiet as to the clause as drafted. It was felt that the provision was sound in principle, but unworkable in practice, for the following reasons:

(i) The clause was complicated and extremely difficult to understand. To this end, it appeared to defeat its own object.

(ii) In order to apply clause 2(2), it was necessary to be able to identify all those provisions of the Act which concerned the arbitration agreement, as distinct from all those that concerned the arbitral procedure. As explained above, if for example English law governed the arbitration agreement, but not the arbitral procedure, by virtue of clause 2(2) only those provisions in the Act which concerned the arbitration agreement (as opposed to the arbitral procedure) would apply. The provisions of the Act had therefore to be individually characterised and separated in this way.

However, the original clause made no attempt to characterise each provision of the Act, precisely because this had proved an extremely difficult and complex exercise. Many provisions concern both arbitration agreements and arbitral procedure, and there appeared to be a divergence of view with respect to many others.

(iii) There was a feeling amongst certain foreign experts that the original clause gave the wrong impression, in that it appeared to endow the English Court with inappropriate extra-territorial powers, when this was clearly not intended.

10. In the light of these difficulties, the DAC decided to recast the whole provision in a different form that would be far easier to understand and that would be entirely workable in practice. The policy behind the section, however, was not materially altered. The final section 2 provides a clear and simple scheme, which was welcomed by all those who had originally expressed concerns.

11. Section 2(1) states the basic rule: Part I of the Act applies to arbitrations which have their seat in England and Wales or Northern Ireland. The concept of a "seat" was referred to in our February 1996 Report, and is defined in section 3 of the Act. The seat of an arbitration refers to its legal place, as opposed to its geographical location. It is, of course, perfectly possible to conduct an arbitration with an English seat at any convenient location, whether in England or abroad.

12. If the seat of an arbitration is in England and Wales or Northern Ireland, the arbitration will be governed by this Act. If, however, a foreign law has been chosen to govern any particular aspect of the arbitration, such as the arbitral procedure or the arbitration agreement, or is otherwise applicable to any such aspect, this is catered for by section 4(5). Therefore, reference may be made to this Act in the first instance, and then back to another law with respect to a specific issue. Whilst a process of characterisation may still have to be done, the combination of section 2 and section 4(5) avoids the dangers that:

— a choice of English law with respect to one part of an arbitration will import other parts of the Act that concern other aspects of the arbitration;
— a choice of England as the seat of the arbitration will necessarily entail the imposition of every provision of the Act.

13. Sections 2(2) to (5) set out a series of deviations from the basic rule in section 2(1).

14. Section 2(2) caters for the New York Convention. Under the terms of this Convention, the English Courts are obliged to recognise and enforce arbitration agreements and foreign arbitral awards. Sections 9 to 11 (stays of legal proceedings etc) and section 66 (enforcement) could not, therefore, be restricted to arbitrations with a seat in England and Wales or Northern Ireland. These particular sections therefore apply even if the seat of an arbitration is abroad. Equally, these sections will apply if no seat has been designated or determined.

15. Section 2(3) extends the power of the Court to grant interim relief in support of arbitrations with a foreign seat, thereby giving effect to section 25 of the Civil Jurisdiction and Judgments Act 1982, as was intended by the original clause 2(3)(b). The power of the Court to exercise these powers is restricted in the last part of this section to appropriate cases. There may well be situations in which it would be quite wrong for an English Court to make an interim order in support of a foreign arbitration, where this would result in a possible conflict with another jurisdiction.

16. Section 2(4) deals with those cases where a seat has still to be designated or determined, but where recourse to the Court is necessary in the meantime. For example, an arbitration agreement may provide that the tribunal, once constituted, will designate the seat of the arbitration. The agreement may also provide that any arbitration must be commenced within a specified time period. If that time period is exceeded, could a party make an application to the English Court pursuant to section 12 of the Act for an Order extending time for the commencement of proceedings (e.g. in order that a seat may be designated)? See e.g. *International Tank & Pipe S.A.K.* v. *Kuwait Aviation Fuelling Co. K.S.C.* [1975] QB 224 (C.A.). Clearly this would not be possible under section 2(1), as long as the arbitration was without an English or Northern Irish seat. It was our view, however, that the English Court should be able to exercise supportive powers if there is a sufficient connection with England and Wales or Northern Ireland such that this is appropriate (i.e. the requirement in section 2(4)(b)), and if there will be no clash with a foreign jurisdiction. For example, there will be cases where it is extremely likely that once a seat is designated, that seat will be England and Wales or Northern Ireland.

17. Section 2(4) therefore gives the English Court powers where that Court is satisfied, as a matter of English law, that the arbitration in question does not have a seat elsewhere. As long as there is no seat elsewhere, there could be no possible conflict with any other jurisdiction.

18. Both sections 2(3) and 2(4) are based on a very clear policy: the English Court should have effective powers to support an actual or anticipated arbitration that does not fall within section 2(1). However, such powers should not be used where any other foreign Court is already, or is likely to be, seized of the matter, or where the exercise of such powers would produce a clash with any other more appropriate forum.

19. Section 2(5) provides that section 7 (separability) and section 8 (death of a party) apply whenever the law applicable to an arbitration agreement is English law, even if the seat of the arbitration is abroad. Without this provision, reference would have to be made to the old English common law with respect to separability and the effect of death in every arbitration where the arbitration agreement is governed by English law, but the seat is not in England and Wales or Northern Ireland, such as to be within Section 2(1). This would be an absurd result.

Section 7. Separability of arbitration agreement

20. As we said in Chapter 6, we suggested that the words "(whether or not in writing)" be inserted after the words "another agreement" in view of the definition of "agreement" in what is now section 5, in order to preclude any argument that section 7 only applies where the other agreement is in writing. This amendment was duly made.

Section 14(5). Commencement of arbitral proceedings

21. Parliamentary Counsel considered that it was not necessary to make the amendment suggested in paragraph 359 of Chapter 6 and we accepted his advice.

Section 16(6)(b) and section 21(4)

22. The Bill used the word "any" after a negative which could thus be read as meaning "all." This was not intended. We suggested a form of wording in paragraph 360 of Chapter 6 but were persuaded that a neater solution was to replace "any" with "a", and this was done.

Section 24(4). Power of Court to remove arbitrator

23. In paragraph 361 of Chapter 6, we drew attention to the fact that the immunity of an arbitrator, under what is now section 29, did not extend to protect an arbitrator from the consequences of resigning, though some protection is available under what is now section 25(3). This we contrasted with what is now section 24, since an arbitrator removed by the Court still enjoyed the section 29 immunity. We thought that this was anomalous and that the Court should be given a discretionary power to make such order as it thought fit with regard to the immunity of an arbitrator it removed.

24. This suggestion was not adopted. After further consideration we concluded that the anomaly was more apparent than real and that the suggestion would undermine the reasons for providing arbitrators with the immunity expressed in section 29. As will be seen from paragraph 362 of Chapter 6, we were against adopting the same suggestion when the parties agreed to remove an arbitrator under what is now section 23. What it seemed to us would be likely to happen if our original suggestion were adopted is that the parties, instead of privately agreeing to remove an arbitrator, would instead apply to the Court in the hope that the immunity would be wholly or partially removed. This seemed to us to be undesirable.

25. It should be remembered, of course, that while an arbitrator retains his immunity if removed by the Court, what is now section 24(4) does give the Court the power to make orders about his fees and expenses, including those already paid.

Section 25(2). Resignation of arbitrator

26. At paragraph 363 of Chapter 6 we noted that the words "in writing" appeared, though by virtue of section 5(1) this was unnecessary. These words were duly removed by amendment.

Section 32, section 45 and section 69

27. The Bill used the words "unless the court certifies." These were changed by amendment to "which shall not be given unless the court considers." This amendment was made to make clear that where an appeal is desired from a decision of the Court, leave must be obtained from that Court itself, and will always be required. Leave may not be obtained from the Court of Appeal. As originally drafted, the incorrect impression was given that leave of the Court may not be necessary where that Court certified the issue as being one of general importance or one which for some other special reason should be considered by the Court of Appeal.

Section 38(3). Security for costs

28. The power for arbitrators to order security for costs was included in the Bill for the reasons set out at paragraphs 189 to 199 of our February 1996 Report. In the Bill as introduced, we included a provision that the arbitral tribunal should apply the same principles as the Court in exercising this power. This was an attempt to meet the concerns of those who considered that since under the existing law arbitrators had no power to order security (unless the parties had expressly agreed to confer such a power), there was a need to set out some principles to guide arbitrators. However, as we explained at paragraphs 364 to 370 of Chapter 6, we concluded in the end that this was not a good idea and that it would be better to amend this part of the Bill, by deleting the references to

Court principles and by making clear that the fact that a claimant or counter-claimant came from abroad was not a ground for ordering security. Our suggestions were adopted. We proposed a specific amendment, but Parliamentary Counsel improved upon it, in particular by not using the word "only" since this might enable it to be argued that the fact that the claimant or counter-claimant came from abroad could be taken into account so long as there were other supporting factors as well. This, of course, was not our intention.

29. It should also be noted that the Bill as introduced used the word "party" in relation to orders for security for costs. This did not matter so long as there was a reference to Court principles, but once this was deleted, it was necessary to change this to "claimant", since it was not our intention to give arbitral tribunals the power to order respondents to provide security. Section 82 defines claimant as including counter-claimant.

Section 46(1)(b). "Equity clauses"

30. Whilst the provisions of Part I of the Act apply to arbitrations commenced after the Act comes into force, regardless of when the arbitration agreement was made (by virtue of section 84), strong representations were made to the DAC that section 46(1)(b) should be commenced differently—in such a way as to preserve the existing law on the validity of "equity clauses" with respect to arbitration agreements that already exist and were made before the Act comes into force. Many existing contracts contain standard clauses which read as if they are "equity clauses", but which have been interpreted differently by the Courts. This is the case, for example, with so-called "honourable engagement" clauses in reinsurance treaties. It was thought that if section 46(1)(b) were to apply to existing arbitration agreements, this would entail a retrospective substantive change in the meaning and effect of existing contracts, different from that which the contracting parties would have contemplated at the time of contracting. The DAC agreed with this view, and decided that section 46(1)(b) should not apply to arbitration agreements that were made before the Act comes into force. Existing case law on the interpretation and effect of "equity clauses" will therefore continue to apply to such agreements. Transitional provisions have been put in place accordingly (see Appendix B).

Section 57. Correction of award or additional award

31. A minor drafting change was made to section 57(3)(b).

Section 66. Enforcement of award

32. In paragraphs 371 to 378 of Chapter 6 we made various suggestions for changes to the provision as it then appeared in the Bill. We were concerned that we had not covered enough of the cases where leave to enforce an award could be refused. We also suggested that it should be made clear that the list was not a closed list. However, on further reflection we concluded that it would be preferable, instead of having a list which would have to be expressed as not closed, to have no list at all; instead relying on the fact (as noted at paragraphs 373 and 374) that the opening words of the provision do not require the Court to order enforcement, but only give it a discretion to do so. Thus what was subsection (3) of the Bill was deleted by amendment. However, it will be noted that in what is now section 81 it is made clear (by an amendment to the Bill as introduced) that any rule of law relating in particular to matters which are not capable of settlement by arbitration or to the refusal of recognition or enforcement of an arbitral award on the grounds of public policy continues to operate.

33. The suggestion that there should be an express reference to an action on the award was adopted and this reference is now to be found in section 66(4) of the Act. This in turn meant that the reference to an action on an award in what is now section 81 was unnecessary and this latter reference was accordingly removed by amendment.

34. In paragraph 378 of Chapter 6 we suggested that where the application was to enforce an agreed award, the Court should be notified of that fact, which should also be recorded in any order for enforcement. Upon reflection, however, it seemed to us that such requirements would be better placed in the relevant Rules of Court, and this, we are informed, will be done.

Section 68. Challenging the award: serious irregularity

35. In the Bill, one of the grounds for challenging an award was expressed as "uncertainty or ambiguity of the award." It was pointed out to us that this wording might encourage attempts to challenge an award under this provision on the grounds that the reasoning of the decision was uncertain or ambiguous. This was certainly not our intention. What we wanted to cover were cases where the result of the award was uncertain or ambiguous. Where the quality of the award was in question, there would only be recourse under the limited right to appeal under section 69. To make matters clear, this part of the section was amended and now reads "uncertainty or ambiguity as to the effect of the award."

Section 70. Challenge or appeal: supplementary provisions

36. In paragraph 380 of Chapter 6 we suggested that the power to order security or that the amount of the award be brought into Court should be extended so as to apply to applications and appeals under what is now section 69, as well as what are now sections 67 and 68. This suggestion was adopted and the appropriate amendments made to Section 70.

37. Subsection 70(6) (security for costs) was further amended in order to bring this provision into line with the amended section 38(3), which has been referred to above.

Section 74. Immunity of arbitral tribunals etc

38. In paragraph 381 of Chapter 6 we suggested tightening the wording of subsection 2. This suggestion was adopted by inserting into this subsection after the word "liable" the words "by reason of having appointed or nominated him." Without this amendment it could have been suggested that an immunity existed even where, for example, an institution conspired with an arbitrator to act partially.

Section 76. Service of notices etc

39. Some minor textual amendments were made to the Bill as introduced, in order to tie this provision with others concerning the giving of notices.

Section 77. Powers of court in relation to service of documents

40. What was subsection (5) of Clause 77 in the Bill as introduced was deleted on amendment as being unnecessary. The point was already covered by section 76(6).

Section 79. Power of court to extend time limits relating to arbitral proceedings

41. In paragraph 382 of Chapter 6 we noted that this provision did not cover cases where the time stipulated was not one having effect in default of agreement between the parties e.g. what is now section 70(3). We suggested an amendment to what is now section 79(1). This suggestion was not adopted, but the point was covered by adding the words "the extending or abridging of periods" to what is now section 80(5).

Section 80

42. The word "appeal" was added by amendment to this provision, so it would cover appeals as well as applications.

43. A minor change was also made to subsection (5) (insertion of the words "the extending or abridging of periods") in order to tie this provision in with relevant Rules of Court.

Section 81. Saving for certain matters governed by common law

44. In paragraphs 383 to 386 of Chapter 6 we made a number of suggestions. First we suggested a reference to privacy and confidentiality. This suggestion was not adopted, since we finally concluded (especially as the law on this topic is in a stage of development) that it would be better to have no express reference at all, and to rely instead as necessary on the general opening words of this section. The second suggestion (namely an express reference to whether a matter is capable of resolution by arbitration) was adopted and the words "matters which are not capable of settlement by arbitration" added by amendment. We also suggested changing the words "common law" in the title, but were persuaded that this was not really necessary.

Sections 82 to 83. Minor definitions

45. In paragraphs 387 and 388 of Chapter 6 we raised a point of drafting on the definition of "question of law." This was dealt with by deleting the words "where the seat of the arbitration is" and inserting in their place the words "for a court."

46. Further minor amendments were made to sections 82 and 83 in the light of the new section 105 that was added (meaning of "court").

CHAPTER 3—PART II OF THE ACT

Sections 85–87. Domestic arbitration agreements

47. In paragraphs 317 to 331 of our February 1996 Report, we set out the reasons why the rules governing domestic arbitration agreements had been grouped together in sections 85 to 87 of Part II of the Act, and our provisional view as to whether or not the distinction in English law between international and domestic arbitration should be maintained. In July 1996, the Department of Trade and Industry published a consultation document on the commencement of the Act in which, amongst other matters, views were sought on this issue. The majority of respondents were in favour of the abolition of this distinction, and the application of the international regime throughout (i.e. a mandatory stay of legal proceedings in all cases, and the ability to exclude the right to appeal on a point of law at any stage in all cases).

48. At about the same time as this consultation document was published, the Court of Appeal upheld the decision of Waller J in *Philip Alexander Securities and Futures Limited* v. *Bamberger and others* (unreported: 8 May 1996 (Commercial Court); 12 July 1996 (Court of Appeal)), in which it was held (in the context of the Consumer Arbitration Agreements Act 1988) that the distinction between international and domestic arbitration is incompatible with European Community law because it amounts to a restriction on the freedom to provide services contrary to Article 59 of the Treaty of Rome and/or unlawful discrimination contrary to Article 6.

49. In the light of the responses to the consultation document, the decision of the Court of Appeal, and the factors we had originally set out in our February 1996 Report, the DAC has since decided that, as matters currently stand, there is no option but to abolish this distinction. Indeed, on one view, in the light of the *Philip Alexander* case, the distinction has already been removed from current English law. However, it is to be noted that (at the time of going to press) an application for leave to appeal the *Philip Alexander* case is pending before the House of Lords, and there remains the possibility that the question will be referred to the European Court.

50. In these circumstances, sections 85 to 87 have not been brought into force by the Commencement Order. The present intention is to repeal these sections by an Order made pursuant to section 88 of the Act, although this may now depend upon the outcome of the *Philip Alexander* case.

Section 85

51. In paragraph 389 of Chapter 6 we noted an anomaly in the definition of "domestic arbitration agreement" and suggested that the opportunity should be taken to correct it. However, in view of the position with respect to the future of the distinction between domestic and non-domestic arbitration agreements, this suggestion was not adopted.

52. Various other minor textual amendments were also made to this section, which now are of no consequence.

Section 88

53. A minor textual amendment was made to this section, in order to reflect the amendments made to the consumer provisions of the Act (the new sections 89 to 91).

Sections 89 to 91. Consumer arbitration agreements

54. Clauses 89 to 93 of the Bill as introduced into Parliament reproduced the Consumer Arbitration Agreements Act 1988. These provisions were removed by amendment, and replaced by what is now sections 89 to 91, which refer to the Unfair Terms in Consumer Contracts Regulations 1994 (implementing EC Council Directive 93/13 EEC). The consumer provisions of the Act were beyond the remit of the DAC, and are therefore not commented upon here. For an explanation of these amendments, reference should be made to Hansard at HL Vol. 571 No. 72, cols. 152–155 (2 April 1996).

Section 93. Appointment of judges as arbitrators

55. Our suggestion in paragraph 390 of Chapter 6 was not adopted.

Sections 94–98. Statutory arbitrations

56. The issue that we noted at paragraph 391 of Chapter 6 concerning the requirement of "independence" in statutory (compulsory) arbitration was debated in the House of Lords (see Hansard HL Vol. 569 No. 51, col. CWH 26–28 (28 February 1996)), but did not result in an amendment to the Bill.

57. The words "or difference" were inserted in section 96(2) by way of tidying up.

CHAPTER 4—PART III OF THE ACT

Section 100(2). New York Convention awards

58. In paragraph 392 of Chapter 6, we recommended that this provision be amended so as to cross-refer to the definition of writing to be found in Part I of the Act, and also to incorporate our recommendation that an award be treated as made at the seat of the arbitration, regardless of where it was signed, despatched or delivered to any of the parties. This recommendation was adopted.

Section 101

59. A minor textual amendment was made to section 101(2), in order to refer to the new section 105, that was added.

Section 102. Evidence to be produced

60. The wording of this provision was amended in order to bring it back into line with the wording of the New York Convention itself.

Section 104. Saving for other bases of recognition or enforcement

61. The concern recorded at paragraph 393 of Chapter 6 did not lead to any amendment.

CHAPTER 5—PART IV OF THE ACT

Section 105. Meaning of "the court": jurisdiction of High Court and county court

62. This is a new section. It was added in order to confer order-making powers on the Lord Chancellor to allocate matters as between different Courts, thereby providing for more flexibility than was provided for by existing rules. Reference should be made to the Allocation Order set out at Appendix B.

APPENDIX A—THE NEW RSC ORDER 73 AND ALLOCATION ORDER

Introduction by His Hon. Judge Diamond, QC

Scope of the order

63. The Order had to govern not only applications to the Court under the Arbitration Act 1996, but also applications under the Arbitration Acts, 1950 to 1979, which continue to apply to arbitrations commenced before 31st January 1997, the date when, by virtue of the Arbitration Act 1996 (Commencement No. 1) Order 1996, the 1996 Act came into force. So as to cater for both classes of arbitration application, the new Order has been divided into three parts and a table has been inserted at the beginning of the Order to indicate to the user which part is appropriate, a matter which depends on the date when the relevant arbitration proceedings were commenced and the date of the application to the Court (see Chapter 7 of this Report). Part I is concerned with applications to the Court relating to arbitrations to which Part I of the 1996 Act applies. Part II of the Order preserves the procedure of the former Order 73 for arbitrations governed by the earlier statutes. Part III is concerned with all applications to enforce arbitration awards (save by action on the award), whether under the 1950, 1975 or 1996 Acts or under certain other enactments.

The general scheme of Part I

64. Part I of the new Order completes and puts flesh on the general scheme set out in the 1996 Act governing applications to the Court. For example the Act provides that in some instances notice of an application is to be given "to the other parties" and in others "to the other parties and to the tribunal". The Order provides how that notice is to be given. In the case of parties (rule 10(1)) this is to be done by making them respondents to the application and by effecting formal service of the proceedings upon them. In the case of arbitrators, notice of applications under sections 24, 28 and 56 of the Act must be given in a similar manner (rule 10(2)) but notice of all other applications to arbitrators may be given by sending the papers to them at their last known address "for information" (rule 10(3)). Similarly, the Order sets out the rights of parties and arbitrators who have been given notice of an application, to appear and be heard in the proceedings or, in the case of arbitrators who are given notice "for information", to make informal representations to the Court or to appear at their option.

Particular features of Part I

65. While it was necessary for the Order to give some guidance as to whether arbitration applications should be heard in open Court or in Chambers, it was considered that this was a matter which depended essentially on the particular circumstances of each application. One consideration is the privacy of the arbitration process; another is whether the application raises points of principle which may be relevant in other cases. Rules 15(2) and 15(3) set out a *prima facie* presumption that all arbitration applications shall be heard in Chambers save for the determination of a preliminary point of law under Section 45 of the Act and an appeal on a question of law under section 69 which should both be heard in open Court. The Court may however order that any arbitration application be heard in open Court or in Chambers depending on the particular circumstances.

66. Part I of the Order contains provisions designed to minimise the cost and delay involved in serving proceedings out of the jurisdiction. Where the respondent to the arbitration application is or was represented in the arbitration proceedings by a solicitor or other agent, the Court may give leave (on an *ex parte* application) for the proceedings to be served on that solicitor or agent (rule 7(2)). While service out of the jurisdiction may still be necessary for the first application arising out of an arbitration or arbitration agreement, subsequent applications by either party can be served at the address for service within the jurisdiction given in the first application (rule 7(4)).

67. When deciding in which Court to bring an arbitration application, the user needs to refer both to the High Court and County Courts (Allocation of Arbitration Proceedings) Order 1996 and also to rule 5 of the new Order 73. Rule 5 also contains provisions designed to ensure that, wherever the application is issued, the Commercial Court is able to preserve some consistency of approach both to the application and to the interpretation of Order 73. All arbitration applications brought in the Royal Courts of Justice are, for this reason, to be issued out of the Admiralty and Commercial Registry (Rule 5(3)) so that the Commercial Court can act as a "filter" and the judge in charge of the Commercial Court may transfer them elsewhere if he thinks fit (rule 5(5)). In the case of applications brought in a Mercantile List or in the Central London County Court Business List, the control of the Commercial Court is preserved by provisions (rules 5(5) and 5(6)) that the application will be reviewed by the judge in charge of the list who, in consultation with the judge in charge of the Commercial Court, may transfer the application to the Commercial Court or to another Court or List.

68. Rule 4(1) introduces a new form of originating process for applications governed by the 1996 Act, called simply an "arbitration application". This supersedes the two different forms of originating summons and the form of notice of motion used under the old procedure (which, however, is retained in Part II of the Order for applications governed by the old law).

General

69. Though necessarily detailed, the new Order 73 is designed to be "user friendly". Users should be assisted by the table, to which reference has previously been made, indicating whether Part I or Part II of the Order is appropriate for a particular application. Similarly, rule 4 attempts to assist users by setting out in table form the most important statutory requirements that need to be satisfied and referred to in any arbitration application made under the 1996 Act.

THE RULES OF THE SUPREME COURT (AMENDMENT) 1996

(1996 No. 3219)

Made	*19th December 1996*
Laid before Parliament	*20th December 1996*
Coming into force	*31st January 1997*

We, the Supreme Court Rule Committee, having power under section 85 of the Supreme Court Act 1981 to make rules of court under section 60 of that Act and under section 84 of that Act for the purpose of regulating and prescribing the practice and procedure to be followed in the High Court and the civil division of the Court of Appeal, hereby exercise those powers as follows—

Citation, commencement and interpretation

1.—(1) These Rules may be cited as the Rules of the Supreme Court (Amendment) 1996 and shall come into force on 31st January 1997.

(2) In these Rules, an Order referred to by number means the Order so numbered in the Rules of the Supreme Court 1965 and a reference to Appendix A is a reference to Appendix A to those Rules.

Arbitration Act 1996

2. The Arrangement of Orders at the beginning of the Rules of the Supreme Court 1965 shall be amended, by substituting for the title to Order 73, the following "Applications relating to Arbitration".

3. Order 11, rule 9(1) and (4) shall be amended by omitting the words "Subject to Order 73, rule 7,".

4. Order 59, rule 1A(7)(a) shall be amended by inserting, after "1979", the words "or under section 69(7) of the Arbitration Act 1996" and rule 1A(7)(b)(iii) shall be amended by inserting, after "section 1(2)", the words "or of section 69(7) of the said Act of 1996".

5. For Order 73 there shall be substituted the following—

"ORDER 73: APPLICATIONS RELATING TO ARBITRATION

Introduction

This Order is divided into three Parts. Part I is concerned with applications to the Court relating to arbitration to which Part I of the Arbitration Act 1996 applies. Part II restates with some necessary adjustments provisions of the existing Order which are to be preserved. Part III is concerned with applications for enforcement under the earlier Arbitration Acts and under the 1996 Act.

The application of the Order to particular proceedings may be determined by reference to the following table. Column 1 shows the date on which arbitral proceedings (if any) were commenced. Column 2 shows the date of the application to the Court. Column 3 shows the appropriate Part of the Order for the application.

Column 1 *Date of arbitral proceedings*	*Column 2* *Date of application to the Court*	*Column 3* *Appropriate Part of Order 73*
not commenced	before 31st January 1997	Part II
before 31st January 1997	before 31st January 1997	Part II
not commenced	on or after 31st January 1997	Part I
before 31st January 1997	on or after 31st January 1997	Part II
on or after 31st January 1997	on or after 31st January 1997	Part I
on or after 31st January 1997	before 31st January 1997	Part II

The other provisions of these rules apply to applications relating to arbitration subject to the provisions of this Order and only to the extent that they do not conflict with it.

See, for example, the following provisions of these rules for the following matters—

Order 10—service of originating process
Order 12—acknowledgement of service
Order 29—injunctions
Order 32—proceedings in chambers
Order 41—affidavits
Order 65—service of documents.

Part I

The overriding objective

1. This Part of this Order is founded on the general principles in section 1 of the Arbitration Act and shall be construed accordingly.

Meaning of arbitration application

2.—(1) Subject to paragraph (2), "arbitration application" means the following—

(a) an application to the Court under the Arbitration Act;
(b) proceedings to determine—
  (i) whether there is a valid arbitration agreement;
  (ii) whether an arbitration tribunal is properly constituted;
  (iii) what matters have been submitted to arbitration in accordance with an arbitration agreement;
(c) proceedings to declare that an award made by an arbitral tribunal is not binding on a party;

(d) any other application affecting arbitration proceedings (whether instituted or anticipated) or to construe or affecting an arbitration agreement,

and includes the originating process by which an arbitration application is begun.

(2) In this Part of this Order, an arbitration application does not include proceedings to enforce an award—

(a) to which Part III of this Order applies; or
(b) by an action on the award.

Interpretation

3. In this Part—

"applicant" means the party making an arbitration application and references to respondent shall be construed accordingly;

"the Arbitration Act" means the Arbitration Act 1996 and any expressions used in this Order and in Part I of the Arbitration Act have the same meanings in this Order as they have in that Part of the Arbitration Act.

Form and content of arbitration application

4.—(1) An arbitration application must be in Form No. 8A in Appendix A.

(2) Every arbitration application must—

(a) include a concise statement of
  (i) the remedy on relief claimed, and
  (ii) (where appropriate) the questions on which the applicant seeks the determination or direction of the Court;
(b) give details of any arbitration award that is challenged by the applicant, showing the grounds for any such challenge;
(c) where the applicant claims an order for costs, identify the respondent against whom the claim is made;
(d) (where appropriate) specify the section of the Arbitration Act under which the application is brought; and
(e) show that any statutory requirements have been satisfied including those set out, by way of example, in the Table below.

Application made	*Statutory requirements*
section 9 (stay of legal proceedings)	see section 9(3)
section 12 (extensions of time for beginning arbitral proceedings)	see section 12(2)
section 18 (failure of appointment procedure)	see section 18(2)
section 21 (umpires)	see section 21(5)
section 24 (removal of arbitrators)	see section 24(2)
section 32 (preliminary point of jurisdiction)	see section 32(3)
section 42 (enforcement of peremptory orders)	see section 42(3)
section 44 (powers in support of arbitral proceedings)	see section 44(4), (5)
section 45 (preliminary point of law)	see section 45(3)
section 50 (extension of time for making award)	see section 50(2)
section 56 (power to withhold award)	see section 56(4)
sections 67, 68 (challenging the award)	see section 70(2), (3)
section 69 (appeal on point of law)	see sections 69(2), (4), 70(2), (3)
section 77 (service of documents)	see section 77(3)

(3) The arbitration application must also state

(a) whether it is made *ex parte* or on notice and, if made on notice, must give the names and addresses of the persons to whom notice is to be given, stating their role in the arbitration and whether they are made respondents to the application;
(b) whether (having regard to rule 15) the application will be heard in open Court or in chambers; and
(c) the date and time when the application will be heard or that such date has not yet been fixed.

(4) Every arbitration application which is used as an originating process shall be indorsed with the applicant's address for service in accordance with Order 6, rule 5.

Issue of application

5.—(1) This rule is to be read with the provisions of the High Court and County Courts (Allocation of Arbitration Proceedings) Order 1996 which allocates proceedings under the Arbitration Act to the High Court and the county courts and specifies proceedings which may be commenced or taken only in the High Court or in a county court.
(2) This rule does not apply to applications under section 9 of the Arbitration Act to stay legal proceedings.
(3) Any other arbitration application may be made—

(a) in the Royal Courts of Justice, in which case it shall be issued out of the Admiralty and Commercial Registry;
(b) in a district registry in which there is a mercantile list, in which case it shall be entered into that list.

(4) Except where an arbitration application is issued out of the Admiralty and Commercial Registry, the Judge in charge of the list shall

(a) as soon as practicable after the issue of the application, and
(b) in consultation with the Judge in charge of the commercial list,

consider whether the application should be transferred to the Commercial Court or to any another list.
(5) Where an arbitration application is issued out of the Admiralty and Commercial Registry, the Judge in charge of the commercial list may at any time after the issue of the application transfer the application to another list, court or Division of the High Court, to which he has power to transfer proceedings.
(6) In considering whether to transfer an application, the Judges referred to in paragraphs (4) and (5) shall have regard to the criteria specified in article 4(4) of the High Court and County Courts (Allocation of Arbitration Proceedings) Order 1996 and the application shall be transferred if those Judges so decide.
(7) In this rule "Judge in charge of the list" means—

(a) a Commercial Judge, where the arbitration application is issued out of the Admiralty and Commercial Registry;
(b) a Circuit mercantile Judge, where the arbitration application is entered in a mercantile list;
(c) a Judge of the business list in the Central London County Court, where the arbitration application is commenced in the business list established at the Central London County Court by Order 48C of the County Court Rules 1981;

but nothing in this rule shall be construed as preventing the powers of a Commercial Judge from being exercised by any judge of the High Court.

Stay of legal proceedings

6.—(1) An application under section 9 of the Arbitration Act to stay legal proceedings shall be served—

(a) in accordance with Order 65, rule 5, on the party bringing the relevant legal proceedings and on any other party to those proceedings who has given an address for service; and

(b) on any party to those legal proceedings who has not given an address for service, by sending to him (whether or not he is within the jurisdiction) at his last known address or at a place where it is likely to come to his attention, a copy of the application for his information.

(2) Where a question arises as to whether an arbitration agreement has been concluded or as to whether the dispute which is the subject-matter of the proceedings falls within the terms of such an agreement, the Court may determine that question or give directions for its determination, in which case it may order the proceedings to be stayed pending the determination of that question.

Service of arbitration application

7.—(1) Subject to paragraphs (2) and (4) below and to rules 6(1) and 8, an arbitration application shall be served in accordance with Order 10.

(2) Where the Court is satisfied on an *ex parte* application that

(a) arbitral proceedings are taking place, or an arbitration award has been made, within the jurisdiction; and

(b) an arbitration application is being made in connection with those arbitral proceedings or being brought to challenge the award or to appeal on a question of law arising out of the award; and

(c) the respondent to the arbitration application (not being an individual residing or carrying on business within the jurisdiction or a body corporate having a registered office or a place of business within the jurisdiction)

(i) is or was represented in the arbitral proceedings by a solicitor or other agent within the jurisdiction who was authorised to receive service of any notice or other document served for the purposes of those proceedings; and

(ii) has not (at the time when the arbitration application is made) determined the authority of that solicitor or agent,

the court may authorise service of the arbitration application to be effected on the solicitor or agent instead of the respondent.

(3) An order made under paragraph (2) must limit a time within which the respondent must acknowledge service and a copy of the order and of the arbitration application must be sent by post to the respondent at his address out of the jurisdiction.

(4) Where an arbitration application has been issued, any subsequent arbitration application made by the respondent and arising out of the same arbitration or arbitration agreement may be served on the applicant in accordance with Order 65, rule 5 (ordinary service: how effected) and similarly any subsequent arbitration application by any party may be served at the address for service given in the first arbitration application or in the acknowledgement of service.

(5) For the purposes of service, an arbitration application is valid in the first instance

(a) where service is to be effected out of the jurisdiction, for such period as the Court may fix;

(b) in any other case, for one month,

beginning with the date of its issue and Order 6, rule 8 shall apply with the substitution, in paragraphs (2) and (2A), of "2 months" for "4 months" and "6 months" for "12 months".

Service out of the jurisdiction

8.—(1) Service out of the jurisdiction of an arbitration application is permissible with the leave of the Court if the arbitration application falls into one of the categories mentioned in the following table and satisfies the conditions specified.

Nature of application	*Conditions to be satisfied*
1. The applicant seeks to challenge, or to appeal to the Court on a question of law arising out of, an arbitration award.	Award must have been made in England & Wales. Section 53 of the Arbitration Act shall apply for determining the place where award is treated as made.
2. The application is for an order under section 44 of the Arbitration Act (Court powers exercisable in support of arbitral proceedings). Where the application is for an interim remedy in support of arbitral proceedings which are taking (or will take) place outside England and Wales, the Court may give permission for service out of the jurisdiction notwithstanding that no other remedy is sought.	None.
(3) The applicant seeks some other remedy or requires a question to be determined by the court, affecting an arbitration (whether pending or anticipated), an arbitration agreement or an arbitration award.	The seat of the arbitration is or will be in England & Wales or the conditions in Section 2(4) of the Arbitration Act are satisfied.

(2) An application for the grant of leave under this rule must be supported by an affidavit

- (a) stating the grounds on which the application is made;
- (b) showing in what place or country the person to be served is, or probably may be found,

and no such leave shall be granted unless it shall be made sufficiently to appear to the Court that the case is a proper one for service out of the jurisdiction under this rule.

(3) Order 11, rules 5 to 8 shall apply to the service of an arbitration application under this rule as they apply to the service of a writ.

(4) Service out of the jurisdiction of any order made on an arbitration application is permissible with the leave of the Court.

Affidavit in support of arbitration application

9.—(1) The applicant shall file an affidavit in support of the arbitration application which sets out the evidence on which he intends to rely and a copy of every affidavit so filed must be served with the arbitration application.

(2) Where an arbitration application is made with the written agreement of all the other parties to the arbitral proceedings or with the permission of the arbitral tribunal, the affidavit in support must

- (a) give details of the agreement or, as the case may be, permission; and
- (b) exhibit copies of any document which evidences that agreement or permission.

Requirements as to notice

10.—(1) Where the Arbitration Act requires that an application to the Court is to be made upon notice to other parties notice shall be given by making those parties respondents to the application and serving on them the arbitration application and any affidavit in support.

(2) Where an arbitration application is made under section 24, 28 or 56 of the Arbitration Act, the arbitrators or, in the case of an application under section 24, the arbitrator concerned shall be made respondents to the application and notice shall be given by serving on them the arbitration application and any affidavit in support.

(3) In cases where paragraph (2) does not apply, an applicant shall be taken as having complied with any requirement to give notice to the arbitrator if he sends a copy of the arbitration application to the arbitrator for his information at his last known address with a copy of any affidavit in support.

(4) This rule does not apply to applications under section 9 of the Arbitration Act to stay legal proceedings.

Acknowledgement of service by respondent

11.—(1) Service of an arbitration application may be acknowledged by completing an acknowledgement of service in Form No. 15A in Appendix A in accordance with Order 12 (as that Order applies by virtue of rule 9 of that Order).

(2) A respondent who

- (a) fails to acknowledge service within the time limited for so doing; or
- (b) having indicated on his acknowledgement of service that he does not intend to contest the arbitration application, then wishes to do so,

shall not be entitled to contest the application without the leave of the Court.

(3) The Court will not give notice of the date on which an arbitration application will be heard to a respondent who has failed to acknowledge service.

(4) The failure of a respondent to give notice of intention to contest the arbitration application or to acknowledge service shall not affect the applicant's duty to satisfy the Court that the order applied for should be made.

(5) This rule does not apply to—

- (a) applications under section 9 of the Arbitration Act to stay legal proceedings; or
- (b) subsequent arbitration applications.

Acknowledgement of service etc. by arbitrator

12.—(1) An arbitrator who is sent a copy of an arbitration application for his information may make

- (a) a request *ex parte* in writing to be made a respondent; or
- (b) representations to the Court under this rule,

and, where an arbitrator is ordered to be made a respondent, he shall acknowledge service within 14 days of the making of that order.

(2) An arbitrator who wishes to make representations to the Court under this rule may file an affidavit or make representations in writing to the Court.

(3) The arbitrator shall as soon as is practicable send a copy of any document filed or made under paragraph (2) to all the parties to the arbitration application.

(4) Nothing in this rule shall require the Court to admit a document filed or made under paragraph (2) and the weight to be given to any such document shall be a matter for the Court.

Automatic directions

13.—(1) Unless the Court otherwise directs, the following directions shall take effect automatically.

(2) A respondent who wishes to put evidence before the Court in response to any affidavit filed in support of an arbitration application shall serve his affidavit on the applicant before the expiration of 21 days after the time limited for acknowledging service or, in a case where a respondent is not required to file an acknowledgment of service, within 21 days after service of the arbitration application.

(3) An applicant who wishes to put evidence before the Court in response to an affidavit lodged under paragraph (2) shall serve his affidavit on the respondent within 7 days after service of the respondent's affidavit.

(4) Where a date has not been fixed for the hearing of the arbitration application, the applicant shall, and the respondent may, not later than 14 days after the expiration of the time limit specified in paragraph (2), apply to the Court for such a date to be fixed.

(5) Agreed indexed and paginated bundles of all the evidence and other documents to be used at the hearing shall be prepared by the applicant (with the co-operation of the respondent).

(6) Not later than 5 clear days before the hearing date estimates for the length of the hearing shall be lodged with the Court together with a complete set of the documents to be used.

(7) Not later than 2 days before the hearing date the applicant shall lodge with the Court—

(a) a chronology of the relevant events cross-referenced to the bundle of documents;
(b) (where necessary) a list of the persons involved;
(c) a skeleton argument which lists succinctly
  (i) the issues which arise for decision,
  (ii) the grounds of relief (or opposing relief) to be relied upon,
  (iii) the submissions of fact to be made with the references to the evidence, and
  (iv) the submissions of law with references to the relevant authorities,

and shall send a copy to the respondent.

(8) Not later than the day before the hearing the respondent shall lodge with the Court a skeleton argument which lists succinctly

(a) the issues which arise for decision,
(b) the grounds for relief (or opposing relief) to be relied upon,
(c) the submissions of fact to be made with the references to the evidence, and
(d) the submissions of law with references to the relevant authorities,

and shall send a copy to the applicant.

Directions by the Court

14.—(1) The Court may give such directions as to the conduct of the arbitration application as it thinks best adapted to secure the just, expeditious and economical disposal thereof.

(2) Where the Court considers that there is or may be a dispute as to fact and that the just, expeditious and economical disposal of the application can best be secured by hearing the application on oral evidence or mainly on oral evidence, it may, if it thinks fit, order that no further evidence shall be filed and that the application shall be heard on oral evidence or partly on oral evidence and partly on affidavit evidence, with or without cross-examination of any of the deponents, as it may direct.

(3) The Court may give directions as to the filing of evidence and as to the attendance of deponents for cross-examination and any directions which it could give in proceedings begun by writ.

(4) If the applicant makes default in complying with these rules or with any order or direction of the Court as to the conduct of the application, or if the Court is satisfied that the applicant is not prosecuting the application with due despatch, the Court may order the application to be dismissed or may make such other order as may be just.

(5) If the respondent fails to comply with these rules or with any order or direction given by the Court in relation to the evidence to be relied on, or the submissions to be made by that respondent, the Court may, if it thinks fit, hear and determine the application without having regard to that evidence or those submissions.

Hearing of applications: open Court or in chambers

15.—(1) The Court may order that any arbitration application be heard either in open court or in chambers.

(2) Subject to any order made under paragraph (1) and to paragraph (3), all arbitration applications shall be heard in chambers.

(3) Subject to any order made under paragraph (1), the determination of a preliminary point of law under section 45 of the Arbitration Act or an appeal under section 69 on a question of law arising out of an award shall be heard in open court.

(4) Paragraph (3) shall not apply to

(a) the preliminary question whether the Court is satisfied of the matters set out in section 45(2)(b); or

(b) an application for leave to appeal under section 69(2)(b).

Securing the attendance of witnesses

16.— A party to arbitral proceedings being conducted in England and Wales who wishes to rely on section 43 of the Arbitration Act to secure the attendance of a witness may apply for a writ of subpoena ad testificandum or of subpoena duces tecum to the Admiralty and Commercial Registry or, if the attendance of the witness is required within the district of a district registry, at that registry at the option of the party.

(2) A writ of subpoena shall not be issued until the applicant lodges an affidavit which shows that the application is made with the permission of the tribunal or the agreement of the other parties.

Security for costs

17. Subject to section 70(6) of the Arbitration Act, the Court may order any applicant (including an applicant who has been granted leave to appeal) to provide security for costs of any arbitration application.

Powers exercisable in support of arbitral proceedings

18.—(1) Where the case is one of urgency, an application for an order under section 44 of the Arbitration Act (Court powers exercisable in support of arbitral proceedings) may be made *ex parte* on affidavit (before the issue of an arbitration application) and the affidavit shall (in addition to dealing with the matters required to be dealt with by rule 9) state the reasons

(a) why the application is made *ex parte*; and

(b) (where the application is made without the permission of the arbitral tribunal or the agreement of the other parties to the arbitral proceedings) why it was not practicable to obtain that permission or agreement, and

(c) why the deponent believes that the condition in section 44(5) is satisfied.

(2) Where the case is not one of urgency, an application for an order under section 44 of the Arbitration Act shall be made on notice and the affidavit in support shall (in addition to dealing with the matters required to be dealt with by rule 9 and paragraph (1)(c) above) state that the application is made with the permission of the tribunal or the written agreement of the other parties to the arbitral proceedings.

(3) Where an application for an order under section 44 of the Arbitration Act is made before the issue of an arbitration application, any order made by the Court may be granted on terms providing for the issue of an application and such other terms, if any, as the Court thinks fit.

Applications under sections 32 and 45 of the Arbitration Act

19.—(1) This rule applies to the following arbitration applications—

(a) applications for the determination of a question as to the substantive jurisdiction of the arbitral tribunal under section 32 of the Arbitration Act; and

(b) applications for the determination of a preliminary point of law under section 45 of the Arbitration Act.

(2) Where an application is made without the agreement in writing of all the other parties to the arbitral proceedings but with the permission of the arbitral tribunal, the affidavits filed

by the parties shall set out any evidence relied on by the parties in support of their contention that the Court should, or should not, consider the application.

(3) As soon as practicable after the affidavits are lodged, the Court shall decide whether or not it should consider the application and, unless the Court otherwise directs, shall so decide without a hearing.

Applications for leave to appeal

20.—(1) Where the applicant seeks leave to appeal to the Court on a question of law arising out of an arbitration award, the arbitration application shall identify the question of law and state the grounds on which the applicant alleges that leave should be granted.

(2) The affidavit in support of the application shall set out any evidence relied on by the applicant for the purpose of satisfying the Court of the matters mentioned in section 69(3) of the Arbitration Act and for satisfying the Court that leave should be granted.

(3) The affidavit lodged by the respondent to the application shall

(a) state the grounds on which the respondent opposes the grant of leave;
(b) set out any evidence relied on by him relating to the matters mentioned in section 69(3) of the Arbitration Act, and
(c) specify whether the respondent wishes to contend that the award should be upheld for reasons not expressed (or not fully expressed) in the award and, if so, state those reasons.

(4) As soon as practicable after the lodging of the affidavits, the Court shall determine the application for leave in accordance with section 69(5) of the Arbitration Act.

(5) Where leave is granted, a date shall be fixed for the hearing of the appeal.

Extension of time: applications under section 12

21. An application for an order under section 12 of the Arbitration Act may include as an alternative an application for a declaration that such an order is not needed.

Time limit for challenges to or appeals from awards

22.—(1) An applicant shall not be taken as having complied with the time limit of 28 days referred to in section 70(3) of the Arbitration Act unless the arbitration application has been issued, and all the affidavits in support have been sworn and filed, by the expiry of that time limit.

(2) An applicant who wishes

(a) to challenge an award under section 67 or 68 of the Arbitration Act; or
(b) to appeal under section 69 on a question of law arising out of an award,

may, where the time limit of 28 days has not yet expired, apply *ex parte* on affidavit for an order extending that time limit.

(3) In any case where an applicant seeks to challenge an award under section 67 or 68 of the Arbitration Act or to appeal under section 69 after the time limit of 28 days has already expired, the following provisions shall apply:

(a) the applicant must state in his arbitration application the grounds why an order extending time should be made and his affidavit in support shall set out the evidence on which he relies;
(b) a respondent who wishes to oppose the making of an order extending time shall file an affidavit within 7 days after service of the applicant's affidavit, and
(c) the Court shall decide whether or not to extend time without a hearing unless it appears to the Court that a hearing is required,

and, where the Court makes an order extending the time limit, the respondent shall file his affidavit in response to the arbitration application 21 days after the making of the order.

Part II

Application of this Part

23.—(1) This Part of this Order applies to any application to the Court to which the old law applies and, in this rule, "the old law" means the enactments specified in section 107 of the Arbitration Act 1996 as they stood before their amendment or repeal by that Act.

(2) This Part of this Order does not apply to proceedings to enforce an award—

(a) to which Part III of this Order applies; or
(b) by an action on the award.

(3) Reference should be made to the other provisions of these rules (except Parts I and III of this Order) for the procedure for any application not expressly provided for in this Part.

Matters for a judge in court

24.—(1) Every application to the Court—

(a) to remit an award under section 22 of the Arbitration Act 1950; or
(b) to remove an arbitrator or umpire under section 23(1) of that Act; or
(c) to set aside an award under section 23(2) of that Act; or
(d) to determine, under section 2(1) of the Arbitration Act 1979, any question of law arising in the course of a reference,

must be made by originating motion to a single judge in court.

(2) Any appeal to the High Court under section 1(2) of the Arbitration Act 1979 shall be made by originating motion to a single judge in court.

(3) An application for a declaration that an award made by an arbitrator or umpire is not binding on a party to the award on the ground that it was made without jurisdiction may be made by originating motion to a single judge in court, but the foregoing provision shall not be taken as affecting the judge's power to refuse to make such a declaration in proceedings begun by motion.

Matters for judge in chambers or master

25.—(1) Subject to the foregoing provisions of this Order and the provisions of this rule, the jurisdiction of the High Court or a judge thereof under the Arbitration Act 1950 and the jurisdiction of the High Court under the Arbitration Act 1975 and the Arbitration Act 1979 may be exercised by a judge in chambers, a master or the Admiralty registrar.

(2) Any application

(a) for leave to appeal under section 1(2) of the Arbitration Act 1979, or
(b) under section 1(5) of that Act (including any application for leave), or
(c) under section 5 of that Act,

shall be made to a judge in chambers.

(3) Any application to which this rule applies shall, where an action is pending, be made by summons in the action, and in any other case by an originating summons which shall be in Form No. 10 in Appendix A.

(4) Where an application is made under section 1(5) of the Arbitration Act 1979 (including any application for leave) the summons must be served on the arbitrator or umpire and on any other party to the reference.

Applications in district registries

26.—(1) An application under section 12(4) of the Arbitration Act 1950 for an order that a writ of subpoena ad testificandum or of subpoena duces tecum shall issue to compel the attendance before an arbitrator or umpire of a witness may, if the attendance of the witness is required within the district of a district registry, be made at that registry, instead of at the Admiralty and Commercial Registry, at the option of the applicant.

Time limits and other special provisions as to appeals and applications under the Arbitration Acts

27.—(1) An application to the Court—

(a) to remit an award under section 22 of the Arbitration Act 1950; or
(b) to set aside an award under section 23(2) of that Act or otherwise, or
(c) to direct an arbitrator or umpire to state the reasons for an award under section 1(5) of the Arbitration Act 1979,

must be made, and the summons or notice must be served, within 21 days after the award has been made and published to the parties.

(2) In the case of an appeal to the Court under section 1(2) of the Arbitration Act 1979, the summons for leave to appeal, where leave is required, and the notice of originating motion must be served and the appeal entered, within 21 days after the award has been made and published to the parties.

Provided that, where reasons material to the appeal are given on a date subsequent to the publication of the award, the period of 21 days shall run from the date on which the reasons are given.

(3) An application, under section 2(1) of the Arbitration Act 1979, to determine any question of law arising in the course of a reference, must be made, and notice thereof served, within 14 days after the arbitrator or umpire has consented to the application being made, or the other parties have so consented.

(4) For the purpose of paragraph (3) the consent must be given in writing.

(5) In the case of every appeal or application to which this rule applies, the notice of originating motion, the originating summons or the summons, as the case may be, must state the grounds of the appeal or application and, where the appeal or application is founded on evidence by affidavit, or is made with the consent of the arbitrator or umpire or of the other parties, a copy of every affidavit intended to be used, or, as the case may be, of every consent given in writing, must be served with that notice.

(6) Without prejudice to paragraph (5), in an appeal under section 1(2) of the Arbitration Act 1979 the statement of the grounds of the appeal shall specify the relevant parts of the award and reasons, or the relevant parts thereof, shall be lodged with the court and served with the notice of originating motion.

(7) Without prejudice to paragraph (5), in an application for leave to appeal under section 1(2) of the Arbitration Act 1979, any affidavit verifying the facts in support of a contention that the question of law concerns a term of a contract or an event which is not a one-off term or event must be lodged with the court and served with the notice of originating motion.

(8) Any affidavit in reply to an affidavit under paragraph (7) shall be lodged with the court and served on the applicant not less than two clear days before the hearing of the application.

(9) A respondent to an application for leave to appeal under section 1(2) of the Arbitration Act 1979 who desires to contend that the award should be upheld on grounds not expressed or fully expressed in the award and reasons shall not less than two clear days before the hearing of the application lodge with the court and serve on the applicant a notice specifying the grounds of his contention.

Applications and appeals to be heard by Commercial Judges

28.—(1) Any matter which is required, by rule 24 or 25, to be heard by a judge, shall be heard by a Commercial Judge, unless any such judge otherwise directs.

(2) Nothing in the foregoing paragraph shall be construed as preventing the powers of a Commercial Judge from being exercised by any judge of the High Court.

Service out of the jurisdiction of summons, notice, etc.

29.—(1) Subject to paragraph (2), service out of the jurisdiction of—

(a) any originating summons or notice of originating motion under the Arbitration Act 1950 or the Arbitration Act 1979, or
(b) any order made on such a summons or motion,

is permissible with the leave of the Court provided that the arbitration to which the summons, motion or order relates is governed by English law or has been, is being or is to be held within the jurisdiction.

(2) Service out of the jurisdiction of an originating summons for leave to enforce an award is permissible with the leave of the Court whether or not the arbitration is governed by English law.

(3) An application for the grant of leave under this rule must be supported by an affidavit stating the grounds on which the application is made and showing in what place or country the person to be served is, or probably may be found; and no such leave shall be granted unless it shall be made to appear to the Court that the case is a proper one for service out of the jurisdiction under this rule.

(4) Order 11, rules 5 to 8, shall apply in relation to any such summons, notice or order as is referred to in paragraph (1) as they apply in relation to a writ.

Part III

Application of this Part

30. This Part of this Order applies to all enforcement proceedings (other than by an action on the award) regardless of when they are commenced and when the arbitral proceedings took place.

Enforcement of awards

31.—(1) This rule applies to applications to enforce awards which are brought in the High Court and such an application may be made in the Royal Courts of Justice or in any district registry.

(2) An application for leave under—

(a) section 66 of the Arbitration Act 1996;
(b) section 101 of the Arbitration Act 1996;
(c) section 26 of the Arbitration Act 1950; or
(d) section 3(1)(a) of the Arbitration Act 1975;

to enforce an award in the same manner as a judgment or order may be made *ex parte* in Form No. 8A in Appendix A.

(3) The Court hearing an application under paragraph (2) may direct that the application is to be served on such parties to the arbitration as it may specify and service of the application out of the jurisdiction is permissible with the leave of the Court irrespective of where the award is, or is treated as, made.

(4) Where a direction is given under paragraph (3), rules 11 and 13 to 17 shall apply with the necessary modifications as they apply to applications under Part I of this Order.

(5) Where the applicant applies to enforce an agreed award within the meaning of section 51(2) of the Arbitration Act 1996, the application must state that the award is an agreed award and any order made by the Court shall also contain such a statement.

(6) An application for leave must be supported by affidavit—

(a) exhibiting
   (i) where the application is made under section 66 of the Arbitration Act 1996 or under section 26 of the Arbitration Act 1950, the arbitration agreement and the original award or, in either case, a copy thereof;

(ii) where the application is under section 101 of the Arbitration Act 1996, the documents required to be produced by section 102 of that Act;

(iii) where the application is under section 3(1)(a) of the Arbitration Act 1975, the documents required to be produced by section 4 of that Act;

(b) stating the name and the usual or last known place of residence or business of the applicant and of the person against whom it is sought to enforce the award respectively;

(c) stating as the case may require, either that the award has not been complied with or the extent to which it has not been complied with at the date of the application.

(7) An order giving leave must be drawn up by or on behalf of the applicant and must be served on the respondent by delivering a copy to him personally or by sending a copy to him at his usual or last known place of residence or business or in such other manner as the Court may direct.

(8) Service of the order out of the jurisdiction is permissible without leave, and Order 11, rules 5 to 8, shall apply in relation to such an order as they apply in relation to a writ.

(9) Within 14 days after service of the order or, if the order is to be served out of the jurisdiction, within such other period as the Court may fix, the respondent may apply to set aside the order and the award shall not be enforced until after the expiration of that period or, if the respondent applies within that period to set aside the order, until after the application is finally disposed of.

(10) The copy of the order served on the respondent shall state the effect of paragraph (9).

(11) In relation to a body corporate this rule shall have effect as if for any reference to the place of residence or business of the applicant or the respondent there were substituted a reference to the registered or principal address of the body corporate.

Nothing in this rule shall affect any enactment which provides for the manner in with a document may be served on a body corporate.

Interest on awards

32.—(1) Where an applicant seeks to enforce an award of interest, the whole or any part of which relates to a period after the date of the award, he shall file a certificate giving the following particulars—

(a) whether simple or compound interest was awarded;

(b) the date from which interest was awarded;

(c) whether rests were provided for, specifying them;

(d) the rate of interest awarded; and

(e) a calculation showing the total amount claimed up to the date of the certificate and any sum which will become due thereafter on a *per diem* basis.

(2) The certificate under paragraph (1) must be filed whenever the amount of interest has to be quantified for the purpose of obtaining a judgment or order under section 66 of the Arbitration Act (enforcement of the award) or for the purpose of enforcing such a judgment or order by one of the means mentioned in Order 45, rule 1.

Registration in High Court of foreign awards

33. Where an award is made in proceedings on an arbitration in any part of Her Majesty's dominions or other territory to which Part I of the Foreign Judgments (Reciprocal Enforcement) Act 1933 extends, being a part to which Part II of the Administration of Justice Act 1920 extended immediately before the said Part I was extended thereto, then, if the award has, in pursuance of the law in force in the place where it was made, become enforceable in the same manner as a judgment given by a court in that place, Order 71 shall apply in relation to the award as it applies in relation to a judgment given by that court, subject, however, to the following modifications—

(a) for references to the country of the original court there shall be substituted references to the place where the award was made; and

(b) the affidavit required by rule 3 of the said Order must state (in addition to the other matters required by that rule) that to the best of the information or belief of the deponent the award has, in pursuance of the law in force in the place where it was made, become enforceable in the same manner as a judgment given by a court in that place.

Registration of awards under the Arbitration (International Investment Disputes) Act 1966

34.—(1) In this rule and in any provision of these rules as applied by this rule—

"the Act of 1966" means the Arbitration (International Investment Disputes) Act 1966;
"award" means an award rendered pursuant to the Convention;
"the Convention" means the Convention referred to in section 1(1) of the Act of 1966;
"judgment creditor" and "judgment debtor" mean respectively the person seeking recognition or enforcement of an award and the other party to the award.

(2) Subject to the provisions of this rule, the following provisions of Order 71, namely, rules 1, 3(1) (except sub-paragraphs (c)(iv) and (d) therefore) 7 (except paragraph (3)(c) and (d) thereof), and 10(3) shall apply with the necessary modifications in relation to an award as they apply in relation to a judgment to which Part II of the Foreign Judgments (Reciprocal Enforcement) Act 1933 applies.

(3) An application to have an award registered in the High Court under section 1 of the Act of 1966 shall be made by originating summons which shall be in Form No. 10 in Appendix A.

(4) The affidavit required by Order 71, rule 3, in support of an application for registration shall—

(a) in lieu of exhibiting the judgment or a copy thereof, exhibit a copy of the award certified pursuant to the Convention; and

(b) in addition to stating the matters mentioned in paragraph 3(1)(c)(i) and (ii) of the said rule 3, state whether at the date of the application the enforcement of the award has been stayed (provisionally or otherwise) pursuant to the Convention and whether any, and if so what, application has been made pursuant to the Convention, which, if granted, might result in a stay of the enforcement of the award.

(5) There shall be kept in the Admiralty and Commercial Registry under the direction of the Senior Master a register of the awards ordered to be registered under the Act of 1966 and particulars shall be entered in the register of any execution issued on such an award.

(6) Where it appears to the Court on granting leave to register an award or an application made by the judgment debtor after an award has been granted—

(a) that the enforcement of the award has been stayed (whether provisionally or otherwise) pursuant to the Convention, or

(b) that an application has been made pursuant to the Convention, which, if granted, might result in a stay of the enforcement of the award,

the Court shall, or in the case referred to in sub-paragraph (b) may, stay execution of the award for such time as it considers appropriate in the circumstances.

(7) An application by the judgment debtor under paragraph (6) shall be made by summons and supported by affidavit.

Registration of awards under the Multilateral Investment Guarantee Agency Act 1988

35. Rule 34 shall apply, with the necessary modifications, in relation to an award rendered pursuant to the Convention referred to in section 1(1) of the Multilateral Investment Guarantee Agency Act 1988 as it applies in relation to an award rendered pursuant to the Convention referred to in section 1(1) of the Arbitration (International Investment Disputes) Act 1966.".

6. After Form No. 8 in Appendix A there shall be inserted the form in Schedule 1 to these Rules.

7. After Form No. 15 in Appendix A there shall be inserted the form in Schedule 2 to these Rules.

Hearsay evidence

8. For Order 38, rules 20 to 34, there shall be substituted the following—

"Application and interpretation

20.—(1) In this Part of this Order the "1995 Act" means the Civil Evidence Act 1995 and any expressions used in this Part of this Order and in the 1995 Act have the same meanings in this Part of this Order as they have in the Act.

(2) In this Part of this Order:

'hearsay evidence' means evidence consisting of hearsay within the meaning of section 1(2) of the 1995 Act;

'hearsay notice' means a notice under section 2 of the 1995 Act.

(3) This Part of this Order applies in relation to the trial or hearing of an issue or question arising in a cause or matter and to a reference, inquiry and assessment of damages, as it applies to the trial or hearing of a cause or matter.

Hearsay notices

21.—(1) A hearsay notice must

(a) state that it is a hearsay notice;
(b) identify the hearsay evidence;
(c) identify the person who made the statement which is to be given in evidence;
(d) state why that person will (or may) not be called to give oral evidence; and
(e) if the hearsay evidence is contained in a witness statement, refer to the part of the witness statement where it is set out.

(2) A single hearsay notice may deal with the hearsay evidence of more than one witness.

(3) The requirement to give a hearsay notice does not apply to

(a) evidence which is authorised to be given by or in an affidavit; or
(b) a statement which a party to a probate action desires to give in evidence and which is alleged to have been made by the person whose estate is the subject of the action.

(4) Subject to paragraph (5), a party who desires to give in evidence at the trial or hearing of a cause or matter hearsay evidence shall

(a) in the case of a cause or matter which is required to be set down for trial or hearing or adjourned into Court, within 28 days after it is set down or so adjourned or within such other period as the Court may specify, and
(b) in any other case, within 28 days after the date on which an appointment for the first hearing of the cause or matter is obtained, or within such other period as the Court may specify,

serve a hearsay notice on every party to the cause or matter.

(5) Where witness statements are served under rule 2A of this Order, any hearsay notice served under this rule shall be served at the same time at the witness statements.

Power to call witness for cross-examination on hearsay evidence

22.—(1) Where a party tenders as hearsay evidence a statement made by a person but does not propose to call the person who made the statement to give evidence, the court may, on application, allow another party to call and cross-examine the person who made the statement on its contents.

(2) An application under paragraph (1) shall be made on notice to all other parties no later than 28 days after service of the hearsay notice.

(3) Where the court allows another party to call and cross-examine the person who made the statement, it may give such directions as it thinks fit to secure the attendance of that person and as to the procedure to be followed.

Credibility

23.—(1) If

(a) a party tenders as hearsay evidence a statement made by a person but does not call the person who made the statement to give oral evidence, and
(b) another party wishes to attack the credibility of the person who made the statement;

that other party shall notify the party tendering the hearsay evidence of his intention.

(2) A notice under paragraph (1) shall be given not later than 28 days after service of the hearsay notice.

Powers exercisable in chambers

24. The jurisdiction of the Court under rules 20 to 23 may be exercised in chambers."

9. Nothing in rule 8 shall apply to proceedings

(a) in which directions have been given, or orders have been made, as to the evidence to be given at the trial or hearing, or
(b) where the trial or hearing has begun

before 31st January 1997.

Miscellaneous amendments

10. Order 29, rule 11(2)(a) shall be amended by substituting for the words "as insurer" the words "an insurer".

Mackay of Clashfern, C.,
Stephen Brown, P.,
Rattee, J.,
Colman, J.,
Bell, J.,
Jean Ritchie.

Dated 19th December 1996

SCHEDULE 1 (Rule 6)

Arbitration application No. 8A (0.73, r.4(1))

Guidance notes for Applicants

1. You should read the following notes carefully before completing the attached form. The form can be used to either—

(a) make an application in existing proceedings; or
(b) begin proceedings (as an originating document).

Notes 2 and 4 are relevant to an application as at 1(a); Notes 3 and 4 are relevant to an application as at 1(b).

2. No acknowledgment of service is required if the form is being used to make an application in existing proceedings. You should delete the notes relating to returning an acknowledgment of service. But you must still complete the address boxes at the end of the form as appropriate.

Service

3. (a) A completed acknowledgment of service must be served with the arbitration application. Notes for guidance attached to that form will tell you how to fill it in.

(b) The application **may not** be served more than 1 month from the date of issue **unless**—
it is to be served on a party outside England and Wales, or
the time for service has been extended by the Court.

(c) You must write in the appropriate time limit for returning the acknowledgment of service. The relevant number of days should be given in the box below paragraph 6 of the notes about service.

(d) If you are an applicant acting in person and you reside at an address which is not in England and Wales, you must give an address for service which is within the Court's jurisdiction.

4. Detach the guidance notes before this form is served.

In the High Court of Justice
Queen's Bench Division
Commercial Court

District Registry Mercantile List

use black ink and capital letters

---

1. (i) In an arbitration application between

Applicant

and

Respondent

of

Respondent

of

Respondent

of

(ii) and in the matter of an (anticipated) arbitration between

Claimant
Respondent(s)

(iii) The arbitrator(s) to whom notice of this application is given are:

give name of any arbitrator(s) listed above as respondents or give full names and addresses where not named as respondents

---

Hearing

(delete (i) or (ii) as applicable)

2. (i) This application is made on notice (ex parte).
(ii) The hearing of this application will take place in court (chambers)

on

at o'clock,

(or on a date to be fixed)

at *(specify court)*

Grounds for application and details of what is being claimed

The grounds for making the application and details of what is being claimed should be set out either in the box below or on a separate sheet attached to this application. The details should include those required by Order 73.

(Set out below the grounds and details of your claim)

The applicant seeks an order for the costs of this application against:

(Set out below the name of the person(s) against whom costs are sought)

Dated ....

Returning the acknowledgment of service

(see also "Notes for arbitrators", at paragraph 5 below)

1. If you are (a) named as a respondent to this application, and
(b) served with a copy of this application
you should complete and return the accompanying acknowledgment of service to the court office which issued it. **You have only a limited time in which to do this.** Full details of the time allowed are set out in the notes for guidance to the form of acknowledgment. **Whether or not you complete the form, and how you complete it, if you decide to do so, will affect your right:**

- **to contest the application; and**
- **to be kept informed or any hearing of future hearings.**

2. If you **complete the form of acknowledgment** and **indicate that you intend to contest the application**, you will **be notified of all hearing dates** relating to this application and **will be entitled to put your case to the Court**. If you wish to put evidence before the Court in response to any affidavit filed by the applicant in support of the application, you must serve your affidavit on the applicant within 21 days after the time limited for acknowledging service (see time for acknowledging below).

3. If you **complete the form of acknowledgment** but **do not indicate that you intend to contest the application**, you will be notified of all hearing dates relating to the application but, unless the court gives permission, you **will not be allowed to put your case to the Court.** The Court will make whatever order it feels is just in the circumstances. If, after returning the acknowledgment, you decide you **do** wish to contest the application, you must **ask the Court's permission to do so.**

4. If you **do not return** the form of the acknowledgment, you will **not be entitled to contest** the application, **or be notified of any hearing dates relating to it.** If you **fail to return** the form of acknowledgment within the time allowed for the purpose (see the notes for guidance on the form of acknowledgment) you must ask the Court's permission to return the form of acknowledgment after the proper time. Unless the Court gives permission, you will not be allowed to put your case to the Court. The Court will make whatever order it feels is just in the circumstances.

Notes for arbitrators

5. If you were or are an arbitrator in the arbitration which gave rise to this application and you are named as a respondent to the application, paragraphs 1 to 4 above apply to you as to any other respondent.

6. If you were or are an arbitrator in the arbitration which gave rise to this application and you are **not** named as a respondent, the application has been sent to you for your information. You need not complete or return the acknowledgment. You may, if you wish, file an affidavit or make representations in writing to the Court. If you wish to do this, you should do so as soon as practicable. You should send a copy of the document which you have sent to the Court to all parties to the arbitration. Alternatively, you may apply to be made a respondent to the application. Any such application should be made to the Court in writing. (*write in 14 days, or where application is to be served out of the jurisdiction the time limit set by the Court)*

The time limit for the respondents to acknowledge service is ☐ days

---

This summons was issued by
of
(Applicant) (Solicitor for the applicant)

(Complete only if you are an applicant acting in person and you reside at an address which is outside the Court's jurisdiction)
Applicant's address for service within the jurisdiction is

SCHEDULE 2

(Rule 7)

Acknowledgment of Service of Arbitration Application No. 15A (O. 73, r. 11(1))

Guidance notes for the Applicant

Read these notes carefully

The notes explain what you have to do before this form is sent to ("served" on) the respondent.

Form heading

You must fill in the heading of the form with:

— the number allocated to the application

— the name of the appropriate High Court Division, for example, Queen's Bench Division, (Commercial Court), or if the arbitration application was issued in a District Registry, the name of the District Registry, and
— the names of the parties (the 'title') as they appear on the application.

Part 3 Please leave blank for respondent to complete

Part 4 Return address

Write in the full address of the District Registry or office in the Royal Courts of Justice to which the form should be returned.

On the reverse of acknowledgment form (Applicant's (Applicant's solicitor's) details.)

Fill in your name and the address to which papers about the case should be sent.
Detach these guidance notes before the form is sent to the respondent.

Guidance notes for the Respondent

Read these notes carefully

They will help you to fill in the form attached and tell you what other steps you need to take.

Act quickly

You have only a limited time to return the form.

Help and advice

You can get help and legal advice from:

— a solicitor, or
— a Citizens' Advice Bureau.

They will also tell you if you qualify for help with your legal costs ("legal aid").

Staff at any District Registry or office in the Royal Courts of Justice (Strand, London) will help you to fill in the form.

Time for returning the form

You have **14 days** from the day you receive the arbitration application to **return the completed form to the court**. The day on which the 14 day period begins depends on how you received the application (how it was "served" on you).

If the application was:

— handed to you personally, the 14 days begins on the day you were given the application;
— delivered by post, the 14 days begins 7 days from the date of the postmark;
— put through your letter box, the 14 days begins 7 days from the day this was done.

If you are a limited company and the application was delivered by post, the 14 days begins:

— on the second working day from the date of the postmark if first class post was used;
— on the fourth working day from the date of the postmark if the second class post was used.

Note: You may have less than 14 days to return the form in certain kinds of proceedings where an early hearing date has been fixed. If in doubt, seek advice.

If the arbitration application was served on you at an address outside England and Wales, the application will tell you how long you have to return the acknowledgment form.

Filling in the form

Read these notes carefully

They will help you to fill in the form opposite and tell you what other steps you need to take.

You can use the same form of acknowledgment for two (or more) respondents provided the form makes this clear and they all wish to reply in the same way.

If you are **under 18 or suffering certain mental disorders** ("under disability") you must ask another person to act for you. That person can be any friend or relative who is over 18 and not a co-defendant in the same claim. But they must act on your behalf with the help of a solicitor. **The solicitor must fill in the form of acknowledgment.**

Part 1

Write in your full name. If your name was incorrect on the summons, add the words "sued as" followed by the name stated on the application.

If you are:

a person trading in a name other than your own, write in your name followed by the words "trading as" and the name under which you trade;

a partner in a firm, write in your name followed by the words "a partner in the firm of" and the name of the firm. **If you are sued as a partner but are not, say so.**

Part 2

Tick the appropriate box to show whether you intend to contest the application, the claim for costs, or neither. Read note 2 below.

Part 3

Unless your solicitor is filling in the form on your behalf, you must sign the form and give an address to which court documents should be sent, and any reference, telephone or fax numbers. If you are being sued as an individual (that is in your own name rather than of your firm or company) the address you give must be one in England and Wales. If you are a **limited company**, the form may be filled in by an **authorised officer** who must state his position in that company, or a solicitor. A solicitor may give his firm's address, an authorised officer must give the registered or principal office of the company.

What to do when you have filled in the form

1. Return the form. Detach these guidance notes and send or take the acknowledgment form to the office in the Royal Courts of Justice or the District Registry which issued the application.

2. Preparing your defence. If you are a respondent and wish to contest the application, you must set out your reasons in an affidavit (a sworn statement). You must send a copy of the affidavit to the applicant, the court and the other respondents. You must do this not more than 21 days after the last day for returning the acknowledgment of service, that is, 14 days after service.

If you are an arbitrator who is not named as a respondent, you may apply to be made a respondent or make representations to the Court. If you wish to make representations, you may do so informally in writing or in an affidavit. You must send a copy to the court and all other parties as soon as practicable after you receive the application.

19 NO

In the High Court of Justice
Queen's Bench Division
Commercial Court
Mercantile List

District registry

use black ink and capital letters

Respondent
Applicant

Part 1

(Your) (Respondent's) full name

Part 2

(Do you) (Does the respondent) intend to contest:

the application? ☐
the claim for costs (if applicable)? ☐
or neither? ☐

Part 3

I acknowledge that (I have) (the respondent has) been served with a copy of the arbitration application.

Signed________________________________Date________________________
Respondent (Solicitor for the respondent) (Authorised officer)

Address to which papers about this case should be sent.

Solicitor's ref. Telephone no. Fax no.

Part 4

When completed this form should be returned to:

Applicant's (Applicant's solicitor's) details
Address to which papers about this case should be sent.

Solicitor's ref. Telephone no. Fax no.

EXPLANATORY NOTE

(This note is not part of the Rules)

These Rules amend the Rules of the Supreme Court so as—

(a) to substitute a new Order 73 (Applications relating to Arbitration) which provides for the bringing of applications under the Arbitration Act 1996 (rules 2 to 7);
(b) to provide a procedure for giving hearsay notices under the Civil Evidence Act 1995 (*rules 8 and 9*);
(c) to make a minor amendment to Order 29, rule 11(2) (*rule 10*).

THE HIGH COURT AND COUNTY COURTS (ALLOCATION OF ARBITRATION PROCEEDINGS) ORDER 1996

(1996 No. 3215)

Made	*19th December 1996*
Laid before Parliament	*20th December 1996*
Coming into force	*31st January 1997*

The Lord Chancellor, in exercise of the powers conferred on him by section 105 of the Arbitration Act 1996, hereby makes the following Order—

1.—(1) This Order may be cited as the High Court and County Courts (Allocation of Arbitration Proceedings) Order 1996 and shall come into force on 31st January 1997.

(2) In this Order, "the Act" means the Arbitration Act 1996.

2. Subject to articles 3 to 5, proceedings under the Act shall be commenced and taken in the High Court.

3. Proceedings under section 9 of the Act (stay of legal proceedings) shall be commenced in the court in which the legal proceedings are pending.

4. Proceedings under sections 66 and 101(2) (enforcement of awards) of the Act may be commenced in any county court.

5.—(1) Proceedings under the Act may be commenced and taken in the Central London County Court Business List.

(2) Where, in exercise of the powers conferred by sections 41 and 42 of the County Courts Act 1984 the High Court or the judge in charge of the Central London County Court Business List orders the transfer of proceedings under the Act which were commenced in the Central London County Court Business List to the High Court, those proceedings shall be taken in the High Court.

(3) Where, in exercise of its powers under section 40(2) of the County Courts Act 1984 the High Court orders the transfer of proceedings under the Act which were commenced in the High Court to the Central London County Court Business List, those proceedings shall be taken in the Central London County Court Business List.

(4) In exercising the powers referred to in paragraphs (2) and (3) regard shall be had to the following criteria—

(a) the financial substance of the dispute referred to arbitration, including the value of any claim or counterclaim;
(b) the nature of the dispute referred to arbitration (for example, whether it arises out of a commercial or business transaction or relates to engineering, building or other construction work);

(c) whether the proceedings are otherwise important and, in particular, whether they raise questions of importance to persons who are not parties, and

(d) the balance of convenience points to having the proceedings taken in the Central London County Court Business List,

and, where the financial substance of the dispute exceeds £200,000, the proceedings shall be taken in the High Court unless the proceedings do not raise questions of general importance to persons who are not parties.

(5) In this article—

"the Central London County Court Business List" means the business list established at the Central London County Court by Order 48C of the County Court Rules 1981;

"value" shall be construed in accordance with articles 9 and 10 of the High Court and County Courts Jurisdiction Order 1991.

6. Nothing in this Order shall prevent the judge in charge of the commercial list (within the meaning of section 62(3) of the Supreme Court Act 1981 (**c**)) from transferring proceedings under the Act to another list, court or Division of the High Court to which he has power to transfer proceedings and, where such an order is made, the proceedings may be taken in that list, court or Division as the case may be.

Dated 19th December 1996 Mackay of Clashfern, C.

EXPLANATORY NOTE

(This note is not part of the Order)

This Order specifies the courts in which proceedings under the Arbitration Act 1996 may be commenced and allocates proceedings between the High Court and the Central London County Court.

APPENDIX B—TRANSITIONAL PROVISIONS

70. As we said in paragraph 315 of our February 1996 Report, we decided to use the precedent of previous arbitration statutes so that the new Act applies to arbitrations commenced after it came into force, whenever the arbitration agreement was made. The transitional provisions reflect this, but of course also have to deal with arbitration agreements and arbitrations which are to remain governed by the pre-existing law.

71. Section 84(1) of the Act is a limiting provision, in that it stipulates that the Act does not apply to arbitrations commenced before the date on which Part I comes into force, and this is of course reflected in paragraph 2(a) of Schedule 2 to the Commencement No. 1 Order.

72. Section 84(2) is an enlarging provision, since it applies the Act to arbitrations commenced after Part I comes into force, even if the agreement is made at an earlier time.

73. The remaining transitional provisions in paragraph 2 of Schedule 2 to the Commencement No. 1 Order, deal with arbitration applications to the Court. Paragraph 2(b) is designed to ensure that the pre-existing law applies to all applications to Court made before Part I comes into force, and that this will remain the case even if an arbitration is commenced after Part I comes into force. Paragraph 2(c) is designed to ensure that applications relating to arbitral proceedings commenced before Part I comes into force are themselves governed by the pre-existing law so as to avoid one law applying to the arbitration proceedings and another to arbitration applications to the Court.

74. Paragraph 4 of Schedule 2 deals with the question of "Equity Clauses" in arbitration agreements, which we deal with in Paragraph 30 of this Report.

THE ARBITRATION ACT 1996 (COMMENCEMENT NO. 1) ORDER 1996

(1996 No. 3146)

Made *16th December 1996*

The Secretary of State, in exercise of the powers conferred on him by section 109 of the Arbitration Act 1996(a), hereby makes the following Order:

1. This Order may be cited as the Arbitration Act 1996 (Commencement No. 1) Order 1996.

2. The provisions of the Arbitration Act 1996 ("the Act") listed in Schedule 1 to this Order shall come into force on the day after this Order is made.

3. The rest of the Act, except sections 85 to 87, shall come into force on 31st January 1997.

4. The transitional provisions in Schedule 2 to this Order shall have effect.

John M. Taylor
Parliamentary Under-Secretary of State
for Corporate and Consumer Affairs,
Department of Trade and Industry

16th December 1996

SCHEDULE 1

(Article 2)

Section 91 so far as it relates to the power to make orders under the section.

Section 105.

Section 107(1) and paragraph 36 of Schedule 3, so far as relating to the provision that may be made by county court rules.

Section 107(2) and the reference in Schedule 4 to the County Courts (Northern Ireland) Order 1980 so far as relating to the above matter.

Section 108 to 110.

SCHEDULE 2

(Article 4)

1. In this Schedule:

(a) "the appointed day" means the date specified in Article 3 of this Order;
(b) "arbitration application" means any application relating to arbitration made by or in legal proceedings, whether or not arbitral proceedings have commenced;
(c) "the old law" means the enactments specified in section 107 as they stood before their amendment or repeal by the Act.

2. The old law shall continue to apply to:

(a) arbitral proceedings commenced before the appointed day;
(b) arbitration applications commenced or made before the appointed day;
(c) arbitration applications commenced or made on or after the appointed day relating to arbitral proceedings commenced before the appointed day

and the provisions of the Act which would otherwise be applicable shall not apply.

3. The provisions of this Act brought into force by this Order shall apply to any other arbitration application.

4. In the application of paragraph (b) of subsection (1) of section 46 (provision for dispute to be decided in accordance with provisions other than law) to an arbitration agreement made before the appointed day, the agreement shall have effect in accordance with the rules of law (including any conflict of laws rules) as they stood immediately before the appointed day.

EXPLANATORY NOTE

(This note is not part of the Order)

With one exception, this Order brings into force the provisions of the Arbitration Act 1996. Those provisions necessary to enable the substantive provisions to be brought into force are commenced immediately. The substantive provisions come into force on 31st January 1997. Commencement is subject to transitional provisions designed to ensure continuity of legal proceedings and to preserve the current law on what are known as "honourable engagement" clauses in relation to existing agreements.

Sections 85 to 87, which make special provision in relation to domestic arbitration agreements, are not commenced.

INDEX

[references to "the Act" are to the Arbitration Act 1996]